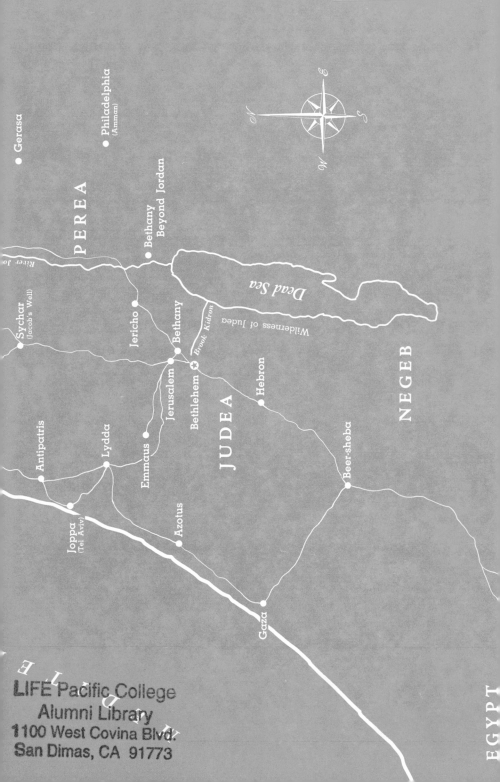

The Holy Land

THE
HOLY LAND

by
G. Frederick Owen

Member of
The American Schools of Oriental Research,
Jerusalem, Amman, and Baghdad

Foreword by
Col. James B. Irwin
Astronaut on the Apollo 15

Beacon Hill Press of Kansas City
Kansas City, Missouri

ISBN: 0-8341-0489-X

Library of Congress Catalog Card No. 77-076289

Printed in United States of America

Contents

Foreword

It has been my very great privilege to go to the moon and to the Holy Land!

As a small boy I gazed at the friendly moon on its best summer nights and almost fancied myself walking over its plains and along the foothills of what seemed to be its mountains. It seemed so very real to me that as a young lad I used to point to the moon and say, "I'm going to go up there someday."

I also attended Sunday school classes and learned of that wonderful country called Palestine and of its interesting places such as Mount Sinai, the Mount of Beatitudes, Bethlehem, Nazareth, and Jerusalem. Abraham, Moses, Joseph, David, and Jonah interested me, but the story of Jesus and how He loved all people —even me—enough to die on Mount Calvary to pay the penalty for our sins touched me very deeply and caused me to want to visit that land where all these things took place. I took part in the Christmas program at our church every year. At 11 years of age I made a public decision for Christ, and my desire to go to the Holy Land increased. Now that I am a man in mid-life and have gone both to the moon and to the Holy Land, I like to parallel the two exploits.

On July 26, 1971, we left the planet earth on Apollo 15 to explore space and the moon. We circled the earth a couple of times at 18,000 mph, then directed our spacecraft toward the moon. At a distance of 50,000 miles, we maneuvered our spacecraft so that the earth appeared in my window. I looked out and couldn't believe my eyes. I called to my colleagues, Dave and Al, and very quickly they floated over. All of a sudden there were 7 three heads—six eyeballs glued to the window—viewing our home—the spaceship earth—looking like a Christmas tree ornament hanging in the blackness of space. It was the most beautiful sight we would see on our voyage—a sight that made us deeply appreciative of the creation of God, keenly aware of *His* precise control, and moved by *His* love.

The major purpose of our landing was to explore the mountains of the moon. We landed at Hadley Base, on the edge of Mare Imbrium (Sea of Rains) and at the foot of the towering Apennine Mountains—mountains that were 15,000 feet above our campsite. I was astonished when I first saw the lofty mountains—I was reminded of a favorite ski resort.

While exploring the area around our campsite, I was conscious of another Force—not visible, but definitely there—a Force that answered prayer, guided our footsteps, and inspired our thoughts to new heights—the very presence of God.

We were guided to the "Genesis Rock"—a unique rock that is said to date back to the earliest beginning of the moon. It was sitting on a dust-covered pedestal rock—glistening white and practically free from dust so that we could see it long before we picked it up. Singularly enough, the rock is composed of a material known on the earth for centuries as moonstone. We found this rock on the Apennine mountain slopes, a long way from our temporary home, Falcon, which appeared like a speck down in the valley.

We returned with a wealth of new knowledge about our moon, but for my personal life the greatest discovery was God's presence on another planet. The total experience caused a deeper spiritual awakening in my life that gave me new direction and a mission when I returned to the spaceship earth. Sharing God and His Son, Jesus Christ, became my new mission on the spaceship earth.

You can imagine my great delight when I learned that I would be able to visit the Holy Land with my family during Christmas, 1972. Since I had never visited the Middle East, where the great religions had their birth, there was a high degree of anticipation—would the spiritual experience be as wonderful as that felt on the moon? This was to be another discovery voyage for Jim Irwin.

As a goodwill ambassador to the Holy Land, there were many semiofficial meetings with government officials and many speaking engagements. We arrived in Amman, Jordan, after an eventful flight—including a forced landing outside Damascus. There was little delay before we began our drive down into the depths of the Jordan Rift Valley, across the Allenby Bridge, by Jericho, and up into the Judean wilderness. I felt like a pilgrim as we wound our way up through the wild, barren mountains to Bethany and on to Jerusalem, the City of God.

We spent our first day traveling to the lowest place on the earth, the Dead Sea, and with Prof. Yigael Yadin as our guide, we visited the magnificent site of Masada with its tragic, breathtaking past. On our return, we inspected the site of Qumran where the far-famed Dead Sea Scrolls were produced and near where they were found.

On Christmas Eve, Mary and I attended a reception held by Mr. Elias M. Freij, mayor of Bethlehem. Mr. Harold Wilson of England and I addressed the reception, representing our countries. That evening I addressed the crowd of pilgrims gathered in Bethlehem square and shared the Christmas story and my personal story. I thought back to my youthful days when I participated in the church Christmas program. I had come a long way. After the program, the mayor took our family to the revered birth site in the Church of the Nativity, where we prayed together as a family in that very holy place.

On Christmas morning I spoke at the Garden Tomb. The stark reality of the empty tomb impressed me anew with the fact of Christ's resurrection.

From Jerusalem, we drove north through Samaria and had a drink from Jacob's well. That night we slept peacefully on the shores of the Sea of Galilee. The next day we lunched on St. Peter fish, and that evening I shared my moon experience with those at Kibbutz En Gev, across the sea.

It was a very winding road to the top of Mount Tabor from where we could see into the Plain of Esdraelon (Armageddon) 9 and to the Mediterranean. We had lunch with the mayors of Upper and Lower Nazareth, and then the Israeli Air Force insisted that I also have lunch with them at a base just west of Nazareth before we flew across the Plain of Armageddon to Tel Aviv. What a beautiful plain for the world's last great struggle! Mount Carmel was a tranquil sight as the sun sank into the Mediterranean.

After two functions in Tel Aviv we drove back to Jerusalem. It was about midnight, a clear desert sky, and a half moon that was just hanging above the steeples and minarets of the Holy City. The moon was inclined so that it appeared to be a golden goblet pouring out its blessings upon the City of the Great King. A most remarkable and memorable sight! When on the moon we had to look directly overhead to see the earth and then it was a half earth—the size of a marble. Now, from the earth, we saw the moon in its stirring beauty.

We had an opportunity to visit with Mrs. Golda Meir and her grandchildren. I presented her a flag of Israel which we had flown to the moon. With her I shared my feeling of the presence of God on the moon. She told me that she had experienced a very similar feeling when on Mount Sinai.

The time went very quickly and before we knew it, it was time to return to Jordan, so we retraced our travel through Jericho.

The people of Jordan were very gracious to us. King Hussein and Prince Hassan took care of our desires, including a flight to Aqaba and then a helicopter flight to Petra. Of course, the final journey into Petra was by jeep. That fascinating city carved from the sandstone canyons captured our imagination, and we were loath to leave. Once back in Aqaba, we visited with the king and Queen Alia at their beach house.

Prince Hassan arranged a personal tour to Hassan Air Base, where I briefed the pilots on my mission. They scheduled a scramble takeoff of two F-104s and a flyby in my honor. I visited the hospital at Aijalon and returned by helicopter to Jordan University, flying over the very well preserved city of Jerash.

10   The final evening was the most exciting opportunity. I addressed the royalty of Jordan and presented to the king the flag of Jordan that we had carried to the moon.

What a privileged and happy man I am to have been to the moon and to the Holy Land. God revealed himself to me on the moon, and many times I felt closer to Him when in the Holy Land because I had walked where Jesus had walked.

As I look back on both experiences, I can see many similarities and differences regarding the moon and the Holy Land. The stark, barren nature of the moon is reflected in the barren badlands of the Wilderness of Judea. The isolation found here provides a place and time to reflect on the purpose of our lives. I can understand why Jesus went into this Wilderness as part of the preparation for the grand ordeal of His life.

Rocks seem to be everywhere—on the moon and in the Holy Land. On the moon, we found the "Genesis Rock"; and in the Holy Land, three of the most magnificent temples in history have been placed on the great rock on Mount Moriah. Only a few men have walked on the mountains of the moon, while many mighty souls have walked upon the heights of the Holy Land, and they are embroidered with the emblems of the most profound history known to man.

The moon is devoid of life in any form. The richest Life on earth was found in the Holy Land. The Son of God came down to visit the spacecraft earth and to impart His plan for our lives. The moon may occasionally cast light on the earth, but the Spirit of Jesus Christ can illuminate all our darkest hours. God has given man the hope and inspiration to "reach out and touch the face of God."

I have now read Dr. Owen's book *The Holy Land* and am much better able to relive my meaningful experiences in that land. I only wish I had had the opportunity of reading this book before I made my trip.

The scriptural injunction is "Go and walk through the land, and describe it," and Dr. Owen has spent a lifetime researching this part of the world and has the talent to give a total picture combining geography, topography, and the rich heritage of its ancient past. The book covers the entire area of the Holy Land 11 —Lebanon, Israel, Jordan, and Syria. It begins, not in Jerusalem, but in the northern city of Ras Shamra. From there you will travel south, going into all sections, sites, and cities of that marvelous land—from Phoenicia to Petra.

I know you will cherish the experience of the Holy Land under the expert guidance of Dr. Owen. I now look forward to another visit because I feel like an expert after reading this book, *The Holy Land.*

—James B. Irwin
Astronaut, Apollo 15

*

The Coastal Plain

*

CHAPTER 1

The Land of Canaan

The land of Canaan!" That is what all Bible readers think of when they think of Palestine in its morning years. And Canaan's land it became when Canaan, the grandson of Noah, came from Babylon about 2900-2800 B.C. and "staked his rights" on the coastal plains north of Mount Carmel. His 11 sons became the progenitors of the people afterwards 14 known as Canaanites.[1]

Sidon, the firstborn son, not only had the honor of having the first Canaanitish city called by his name, but inherited all the originally inhabited coastal strip and ruled over the Sidonians, who later were called Phoenicians.[2] His 10 brothers settled over Palestine and Syria, each taking homesteads wherever it seemed to please his fancy and suit the convenience of all concerned. Wherever they went, they were known as Canaanites, and the entire country became known as "the land of Canaan."

Eight centuries of occupation and expansion had firmly fixed this in every mind when Abraham came this way.[3] For nearly 1,000 years they wrote with Babylonian cuneiform script, then either borrowed or carved characters of their own and formed them into the Phoenician alphabet and passed them on to the world.

The Sidonians planted a string of cities and built highways along the seaside from Mount Carmel in the south to Byblos and Ras Shamra in the north. Fertile but narrow was their coastal strip. The snow-crested mountains shut them in on the east; the Great Sea crowded them on the west. Necessity nudged and opportunity urged. From the sea they caught fish; from the sands they made glass; from the murex shells they extracted dye; and from the worms they obtained silk. The challenge of the sea was accepted when they hewed timbers for their ships, carried cargoes and mails, established commercial relationships with the peoples of the then known world, and courageously sailed the seas until trade became their delight and glory.

The Phoenicians founded proud and prosperous colonies in Carthage, Malta, Sardinia, Tunis, and Spain; then broke out of the Mediterranean and sought their fortunes beyond the Gates of Hercules. The Azores, Madeira, the British Isles, and other faraway shores saw their sails, heard the keen barter of their merchantmen, and recognized them as the most famous mariners of ancient times. But their religion was that of Baal and Ashtaroth (Astarte). To these deities they "made horrible sacrifice of manhood, feminine purity, and child life."[4] Their religion destroyed them. Succeeding generations have admired their genius but revolted against their religion.

15

Some of the chief cities and leading points of interest in Phoenicia are: Ras Shamra (Ugarit), Arvad, Byblos, the Dog River, the Pass of the Conquerors, Beirut, Sidon, Zarephath, the River Leontes or Litany River, Tyre, and the Ladder of Tyre.

Ras Shamra, known in ancient times as *Ugarit,* was a thriving commercial and religious center with its Canaanite beginnings in the Early Bronze period—probably about 2900 B.C. It was located on a hill a half mile from a small harbor and served as a seaport junction between the Mediterranean and the Euphrates. Copper, tin, timber, purple dye, and other riches of the then known world passed through its port for long generations. In the 15th and 14th centuries B.C. it enjoyed unusual prosperity, but about 1350 B.C. it was shocked by an earthquake which devastated the city and port. Afterwards it recovered and enjoyed a measure of prosperity under Hittite and Egyptian influence until about 1200 B.C., when it was invaded from the north and left in ruins.

In modern times it appeared as an attractive mound three-fifths of a mile in diameter and 65 feet in height. In 1828, a Syrian was cultivating his field on top of the mound when his plow struck the roof of a fine-vaulted tomb containing many valuables. This led to 10 carefully directed archaeological campaigns which uncovered temples for worship, schools for learning, a palace with its royal archives, counting houses for commerce, a wealth of materials in storage jars, magnificent vases, many kinds of weights, a pantheon of gods, a pile of 74 well-preserved tools and weapons, and a temple library containing hundreds of clay tablets written during the 15th to 14th centuries B.C. Many of these tablets were written in the conventional cuneiform script, but more than 600 tablets were written with 30 characters or letters which formed an alphabet of the early Semitic language closely related to the Hebrew. Many of the homes were built around an open court and had many rooms, including bathrooms and other sanitary facilities.

Arvad, now called Ruwad, was an ancient Phoenician city, located on a small island two miles off the coast, directly south of Ras Shamra. The Arvadites were descendants of Canaan—close relatives of the people of Tyre, for whom they served as mariners, pilots, and guards (Ezek. 27:8, 11). The city was first mentioned in the Amarna letters of the 14th century B.C. and later appeared engraved on the Assyrian Bronze Gates of Shemaneser III (858-824).

Byblos, 25 miles north of Beirut, was a small settlement as early as 2900 B.C. and was among the first cities developed by the Canaanites. It had a small but adequate harbor. In the Bible it was known as Gebal (Ezek. 27:9). In Phoenician mythology, the nearby castle-crowned rock was where the strikingly handsome Adonis lived and was loved by Astarte, the beautiful goddess of love and fruitfulness. While hunting, Adonis was wounded by a wild boar and perished before Astarte could save him. Here in later years, the Phoenicians and Greeks of the Adonis cult gathered each autumn to mourn with Astarte over the death of her lover, and each spring, when the goddess of fertility prevailed, they met for mystic festivals.

> *Astoreth, whom the Phoenicians called Astarte,*
> *Queen of heaven, with crescent horns;*
> *To whose bright image nightly by the moon*
> *Sidonian virgins paid their vows and song.*

Byblos was the intellectual center of the ancient Phoenician world and was known as the City of Books because the Phoenicians imported crude papyrus from Egypt and refined it into writing materials for documents, accounts, and chronicles. In Greek the word *byblos* meant papyrus, and this city was the intermediary source of their papyrus supply; therefore they called it Byblos. And later through the Latin *biblia* came our word *Bible*—the Book of Books. Thus the papyrus industry at Byblos gave to the world the word *Bible.*

From here, during the 14th century B.C., the governor of Byblos wrote 13 of the Tell El Amarna letters to the ruling Pharaoh of Egypt. Here the medieval Crusaders first tasted sugarcane.

The excavations carried on in the ruins of this ancient city have disclosed some most interesting facts that have to do with the language, religion, commerce, and customs of the people— especially during the 14th to 12th centuries B.C. In the necropolis royal tombs were found containing funeral offerings—of gold, silver, bronze, and alabaster. On the sarcophagus of Ahiram, king

17

of Gebal (1000 B.C.), was an inscription in the earlier form of Hebrew writing, and at other places in the ruins were found inscriptions in the cuneiform and hieroglyphic scripts.

Some miles southward from Byblos, the **Dog River** penetrates a picturesque mountain defile and empties into the beautiful Bay of St. George. The spot teems with historic interest, but the interest centers not in the river itself nor in the valley through which it flows. On the cliffs facing the sea, upon the ragged faces of which have been carved a series of wonderfully fascinating inscriptions, are memorials of "the conquerors of antiquity who

18

High on the cliffs south of the Dog River are a series of carvings and inscriptions, apparently memorials to various conquerors.

have passed this way, and, in passing have stopped to leave the indelible stamp of their achievements."

There are upward of a dozen inscriptions, one or two in Latin and Greek, but the majority commemorating the valor of the Assyrian monarchs, among whom are Shalmaneser II and Tiglath-Pileser III. In a panel cut deep into the rock is the seal and unmistakable hieroglyphic inscription of Rameses II, who passed in his triumphant progress against the Hittites to Kadesh and dedicated tablets to the great gods of Egypt. Singularly enough, beside the finest of Rameses' Egyptian panels, there was added, about 670 B.C., that of the Assyrian King Esar-Haddon in cap and curly beard, who passed in the reverse direction with his Assyrian host to overrun Palestine and enslave Egypt.

The Crusaders, the Saracens, the Turks, the French, and the British have inscribed tablets which tell of their military achievements. Here, side by side, graven upon this towering rock cliff, some of these have "looked out over the same restless sea for almost three millenniums—mid springtime and harvest, dawn and sunset, storm and calm."[5]

What an illustration is here given of the march of the military might of the ages; yet the slow, passing centuries have exacted their due. In many instances, while the general outlines are very apparent, the cuneiform characters of Babylon and the hieroglyphics of the Pharaohs are now scarcely discernible.

Some few miles southwest of the passageway of the conquerors, lifting itself tier upon tier above the Mediterranean Sea, lies the port city of **Beirut** upon which nature has lavished rich gifts. Myriads of fronded palms stand here in their stateliness. Pine, fir, and cedar are reminders of the distant past. Orange, almond, and oleander blossoms waft their fragrance out over the sea, across the colorful landscape, and up the snow-capped Lebanons which serve as a distant, though fitting, background.

On the seaward side the azure bay—resting in its quiet beauty; or tossing its white, billowy, spray like dust into the air; 19 or heaving its great swells to the consternation of landing tourists —completes a picture of irresistible charm for all types and moods of humanity. One contemplates the past with all its grandeur and glory, as well as its wreckage and its ruin.

Beirut was old even among the Phoenicians, being surpassed in age only by Sidon and Byblos. Some think it the Beroth of Samuel and Ezekiel. Alexander the Great captured it from the Phoenicians. The Romans named it Berytus after the daughter of Emperor Augustus. She must have been possessed of exquisite charm and beauty that this place should have reminded them of her.

It is mentioned in the Tell El Amarna tablets of the 15th century. Strabo, Pliny, Ptolemy, and Josephus attest its importance in their time. Under the Romans, Beirut became a mighty military center, the seat of the celebrated school of law, and an outpost of Latin culture in the Greek-speaking and Hellenized Orient. To it students flocked from almost all parts of the known world. Some were said to have passed by Athens and Alexandria to study law at Beirut. It continued as a seat of learning until A.D. 551, when the city was largely leveled by an earthquake, followed by a tidal wave.

In afteryears the city was rebuilt and steadily grew in importance to a position of first place among Syrian and Palestinian cities as a commercial, religious, and educational center. Thousands of young men and women came to study at Beirut's four main universities: Lebanese, French, Jesuit, and American. The last was the largest in the Middle East; in the years immediately preceding the civil war, it had more than 3,000 students from 44 countries and 20 different religious groups. The Syrian Protestant College and many other smaller institutions of learning also have constituted an important factor in the development of the entire Levant.

Cultivated and earnest professors and teachers have devoted themselves with marvelous diligence, ability, and fidelity to the work of educating the young men and women who came here from all areas known as Bible lands. Teachers, ministers, doctors, lawyers, and businessmen are now scattered throughout these eastern Mediterranean countries, and the majority are the products of these splendid institutions of learning. Beirut became recognized as an educational center second to none in the Middle East, and it is hoped that the devastation of the war will not have crippled beyond recovery this monumental facet of this once beautiful city.

Not long ago, Beirut had also become an "oasis of pleasure," with its 86 banks, 15,000 hotel beds, hundreds of dazzling new apartment buildings, along with 500,000 visitors who spent some $50 million each year in Beirut and the surrounding country. That picture has changed drastically and tragically but hopefully not beyond the possibility of recovery.

Leaving the city and going south along the Phoenician Plain, one passes through that fair forest of pines—the famous "snow-bar" which yields some of the world's most delicious pine kernels.

Stretches of red sand which skirt Beirut to the south, lead on to the vast olive garden reputed to be the second largest in the world. Numerous villages, made picturesque by pines, dot the plains or cling to the hillsides. Pastures and grainfields cover the floor of the valley. Millions of leafy mulberry trees, kept to a moderate height, remind one that he has come to the home of the renowned silk industry of Lebanon. But alas! The scientific process by which "silk" is manufactured has all but put the silkworm out of business. Many of the hillsides are carefully terraced and sown with wheat and barley or planted with vines, figs, or mulberry trees.

Passing through a scenic area broken here and there by villages, olive gardens, and orange groves, the road enters the village of *El-Jiya*, where the Mohammedans have a white-domed shrine in honor of the prophet Jonah, whom they say was cast up onto the shore in this vicinity by a whale. From here he is said to have taken the most direct road to Nineveh.

On nearing the city of *Sidon*—20 miles south of Beirut—the plain widens to almost five miles. The city and its environs lie in an almost Edenic setting of green gardens, grain, and orchards, watered by the aid of a great waterwheel slowly turning its 21 ponderous wooden frame, raising its jars from hidden depths, and emptying them in wearisome succession into a small tank.

From here the water is led off to nourish the growths of palms, pomegranates, plums, almonds, bananas, apricots, figs, olives, melons, citrons, pears, peaches, cherries, apples, and oranges.

Beautiful for situation is this mother city of the Phoenicians. Three streams flow into the plain, bringing the elixir of life worth millions. In older times an aqueduct came down from the mountains, bringing an abundant supply of cool, refreshing water from the copious spring known as the Fountain of the Cup. The display of skill evidenced in this ruined water system shows advanced knowledge of engineering in those distant days.

Sidon was one of the older cities of the world, being mentioned both in the Book of Genesis and in the Homeric poems. It was celebrated for its purple-dyed fabrics, its silverware, its manufacture of glass, and its shipbuilding industry. In Solomon's time there was none that had "the skill to hew timbers like the Sidonians."[6] They assisted Solomon in his preparations for the building of the Temple. They also brought cedar trees from Lebanon to the sea and sent them on rafts to Joppa for the building of both Solomon's and Herod's temples.

Homer extols the purple-dyed garments woven by the Sidonian women, and praises the silver and metal work as famous beyond all others of the kind in the world.[7] These luxuries were used by the rich of Europe, Asia, and Africa.

According to Strabo, Sidon early achieved fame because of its proficiency in philosophy, science, and art—but especially in astronomy. For wealth, commerce, luxury, vice, and power it was unequalled in the Levant until Tyre outstripped it, and Shalmaneser conquered it in 725 B.C.

Paul came by Sidon when on his way to Rome and was allowed "liberty to go unto his friends" there and to eat and drink with them.[8] During the two centuries of the Crusades, Sidon was in the hands of the Christians several times, once for 25 years, but in A.D. 1291, it passed into the hands of the Mohammedans.

22   Archaeologists have unearthed a remarkable sepulchre near here containing a number of exquisitely carved marble sarcophagi. They are believed to belong to some of Alexander's

high military officials who fell in the Battle of Issus and the Siege of Tyre. One especially fine sarcophagus is thought by some to have belonged to Alexander himself. It is now displayed in the Constantinople Museum as the "sarcophagus of Alexander the Great."

Successive waves of conquest have swept away almost all signs of the ancient city. "Sidon the Great," as it was called by Joshua, has long since been spoiled. Only the ruins of the fine old 13th-century castle of Louis in the upper portion of the town, a few columns, broken statues, sarcophagi, and smaller bits of architectural remains attest the city's former fame. Encircled by the sea and standing on a rock a little way from the mainland are the ruins of a 12th-century fortress, *Qal-at-el Bahr,* which can be reached only by a narrow bridge of stone.

The Sidon of a few decades ago was so poorly maintained that travelers frequently spoke of it as the place where the "king of fleas" held world court. But conditions have steadily improved until Sidon (Saida) is now a growing town where some 40,000 people carry on various forms of light industry and cultivate extensive gardens and orchards which produce vast quantities of fruits and vegetables. Considerable credit is due Gerald Institute, a unit of the Syrian Protestant Mission; two American high schools; and Dr. Shabb's excellent, 24-bed hospital—all founded under Christian and American auspices.

Along the old Roman thoroughfare, eight miles south of Sidon, is **Zarephath** or **Sarepta.** Zarephath means "Melting Houses," which indicates it as a place of furnaces—a chief center for the far-famed glassworks of ancient Phoenicia. Its greatness, however, lies in the noble lesson of faith taught by the plain, rugged prophet Elijah and the obedient, generous-hearted widow. Here in an atmosphere rank with Baalism, the Lord, through Elijah, multiplied the barrel of meal and the cruse of oil, neither of which failed for a full year; and here the prophet raised the widow's son to life. Oh, what divine loftiness alongside low, groveling, licentious Baalism!

23

God might have sent Elijah to be entertained by one of the glass magnates or a wealthy merchant of Zarephath, but why should the Almighty do rash things? Their smug smartness would have caused them to reveal the secret and fail to receive the honor of feeding and concealing the plain preacher, thus spoiling God's plan. What blessing and renown they missed! What fame the widow received! And, a lesson of obedient faith she taught the more sophisticated world.

Sarepta (Zarephath) is located on a promontory within a small but attractive plain close to the shore. Its ruins are scattered over the plain at intervals for more than a mile. A rather flourishing city it must have been in its glory days. But now its human habitation has all gone. A new village called Serepta lies two miles inland under the shelter of the hills. Kind nature spreads its mantle over the environs of the old site. Its crops, its flocks, and its flowers give it a pastoral scene of beauty and restfulness that impress the many who pass this way.

The way now becomes sacred ground, consecrated not only by the touching visit of the great prophet of Israel "unto a woman that was a widow," but still more by the footprints of One greater than Elijah, who came into the Gentile region of the coasts of Tyre and Sidon and awakened in the Phoenician mother that instance of noble and persistent faith. "Have mercy upon me, O Lord, and heal my child," her plea continued, until her body, like a filthy rag, was humbly thrown at His feet, while her brown, fevered lips uttered that effective plea, "Lord, help me."

On being advised of her lowly station, she gave ready assent, yet in her persistence made the most humble plea ever recorded: "The dogs eat of the crumbs which fall from the master's table." Christ's immediate commendation and verdict was, "O woman, great is thy faith: be it unto thee even as thou wilt."[9] Her plea was granted; her child was saved. With what emotion one reads of this Syrophoenician woman and of the great multitudes from Tyre and Sidon who followed Him. Only eternity will reveal the enduring results of that divine visit to Phoenicia!

The landscape holds one's interest with irresistible force as you proceed southward. On the right hand are the deep blue waters of the Mediterranean, while the left is bounded by the majestic Lebanon Range "crested by *Jebel Sunnin* with its whitened crown." Patches of barley and wheat green the landscape. Halfway between Zarephath and Tyre the **Leontes** or **Litani** River empties into the sea. It is the finest river in all Phoenicia but is little utilized, except in its upper reaches where only a small portion of water is taken from it as it flows southward from Baalbek through the fertile Valley of Beka'a, between the Lebanon and Anti-Lebanon ranges.

The main street of ancient Tyre

It is with mingled emotions that one looks upon **Tyre,** the "crowning city situated at the entry of the sea." Being founded by a colony from the city of Sidon, this proud imperial mistress of the commerce of the then known world was called "The daughter of Sidon . . . whose antiquity is of ancient days."[10] The murex shell, from which they extracted the world's most famous dye, was found here in abundance in ancient times, and so great was the production and sale of the royal dye that it is usually thought of at the mention of Tyre.

25

Who has not heard how Tyrian shells
Enclosed the blue, that dye of dyes
Whereof one drop worked miracles,
And colored like Astarte's eye
Raw silk the merchant sells?

In Joshua's day it was "the strong city."[11] During the days of
David and Solomon, Tyre enjoyed the time of her greatest power
under Hiram, whose wisdom and sagacity "enhanced her reputation as a powerful commercial center and as a good and peaceful
neighbor." Hiram not only made a league of mutual friendship
and assistance with David, but established splendid trade relations between Tyre and Israel. He furnished both material and
men for the construction of Solomon's Temple at Jerusalem, and
every three years Hiram's and Solomon's fleets sailed together to
foreign lands and returned with "gold and silver, ivory, apes, and
peacocks." In Ahab's day there was no belle that suited him for a
wife like Jezebel, the daughter of the king of Tyre.

One of the later kings of Tyre, Pygmalion, gave his sister
Elissa or Dido in marriage to a priest of Astarte. The priest attempted to usurp the throne but lost his life. His widow and a
party of sympathizers fled by sea to the north coast of Africa,
where they bargained for land and founded the city of Carthage,
famous in the Punic Wars and in the period of the Early Church.

The situation of Tyre seemed, in many respects, the most
ideal in all the ancient Levant. A small island largely composed
of rock, about three-quarters of a mile from the mainland, not
only gave the city its name—"the rock"[12]—but made possible a
port and a place of refuge such as were denied other ports in
much of this eastern Mediterranean world.

The original Tyre was built on the mainland, but New Tyre
soon raised its proud and defiant ramparts on the island. The
builders made use of limestone from nearby quarries, cedars
from the Lebanon mountains, red and gray granite from Egypt,
ivory from Chittim, and "every precious stone gathered from
afar." The best engineering and architectural skill of the day
made of it a city of strong walls and high towers, and a thing "of
perfect beauty."[13]

26

A dip in the rocks from the hills enabled the engineers to send a vigorous subterranean streamlet under the sea to the rock island, where it was brought to the surface and furnished a never-failing supply of cool, refreshing water, in time of both peace and war. The island city was never troubled by want of water and therefore could withstand the longest and most severe sieges.

From its position, Tyre outstripped Sidon, its parent city, and became the mart of nations and a "merchant of the people for many isles." Its ships were among the most beautiful ever seen in the blue waters of the Mediterranean. The boards were of fir, the masts of the cedars of Lebanon, the oars of the oaks of Bashan, the decks of ivory, and the sails were of the costly blue and purple linens of Egypt and the isles of the sea. Many of their mariners were renowned for their knowledge of sails and the sea, some were scientists and philosophers, others were soldiers. Above all they were tradesmen and merchants of the first rank.

With various foreign lands they trafficked in slaves, horses, mules, sheep, goats, apes, peacocks, gold, silver, ivory, ebony, tin, lead, acacia wood, purple-dyed fabrics, and cedar chests in which to place them; also wheat, barley, oil, honey, precious spices, balm, wine, and wool.[14] So famous did the merchant city of Tyre become and so glorious, that seafaring men of other countries joined her marine and became her men of war. She became "the renowned city, which was strong in the sea"—a perennial "world's fair" into which came the merchandise of the then known world.

The greatness of their riches, the volume of their merchandise, the beauty of their city, and the keenness of their wisdom caused the heart of her king to be lifted up in pride. He said, "I sit in the seat of God in the midst of the seas." And as it was with the prince, so with the people. In their pride, in their loftiness, they became jealous of God's chosen people, they rejoiced at Hebrew adversity. With Jerusalem's fall, Tyre burst forth in a song of exultation: "Aha! She is broken that was the gate of the people, her traffic and her wealth are turned to me. I shall be replenished now she is laid waste."[15]

The merchants of Tyre even purchased Hebrew captives and

sold them as slaves. These insults sealed her doom with God. Their proud, haughty spirit only presaged their fall. Ezekiel prophesied that Tyre was to be fought against, decline, and be destroyed.

In keeping with this prophecy came Shalmaneser III, king of Assyria, in 725 B.C., and besieged Samaria, then came up to Tyre and destroyed its mainland; but even with five years' effort was unable to crush the island city. Following this unsuccessful siege, the people rebuilt all that Shalmaneser had destroyed and enjoyed prosperity for 150 years.

Then came Nebuchadnezzar, king of Babylon, in the year 571 B.C., with a vast army well supplied with horses, "engines of war," and with ships. Mighty was that army that strove year after year for 13 years. The mainland city went down, and many maidens and men were taken, and "every head was made bald and every shoulder was peeled." The siege was exceedingly severe, yet out on the fortified rock the flag of Tyre waved proudly to the end. Tyre was humbled, but Nebuchadnezzar gained not the "crowning city . . . for the service that he had served against it."[16]

Under the Persians, who succeeded the Babylonians, the glory of Tyre "was sadly dimmed." Then, in 332 B.C., the city was besieged by Alexander the Great. With comparative ease he took charge of Tyre on the mainland, but the inhabitants retired to the island stronghold, and having command of the sea, defied all the efforts to take their city. Surrounded by mighty walls and with ramparts fronting the mainland to a height of 150 feet, withdrawn from the shore, the task seemed no small one even for Alexander.

A general of the land, Alexander, began the stupendous task of filling up the channel between the island city and the mainland. In this he employed the materials which had made up the mainland city, and in so doing, the prophecy of Ezekiel was fulfilled: "They shall lay thy stones and thy timber and thy dust in the midst of the water."[17] The site of the old city was left bare, yet the causeway was not entirely completed.

A storm destroyed much of the causeway. The forces of nature seemed to fight against the famous conqueror, but he pushed the work with even greater vigor. Immense quantities of trees were used in the new structure, but opposing Tyrian divers swam out and attached grappling hooks with which the defenders then pulled them away into deep water. Fireships were floated against the wooden causeway, and when they crept up near, the defenders poured molten lead and red-hot sand upon Alexander's men. But alas, despite all setbacks, the causeway was finished and Alexander's legions ascended towers and scaling ladders and poured into the place where no other soldiers had been able to enter. A few of the inhabitants escaped by boat, but immense numbers were massacred, 2,000 were crucified or hanged on the seashore, and 30,000 were led away captive and sold as slaves. Fuller says that Alexander's armies "which did fly into other countries were glad to creep into this city."

Rising again from its wreck and ruin, the city staggered to a respectable position but never again enjoyed the prominence it once held. Christ considered it a city of the past. Many people did live here, however, some of which heard Christ and became His followers. Paul, when on his way from Ephesus to Jerusalem, tarried here seven days; and when he departed, the Christians accompanied him until they were out of the city; then, after a prayer on the seashore, they returned home while Paul went on to Jerusalem where he should be bound.[18]

The Moslems took the place during the 7th century; the Crusaders wrested it from them during the 12th; and it remained in their hands for more than a century and a half. When the Crusaders lost Palestine, Tyre was among the last strongholds to be surrendered; but when they saw they were losing all, they had prayers and left the city "without the stroke of a sword, without the tumult of war," and embarking in their vessels, abandoned the city to be occupied by their conquerors. On the morrow the Saracens entered, "no one attempting to prevent them, and they did what they pleased." The fortifications were razed to the ground, and from this blow Tyre has never recovered.

Approaching Tyre today, one will find a small, poorly arranged town located, for the most part, on the sands covering the mole or causeway built from the mainland by Alexander. The inhabitants are chiefly fishermen who make the rocks and sands "a place for the spreading of nets." The crowning city, with "heaped up silver as the dust, and fine gold as the mire of the streets," is all changed now. Her walls are destroyed; her towers are broken down. Her markets and her merchandise, and her stately ships, with masts of cedars from Lebanon, benches of ivory, and sails of blue and purple from the isles of Elishah, are no more.

Only shafts of gray and red granite columns, capitals of many kinds of marble, and fragments from the buildings of many generations protrude from the debris, lie in the water, or are buried in confusion. Three cities of the Crusaders lie beneath several feet of debris; below this is what remains of Mohammedan and early Christian Tyre. The Tyre of the Phoenicians and early Canaanites lies below these ruins.

The glory of Tyre thus departed. The prophetic voice has been verified: "I will cause the noise of thy songs to cease; and the sound of thy harps shall be no more heard. And I will make thee like the top of a rock: thou shalt be a place to spread nets upon: for I the Lord have spoken it, saith the Lord God."[19]

> Now on that shore, a lonely guest,
> Some dripping fisherman may rest,
> Watching on rock or naked stone
> His dark net spread before the sun,
> Unconscious of the dooming lay
> That broods o'er that dull spot, and there
> Shall brood for aye.

In the neighborhood of Kanah, a village just a few miles southeast of Tyre, there is a large Phoenician sepulchral monument known as the Tomb of Hiram, King of Tyre.

The pedestal of the tomb is made of three layers of grey limestone, each three feet thick, the top stone extending slightly beyond the other two. The tomb or sarcophagus which rests upon the pedestal is 12 feet long, 6 feet wide, and 6 feet high, and is made of a single block of stone. A heavy lid, which consists of one solid block three feet thick, rests upon the sarcophagus. A large hole in the eastern end of the tomb indicates that vandals have broken into it, probably to secure the royal jewels and precious stones that were interred with the body. Here is the way they entombed Hiram, king of Tyre.

Ras el Nakoura, or "The Ladder of Tyre." Some few miles south of the site of the ancient city the rough hills crowd the sea in bold cliffs, thus forming the natural boundary between modern Lebanon and Israel. Once the steplike passage across these steep, jagged rocks overhanging the sea gave name to the place. Conquerors have marched their men and pulled their chariots and war machines across the Ladder, and travelers have dreaded the crossing; but today one passes on a well-surveyed road which robs it of its old-time dangers. You ascend on the Syrian side and descend into the beautiful Plain of Acre, on the Israeli side.

CHAPTER **2**

The Beautiful Plain of Acre

At *Ras el Nakoura*, one
reaches the border line between Lebanon and modern Israel.
Soon after leaving the custom house and the border patrol station, you enter the Plain of Acre which sweeps southward for
some 20 miles until Mount Carmel lies athwart the way.

The Plain of Acre derives its name from the ancient and
32   picturesque city of Acre. Being 20 miles in length, and having an
average width of about 5 miles, the entire area comprises some
60,000 acres. Its eastern boundary is formed by the foothills of

the Galilean mountains, its western boundary by the Mediterranean Sea and the beautiful crescent-shaped shoreline of the Bay.

Out across the plain eastward, many springs and two rivers leap from the Galilean hills, or enter from the far-famed plain of Armageddon. The once famous *Belus River,* now known as *Nahr Naman,* is about 3 feet deep and 100 feet wide. It rises in the upland region north of Nazareth, meanders across the north central portion of the plain, drives a number of mills, and finally flows into the bay a few hundred feet south of Acre.

Entering in from the Plain of Armageddon through the pass at *Tell el Kassis* is the *Kishon,* "that ancient river" which runs close by the foot of Carmel, then breaks away for the last two miles and leisurely enters the bay just northeast of Haifa.

The volume of these streams varies with the wet or dry seasons, yet they are always augmented by living springs which rise from the nearby hills. Other splendid springs have, through the recent centuries, been permitted to run uncontrolled over the plain and create unhealthy marshland. Reeds and rushes, thorns and thistles, wild flowers, shrubs, and a few date palms have encumbered the ground and made it famous for its beauty, its fertility, and its longtime idleness.

Between the bay and the plain a broad belt of yellow sand forms a smooth beach, which for centuries has constituted a hard and firm roadway over which kings and conquerors have often led their armies, and pilgrims have trudged on toward the fulfillment of their sacred ambitions.

The history of the Plain of Acre dates back to the earliest Canaanitish settlements on the shore of the Mediterranean. Following the Hebrew Conquest, many of those fertile acres were assigned to the tribe of Zebulun. "Zebulun shall dwell at the shore of the sea, and he shall be a shore for ships."[1]

In a larger sense, however, it may be said that the plain lay within the territory of Asher. Perhaps there was too much of the trader instinct in the seacoast tribesmen and too little of the tiller of the soil, for the people of Zebulun and Asher dwelt among

33

the Canaanites and apparently made little use of these fertile farmlands.

The Phoenicians recognized many things of value about the plain and put it to fair use. Their principal industries were the making of purple dye from the murex shells, and the manufacture of glass from the white sands found in such great abundance along the beach of the Bay of Acre. Pliny, the historian who wrote about A.D. 60, says that the Phoenicians discovered the value of these sands for glassmaking when a merchant ship landed near the mouth of the river Belus.

The ship's cargo consisted of natron, a natural alkaline crystal, usually called saltpeter, found in Egypt. When the crew lighted a fire, they used lumps of natron from the cargo to prop up their kettle. What was their surprise to find afterwards a stream of crystal running from their campfire! The heat acting on the natron and on the sand had caused them to fuse and form glass.[2] This, however, could not have been more than the beginning of the glass industry among the Phoenicians, for the art of making glass was well known in Egypt from much earlier times. But the industry grew to large proportions and was widely used by the Phoenicians as shown by the large quantities of beautiful glassware found in excavations, and wherever Phoenician tombs have been opened. Acre was probably a principal center for the industry, as debris from the glass furnaces is frequently found about the city, particularly in the wadies between Acre and *Kafr Yasif.*

During the Maccabean Wars of the second century before Christ, the Maccabean leaders and the kings of Syria had various encounters on this plain. Paul passed this way as he went to Jerusalem in A.D. 60.[3]

During the Middle Ages vast numbers of pilgrims came this way. In 1163, Benjamin of Tudela visited Acre, where he found nearly 200 Jews. In Haifa he found Jewish tombs but no Jews. On the plain he found no Jews, no tombs, and few signs of life at all.

34 The plain often played a large part in romantic war episodes of men of the Cross. In 1192, Richard the Lion-hearted encamped on the plain in the well-known palm grove where he contracted

a malarial fever which detained him four weeks and gave rise to reports of his death.

During the four centuries of Turkish rule in Palestine (1517-1917), Omar Zahar and Ahmed Pasha el Jezzar made themselves famous as rulers in this area. The latter developed the plain, brought water to Acre by means of a very fine aqueduct, constructed the great White Mosque, built an enduring Turkish bath and the splendid White Market, and became responsible for strengthening of the massive stone fortifications and port facilities, much of which stand today as a mute testimony to the enduring quality of his work and that of the Crusaders.

Napoleon Bonaparte fought on this plain in the year 1798, but he and his 13,000 men faced failure and left these plains in the hands of Ahmed Pasha el Jezzar, who died in 1802 and was buried in the great mosque of Acre. When the British assumed control in 1918, the plain was unoccupied save for those who lived in Haifa and Acre and small groups of malaria-stricken Bedouin, with a few *fellahin.*

In 1881, Menahem Ussishkin visited Palestine and dreamed of a day when Jewish people would purchase the lands constituting the Plain of Acre. The lands, he said, should receive back the biblical name—*Emek Zebulun*—according to Gen. 49:13. He was annoyed by the Germans in Haifa who told him Jews could not work the land! He felt they should at least have a chance to try.

Theodor Herzl, the father of modern Zionism, envisioned a day when great ships would lay anchored in the roadstead between Acre and the foot of Carmel. Cupolas, minarets, and grey old castle walls would outline in delightful Oriental silhouettes against the morning skies. The gracefully crescent-shaped bay would be unchanged. But to the south there would be thousands of white villas in green gardens. The whole area from Acre to Carmel would be one great park. The summit of Carmel, too, would be crowned with beautiful homes. A magnificent city would be built beside the sapphire blue Mediterranean. The 35 massive stone which went into the construction of the harbor would make it the safest and most convenient port in the eastern

Mediterranean. Every kind of craft, flying the flags of all nations, would lie sheltered there.

When the late Sir 'Abbas Effendi 'Abdu'l Baha stood on Mount Carmel on February 14, 1914, and looked across the Plain of Acre, he said:

> In the future the distance between Acre and Haifa will be built up and the two cities will join and clasp hands becoming the two terminal sections of one mighty metropolis. As I look now over this scene, I see so clearly that it will become one of the first emporiums of the world. This great semicircular bay will be transformed into the finest harbor, wherein the ships of all nations will seek shelter and refuge. The great vessels of all peoples will come to this port, bringing on their decks thousands and thousands of men and women from every part of the world. The mountain and the plain will be dotted with the most modern buildings and palaces. Industries will be established and various institutions of a philanthropic nature will be founded. The flowers of civilization and culture from all nations will be brought here to blend their fragrances together and blaze the way for the brotherhood of man. Wonderful gardens, orchards, groves, and parks will be lighted by electricity. The entire harbor from Acre to Haifa will be one path of illumination. Powerful searchlights will be placed on both sides of Mount Carmel to guide the steamers. Mount Carmel itself, from top to bottom, will be submerged in a sea of lights. A person standing on the summit of Mount Carmel, and the passengers of the steamers coming to it, will look upon the most sublime and majestic spectacle of the whole world.[4]

As a first step toward reclaiming this unusual plain, the government set aside a large acreage in the well-drained area northeast of Acre, where they established a very large and up-to-date experiment station for the encouragement of agriculture, horticulture, and animal husbandry. The very finest breeds of horses, mules, cattle, hogs, sheep, goats, turkeys, chickens, and ducks are kept and cared for along scientific lines for the express purpose of lending every encouragement possible to the people of the country who will accept any help toward improving their herds, their poultry, their fruits, and the grain of their fields.

36

During the years in which this experiment station has been in operation, they have proved that bananas, dates, oranges, olives, almonds, grapes, figs, and loquats are well adapted to this section. Both large and small grains and a great number of vegetables thrive on the plain, some of which may be produced for export.

The outstanding move, however, to reclaim the Plain of Acre had its beginning in 1925 when the Haifa Bay Development Company purchased 11,750 acres of this land between Acre and Haifa, and in 1928 resold it to the Jewish National Fund and the Palestine Economic Corporation. It was to be held for the Jews for all time and there was to be no speculation.

The Jews named it Emek Zebulun in conformity with the biblical dictum, "Zebulun shall dwell at the haven of the sea."[5] They took upon themselves the heroic task of reclaiming the plain. This required courage and skill, seeing much of the area was little more than "an oasis of scrub in a wilderness of malaria," a place where millions of mosquitoes carry death as they wing their way across the plain.

Bronzed young Jews, with pickaxe, spade, and dredging machine, dug channels, lined them with concrete, and forced the waters to obey the orders of engineers. Thus the swamps and marshy wastes were drained, death-bearing mosquitoes were destroyed, and the plain leveled and rendered healthy and habitable.

They then employed Prof. Patrie Abercrombie of Liverpool University, who mapped the entire area, surveyed a road across the plain, and divided the land into three zones. Nearest to Haifa was the industrial zone of 4,000 acres, which included about one-third the area. Here they constructed a variety of plants, including oil refineries; steel, concrete, chemical, and glass works; foundries; railway and machine shops; flour mills; woolen mills; canneries; and many other manufacturing and industrial concerns.

The second area was given over as a residential zone where, far from the maddening crowd and away from the noise and bustle of the busy city, the tired worker might occupy his own home in the workers' suburb, while next to him was a settlement for a "middle class," and on beyond was a settlement for the

German Jewish families. Beyond the residential zone is located the agricultural land from which come a rich variety of fruits, vegetables, and dairy produce for the town and residential neighborhoods.

A strip of green trees lies between the industrial and residential zones. This serves as a park, stretching for more than a mile, accomplishing much toward keeping out the smoke and smell of industry from the homes as well as providing a place of rest and quiet when the day's work is done. A splendid drainage system has been completed, the scourge of malaria has fled, the sand hummocks near the sea are being utilized, and practically all of the plain is reclaimed and presents a most charming spot.

The plain, as it now appears in its springtime freshness and buoyancy, presents a *partial* fulfillment of the dreams cherished by the Jews, the Persians, the Frenchmen, and other farsighted world leaders.

When seen from Mount Carmel, there is the highly industrialized area with its hum of economic activity; the pleasant residential sections with their groves of lofty cypress; the rich orchards; the fresh streams; the long reach of perfectly level beach, with men and animals and machines diminishing in the distance; and the broad bay, with its boats and ships, opening out upon the boundless sea. All these combine to excite the mind, enliven the scene, and impress one with the pathos of prophecy.

When out on the higher, less-developed portions of the plain, one feels an irresistible fascination in the enjoyment of a wild beauty spread far and near. Here and there are somewhat broken low ridges, as if to show that nature loves variety. In the springtime there are patches of wheat and barley; then thick bush, arbutus, and wild flowers of the most exquisite red, blue, and yellow spring up in rich luxuriance among the emerald carpet. Along the eastern border are a number of native villages, both in the plain itself and on the slopes of the hills. Thus there meet on this beautiful plain the ancient and the modern—the intriguing past, and the prospect of the future luring man on to a nobler place to live and love and labor.

The three better-known cities of the plain are: Achzib, Acre,

38

and Haifa. **Achzib,** now known as *Es Zib,* is an ancient Phoenician port which crowds the shoreline north of Acre. Twice mentioned in the Bible, this town was regarded as the northern limit of the Holy Land after the return from the Babylonian Captivity. Today it is a native village with little order and less ostentation. Nearby is a thriving Jewish colony.

The ancient city of **Acre,** sometimes called *Acco,* occupies the northern promontory of the Bay of Acre. When viewed from a distance, it is the most picturesque city of Palestine. Historical associations carry its story back to the days before the children of Israel were in Palestine. It is listed on the Egyptian monuments as one of the towns that Thotmes III conquered when he made his famous and exceedingly successful campaign against the Canaanites just after 1500 B.C. Later it was mentioned in the Tel el Amarna letters. And Sennacherib enumerates it among the Phoenician towns he took in 702 B.C.

Acre, along with its surrounding plain, was allotted to the tribe of Asher, but the Israelites were unable to drive out the inhabitants of the place. It never fell to the Jews until during the Maccabean Wars. It was at Acre where Jonathan Maccabaeus met his enemy, Trypho, for an interview, was made a prisoner, and his bodyguard of 1,000 men was massacred, and Jonathan himself was later put to death.[5]

When Pompey invaded Palestine, he made it, along with several other coast towns, a free Greek city-state. Paul refers to his stay in the city of Acre on his way from Damascus to Jerusalem. During the years from A.D. 67 to 70 Vespasian and Titus used Acre as a port of landing and an important military section in their campaign against Galilee and Judea. Josephus mentions the city many times, for it was in nearby Jotapata that he lived and was eventually taken captive by the Romans. Al Harira, a famous Arab poet of about A.D. 1100, praised Acre as "a pleasant meetingplace of the ship and the camel, where lizards may watch the leaping sea-fish, where the camel-driver communes with the sailor, and the fisherman astonishes the tiller of the soil with stories of the sea."

The Crusaders made of it their chief port of invasion and

principal base of supplies. Here they fought some of their fiercest battles and eventually suffered one of their saddest defeats. For it was near here that Khalil, the Mameluke Sultan, who reigned in Cairo, swore by the name of Allah in 1291 that he would exterminate the last of the Christians within the limits of his dominions. Gathering an army of 200,000 men, he pitched his camp before the walls of Acre. The Christian forces defending the city were sufficient in size, but division of counsel, confusion, and feverish excitement so enfeebled their efforts and weakened their wills that they turned to the sea for escape.

Thousands gathered their few belongings and hastened to

The fortified seawall of Acre (ancient Acco)

the wharf where they embarked. Only 12,000 knights and warriors were left to defend the stronghold. These held out for 33 days until the Mameluke warriors effected a breach in the walls and began to pour into the city. The inhabitants left in the city were quickly butchered or seized as slaves. The knights fought until there were only seven left to tell the tale of destruction. Thus the fate of the Crusader Kingdom was sealed with the final fall of Acre.

The present city covers an area of 50 acres and is surrounded by walls and fortifications which date from 1750 to 1840 but are for the most part built on Crusader foundations. The only entrance is through the Tower Gate to the southeast.

The strong seawall along the south front of the city is built of very large stones, many of which bear the marks of the Crusaders. The bold western seafront with its loopholed battlemented walls is strong, long, and impressive. Both the north and the east walls have a double line of fortifications and are surrounded by a moat. Places of interest to be seen inside the city are: the Crypt of the Church of St. John (13th century), the Great Mosque of Jezzar Pasha, and the arsenal containing large stones of early 19th-century munitions of war.

A beautiful white marble gateway, novel in style, stood before one of the Crusader churches in Acre. But after a siege of one month, in A.D. 1291, Sultan Khalil of Egypt stormed Acre and carried the gate away to Cairo, Egypt, where it now spans one of the main thoroughfares of that city. The gateway is especially interesting, seeing it is the only perfect relic now left of the many churches built by the Crusaders at Acre.

The external appearance of Acre today is "preeminently picturesque" when viewed from Mount Carmel across the bay, from the deck of a ship, or on a calm, bright, moonlight night when God's lanterns are in the sky.

One mile east of Acre is "Mount Turon," an artificial mound 96 feet high, which dominates the city of Acre and overlooks the plain. Here the great Crusader, Richard the Lion-hearted, encamped in 1191, and here Napoleon planted his batteries in vain in 1799.

Looking across the city of Haifa and its beautiful harbor from the slopes of Mount Carmel.

Haifa, "The Gateway to Israel and the Middle East," is situated between Mount Carmel and the southern end of the Bay of Acre, and not far from where the ancient river Kishon merges into the bay.

Its situation, from a commercial point of view, is the most ideal of all cities in Palestine or Syria. It has before it the most beautiful bay in eastern Mediterranean countries; to its rear is the magnificent Mount Carmel range which juts far out into the sea, forming the best natural breakwater of the entire Levant. Nearby is the fertile Plain of Acre extending away to the foothills where an unlimited supply of fruits and vegetables may be produced.

Many have marveled that the ancients constructed no large city here to accommodate their imports and exports. But such seems to be the case, for there is no certainty that either the Canaanites or the Hebrews had any kind of a city at this exact location. The Greeks and Romans had a small place called Sycaminum (Sycamore) somewhere in this area. The Crusaders, under Tancred, besieged and stormed a comparatively small town here in A.D. 1100. Eighty-seven years later it fell into the hands of Saladin,

42

but was afterwards assaulted and destroyed by Richard the Lion-hearted. Traces of these ruins remain to the present time in the excavated mound of ancient Shikmona.

The present city, however, owes its origin to Omar Zahar, the leader of a strong Bedouin group, who, in 1761, established his seat of government at Acre. Marching his army along the curvature of the bay, he attacked and destroyed a small rebellious town situated just below the northwest point of Mount Carmel, and transported the survivors to the present location, where he built a castle and surrounded the town with a wall. The gates and portions of the old wall stand today, and in this section there are native bazaars conducted in real Oriental style.

The city of Haifa made phenomenal progress during the British occupation from 1918 to 1947. Seeing its possibilities as a commercial city for imports and exports, the British made soundings in the bay and decided on Haifa as the deepwater port of Palestine.

In 1927, the contract for a very fine harbor was let to Messrs. Rendel, Palmer, and Tritton for a consideration of £1 million sterling (then U.S. $5 million). After further surveys and an elaboration of plans, one-quarter of a million pounds was added to the original contract price. The first steps toward building the port were taken in 1929, when the engineers opened the stone quarries near Athlit, the Crusader stronghold south of Mount Carmel. The work was fairly well completed in 1933, but has since been extended so as to provide quay space for more ships.

The main breakwater of the harbor is about a mile and a half long. The cost of this breakwater was the largest item of the project. It is formed of natural blocks of quarried stone, graded according to size, the largest weighing some 12-15 tons, being placed on the seaward side. It contains more than 1 million cubic yards of stone and is surmounted by a concrete parapet, with ballards at intervals for end-on moorings for cargo steamers. The other breakwater, known as the lee breakwater, is formed by prolonging the existing railway jetty, and is about half a mile long. It is of less massive structure than the main breakwater. In all, the breakwaters total nearly two miles in length and inclose an area of nearly 300 acres of sheltered water, within which a score of steamers, up to 30,000 tons, can lie at moorings.

A deepwater berth about 1,400 feet long, to accommodate three or four large steamers, was provided, and at the eastern end an oil dock was formed to accommodate the famous Iraq Petroleum Company and other large oil concerns. The port has ample rail and road access, and a site is reserved for a maritime station, which, in time, is to act as the terminal for the proposed Haifa-Baghdad railway. Huge transit sheds allow orange growers to load and unload in stormy weather with little risk to their wares.

The sands dredged from the harbor were placed between the city and the harbor, thus forming a considerable area of newly made land. This was arranged according to modern methods of town planning, and in time the wide streets were lined with some of the world's most beautiful and most modern commercial buildings. Thus traffic was relieved in the congested streets and alleys of the old city, more spacious shopping and social centers were provided, and a new and striking appearance given the city of Haifa. As Israel's northern metropolis, Haifa is now the largest in area and second largest in population.

To enter this beautiful Holy Land harbor, in the eventide of a spring day after a long voyage, one is half encircled by the yellow and white sands of the crescent-shaped bay and sees Mount Carmel like a sentinel on guard keeping watch above the hush of the waves. He feels the soft winds of this congenial clime and is overwhelmed with the consciousness of having come to a pleasant port.

CHAPTER 3

The Excellency of Carmel

Jutting out into the Great Sea and lying between the Plain of Acre and the Plain of Sharon is a long, bold promontory known as Mount Carmel. In naming it Carmel, the ancients regarded it as "The Park," or "The Garden of the Lord." Its excellency was proclaimed in story and in song.

Carmel runs inland from the sea 15 miles and is from 3 to 8 miles wide. At its extreme northwestern point, which extends out into the sea, it is 500 feet high; and about a mile and a half due south of Esfiya, 10 miles away to the southeast, it reaches its high-

45

est point of 1,810 feet. From there it gradually falls away to the Plain of Armageddon.

Its general shape is that of a triangle with its apex pointing northwest, but this is seldom noticed, seeing the important portions of the mountain appear as a long, rugged ridge oriented northwest to southeast. Its massiveness reminds one of a huge, houndlike creature which, having crossed the great Plain of Armageddon, has lain down beside the Kishon "with a firm foothold upon the sea."[1] But this creature impression is gained only from its general form when one views it from afar. At close range it pleases and fascinates.

A high road runs along its central watershed, and from this extend fairly long parallel spurs, divided in places by narrow, winding valleys. All along the top of this rugged ridge one finds outcroppings of a thin layer of chalky limestone overlaid by a thin layer of soil, studded here and there with stunted pine and scattered flowering bush. Farther down the mountainsides one finds hard, gray limestone, covered for the most part by a rich, red soil which is remarkably productive. Here grow a few large oaks—reminders of its ancient glory. Anxious to preserve these, the government has set aside this area as the Haifa-Carmel National Park.

In ancient times the royal vineyards of King Uzziah were located on Mount Carmel, and it was used for the production of fruits and flowers for various purposes. Throughout the Old Testament, Carmel stood as a symbol of vast productiveness and quiet, fixed beauty enveloped in an atmosphere of refined sacredness. It received unstinted praise, and its beauty and usefulness were far famed.

Along with Sharon, Lebanon, Tabor, and Bashan, it was regarded as reflecting the favor of the Lord. Of all the praise given, it was quite deserving; for it alone, of all mountains of the Levant, extended far into the sea and formed a natural, crescentlike bay which was one of the finest and most beautiful known to man.

46 Carmel was the first of Israel's highlands to receive the moisture that came from the Mediterranean Sea, and its dews were usually quite heavy throughout the summer months. Therefore

in Israel's glory days it was clothed with grand forests, vast olive orchards, productive vineyards, flowering shrubs, and myriads of wild flowers.

Much of its grace and parklike beauty passed when men of various wars and Turkish axmen cut away its fine forests, thus permitting heavy rains to wash much of its soil to lower levels. Yet just as time heals the hurt of life, so nature has slowly, yet faithfully, worked toward restoring its beautiful trees, renewing its soil, and replacing its flowering bushes and shrubs, while more and more wild flowers have ever sprung up with the passing seasons.

Today there are ruined sites, ancient cisterns, millstones, and oil and wine presses to attest its former productiveness. And, too, there are olive groves and vineyards, carob and oak, pine and plane trees which thrive at various places on the mountain. Carmel's wonderful array of flowering and perfumed shrubs, such as bay, storax, linden, arbutus, and innumerable others, waft their fragrance through the air and verily set the mountain-sides aflame with beauty throughout the spring and far into the summer. A thousand glades on Carmel are graced with flowers of every hue; such as crocus, cyclamen, tulip, and "the lily of the field" which bloom in wild profusion. The best of Carmel's beauty comes in the spring, yet it remains quite green and beautiful throughout the year; for when the rain-bearing winds from the Mediterranean cease in May, then come the heavy dews which keep it refreshed throughout the summer months.

Otto van Richter declares, "There is no mountain in or around Palestine that retains its beauty as Carmel does; its groves are few, but they are luxuriant; no crags are there, nor precipices, nor rocks for wild goats." And the famous Belgian traveller, Van de Velde, declares, "I have not found in Galilee nor along the coasts nor on the plain any flower that I did not find on Carmel." The wild flowers of Carmel, when properly dried and pressed, never lose their color. Pope sang of it: "Carmel! thy flowery top perfumes the skies."

Solomon beheld Carmel's graceful form and verdant beauty and likened it to "the head of a bride." "Thine head upon thee is like Carmel, and the hair of thine head like purple; the king is held in the galleries."[2]

Mount Carmel's natural beauty, however, was but a dim shadow of its spiritual beauty and fertility, for its chief renown was as a *place of worship*. It was considered a fit sanctuary for those who stood in awe before nature at its best, or for those who bowed down before the Maker of heaven and earth and the beautiful sea that sang at the foot of that glorious headland which lifted itself far out above the waters of the beautiful Mediterranean.

Here came the ancient Canaanites worshiping their gods on the quiet and sunny summit of Carmel. Then came the mighty prophet Elijah who established a school of the prophets here and trained many young men for the work of the Lord.

Along the coast northward at Sidon, Baal and Ashtaroth were worshiped without restraint in all the abominations of those foul, debasing, and immoral idolatries. The king himself was the priest, and his royal daughter the priestess. And in order not to marry out of royal line, Ahab, the young king of Israel, passed by the daughters of Israel and yielded to the flirtations of Jezebel, the worldly, fastidious daughter of the king of Tyre. He took the heathen enchantress to wife. When at the royal courts at Samaria and Jezreel, she lived in luxury but not in idleness. She sat down to her table to eat and to drink; she rose up to pervert the truth and to seduce the people away from what pure worship of God as remained among them.

Temples of Baal were created, priests with highly colored robes burned incense, "high places" were built, images were set up, altars of Baal and Ashtaroth became numerous both at the court and upon those picturesque hills and mountains of Samaria.

When this Baal worship had almost ruined Israel, then came Elijah, that stern yet holy man of God, representing God's prophets, as Moses had represented God's law. With a mission from God to Ahab and Jezebel, this strange yet powerful prophet came to check the widespread abominations of the court and the people. Suddenly, without warning, he confronted the king and declared: "As the Lord God of Israel liveth, before whom I stand, there shall not be dew nor rain these years, but according to my word."[3] When no dew nor rain had come for three years and six months, and Ahab and Israel had time to think, then Elijah reappeared as suddenly as he had gone away.

In dramatic style, Elijah said to Ahab, "Now therefore send, and gather to me all Israel, unto Mount Carmel, and the prophets of Baal four hundred and fifty, and the prophets of the groves four hundred, which eat at Jezebel's table." The king obeyed the request of the plain, powerful man of God. In brief time there were gathered all the 850 leaders of the Baal cult and a vast concourse of the people along with Ahab to a vast natural amphitheater on the southeast brow of Mount Carmel.

Here on this mountain, poised between the countries of Israel and Phoenicia, the lone prophet of the Lord stepped before the king and the vast assemblage of people and said, "How long halt ye between two opinions? If the Lord be God, follow him: but if Baal, then follow him." The people being speechless, Elijah continued,

> I, even I only, remain a prophet of the Lord; but Baal's prophets are four hundred and fifty men. Let them therefore give us two bullocks; and let them choose one bullock for themselves, and cut it in pieces, and lay it on wood, and put no fire under: and I will dress the other bullock, and lay it on wood, and put no fire under: and call ye on the name of the Lord: and the God that answereth by fire, let him be God.[4]

The altars were prepared, and there followed the strange, weird scene of the priests hysterically calling in vain upon Baal. They leaped upon the altar, they cut themselves, and cried out hour after hour for the fire from heaven, but none came. Then near the time of the evening sacrifice, while the sun was lowering over Mount Carmel and the Mediterranean, Elijah repaired the altar and calmly stood before God and quietly prayed, "Hear me, O Jehovah, hear me, that this people may know that thou, Jehovah, art God."

Then the fire fell from heaven, and the water with which the sacrifice had been drenched was licked up, and the burnt offering and the wood were consumed. The awe-stricken people fell on their faces and cried out. "The Lord, he is God! The Lord, he is

God!" At the foot of the mountain where ran the river Kishon, the priests of Baal were slain, and the water ran red with their unhallowed blood.

The prophet withdrew from the crowd and bowed himself to the earth in prayer. After a time he asked his servant to go to the highest point on the mountain and look toward the sea for signs of rain. Over and over he went and returned until on his return the seventh time he reported seeing a small cloud arising out of the sea "like a man's hand." Elijah then said to him, "Go up, say unto Ahab, Prepare thy chariot, and get thee down, that the rain stop thee not."

Then the heavens grew black with clouds and wind, and there was a great rain, and Ahab mounted his chariot and drove off in furious haste toward Jezreel. "And the hand of the Lord was on Elijah: and he girded up his loins, and ran before Ahab to the entrance of Jezreel."[5] How vivid the landscapes into which the narrative fits perfectly!

High up on the southeast brow of Carmel, 1,685 feet above sea level and 13 miles from the sea, is a natural amphitheater and a rude quadrangular structure of hewn stones known by everyone as *El Mukhrakah,* or "the burning of the Lord." There, says tradition, is the place where Elijah met the idolatrous priests of Baal, the favorites of Ahab and Jezebel, and gained the day for the Lord Jehovah. Nearby is the spring from which the water for sacrifice was obtained. Beneath flows the river Kishon, which the Arabs call *Nahr el Mukhattar,* "The River of the Massacre," which, of course, harks back to the slaughter of the priests of Baal, and perhaps also to the destruction of Sisera's host.

At the bend of the stream, at the nearest point to the place of sacrifice, there is a "tell" or ancient townsite, which is called Tell el Kassis ("The Hill of the Priests"), and this most probably was the place where they either executed or buried the priests of Baal.

Traditions and miraculous stories of the prophet Elijah became so common during succeeding centuries that he readily became the patron saint of various Jewish, Christian, Mohammedan, and Druze communities over Palestine and elsewhere.

Mount Carmel itself, because of the mighty manifestations of divine power, became a kind of memorial to Elijah, a symbol of religious power, a shrine and a place of retreat to which many would resort. Pythagoras, the Greek philosopher and astrologer, spent some time here during the fifth century B.C.; and Tacitus, the Roman orator and historian, tells us that an altar to the God of Carmel stood on top of the mountain, and that Vespasian caused the oracle to be consulted in A.D. 69, while on his Palestinian campaign.

The northwestern promontory overlooking the sea came to be considered one of the most sacred parts of the mountain. Here, it is said, the prophet Elijah, "wearing the yellowed shawl of wisdom" and bearing the mighty presence of God, chose these heights overlooking the sea and built a school of the prophets. The spot now held in greatest veneration by Christians, Arabs, and Druzes, is a "grotto" about 15 feet long and 12 feet high, where the prophet is said to have resorted for prayer and security. Over this grotto there now stands a magnificent church, and adjoining it is the Carmelite Monastery. Farther down the mountainside toward Haifa is the great gilt-domed Temple of the Bahia—one of the quietest and most picturesque spots of this area.

Being a place of beauty, where grow so many trees, flowering shrubs, and wild flowers, and extending out into the sea and lifting its head 500 feet above the water, Mount Carmel is by nature a cool, quiet retreat and an ideal residential area for those who can afford such luxury of life, and for thousands of others who come for a brief time to escape the midsummer heat of other less-favored sections of Palestine. A number of Jewish towns and villas are located on the sides or on the summit of Carmel, the most flourishing of which is villalike Carmelia with its beautiful homes and contented people—in fact, the entire central and western portions of Mount Carmel are now well settled with elegant homes, hotels, and pensions.

Hadar Hacarmel, "the splendor of Carmel," is built on the 51 slope of Carmel and at the same time is really within the municipal boundaries of Haifa. The first step towards the forming of

Hadar Hacarmel was the erection of the Hebrew Technical Institute building in 1912. Other educational institutions of various types, including public and private kindergartens, elementary and secondary schools, colleges of music, and public libraries, soon followed. The first homes in Hadar Hacarmel were built in 1920. Then from 1924 to 1939, its population grew to 36,000. Today it is a large, compact, garden, resident city of detached villas of individual design with front lawns, clean concrete houses, tree-lined boulevards, comfortable boarding houses, hotels, hospitals, and thousands of dwellings. It is one of the chief centers of Jewish public and cultural life for Haifa and the surrounding area.

Somewhat higher on up Carmel lies Achuzat Sir Herbert Samuel, named after the first high commissioner for Palestine, and known simply as *Achuza.* It is a gardenlike settlement with about 5,000 inhabitants and a great future.

Yaarot Hacarmel, the settlement highest on the mountain, has an area of 2,000 acres, where enterprising laborers cultivate the soil and work to acquire plots of land of their own. Other newer homes and building projects almost completely take up all available building sites on the western half of Mount Carmel. Two or three picturesque Arab villages stand well back eastward on the mountain.

A rare experience is in store for any who may on a spring day stand on Mount Carmel, at one of its highest points, and forgetting self and life's small demands, just open wide the heart and eyes and see one of the grandest countrysides that may ever fall into man's view. Northward lies the picturesque Bay of Acre with its crescentlike beach of yellow sand; and on beyond the ancient city of Acre with its massive gray walls, rare-lit domes, white minarets, and gleaming cupolas, one sees through the haze the white Ladder of Tyre. To the northeast are the fertile hills and vales of northern Galilee, the Lebanon mountains, glistening in their whiteness, and snow-clad Mount Hermon standing in its majesty —the "chief" of all the mountains of the Holy Land.

Eastward is the grand sweep of the Plain of Armageddon, the hills of Lower Galilee, the wooded slopes of Tabor, Mount

Moreh, Mount Gilboa, with here and there between the gaps, the mountains of Bashan and Gilead on the other side of Jordan.

To the southeast lies the imposing mound of mighty Megiddo and the hilltops of Samaria, with the mountains of Ebal and Gerizim standing out in bold relief.

To the south is the lovely Plain of Sharon with her scattered forest, her vast orange groves, her thriving colonies, and her coast of yellow sand glistening in the sunlight. Southwestward, almost at your feet, lies the battered ruins of Athlit, the last stronghold of the Crusaders.

Westward is the boundless expanse of the Mediterranean Sea; stretching on out as far as the curvature of the earth will permit the eye to see are the blue green waters, shadowed by passing clouds and brightened by the many white sailing ships that gracefully pass during the course of the day. Then at eventide, when the sun dips into the waves, the firmanent is fired to a burnished gold, then turns to a lilac and purple, while one dark streak of crimson lines the horizon and fades as the sun sinks into its reddened sea and the glory of the day passes away.

> So when, deep sinking in the rosy main,
> The western sun forsakes the Syrian plain;
> His watery rays reflected luster shed,
> And pours this latest light on Carmel's head.

CHAPTER **4**

The Fertile Plain of Sharon

The Plain of Sharon begins just south of that western portion of Mount Carmel that juts out into the sea. It sweeps southward for some 62 miles to the river Rubin, 7 miles south of Joppa (Tel Aviv). At first the plain is only a few hundred yards wide, then widens to from 1 to 4 miles for about 18 miles, until one approaches the ancient city of Dor,[1] after which there is a gradual increase in width to 10 or 11 miles. This increase in width is maintained until just north of the city of Lydda, where the plain broadens to 13 miles as it connects with the Valley of Aijalon.

Sharon is the largest and finest plain west of the Jordan River. Much of its surface is level and well watered; other portions are agreeably varied by sandy ridges, isolated hills, or even chains of hills which afford slightly elevated positions for villages, upland fields, and forests.

Its western border is fringed by the white foam of the sea. But under that foam, the entire coast is underlain with, and composed of, deep beds of coarse, soft sandstone. The perpetual wash of the waves disintegrates and crumbles it into sand and pushes the sand onto the shore, where it is dried by the sun and driven inland by the wind. For long centuries this process has continued, until an almost unbroken ridge of yellow sand stretches along the coast, tending to obstruct the outflow of streams. It is gradually creeping inland at the rate of approximately 3 feet per year. At some points it rises as high as 50 to 60 feet and has covered almost everything in its path for as much as two to four miles. Seeing the steady inundation of the Holy Land's most valuable acres, the Jews in recent decades have become alarmed and planted trees in its path and in places constructed walls and other obstacles to halt the oncoming scourge.

From the sea to the mountains there is a fairly gradual ascent of nearly 200 feet in the elevation of the plain. When the extreme eastern limits of the plain are reached, a fringe of olive groves beautifies the border and demonstrates nature's kindly manner of modifying abruptness.

The Plain of Sharon is traversed by a number of streams of considerable size, which rise in the mountains and flow westward across the plain. The most important of these are the *Crocodile River,* the *Dead River,* the *Salt River,* and the *Auja River.* These four streams are perennial, being fed by springs either far up in the mountains or at their foothills.

The **Crocodile River** rises in the southwestern extremity of Mount Carmel and, from the marshes of the Plain of Dothan, flows westward through wide pastures, by flourishing farms until in its meandering it has crossed most of the plain, then turns 55 slightly northwestward and flows into the sea five miles south of Dor and two miles north of the ruins of Caesarea. The natives call it the *Zerka* or Blue River. Several mills are located on this fine stream, fish abound in its waters, and crocodiles were taken from it as late as 1902.

Now the marshes have been drained and the celebrated Crocodile River canalized. The climate of this region resembles that of Egypt, and the Jewish people grow rice and sugarcane. Here was once located the Roman circuit of the town of Crocodipolis, and many antiques can still be found in the area. The colonists have made a little museum which grows from year to year.

The **Dead River,** known by the natives as *Nahr el-Mefjir,* has its rise on the Plain of Dothan. After flowing across the Plain of Sharon, it empties into the sea two miles south of Caesarea.

The **Salt River,** known by the Crusaders as *Iskanderuneh,* or Alexander's River, drains the center of the plain and enters the sea two miles south of the Jewish colony of Natania.

The **Auja River** is known as the shortest river in Palestine, being less than 10 miles in length, yet it is also the largest river west of the Jordan. It is formed by the confluence of a number of lesser streams, but it has its main source at the large, fine spring at Antipatris, known as *Ras el-Ain.* It is a deep stream with flowers and Syrian papyrus along its banks, and the only genuine pines in Palestine dot the higher banks of its upper course. For long centuries it has had sufficient depth for sailing vessels to make their way some miles inland up this stream. Now much of its waters are being pumped in large pipes southward to irrigate the Negeb.

The river *Rubin* properly belongs to the Plain of the Philistines, as it touches the Plain of Sharon only at its outlet to the sea.

"Sharon" means "The Forest Country," or "The Plain of the Forest." Josephus describes the Plain of Sharon as "The Place Called the Forest." Strabo is said to have called it "a great forest," while the Crusaders called it "The Forest of Assur." Even as late as Napoleon's day, he called it the "Forest of Meski," from the village of Miskieh.

Of the forests which were so very dense in those distant days, there remains only one large oak grove covering an area of about eight square miles in the extreme northeast section of the plain. In going southward, however, one encounters scattered clumps of oak, carob (husks), tamarisk, willow, cyprus, sycamore, eucalyptus, ash, and palm trees. Smaller shrubs are more plentiful.

The soil on most of the plain is now extremely rich, varying from bright red through chocolate brown to deep black, with a few breaks and gullies between low-lying hills. Ninety percent of the area, aside from the sand-blown coastline, lends itself to intense cultivation. And like California and Italy, both its climate and soil are favorable to the growth of cereals, melons, citrus, grapes, olives, and almost every kind of fruits, and flowers. Their specialty is the production of the far-famed Jaffa oranges. Normally the citrus fruit industry exports $75 million to $80 million worth of citrus fruit annually, and more than half of this is grown on the Plain of Sharon.

Millions of flowers of various kinds are cultivated for the

57

Packing the famed Jaffa oranges for shipment

A field of commercial flowers on the Plain of Sharon

markets, and a great variety of wild flowers are scattered over the fields and meadows of the plain—poppies, anemones, narcissus, gladiolus, phlox, daisies, myrtle, and pimpernels. During the spring months the air is well populated with bees and butterflies. The rose of Sharon and the lily of the valley once grew here, but no one now is quite able to positively identify either of these flowers. The word translated "rose" in our Bible is believed by some to have been the narcissus. It blooms here in abundance and is carried around for the benefit of its perfume, yet it is not a true rose. The general consensus is that the lily of the valley is the scarlet anemone, which colors the ground in unforgettable beauty here and elsewhere in Palestine in the late winter and spring. The name *shushan,* translated "lily" in the Scripture, is now used by many of the people as they speak of this flower.

The beginning of man's habitation on this fertile Plain of Sharon is somewhat obscure, yet here and there one finds indication of Egyptian, Canaanitish, and Babylonian influence from two to three thousand years before Christ. In the middle of the 16th century B.C., Egyptian history mentions a conquest of Palestine which is followed some 35 years later by another. During the early 14th century B.C. the Tell El Amarna letters show Palestine to be still subject to Egypt, but they speak of the *Habiru* or Hebrews who were then entering and overrunning the country.

For a time, during the second millenium before Christ, the Philistines and Canaanites occupied this plain, depending on which was the stronger. In time, however, the Philistines overcame the Canaanites and completely ruled the plain. The Isrealites gradually settled here.

During the reign of King David, around 1000 B.C., the Plain of Sharon was the feeding grounds for the royal flocks and herds, and during Solomon's reign the king's table was supplied with meat and other delicious foods from this fertile plain (1 Kings 4:11; 1 Chron. 27:29). Isaiah describes Sharon as a fold for flocks, and its prosperity and excellency was symbolic of the excellency of God.

With Alexander's invasion the Philistine coast and cities were opened to Greek influence. Greek trade came through the harbors; Greek men settled in all the cities; Greek institutions arose; old deities became identified with Greek gods. Though the ancient Philistine stubbornness persisted, it was exercised in defense of civic independence from Greek ideas, Greek manners, and Greek morals.

Coming in 63 B.C., the Romans built roads, drained various areas, sowed fields, protected the forests, planted a string of cities, and developed the plain until under Herod the Great it became the pride of the country. From being merely a place for game, farms, and fruit, it arose to almost first place of importance. Even the capital of Palestine was moved to Caesarea, which was sometimes called "Little Rome."

Across this plain ran the great highway of the nations, and connecting roads were built between such important cities as Jerusalem, Neapolis, and Sebaste in the interior, and Acre on the north and Gaza on the south. The commerce of Damascus, Persia, and India passed this way to Egypt and the colonies of northern Africa. This traffic, along with the constant movement of troops backward and forward, must have made this plain one of the busiest and most populous regions of Syria.

Few places in Palestine are so closely connected with the apostolic history as this tract of coast between Gaza and Acre, and especially the neighborhood of Caesarea.

However, the glory of Rome finally collapsed and the rising power of the Arabs seized the glorious Plain of Sharon in the seventh century. Together with overthrowing the excellency of Rome, the Arabs overthrew the glory and excellency of Sharon, for under the Arabs the plain greatly deteriorated and fell to ruin.

Again deterioration swept over the plain as the Turks, in A.D. 1517, conquered all the lands in the Near East. The Turks permitted the Arabs to occupy the plain, and little effort was made to rebuild it or even to maintain the cities and fields already developed. The rivers and wadies stagnated in many places as debris and sand stopped their flow. Mosquitoes and other insects thrived in these swamps, and soon entire sections of the plain became malaria-infested. The plain deteriorated still farther, being sparsely inhabited by people who only took from the land and did nothing to replenish the woods or fertilize the soil.

The Plain of Sharon is strewn with the wrecks of bygone centuries. Ruined cities, red and gray granite columns protrude above the sands or lie sprawled in the water's edge. These ruins carry us deep into the historical past. Mighty civilizations have been there, but now the Jews are constructing many cities and making a veritable garden spot of most all the plain from north to south. Its cities during the past and present have played and are now playing a large part in the history and development of the plain.

Of the past, there remains the memory and the historic ruins of such cities as Athlit, Dor, Caesarea, Antipatris, Joppa, Lydda, and Ramle. The present modern cities include such important places as Tel Aviv, Benyamina, Hadera, Herzliya, Tulkarm, Raanana, Sarona, Petah Tikva, Mikweh Israel, Rishon Le Zion, and scores of thriving colonies and picturesque villages.

Athlit is located eight miles south of Mount Carmel, slightly

60 west of the coastal road from Acre to Jerusalem. The city site is on a cape which projects about a half mile into the sea, terminating in a compact and rocky promontory. Some have seen in it the

appearance of a "clenched fist"—a grim headland thrust out in perpetual defiance. And much of the history of the place would harmonize with such a thought.

Athlit was the last stronghold of the Jews in their fight for independence in A.D. 130, but with the Jewish defeat all was left in ruins until the coming of the Crusaders, who saw it as an ideal location at which to check the enemy's forays from Mount Tabor, some 30 miles east. In 1217, they began the construction of one of the most important crusading strongholds in Palestine, the Castle of the Pilgrims, which, when finished in 1218, was one of the strongest and finest of the Latin castles.

This imposing four-story castle fortress, of which ruins remain today, stood in the center of the rocky promontory between two bays. This site afforded a double port facing north and south and forming a natural breakwater, the only such port possible along the Palestinian coast. A stage on the road from Acre to Jerusalem, it was at times used as a port of entry for pilgrims, whom the Templars escorted inland.

The huge outer walls of the castle were of sandy, porous limestone, 15 feet thick and 80 feet high. They were strengthened by great towers and pierced by three impressive gates. Graceful arches adorned the spacious rooms, from which large windows opened toward the sea. On the highest point of the rocky promontory these men of the Cross carved out of the solid rock a beautiful, spacious banqueting hall, then crowned the lovely place with a magnificent church. One great wall shut out these buildings from the mainland, and outside this great wall ran a deep moat into which the sea flowed, completely surrounding the stronghold.

The place contained extensive stables accommodating 250 horses. Iron horseshoes have been found in the ruins. There were also good wells of water. The surrounding country was well watered and possessed vineyards, orchards, and pasturelands. The nearby waters were well stocked with fish, the coast held splendid salt pans, and the forest afforded an abundance of game and fuel.

The place contained extensive stables accommodating 250 and fuel.

Around the harbors and about the castle grew up the city of

61

Athlit, which became a town of considerable importance. Its contented and prosperous inhabitants were not exposed to the ravages of war, for the place was never besieged and scarcely threatened. At last, however, when the battle of Hattin had been lost and Acre had fallen, Athlit could not resist independently. The Crusader leaders assembled in the great banqueting hall for their last conference. After praying earnestly and committing themselves to the care and protection of Almighty God, they embarked in their ships on that August night of 1291 and sailed away for Cyprus.

Dor, now known as Tanturah, six miles south of Athlit, occupies the site of the ancient city of Dora, as it was called by the Romans. In early times it was a Sidonian colony, but later became a royal Canaanitish city with several outlying towns. Its soldier inhabitants fought against Joshua in the battle of Hazor. Dor, along with its daughter towns, was allotted to the children of Manasseh, who were unable to expel the Canaanites, but who finally compelled them to pay tribute (Josh. 17:11-13). The city was much fought for because of its coastal position and its rich supply of murex shellfish, so valuable in the manufacture of the famous Tyrian purple dye.

During Solomon's reign, "Judah and Israel were many, as the sand which is by the sea for multitude, eating and drinking, and making merry," and the demands of the king's table for one day was "thirty measures of fine flour, and threescore measures of meal, ten fat oxen, and twenty oxen out of the pastures, and an hundred sheep, beside harts, and roebucks, and fallowdeer, and fatted fowl." The wise king had 12 officers who lived in as many districts of Palestine, and were each responsible for one month's provision for the king and his household. One of these officers was *Ben-Abinadab,* who lived in Dor, and was son-in-law to Solomon. His must have been a comparatively easy and pleasant task, seeing the fertile fields about Dor produced so abundantly, the pastures sustained such vast flocks of sheep and herds of cattle, and the nearby woods abounded in wild game of almost every kind (1 Kings 4:11, 20, 22-23).

A wild beauty pervades the environs of the place today. Old

ruins protrude, tombs and quarries abound, with here and there a low, wet bog. Stretching away eastward are fields and woods, and strewn on the nearby beaches are many murex shells which remind one of the ancient glory of the city.

Caesarea. Two hundred years before Christ, Caesarea was known as "Strato's Tower," and today the ancient name in the Arab form, *Kaisariyeh*, still clings to the ruins on the seashore about 30 miles north of Jaffa, 25 miles south of Mount Carmel, and 55 miles northwest of Jerusalem. The change from "Strato's Tower," where some few ships landed, to the Caesarea of which Tacitus speaks in the first century A.D. as being "the head of Judea," was made by Herod the Great in his desire to build a strictly Roman town on the seaside that would be suitable for a port and a stronghold of naval power, as well as the capital of the country.

The city was begun in 25 B.C., and its construction required 12 years.

Herod was known for enlarging and beautifying cities, but his special care was bestowed on Caesarea, for he named it after Caesar, and made it a model of Graeco-Roman civilization. It was to become the official residence of the Herodian kings, and of Festus, Felix, and other Roman procurators of Judea, as well as the headquarters of the military force of the province. Under the Roman governors, Caesarea was a vast and crowded metropolis.

The city was constructed of white marble, red and gray granite, and other expensive materials brought from afar. King Herod spared no expense. Most sumptuous palaces, spacious public buildings, airy courts, attractive bazaars, and long, wide avenues were characteristic of the place.

In the north part of the city was constructed a magnificent theater building; in the south quarter, a great amphitheater accommodating 20,000 spectators; and near the east gate, in a slight depression, a hippodrome 1,000 feet long. The Romans were eager for sports, and Herod intended that ample provision should be made for their overdeveloped instinct in this direction. 63

Herod erected spacious quarters for those who sailed the seas and an appropriate base for the Roman legions of the Levant.

Crowning all was a grand palace for himself and those Roman governors who should rule after him. An abundant water supply was brought to the city by two aqueducts; one was a double conduit of great size. Nor did he neglect to provide sanitation and convenience, for a complete system of underground sewerage carried the refuse into the sea. An elaborate subterranean passage for both people and transport led directly down to the wharf and the seaside. The substantial walls of this Herodian city enclosed 400 acres. Outside the walls were villas and gardens, for peace was assured when Rome ruled.

But "the greatest and most laborious work of all" was the magnificent harbor, "always free from the waves of the sea." To make amends for the absence of a natural haven, Herod had his engineers pass out to where the water was 20 fathoms (136 feet) deep and let down "vast stones" 50 feet long, 18 feet broad, and 9 feet thick, and thus effect the construction of a double harbor 200 yards each way. It was excellent workmanship, and all the more remarkable because the place itself was not suitable for such noble structures. The whole coastline is singularly ill-fitted for the formation of harbors.

A pier was also constructed, 130 yards in length and 200 feet wide, which was adorned with splendid pillars and several towers, the largest of which was called *Drusus,* after Drusus, the son-in-law of Augustus Caesar. There were also arches formed in honor of the seamen, and nearby residences constructed for their convenience.

Around the entire haven was a splendid walk which was most appropriate "to such as had a mind to that exercise." Along this elevated circular haven there were many edifices constructed of highly polished stone, and towering above them all was a temple that stood out in bold relief—a spectacle for all who sailed near Caesarea.

Caesarea was a great city during the lifetime of Jesus and Paul. Its harbor, its buildings, and its fine streets were famous among the world's seaports. All its streets led to the harbor and were intersected by straight, parallel avenues.

It was the military, commercial, political, and sporting capital

Portside ruins of what was once the magnificent harbor of Caesarea

of Palestine, and as such was to harbor many a strange person and event. Built with unheard-of pomp by Herod the Great, it was further embellished by Herod Agrippa for Bernice, for whom this city was a favorite resort. She came here with King Agrippa to hear Paul tell of his conversion experience on the Damascus road; she also came here with Titus.

It was here that Cornelius, the devout Roman centurion, heard from heaven and sent for the Apostle Peter (who was at Joppa, 31 miles down the coast) and became one of the first Gentile converts to Christianity.

65

Here, too, Herod Agrippa donned the robes of silver tissue,

entered the theater, and made an oration before the people who flatteringly hailed him as a god. Proud to be accorded divine attributes, the king accepted the blasphemous homage only to be stricken down in violent pain and carried from the theater (that his grandfather had built) to his palace, where after five days he died, "worn out with pain."

Here Paul stopped for a few days in the home of Evangelist Philip, who had four daughters that prophesied. Later he was brought here as a prisoner and kept for two years, previous to his going to Rome. It was here before Felix and Drusilla, the Roman governor and his attractive wife, that he made a noble defense in which he "reasoned of righteousness, temperance, and judgment to come," and received that pathetic answer from the governor, "Go thy way for this time; when I have a more convenient season, I will call for thee." And later, before Festus and King Agrippa, he delivered that celebrated oration which made Festus declare that much learning had made him mad, and Agrippa say, "Almost thou persuadest me to be a Christian" (Acts 26:28).

It was here that Vespasian, the father of Titus, was proclaimed emperor. Here, in the old circus building, Titus, after the fall of Jerusalem in A.D. 70, celebrated his victory with games and contests in which over 2,000 Jewish prisoners were killed as gladiators in the arena.

The dissensions between the Jews and the Syrians here led to a great massacre of the former, which brought on the rebellion and the Roman war. A council was held here in A.D. 95, when the city was the seat of an archbishop. In the third century it became the metropolis of the Christian bishops of Palestine and the home of Origen and of Eusebius, the illustrious church father, and the author of Onomastikon, an important research work on Palestine geography. In A.D. 548, the Jews and Samaritans united in taking up arms against the Christians. In the year 639, the city was taken by Abu Obeida and remained in Mohammedan hands for nearly 500 years.

66   In the year 1035, it was visited by the traveller Nassiri, who describes it as an agreeable city, irrigated with running water and planted with date palms and oranges, sweet and bitter. It

was surrounded by a strong wall, either built or restored by the Mohammedans during their first occupation.

In 1101, King Baldwin seized Caesarea, put the inhabitants to the sword, and among the booty *discovered a green glass bowl,* made of a single large emerald, which he and his fellow Crusaders believed to be the veritable Holy Grail used at the Last Supper.[2] The Crusaders then settled in the place in their own manner, making a portion of the city into a small medieval fortress. Saladin took it from them in the year 1187, but the Crusaders recaptured it in 1191. Louis rebuilt the citadel and the walls, and it stood for long years. But Sultan Bibars of Egypt took it in 1256 and partially destroyed both its walls and buildings. At times it has tried to rise again but has failed.

Today Caesar's city, built with unheard-of pomp by Herod the Great, lies in extensive and intricate ruins. Across its fields of sand lie broken pottery, fragments of granite and marble columns, shattered portions of gates and castles. Desolation "laughs at the mightiest works of man, turning beauty to ashes and strength to destruction." Among the many things of interest found during excavations at Caesarea were: a Roman amphitheater, a Crusaders' cathedral, a cache of 3,700 bronze coins at the site of a 3rd century B.C. synagogue, two crusader seals of the 13th century, and an inscription bearing the name of "Pontius Pilate," the infamous governor who washed his hands before the multitude and permitted the mistrial of Jesus the Messiah.

Antipatris (Ras el 'Ain). On the eastern side of the Plain of Sharon, just above the large collection of fountains which serve as the main source of the Auja River, lies a high mound which holds the remains of ancient Antipatris. It was built by Herod the Great as a pleasant residence town and named after his father, Antipater.

Lying as it did, 42 miles along the Jerusalem highroad which led down to the seaside capital of Caesarea, it afforded a most convenient place for statesmen, churchmen, and military personnel to break the journey when traveling between these two 67 most important cities.

Seventy mounted troops and 200 foot soldiers accompanied

the Apostle Paul when he was sent as a prisoner along this road. After a rest at Antipatris, the foot soldiery returned to Jerusalem, while the 70 horsemen continued with Paul to Caesarea, 26 miles away. Parts of the old Roman road have been uncovered near Antipatris and remain unto this day. Water from the fine springs here irrigate nearby fields and gardens, and some is pumped to Jerusalem for part of its water supply. And a larger volume is carried away in a huge 48-inch concrete pipe to furnish water for the thirsty Negeb more than 40 miles southward.

Joppa, one of the oldest cities in the world, is said to have derived its name from the Hebrew y*afe,* which means beautiful. Others say it was named after Japheth, son of Noah, who established the city after the Flood. It is situated on a 116-foot-high promontory which juts out into the Mediterranean Sea and appears like a flower garden nestled among great orange gardens, fig trees, and date palms. For long centuries Joppa has been a strange place and thoroughly Oriental.

It is mentioned by the *Mohar* of Egypt, who travelled in Palestine during the 14th century before the Christian era, and in the Tell El Amarna tablets of the 15th century. It is among the list of towns enumerated in the Temple of Karnak as having been conquered by Thotmes III during the 16th century. One record describes what is probably the origin of the Ali Baba story, of a general named Thutia, who commanded the army of Thotmes III and introduced 250 picked warriors into the city, concealed in earthen jars. These warriors bound the garrison and let in the beseigers.

Only occasional mention is made of the city in the Bible. Josh. 19:46 mentions the city as bordering on the territory of Dan.

Joppa was the port where the prophet Jonah took passage for Tarshish, when he was running away from the job which the Lord had assigned him. Cuneiform inscriptions have been found recording Sennacherib's capture of the city in 702 B.C.

In Solomon's time, Joppa was the port of Jerusalem, to which Hiram, king of Tyre, sent the cedars of Lebanon on rafts, and from there King Solomon's men took them up to Jerusalem. Again in the days of Zerubbabel, when the second Temple was built, "cedar trees were brought from Lebanon to the sea unto Joppa, according to the grant that they had of Cyrus, king of Persia" (2 Chron. 2:16; Ezra 3:7).

Alexander the Great stormed the town in 333 B.C., after which it passed from hand to hand. During the Maccabean Wars the local inhabitants turned upon the Jewish residents in the city and took 200 of them out to sea in boats and solemnly drowned them. This event caused Judas Maccabaeus to lead his army down and avenge them by burning the ships. Jonathan and Simon fortified the place and dug a harbor for foreign trade. Joppa soon became the most Jewish town on all the coast, and the only seaport the Jews possessed.

In 135 B.C., Antiochus took Joppa, but the Roman Senate ordered him to restore the town and its port to the Jews. In 63 Pompey took Joppa from the Jews and made it a free town, but Julius Caesar ordered all that had previously belonged to the Jews to be given back to them, and Joppa was restored to the high priest Hyrcanus. In the struggle between Herod and Mattathias II, Joppa remained faithful to the Jews; and when Herod returned from Rome to become king of Judea, it was necessary for him to take Joppa by storm.

In New Testament times Joppa was chiefly associated with the work of the Apostle Peter. It was here that he raised Dorcas to life and later received the great vision of clean and unclean beasts, together with his call to Cornelius at Caesarea and the Gentile world at large, while lodging in the house of Simon the tanner. The house now shown as the original is probably on the site of the one where Peter lodged.

After Herod built Caesarea with its spacious harbor, Joppa fell from its position as chief harbor of Palestine. Being a purely Jewish town, however, and maintaining close relations with Jerusalem, it continued to be a prominent place until the fall of Jerusalem in A.D. 70. After this it became a rendezvous for pirates and was finally destroyed by Vespasian.

It soon rose up again and became the seat of a Christian 69 bishop, but was captured by the Arabs in 636, after which it sank to the level of a small and insignificant place. Being on the coastal road along which the Christian and Moslem armies marched, it experienced many a bloody conflict during the period of the Crusades. It was here that Richard the Lion-hearted is said to have jumped into the sea in full armor and fought his way to land. Following Crusader days, the place suffered varying fortunes and misfortunes, but once again became the harbor of Jerusalem in the latter part of the 18th century.

Napoleon Bonaparte captured the city in 1799, and was faced with a predicament upon finding 2,000 prisoners surrendered to him after a gallant resistance. His generals and soldiers objected to sharing any of their limited food with these "Arabs and Jews." He was pressed for time, too. Influenced more by the clamor of his men than by the appeals of his prisoners, he lined them up on the beach and had them massacred. Returning later on his retreat, he occupied Joppa again, and by chance or fate the regiment which did the massacring was quartered in the hospital and ground recently used by lepers. The horrible disease fastened on them, and only seven escaped.

Joppa has been dealing with the outside world for many centuries, but the native life here has not seemed to have been affected. There are many narrow streets in which the merchants have their tiny shops, funished with small stools upon which men sit smoking their curious pipes (narghilas), bargaining and gesticulating. The bazaars present a lively picture, teeming with life from all Asia Minor and bringing together so many races and languages and products that one cannot help but be interested.

The gardens of Joppa, surrounded with stone walls and cactus hedges, stretch inland about a mile and a half and are over two miles in extent north and south. Palms, oranges, lemons, pomegranates, figs, and bananas are grown in profusion, water being supplied by means of numerous deep wells.

The gardens are skirted by vineyards on the south. On the southeast is the land belonging to the Mikveh Israel, or Jewish Agricultural Alliance, 780 acres in all, of which a third is reclaimed land. The work here has developed into one of the finest agricultural colleges in Israel.[3]

On the way from Joppa to Lydda, about half a mile out, is a

fountain which is one of the finest specimens of Saracenic architecture in Palestine and a memorial of a thoughtful and kindly governor, Abu Nabat. It is built of white stone in the form of a parallelogram, and *inside the center cupola* lies the sarcophagus of the founder with an inscription in Arabic calling upon all who gather about to offer a prayer for him who provided this fountain for the free use of every passerby.

Jaffa is said to have had a population of about 8,000 before it was taken over by the Jews in 1948, a majority of whom were Moslems, but Greeks, Latins, Armenians, Maronites, Protestants, and Jews were found there. The place had a trade with Egypt and the north in silk, oranges, sesame, and other such products. The annual value of the fruit crop alone was said to be $10,000. However, since the Jews took control, much of the city is being rebuilt. Only a small portion retains its ancient appearance, and only a few thousand Moslems and Christians live here.

The Plain of Sharon, as a whole, is now thickly dotted with modern cities, towns, and colonies. These colonies began to be planted on the plain during the latter part of last century. Now there are more than 100 colonies—mostly Jewish; yet there are two Christian German colonies and one Greek colony, along with some Arab villages. The most of these began as agricultural colonies but in time developed some kind of an industrial quarter to supplement the colonists' income. *Herzliya* built luxury hotels; *Natanya* developed its picturesque beach to attract tourists and became famous for its diamond-cutting and polishing industry; *Michmoret* went in for fishing; *Mishmar-Ha-Sharon* grew gladiolus for export; *Ramot-Hashavim* became famous for its poultry farms.

Other colonies constructed hotels, rooming houses, restaurants, cafes, and established factories for producing cement, wine, and olive-wood products. A few of the colonies have grown into flourishing towns and cities. In between the colonies are rich and fertile citrus groves, olive orchards, and grape vineyards. And there are people, many people on the Plain of Sharon. One Jewish physician said to me, "Almost everybody.desires to live beside the sea." 71

CHAPTER 5

The Plain of the Philistines

The Philistines! Strange how that people who passed along the highway of history so long ago should cling to our modern-day thinking, and the name be perpetuated by modern sociologists who suppose they find the Philistines' counterpart in a certain nondescript group who infest modern social circles. From whence those ancient Philistines came, and whither they went, has offered about as much inducement for speculation as has any people of ancient time.

72   No final word has been spoken, yet after decades of patient

research it has about become the consensus that these people descended from one Mizraim, the son of Ham, whose two sons, *Casluhim* and *Caphtorium,* settled on a Mediterranean island which became known as Caphtor or Crete.[1] Some unknown catastrophe left only a remnant of them, who migrated to their distant kinsmen, the Egyptians, who permitted temporary settlement on their coast.

Being soon sized up as desirable frontier fighters, they were offered a free hand by shrewd Pharaoh for conquest in southern Canaan, with the understanding that they would become the guardians of Egypt's north frontier.[2] Varying fortunes accompanied the Philistine effort at conquest, but in time the country which became known as the Philistine Plain was a strip of land which extends from river Rubin *(Nahr Rubin)* to the river of Egypt *(Wady El Arish),* a distance of about 50 miles. Its average width is 12 to 16 miles, or slightly greater than that of the Sharon Plain, especially that portion which lies between Gaza and the *Wady El Arish,* which is the famous pastoral region known as the kingdom of Gerar in the time of Abraham.[3] The well-known trade route from Asia to Africa ran directly through the center of their country and passed by their leading cities; thus the Philistines could justly be styled "the guardians of the gate to Egypt." The Philistines were a tall, well-proportioned, warlike people. They went to battle in chariots of iron, armed with helmets, shields, swords, and other weapons of artistic workmanship.

Israel avoided their way as danger-fraught and God-forbidden, when she left Egypt for Canaan. Such a formidable enemy to be met after a long desert trek was too much, even for Israel. But later, when Israel had entered by the east, she listened to Joshua's final address, and then, in the fresh rush of enthusiasm, took Ekron, Askelon, and Gaza. But they soon lost these because they could not drive out the intrepid Philistines who fought with "chariots of iron."[4]

Amos declares that the same Power planted the two nations in the land—the one on the coast and the other on the Central Mountain Range—yet they never seemed to be at peace with one another.[5] Their outlook, their ideals, and their mission in life were poles apart. War, commerce, agriculture, stock raising, pagan worship, and the pursuit of personal pleasure absorbed the Philistine mind. Israel seemed destined for a higher purpose; yet the Bible makes no mention of a Philistine being changed at heart and taking the upward path that leads to nobler achievement here and eternal life hereafter. Too often they are merely represented as the proverbial enemies of Israel.

The Philistines pushed and horned the Israelites at intervals and grew so strong and independent that Ramses III attacked them in battle about 1190 B.C.[6]

The Plain of the Philistines is drained from east to west by four principal streams: *River Rubin, Sukerir River, Wady el-Hesy,* and *Wady Ghazzeh* with its tributary, *Wady esh Sheriah.* Some of these streams are perennial, but none are very large, except when swollen by winter rains. Much of the water from these winter rains, however, makes its way toward the sea along the top of the underlying rock. In a few places these waters break out and come to the surface as springs, but for the most part they remain 25 or 30 feet underground, which means that an inexhaustible supply of fresh water is found by digging wells of moderate depth.[7] Abraham and Isaac, in their day, dug wells in the Gerar section, but today there are thousands of wells scattered over the plain, and more will be dug as needed.

The soil on the plain is generally fertile, suitable for the production of grain, melons, grapes, figs, olives, dates, and the various citrus fruits. The crop for which the plain has long been known, however, is that of grain, the plain from Ekron to Gaza being one of the best grain districts in Palestine. In ancient times cargo ships from Greece and other countries put into the old port at the mouth of *Wady Ghazzeh* and were loaded with the grain of this plain. In fact this district was long known as "the granary of the Near East."

74   In ancient times there stretched for many miles, in every direction, a sea of grain, which in the warmer days of late spring, as harvest approached, would be like so much tinder.[8] It must have been into such fields as this that Samson loosed the foxes

with firebrands tied between their tails and burned the grain-fields of the Philistines.

The land of the Philistines was originally divided into five districts, over which five "lords" ruled in as many cities—*Ekron, Gath, Ashdod, Askelon,* and *Gaza.* Each of these cities had a cluster of "towns" about it which were subject to the ruling city.

Ekron, celebrated for the worship of Beelzebub, stood in the center of the plain, slightly north of the ancient valley of Sorek.

There seems no reason for doubt that the present Arab village of *'Akir* answers to the ancient Ekron. That city was the northernmost of the five cities of the lords of the Philistines and was situated near the southern border of Sharon; while the other four cities lay well within the territory usually ascribed to the Philistines. Here, in ancient Ekron, Samson was betrayed by Delilah, the infamous Philistine beauty.

Afterwards it became remarkable in connection with the capture of the ark by the Philistines, which was sent back from Ekron upon a new cart drawn by two milch cows. These being left to their own course took the "straight way" to Beth-shemesh, the nearest point of entrance to the mountains of Judah. In coming, therefore, by the present road from Ekron to Beth-shemesh, one almost follows the track of the cart on which the ark was thus sent back. After David's victory over Goliath in the Valley of Elah the Philistines were pursued to Ekron. At a later day, the prophets uttered denunciations against it, along with the other cities of the Philistines.

The Ekron of the Bible was built of unburnt bricks, which within a comparatively few years were reduced to dust. The only remains of the ancient city are represented in the stones of hand-mills, two marble columns, and a stone press. The present Ekron was only a mud hamlet until a few years ago when the Jews purchased the ground, where they have built a thriving colony which they call by that name.

Gath was the home of Goliath, the famous giant whom David slew with a sling and a stone. The place fell into disrepute and has been so much forgotten that its name has disappeared, and the site cannot be, or has not been, definitely ascertained. Tell-es- 75

Safiyeh, a fine mound in the western portion of the Valley of Elah, has long been pointed out as the probable location, but considerable uncertainty abounded and no excavations were ever carried forward there. In 1955, the Jews founded Kiryat-Gat (town of Gath) far south of here, near a conspicuous mound which they supposed to be the biblical Gath.

Ashdod, the military pride of the Philistines, was located midway between Ekron and Askelon, on a low, rounded hill overlooking the sea. Being known for its military strength and for its sacredness in connection with the temple of Dagon, the Philistines, on capturing the ark of the covenant, hurried the ark to their temple. The following morning the people found the image Dagon fallen and broken to pieces; thereafter they had less faith in it.

In 760 B.C. the prophet Amos denounced Ashdod's inhabitants.[9] Isaiah says that Sargon, king of Assyria, sent Tartan, his general, who took the city of Ashdod.[10] For a long time the critics disputed this positive statement, because of secular history making no mention of such a king; then, in 1842, M. Botta began excavations at Khorsabad. The first monuments brought to light were those of this vanished Sargon. As one of the most magnificent of the Assyrian conquerors, he possessed a palace which was scarcely excelled in ornamentation by any royal edifice. Later, Mr. George Smith discovered an octagonal cylinder recording the very conquest mentioned by the Hebrew prophet. Sargon's inscription read: "In my ninth expedition to the land beside the great sea, to Philistia and Ashdod I went . . . the cities of Ashdod and Gimzo of the Ashdodites I besieged and captured."[11]

Ashdod withstood siege longer than any city in history, when Pharaoh Psammeticus (633-609 B.C.), the first king of the 26th dynasty, kept his armies before its gates for 22 years ere the standard of Upper and Lower Egypt flew over the city. How strange are the vicissitudes of war. Men and maidens were born "with the enemy at their gates, grew to maturity, married and had their families—all with the menace of red death ever before them. Shut up within the city, the camp fires of the Egyptian glimmering every night in the warm dusk of the Philistine evening, or sputtering beneath the lash of the heavy rains of winter."[12]

Likewise young men entered on their military career in the Egyptian army, were assigned trench duty at Ashdod, finished their full years of service with their initial venture yet unsuccessful. Such sieges went far toward breaking up the military might of the Philistines. And of fulfilling the prophecy of Amos who, as God's prophet, had said, "And I will cut off the inhabitants from Ashdod . . . and the remnant of the Philistines shall perish" (Amos 1:8).

In the year 163 B.C. Judas Maccabaeus cleared the city of idols, and 15 years later Jonathan and Simon burnt the old temple of Dagon.[13]

During the Greek and Roman period Ashdod was known as *Azotus,* and it was here that Philip began his evangelistic tour after he had brought about the conversion and baptism of the treasurer of Ethiopia, "a eunuch of great authority under Candace, queen of the Ethiopians."[14]

Today the city mound rises high over the surrounding country, being covered on its very top with fields of lentils, and bordered with olives, figs, and other semitropical fruits. The secrets of the interior remain yet to be divulged by a thorough archaeological expedition, the process of which would be thrilling and the results enlightening. An Arab village nestles at the foot of the mound eastward. But in 1958, the Jews began to build a new town four miles north of the biblical mound, and to make of Ashdod Israel's newest Mediterranean port. Large docking facilities were built, and soon its population grew to 24,000 with splendid prospects for the future.

Askelon, 10 miles north of Gaza, was the second seaport city of the Philistines. Having no inlet of the sea or natural harbor in which vessels might be sheltered, its walls were so arranged as to stretch around the water's front like "a deeply bent bow" with the sea in the position of the bowstring.

Askelon was wealthy and had a varied history. It was here that Samson collected the necessary articles to pay his wager with the Philistines. Here the mayor of the city made golden figures of mice to send with the ark of the covenant to Jerusalem, in an effort to propitiate God in relieving the Philistines of an awful scourge that must have been similar to the bubonic plague.[15]

Out from the port of ancient Askelon went large stores of food and provision shipped to Egypt, Greece, and other Mediterranean countries. Among the Tell El Amarna tablets there is a letter from "Ita, prince of Askelon," informing his overlord, the king of Egypt, that he had furnished all the "victuals, drinks, cattle, sheep, honey, and oil" that he had required. Considering it a central city of extreme importance, David, in his lament over Gilboa's tragedy, said, "Tell it not in Gath, publish it not in the streets of Askelon."[16]

Just previous to the Christian era, the place became famous as the birthplace of *Herod the Great,* who honored his native city by erecting magnificent buildings, "baths, costly fountains, and a cloistered court." But Askelon's history was not to be written in such peaceful paragraphs. Fierce and bloody battles were to be fought around and within those half-circled walls. The conflict between the cross and the crescent brought days of trial and disaster, when both Godfrey and Richard held it for a time, then Saladin. The city being lost and won like a pawn, and destroyed and rebuilt like a plaything, its ruin was at last sealed, and it never arose to any prominence. The city whose name had been known in every land in Europe came to be known as a place of "utter desolation," where fragments of massive walls marked outlines of the once proud and famous city of the Philistines and of Herod the Great.

A few years ago, an Arab owner of land within the ruins of Askelon was cutting a towing path to enable a camel to draw water from a well when he found some bronze figures. Subsequently, Mr. J. Ory, inspector of the Department of Antiquities, carried out soundings and found a hoard of bronzes, including human figures, animals, and weights. One figure, thought to represent Isis nursing Horus, still had on its face the original gold leaf with which it was covered. It was thought probable that most, if not all, the figurines were similarly gilded.[17] Further excavations laid bare so many walls and interesting ruins that historical

Askelon has now been made a national park to which visitors pay an entrance fee.

Gaza, the most famous of the five Philistine confederate cities, and one of the oldest cities in history, was located two and one-half miles from the sea, on a well-rounded hill rising some 60 feet above the surrounding plain. Situated on the great coastal highway between Egypt and Mesopotamia and at a junction of the trade route from south Arabia, it was one of the ideally located caravan cities and an important commercial and military center when Moses led the Israelites out of Egypt to Canaan.

Markets, traffic, and trade have always been the very life of the city; yet Gaza exported more than she imported, for the gardens, orchards, olive groves, and extensive grainfields north and east, stretching away for miles and billowing like the waves of the sea, supplied the local demand and furnished cargoes for the outgoing ships bound for Phoenicia, Greece, and the islands of the sea.

It was here that Samson took one of his first steps on the downward road. Here, when the Gazites attempted to trap him, he "took the doors of the gate of the city, and the two posts and went away with them, bar and all, and carried them to the top of a hill," which tradition says is the prominent but isolated hill of *El Muntar,* southeast of Gaza. Here, too, he was forced to come when the Philistines "put out his eyes, brought him down to Gaza," and "he did grind in the prison house." Often he must have thought of his godly mother and the angel who talked to her of God's plan for his life—"If I only had . . ." Here he made vows to God and his strength returned. Then one day while making sport for the Philistines, he asked to be led to the two principal pillars of the great temple of Dagon. On removing these, the building crashed and killed both himself and the leading lords and ladies of the Philistines (Judg. 16:20-30).

The Philistine gods were Dagon, Baal-Zebub, and Astarte. The manner of worship directed toward these false deities debased and sensualized the worshippers. Unchaste goals and gross materialism gradually swallowed up the Philistines. Their cities are now but dust and their name a curse, while noble ideals and a sense of the sacred mission not only preserved Israel but caused them to give to the world sacred law, ennobling literature, fearless prophets, and the Messiah who pointed the path to higher realms and imbued men's minds with a spiritual ideal that should outlive the ages.

Gerar, where both Abraham and Isaac sojourned for a time, dug wells, and prospered under the generous treatment of "Abimelech king of Gerar" (Genesis 20 and 26), has long been identified with *Tel el Jemmeh,* about eight miles south of Gaza. The mound was partially excavated by W. J. Phythian-Adams (1922) and Sir Flinders Petrie (1927). In the former excavation four city levels were found, extending from the Patriarchal to the Roman period. In one short season Dr. and Mrs. Petrie uncovered seals, scarabs, jewelry, idols, weapons, household utensils, agricultural tools, grain pits, a "sword furnace" where iron implements were sharpened, and a large variety of pottery. Nothing was found that identified the site as Gerar.

More recent surveys have led many very good authorities to believe that Gerar should be identified with *Tell Abu Hureira,* which lies on the banks of Wady esh-Sheriah, 11 miles southeast of Gaza. On this 40-acre mound is found an abundance of pottery which indicates prosperity during the Patriarchal period. Anywhere one may dig here he will find an abundance of water 20 to 30 feet beneath the surface.

CHAPTER **6**

The Shephelah

The term *Shephelah* means the "low hills" and is applied to the group of irregular hills lying between the Plain of the Philistines and the central range of the mountains of Judea. The term "the hills" was first applied to this section in the Book of Joshua,[1] and later the Talmud merely designated it "the Shephelah."[2] The Bible refers to this section 18 or 20 times under the general name Shephelah. In this wide sense Shephelah included much of the territory originally given to the tribe of Dan.[3]

This region measures about nine miles from east to west, and extends from the Valley of Aijalon on the north to Wady esh-Sheriah on the south. It is entirely separated from the Central Mountain Range of Judea and has a topography different from that of any other section in Palestine. Its hills, with open valleys between, vary in height from 500 to 1,000 feet above sea level and are usually covered with marl, clay, pebbles, and soft, chalky limestone, with here and there an outcropping of fragments of black like flint.[4]

The Shephelah is more than barren hills. Its agricultural life, its historical background, and its valleys with their cities teem with interest.

The inhabited villages and cities of the Shephelah are frequent. The soil, in its own way, is some of the richest and most productive. Its special adaptation is to olive groves and grain. The olives are usually grown on terraced hillsides which have been built up with stone retaining walls. Grainfields abound on the more level areas. There are also a few mulberry, sycamore, and scrub oak trees growing here and there. In recent years the rougher areas have been reforested with a variety of trees.

The Shephelah is refreshed by the sea breezes, receives a fair amount of rainfall, and is blessed with numerous springs in areas where there is an outcrop of hard limestone. In fact, almost all the area is underlain with a sheet of very fine water, and any number of wells may be dug only a few feet below the surface of the ground and will yield an abundant supply of spring water.

The great number of ruined sites indicate that a heavy population once lived there, and agree with the large number of towns mentioned in the Bible and other ancient literature. Even the caves seem to have been used at times for living and other purposes. There were continual Philistine raids in the springtime to rob the threshing floors when the people were busy during the harvest treading the grain, winnowing it of chaff, and placing it in the garners. Such harvest scenes as those enacted 3,000 years ago are plentiful today within the same valleys and on the same plains.

Today there is peace in the Shephelah, with no thought of

marauding bands to carry away the golden harvest. But it has not always been so, for this territory more justly deserves the name of "The Hills of Conflict" than most any other in Palestine.

Those who have lived here in times past have been accustomed to war and invasion which have come at frequent intervals. Here Israel and the Philistines frequently met in conflict and fought their bitter and often decisive battles; here the Maccabeans were nurtured and breathed the air of conflict, meeting their Hellenistic enemies and overcoming them with inferior numbers. Here the British yeomanry under Allenby forced the Turco-German forces along through these narrow mountain defiles before they were well aware that the British would not be content to camp in the Plain of Philistia and Sharon below.

There are four valleys that descend through these hills through which the tides of war have surged during the centuries. They are the Valley of Aijalon, the Valley of Sorek, the Valley of Elah, and the Valley of Zephathah.

The Valley of Aijalon begins at the Plain of Sharon and rapidly ascends to the foot of the Central Mountain Range. Here the high walls of rock seem to forbid further passage, except where three gorges break through and ascend as narrow defiles up past the two Beth-horons to the plateau at Gibeon, five miles northwest of Jerusalem.

The Philistines came up this valley to get at Israel; and here the Maccabeans, the Greeks, the Romans, and the Crusaders fought some of their most noted battles. The narrow defiles proved an aid to the defenders, and defeat became so common here that military leaders came to shun the place or carefully study the terrain when they made a drive on the uplands of Palestine. General Allenby is a classic example, for he carefully studied the Bible, Josephus, and George Adam Smith before his final drive on the uplands of Judea.

The Valley of Aijalon will ever be memorable because of Joshua's experience there. When the long-drawn battle was turning to victory and time was getting short, lest darkness come on and limit the victory, the leader of the Lord's host called on Jehovah to stay the sun in its course—that the sun no longer whirl the 83 earth about in the usual manner. God stayed the earth in its course, and since then men have been saying that if need be, God will do almost anything to help His people who will dare ask largely and trust Him implicitly.[5]

The Valley of Sorek lies south of Aijalon and at present is known as *Wady Surar.* As the second approach to the mountains of Judea, it springs away from the Plain of the Philistines near Ekron and Gezer and advances broadly through the hills of the Shephelah, narrowing as it approaches the Judean uplands a few miles west of Jerusalem. In its lower places it is one of the most fertile portions of the Shephelah.

It was up this valley that the Philistines sent the ark of the Lord on a cart drawn by lowing milch cows that, as if by divine compulsion, took the "straight way" from Ekron to Beth-shemesh where the people reaping in the fields saw the ark coming up the road, and went out to meet it.[6]

The Valley of Sorek will ever be associated with Samson the strong man. It was at *Zorah,* overlooking this valley, that his parents lived and worshipped God when an angel announced that a son would be given them, who should be dedicated to the Lord for the express purpose of "troubling the Philistines." After coming to manhood, he crossed and recrossed this valley time and again as he went down into the Philistine plain.

Today the valley is well covered with grainfields, possesses a number of thriving Jewish colonies, and has running directly through it the railway that connects Jaffa to Jerusalem.

The Valley of Elah is the third approach through the Shephelah to the Central Mountain Region of Judea. At Tell es-Safi, which is thought by some to be Gath, the native city of Goliath, the valley leaves the Plain of the Philistines and ascends eastward until it reaches the great watershed of Judea southwest of Bethlehem. This valley offered a fairly convenient pass for the Philistines, and they often endeavored to make use of it in their warfare against the Israelites.

84   The Valley of Elah will always be remembered as the scene where God proved that fearless faith in Him was not without reward. For it was here that David, the shepherd lad, met and

overcame Goliath, the giant, with a simple sling and a smooth stone and sent the Philistines through this very opening near Gath back to the gates of Ekron. In the streambed running through the center of this valley are thousands of stones—"round and smooth" like the five stones which David chose and placed in his scrip as he went out to meet Goliath.[7]

The Valley of Zephathah, now called *Wadi Zeita,* is the fourth and final approach through the Shephelah. This valley has its beginning just west of the fine old fortress of Beth-zur which guarded the highroad to Jerusalem. The pass through this beautiful valley vibrated to the tread of military men of Egypt, Babylon, and Europe, but perhaps the most famous and startling event of this valley took place when Nebuchadnezzar of Assyria captured Lachish in 701 B.C., and used it as a base of operation against Judea.

Also, there are two wadis which penetrate the Shephelah: Wadi Hesi and Wadi Sheriah.

Wadi Hesi rises in the mountains some six miles southwest of Hebron and finds its way to the sea between Gaza and Askelon. On this watercourse is located the important site of *Tell el Hesi;* and up this way was an important roadway leading into the highlands.

Wadi Sheriah rises far south of Debir (Kirjath Sepher), and after flowing some miles, it joins the more famous Wadi Ghazzeh, and then flows into the sea four miles south of Gaza.

It was inevitable that the people who fortified and held these four southern passes would control the highlands of central Canaan. It was likewise inevitable that the Shephelah, the immediate approach to these passes, would constitute disputed territory and a battlefield. The history of the region is a story of continual struggle gathering round the names of the Philistines, Hebrews, Greeks, Romans, and others who dared to invade the hill country of Judea or to descend from the highlands in formidable attacks on the plainsmen. To visualize these valleys is to better understand the wars which have been waged in this area from Joshua's time to Allenby's. 85

Six of the more famous cities of the Shephelah were Aijalon,

Zorah, Timnath, Gezer, Maresha, and Lachish. These cities are not inhabited now. Some have been excavated, and the others which have not are just mounds.

Aijalon is the town from which the Valley of Aijalon derives its name. Near here Joshua was able to complete the routing of the five kings because of the miraculous prolongation of daylight.

Zorah will ever be associated with the strange, strong man, Samson. Near here, out in the field, an angel talked with a wonderful woman, the wife of Manoah. Nearby is an ancient rock altar which could well be the one upon which Manoah offered a "meat offering," and "the angel of the Lord talked with Manoah, then ascended in the flame above the altar."[8] Here Samson was born, and here he gave the first indication of his great mission to liberate Israel from the yoke of the Philistines. After the tragic death of Samson at Gaza, his body was returned and buried here near Zorah. A two-room home, with walls constructed of solid stone, is now shown visitors as the "home of Samson."

The spies and raiders of the Danites started from Zorah when they went in search of a place to settle in another section of Palestine—and eventually settled permanently at Dan.[9]

Four miles southwest of Zorah, on the crest of the ridge opposite, are the ruins of **Timnath.** This is the home of the Philistine woman to whom Samson was married. While on his way to see his love one day, a lion roared at him from out of the thickets. Samson killed the lion with his own hands, and bees built in the lion's carcass and there stored their honey. On passing by later, Samson observed the unusual phenomena and formed the riddle, "Out of the eater come forth meat, and out of the strong come forth sweetness."[10]

Gezer, now called *Tell el Jazar,* commanded the entrance to the Valley of Aijalon, and was one of the older sites known in Palestine. Its name is said to mean "precipice," which seems suggestive of its isolated position high on a hill in the extreme northwestern section of the Shephelah.

Excavations revealed a well-built stone wall about 16 feet

thick surrounding the city. On the south stood a massive brick gateway. Within the very heart of the city there is a great tunnel about 200 feet long, with a vertical depth of 94 feet. Here along this descending stair-cased tunnel were smoke-stained niches wherein had set olive oil lamps to give light. At the bottom of the tunnel was a living spring that furnished a never-failing supply of water for the people both in time of peace and in time of siege. This tunnel was constructed about 2000 B.C. and abandoned about 1400 B.C.

The area around Gezer is quite fertile and well watered. On these hillsides immediately surrounding the city mound can be found literally hundreds of threshing floors where the people and their animals tread the grain and winnow it of chaff just as they have done for centuries.

Maresha, one mile south of Beit Jibrin, was the home of the prophet Micah, who said God would be compassionate and "cast all their sins into the depths of the sea."[11]

Lachish and Azekah were the last cities in Palestine to fall during the Babylonian conquest. Lachish is seven miles southwest of Beit Jibrin on the road from Gaza to Hebron. For long centuries it has been but a tell or mound known by the natives as *Tell Duweir.*

An excavation was carried on in the season of 1932-35 to try to trace the sources of the various foreign contacts which influenced the development of Palestinan culture. There is ample evidence of influence from Egypt.

Under the Jewish monarchy Lachish was not so important as a city, but continued to be one of the principal fortresses. It was enclosed by a double wall connected by a double gatehouse. However, the city came to a violent end, being twice destroyed by fire within a few years. These two destructions have been connected with the two invasions of Nebuchadnezzar in 597 and 586 B.C. Between the two destructions the fortifications seem to have been somewhat restored. After the final capture there seems to have been a governor's official residence here during the Persian period, for there are remains of such a structure. From this point Lachish disappears from history as shown by the excavation.

87

The tell, or mound, covering the ancient fortified city of Lachish along the road from Hebron to Gaza.

For the Bible student, however, the main interest lies not in its history as a fortress of Judah, but in objects found in excavations carried on here. One of these was a tall water vessel with writing in Phoenician or proto-Hebrew characters; also a blade of a Hyksos dagger with four pictographic characters suitable to the age of Hezekiah, and a clay seal bearing on its back the impression of the fibers of the papyrus document to which it must have been attached when found, although proof of identity is impossible. Of greater significance, however, are the "Lachish Letters" which were found.

Even though these excavations may not add much to our definite knowledge about Lachish, there is no doubt that they add life and color of detail to the books in the Bible.

*

The
Central Mountain
Region

*

CHAPTER **7**

The Beauty of Lebanon

*L*ebanon, the "White Mountain," is the most northern zone of the Central Mountain Region. The range is nearly 100 miles in length, from north to south, but usually no more than 15 to 20 miles in width. *Leban* means "white," and the name in this instance is derived from the gleaming white limestone rocks and its ramparts of perpetual snow that in the winter season makes it to appear like a great white ghost silhouetted against the horizon. During other seasons of the year there is snow in places, yet the mountain has miles of greenery and is marvelous for its massiveness and its sheer loveliness.

90

The Lebanon range is largely made up of long, broad, east-west ridges, broken by hundreds of hills which are eventually dwarfed into insignificance by the wind-swept summits along the divide, or by the great peaks which rise behind them. *Mount Sunnin* stands 8,557 feet in its majestic beauty in the high ranges northeast of Beirut—the pride and joy of all who live in this area. On farther north is *Kornet es Sandra,* which rises to an elevation of 11,032 feet above sea level, the highest peak of the entire range.

One cannot traverse this region from north to south without meeting constant obstacles in the way of rugged ridges to be climbed or gorges and turbulent rivers to be crossed. The only possible routes from end to end of this famous mountain range is along the Mediterranean coast or along the valley of Bekaa, east of the range.

To penetrate the Lebanons from the west or the east, one must walk or ride a donkey through deep valleys, by charming glens, and along turbulent streams which leap from limestone caves and roar along in their white swiftness, now under a natural bridge, and then to cascade from terrace to terrace on toward the sea.

The worth of the Lebanons cannot be better described than as "a great treasure-house of interest" in its history, geography, geology, botany, ethnology, and archaeology. Its lofty summits, its frightful chasms, its deep caverns and subterranean lakes, its magnificent fountains and cascades, its noble cedars, its vineyards; its orchards, walnut and olive groves; its ruined temples and nameless vestiges of hoary antiquity; its monasteries, churches, Druse chapels, and palaces; its picturesque villages; and the daily practices and beliefs of its people combine to make it a fruitful theme of study and an endless delight to the passing traveler and the most scholarly and patient explorer.[1]

In viewing Lebanon, crowned with its diadem of cedars, one becomes enraptured and delighted by the different tints of azure, which, shaded by the diversity of distance, blend together between sea and sky. He breathes a soft and balmy air, and the soul itself becomes subdued and filled with reverence before this land of ancient renown which God bequeathed to His chosen people when He divided the world among the nations. The land which Moses desired to see, but never entered; one which King Solomon knew intimately, and other Hebrew people visited frequently.

Its picturesque landscapes with their varied splendor always astonish visitors. The plains, the uplands, the valleys, and the mountains make the country look like a small universe.

The Bible, finding no more appropriate criterion of beauty than Lebanon, extols its perfumes, its flowers, its cedars, its meadows, and its beautiful views.[2] Its soft-flowing waters, green trees, plants, attractive shrubbery, and brilliant shades truly make it a revelry of beauty. Under a cloudless sky and a golden sun everything testifies to the terrific force of the Word of God. Peaks pierce the sky at a prodigious height; crests, bolder still, rise beyond and appear as though eternally on fire in the midst of the sun-struck snow. Below, in the deep valleys, flow the famous waters of ancient and celebrated rivers. Above these rivers tower masses of rock, some of which are sharp like titanic blades of stone, and others massive and round like gigantic cannonballs; and on yet higher is the perpetual whiteness of its ever melting, yet eternal, snows. The people who live here say that Lebanon bears winter on its head, spring on its shoulders, summer on its bosom, while autumn lies slumbering at its feet.

No city of any size is found in these mountains, yet there are Roman-built bridges which span streams, and there are more than 1,300 villages and rural towns which nestle along these valleys, cling to hillsides, or perch high on mountainous tablelands. Some live in the midst of this indescribable beauty, work their gardens, tend their orchards, and ply their simple trades, yet seldom sense the wealth which lies all about them. Others do realize the wonders of their country, for when they pray, they say, "Thank God for this beautiful land. It must be beautiful or folks wouldn't come so far to see it."[3]

The *Cedars of Lebanon,* which have adorned the mountains from time immemorial, have always been renowned in literature and history as the emblem of majesty, strength, and beauty. In

A few of the famed "Cedars of Lebanon" which are not nearly as plentiful as they once were.

size they are somewhat like our redwoods of California, but not so tall. Isaiah speaks of them as "the cedars of Lebanon that are high and lifted up, the glory of Lebanon." The Psalmist says that "the righteous shall grow like a cedar in Lebanon."[4]

In the course of his warning message to Pharaoh, Ezekiel uttered an allegorical dirge over the king of Assyria whom he compared to a cedar of Lebanon which had prospered until "no tree in the garden of God was like unto him in his beauty," but when his "heart was lifted up" in pride, God delivered him to the woodsman who came and laid his branches low (Ezek. 31:1-14).

In ancient times the Lebanon mountains, for 100 miles along their higher ranges, were covered with cedar forests whose trees were known to be suitable for carving, to be heavy with resin, to emit a fragrance, to take a high polish, to resist termites, and to be exceedingly durable. Kings and rulers and craftsmen and military men used them freely in shipbuilding, coffin construction, idol manufacture, siege engines, and the ceilings of temples and palaces in all the Middle East countries.

From about 2850 to 1350 B.C., Egypt got its supply of resinous woods from here, and with these they ceiled and adorned their famous temples. The Assyrians began making use of them about 1100 B.C., and shortly before 700, Sargon II made especially heavy demands on them. King David built himself a palace of cedar wood (2 Sam. 5:11). Solomon, Zerubbabel, and Herod used them to roof, ceil, and adorn their magnificent temples at Jerusalem. Nebuchadnezzar, the mighty monarch of Babylon, in an inscription dug from the libraries of that mighty city, says:

> At that time the place—my royal abode—I rebuilt in Babylon. Great cedars I brought from the beautiful forest of Lebanon to roof it. A great wall of mortar and brick I threw about them. . . . The great gates of both Imgur Bel and Ninitti Bel. . . . With burnt brick and brilliant blue glaze tile on which bells and serpents were engraved I made them skillfully. Great cedars for their covering with bronze. Those great gates I ornamented to the astonishment of men.[5]

Almost all the famous temples throughout the Near Eastern countries, including that of Diana of Ephesus, were ceiled with these cedars. Tiglath-pileser visited the Lebanons for the purpose of obtaining cedarwood to adorn the temple and palaces of Ashur (now called *Kalat Shergat*) in ancient Assyria. Alexander got the timber supply for his siege of Tyre in the Lebanons, and other generals of military might have used this area as their base of supply.

It was long supposed that the supply of timber from these forests was inexhaustible, but time has proven otherwise. Of their former magnificence all that now remains consists of a few groups, scattered at wide intervals over the mountains. In all these groups, with a single exception, the trees are comparatively young and of small size. The only grove of any size and age is the far-famed group of some 600 which are about 40 miles northeast of Beirut. They stand nearly 7,000 feet above the level of the sea, and 2,000 feet below the summits of Lebanon. Among these 600 trees, there are about 12 which are the remaining representatives of the ancient forest.

These time-honored trees grow to 100 to 120 feet in height. The trunks of the older trees are of enormous girth. Several are from 6 to 10 feet, and one is 42 feet in circumference measured a short distance above the ground, at which point it sends off five immense branches, each from 3 to 5 feet in diameter, thus, in reality, constituting five trees of immense size. This tree with its branches measures two or three hundred feet in circumference.

No certain estimate can be formed of the age of these trees, but the largest of them, known as the "Guardian," is reputed to be at least 2,000 years old—some say as much as 3,000. Certainly the oldest of these trees waved in their wild way when Christ was born at Bethlehem, when Rome declined, and when the Crusaders passed by to recover the tomb of Christ. For centuries they have stood as silent sentinels of the far-famed Lebanon, and a remnant of those "cedars of the Lord" which went into so many sacred edifices which are famous wherever the Bible and ancient history have been read. Long the symbol of peaceful life they are now the political emblem of the Republic of Lebanon.   95

The country of Lebanon is an ideal summer resort. The mountains are cool, and there is no rain between June and October. The sea breezes combined with the cool mountain atmosphere lend health and vigor which is surpassed by few other places on the globe. Tourists never tire of the ever-changing beauty of the scenery, the lusciousness of its fruits, the courtesy and hospitality of the people. No matter what village you visit, there is always someone to show you around.

It is little wonder that Lady Hester Stanhope, the niece of the great William Pitt, should become enamored of these gorgeous mountains. With her uncle gone, and Sir John Moore—Britain's most efficient military general, and the only one she ever loved—dying with her name as the last words on his lips, she packed up and traveled in Eastern lands to finally purchase a mansion on a mountaintop 12 miles northeast of Sidon. Here she added 25 rooms and spent a fortune on horses, guards, servants, and just living the last 20 years of her life; to finally die on June 23, 1839, and be buried on the hilltop midst the trees, the flowers, and the singing birds.

CHAPTER **8**

Upper Galilee

Upper Galilee begins with
the Leontes River as its northern boundary line, and continues
southward to an irregular line running from the north end of the
Sea of Galilee by *Wady Maktul* leading up from the Plain of Gennesaret to the canyon just south of Safed, and thence westward
to the Plain of Acre. It is actually a continuation of the Lebanon
mountain chain, and is made up of a series of broad mountain
plateaus which rise in elevation from 2,000 to 4,260 feet above sea
level. The highest and most noticeable point is *Mount Jermuk,*

which is the principal landmark of the entire section—the highest point west of the Jordan.[1]

The numerous valleys and narrow passes of this highland territory are made fertile by a rich red loam soil, much of which has for centuries been protected and kept moist by a growth of entangled shrubbery. The rainfall here is heavier than elsewhere in Palestine, wells are numerous, the climate equitable, and the mountains well wooded with such trees as oak, pine, beach, carob, myrtle, bay, and maple. Here also are olive orchards, fruit trees of various kinds, and many grainfields which usually produce an abundant harvest. The wealth of olive trees made Galilee literally a country flowing with oil. "It is easier," says the Talmud, "to raise a legion of olives in Galilee than to bring up a child in Palestine."

The terrain of certain sections of Upper Galilee is marked by extinct craters, ancient basaltic dikes, and bubbling hot springs, all of which show unmistakable signs of former earthquakes and volcanic activity.

Though the ancient Galileans for the most part were a quiet, peaceful, simple, hill-country folk, they were proud of their country; and when liberty was challenged, they went forth lion-hearted to fight for their homeland against the Roman oppressors. Josephus writes, "The Galileans are inured to war from their infancy . . . nor hath the country been ever destitute of men of courage or wanted a numerous set of them." Also, excavations have uncovered the ancient remains of great pillars and fine capitals, beautifully carved stones, ornamental decorations, and inscriptions, which indicate that they were a people who excelled in the building craft.[2]

Cities and villages have long dotted the Galilean hillsides. Here lay the "twenty cities" which Solomon gave Hiram in return for the cedars of Lebanon, which had been carried to Jerusalem for the purpose of ceiling Solomon's new palace and Temple.

At certain intervals through the past centuries, the country has been ravaged by earthquake and war. It was the vanguard in the fight against Rome and the battleground in the fight for the preservation of the ancient synagogues of that time with their

A shepherd with a flock of fat-tailed sheep in Upper Galilee

Jewish symbols and Hellenistic art forms. It was in Upper Galilee that the Jews showed such self-sacrifice for their culture, their country, and their homes. Almost every acre there is a reminder of those events.

After the fall of Jerusalem the bulk of the Jewish people concentrated in Galilee; and it became for many centuries onward, until the Arab conquest, the center of Jewish political and religious life. Principal among the ancient and present cities are the following: *Abel-beth-maachah, Safad, Meron, Gischala, Zebulun, Kedesh, Hazor, Rosh Pina, Metulla,* and *Kfar Gilaid.*

Abel-beth-maachah ("meadow of the house of oppression") was a city of importance in the extreme northern portion of Palestine, which played a rather important although somewhat tragic role in ancient Bible times. It was to this fortified city that Joab pursued Sheba, son of Bichri, and the "wise woman" tossed the rebel's head over the wall and saved the city (2 Sam. 20:14). It was taken by the Syrians under Ben-hadad (1 Kings 15:

20), and later by the Assyrians under Tiglath-pileser (2 Kings 15:29). In Roman times it was known as Abila. Today it is known as *Tell Abil,* and is a typical unexcavated city mound rising out boldly on an upland plain some six miles west of Dan, overlooking the Lake Huleh lowlands that stretch away to the southeast.

Safad, one of the four "holy cities" of the Jews, and supposedly the city to which Christ referred when He said, "A city that is set on a hill cannot be hid," proudly curls about the top of Mount Safad, 16 miles north of Tiberias and 3,400 feet above the Sea of Galilee.

Within the city are narrow streets, flights of steep steps, whitewashed houses with extended balconies, and synagogues on which appear mysterious Cabalistic signs. About the place are large olive plantations, fruitful vineyards, and the strangest mystical charms pervading the atmosphere—deep rooted in the past, yet ample to entertain the eye of the present. On a clear day, much of Upper and Lower Galilee and the Sea of Galilee may be seen from this tableland city.

In the glory days of the kingdoms of Israel and Judah it was called Tsafet, or Zefat, which means the "place of outlook." From it a beacon light was lighted announcing the rising of the new moon, which was first proclaimed in Jerusalem on the Mount of Olives and relayed from high point to high point until Safad's beacon served as a signal for northern Palestine.[3]

Safad excites an attitude of reverence in the hearts of the Jews; for it was the refuge of many ancient rabbis after the fall of Jerusalem and the bitter defeat of Bar Cochba at Bittier in A.D. 132; and as a scholar's retreat it became the seat of a great Talmudic school, a center of Judaic and Cabalistic lore. It is even probable that the celebrated *Midrash Ha Zohar,* the Book of Splendor, the Bible of the Kabala, attributed to Simon ben Yohai, was edited here by a Spanish rabbi who flourished about A.D. 160. It was also the residence of Joseph Caro, author of the *Ahulchan Aruch,* the last codification of the Jewish law; and his

100 pupil, Rabbi Jacob Berov, who endeavored to reestablish Palestine as the center for rabbinical ordination.

In the 16th and 17th centuries, Safad became the center of

immigration from Spain and the rendezvous of the Jews for the study of Cabalist mysticism. Jewish poetry saw its revival when Alkabetz wrote the famous Sabbath Eve hymn, "Come, My Friend, to Meet the Bride." At this time the first printing press of all Asia was set up, and the first Hebrew book printed in Palestine.

In 1607, there was reputed to be in Safad 300 rabbis, 18 rabbinical colleges, and 21 synagogues. Because it housed this great rabbinical school, Safad earned for itself among the Jews the high distinction of being one of the four holy cities of Israel.

Here the Jewish mystics dreamed dreams, saw visions, and compiled the *Zohar*, in which it was stated that the Messiah would appear first in Upper Galilee. Isaac Luria stands out as the giant and genius of all these mystics, and the grandest figure of Safad legend, and his pupil, Rabbi Haim Vital, almost as famous. It was the mystics' dreaming which made possible the messianic movement that had its strange fulfillment in the Shabbathai Zevi, and which also bore fresh fruit in more recent years when the modern dream of the return to Palestine stirred the heart of Israel.

An earthquake occurred at Safad in 1765, in which most of the inhabitants were killed; but the town was resettled so that by the early 1800s it housed 4,000 Jews. Unfortunately another disastrous earthquake occurred in 1836 and once again took the lives of most of the community. Since this disaster the city fell from its proud Jewish pinnacle, and its schools and synagogues no longer had preeminence. However, it is now flourishing again under the new Israeli government and is known especially for its "artists' colony."

Meron, four miles northwest of Safad, is a small village located in a picturesque setting of fine groves of olive and fig trees. It is frequently mentioned in the Talmud and is revered by the Jews as one of their most sacred shrines, because it was here that the famous rabbis and celebrated Jewish sages of centuries past, who lived at Safad and elsewhere, were buried: Rabbi Simon ben 101 Yohai, the one whose teachings inspired the Jewish revolt against the Romans; his son Rabbi Eleazar; Rabbi Jochanan Sanderlar, a distinguished disciple of Rabbi Akiba, who would accept no payment for his teaching but made a living by repairing the sandals of his students; and of Rabbis Hillel and Shamai, the two most celebrated scholars who were famous for their interpretation of the Law and their teaching of the Talmud. Even the prophet Obadiah is said to be buried here.[4]

Once a year, on the anniversary of the death of Rabbi Simon ben Yohai, vast crowds come in procession from Safad, carrying decorated scrolls of the law. They throng the way to the tomb of Simon and light festive fires into which silks, jewels, and other valuables are thrown as sacrifices. Hundreds of candles burn in front of the tomb while young and old in glad abandon dance in ecstasy their religious dances from sunset to dawn. At midnight the sound of prayer mingles with the sound of song, and the sound of song accompanies the stepping of the dance, and the stepping of the dance keeps in time with the blazing of the fires and the words

Rabbi Simon ben Yohai,
He will never die;
His name is glorified on high,
Rabbi Simon ben Yohai

rise to the star-laden sky from the lips of Jews who have come from every quarter of the globe to Meron of Galilee to give expression to that more intense longing for a communion with God by means of ecstasy.

Gischala, now called El Jish, is located five miles northwest of Safad. It was a prosperous city in the time of Christ and is thought by some to be the original home of Paul's parents. It was the native home of John of Gischala who tricked the Romans in A.D. 67. This was the last of the Galilean fortresses to hold out against the Romans. The army had surrounded the city and offered John protection for surrender, but he begged that they would recognize the sacredness of the Sabbath day and withdraw their army until the following day when terms could be formally concluded.

When Titus, in all good faith, withdrew his troops for the

night, John of Gischala and his band of Zealots marched out of the city under cover of darkness and made their way to Jerusalem. On Monday the Romans took the city without its leaders. At a later date Gischala was totally destroyed by an earthquake; not a house of any kind was left standing. However, the village has been partially rebuilt.

Zebulun, now called Neby Sebelan, is only a few miles southwest of Gischala and is wedged between the southern half of Naphtali and Asher.

Kedesh or *Kedesh-Naphtali* was one of the six cities of refuge in Old Testament times, the birthplace of Barak (Judg. 4:6), and the traditional burial place of Naphtali, Barak, Deborah, and Jael. The site of ancient Kedesh is now partially occupied by a small Arab village located on the end of a ridge overlooking the Kadesh plain. The ruins about the place are quite extensive, the most imposing of which are those of a structure called the Temple of the Sun.

Hazor is situated three miles south of Kedesh, at the head of one of the most rugged ascents in Palestine. It is in a strong position, occupying a full 200 acres on top of the mound. Once a royal town, but in recent times a rocky hillock honeycombed with broken cisterns, it is surrounded in places by broken walls and partially filled moats.

It was destroyed by Joshua during the great battle with the Canaanites but was rebuilt and became the capital of another Jabin, who long oppressed the northern tribes. He was finally overthrown in a crushing defeat in the great battle of Tabor, when Deborah and Barak led the Hebrews. Extensive excavations have been carried on at Hazor, since 1955, by Dr. Yigael Yadin. Ten city levels were found on the mound of the acropolis, one of which was identified as the "Solomonic level."

Rosh Pina, the "Mother of Colonies," is situated on a parcel of land at the foot of Mount Canaan, just a short distance east of Safad. It was founded in 1882 by about 50 Jewish families from Romania who walked or rode camels from Beirut to the site which had been purchased by Reb Davis. On seeing the rock and boulder-crowned area, they were overwhelmed by its grandeur and exclaimed, "The rock rejected by the builders became the cornerstone [Rosh Pina]" (Ps. 122:18). They made a covenant of peace with the Arabs and built with this verse reverberating in their ears.

In the following year they celebrated their first Harvest Festival and made a covenant between man and the soil by their first marriage. Unfortunately an Arab construction worker was accidentally killed by a shot fired in honor of the bride. After considerable compensation and intercession, peace was finally restored at a great "feast of forgiveness," and the next of kin renounced their right to avenge the death of their kinsman.

The settlers were often plagued by drought, malaria, mosquitos, pernicious illness, and death. They became discouraged and talked of abandoning the place and returning to Romania. But when the more courageous members had convened the settlers in the synagogue, one mother who had lost her only son cried: "Are you not ashamed to leave the graves of your beloved ones here and shamefully return to your 'airy-business' in Diaspora?" They reconsidered and took an oath on the Torah scroll not to abandon the colony, and to excommunicate the "traitors and cowards" who dared to do so.

Shortly thereafter Baron Edmund Rothschild took Rosh Pina under his wing and furnished money, new homes and courtyards, a large schoolhouse, a beautiful synagogue, and shelters for their livestock. The settlers piped water to their homes, planted vineyards and mulberry trees for cultivating silkworms, and built factories for silk manufacture. Other families came, and the colony has prospered ever since.

Metulla, the northernmost Jewish settlement, noted for its healthful and invigorating mountain air and excellent view of the upper Jordan Valley, is located west of Mount Hermon and the ruins of the ancient Jewish city of Dan.

104   It too was founded by Baron Rothschild in 1896. Its main industry is grain, and cattle, with vineyards, almonds, and fruit trees being added more recently.

Kfar Gilaid with its surrounding grainfields and its hillsides decked with various fruit trees appears as a blooming garden spot or oasis in the desolation of the surrounding country.

It was originally founded in 1917 as two separate colonies on land belonging to Baron Rothschild, but was eventually merged into one. The settlers were all former members of the famous organization, "The Guard," which rendered wonderful service to the Jewish settlements of Palestine in the days of the early colonization movement.

Upper Galilee is a pleasant land with good soil, many trees, an excellent climate, and reasonable rainfall. It has long had farms and villages inhabited by Moslems, Druzes, and Christian Arabs. This century has brought a number of Jewish settlements which have done very well with olives, grain, dairying, poultry raising, bee-keeping, fishponds, and other means of livelihood, yet the country is sparsely settled, and could well become the home of many other tens of thousands of industrious home seekers. The one thing needed here, and throughout the Holy Land, is PEACE.

CHAPTER **9**

Lower Galilee

Lower Galilee is situated just south of Upper Galilee and is north of the Plain of Armageddon and the Valley of Jezreel. To the west lies the Plain of Acre, while the Sea of Galilee makes up the eastern boundary.

This picturesque and beautiful country is largely composed of a series of low, long, parallel mountain ranges with broad plateaus broken by wooded glens; wide, fertile valleys; meandering brooks; and soft marshland. The rolling hills of Lower Galilee are not as rugged as those of Upper Galilee, and the valleys and plains are wider; and in season their fields of wheat and barley, with alternate stretches of fallow land, mark a checkerboard on the plains and along the lower reaches of the hills and mountains.

The soil in most of Lower Galilee is very fertile. Flowers of many varieties grow bountifully, and it is known for its great variety of fruits, melons, grain, and vegetables. There are forests of oak, orchards of olive and fig trees, and the evergreen cactus hedges which show off well against numerous white walls.

The villages in Lower Galilee are many, but its principal cities of historical interest are Nazareth, Sepphoris, Jotapata, Cana, Nain, and Endor.

Nazareth nestles within a circular vale and on the surrounding mountain slopes just above the Plain of Armageddon. It was never mentioned by name either in the Old Testament nor by Josephus, but it has a prominent place in the New Testament. Inwardly and silently the life of the Master, in His formative years, unfolded itself at Nazareth. Thirty out of the 33 years that He lived on the earth were here, and that life in those few years stamped the city with a sacredness which will last until the end of time.

It is sometimes said that Nazareth was an obscure place, but this is an inaccurate statement. The city, in Christ's day, was little more than a mile long and a half mile wide, and was almost completely shut in by surrounding hills. This provided seclusion, yet it was not an out-of-the-way place, for along the hilltops a few hundred yards east of the city there ran a much traveled branch road, and five miles east was the highway from Assyria to Egypt, over which went caravans of all kinds and men of every nation and tongue. As a young man Jesus could climb the high hill back of Nazareth and see the great Plain of Armageddon, Mount Carmel, the Mediterranean Sea, Mount Tabor, the Jezreel Valley, Gilboa, and the great international highway.

Jesus was a carpenter in Nazareth until that day He left the shop to enter His period of active ministry. Yet being a carpenter then meant some things different from now. Someone has sug- 107 gested that the imagery of His teachings and His parables carry an atmosphere of the life of the soil—of nature and the farm such as you would expect to find in the country, rather than that of the carpenter shop. However, in those days—as in rural Palestine today—the carpenter made plows, yokes, and goads for field work, and made or mended carts, wagons, and chariots for the highways. These were made of wood, while most homes were made almost entirely of stone or of adobe brick and were constructed mostly by the masons.

As a carpenter, Jesus made yokes, and deep was the meaning of His words, "Take my yoke upon you, and learn of me . . . For my yoke is easy, and my burden is light" (Matt. 11:29-30). As a minister, Jesus Christ returned "in the power of the Spirit" into Galilee and taught in their synagogues. He came to Nazareth, where He had been brought up, and as usual went into the synagogue on the Sabbath day. It was there He read from the scroll of the prophet Isaiah the words:

> The Spirit of the Lord is upon me, because he hath anointed me to preach the gospel to the poor; he hath sent me to heal the brokenhearted, to preach deliverance to the captives, and recovering of sight to the blind, to set at liberty them that are bruised, to preach the acceptable year of the Lord (Luke 4:18-19).

When the people endeavored to stare Him out of countenance, He added, "This day is this scripture fulfilled in your ears." At that the people hustled Him out of the city and to the brow of the hill where they intended to throw Him headlong to His death. But He evaded them and left unnoticed. No record was ever kept as to the exact precipice, but a steep defile southeast is now called the Mount of Precipitation and is pointed out as the place where Christ's enemies had thought to end His career.

After Christ's time, there is little of importance on record about Nazareth until the time of Constantine, when the first Christian church was built there in A.D. 330. Then Nazareth became an object of great interest to which pilgrims flocked from all parts of the Christian world.

In Crusading times it became the seat of bishops, eight of whom are mentioned. In A.D. 1187 it was taken by Saladin, and his successors destroyed its churches, reducing it to an insignificant village. It was visited by Sir John Maundeville in A.D. 1332. In A.D. 1620 the Franciscans tried to establish themselves there, and in 1730 their first church, the Church of the Annunciation, was consecrated. Many Christians, chiefly Maronites, from Mount Lebanon began to make pilgrimages to it; and also Orthodox Christians from the Hauran in Transjordan.

Today Nazareth is a city of some 44,000 people, and as one passes along the narrow, yet attractive, streets, he hears the clang of hammers of the artisans who beat out brass and copper goods which lie on the ground both without and within the dark recesses of the shops. He may pause at the carpenter's shop where plows, yokes, tables, and stools are made, and the odor of sandalwood, wafted from the shops of curio makers, will remind one of the distant days when the Master was a woodworker in this selfsame place.

At the top of the principal Suke, the road turns abruptly to the left where the clothiers, the saddlers, and the drapers have their shops. The street is very attractive, and it is difficult to pass along it quickly without stopping to look, question, and purchase. The saddlers are particularly fascinating for, instead of plain brown leather, they deal in girths and reins of woven black, yellow and blue, and hung with woolen tassels.

Farther on, the grocery shops begin and the passerby has to push past trays of coffee beans and sugar and pink and white sweetmeats, big tins of paraffin, baskets of walnuts or almonds all crowding out of the shops onto the pavement, making the narrow street narrower still.

The chief water supply for the city of Nazareth has long been the Virgin's Fountain, which is the only living spring of water in or near the city. The women and girls fill their jars here morning and night. This sight, and the fountain itself, does much to give one a true picture of what occurred on many a day while Christ lived here in the long ago.

The houses in the main part of town are of gray limestone and are crowded close together from the base to near the summit of the hill; these are interspersed with fig, tamarisk, and carob trees. Olive groves and green cactus hedges enliven the landscape and give the little mountain town a picturesque appearance which is not easily forgotten by anyone who has looked upon the place. Some of the numerous "holy places" here could be false, but Nazareth is real; and that being true, it is holy ground. The events that took place here have made it such. However, for those who desire to see what church leaders have to show in the way of traditional "holy places," there is a church building to mark each place.

First, in size and importance, is the *Church of the Annunciation* which is a new church (completed in 1966) which is said to be the largest Christian church in the Holy Land and one of the most holy shrines in the Christian world. Some regard it as the very cradle of Christianity. It is built over the site of a church which stood here from 1730 to 1955, and which itself was built over a Crusader foundation of the 12th century. The church stands on the site where, according to Christian tradition, the angel appeared before Mary to announce the birth of Jesus:

> The angel Gabriel was sent from God unto a city of Galilee, named Nazareth, to a virgin espoused to a man whose name was Joseph, of the house of David; and the virgin's name was Mary. And the angel came in unto her, and said, Hail, thou that art highly favoured, the Lord is with thee: blessed art thou among women. . . . Fear not, Mary: for thou hast found favour with God. And, behold, thou shalt conceive in thy womb, and bring forth a son, and shalt call his name JESUS. He shall be great, and shall be called the Son of the Highest . . . and of his kingdom there shall be no end *(Luke 1:26-28, 30-33)*.

The Grotto of the Annunciation is in the basement, and the altar there is inscribed with the words: "Verbum caro hic factum est"—Here the Word was made flesh.

The Church of Joseph, or the Church of the Holy Family, is supposed to occupy the site of the home of Mary and Joseph, with Joseph's carpenter shop in the basement. In the basement the altar bears the inscription: "Hic erat subditus illis"—Here He became subject to them. Excavations have been carried on here for some time, but as yet no final proof has been brought forth that this was the site of the home and the shop in which the Great Carpenter lived and worked.

The Synagogue Church is located in a market lane, and the ancient church beside it is the one which, according to tradition, is the synagogue Jesus attended.

The Basilica of Jesus the Adolescent is a beautiful church on the mountain overlooking Nazareth from the west. Adjoining it is the seminary usually known as the "Boy's School." This is well worth seeing, and the view from the top of the hill is one of the finest in the Holy Land—a point of view from which Jesus must have feasted His eyes many times.

Kiryat Natsrat is the name of the new Jewish suburb built on the top of the hills which tower above the city on the northeast.

Sepphoris, three miles northwest of Nazareth, was the Roman capital of Galilee during Christ's time. Through Sepphoris ran one of the great high roads from the Mediterranean coast to Damascus. Tradition suggests that Sepphoris was the original home of the parents of Mary, mother of Jesus. At one time it was the headquarters of the Jewish Sanhedrin, and here the Romans crucified many a Jew while Jesus was a boy. Sepphoris is surrounded with olive trees, and about a mile to the south is Kustul Seffurieh, with the fine large springs, where the army of the Christians encamped before the battle of Hattin. The city now lies in ruins.

Jotapata, now called *Khurbet Jefat,* is a ruin five and one-half miles north of Sepphoris. It is thought to be the town which gave name to the Valley of Jiphthahel mentioned in Josh. 19:27, but its fame is bound up with Josephus, the famous Jewish historian. It was here that Josephus fortified himself and his army for his last stand against the Romans in A.D. 67. Water was then scarce but provisions were plentiful, and the city was on a high precipice only accessible from the north. Here it was protected by a high wall.

Vespasian, the Roman general, built a bank against the wall, but the defenders built the wall higher and poured down boiling oil on the Roman soldiers. Then the Romans built 50 strong towers near the walls, whence, out of reach of the boiling oil, they hurled stones and threw javelins. Jotapata held out 47 days; then, during a surprise attack at early dawn on the morning of July 1, A.D. 67, a huge battering ram made a breach in the wall, and the Romans poured in and took control of the strong city. The women were taken as slaves, 15,000 men were killed, and 2,000 were sent to help cut the canal of Corinth. Josephus and four companions jumped into a dry well and from thence went into an underground cavern. When they were discovered and asked to surrender with a promise that they would be spared, Josephus desired to do so, but his companions were unwilling. They formed a death pact, drew lots, and killed each other, till only Josephus and one companion were left. Then by mutual consent the two walked out and surrendered themselves to the Romans.

Assuming the role of a prophet, Josephus advised them that Vespasian would soon become the emperor of the Roman Empire. The Romans thereafter used Josephus as an advisor and historian in the Palestinian campaign. The hill on which Vespasian camped is half a mile to the north.

Cana lies about four miles northeast of Nazareth. It is the hometown of Nathanael, the disciple of Jesus, and has become famous as the place of the wedding feast where Christ performed His first miracle by turning water into wine for the guests. Cana is a large village with well-built houses, but with few special marks of antiquity. The place is known as *Kefar Kana* to all the people in this region. It stands amidst many pomegranate, orange, and olive trees, along with arbors of grapevine. Nearby is a spring which is called the "Source of Cana."

The town itself nestles among the stony hills as so frequently characterizes the hillside villages of Palestine. Cana has two churches, both claiming to be built upon the site of the marriage feast. One is Latin, the other Greek. The Latin church, however, is the older of the two. Each of the churches displays two large water jars, declaring them to be the identical waterpots Christ used at the wedding feast. One may walk along a narrow path leading by stone houses and mud hovels to the center of the village, which looks very prosperous. An ornate marble sarcophagus does duty as a water trough, and women can be seen filling their pitchers from its contents.

Nain, now called Nein, lies on the northwestern slope of Mount Moreh, overlooking the lovely expanse of the northern arm of the Plain of Esdraelon, out of which, just opposite, rises the majestic Mount Tabor.

Here our Lord restored the widow's son to life and thus proved himself Lord of life (Luke 7:11-15). The city of Nein is now a small village of about 20 huts on a rocky slope in the midst of extensive ruins. There is a small modern Latin chapel that lies in the midst of a Moslem population. Four miles to the east of Nein is the village of Endor.

Endor is obviously the Endor of the Old Testament, assigned to Manasseh, though lying without the borders of that tribe. It is mentioned also in connection with the victory of Deborah and Barak, but is chiefly known as the abode of the sorceress to whom King Saul made his way and consulted on the eve of the fatal battle of Gilboa. Demoralized and despairing, he skirted the enemy camp by night and heard his own doom foretold (1 Sam. 28:3-25). The name does not occur in the New Testament; but in the days of Eusebius and Jerome, Endor was still a large village four Roman miles south of Mount Tabor, corresponding to the present site. It was recognized in the time of the Crusades and is mentioned by Brocardus, but appears afterwards to have been again lost sight of, at least partially, until the 17th century.

The famous *mountains* of this section are: Mount Tabor, the Hill of Moreh, and the Mount of Beatitudes.

Mount Tabor, the finest and most beautiful of the mountains of Galilee, rises out from the Plain of Tabor to a height of 1,843 feet above sea level. It is located five miles southeast of Nazareth, and is in the triad of sacred mountains—Hermon, Tabor, and Carmel—so often referred to in Scripture (Ps. 89:12; Jer. 46:18). When the Psalmist exclaims: "Tabor and Hermon shall rejoice in thy name," he selected these two as the representatives of all the mountains of Palestine: Mount Tabor was the most graceful, and 113 Mount Hermon the loftiest.

As a symbol of beauty, of grace, and of strength, Tabor

A patchwork of cultivated fields in Lower Galilee as seen from Mount Tabor.

carries its symmetrical outlines and proportions upward from its base to its crown. When viewed from the south, it appears like a huge sugarloaf or a hemisphere; but when seen from other directions, it has the appearance of an arched mound or dome—depending upon the direction from which it is viewed.

Its graceful slopes are dotted with trees, and its picturesque coves are grown over with groves of oak and other greenery where fallow deer may occasionally be seen. Into one of these coves Deborah and Barak rallied 10,000 men who, at the proper time, swept down upon Sisera and his Canaanite army and threw them into confused flight (Judg. 4:6-17). Here, on Mount Tabor, Zebah and Zalmunna, kings of Midian, killed Gideon's brothers (Judg. 8:18-21). Here, through the ages, many forces have struggled for possession of the mountain, and here on its summit many temples, forts, and churches have been built and destroyed.

In former years, access to the top was by thousands of steps cut into the steep slope, but now a narrow roadway ascends the mountain in a series of hairpin curves. The summit is a half-mile-wide rounded cone crowned by the beautiful Franciscan Basilica of the Transfiguration, with its adjoining pilgrim hostel, the Greek Church of St. Elias, and many ancient ruins.

From the summit of Tabor (some stand on top of the high Crusader wall) a fine view is afforded—the eye taking in the snowy top of Mount Hermon, Safad, the Sea of Galilee, Mount Carmel, the Plain of Esdraelon, Gilboa, the Jordan Valley, and the land beyond the Jordan.[1] An early tradition placed the scene of Christ's transfiguration on Mount Tabor, and vast numbers of pilgrims have visited the place with this in mind. But the tradition has been suspected as a fourth-century convenience, seeing it does not agree with the account given in the Gospels, nor with the fact that it was permanently occupied by a Roman garrison during the time of Christ. Most all students of the Bible agree that the Transfiguration must have taken place on Mount Hermon, for the events before and after took place around the base of Hermon.[2]

Mount Moreh or the **Hill of Moreh** is more or less insignificant as to appearance, yet its prominence in location has caused it to play a conspicuous part in various events of history. Not that the mountain itself has often been utilized, but many incidents have taken place at various points about its base, and many armies have camped nearby. The villages of Shunem, Endor, and Nein nestle at its feet; on its crest is a Moslem *weli* to which the faithful make pilgrimages; and about its foothills a number of thriving colonies are now located.

This mountain has sometimes been called "Little Hermon" but is in no way to be confused with Mount Hermon. The strange designation began in the fourth century when it was difficult for the zealous pilgrims to visit the true Mount Hermon far away to the northeast; the accommodating monks found it desirable to show this as Mount Hermon. The identification was exceedingly unfortunate, for there is no authority whatsoever for calling it any other than Mount Moreh.

Belvoir, the famous Crusader castle-fortress, occupies one of the most picturesque scarps extending eastward from Mount

115

Moreh. It rises 1,400 feet above the Jordan Valley and is so situated that one standing on its heights may see the movements of men much of the way between Tiberias and Beth Shean. It commands a view of two highways ascending from the Jordan Valley westward into the interior: one by the Jezreel Valley and the other by way of the Tabor Valley.

In Roman times the fort of Agrippina stood here. In 1168, the Crusaders purchased the site and erected Belvoir, one of their famous castle-forts which held off strong Moslem forces until January, 1191, when the eastern tower was undermined and destroyed. Seeing the hopelessness of continuing the struggle, the Christian forces sued for peace and were permitted free passage to the city of Tyre. Belvoir was dismantled in 1241, and eventually an Arab village rose amid its ruins. However, it too was abandoned in 1948. In 1966-67, excavations were carried out at the site by M. Ben-Dor on behalf of the National Park Authority. Stables, storerooms, cisterns, a kitchen, a very fine hall with pillars, and capitals made of black basalt stood next to the church.

Kurn-Hattin, "The Horns of Hattin," four miles northwest of Tiberias, has been known to the world since the time of the Crusades as the **Mount of Beatitudes,** from which Christ delivered His matchless sermon as recorded in the Gospel of Matthew. No really authentic history confirms the Crusaders' conclusion, yet there is a fine natural amphitheater there, and no other mountain or peak in the vicinity answers to the Gospel description so well as this place; therefore with some the tradition has passed almost unchallenged.

At its eastern end is an elevated point or horn, rising about 100 feet above the plain; and at the southwestern end another rocky ridge almost as high. Between the two is a natural depression, which gives to the mountain at a distance the appearance of a huge saddle. The place is called "Horns of Hattin" because of this appearance. When viewed from the west, this place has the appearance of two great horns protruding in the air only a little way above the gradually rising land elevation, while on the north there is a very steep descent of 800 feet to another plain,

116

which again terminates at the Sea of Galilee. The mount itself, with its twin heads, rises 1,038 feet above sea level.

The natural depression between the horns makes up a very natural amphitheater which would accommodate a few thousand people. Here, with its naturelike arrangement, the multitude were gathered eager to catch Christ's words and to receive His gifts.

Having spent the previous night in solitary prayer, Christ stood forth, amid the scenery of the mountains, with majesty on His brow, love in His heart, and truth on His tongue. Alluding

117

The "Horns of Hattin" looking east toward the upper end of the Sea of Galilee.

to the fowls of the air, He looked up, and, behold, they were hovering near Him at the moment of speaking. Referring to the grasses and lilies, they were flourishing at His feet and perfuming the breeze just as they do today. To the north, situated on the edge of a high hill, was the little town of Safad. His message was so wise and so divine that its sentences burned like fire in the human hearts. It was like a flood that swept everything before it. No one has endeavored to contest the simple statements or deride the sweet spirit in which this sermon was pronounced, or to render illogical the underlying basis of the whole. It easily rates as the greatest message ever spoken.

Therefore, it is not considered strange that many modern pilgrims have stood here and read: "Blessed are they which do hunger and thirst after righteousness"; "Let your light so shine"; "Love your enemies . . . pray for them which despitefully use you . . . that ye may be the children of your Father which is in heaven"; "Is not the life more than meat, and the body than raiment?"; "Seek ye first the kingdom of God."

Aside from its scriptural associations, Hattin is a historical center to which the terminal lines of the Crusades point. Here, in July, 1187, the Crusaders were marshalled under King Guy and the grand master of the Knights Templars, and were opposed by the Mohammedan forces under the gallant Saladin. Around the Horns of Hattin the battle raged until King Guy was taken prisoner, the grand master was slain, and the heroic knights either slain or made prisoners. The cross gave way to the crescent, the flower-embowered mountain was bathed with the blood of martyrs, and the might of the Crusaders was forever broken in Palestine.[3]

When on the summit of Hattin, all nature seems silent yet eloquent. Lying spread out like a carpet before one are fields of varied hues. On the north down the steep declines nestles the peaceful city of Hattin. On the northeast one sees the forbidding brow of the Robber Hill, and on beyond the northern part of the Sea of Galilee and on its western shore the beautiful Plain of Gennesaret.

At the present, Lower Galilee is undergoing intense settlement and development by the Jewish people. Agriculture, poultry, and cattle raising promise a great future for thousands of happy and industrious families.

CHAPTER 10

The Plain of Armageddon

The Plain of Armageddon, frequently called *The Plain of Esdraelon,* or simply *The Emak,* is a vast inland basin—a great fertile plain in the midst of the land.

From the landward slopes of Mount Carmel near *Tell el Kassis* the plain rises gradually to the southeast and continues far into the curving cove at the foot of Mount Gilboa. On its northeast it continues to Mount Tabor. The Galilean mountains form a northern boundary, and the Samarian mountains bound the southern limits. The plain itself is from 5 to 14 miles wide, and approximately 22 miles long at its greatest length.

The word *Armageddon,* or *Harmageddon,* is the Greek form for "The Mountain of Megiddo," or "The Hill of Megiddo." Megiddo means a "place of troops," and the plain takes its name from the city of Megiddo which lies on a hill, guarding the entrance to the pass of Megiddo on the southwestern border of the plain.

The plain has an average altitude of 250 feet and is hollowed out slightly so that it catches the drainage from the surrounding chains of mountains. These mountains rise to a fair height on all sides and slope gradually away to the plain far below.

The *river Kishon* drains the Plain of Armageddon. It rises in the northern hills of Samaria—around the foothills of Gilboa and the Springs of Jenin—and flows northwestward through the Plain of Armageddon, and empties into the Mediterranean under the brow of Mount Carmel. It is a sluggish river in the summertime but often becomes a roaring and dangerous torrent during the winter. As a river, the Kishon is second only to the river Jordan in Palestine and has played a prominent part in the varied events of the plain.

At intervals for more than 30 centuries the plain has been

The vast plain of Armageddon (Esdraelon) as seen looking east from Mount Carmel.

used as a common battleground of nations. Being the middle ground between Asia and Africa, and stretching out for many miles, it has afforded ample terrain for chariots and horses and men to spread themselves. Therefore military men of many nations met here to fight their decisive battles and endeavor to settle their differences, until historians have regarded it as the world's classic battlefield.

Physically, the plain is like a vast stage set for peace or for war, with five natural openings or passes carefully arranged for men of peace or for armies to make their entries and their exits. At the western end is the *Pass of Kishon* through which the Kishon River breaks through low-lying hills to enter the sea in Haifa Bay; halfway along the southwestern side, Megiddo guards the *Pass of Megiddo,* through which comes the highway of the nations between the rich clime of Egypt and the populous nations of Asia; the *Pass of Jenin* at the southeastern corner accommodates the central highway from Judea and Samaria; the *Pass of Jezreel* leads from Arabia and the Jordan up by Bethshean through the Valley of Jezreel; and at the northeastern corner is the *Tabor Pass,* where the immemorial road from Damascus and Tiberias skirts around Mount Tabor and enters the plain.[1]

Long and impressive is the list of military conquerors who have entered through these passes and made battle on this historic plain. Names familiar in history, such as Thotmes III, Ramses II, Nebuchadnezzar, Sargon, Sennacharib, Pharaoh-Necho, Alexander the Great, Titus, Richard I, Saladin, Napoleon Bonaparte, and Allenby of the British Army are but a few of those who have entered into military engagements in this arena of war. Thus, the Assyrians, the Babylonians, the Persians, the Jews, the Egyptians, the Crusaders, the Arabs, the Turks, the French, as well as the British, and warriors from other nations have fought and had their fate to hang on engagements here.

No section of land on the face of the earth attracts more attention from biblical and prophetic students than does this plain. For the Jews it has held a place in their history since the origin of their race. It has demanded the attention of the Christian Church since the time of John and gathers climactic interest in the closing chapters of the Book of Revelation.[2]

The earliest battle fought by Israel on the plain of Megiddo was when Sisera, the captain of King Jabin's Canaanitish forces, came against Israel with 900 chariots of iron. Deborah and Barak rallied Israel in a wooded glen well up on the side of Mount Tabor, where they "watched till the lengthening line of the enemy's chariots drew out the western angle at Tell el Kassis and stretched opposite to them with Ta'anach and Megiddo behind them," then Israel gave them battle in a fierce highland charge, while God sent a heavy rainstorm, confusing and frustrating the invaders. The river Kishon filled to overflowing, the battlefield was turned into a sea of mud, and the chariots bogged to a standstill.[3]

Crazed with fear, their drivers and the accompanying infantry raced on foot westward for the Pass of Kishon at Tell el Kassis where the Kishon flows out to the Plain of Acre and to the Haifa Bay. Here the overflowing waters surged in swirling torrents through the pass and swept the proud Canaanites to their ruin. After this great victory, Deborah and Barak sang a song of thanksgiving unto God:

> They fought from heaven; the stars in their courses
> fought against Sisera.
> The river Kishon swept them away, the ancient river,
> the river Kishon. O my soul, march on with strength.[4]

One of Judah's sad, tragic battles was the one in which the good King Josiah went out very unwisely to stop Pharaoh-Necho of Egypt, and was slain at the Pass of Megiddo. In defeat and deep sorrow they returned with him in his chariot to Jerusalem and buried him in his own sepulchre. Then Jehoahaz was anointed king in his father's stead at the age of 23.

The British advance upon the plain by General Allenby in September, 1918, was one of the most skillfully planned of any battle ever to be fought in the Middle East. Allenby prepared by leading the enemy to believe that the main attack on them was to come from east of the Jordan—from the forces of Feisal and

123

Lawrence—and from the west bank of the Jordan, where in reality only a huge sham camp and a skeleton force was maintained. Allenby's surprise attack actually came from the Plain of Sharon directly through the Pass of Megiddo onto the plain. The enemy was thoroughly unprepared to receive an attack from this direction; therefore their forces crumpled up, the two German-Turkish armies were destroyed, thousands of prisoners taken, and Allenby's conquest virtually completed.

Generally the Plain of Armageddon or Esdraelon has been associated with thoughts of war, yet there have been periods of time—decades, even centuries—in which peace and prosperity has reigned; and during these times there have been peaceful pursuits, and through these passes and across this plain have come caravans and merchantmen, patriarchs and prophets, the master seeking the lost, and the prodigal son returning home from a far country.

The soil of the plain is largely composed of volcanic deposits that have poured into the plain for centuries. The subsoil is basaltic in nature. Together, through decomposition, these have given the plain a marvelous fertility. In the ancient past the rich plain was the breadbasket of northern Palestine, and a source of animal forage and food for the many caravans that passed by that way. The Midianites and other ancient peoples sometimes came and carried away its abundant harvests. An inscription on the wall of the Temple of Amon at Thebes tells how King Thotmes III, during the 15th century B.C., fought against Megiddo and carried away 924 chariots, 2,238 horses, and how he sent his army up to the Plain of Megiddo every year to cut grain necessary to keep the horses of his cavalry. On one of these expeditions he carried away 150,000 bushels.

At the close of the First World War the plain presented one of the poorest potentials of all places in Palestine. Then in 1921, the Jewish National Fund purchased the plain and made it their first big reclamation project. Swamps, marches, mosquitoes, and malaria were so prevalent that among the Arabs it was a common saying that a bird could not fly over it without becoming contaminated. Yet wise men knew that beneath all this noxious organic matter there was fertility. Men and women entered the plain with machines, with brawn, and with determination. They cut ditches, laid underground pipes, drained swamps, leveled land, harnessed springs, and planted trees until within a few years the marshes were gone, the mosquitoes killed, malaria stamped out, and the land restored to its normal productiveness.

Nahalal, the first settlement, was founded in 1921, and built in a circle—like a wagon wheel. In the center were such public buildings as the synagogue, the agricultural school, the communal center, warehouse, chicken runs, and dairy barns. Out from the central circle radiated 75 strips of land like slender slices of pie. Each strip of land contained 25 acres which was the home of a family who owned it as a corporate, independent, small holder. Members bought supplies and sold their products as a group, and helped each other in time of need. They marketed beef, milk, poultry, eggs, fruit, and vegetables.

125

The wagon-wheel arrangement of the Nahalal farming community on the Plain of Esdraelon.

Slowly but surely *Ginegar* and a dozen other colonies were laid out. Germans, Poles, Russians, and peoples from other lands filled the new settlements until today the Plain of Armageddon is dotted with colonies and villages and is crisscrossed with grain-fields, gardens, vineyards, fruit orchards, and dairy farms which extend over most of the plain. Then there is the thriving city of *Afula*—crossroads for many ways. Water from the river Kishon, from 50 or more mountain springs, and from deep wells provide for considerable irrigation.

As seen from the heights, there are fields of wheat, barley, maize, millet, sesame, and fruit which form the checkerboard pattern on the plain and give it the appearance of being one of the most cultivated, fertile places in all the world. Varicolored strips of fallow ground break up the design made by these patch-work fields. The lower foothills on the outer edges of the plain are mottled by groves of fig and olive trees. In the northwest corner is the great Balfour Forest near the Jewish colony of Ginegar.

O Armageddon, what variables of human activity you have accommodated! On thy bosom great empires, races, and faiths have contended with each other, then marched on to judgment. Yet thy future is bound up with prosperous, peaceful settlements, and in the end, "the battle of that great day of God Almighty." As in John's vision, an angel "gathered them together into a place called . . . Armageddon . . . and there came a great voice out of heaven, from the throne, saying, It is done. And there were thunders, and lightnings, and a great earthquake, such as was not since men were upon the earth. . . . And every island fled away, and the mountains were not found" (Rev. 16:14-20).

CHAPTER **11**

The Valley of Jezreel

This narrow, yet exceedingly important valley is a beautiful, meadowlike expanse, from 2 to 3 miles wide and 11 miles long. It begins about a mile east of Afula, just northwest of ancient Jezreel, where there is a sudden fall of ground level eastwards, which visibly separates it from the Plain of Esdraelon or Armageddon. It breaks "as visibly as river from lake and has the slope and look of a current upon it." It passes below sea level about two miles from the Esdraelon plain; and with Mount Moreh on its left and Mount Gilboa on its right, it gently descends southeast for nine miles to Beth-Shan, where it falls over a ledge and 300 feet below merges with the Jordan Valley. Thus it separates Galilee from Samaria, and is a link between the Plain of Armageddon and the Jordan Valley.

It is also a transitory zone between the two in soils, climate, and living conditions. The valley is open throughout and offers a natural route for the high road from Damascus through this valley and over the great Plain of Armageddon, then on to Egypt.

Beautiful Jezreel Valley was the scene of considerable Bible history. It was intricately bound up with battles which often left its fertile acres strewn with war implements and soaked with blood. Here was fought the celebrated battle of Gideon and his 300 against the Midianites and their allies. At harvesttime the Midianites, along with other nomadic tribes, often made incursions through the Valley of the Jordan up to the Valley of Jezreel and on to the Plain of Armageddon. By sheer force of numbers, they took over the fields and reaped the harvest; they permitted their flocks and herds to trample down the fields; they plundered vineyards and gardens; and they seized cattle and robbed men and houses.

At a time when Israel had become morally weak by erecting altars to Baal on the high mountain peaks of the country, the foreign forces entered the country, encamped with headquarters at Shunem, and threatened all the land of Israel. In this midnight hour of Israel's hope, the Spirit of the Lord came upon Gideon. He blew a trumpet and collected a 32,000-man army at *Ain Harod* —a fine spring at the foot of the northern slope of Mount Gilboa. From the position of this spring, the vast host of the children of the east could be seen lying along the valley "like grasshoppers for multitude, and their camels were without number as the sands of the sea for multitude."

Most generals would have called for more soldiers, but, at God's word, Gideon called for less. Twice did he winnow his forces. Then when left with only 300 who had taken the water in their hands and lapped it as they went forward, he armed them with trumpets, pitchers, and a flaming torch within each pitcher. In the dark hours of that night, his valiant little army charged the enemy hordes from three sides, blew their trumpets, broke their pitchers, shined their lights, and shouted, "The sword of the Lord, and of Gideon." The enemy went into a riot, fleeing headlong down the valley, and the world's military classic for night charges was in full force (Judg. 7:1-25).

Across this same valley went despondent Saul, king of Israel, to the witch of Endor. There on Mount Moreh's northern slopes a ghostly realism mocked his empty soul, not with a thrilling pancake story but a pronouncement of his own doom, and he

> rose up dumb and mighty—pale
> and terrible in blood stained mail,

and went back around the Mountain of Moreh and across the Valley of Jezreel to await the issues of the oncoming day, when

> Enthralled, past knowing cold or heat,
> or hearing thunder of the feet
> of armies,

his host was attacked on the rear flank, and he went down to an ignominious defeat and death on Gilboa's height. Soon the enemy came to strip the slain; and before the sun was set, King Saul's body hung on a wall at Beth-Shan.

This valley takes its name from the ancient city of Jezreel, which was situated on a low spur projecting westward from Mount Gilboa. Here at Jezreel was located the choice vineyard of Naboth which Ahab, the most unrestrained of all Israel's kings, lusted after until he lay upon his bed aflame with a fire of unsatisfied desire and would eat no bread. Jezebel, his doubly insidious, prophet-slaying wife, soothed him with the sinister promise, "I will give thee the vineyard of Naboth." Therefore, she hurriedly wrote letters in Ahab's name, sealed them with his signet, and said that Naboth had blasphemed God and the king. As phony witnesses she sent two men to testify at court who were "children of Belial," and then announced to the king, "Naboth is stoned, and is dead."

Ahab, while strolling in his stolen vineyard, was suddenly confronted by Elijah, and exclaimed, "Hast thou found me, O mine enemy?"

129

The Valley of Jezreel as seen from famed Mount Gilboa

Elijah's reply was, "Thou hast sold thyself to work evil in the sight of the Lord. . . . In the place where dogs licked the blood of Naboth shall dogs lick thy blood. . . . And the dogs shall eat Jezebel by the wall of Jezreel." All things spoken by the prophet came to pass—Jezebel's tragic end here in the city of Jezreel, overlooking the Valley of Jezreel.

The prophet Elisha oft made his circuit through this valley. And so it was that as he passed by, he turned into Shunem to eat bread. Here he was invited into the home of a good, kind Shunammite woman and her husband who made a little room on the wall and set there a bed, a table, a stool, and a candlestick that the prophet might freely pass in and out. Here was enacted the

tender scene when the prophet raised the dead son of his bene-
factress to life.

At the eastern entrance of the Valley of Jezreel, near its junc-
ture with the Jordan Valley, the historic city of *Beth-Shan* was
strategically located. It was perched on a high mound that made
it like a "toll keeper" on the much traveled route between
Damascus and Egypt. From its splendid position it dominated the
country for miles around. It was here, when after defeat by the
Philistines on Gilboa, the bodies of Saul and Jonathan were hung
high upon the walls until the men of Jabesh Gilead arose and
went all night and took them down and buried their burnt bones
at Jabesh Gilead (later they were reburied at Zelah, just west of
Rachel's tomb).

With the decline of the country, this fruitful valley became
lost to the outside world. Caravans of camels with tinkling bells
passed this way, but little notice was taken of them.

However, the Valley of Jezreel still lies there, overlain with
black, alluvial swamp soil, rich in organic components. It is now
given to the plowshare and is quiet from the forays of Midianites,
Philistines, and other marauders.

The little village of Shunem stands at the northwest portion
of the valley as of old, and many view it with thoughts of the
prophet Elisha and the "great woman" and her husband who
provided for "the man of God." Rich and prosperous kibbutz
colonies occupy the land today—Merhavya, Ein-Harod, Tel-
Yosef, Gide'ona, Geva, etc. Ain Harod, the fine, strong spring,
still flows from the enormous cave at the base of Gilboa. A youth
hostel stands on the banks of the spring whose waters go mostly
through underground channels to the surrounding colonies.
Only a small stream is now allowed to flow into its natural bed
known as the river Jalud which, since ancient times, has coursed
its way down the valley.

Far down the valley, on its south side, the fine mound of
Beth-Shan looms high on the horizon, and nearby is the Arab 131
village of Beisan which provides a splendid market for all kinds of
native needs.

CHAPTER 12

Samaria, Land of Places and Personalities

Samaria, sometimes referred to in the Old Testament as "Mount Ephraim," or as "the mountains of Samaria," is one of the most extensive as well as one of the most interesting of all the many sections of Palestine—interesting largely because of its places and people. Its northern boundary begins at the southeast foot of Mount Carmel and runs southeast along the southern edge of the Plain of Armageddon, then swinging northward includes Mount Gilboa and the adjacent mountains to the Jordan Valley. Its southern boundary begins with the Valley of Aijalon and runs eastward along a line just south of Bethel to the deep gorge of Michmash and thence to the Jordan Valley. It comprises an area of approximately 40 by 50 miles, which, for the land of Israel, is quite large. It was the true geographical center of Canaan, and in those early days was thickly wooded (Josh. 17:18).

Although it adjoins Judea geographically, the difference existing between the two is amazing. Whereas Judea is of rugged, arid terrain, and its mountains are almost impassable, Samaria is a land of beauty and symmetry. Its graceful mountains, fertile valleys, flowing fountains, flowering shrubs, trailing vines, and millions of wild flowers make it an exceedingly desirable land. The average elevation is 2,000 feet, with a few mountain heights as much as 3,000 feet. The topography is made up of a series of high ridges with intervening elevated valleys and plains. The land is easily accessible in the northern portion, but the southern half is bordered by precipitous banks and rugged wadies. The descent to the Jordan depression is very steep. In one place the drop is 2,800 feet in nine miles. On the western side the land has a gradual slope toward the maritime plain.

Agricultural potentialities are unusually fine due to the fertility of the land. Grapes, olives, pomegranates, plums, peaches, passion fruit, apricots, and nectarines are produced here in abundance. Pastures, shut in by the surrounding mountains, yield an abundance of grass; and the goats, sheep, and cattle are quite famous for the quantity and the quality of their milk and meat.

The land of Samaria has mountains and plains and city sites which are rich in historical setting—and made so by certain personalities. The more important of these places are: Shechem, Jacob's Well, Sychar, Joseph's Tomb, Joshua's Tomb, Mounts Ebal and Gerizim, Nablus, Tirzah, City of Samaria, Dothan, Jenin, Mount Gilboa, Megiddo, Shiloh, Ai, and Bethel.

Shechem, now identified with *Tell Balata,* is a mile and a half east of Nablus, between Mount Ebal and Mount Gerizim. It stood guard over the crossroads here and was the religious and political center of Palestine during early Old Testament times. It is midway 133 between Dan and Beersheba, and almost midway between the sea and the Jordan.

Shechem was the site of Abraham's first encampment in the Promised Land, and the place where he erected the first altar "unto the Lord, who appeared unto him" and renewed His covenant promise (Gen. 12:6-7). On returning from his 20-year sojourn in Haran, Jacob was kindly received by the people of Shechem who sold him land on which he and his servants dug a well. Here he received from the people their "strange gods . . . and their earrings" and buried them under an oak which was by Shechem (Gen. 35:1-4). Joseph came here in quest of his brothers, whom he later found at Dothan (Gen. 37:12-17). Joseph's body was brought from Egypt and buried at Shechem.

The Israelites, under the leadership of Joshua, were gathered here to reaffirm the covenant; and here long years afterwards, when Joshua was "old and stricken in age," he gathered all Israel and made his farewell address in which he uttered that ringing challenge, "Choose you this day whom ye will serve. . . . as for me and my house, we will serve the Lord." In reply the people said, "We will serve the Lord our God . . . and his voice will we obey." Then Joshua "made a covenant with the people and wrote these words in a book . . . and took a great stone and set it up there under an oak" (Josh. 24:14-26).

Shechem was one of the cities of refuge in the days of the judges.

Here at Shechem, after the death of Solomon, all Israel came together to make Rehoboam king, but his exorbitant demands for more taxes and greater service split the kingdom and sent him speeding in his chariot to Jerusalem, where thereafter he ruled over only 2 tribes. Jeroboam became king of the 10 northern tribes, rebuilt Shechem, and made it his court for a time, but later moved the capital to Tirzah.

134 The Assyrian invasions of 724-721 B.C. completely destroyed Shechem, but it was rebuilt by the Samaritans and became a prosperous city. Even a temple was built on Mount Gerizim, and the city became a rival to Jerusalem. John Hyrcanus brought about

the final destruction of Shechem in 107 B.C., and along with it, thousands of Samaritans were put to death.

A team of archaeologists, under the direction of Dr. G. Ernest Wright, has excavated here for a number of seasons. Gates, walls, temples, and a wealth of pottery, coins, tools, and other smaller objects have been found, and considerable history has been confirmed—both secular and biblical.

Jacob's Well is one mile southeast of Shechem, on the high road from Jerusalem where it curves westward to enter the valley between Mount Gerizim and Mount Ebal. Situated on the ground purchased by Jacob "for an hundred pieces of money" from the sons of Hamor, the father of Shechem, this wayside well is one of the most authentic sites in all Bible lands (Gen. 33:18-19). Samaritans, Jews, Christians, and Mohammedans revere it as the very well which Jacob dug, and the one on whose curb Jesus sat when He talked to the woman of Samaria, who had come there to draw water.

Samaritan tradition dates back more than 23 centuries and was repeated by the Samaritan woman who said to Jesus, "Our father Jacob gave us the well" (John 4:12). Christian tradition dates from 333 when the Bordeaux Pilgrim visited the well, over which a small Christian church had just recently been built by Queen Helena. The Crusaders found the church in ruins and rebuilt it, but their church was destroyed during the 12th century. Its ruins, as a "heap of brown stones," lay for long years over the well.

In 1838, Dr. Robinson found the entrance to the well's mouth, measured the well, and found it to be 105 feet deep. In 1881, Dr. C. A. Barclay cleared away the mass of accumulated rubbish about the original mouth of the well and found that debris had fallen or been thrown into it until it measured only 67 feet deep.[1] Later the well was cleaned out to its bottom and found to be, in fact, 105 feet deep. But so many tourists, and others passing by, threw or pushed stones into it in order to hear how long it would take for a stone to splash in the water below, that it gradually filled again until it was only 75 feet deep.

In 1912, the Russian Orthodox church began building an

enormous basilica church around the well, but the work was stopped during the First World War. Later the place was purchased by the Greek Orthodox church, but it would require so much to complete the church that it has never been finished. Directly over the well is a small, richly adorned chapel, with walls covered with old paintings and icons, mostly depicting Jesus and the woman at the well.

The ancient well curb is many feet below the present level and shows deep grooves worn by the ropes by which the waterpots or waterskins were drawn up. The well measures 7 feet 6 inches in diameter. Its upper portion is lined with masonry, but the lower portion has been dug through solid stone. The water is cool, soft, and refreshing—much more palatable than the hard or "heavy" spring water that gushes from the limestone strata at Sychar. It is both a cistern and a spring—that is, it is fed both by infiltration through its sides and by an underground spring. Under present management, water is sold to tourists in small bottles and taken to most parts of the world. For those who desire it, the attending priest draws water for a drink and also lets down a steel platter with lighted candles so that one may see along the walls of the well down to the water level.

The associations of the well carry us back in the world's history to pastoral scenes, to patriarchal customs, and to the beginning of Jesus' ministry. By this wayside well He revealed His divine self to the perplexed Samaritan woman and spoke the profound truths: "They that worship [God] must worship him in spirit and in truth," and "Whosoever drinketh of the water that I shall give him shall never thirst; but the water that I shall give him shall be in him a well of water springing up into everlasting life" (John 4:24, 14). The sequel to it all was that the Samaritan woman accepted Christ and led many of the townspeople to know and accept Him, who in turn "besought him to tarry with them, and he abode there two days and many believed."

Sychar, the hometown of the woman who talked with Jesus at the well, is identified with the Arab village of Askar, which is about three-quarters of a mile north of the well. It lies at the foot of Mount Ebal and is built over the ruins of the ancient town of

Sychar. It has a spring, but the water is not as palatable as that in Jacob's well.

Joseph's Tomb. On a slight elevation about 400 yards northeast of Jacob's well is a walled-in, white-domed chapel tomb about 12 feet square. Inside the small chapel is a simple tomb about three feet high, and an inscription stating that in 1860 the place was restored by a British consul.

Here lie the embalmed, mortal remains of Joseph, whose character and faith in God were such that, when faced with fiery temptation, he said, "How can I do this great wickedness, and sin against God?" For his refusal to do wrong he went to prison, but God was with him, and soon he was called to the throne to be Egypt's prime minister.

At 110 years of age, he said to his kinsmen, "God will surely visit you, and ye shall carry up my bones from hence." "And the bones of Joseph, which the children of Israel brought up out of Egypt, buried they in Shechem, in a parcel of ground which Jacob bought of the sons of Hamor, the father of Shechem, for an hundred pieces of silver: and it became the inheritance of the children of Joseph" (Josh. 24:32).

This is one of the three places—along with the Cave of Machpelah at Hebron, and the Temple site at Jerusalem—that religious Jews claim is historically theirs by right of documented purchase.

Joshua's Tomb. Nine miles southwest of Shechem, in a rather rugged mountainous area, is Timnath Serah (now called Kefer Haris) where is located three domed tombs, which Jewish, Samaritan, Christian, and Moslem traditions say belong to Joshua, Caleb, and Nun. Other tombs, both here and in the Shechem area, are held sacred because they are said to belong to other old heroes of the Hebrew invasion.[2]

Ebal and *Gerizim,* twin mountains in the physical center of Samaria, are separated from each other by the beautiful Vale of Shechem. These mountains rise up on either side of the valley like lofty walls—Ebal on the northeast to a height of 3,044 feet, and Gerizim on the southwest to 2,870 feet above sea level.

From the slopes of these mountains the tribes of Israel assembled under Joshua, in fulfillment of Moses' command. On

Gerizim—the "Mount of Blessing"—stood the tribes of Simeon, Levi, Judah, Issachar, Joseph, and Benjamin. On Ebal—the "Mount of Cursing"—stood the tribes of Reuben, Gad, Asher, Zebulun, Dan, and Naphtali. In the midst of the valley separating the two mountains stood the ark of the covenant and the priests.

With the elders, officers, and judges arranged about the sacred symbol, and the vast multitudes covering the mountainsides and filling the plain below, the loud-voiced Levites turned their faces Gerizim-ward and uttered the blessings that would certainly visit the lives of those who lived righteously. Then, turning their faces Ebal-ward, they uttered the evil that was destined to descend upon those who transgressed the law. A tremendous AMEN! arose from the mighty congregation, 10-fold louder as it reverberated from Ebal to Gerizim and from Gerizim to Ebal. The scene was impressive and the effect upon the vast assembly was extremely wholesome.[3]

Jotham's parable of the trees was later spoken to the men of Shechem from a prominent ledge well up toward the top of Mount Gerizim. A certain ledge here is now popularly called "Jotham's pulpit" (Judg. 9:4-21).

Nablus, whose name comes from Neopolis, the "new city," is located between the mountains of Ebal and Gerizim, just southwest of the site of ancient Shechem. It was founded in A.D. 72 by the veterans of the armies of Vespasian and Titus. For a long time the inhabitants here were Romans, and from these was born, in the beginning of the second century, Justin Martyr, a philosopher, carefully trained in the schools of Greek philosophy. In his search for truth concerning God, he met an old man of venerable appearance who referred him to the apostles and prophets. He not only studied these but watched the Christians and decided they were not guessing at the truth, neither were they demonstrating divine things by reason, but were witnesses to the truth which they had themselves experienced.

Justin Martyr became a Christian and his knowledge widened, his love deepened, and his life was enlarged and intensified. The mirror of his soul became burnished, and his mind luminous and symmetrical. He devoted himself to the work of teaching and writing in defense of the Christians and of their faith. When a wave of persecution of the Christians broke out under Antoninus, Justin felt the destiny of a people hung on what he did; therefore he made a contribution to his own generation and to the world's betterment by presenting to that emperor an admirable apology in the Christians' behalf, which had the desired effect. In A.D. 165, he defended the Christians to Marcus Aurelius, but for this he was rewarded with a martyr's crown.

After the Crusades in the Middle Ages, the population of Nablus became more and more Arabic. Today Nablus has a population of 45,000, of which there are some 44,000 Moslems, 750 Christians, and 250 Samaritans. These Samaritans live in a small colony to themselves and have a high priest and a synagogue, in which is the ancient Samaritan Pentateuch. Each high priest is required to keep a record of the chief events transpiring during his term of office, and these records reach far back into the past. Rev. Youhannah El Karey, a native Baptist missionary of Shech-em, says he inquired as to whether there was any reference to Jesus Christ in those high-priestly records. He said that two such references had been discovered—one to the effect that Jesus Christ had come to their town and done many wonderful works, and another that He had been crucified in Jerusalem. Once each year the high priest leads his congregation up Mount Gerizim where they kill seven white lambs and observe the Feast of the Passover.

Many wealthy citizens have built their homes on the slopes of Mount Gerizim and Mount Ebal, and the place enjoys an atmosphere of prosperity. Fruit orchards, vegetable gardens, and olive groves have long characterized the environs of Nablus. The people sell fruit and prepare fruit juices for the markets, but the chief local industry is the manufacturing of an especially high grade olive-oil soap, which they export to various neighboring countries. Other modern industries are now adding to the prosperity of the area.

Tirzah, now identified with a large mound known as Tell el Farah, lies seven miles northeast of Nablus. At an indefinite time,

139

after the division of the monarchy, Jeroboam made it the capital of his kingdom (1 Kings 14:17), but after his death it suffered from many years of turbulent history. Omri besieged and captured the place in 884 B.C. and reigned there for six years before he moved his capital to Samaria.

Excavators have found four periods corresponding with the biblical history of Tirzah. Period I (that of level III in the tell) came to a sudden end about the time Omri captured the place. During the period of Omri the house plans included courtyards and were quite substantial. Each represented the house of an Israelite family. Large administration buildings were shown to have been begun but not completed. This the excavators thought represented the city at the time Omri abandoned the place and moved his capital to Samaria.

Samaria. After reigning at Tirzah for years, King Omri negotiated a deal with Shemer for a beautiful site eight miles northwest of Shechem. Here, on this well-rounded hill 400 feet above the surrounding valleys, he constructed his royal palace

The hill country of Samaria

and named it Samaria, after Shemer. Ahab, his son and successor, married beautiful, wordly, wicked Jezebel, and in selfish luxury constructed an ivory-veneered palace, and "reared up an altar for Baal in the house of Baal, which he had built in Samaria. And Ahab made a grove" (1 Kings 16:31-32).

During his lifetime—most of which was spent at or near Samaria—Ahab was "busy here and there" with things which crowded God from his life, but when he died in battle, his body was brought to Samaria where "one washed the chariot in the pool of Samaria; and the dogs licked up his blood . . . according to the word of the Lord" (2 Kings 22:34-38). Here Jehu slew all the seed of Ahab; destroyed the prophets, the priests, and the servants of Baal; and went to the house of Baal and brought forth the images and burned them publicly. The temple, also, was demolished and laid even with the ground (2 Kings 10:24-27).

The city of Samaria was destroyed and rebuilt time after time. In 724, Shalmaneser, king of Assyria, gathered his armies and came into Israel to collect tribute. The cities about the plain of Esdraelon surrendered, or the inhabitants fled to the capital. Hoshea prepared for a long siege with the hope of receiving help from Egypt, but for this he looked in vain. The siege of Samaria continued for two years—724 to 722 B.C.—under Shalmaneser V; then Sargon II, his successor, continued it for a short time.

At last Samaria's heights were stormed, King Hoshea was led away to spend the rest of his life in an Assyrian prison, and the people were deported to Assyria, where they were sent to various sections of the country to be absorbed by the people among whom they dwelt, or finally to journey to other lands.[4] Captives from other countries were settled in Samaria—these mingled with the Israelites left there, and afterwards made up those who became known as "Samaritans."

Alexander the Great destroyed the city of Samaria in 331, and again it was destroyed by John Hyrcanus in 108 B.C. It was rebuilt by the roman general Pompey in 63 B.C. Then, in 27 B.C., Emperor Augustus gave it to Herod the Great, who fortified the city, rebuilt it on a magnificent scale, and gave it the name of *Sebaste*, in honor of his patron, the Emperor Augustus. Herod built a palace, into which he brought his beautiful Mariamne, whom in jealousy he afterwards murdered, along with two of his sons. What a sordid, checkered past for a city which had been built on such a charming site. But for nearly 900 years it had been known as the center of idolatry. However, there was to be a better day with the coming of Jesus Christ.

Here Philip the evangelist preached Christ, "and the people with one accord gave heed unto those things which Philip spake . . . And there was great joy in that city." Even Simon the sorcerer "believed" and was baptized. Then came Peter and John who taught the people about the Holy Spirit, and "preached the gospel in many villages of the Samaritans" (Acts 8:25). Christianity continued in Sebaste (Samaria), for in the fourth century the city possessed a bishopric, and in 1187 the Crusaders built a cathedral there, the ruins of which now serve as a mosque.[5]

The city of Samaria has been excavated. Gates, walls, columned streets, foundations for palaces, temples, and other structures have been found which adequately confirm history as recorded in the Bible and other sources—even a collection of several thousand pieces of ivory of great variety and design. Some pieces were cut to receive color inlay, other pieces were overlaid with gold or inlaid with lapis lazuli. These, the excavators thought, were originally mortised into the throne, into beds, couches, tables, cabinets, and in the paneling of the walls and ceilings of the palace—all of which gave substance to the account in 1 Kings 22:39 which lists the ivory house as one of the great achievements of Ahab.

Jenin, the ancient En-Gannim (garden spring), lies on the southeast rim of the Plain of Armageddon, beside the pass from the Plain of Dothan. It has a strong spring which supplies all its domestic needs; then after watering vegetable gardens, fruit orchards, vineyards, olive groves, and a few palm trees, it passes on north and west to become one of the chief tributaries of the Kishon River. Josephus mentions it as being located on the border between Samaria and Galilee. Some believe Jenin to be the place where Jesus healed 10 lepers, one of whom was the Samaritan who returned to give thanks (Luke 17:11-19). Ancient *Ibleam,*

142

identified with modern Belameh, lies about a mile to the south of Jenin.

Dothan, now known as *Tell Dothan,* is located 5 miles southwest of Jenin and 12 miles north of the ancient city of Samaria. It is an isolated city mound which rises 175 feet above the plain, and has 10 acres on top and 15 acres on the slopes. An Arab village is now on the southern slope of the mound. Dothan means "two wells," and here they are today on the plain south of the mound—about 100 yards apart. Flocks of sheep and goats and some cattle still come here for water.

It was here that Joseph, after passing through Shechem, found his brothers, who, while he was yet "afar off," said, "Behold, this dreamer cometh. . . . now . . . let us slay him . . . and we shall see what will become of his dreams." Eventually, they sold him for 20 pieces of silver to a passing caravan of Ishmaelites and Midianite merchantmen, who "brought Joseph into Egypt . . . and . . . sold him . . . unto Potiphar, an officer of Pharoah's, and captain of the guard" (see Gen. 37:12-36).

Here the king of Syria laid siege to the city in an attempt to seize the prophet Elisha. When Elisha's servant arose early, he saw the horses and chariots, and the great host, and cried out, "Alas, my master, how shall we do?" When Elisha had prayed, the Lord opened the eyes of the young man. "And, behold, the mountain was full of horses and chariots of fire round about" —far more than those that composed the Syrian army (see 2 Kings 6:8-23).

Excavations conducted here since the spring of 1953 by Dr. Joseph P. Free of Wheaton College have revealed 11 levels of successive occupations from Early Bronze (3000-2000 B.C.) to the Middle Iron Age (900-586 B.C.). Special attention was given to Middle Bronze level (2050-1550 B.C.), the city of Joseph's day, and the Middle Iron level (900-586 B.C.), the city of Elisha's day. In this latter level, 15 pieces of silver was found stored in a pottery box—evidently the savings of some individual who was obliged to leave them.

143

Megiddo. Leading northwest, up to the southeast foothills of Mount Carmel, is a 20-mile chain of very important Samaritan hills—a veritable southwestern backdrop for the Plain of Esdrae-lon or Armageddon. In those hills and on the border of the plain there are now many modern Jewish colonies, but in ancient times there were four very important fortress towns—Jokneam, Megid-do, Taanach, and Ibleam. These dominated the four passes which connected the Plain of Sharon with the Plain of Armageddon.

Of these four, Megiddo guarded the famous Pass of Megid-do, through which ran the great highway or military artery which connected Egypt and Assyria. Thotmes III, king of Egypt, came this way in 1468 B.C. to conquer the kings of Canaan. King Solo-mon, in the 10th century B.C., made Megiddo a bulwark for the defense of the kingdom, using it chiefly as a chariot city of which excavations have revealed the remains of extensive stable com-plexes. In each stable, a central passage was flanked on each side by rows of pillars serving as supports for the roof and as hitching posts. Between the pillars were mangers. Each section of stables accommodated about 24 horses.

Pharaoh-Necho came through this pass in 610 B.C., on his way to aid the king of Assyria at the Battle of Carchemish. In his effort to stop him, the good King Joash lost his life (2 Chron. 35: 20-24). The armies of Alexander the Great passed here on the way to Egypt; Napoleon on his way to Acre; and General Allenby in pursuit of the Turco-German forces, whom he was driving from the Holy Land. This phase of his work was so significant that later he was knighted as Lord Allenby, Viscount of Megiddo.[6]

The Mountain of Gilboa. Just south of the Valley of Jezreel lies the farthest northeast portion of Samaria. It is a curving, bar-ren mountain ridge, 1,700 feet high and 10 miles long. Here, on Gilboa's height, was fought the fatal battle with the Philistines in which King Saul was disastrously defeated, and he and his sons were slain. On hearing of the tragedy, David's great soul was stirred to its depth, and he wrote that touching lament:

> The beauty of Israel is slain upon the high places: how are the mighty fallen: Tell it not in Gath, publish it not in the streets of Askelon: lest the daughters of the uncircumcised triumph . . .
> Ye mountains of Gilboa, let there be no dew, neither let

144

there be rain upon you, nor fields of offering: for there the shield of the mighty is vilely cast away, the shield of Saul, as though he had not been anointed with oil. . . .

Saul and Jonathan were lovely and pleasant in their lives, and in their death they were not divided: they were swifter than eagles, they were stronger than lions. . . .

How are the mighty fallen in the midst of the battle: O Jonathan, thou wast slain in thine high places.

I am distressed for thee, my brother Jonathan: Very pleasant hast thou been unto me: thy love to me was wonderful, passing the love of women.

How are the mighty fallen, and the weapons of war perished! *(2 Sam. 1:19-27)*.

Shiloh, where Israel first set up the Tabernacle sanctuary in the Holy Land, is situated on a low-lying hill in a secluded upland valley 10 miles south of Shechem. The place is now called Seilun, and the location fully agrees with that given in the Book of Judges which places it "on the north side of Bethel, on the east side of the highway that goeth up from Bethel to Shechem" (Judg. 21:19).

Here Joshua completed the division of the land among the tribes of Israel, and here the Tabernacle remained for more than 200 years.

Here Hannah prayed earnestly to God for a "man child," and vowed that he would be given "unto the Lord all the days of his life." Here Eli ministered as high priest, and here the child Samuel was dedicated to the Lord and grew up in the service of the sanctuary. Here "the Lord came, and stood, and called, Samuel, Samuel," and that fine lad answered, "Speak; for thy servant heareth" (see 1 Sam. 3:1-21).

Excavations were begun in 1922 by Dr. Schmidt, a Danish scholar. Among other things, he discovered the pottery remains and fragments of utensils used by the Israelites. The period of their occupation came to an end in the 11th century B.C. No traces of occupation of the site were found after the 9th century B.C.[7]

Bethel (Beth-el = house of God) is the place where Abraham built his second altar. It is where Jacob slept with a stone as his pillow and in his dream saw a ladder which reached from earth to heaven, and the angels of God ascending and descending. The Lord said, "I am the Lord God . . . the land whereon thou liest, to thee will I give it, and to thy seed . . . and in thee and in thy seed shall all the families of the earth be blessed." And Jacob said, "Surely the Lord is in this place . . . this is none other but the house of God, and this is the gate of heaven" (Gen. 28:10-17).

The legend of the old historians says that this stone on which the patriarch Jacob laid his head was brought to Spain, then transported to Ireland where Simon Brech was crowned on it about A.D. 700. It was then transferred from Ireland to Scotland and placed in the Abbey Church of Scone in A.D. 850, where the Scottish kings were crowned until 1296. At that time King Edward I carried it to England and placed it in Westminster Abbey where it was fixed under the seat of the coronation chair. It is called the "stone of Destiny" or "Scone Stone," and upon it all kings and queens of England have been crowned for almost 700 years.

Samuel came to Bethel once a year to judge the people (1 Sam. 7:16), and there was a school of prophets at Bethel when Elijah and Elisha were en route to Elijah's translation. On the return trip occurred the episode of the large crowd of young fellows who attempted to make sport of Jehovah's chosen prophetic leader. God challenged their rude and irreverent insults by permitting two she bears to come from the woods and maul 42 of those who had blatantly dishonored His chosen servant (2 Kings 2:23).

Jeroboam set up a golden calf and made an altar in Bethel, and "sacrificed unto the calf which he had made, and the priests cried, Let the people that sacrifice kiss the calf." By this altar stood Jeroboam, and his hand was withered and "the altar was rent" when he stretched forth his hand to seize the prophet of Judah who cried against the altar (see 1 Kings 12:28-33; 13:1-7). Here, later, came Amos, on one of the calf-cult's high days, and

condemned the oppession of the poor, the perversion of justice, and the taking of bribes. He condemned their shams, cried against their substitutes, and declared, "The Lord stood upon a wall . . . with a plumbline in his hand" (Amos 7:7) and that "Beth-el shall come to nought" (5:5). This prophecy was fulfilled; for, until the beginning of the 19th century, Bethel's site was unknown.

Baal-Hazor *(Tel Asur),* a mountain 3,334 feet high, nine miles northwest of Bethel, is where Absalom gave a dinner party and made his half brother Amnon drunk, then had him murdered in revenge for dishonoring his sister Tamar. The king's sons then mounted their mules and hurried back to Jerusalem, while Absalom fled to his mother's kinsmen in Geshur (Jedure) (2 Sam. 13:23-38).

Ai, the second place attacked by the incoming Israelites under Joshua, has usually been identified with Et Tell (the ruin), two miles east of Bethel. However, incomplete excavations there have thus far shown no definite traces of a city of Joshua's time. The biblical Ai could well have been little more than a temporary wooden fortification, manned by the men of Bethel and Ai, and such fragile strata as was left there could have been removed by erosion. Or, perhaps the Ai of biblical fame will be located elsewhere.

CHAPTER **13**

Judea, Land of Redemption

Blest land of Judea! thrice hallowed of song,
Where the holiest of memories pilgrim-like throng:
In the shade of thy palms, by the shores of thy sea,
On the hills of thy beauty, my heart is with thee.
                                        —Whittier

148   Judea has ever been, and
always will be, regarded as the principal stronghold of Israel, the
home of her chief prophets, the site of her Temple, the sanctuary
of the Holy Land, and the soul of the Old and New Testament

world. Judea is the land of worship, of romance, and of tragedy; but beyond all, it is the land of redemption—God and man met in the Temple on Moriah; Jesus the Saviour was born in Bethlehem; He died and rose again for our sins in Jerusalem; and the Holy Spirit came to those who tarried in the Upper Room. The entire area is rich beyond other lands in hallowed memories and stirring sacred events.

Judea came to include all the lands originally assigned to Benjamin and Judah. It begins a few miles north of Jerusalem near Beeroth and Ramallah, and extends southward for about 50 miles to the region where the foothills of the Judean Mountains fade away into the plain a few miles north of Beersheba. The entire territory is only about 35 miles wide from the Shephelah to the Dead Sea—much *less* when the Wilderness of Judea is not considered. It is a rugged, mountain land with many valleys, and a few brooks here and there. Piled high in its very center is the great watershed which runs from north to south and drains the water eastward to the Jordan and westward to the Mediterranean. Along this watershed runs the high road from Nazareth to Beersheba.

The whole area of Judea possesses an average height of 2,500 feet above sea level. The greatest elevations of the range are in the vicinity of Hebron where a height of 3,340 feet is reached just north of the city. At Jerusalem the elevation reaches 2,585 feet; while Neby Sam'wil is 2,942 feet above sea level—the highest point in the environs of Jerusalem and northern Judea.

A great part of the eastern portion of Judea is desolate and stony with few trees and slight vegetation, while the western slope is hilly and stony; yet it receives more moisture, and the rocky, limestone composition of the hills is easily converted into soil. When terraced and cared for, they are beautiful beyond compare and produce olives, rich vineyards, and an abundance of deciduous fruits of most every kind. But when neglected, these hills become desolate.

During the winter season, Judea's valleys are turned into rushing riverbeds as the water falls in sheets and rushes swiftly away to the Jordan Valley or to the Mediterranean Sea. Throughout this region one will find only six or eight perennial streams. Springs are very rare and true water-bearing wells are almost unknown. Covered cisterns, in which rainwater is collected and stored, supply man and beast during the long, dry, summer months. Added to this is the generous amount of dew which refreshes all living things from night to night.

The soft limestone formation has resulted in numerous caves and caverns. These have been used by the people for habitation and defense. They furnish an abode for the poor and, in summertime, protection from the heat. In time of danger the Isrealites hid themselves in the caves and dens. They were also used as cemeteries, for storage, and folds for flocks. Some caves were so important that they became historical landmarks.

One may stand on the height of Neby Sam'wil and survey a very large portion of Judea, and in some instances see even far beyond its confines. Thus Judea was a very small country—so small, in proportion to her enemies, that she could hope to exist only by the miraculous power of God. This is why almost every square mile of her territory, as well as every mountain and place, is associated with some important biblical event. The more important of these are: Hebron, Jerusalem, Ain Karim, Bethany, Bethlehem, Rachel's Tomb, Kish's Tomb, Solomon's Pools, Tekoah, Neby Sam'wil, Gibeon, Gibeah of Saul, Ramah, Ramallah, and Beeroth.

Hebron, one of the oldest cities in Palestine, will always be associated with Abraham, "the friend of God." Some 3,900 years ago Abraham pitched his tent in the Grove of Mamre, where now stands an ancient tree, which at least since the 16th century has been known as the Oak of Mamre (Gen. 13:18). Its short, gnarled trunk is over 30 feet in circumference; its twisted limbs are almost entirely bare of leaves and so weak that they have to be propped up by heavy iron beams; while around the ancient oak is a strong iron fence, designed to keep goats from nibbling the bark, and tourists from carrying away the whole tree piecemeal. It was here, while sitting in his tent door, that Abraham saw three men approaching him, and on offering them hospitality, found he was entertaining angels unawares (Gen. 18:1-33).

150

In the nearby fertile vale, 3,000 feet above the sea, lies Hebron, where Abraham settled after Lot had departed from him. Here Isaac was born; and here Abraham purchased the *Cave of Machpelah* in which he, Sarah, Isaac, Jacob, Rebecca, and Leah were buried. It was "out of the vale of Hebron" that Joseph was sent to deliver a message to his brethren. Here David reigned over Judah seven and a half years, until he was anointed king over all Israel; and here ungrateful Absalom raised the standard of rebellion against his royal father.

There are two ancient reservoirs in the south part of Hebron. The largest of these is 135 feet square and quite deep. It is thought that over this pool King David's young men hanged up the hands and feet of the murderers of Ishbosheth (2 Sam. 4:12).

The most interesting as well as the most conspicuous object in Hebron is the Cave of Machpelah, which Abraham bought from Ephron the Hittite for 400 shekels of silver. The object which looms large is in reality the "Great Mosque," a massive, castlelike structure 200 feet long, 115 feet wide, and 58 feet high, built over the cave. The building is very old, and the stones in the lower courses are beautiful and very large—one stone measures 24 feet in length, and another 38 feet long and 3½ feet high. These lower courses of masonry are marginally drafted after the style used in cutting stones during the time of Herod the Great, and Josephus mentions the beauty of the building in his day. Therefore, it is reasonably certain it was built by Herod. Arab tradition, however, insists that it dates back to King Solomon.

To reach the supposed burial place, you move up a long stone staircase beside the mosque, pass under a great arch, and enter a plain, many-sided hall. To one side, in a recess behind an iron grill, is a large, tomblike structure covered with costly embroidered tapestries, faded with age. This is the cenotaph of Abraham. Opposite, under a similar pall, is that of Sarah. To the southeast are the cenotaphs of Isaac and Rebecca, and to the northwest, Jacob and Leah. In each case the cenotaph is supposed to be directly over the actual tomb below the floor in the cave. 151

The Cave of Machpelah is revered by the three great monotheistic religions—Jews, Christians, and Moslems—yet for generations the Moslems would not allow the Jews to ascend any farther than the seventh step on the stone steps beside the mosque. Above the fourth step to the left is a deep cleft in the wall, which many Jews believe to extend through the wall and to emerge into the burial chamber itself. Here, in this cleft, the Jewish pilgrims placed small notes with intimate requests which they hoped would be granted by the patriarchs. Nowadays multitudes of Jews come to Hebron, ascend the steps, and eagerly enter the cenotaph hall. Some merely stand in thoughtful reverence. Others touch the iron bars reverently, pray, and smile as though they were meeting someone they had once known well, and were seeing them again after a long, long time. No one is ever permitted to descend into the cavern beneath the floor, for fear of disturbing the rest of the saints.

Jerusalem, the city of the soul, the city where man's redemption was achieved, and the city that makes all men think of the Bible and of heaven, is located on a 1,000-acre plateau in the central Judean mountains.

Numerous significant events took place in Jerusalem, or outside its gray walls. The ones which had to do with our redemption are, of course, the more momentous. The magnificent Temple with all its deeply meaningful parts—beginning at the Beautiful Gate and climaxing with "the place of the mercy seat"—was the most revered. Here in the most holy place, God, in His Shekinah presence, met man in mercy and atonement as the high priest came with blood, once each year, representing the people. And just outside the city wall, Jesus Christ, the God-man, gave His life on the lone gray hill of Calvary to "put away sin by the sacrifice of himself"—the true Offering and Atonement of which every sacrifice in the Temple was only a type.

Illustrious lives have left their imprint on the Holy City—Melchizedek, Abraham, David, Solomon, Isaiah, Jeremiah, Nehemiah, Judas Maccabaeus, Gamaliel, and Jesus Christ in whose honor Jerusalem came to be called "The City of the Great King."

152

The story of the glorious city extends over a period of 4,000 years and is told in some detail in the author's 180-page book,

Jerusalem,[1] but the following chapter of this present volume gives a capsule study of this most famous of all cities. But first we will consider some of the other significant sites in the area.

Ain Karim, according to tradition, is the "City of Judah" two miles west of Jerusalem where John the Baptist was born to Elizabeth and Zacharias the priest. The traditional site of their home is covered by the convent and church of St. John, within which is a small circular chapel, or grotto, cut in the natural rock, to which you descend by seven steps. Over its entrance is written in Latin the first words of Zacharias' prophetic benediction, "Blessed be the Lord God of Israel." An inscription on a marble slab in the floor states that "here the forerunner of our Lord was born."

The paintings on the walls give many details of his eventful life—his birth, his teaching in the wilderness, his baptizing of Christ, and his tragic death. One picture, as an altar piece, depicts the virgin Mary's visit from Nazareth to her cousin Elizabeth.

Bethany, the quiet village where Mary, Martha, and Lazarus lived, is two miles east of Jerusalem, on the southeastern slope of the Mount of Olives. From the earliest ages the name and places here have had a peculiar charm for the Christian heart, because here in the quiet home of this good family, Jesus revealed so much of both the human and divine side of His unqiue nature. Here He taught of the many aspects of life, here He raised Lazarus from the dead, and from some spot overlooking Bethany He ascended "into heaven, and sat on the right hand of God."

Eusebius (265-340) is said to have seen the "tomb of Lazarus" at Bethany (Jerome, *Onomastikon*); it was shown to the Bordeaux Pilgrim in A.D. 333; and Paula visited it just after 400. Moslems and Christians have marked many sacred sites here, and Christians built churches over some of them in the sixth century and during the Crusades; but these churches and other markings of more or less certain sites are all gone now—even the highly endowed nunnery established by Melissinda, the queen of King Fulco.

The ruined tower shown as the remains of the "house of Simon the Leper" dates no further back than the Crusaders; and the "grave of Lazarus," reached by descending 22 slippery steps, has no certain marks of an ancient Jewish grave. Though there is little about the center of the village to impress the earnest Christian, yet it is when you move out in the serene landscape, among the pine and olive groves, and see the sheep grazing on the hillsides, that you are reminded of the dignity, sacredness, and undying interest which Christ imparted to the area. The Mount of Olives is in its proper relative position, and there can be no doubt about the correctness of the identification of Bethany.

Bethlehem, so familiar to all, lies six miles south of Jerusalem. It, along with Jerusalem, is one of the most famous cities known to man, and a focal point of pilgrimage for the entire world. Jacob knew it as "Ephratah" (the fruitful), and buried his beloved Rachel in its suburbs. Ruth gleaned in the nearby fields of Boaz and became the ancestress of David and of our Lord. David was born here and later was anointed to the kingship by the saintly Samuel. And here Jesus Christ the Messiah, the Saviour of the world, was born.

The name Bethlehem in Arabic means "House of Meat," and in Hebrew it means "House of Bread"—bread for the body, bread for the mind, bread for the emotions, and bread for the soul. At every Christmas the hearts of all Christendom are turned here, and old men rejoice with littel children over the Gift of gifts, the Bread of Life from heaven.

What sacred mystery surrounds Bethlehem, and what mighty influences for good have gone forth from this lovely place during the past centuries! Because man could not climb the long road to a faraway heaven, the God of love came down to man and was born of the virgin Mary in Bethlehem of Judea. Angels sang "Glory to God in the highest, and on earth peace, good will toward men." Shepherds came to see the young Child and returned to glorify and praise God, and wise men came from the east to worship Him and to present Him gifts: gold, frankincense, and myrrh.

Bethlehem was reverenced by Christians from the earliest times—especially the grotto of the manger where Christ was born. So devoutly was the place venerated during the early part of the second century that Emperor Hadrian (76-139), in his attempt to wipe out Christian worship, built over the place of the manger a temple and placed within it a statue of Adonis.

In A.D. 328, when Helena, the mother of Emperor Constantine, came to Bethlehem to erect a church over the place of Jesus' birth, the location presented little or no difficulty, for, ironically, the ruined temple of Adonis marked the place. With ample funds furnished by her emperor son, she completed and dedicated the Church of the Nativity in 332. The Pilgrim of Bordeaux, who came in 333, and many other pilgrims who came later, mention its beautiful interior ornamented with gold, silver, marble, mosaics, embroideries, and paintings. Emperor Justinian (527-565) rebuilt the church, and in the operations the floor level was raised, a stone pavement laid, and the colonnades reset.

The soldiers of Chosroes of Persia, who in the year 614 destroyed other churches in the Holy Land, spared the Church of the Nativity when they saw the mosaics of the wise men in Persian dress. Justinian's church stands today, but with many restorations carried out by the Crusaders in the 11th and 12th centuries. It is regarded as the oldest Christian church extant. In appearance it is like a citadel. The large original entrance has been closed down with masonry until now there is only a low opening, especially made in its present form about 1500, to prevent intruders on horseback from desecrating the church. Above this entry may still be seen the original pointed Crusaders' arch.

In 1934, Mr. William Harvey carried on limited excavations, and about 18 inches under the floor of the present church, he discovered portions of the mosaic floor of the original church built by Helena and Constantine. Some of these mosaic designs were of flowers, fruits, and birds; others were geometric in design. No religious scenes were used in these floor decorations since they would be trodden underfoot.

155

Three Christian faiths share rights in the large Nativity complex—Roman Catholic (Franciscan friars), Greek Orthodox, and Armenian. Each has its own chapel and altars. The Protestants are allowed to sing carols and conduct a brief service on Christmas Eve in the open courtyard. Next to the basilica of the Church of the Nativity is the commodious Chapel of St. Catherine, from whence the Latin Mass is broadcast and televised on Christmas Eve.

Below the eastern end of the nave of the main basilica of the church, two stairways lead through bronze Crusader doors down into the "grotto of the Nativity," 20 feet below the floor level. This cavelike chapel room measures 12 by 40 feet, the marble walls are completely concealed by tapestries, and ornate lights hang from the ceiling. At the eastern end of the chapel is a small crypt, the marble floor of which is inlaid with a vermillion silver star, lighted by 16 silver lamps. A simple inscription in Latin announces the most stupendous event in all history: "Here Jesus Christ was born of the virgin Mary." Nearby is a manger which

156   The marble floor of the "Grotto of the Nativity" in Bethlehem. The inscription on the silver star reads: "Here Jesus Christ was born of the Virgin Mary."

completes the setting for the profound statement: "And she brought forth her firstborn son, and wrapped him in swaddling clothes, and laid him in a manger; because there was no room for them in the inn" (Luke 2:7). People of the most widely divergent temperaments and degrees of culture and stations of life have knelt devoutly at this shrine and lifted their hearts in unfeigned gratitude to God for this best Gift of His love.

From one end of the grotto a passage leads to several small, subterranean, chapellike caves. One contains the altar and cave of the Holy Innocents before which the Franciscan friars in their daily rounds sing the old hymn *"Salveta Flores Martyrum"*—"All Hail, Ye Little Martyr Flowers." This is in memory of the innocent children's martyrdom by Herod. The English rendering is as follows:[2]

> Hail! flowers of martyrs, whom, on the very threshold of life, the persecutor of Christ cut down, like tender rosebuds scattered by the wind. Hail! first victims for Christ, tender lambs offered to Him; with childlike innocence you play around His altar, with palms and crowns the sign of your martyrdom.

Close to the altar of the Holy Innocents is the *Chapel of St. Jerome,* which was once the study of this illustrious scholar. Here he spent 30 years (390-420) in prayer, fastings, and study, to finally complete his monumental work, the Vulgate, which was the Bible translated from the Hebrew and Greek into the Latin —the language of the Romans. This translation not only enriched the lives of the people, who previous to this time had only a scanty knowledge of the Word of God, but it was of inestimable value also to the Reformers and Protestant translators of the Bible.

In the fertile plain below about a mile east from Bethlehem on a green slope is a group of ruins and a grotto surrounded by olive trees, where the angel of the Lord is said to have appeared to the shepherds with the glad tidings of great joy. Over those fields the heavenly host sung the first Christmas carol which was to resound through all ages in all lands of Christendom:

> Glory to God in the highest,
> And on earth peace, good will toward men.

Today Bethlehem is one of the world's most popular tourist centers. Some 20,000 people live here, of whom about one-half are Christians. At Christmastime they very graciously receive the world as their guests. However, an unknown poet has well said:

> *Though Christ a thousand times*
> *In Bethlehem be born,*
> *If He's not born in thee,*
> *Thy hope is all forlorn.*

Rachel's Tomb. Beside the high road that runs through the center of Palestine, less than a mile from the city of Bethlehem, is Rachel's tomb. Beautiful Rachel, with whom Jacob fell in love at first sight at the Padan Aram well, and for whom he served a double seven years ("they seemed unto him but a few days, for the love he had for her"). The romance had continued for more than a quarter of a century. Joseph had been born, and they had gone many places together. But as their caravan journeyed on the high road "from Bethel; and there was but a little way to come to Bethlehem, Rachel travailed . . . and the midwife said unto her, Fear not; thou shalt have this son also." And as her soul

158

Entrance to Rachel's tomb near Bethlehem

was departing, she called his name Ben-o-ni, but his father called him Benjamin, "the son of my right hand." And Jacob buried her there "on the way to Bethlehem . . . and set a pillar upon her grave" (Gen. 35:19-20).

The tomb has undergone many changes in the course of generations. Origen (A.D. 185-254), an early Church Father, first mentions the tomb. Jerome described it as a pyramid of 12 stones representing the 12 sons of Jacob. In the 12th century the Crusaders erected over it a domed room 24 feet square. In the 15th century the Moslems reconditioned the building and constructed a modern masonry-cenotaph over the site.

In 1841, Sir M. Montefiore purchased the grounds and monument for the Jewish community, added an adjoining prayer vestibule, and reconditioned the entire structure with its white dome and quiet reception or prayer room. In the middle of the burial room is the large concrete cenotaph, painted in battleship gray—no name, not an ornament, nor a carving. On Fridays and holidays the Jews come in large numbers to quietly revere the place, to pray, or, led by a young rabbi, chant the prophet Jeremiah's lovely lament: "A voice was heard in Rama, lamentation and bitter weeping: Rachel weeping for her children and would not be comforted, because they were not."

A motherly woman may stretch out her arms, embrace a corner of the gray cenotaph, and passionately kiss it again and again. The group may move around the tomb, touching, kissing, stroking its cold surface with affectionate hands, until all have made the full circuit. Then, with eyes shining, they file out into the sunlight.

At *Zelah,* about a half mile west of Rachel's tomb, on a low hilltop near a large and beautiful grove of olive trees is located the family burial **tomb of Kish,** where Saul and Jonathan are buried. At David's command, the bones of Saul and Jonathan were brought from Jabesh-gilead and buried here in the family sepulchre of Kish, Saul's father (2 Sam. 21:12-14).

The Pools of Solomon. Three miles south of Bethlehem, near the head of the Valley of Urtas, are three large reservoirs known as the "Pools of Solomon." They are chiefly hewn out of the native rock and partly built of squared stones. The pools are about 150 feet apart, and the bottom of each is higher than the top of the one below it. They are strengthened by buttresses and connected by well-cut channels. The upper pool is 380 by 229 feet, and is 25 feet deep; the middle pool is 423 by 230 feet, and is 39 feet deep; while the lower pool is 582 by 207 feet, and is 50 feet deep. To enable the pools to be cleaned and water to be drawn when not full, there are flights of steps inside the lower end of each. They show signs of having been repaired, and at least partially lined with cement from time to time.[3]

These reservoirs are supplied by surface drainage from the nearby hills, by *Ain Saleh* (a splendid spring flowing from an enclosed rock chamber known as the place Solomon referred to as "a spring shut up, a fountain sealed"), and by three other smaller springs. Below the lower pool is an ancient, rock-laid aqueduct leading to Jerusalem about eight miles away and 82 feet lower. A second aqueduct leads toward Herodium, east of Bethlehem, where Herod had a palace. The village of Urtas lies near the bottom of the valley, about a mile east of the pools.

The entire area of luxuriant verdure fits very well into the setting of ancient Etam where King Solomon is said to have made a paradise of pleasure—"planted vineyards, made gardens and orchards, and planted trees of all kinds of fruits . . . and made pools of water to water the wood that bringeth forth trees" (Eccles. 2:5-6). Josephus amplifies the account by telling us that Solomon clothed himself in white, and in a gold-lined chariot drove to his fine gardens at Etam each morning.[4]

The Romans made use of these pools, along with the *Ain Arroub* springs farther south. Their aqueduct connected the two water sources as it trailed around the hills to finally enter the Great Sea under the Temple area at Jerusalem. It is quite possible that the Roman reservoirs were enlargements and restorations of the pools originally prepared by Solomon.

The Palestine government, following World War I, repaired the pools and installed a large pumping station below the lower pool. A pipeline from the springs of Ain Arroub leads to the pools, and all the water is now pumped on to Jerusalem.

Tekoah is the home of Amos the herdsman prophet who, at the call of God, arose up and went to Bethel where he preached plain yet profound truth for all men for all time. It was also the home of "the wise woman" whom Joab employed to induce King David, by a parable, to recall Absalom from banishment (2 Sam. 14:1-22).

Tekoah was the eastern outpost of Judah, five miles southeast of Bethlehem and 10 miles south of Jerusalem. It was on the dividing line between the desert and the arable land. To its east was the Wilderness of Judea, and to its west the lands which lay along the high road which led through Hebron, Bethlehem, and Jerusalem.

Being located on the perilous caravan route from En-Gedi to Judah, and situated on an elevated plateau, it was the signal-station where the trumpet was blown and the fire signals set up in time of potential danger ("blow the trumpet in Tekoa, and set up a signal of fire"). Well did these warning signals work for Jehoshaphat when Edom, Moab, and Ammon was observed marching around En-Gedi up toward Tekoah. Then Jehoshaphat called the people to prayer, and was advised by the prophet Jahaziel, the son of Zechariah, "Ye shall not need to fight in this battle ... the Lord will be with you." The following day Israel only sang while the Lord brought consternation and defeat to the enemy armies in the narrow pass east of Tekoah, and the place was called "The Valley of Berachah" (2 Chron. 20:1-26).

Neby Sam'wil is a conical hill, 2,942 feet above sea level, five miles northwest of Jerusalem. It is the most conspicuous promontory in northern Judea, and believed by Edward Robinson, G. A. Smith, and W. F. Albright to be the *Mizpeh* of Benjamin. (Others think Mizpeh should be identified with Tell en-Nasbeh, eight miles north of Jerusalem.) Popular tradition has long designated it as the burial place of the prophet Samuel, and during the Middle Ages the Jews gathered in large numbers to hold solemn celebrations at the shrine—although the records state that Samuel was buried at Ramah (1 Sam. 25:1).

161

The Crusaders called the place Mount Joy, because from the top of this mount they had their first glimpse of the Holy City.

The summit is crowned by a dilapidated mosque, once a Christian church, within which is shown a comparatively modern Moslem tomb as the tomb of Samuel. One of the most extensive and interesting views in all Palestine is obtained from the top of the mosque's minaret.[5]

Gibeon, one mile northwest of Neby Sam'wil, is the home of the ancient Gibeonites who tricked Joshua and the incoming Israelites into making a perpetual league with them, and the place where the Tabernacle was set up after the slaughter of the priests by Saul. Here also the Lord appeared to Solomon in a dream by night, and asked, "What shall I give thee?" and Solomon answered, "Give . . . thy servant an understanding heart to judge thy people, that I may discern between good and bad" (1 Kings 3:9). The area has been excavated by Dr. Pritchard.

Gibeah of Saul is perched on the summit of a lofty, limestone hill, on the east side of the highway, three miles north of Jerusalem. The Arabs call it *Tell el-Ful* (Hill of Beans), but in reality it was King Saul's royal palace and citadel where young David came to console the king with sweet strains of harmony from his harp, and to hold high friendship with Prince Jonathan. Excavations have revealed that Saul's well-constructed, two-story fortress-palace measured about 115 by 170 feet, or nearly 20,000 square feet for each of the two floors. His audience room where he contracted state affairs, and where David probably played his harp, "barely equaled the modest modern living room, 14 by 23 feet." Wine, oil, and grain jars showed that the basement rooms were stored with food. The 2,758-foot hilltop is now crowned with the abandoned shell of a new palace, which was begun for King Hussein.

Ramah, the native home, official residence, and burial place of Samuel the prophet, was located north of Jerusalem in the midst of that most interesting cluster of towns including Gibeah, Gibeon, Mizpeh, Beeroth, and Bethel, yet no one is certain of its exact location. Seven different places have been suggested.

162   After many years of study and research, the present writer has come to believe we are justified in considering Ramah and Ramallah as one and the same place.

Ramah is derived from the Hebrew and means "the height"; *Ramallah* is derived from the Arabic and means "the height of God." Ramallah is 2,930 feet above sea level, the highest and finest eminence in this area (aside from Neby Sam'wil, which is somewhat to the west). Ramallah overlooks the entire region and therefore the government broadcasting station is now located there.

Samuel is described as living by a very important hilltop, or high and holy place where he had built an altar, to which the people came to worship God. It was customary for them to wait for him to ascend the hill and pronounce a blessing before they partook of solemn feasts. Around this high portion of Ramah, in the center of town, there prevailed a profound sacredness, and many wonderful things took place there. Samuel was one of the most godly men history has known, and Ramah plus Samuel was the epitome of sacredness—the focus of spirituality for those times. After Samuel had anointed Saul, he said, "Thou shalt come to the hill of God . . . and the Spirit of the Lord shall come upon thee, and thou shalt prophesy with them, and shall be turned unto another man" (1 Sam. 10:5-6). As a judge, Samuel went year by year on a circuit to Bethel, Ramah, Mizpeh, and Gilgal. Then he would come back to his home at Ramah.

Ramallah, along with Bethlehem, has long been known as one of the cleanest, safest, and finest small cities of the Holy Land. It is now an educational and commercial center of some 25,000 people—the largest city between Nablus and Jerusalem. It is a Christian city—largely Protestant because of the splendid Quaker college located there.

The splendid springs at Ramallah are not only adequate for all local needs, but water is piped from there to Beitin (Beth-el) and to Der Dibwan, prosperous Arab villages to the northeast.[6]

Beeroth, now called *Bireh,* lies just across the highway east-ward from Ramallah. It derives its name from the copious springs at the southwestern corner of the town, where some 13,000 inhabitants, all Moslems, now live. These springs serve the same purpose as the village well, where in the morning hours the women gather for gossip, then fill their waterpots and gracefully bear them away for the day's water supply. They gathered here after this fashion 2,000 to 3,000 years ago. I first saw them gather here in 1926, and purchased a choice "dowry coin" from one of them—a Maria Theresa coin minted in 1780.

Because of this splendid watering place, ancient Beeroth was the customary resting place of pilgrim bands on their return from the great feasts at Jerusalem, for it was a short day's journey from the Holy City. Tradition has it that Joseph and Mary first missed their 12-year-old Jesus here, and tracing their steps backward, found Him "in the temple, sitting in the midst of the doctors [teachers], both hearing them and asking them questions" (Luke 2:41-46).

CHAPTER **14**

The City of Jerusalem

Jerusalem, whose history reaches back some 4,000 years, and whose name awakens more mystery and sacred memories to more people than any other place on earth, has been called "The City of Peace," or "The City of the Great King." Others think of it as "The City of God," "The City of the Soul," or as "The City of the Book." It is located on a 1,000-acre plateau, next to Gihon Spring in the central Judean mountains. It slightly slants toward the southeast and is encircled by the Kedron and Hinnom valleys. A lesser valley known as "the

Tyropoeon" drains central Jerusalem and divides the "Lower City" from the "Upper City." In Jesus' day this valley was spanned by broad and beautiful bridges supported by immense arches, but in the intervening centuries it has been largely filled up.

Jerusalem has long been surrounded by gray stone walls, varying in height from 30 to 80 feet, and in length from two to five miles. Only remnants of its ancient walls remain. These lie below the present ground level, or form the foundation for later walls. The present walls were built by Suleiman I, "The Magnificent," from 1538 to 1542, and are pierced by eight well-known gates —Jaffa Gate, the New Gate, Damascus Gate, Herod's Gate, St. Stephen's Gate, the Golden Gate, Dung Gate, and Zion's Gate. There are a number of minor gates which are closed.

Within those walls are five famous hills—Mount Ophel, Mount Moriah, Mount Zion, the Northwestern Hill, and Bezetha. Three temples were built on Mount Moriah—Solomon's Temple, Zerubbabel's Temple, and Herod's Temple. The temple area covered 35 acres. The deeply cloistered and colonnaded Outer Court was for the people—among them Gentiles from many lands. The Inner Court had at its center the magnificent Temple proper. On Mount Zion, on the Day of Pentecost, the Holy Spirit came to purify, empower, and guide individuals and the Church.

Modern Moriah, called "the Temple Mount," now has the Dome of the Rock, a Moslem shrine, with its fine grain marble, its beautiful blue Persian tile, its ornate Arabesque script, and its golden dome—altogether, one of the world's finest architectural masterpieces in detail, color, and contour. Directly underneath the dome lies the rough and partially tooled sacred rock in all its massiveness—a huge ledge of gray limestone 57 feet long and 43 feet wide, which is unquestionably the summit of Mount Moriah, where once stood the temples of Solomon, Zerubbabel, and Herod.

Directly south, against the southern wall of the Temple area, is the richly carpeted Mosque of *El Aksa*, Islam's holiest shrine after Mecca and Medina, where worshippers kneel for prayer in the direction of Mecca.

Solomon's Stables, a vaulted structure of 12 parallel rows of

The Western Wall or Wailing Wall in Jerusalem

aisles 200 feet long with 88 supporting columns, lies *under* the southeast corner of the Temple area. Apparently these were built by Herod, since most of the stones are of the Herodian pattern. Portions of the basic structure could have been built by Solomon. They were reconditioned and used by the Crusaders. Some of the rings to which they tethered their horses still exist.

West from these "stables" are *ancient underground water reservoirs* now in use. One known as the Great Sea has an estimated capacity of 2 million gallons. The water for these reservoirs comes from Solomon's Pools, seven miles away.

Solomon's Quarries are stone quarries which extend some 700 feet beneath the northern section of the Old City. Markings

167

in the side and end walls show the very shapes of large building stones which were removed. Throughout the quarries are small rock shelves on which the ancients placed earthen lamps that gave light to the laborers.

The *Wailing Wall,* which the Jewish people prefer to call "The Western Wall," is a part of the retaining wall bordering the outer court of Herod's Temple—a grand architectural fragment whose proximity to the Temple sanctuary has made it an object of veneration and Jewish pilgrimage since soon after the destruction of the Temple more than 1,900 years ago. Many of the carefully marginal-drafted stones in the five lower courses of this wall are so old and so strikingly beautiful that they are regarded as some of the world's finest and most venerable stones.

But the tens of thousands who frequent this wall each week come not to worship an ancient architectural relic, but to pray in deep earnestness and devotion to Almighty God. Their prayers are as varied as human needs and desires. Some write their prayer petitions on a slip of paper and insert them into cracks in the wall. Sometime ago Moshe Dayan wrote his personal prayer and placed it in the wall. It read simply, "Shalom"—Peace. How appropriate, for the Scripture enjoins men to "pray for the peace of Jerusalem."

The *Citadel,* or "Tower of David," is the oldest and most impressive of Jerusalem's ancient buildings. It is located immediately south of Jaffa Gate, and is usually the first of the ancient buildings to be seen by a visitor or pilgrim to the Holy City.

In 24 B.C. Herod the Great built his beautiful palace adjoining this site on the south, and as a means of protection erected three huge towers which he dedicated to Phasael, his brother; Meriamne, his wife; and Hippicus, a friend. When Titus razed the city in A.D. 70, he was impressed by the size of these towers and left them standing as a protection for the legion left to garrison the place. Later destructions took away two of the towers, and much of the third. What we see today is the base of the Phasael Tower and reused stones from the other structures. The major portion of the remains which belonged to Herod's palace, and the towers, are buried beneath a mass of rubble more than 30

168

Looking over the northern wall into the old city of Jerusalem at the Damascus Gate.

feet deep. Some stones here are earlier than Herod's time; others are much later. We do not know if King David ever had a tower here.

The building, as we now know it, was rebuilt and remodeled by the Crusaders in the 14th century, by the Turks in the 16th century, and more recently by the British in 1929, at a cost of some $30,000.

The *place where Jesus Christ was crucified* has deeply concerned Christians from the earliest times. The apostles and thousands of others knew the place quite well. Then, in A.D. 70, the dark holocaust came with the destruction of Jerusalem by Titus. The people were killed or led away into slavery, and for some 60 years the Holy City lay in ruins. When it began again to be rebuilt, it was under a pagan regime, and neither Jews nor Christians were allowed to enter the city. When the Christians finally returned, none knew the place of the Crucifixion.

Helena, the mother of Emperor Constantine, came to Jeru-

170

The Garden of Gethsemane looking across to the city wall and the Eastern or Golden Gate.

salem in 326, and by the aid of Eusebius, bishop of Caesarea, and Macarius, bishop of Jerusalem, searched for the place where Christ was crucified and buried. Eventually they decided on the place where now stands the Church of the Holy Sepulchre. Few if any sites of the world have been regarded with such awe and treated with such reverence.

Others, in more recent times, have settled on a three-acre gray hill, just a few hundred feet outside Damascus Gate, as the probable Golgotha or Mount Calvary. It rises some 50 feet above the surrounding terrain and on its side toward the city bears a "certain fantastic likeness" to a human skull. Nearby is a garden and a tomb which is called "The Garden Tomb."

"The tomb is without ornamentation or ostentation, and for all that is the more impressive. No one worships the place, and it is to be hoped none ever will, but many notable Easter services have been conducted here." Among the speakers have been Dwight L. Moody, Dewitt Talmage, and Billy Graham. Thousands gather here from the many countries of the earth and in a small measure feel the force and simplicity of the angel's words: "Come, see the place where the Lord lay."

Other places of interest outside the walls of Jerusalem are: The Hill of Evil Counsel; The Potter's Field; Gihon Spring (the Virgin's Fountain); En-rogel (Job's Well); the Village of Siloam; the Mount of Offense; the Mount of Olives; the Garden of Gethsemane; the Chapel of St. Stephen; Jeremiah's Grotto; and "the Tomb of the Kings."

Jerusalem is rapidly becoming a great metropolitan city—composed of Ancient Jerusalem, the major portion of which is surrounded by walls and largely Arab in population; New Jerusalem, the Jewish city; and East Jerusalem, which is largely made up of Arabs. The last two sections mentioned are being rapidly filled with high-rise buildings which tend to obscure the skyline of the Holy City as it has been known for the past centuries. Yet more and more people come here to live, and about a half million tourists visit the city each year.

CHAPTER 15

The Wilderness of Judea

The Wilderness of Judea has long been known as the badlands of Palestine—"the Scapegoat Wilderness" into which the scapegoat was led "by the hand of a fit man," after the iniquities of the people had been confessed and put upon his head. It lies between Judea and the Dead Sea. Its northern boundary line is *Wadi Kelt,* and it reaches southward to the Negeb. It is some 15 miles wide and 50 miles long.

This "wilderness" is a dry, parched, eroded land, full of white, steep, rugged ridges, and is savagely cut from west to east

172

by hundreds of deep, torturous ravines and canyons which descend abruptly toward the Jordan Valley and the Dead Sea. The hills are largely made up of soft, chalky marl and other limestone compositions, and are bald and smooth and white, without a tint of green, other than soon after the scanty rainfall of the brief rainy season. At other times there is a startling desolation and an oppressive heat—almost like an oven. Occasionally there is flying dust which, when driven by the wind, sweeps the wilderness in blinding fury.

Its great gorges are black and yawning, and its precipices so steep as to make one shudder. All about there is barrenness, chaos, emptiness, isolation, and unfriendliness. These wild wastelands are so dry and sterile and unproductive that one cannot hope to produce any crop. Yet a few plants of retem, some thorns, a bit of grass, and a few flowers do grow here for a brief

173

Typical view of the rugged Wilderness of Judea

time after the winter rains. Also there are a few pleasant days during the year. David in his younger years occasionally grazed his flocks here, and in modern times three Bedouin tribes claim jurisdiction, each in their respective areas. Many groups of people have lived at certain places in this desert from time to time so that the Judean Wilderness becomes a place of singular interest. The places which for one reason or another have fascinated men and caused them to use them or to live here are *Wadi Kelt*, the *Mount of Temptation*, the *Jericho Road*, *Cave of Adullam*, *Herodium*, *Mar Saba*, *Masada*, *En-Gedi*, *Qumran*, and certain cave areas.

Wadi Kelt, through which flows the traditional "Brook Cherith," is a deep, wild ravine which forms the northern boundary of the wilderness. It rises six miles northeast of Jerusalem (where at first it is called Wadi Farah), and flows eastward for some 10 miles until it enters the Jericho plain. It is fed by three strong springs—*Ain Farah, Ain Fowar,* and *Ain el Kelt*—which ordinarily would make it a perennial stream, only that the water from Ain Farah is pumped back to Jerusalem, and an aqueduct conducts the water from the other two springs down to the Jordan plain for irrigation.

In its lower reaches, where it deepens to almost unthinkable depths, it is known as "The Valley of the Shadow of Death" made famous by David's Shepherd Psalm. Also, it is thought to correspond with the "Brook Cherith" of 1 Kings 17:3-5, where Elijah drank of the brook and was fed by the ravens. Here, its sheer walls of rock, sometimes only 12 to 20 feet apart, rise to as much as 200-300 feet and make it practically inaccessible to other than the hardiest of men. Built high upon the wild cliff, where a cavern was said to have been Elijah's lodging place, is the Greek Orthodox Monastery of St. George, where for 1,600 years have come thousands of monks to meditate and pray.

Some years ago, when the British ruled and there was peace in Palestine, the writer went through this "Valley of the Shadow of Death," armed with no more than a camera. We lunched at beautiful *Ain el Kelt* and began our descent of the valley. For the first half mile grass covered the sloping hillsides and shepherds pastured their flocks. Then passing down over a precipice, the valley grew deeper and wilder. In places it was only as wide as the stream bed. We had read of ravens, wild dogs, wolves, and hyenas being here, but on our trip we encountered only one wild dog who charged three times. Our defense was with stones which we drove at him with sufficient accuracy that he finally went away and bothered us no more. Near the lower end of the gorge we met up with two shepherd boys who were leading their flocks home as the shadows were deepening in the Valley of the Shadow of Death.

Mount Quarantana, the traditional **mount of Christ's temptation,** with its cells, its chapels, and a ruined church on its peak, towers up nearly 1,000 feet some two miles west of Jericho. "He was there in the wilderness forty days, tempted of Satan, and was with the wild beasts; and the angels ministered unto him" (Mark 1:13).

What appointments are here indicated, for when Jesus had finished His 40-day fast and was "afterward hungered," the angels "ministered unto him," and not far away was Wadi Kelt (Brook Cherith), where when Elijah was hungry, he was fed by the ravens. Ravens and angels spreading a feast! Surely the Lord can "make a feast in the wilderness."

The Jericho Road spans the distance between Jerusalem and Jericho—about 13 miles. It is the only real road which runs through this wild, wilderness land. Four ancient Roman milestones and numerous ancient land markings indicate that the Turkish road of 50 years ago, and in some places the present road, takes much the same course as the ancient Roman road on which "a certain man went down from Jerusalem to Jericho, and fell among thieves, which stripped him of his raiment, and wounded him, and departed, leaving him half dead." A priest and a Levite passed him by, heedless of his hurt. But a certain Samaritan, "as he journeyed, came where he was; and when he saw him, he had compassion on him, and went to him, and bound up his wounds, pouring in oil and wine, and set him on his own beast, and brought him to an inn, and took care of him" (Luke 10:30-34).

Multitudes of happy pilgrims journeyed over this road to

Jerusalem to break the unleavened bread at the festival of the Passover, and Jesus was the Center of attraction on certain of those occasions. At one point are the supposed ruins of the Good Samaritan Inn, and at another is the Apostles' Well. The United States furnished funds for construction of the present modern road.

The Cave of Adullam, which gave refuge to David and his followers when fleeing King Saul's jealous opposition, has for many centuries been identified with a large, impressive cliffside cave in the Wilderness of Judea, four miles southeast of Bethlehem. Located in the rough ravine of *Wadi Khureitun* with its rugged, precipitous sides several hundred feet deep, and the cavern's partially obscured entrance nearly 200 feet up on the rock wall of the canyon, there is a strange seclusion and wildness about the place.

It would seem all but impossible to reach the entrance. But a huge boulder has fallen from above and lodged within a few feet of the opening, so if by strenuous effort you gain a footing on the boulder, a wild leap will land you within the rather crudely chiseled doorway.[1]

You then enter a narrow, low passage leading to a small cave, from which a winding gallery leads to the great cave—a natural grotto 120 feet long by 40 feet wide and 40 to 50 feet high. It is probably the largest natural cave room in Palestine. Numbers of passages—one about 100 feet long—branch out in all directions, often leading to other fair-sized rooms, some of which are partially artificial. Through some of these caverns there are steep descents into a lower series of rooms, and from these there branch out still other caverns and rooms—some as much as 600 feet from the entrance. Parts of the cave have never been investigated.

Nearby is a copious spring of cold, fresh water, falling quietly into a small, rock-hewn basin—sufficient to supply the needs of David's 400 followers. The place matches well the details of the scriptural account.

Herodium, "The Mountain of Paradise," is a 600-foot high, cone-shaped hill standing out boldly on the plain three miles southeast of Bethlehem, and one mile north of the Cave of Adullam. It may have been the Beth-haccerem or "Beacon Mountain" of Old Testament times, from whence "fire signals" were sent, but in known history it is connected with Herod the Great. Desiring a country estate for his own pleasure, and having ample funds at his command, he raised the hill still higher, then on the very top he erected a massively fortified castle and a luxurious royal palace of great strength and splendor. The only way of access to this top level was by way of a superb stairway of hewn stone.

At the foot of the hill and on the surrounding plain, Herod laid out a beautiful town in Roman style, including a palace for himself and beautiful homes for his friends. The place was ornamented with trees and beautiful gardens. To insure an adequate water supply, he had an aqueduct constructed from the spring at Etam (near Solomon's Pools) to a central fountain at Herodium. From here it was channeled to various buildings and to the gardens. When all was complete and in operation, the natives called it "Jebel Fereidis" ("Mountain of the Little Paradise"). Herod used it as a quiet place of enjoyment with his friends and as his base when he took off on expeditions for hunting partridge, ibex, and other game in the wilderness. Herodium was also a signal light station where communication could be received from or sent to the Mount of Olives, Masada, Machaerus, and Alexandrium, north of Jericho.

The Christians frequently call it "Frank Mountain," from a 15th-century tradition that it was defended by the Crusaders for a long time against the Saracens, after the loss of Jerusalem. Recently it has been made into a national park.

Mar Saba Monastery is one of the strangest and most extraordinary places it is possible to dream about. Certainly you can hardly believe your eyes when you view it in reality. Partly hewn in the rock and partly built on strongly buttressed ledges, it rises up tier upon tier and tower upon tower from the south cliffs of the blasted and desolate *Wadi n-Nar* ("Valley of Fire"), which is the channel down which the Kedron flows to the Dead

Sea. No other place in the world is more weirdly situated, and no other place in the Judean Wilderness is more shrouded with mystery than this monastery of Mar Saba, located at sea level, four miles east of Bethlehem. From one outlook on the wall it is 590 feet down to the bed of the Valley of Fire.

St. Saba, a native of Cappadocia, who was famed for his sanctity, his learning, and his power to work miracles, penetrated this desert and became fascinated with the idea of founding a monastery in this wild gorge. In A.D. 483, at the age of 44, his dream was fulfilled when he gathered around him hundreds of deeply religious men under the rule of St. Basil, and began the construction of *Mar Saba* as a Greek monastery by authority of the patriarch of Jerusalem.

The foundations for the structure were and have ever been a marvel of engineering, for the stone ledges and the pinnacled piers and pilasters seem as one. The many towers, terraces, balconies, courtyards, chapels, shrines, rock-hewn cells, rooms, iron rails, and winding stairs all cling to and blend with the gray cliffside like a huge and intricately built swallow's nest.

In addition to its multiplicity of accommodations for monastic living and practices, it has an ornately decorated chapel with its stalls, walls, screen, and chancel gorgeous with gilding and paintings.

Mar Saba's library is reputed to contain rare manuscript treasures, but only such men as Curzon and Tischendorf have been permitted to examine them. Curzon reported seeing about 1,000 manuscripts, several of which were of great interest—among them a copy of the first eight books of the Old Testament, and a copy of Homer's *Iliad*.

It is said that at one time more than 3,000 monks and hermits lived at this monastery and in surrounding areas. Now there are only a few.

The entrance by which travelers are received is marked by a large tower with dilapidated battlements. Here, at a small, iron-barred door, travelers must present their credentials and be carefully scrutinized before admission. No ladies are admitted, but for their reception the tower outside is provided where they are supplied with simple fare and a night's lodging.

Masada, a majestic 23-acre flat-topped mesa, two and one-half miles off the west shore of the Dead Sea, is one of the world's most startling natural fortifications. Shaped like a great ship 2,000 feet long and 1,000 feet wide in the middle and tapering to narrow promontories at the northern and southern tips, its sides are composed of almost sheer rock cliffs which rise 1,000 feet above the barren wilderness of Judea, and 1,300 feet above the

Looking down on the fortress of Masada showing the three-tiered palace of Herod clinging to the northern slope.

waters of the Dead Sea. Stark, forbidding, and almost inaccessible, it was chosen by Herod the Great, in 37 B.C., as a site for his wilderness palace and fortress—a place of retreat and refuge in case of possible attack by Cleopatra of Egypt, by his own subjects, or by armies from the desert.

He encircled the entire top of the plateau with a great white wall 4,250 feet long, 20 feet high, and 13 feet wide. It had three gates and 38 towers. As his residence, he erected the "Western Palace," which was a very large and wonderfully fine place with throne room, living and reception quarters, luxurious baths, colored mosaic floors, and sumptuous apartments. About his palace, and at other places on the mesa, where colonnaded porticos, cloisters, walkways, cisterns, groves, gardens, and storerooms for both arms and provisions sufficient to supply 10,000 men for many years—"And thus was the citadel fortified by nature and the hands of men."

Later, to make his retreat doubly secure, more pleasant, and more impressive, he moved the sphere of his architectural activities to Masada's northern precipice, and there erected his three-tiered "hanging palace"—the architectural wonder of the ancient world. On the upper terrace were four spacious and highly decorated apartment rooms with a semicircular court extending out to the very edge of the cliff. The middle terrace, 60 feet below, was a circular pavilion and a colonnade. The lowest terrace was an elaborate apartment with its rooms and baths built on a 54-foot square, surrounded by a double colonnade. The wall frescoes were of imitation marble and precious stones. Inner staircases connected the three terraces.

But Herod was never to use Masada, except for possibly a few vacation trips. After his death, in 4 B.C., a Roman garrison was stationed at Masada, and this occupation continued until A.D. 66, when a large-scale Jewish revolt broke out all over the land. At this time the Jews made a lightning raid on Masada, destroyed the Roman garrison, and took charge of the plateau with its fortifications and palace complex. As fighting continued throughout Palestine, many more zealous Jews came to Masada and strengthened the Jewish garrison.

After the fall of Jerusalem to Titus, in A.D. 70, the Jews gathered their remnants and prepared to stage their last desperate resistance at Masada. Titus' deputy general, Flavius Silva, came there in the autumn of 72 and laid siege to Masada, which was then defended by Eleazar ben Yair, the leader of the Zealots.

For long months they defended themselves in their natural fortress. But the Romans erected a huge ramp or causeway on the western side over which they could reach the rim of the plateau. At its head they built siege towers, catapults, and battering rams, and in the end attacked with flaming torches. Then, when the Jews could resist no more, Eleazar made a speech in which he set forth the horrors of the fate that awaited them as prisoners to the Romans, and begged them to kill themselves rather than submit. The garrison consented.

Embracing their loved ones, with sword and dagger they dealt the fatal blows. Personal treasures were collected in piles and burned. Finally they chose 10 men by lot to slay all the rest. When these 10 had done the deed, they in turn cast lots among themselves to determine who should kill his 9 companions and afterwards slay himself. Thus, in silence so the enemy should suspect nothing, one of the most touching tragedies in the annals of human history took place.[2]

The next day, April 15, A.D. 73, when the Romans at last got into the fortress they had besieged so long, they found two women and five children who had concealed themselves, and a mass of 960 dead bodies. An awful silence took the place of the clamor they had expected. Masada! O Masada of the Wilderness![3]

Yigael Yadin and a very large number of volunteers excavated Masada in two campaigns, one of seven months and one of four. In the Western Palace they found the throne room, reception halls, bedrooms, bathrooms, service quarters, and storage rooms in which were hundreds of broken storage jars containing remnants of food. Many of the jars bore labels describing their contents in Aramaic or Hebrew. In some of the Zealots' rooms 181 they found domestic utensils, mats, shoes, and clothing.

Many bronze and silver coins were found, including "great

hoards" of silver shekels inscribed "Jerusalem the Holy—Shekel of Israel." Beneath the floor of the synagogue were found two biblical scrolls—parts of Ezekiel and Deuteronomy.

Today hardy souls may take the three-mile "serpent's trail" to the top; others not caring for the extreme exertion may now go up in an electric cable car. On the top of Masada, Jewish soldiers are initiated into the Israeli Army with the significant words, "It shall not happen again."

En-Gedi (Ain Jidy—"The Fountain of the Kid") is a small oasis halfway along the west shores of the Dead Sea. Here, almost 500 feet above the sea, an immense spring of warm water leaps from the base of a towering rock cliff and splashes from terrace to terrace down to a small but very fertile plain, half a mile broad and a mile in length.

As early as the reign of Solomon, En-Gedi was one of the richest areas in Palestine. Here were vineyards, date palms, camphire, gum arabic, myrrh, sugarcane, melons, and many other edible fruits, spices, perfumes, and plants that made up one of the world's famed garden spots. Josephus suggests that balsam saplings were among the presents brought to Solomon by the queen of Sheba. Apparently the cultivation of balsam was begun here by the king.

Above and around the fountains are lofty cliffs, deep ravines, and a wild desolation called "the wilderness of En-gedi," which one could not well overrate as a place of refuge. There are numerous natural and artificial caves and sepulchers in the area, some of which sheltered David and his followers when they dwelt here for some time in the "strongholds at En-gedi" (1 Sam. 23:2). Solomon exclaimed, "My beloved is to me as a cluster of camphire in the vineyards of En-gedi" (Song of Sol. 1:14). En-Gedi continued, with varying fortunes, until its destruction in the Arab invasion of the seventh century. Since than it has lain in ruins until recently a pioneering group of young people from Israel have planted a thriving colony here.

182

Khirbet Qumran, bordering the northwest shore of the Dead Sea, is where, about the year 150 B.C., the Essenes removed themselves "from the evils and wrongs which surge up in cities," and built their own colony.

Here for almost two centuries they lived quiet and extremely simple lives and "devoted themselves to agriculture and other peaceful arts." Among their arts was copying the Scriptures and other sacred scrolls. They were so deeply imbued with a spiritual ideal that they lived in anticipation of the kingdom of God.

Finally, Rome came about A.D. 68 and destroyed or dispersed the Essenes, leaving only the ruins of their city. But before destruction came, they had hidden thousands of sacred scrolls in nearby caves. These were discovered in 1947 to 1956, and constitute the greatest archaeological discovery of modern times.

Oh, the wilderness! This Judean Wilderness! What thoughts it all conjures up! On its border have lived mighty men of God —Amos, Jeremiah, and John the Baptist. And in its wild wastelands Jesus, the Son of God, fasted, was tempted, said no to the devil, and angels ministered to Him. Here Herod built a "little paradise" at Herodium and at Masada, the mightiest fortress and palace of the Near East. And here the Essenes lived and left thousands of copies of the Bible for modern men.

CHAPTER **16**

The Negeb, or Southland

The Negeb, or dry southland, is that large, inverted land triangle with its base on an east-west line just north of Beer-sheba, and its apex at Elath on the Red Sea. In many respects the Negeb (or Negev) is a highland plateau made up of sandy plains, rolling hills, small fertile wadies, craters, and fantastically shaped mountains which rise here and there in irregular disorder. All of its annual rainfall of five to eight inches comes between December and March. During spring months the atmosphere is fresh and clear, the flowers bloom, and one hears the whistling of the quail, the song of the lark, and the warbling of smaller birds. At other seasons much of the land assumes the features of a desert—dry, wadi-cut, and sand blown.

In ancient times the Negeb was one of the fertile and fascinating sections of Palestine—one to which the Hebrew patriarchs went and spent much of their lives. Here they dug wells, erected altars, called on the name of the Lord, planted groves, tilled the land, and reared their families. Over these swelling hills and within these valleys their flocks and herds roved by the thousands.

It was in the desert lands of this southwestern Negeb that Hagar wandered with her son Ishmael when driven from Abraham's tent encampment.

From here Abraham journeyed with Isaac to Mount Moriah, to offer him up there in sacrifice. During the lifetime of Samuel, his sons were made judges, lived at Beersheba, and judged the Israelites who lived in this southland of Palestine.

Elijah, when fleeing from the fury of Queen Jezebel, came to Beersheba and, leaving his servant, went a day's journey southward into the wilder portions of the Negeb. There he "sat down under a juniper tree" and asked the Lord to let him die. This juniper tree, known as *Retem,* is a species of the broom-plant and is still the largest and most conspicuous shrub of these deserts, providing the traveling Arab with shelter from the wind at night and from the sun by day.

More advanced forms of civilization in the Negeb began with the Nabateans, an Arab people of the first century before Christ. The pressure of large, dynamic populations was so great in the Edom area that thousands were forced to seek sustenance and shelter in these less-favored lands, where other large civilizations less trained in the arts of life must have miserably perished because of a lack of knowledge of how to conserve the natural water supplies. But here the Nabateans not only survived, but built up a civilization that evoked the admiration of all who saw or heard of their exploits. They conserved rainwater by a system of dams and cisterns, and a network of cut channels along which they directed runoff water from the hills, built towns along the caravan routes, "worked out the refinements of soil and water management" so that there was ample provision for agricultural pursuits as well as for domestic purposes.[1]

When the Roman conquerors took over, just previous to and during the early Christian period, this district underwent further and more extensive development. They dug wells, built reservoirs, and constructed aqueducts to lead water for long distances to irrigate lands which would otherwise have lain fallow. They erected public buildings, established garrisons, and built a civilization that will always impress those who see these lands and gain a fair acquaintance of the climate and history of the country.

Civilization in the Negeb reached its peak under the Byzantines who succeeded the Romans. Taking over the entire Roman development, they further improved the country by constructing stone walls for terracing and conserving the soil. They built vast rock cisterns and immense dams for conserving the water. The peak of this civilization was under Emperor Justinian during the sixth century A.D. During this time the Negeb developed a population of around 100,000 people who enjoyed improved roads and a flourishing trade. Then, in the seventh century, the Arabs took over in the Negeb, and civilization gradually dwindled, to finally suffer its deathblow under Turkish misrule.

With the passing of the centuries the face of the land changed. The reservoirs and other water controls were permitted to be destroyed, the rock terraces to deteriorate, and the soil to wash away by seasonal rains. Sand-blown deserts replaced a notable civilization. Only here and there vestiges of destroyed cities, remnants of ruined reservoirs, and fragments of sculptured stone remained to tell the tale of the glorious past.

With the beginning of this century the once fertile parts of the country were largely made up of fields of sand and crumbling ruins over which lizards glided by day and jackals crept with the coming of twilight, while hoot owls broke in upon the deathlike stillness of the night. A few scattered Bedouin tribes encamped here and there in their black, sackcloth-of-hair tents, grazed their sheep, goats, horses, and camels wherever they could find water

186

A typical Jewish kibbutz (colony) in the Negeb

and sufficient herbage, and clung to their ancestral modes of life.[2]

In 1942, a committee of experts from the Land and Afforestation Department of the Jewish National Fund explored the Negeb and carried out tests to ascertain its water resources, weather, soil, and flora. Of the 2,375,000 acres comprising the area, they advised that 400,000 acres were suitable for cultivation and another 400,000 suitable for reforestation. In 1943, therefore, the Jews established three experimental settlements south of Beersheba—at Revivim, Gevulot, and Beit Eshel. These served as the "agricultural bridgeheads" of the Negeb. One night in October of 1946, after the Yom Kippur fast, convoys of secretly loaded trucks went rumbling into the Negeb, and by daylight next morning 1,000 veteran settlers had set up 11 new settlements, each complete with prefabricated wooden huts, including stockades and watchtowers. Ever afterwards the activities of that night were known as "Operation Negev."

By 1948, there were 26 settlements in the Negeb. Then with the coming of statehood, and the large influx of immigrants looking for living space, the Israeli authorities were obliged to further open the way for large-scale settlement in this great southland. Planning for the Negeb was no longer on the piecemeal order but as a part of a concerted, all-embracing effort to bring as much of the area as possible back to fertility and usefulness. Almost every week a new settlement sprang up.

By 1959, these efforts to reclaim the Negeb were further aided by Prof. Michael Even-Ari, professor of botany at the Hebrew University. He and a team of Israeli botanists and agrarian experts took the lead in endeavoring to follow the farming patterns of the ancient Nabateans in constructing fields; building systems of dams, cisterns, and canals; growing the same crops by the same methods. They were thus using the same water conservation and irrigation techniques used in past ages, all of which proved practical, indeed.

188   Furthermore, in their conquest of the Negeb, the Jews laid a 108-inch pipeline which brought water from the northwest shore of the Sea of Galilee across Lower Galilee, and along the Plain of

Sharon to the Negeb—160 miles—to aid them in the irrigation of the land. A second water pipeline was laid from the headwaters of the Zerkon River at Antipatris.

Armies and crews of khaki-clad young men and women, along with others who were not so young, then moved into the Negeb. Working under the instruction of these experts, they made surveys, operated bulldozers, built houses, bored wells, dug ditches, laid pipelines, constructed huge stone catchments, planted trees, put in forage crops, arranged gardens, planted grain, and cultivated the rolling plains. Within two years, over 1 million tamerisk, eucalyptus, and other trees were planted in the forest areas, and tree shelter belts (or windbreaks) were planted in crisscrossing rows for a total length of about 500 miles.

A strange romance grew up about converting desert lands into homes—one of the world's most exciting battles between man and nature. Soon there were nearly 50 towns and settlements in the Negeb, and the work of creating new settlements, arranging new farms for new families, building schools for Bedouins and Jews, locating chemicals, and restoring the wastes of the great southland went forward with a pioneering zeal that was without parallel in modern history. The 18 tribes and subtribes of Bedouin Arabs—numbering in all some 15,000—were, as far as is possible, given title to certain areas of the land and gradually came to lead more settled lives.

The story of the founding of each of the colonies and the growth of some into fair-sized cities is absorbing and sometimes heartrending. We briefly recount the fortunes of four of the places: *Beersheba, Dimona, Sede Boker,* and *Avdat.*

Beersheba, the true capital of the Negeb, and the famous center of patriarchal life, signifies "the Well of the Oath," for here Abraham dug a well and gave seven ewe lambs to Abimelech in token of an oath of covenant between them. He then "called the place Beersheba," planted a grove, and "called on the name of the Lord, the everlasting God." Here Abraham received the strange yet deeply meaningful command to sacrifice his son Isaac, and from here journeyed to the land of Moriah in unquestioned faith and obedience to the divine direction.

(Above) A view of a portion of the Bedouin market at Beersheba. (Below) The author bargains with a Bedouin in the Beersheba market for a string of miniature camels.

Here Isaac built an altar and "called upon the name of the Lord," and his servants digged a well. To Beersheba Rebecca came as a bride, and here their children were born. Here Esau forfeited his birthright, and Jacob obtained by fraud the coveted blessing (Gen. 25:34). And Jacob "went out from Beersheba, and went toward Haran."

To the Beersheba sanctuary Jacob came once more, when an old man, on his way to Egypt, and here God spoke to him in a vision of the night and dispelled all his fears, promising to bring him up again to the land after that his son Joseph "should have put his hand upon his eyes" (Gen. 46:1-4).

A strange sacredness pervades the atmosphere about these ancient ruins and about the ancient wells which are yet in use. Tradition says two of them are the very wells which the patriarchs and their servants dug. In this case tradition could very well be right. These wells are circular, and the larger one is 12½ feet in diameter and about 45 feet deep. The old stone curb, deeply grooved by the ropes of many centuries, has now been replaced by a newer well-mouth somewhat higher up. Yet, until recent years, many herds of camels, cattle, and sheep drank here daily from stone and cement troughs.

Present Beersheba gradually grew up two miles west of the wells but had a population of only 2,000 when General Allenby's forces captured it in the summer of 1917 and left a neat military cemetery at the edge of the town. The place had small growth, however, until the Jews took over in 1948. It then became the true capital of the Negeb, as it mushroomed into a frontier city of 85,000.

It is amazing to see modern Beersheba, with its attractive residences; its modern hotels; its schools, hospitals, shops, museums, industrial areas; its many blocks of apartment buildings; and its university of 550 students. Perhaps most colorful of all is its Thursday morning Bedouin Market, when the tribes of the nearby areas come to sell their camel colts, lambs, goats, young donkeys, chickens, turkeys, copper and silver ware, fine needle work; and to buy cloth, flour, rice, coffee, sugar, and other basic needs. Their clothing, their manners and customs, 191 and their unhurried bargaining in buying and selling make your dreams suddenly have relation to reality. Bible characters take on flesh and blood and live before your very eyes—especially when you see camels, goats, and sheep being watered from ancient wells, women wearing long black veils, men dressed in sweeping robes, and white kaffiyehs—much as they did in Abraham's day.

Dimona, a colony 20 miles southeast of Beersheba, was started in 1955, when a small group of immigrants pitched their tents, laid out a townsite, began to build simple wooden homes, and went forward with the construction of water, sewer, and electric light systems.

In time a textile plant and an atomic reactor were built. Then other immigrants came and sturdy stone houses became the vogue. Fortune further favored the Dimona settlers when the phosphate mines opened at Oron, a few miles south, in the Big Crater. Many substantial dormitories arose to serve the commuting workers, until today the population of Dimona stands at around 24,000 and bids fair to increase.

Sede Boker (Field of the Rancher), 30 miles south of Beersheba, was established in 1952 by a group of 16 young men and 3 young women whose aim was to raise sheep and cattle. From the very first year they prospered, yet suffered a tragedy when one of the girls was murdered by Arab marauders.

In 1954, Prime Minister David Ben-Gurion brought great encouragement to the colony when he went into temporary retirement and with his wife, Paula, not only built their permanent home here, but sponsored the construction of the Sede Boker Institute of Negev Studies—a sort of University of the Desert. Its complex of buildings houses a regional high school, a teachers' training college, and an institute for special seminars on desert farming, architecture, and general living. During its 25 years the colony has inaugurated a splendid water system and successfully developed fields, gardens, orchards, and pastures to meet their needs. During the summer season they operate a roadside stall where fresh grapes, plums, apples, and peaches, neatly packed in plastic bags, are sold to grateful travelers.

Avdat, or Abde, eight miles south of Sede Boker, offers a

An aerial view of the excavated ruins of the ancient Nabatean city of Avdat in the Negeb.

flavor of the ancient. Perched high on a flattened hilltop are the restored ruins of a small, acropolislike city with its graceful Corinthian columns rising in the clear desert air, and its houses tumbling down the sides. The place was founded by the Nabateans in the third century B.C., and for 1,000 years continued with varying fortunes under the Nabateans, the Romans, and the Byzantines.

193

It fell to the Arabs without resistance during their conquest of the Negeb in A.D. 634, and gradually declined until the 10th century, when it was abandoned for another 1,000 years. The network of ruined dams, cisterns, and hillside channels attest the engineering abilities of the Nabateans 2,000 years ago, and serve as models for modern engineering. Extensive excavation and large-scale restorations began in 1959, under Professor Even-Ari of the Hebrew University, and are now completed. The ancient dam has been rebuilt, the run-off water system revived, a roadside cafe brought into service, and a small museum that displays statuettes, pottery, and inscriptions of the people who lived there during those long yesteryears.

CHAPTER **17**

Sinai, Land of Revelation

The Peninsula of Mount Sinai," says Dean Stanley, "is, geographically and geologically, one of the most remarkable districts on the face of the earth. It combines the three grand features of earthly scenery—the sea, the desert, and the mountains. It occupies also a position central to three countries, distinguished for their history and geography among all other nations of the world—Egypt, Arabia, and Palestine. It has been the scene of a history as unique as its situation; by which the fate of the three nations which surround

195

it have been decided and through them the fate of the whole world."[1]

In form, the Sinai Peninsula is somewhat like a great inverted land triangle, which lies between the two arms of the Red Sea known as the Gulf of Suez and the Gulf of Aqaba, and between the Suez Canal and the Negeb. Its irregular baseline along the north is some 150 miles, and it measures about 240 miles to its southern point. When seen from high in the air, or as a three-dimensional map, it has the appearance of a huge stony heart—a 20,000-square-mile mass of sand, sandstone, limestone, and granite mountains broken up into very irregular and fantastic forms.

At its baseline, along the Mediterranean coastal belt, it is barren and sandy with long stretches of 200-feet-high sand dunes, interspersed here and there with salt marshes and well-watered oases with their picturesque groves of date palms. Here passes one of the most ancient roadways in the world: the "Way of the Sea," which for millenniums has served as a link between the two great empires of Egypt in Africa and Assyria-Babylonia in Asia. In olden times it was known locally as "The Way of the Land of the Philistines" (Exod. 13:17), and Moses was told not to bring the children of Israel by that route when they left Egypt because of the warlike tribes they would meet around the Gaza district.

Through the ages, caravans of merchants have crossed this way in time of peace, and colorful armies in time of war—the Pharaohs, Alexander, Napoleon. The British Expeditionary Forces improved the roadway and brought a railway and a water line through here in 1917 on their way to Gaza. Some felt the prophecy of Isaiah was beginning to be realized: "In that day there shall be a highway out of Egypt to Assyria" (Isa. 19:23).

At the center of the peninsula is the great *Plateau of the Tih,* which rises to a height of 4,000 feet above the sea and consists of a vast plain, broken in places with mountain ranges, and drained toward the north in slightly depressed stream beds, or "seils." These converge on the so-called "River of Egypt," or Wadi El Arish. Over this arid tableland runs a roadway from Elath to Suez. On this road is Nakhl, a famous watering place for caravans of all kinds. To the west of Nakhl is Mitla Pass which has figured prominently in recent Arab-Israeli wars.[2]

In the south central portion of the peninsula is a striking group of peaks—Mount Serbal, Mount Katherine, Mount Shomer, and Mount Sinai, of which 7,363-foot Mount Sinai (known through the centuries by the natives as *Jebel Musa*, or Mount Moses) holds chief attraction. On its surface here, the whole face of nature is wild and rugged and naked—appearing like the "Alps unclothed." Yet the very nakedness of the peaks imparts to the scene a grandeur, a solitude, and a beauty peculiarly its own.

Straight from the miraculous crossing of the Red Sea at Suez, past the copper and turquoise mining center at Serabit el Khadim, came Moses leading the vast concourse of Israelites along with the "mixed multitude," and encamped them before Mount Sinai on a long, broad plain since known as "the Plain of the Tribes." Having a previously arranged appointment for an encounter with God, Moses went up where "the glory of the Lord covered the top of the mountain like devouring fire." On the third day there were thunders and lightnings, and a thick cloud upon the mountain. A trumpet sounded long, and waxed louder and louder.

> And God spake all these words, saying,
> I am the Lord thy God . . . Thou shalt have no other gods before me.
> Thou shalt not make unto thee any graven image, or any likeness of any thing . . .
> Thou shalt not take the name of the Lord thy God in vain . . .
> Remember the sabbath day, to keep it holy. . . .
> Honor thy father and thy mother . . .
> Thou shalt not kill.
> Thou shalt not commit adultery.
> Thou shalt not steal.
> Thou shalt not bear false witness . . .
> Thou shalt not covet (*Exod. 20:1-4, 7-8, 12-17*).

197

And "he gave unto Moses, when he had made an end of communing with him on Mount Sinai, two tablets of testimony, tablets of stone, written with the finger of God . . . the words of the covenant, the ten commandments" (Exod. 31:18; 34:28).

How simple, yet how profound! What depth of wisdom—the Creator and Governor of the moral universe giving to man righteous laws. These were to be his guidelines to help him discern the structure of the moral universe, to keep him in the good way, and to guard him from the consequences of evil. No wonder these laws of Sinai have become the "cornerstone of all morality," the basis for the laws of all good governments, the very pillars of respectable society.

The Monastery of St. Katharine at the foot of Mount Sinai where the famous Codex Sinaiticus was found in 1844.

It was here at Sinai that the people brought in their gifts, and the craftsmen constructed the Tabernacle exactly as God had laid down the plans. Here, too, many centuries later, God spoke to Elijah with a "still small voice" that was stronger than wind, earthquake, or fire (see 1 Kings 19:4-18). In a vale, at the foot of Mount Sinai, is the *St. Catherine Monastery,* a Greek Orthodox institution, built here in the desert solitudes by Emperor Justinian in A.D. 527. Its massive walls and square, squat design give it the appearance of a fort, yet when within, one readily gains the impression of a treasure house of decorative art and of gruesome antiquity. Its banner-hung church, its many cells, its 50 guest rooms, its library of precious manuscripts, its crude cymbals which call to prayer, and its charnel house where the bones of those who have served here before are laid out in rows—from skulls to skeletal feet. In one instance the skeleton of an abbot, in full clerical dress, watches over his lifeless flock. Over the monastery the standard of the Lamb and the Cross is on its highest towers, and with the proper credentials one will find a whole-hearted welcome here, along with frugal fare.

Kadesh-barnea, the place next in importance to Mount Sinai, was for the children of Israel "eleven days' journey" northward, on the northeast border of the peninsula. And so it is today, for just 50 miles southwest of Beersheba, in a lush little valley, near a branch of the River of Egypt, is "the powerful spring" of *Ain el Qudeirat* which flows all year; and the oasis which it creates tends to remind one of how, in a small way, the Garden of Eden must have looked. Within this area are two more splendid springs: *Ain Qudeis* and *Ain Qoseimeh.*

Ain el Qudeirat is the strongest of the springs, and is generally regarded as the original Kadesh-barnea. The other springs, with their oases, are nearby—*Ain Qudeis* five miles to the southeast, and *Ain Qoseimeh* some two miles to the west. The Israelites would have made use of the whole group of springs with their oases and extensive pasturelands, for it would have required much water and land to sustain so great a throng of people. The topographical requirements of the biblical narrative are well suited to this area.

Many men have searched for Kadesh-barnea—John Rowland, H. C. Trumbull, C. Leonard Woolley, T. E. Lawrence, Jonathan Cape, Nelson Glueck, Y. Aharoni, and others—and all have concluded that here in this area is to be found the historic spot where the Israelites encamped during much of their sojourn in the wilderness. It was from here that Moses sent the 12 men to spy out the land; here Miriam, Moses' sister, died and was buried; and from here Moses sent a delegation in vain to the king of Edom, asking permission to pass through the territory of Edom on their way to Canaan.

199

Many armies, expeditions, and caravans have crossed and re-crossed Sinai, yet the people who live in these parts seem to remember but the one. Their mountains, valleys, springs, and places of encampment are named after Moses, Aaron, and Jethro, and you will not talk to them long until they will speak very reverently, respectfully, and enthusiastically of the children of Israel as though just last year they had passed through.

Sinai "is no ordinary land of broken plains and naked ranges, and scanty water" and copper, and silver, and turquoise, and oil. "God walked abroad in it and divine purpose was made manifest there of old. It has always been . . . a sanctuary of revelation and reformation, with the spirit of the Holy pervading the very atmosphere."[3]

*

The Jordan Rift Valley

*

18

The Beka'a,
or Valley of Lebanon

Lying between the Lebanon and Anti-Lebanon mountain ranges is the broad rift valley which is known in the Bible as "the valley of Mizpeh," or simply as "the valley of Lebanon" (Josh. 11:8, 17). Ancient writers knew it as "the Entrance of Hamath" or as the Coele-Syria (Hollow Syria), while in modern times it is usually known as the Beka'a (the valley).

The valley is 205 miles long, from 3 to 10 miles wide, and is drained by two well-known rivers—the Litany and the Orontes. The *Litani* rises just north of Baalbek and flows southward to a

A vineyard in the Valley of Lebanon, with the Lebanon mountains rising behind.

point just west of the headwaters of the Jordan, where it turns sharply to the west and passes through the Lebanons by a narrow gorge, and finally discharges its waters into the Mediterranean five miles north of Tyre. The *Orontes* river rises just north of the sources of the Litany, and flows due north through the great plain within and beyond the Lebanons, for a distance of about 130 miles; then, like the Litany, it turns sharply to the west and pours its flood of waters into the sea.

This beautiful and exceedingly fertile valley lies at an average of 3,000 feet above sea level and at one point attains an elevation of about 4,000 feet. In the winter it is sometimes covered with snow, but in the springtime its great fields of plowed earth, of flowers, and of ripening grain coupled with its lush orchards present a pattern of rich reds, browns, greens, and yellows which, in the south, spreads out for more than 70 miles between the two mountain ranges.

On entering the valley, one may think of it as a secluded mountain retreat, but such is far from the case. For, from time immemorial, there has run through it the far-famed highway which links Mesopotamia with Egypt. Over this route and

203

through this valley have passed numberless caravans, many military expeditions, and multitudes who have gone on state errands and missionary enterprises. Abraham passed this way as he "came into Canaan"; Eliezer went to Mesopotamia and returned through the valley when on his mission to obtain a wife for Isaac. Jacob passed along this way in going to Padan Aram where he married beautiful Rachel, and returned by the selfsame road some 21 years later.

The cities of this valley which played a large part in the sacred and secular history of the ancient world were Hamath, Riblah, and Baalbek. Imposing mounds stand today to attest the importance of the first two of these cities, and the impressive ruins of Baalbek bring forth the admiration of all who see them.

Hamath was on the Orontes River, near the northern entrance into the Land of Promise—thus "the entrance of Hamath" (Num. 34:8). Its king sent presents to David when he defeated the king of Zobah (2 Sam. 8:6), and it was frequently mentioned in the Bible as Israel's ideal northern border. Dan, however, was actually the north limit most of the time. It was only at brief intervals, under David, Solomon, and Jeroboam that the country about Hamath was subject to Israel.

Riblah, now called Ribleh, is located on the Orontes, 35 miles north of Baalbek, where the old caravan route from the coast intersects the main highway, then passes on eastward to Palmyra (Tadmore). Being so strategically located from a military point of view, and being so near the vast forests of the cedars of Lebanon which were essential for building machines of war, the military leaders of Babylonia and Egypt used Riblah as a camping ground, a base of supplies, or center of operations while carrying on war in Syria and Palestine.

While encamped here with his army, just previous to the battle of Carchemish, Pharaoh-Necho deposed Jehoahaz of Judah and put him "in bonds" (606 B.C.). After Necho's withering defeat at Carchemish, he took the Judean king back to Egypt where he died (2 Kings 23:32-34). When the Babylonian army made a breakthrough in the siege of Jerusalem in 586 B.C., King Zedekiah and all his men of war fled out of the city by night.

204

But the Chaldeans' [Babylonian] army pursued after them, and overtook Zedekiah in the plain of Jericho: and when they had taken him, they brought him up to Nebuchadnezzar king of Babylon to Riblah in the land of Hamath, where he gave judgment upon him. Then the king of Babylon slew the sons of Zedekiah in Riblah before his eyes: also the king of Babylon slew all the nobles of Judah. Moreover he put out Zedekiah's eyes, and bound him with chains, to carry him to Babylon (Jer. 39:5-7).

Baalbek, the "City of the Sun," is situated at an altitude nearly 4,000 feet above sea level, and is the most ideal spot in the entire valley, or as it is generally regarded, one of the grand spots of the world. Here the climate is ideal, the soil excellent; and clear, cool, spring water breaks forth at various places in or near the city. During much of the year the trees put forth their shade and fruit, flowers bloom, and a variety of birds sing their sweetest lays. Thus, from time immemorial Baalbek, with its natural advantages, has been a miniature earthly paradise to which people from far and near have resorted.

The tradition persists that Baalbek was one of King Solomon's summer resorts, that it was the "Baalath" which he built as a center of commerce on the caravan route to Mesopotamia, and that here he built the magnificent "house of the forest of Lebanon" (1 Kings 7:2-5). It could well have been, for in Solomon's day it was a place of beauty, and a place that for natural advantages outranked all other places in this section of the country.

However, the present magnificent ruins of the temple of Jupiter and the temple of Bacchus, as we now know them, were begun by the Roman Emperor Antoninus Pius (A.D. 138-61) and continued by Septimus Severus and other rulers down to Caracalla (A.D. 211-17). As a center of sun worship, Baalbek acquired renown as the seat of an oracle and was visited by leading rulers and prominent people from far and near. Under Constantine the temples became Christian churches, but when captured by the Arabs in the seventh century, they were turned into fortresses and served as such during the Middle Ages. In 1664 and again in 1795, these buildings were shaken by violent earthquakes, from which they never recovered.

This 1,500-ton building stone, 70 feet long and 14 by 13 feet on the end, apparently never reached its destination in the building of the city of Baalbek.

Some of the enormous blocks of stone used in the construction of the Temple of the Sun (Jupiter) measured 60 feet long by 12 thick, and its 54 columns, of which 6 are still standing, were 72 feet high and 22 feet in circumference. In a quarry, just a half mile south of the Acropolis of Baalbek, lies a block of stone said to be the largest in the world. It is 70 feet long, 14 feet high, and 13 feet wide. Its weight is estimated to be about 1,500 tons. However, at one end it is not entirely loose from the quarry.

A great chain of inland cities—Antioch, Aleppo, Homs, Hama, and Baalbek—occupy the valley today, and enjoy a prosperous civilization which is all but unique.

CHAPTER **19**

The Rise of the Jordan

The Jordan, most famous of all rivers, finds its origin in the vast reservoir of snow and ice which perpetually covers the summit of Mount Hermon. This melts and sinks down through secret caverns to form subterranean springs which come to the surface in the lower foothills of the mountain. These abound all about Hermon, but at four places on its west and south, springs converge and break forth in the form of powerful fountains, each a river almost full grown from the beginning of its course. The four are found at Hasbani,

Dan, Banias, and Nahr Bareighit. These constitute the main sources of the Jordan River.

1. **The Springs of Hasbani** are the first, the highest, and the most remote source of the Jordan. They are located in the western foothills of Mount Hermon, 1,700 feet above sea level, and a half mile northwest of the village of Hasbani. Coddled here in the hills and watched over by great Hermon, where olive and oleander thrive and wild flowers bloom in profusion, there are some 20 crystal clear fountains which, with a low, gurgling sound, flow upward, in artesian style, from a small islandlike area next to a steep and rugged, yet beautiful, limestone cliff. The water from these fountains flows in all directions immediately after boiling up from the earth, but they soon settle into a beautiful pool. From there they gracefully flow over a moss-grown dam of strongly stratified rock some 30 feet wide and 5 feet thick, and start southward on their 115-mile trip to the Dead Sea.

At first the stream takes the name of Hasbani, as if it were too small to be called the Jordan. In winter and spring, however, the

208

The Springs of Hasbani, the first and most remote source of the Jordan River.

stream is rather strong and sometimes boisterous as it meanders through a picturesque country, passing villages, turning mills, and is finally joined by other tributaries.

2. At the city mound of ancient *Dan* is the **Fountain of the Leddan,** which is the second and *largest* source of the Jordan River. This place was first known as *Laish,* where lived a small colony of people from Sidon. Their manner of life was quiet and carefree, and they felt secure in this place where "there was no want of any thing that is in the earth" (Judg. 18:7, 10). But all this was changed when the tribe of Danites charged them on a dark night, scaled the walls, set the city on fire, and destroyed the inhabitants (Judg. 18:27). The city was then rebuilt and called Dan after the father of the conquering tribe. Ever after it marked the northern boundary of Palestine, which gave rise to the proverbial expression "From Dan to Beersheba." Here King Jeroboam built a temple and set up in its shrine one of his golden calves as an idol-god to be worshipped by the Israelites who lived in the northern portions of his kingdom. The place is now known as *Tell el-Kadi,* the "Mound of the Judge." Jacob, when in prophetic mood on his deathbed, said, "Dan shall judge his people"; and to the Arab, the place where Dan dwelt will ever be the "Mound of the Judge."

The city mound is now without inhabitants but is a most interesting site. It rises from 30 to 80 feet above the plain and is nearly 1,000 feet long and over 700 feet wide. In places the uneven summit has many trees such as acacias, oaks, poplars, wild figs, and wild olives. At the southwest corner of the mound a pair of exceedingly large trees, one an oak, the other a terebinth, mark the traditional site of the sacred area, where may have stood the golden calf. One of the trees measures 19 and the other 21 feet in circumference. These shade the tomb of an unknown Mohammedan saint and are hung with small strips of cloth—each rag representing the prayers of a pilgrim who has journeyed and prayed there.

Dense jungles of bush and briars, as well as ruins of bygone civilizations, cover portions of the mound. A few small garden patches grow where water can be had from a small spring which flows from the jungle of reeds and bushes well up on the mound. Underneath the surface of the mound many objects of antiquity lie hidden, awaiting the spade of the archaeologist.

The main Fountain of the Leddan rises under the western shoulder of the city mound. Fresh from the deep caverns of towering Mount Hermon, these waters come bubbling and whirling out from under a screen of wild figs and vines, forming a pool of pale, clear blue, 100 feet in diameter. Out of this bubbling basin the newborn river rushes, foaming down the hillside through lines of oleanders, flowering bushes, and overhanging willows toward the plain. This is the largest of all the fountains of Palestine and is considered to be the largest in the world. It is 500 feet above sea level and its immense volume of water entitles it to be regarded as the *chief source of the Jordan.*

3. The third and most impressive source of the Jordan is the **Springs of Banias,** at the village of Banias, three miles southeast of Dan. Here, directly under the southern base of Mount Hermon, 1,000 feet above sea level, is a 100-foot cliff of ruddy limestone with niches and shrines and inscriptions carved on its face. At the bottom of this rock cliff is a dark cave whose mouth is partly filled with loose stones; and over these stones a foaming "full-born river" flows out and glides southward through a luxuriant, cavelike depression where a pastoral paradise is formed of towering oaks, trembling poplars, splendid sycamore, gray green olives, wild figs, trailing vines, drooping maidenhair fern, and myriads of wild flowers.

It is little wonder that through the centuries people, creeds, nations, and religions have longed to have a village, a shrine, or a city here at Banias, for it is one of the world's outstanding beauty spots. It has about it a strange mystery that has always cast its spell over the imaginations of men. Here the Phoenicians established the idolatrous worship of Baal and revelled in their splendid possessions until Joshua drove them out. The Canaanites dedicated the place to Baal-gad, to whom they paid their reverence in the presence of the gushing waters. For the Greeks, no finer or more ideal place could be found for the abode of Pan, the flute-playing god of the hills and woodlands, of the shepherds and hunters. Therefore they built a shrine to Pan and called the place Paneas. There the rites of Pan and all the nymphs were celebrated. A Greek inscription carved in the face of the cliff still exists, declaring, "Pan and his nymphs haunt this place."

When Rome conquered the territory, Herod the Great built here on the shelf rock above the cave a beautiful white marble temple in honor of Emperor Augustus Ceasar. Herod's son Philip made the city more beautiful and named it Caesarea Philippi to distinguish it from the coast city of Caesarea. Subsequently it went by various names, but eventually came again to be called Paneas. Arab inability to pronounce the letter *p* caused them to call it Banias.

It was here at Caesarea Philippi in this "paradise of nature" that Jesus withdrew with His disciples for quiet rest, and asked of them, "Whom do you say that I am?" And here, where so many had vainly worshiped Baal, Pan, and Baal-gad, the stalwart Simon Peter made the great declaration, "Thou art the Christ, the Son of the living God" (Matt. 16:13-16).

On a lofty mountain spur, 1,500 feet above the springs and village of Banias, stands the great and mighty castle known as "The Castle of Subeibeh." It was originally built either by the Phoenicians or the Romans, and rebuilt in turn by the Crusaders, the Arabs, and the Turks. Deep valleys defend this fine, old, ruined castle on its north and south; while on its west, at the end of the spur, is a deep, rock-cut ditch or moat, which makes it inaccessible. Only from the east can it be approached, and then one is obliged to pass along a narrow and difficult path and over a bridge entirely open to the view of the defending garrison.

The castle is surrounded by walls 10 feet thick and in some places nearly 100 feet high, with numerous round towers, built with identical blocks of stone two feet square. The interior of the fortress is an uneven area of four or five acres, dotted here and there by houses, cisterns, huge walls, and wide courtyards. At the eastern side of the castle area and 150 feet above it stands the citadel with a great wall and moat of its own, so that, as Josephus said, the garrison could retire into the citadel and make a protracted defense even after the main castle had been taken by an enemy.

Within the castle are numerous subterranean rooms, vaults, and passageways. At the western end is a stairway cut in the rock, descending at an angle of 45 or 50 degrees. Popular belief regards this stairway as extending down to the fountain of Banias, but it may only lead to subterranean reservoirs for water. This great old castle commanded the highway leading from the Jordan Valley to the Plain of Damascus. It was so strongly built, so strategically located, and so well defended that it has been rightly called "the Gibraltar of Palestine."[1]

The waters of Banias, after passing through the parklike verdure about the village of Banias, soon veer southwest and hurry on to meet and converge with the river Leddan some six miles from Dan. Then, as one, the waters of Dan and Banias move on to meet and merge with waters from Hasbani.

4. *Nahr Bareighit,* the fourth and westernmost source of the Jordan, is the small mountain stream which rises as a strong spring in the "Meadow of Ijon"—the Ijon of the Scriptures, and the most northern possession of the tribe of Naphtali (1 Kings 15:20). Through the middle of this beautiful valley, five miles long and two miles wide, this gentle stream meanders. As it approaches the southern end (not far from the Jewish colony of Metullah), it deepens its bed and passes through the ridge by a remarkably deep and narrow chasm and, in the form of waterfalls, pitches over the precipice and moves along to join the river Hasbani about three-quarters of a mile above the point where the Hasbani joins the junction of the Leddan and Banias streams. The confluence of these four perennial streams form the Jordan, which travels sluggishly through what was once dense papyrus growths and enters the now greatly reduced Lake Huleh.

CHAPTER **20**

The Grand Huleh Basin

The Grand Huleh Basin is located between the southern foothills of Mount Hermon and the Bridge of Jacob's Daughters. It is 5 miles wide and some 15 to 20 miles long from north to south. From time immemorial it has been known for its broad, fertile, grazing plains in the north; its amazing variety of its plant life and all but impenetrable papyrus marshes in the south central; and its small but unusual lake, known as the Waters of Merom, or Lake Huleh, in the south. It is the first and highest of the three lakes in the Jordan Rift Valley. Into this lake pours the waters of the Jordan, which later run into the Sea of Galilee, and later still into the Dead Sea about 1,300 feet below sea level.

It was here, by the Waters of Merom, that Jabin, king of Hazor, and the combined military forces of the north "came and pitched together to fight against Israel." The Lord said unto Joshua, "Be not afraid because of them: for to morrow about this time will I deliver them up all slain before Israel," and so it happened. "Joshua turned back and took Hazor: for Hazor was the head of all those kingdoms" (Josh. 11:5-11).

The soil of the upper plain of this basin is deep, loose, and in places sandy, and is well watered. In ancient times the city of Dan stood on a low hill near the head of the plain. But for long centuries the area has been sparsely occupied by seminomadic tribes whose chief occupation was the raising of cattle, principally water buffalo. These large, black creatures could well be the "behemoths" of the Bible. In large herds they graze this plain during the early morning hours, and during the heat of the day lie in the water "among the willows of the brook" with their mouths "all turned upstream" on a level with the surface, as if, like Job's behemoth, "he trusteth that he can draw up Jordan into his mouth" (Job 40:15-23).

The Marshland is the center area of some 10 to 15,000 acres of wet sediment land immediately north of Lake Huleh, which has been built up as century after century the Jordan has crept sluggishly into the lake. The dense masses of growth here are cane, bush, water lily, and the papryus plant (of which paper was first made). These have formed an almost impenetrable jungle where crows form rookeries, rear their young, and from which they come and go in droves that number in the hundreds and even thousands. In these jungles wild boars, panthers, wolves, jackals, foxes, and many other animals and birds, great and small, hide away at certain seasons of the year and make the place an ideal rendezvous for hunters. Here, during his earlier years, came Herod the Great to hunt the game swarming in the papyrus thickets, and to distinguish himself with his javelin-throwing.

Lake Huleh, known in the Bible as the "Waters of Merom," lies 12 miles south of Dan, and is seven feet above sea level. Originally it was about 3 miles wide and 4 miles long—little more than an enlargement of the Jordan which flows into it on the north

A Jewish shepherd boy in the lush Huleh Basin

and out of it on the south. The lake has long been blessed with an abundance of fish of many kinds, and was an ideal refuge for waterfowl. Some of the birds were permanent residents, while tens of thousands of others were migrants on their way between northern Europe and tropical Africa. Therefore, in the spring and late autumn the lower end of the lake was almost completely covered with ducks, geese, cranes, brants, bitterns, storks, pelicans, and other forms of bird life. Dragonflies hummed over the lake, and kingfishers swooped down for fish. The lake was of little use to man but offered seclusion for wildlife.

When Israel became a state in 1948, one of her first thoughts was to reclaim the Huleh Basin. The Jewish National Fund purchased the land, and in 1950, the work began. During these years a dramatic transformation has been taking place. The channel of the Jordan River below Lake Huleh has been broadened and deepened, and the two large channels passing through the marshland above have been widened, deepened, and so directed as to meet in a V form in the center of what was Lake Huleh. Drainage canals have been dug to drain the waters from the swamps into the new river channels. The size of the lake itself has been reduced, so that it is now little more than a fish pond, through it is still a bird refuge. Some 18,000 to 20,000 acres of the marshland and lake area have been drained sufficiently dry to be leveled, plowed, and cultivated. In the very area where until not long ago the malaria-carrying mosquito, the black buffalo, and the wild boar reigned supreme, scores of new settlements have now been established. The rich, black soil is said to be capable of producing food for 100,000 people. Malaria, the curse of marshlands, has almost altogether disappeared since the importation of topminnows—native American fish that live chiefly on mosquito eggs.

The principal crops which are proving suitable to this area are cotton, sugarcane, wheat, sorghum, ground nuts, tulip bulbs, feed crops, and mixed vegetables. Sugarcane thrives in many parts of Israel, but the cost of water has limited its planting. Here in this water-surplus area its production promises to be a genuine boon to the country. Vegetables grown here ripen early and are among the finest. Tulip bulbs mature in one season, rather than in two or three, and the Dutch pay well for the service. Rice does well here, and some is grown, although the government discourages its cultivation because it is conducive to mosquito breeding. Carp ponds abound in the region. Also in a section of Huleh's marshland, there are 3,750 acres of peat land —one of the richest peat deposits in the world. As this is exploited, it will be used to enrich worn-out soils in other parts of the country.

The climate in the Huleh Valley is fairly mild with an average annual temperature of 68° F. The direction of the winds in the summer are generally from perpetually snow-covered Mount Hermon in the north. During the rest of the year the directions vary. There are an average of 100 cloudy days during the year, of which about half are rainy days. During the rest of the year the skies are "a canopy of clear blue."

Reclaiming the Huleh area from decay and disease and making it bountiful for Jew and Arab has been styled "the crowning achievement" of the Jewish National Fund. Now the area is being called "The Huleh Plain," in Upper Galilee.

About two miles below the lake site, the river is crossed by an ancient bridge, built of black basalt, which the Arabs call *Jisr-Benat-Yacob* (Bridge of the Daughters of Jacob). The name often puzzles travelers and archaeologists, but probably derives from an early but mistaken tradition that Jacob and his family crossed the Jordan here on his return from Padan Aram. However, the crossing is of ancient origin, for at the eastern end of the bridge is a ruined khan, and the remains of an old road paved with basaltic blocks, which goes on toward Damascus. In all probability Saul of Tarsus crossed the Jordan here as he journeyed to Damascus and his rendezvous with the Lord.

Down a narrow depression, fringed with willow and oleander, the Jordan descends at the rate of 90 feet per mile for 9 miles, through wild and beautiful scenery until it reaches the Sea of Galilee, where it is hushed to rest for a time in the bosom of this quiet and beautiful sea.

CHAPTER 21

The Beautiful Sea of Galilee

The Sea of Galilee lies 682 feet below sea level, in the upper portion of the great Jordan Rift Valley. It is shaped somewhat like a pear and is 13 miles long and 6½ miles wide. Its water is clear and sweet, and varies in depth from 60 to 156 feet. Through it runs the Jordan River— entering in at the northeast corner and flowing out at the south- 218 western end. Around most of the 50-mile shoreline of the sea there is a broad, pebbly beach, mingled with a generous sprin- kling of small, conical-shaped shells. For almost 3 miles, from

Magdala northward, the beach is almost entirely made up of these white shells.

About the sea there are hot mineral springs, the strongest and most famous being the three which are located a mile south of Tiberias. Herod the Great, Cleopatra, Herod Antipas, and many other historical characters are said to have taken health baths here. Today it is the center of a much patronized health resort. Close by is the white-domed tomb of Rabbi Meir.

The waters of this sea are a deep blue, its atmosphere is invigorating, and the whole environment speaks peace—except for an occasional storm that sweeps down through the great gorge, lashing the surface of the lake into white-capped waves.

About this sea, the myrrh-scented hills rise easily and slope away in such a fashion as to impress the beholder with the elegance of the setting so appropriately provided by nature. The fertile acres of the far-famed, crescentlike plain of Gennesaret favor mankind with a "garden that has no end." Here in the springtime the birds sing their sweetest lays, the flowers bloom in wild profusion, while out over the sea the glistening white sails gracefully hoisted above the sailing vessels carry the fishermen or the travelers to their desired havens. Of all places in the whole world this, more than any other, lends itself to quiet, peaceful rest.

It was about the shell-strewn beaches of this lake that Jesus walked when His voice fell upon the ears and restless souls of many of those disciples who were to make up the apostolic group. For the most part they were simple fishermen who netted the fish of this beautiful sea. That tender voice and those striking words, "Follow me, and I will make you fishers of men," first heard about blue Galilee, challenged their attention, quieted their fears, enchanted their souls, and empowered their lives until they cared only to follow Him with an undying devotion. Some, like Him who called them, were to go to a cross; some, to be dragged to their deaths through the streets; some, to the arena where they would be done to death by wild beasts. But go where they would, experience what they might, His voice, first audible in Galilee, could not be forgotten nor confused with other voices.

"Follow me," I heard Him cry;
I saw the stalwart men;
I read the answer in each eye,
Such as had never been.

It was on the hills and mountains about this sea that Jesus spent nights of prayer, taught the multitudes, and pointed out the most profound lessons known to man. Here He healed the sick, unstopped deaf ears, cast out unclean spirits, raised the dead, and set the captives free. Here 19 of His 32 parables were spoken, and 25 of His 33 recorded miracles were performed. Here He challenged the attention of man as none other has challenged him; unfolded the plan whereby sinful souls might become the children of the Most High; and pointed the way to the celestial gathering place.

These waters He loved and controlled at will. Upon them

220

Looking across the northern end of the Sea of Galilee from the vicinity of Tiberias.

He walked. At His command the wild winds were subdued and boisterous waves became calm. "What manner of man is this that even the wind and the sea obey him?" asked His disciples when they perceived how familiarly He directed these waters.

The sight of this lovely Lake of Galilee, sleeping in its "deep blue beauty" amidst its beautiful plains and ringlet of low-lying mountains, enchants the beholder and produces a devotional fascination that no tongue can tell and no pen can describe. Here the Christian senses the fragrance of the Christ life and becomes more fully absorbed in the spiritualities of the past than at any other place in the world. Away to the north towers Mount Hermon, hoary and high, standing as a silent sentinel guarding the majestic scene—the most sacred and the most famous sea known to men.

The rabbis of old used to say that after God had made the seven seas, He made the Sea of Galilee for His own particular pleasure. In Leslie Savage Clark's inquisitive lines is the same thought, "Of all the seas in the East and West, did God, perhaps, love Galilee the best?"

When Christ was in Galilee, nine cities formed an impressive and almost continuous circuit about the shores of the sea. They were Tiberias, Magdala, Capernaum, Chorazin, Bethsaida, Gergesa, Gamala, Hippos, and Taricheae. And one could stand on some eminent point and at a glance see them all—the entire theater of His Galilean ministry. How indelibly it fixes itself upon the mind of the one who has seen it—the sea, the shore, the hills, and the sites of the cities where He lived and taught and drew from common things His lessons that have changed the thinking of much of mankind, and transformed the lives of millions.

Tiberias is situated on a sloping plain about midway up the west shore. Herod Antipas (the son of Herod the Great) surveyed the walls and began construction of the place as the capital of his Galilean province when Jesus was 21 years of age, and completed it when the Master was 27. Herod named the city in honor of the emperor Tiberius.

221

For more than two miles the city arose along the lake front behind a low, strong seawall. There were temples, palaces, theaters, amphitheaters, baths; a forum, a praetorium, a racecourse, a strong citadel, and many elegant houses. Then to please the Jews, he built a large and beautiful synagogue. They eyed the city narrowly, however, and the stricter Jews chose not to live in it, since portions of the place were built over the site of an ancient cemetery. Besides, many of its luxurious buildings were adorned with costly works of art which they considered "idols." Christ went near the city many times, but we have no record of His ever entering it, unless it was involved in His having preached "in all the cities round about."

Jewish attitude was changed, however, following the revolt led by Bar Kochba and the final destruction of Jerusalem in A.D. 132. Tradition says that Simon ben Yohai, the supposed author of the Zohar, bathed in the hot springs in the southern suburbs of the city and was cured of a sickness which he had acquired while hiding away from the Romans. Out of gratitude he declared Tiberias a fit city for the habitation of the Jews.

In due time the chief rabbis moved to Tiberias, where they produced the Mishnah, reestablished the Sanhedrin, and completed the Palestinian Talmud. They not only made Tiberias a center of language and literature, but one of the four sacred cities of Palestine, the other three being Jerusalem, Hebron, and Safad. In time, several Jewish rabbis and scholars, whose tombs are venerated, were said to have been buried in this vicinity. Among them were Maimonides (1135-1204), the Spanish Jewish rabbi, theologian, philosopher, commentator, and one-time physician to Saladin.

Tiberias is now a modern Jewish city, a "caldron of cultures in which new Western ways and old Oriental ones mix comfortably and colorfully." Its streets are lined with bulging markets, its avenues with gleaming hotels, and its hills with elegant homes. In its midst, as a chief landmark, stands the old Scottish mission, which has been dispensing the gospel and medical care to all classes of people for more than 50 years.

222   *Magdala* and the Plain of Gennesaret. The former home of Mary Magdalene was a seaside village three miles north of Tiberias, at the southern end of the beautiful Plain of Gennesaret.

The name Migdal-el meant "The Tower of God." All who have gone there during the past century have spoken of it as a ruined and unattractive, mud-and-stone village whose rock tower was rent asunder by a deep chasm. Yet romantic indeed must have been its situation in Christ's day, with palms and balsams, fruits and flowers around it, the blue lake in front, the precipitous Wad el Hamam (Valley of Doves) behind, and beside it the fertile Plain of Gennesaret with its extensive fields of fruits, flowers, vegetables, grain, and groves flourishing everywhere. Josephus called it "the ambition of nature where there is not a plant that does not flourish there." Near Magdala a Jewish colony has been built, and the Jews are responsible for restoring to the plain its original gardenlike quality.

At *Tabgha,* northward along the shore there is a grove; three clear, cool streams; some pools; the remains of an ancient mill; and beloved Father Tepper with his tiny hospital and comfortable hospice. Here, in the mosaic floor of a fourth-century Byzantine church, is pictured the story of the miracle of the loaves and fishes—a basket of bread set between two fish (though the actual miracle probably took place near Bethsaida, several miles east). Nearby is depicted peacocks, storks, ducks, and geese, along with gaily colored birds perched on lotus flowers.[1]

Above Tabgha, on the traditional site of the Sermon on the Mount, is a church, a monastery, and the Mount of Beatitudes hospice. The view of the Sea of Galilee from here is one of the best and the biblical scenes as vivid as one could desire.

Capernaum is identified with the ruins of Tell Hum, five miles northeast of Magdala and three miles west of where the Jordan River enters the sea. It was once the commercial metropolis of all northern Palestine, and was the hometown of Simon Peter, James, and John, and of Matthew, the customs official who "rose up and left all" to follow the Man of Galilee. And more wonderful yet, it was the adopted home of Jesus, who "on the Sabbath day entered into the synagogue and taught" (Mark 1:21). The partly restored ruins of a magnificent successor to this original synagogue, built sometime later (presumably during the second century A.D.), can be seen at Capernaum today. The walls

223

were decorated with lovely friezes depicting palms, vines and grapes, acanthus leaves, pomegranates, and garlands. Cut in the marble floor and elsewhere are the traditional symbols such as the seven-branched candlestick, the six-pointed Star of David, and a shofar, or ram's horn. An Aramaic inscription scratched on a limestone pillar reads: "HLPW, the son of Zebidah, the son of Johanan, made this column. May blessing be his." "Those names," says Dr. Glueck, "correspond roughly to the New Testament Alphaeus, Zebedee, and John, mentioned, by an interesting coincidence, in the list of Jesus' disciples and their families" (Mark 3:17-18).[2]

Here, in those days, ran the great highway of nations—the Roman road known as the "Way of the Sea." It ran down from Damascus and across the Lower Galilean hills, dipping down to the lakeside at Capernaum on the way across Armageddon to the maritime plains and Egypt. Here at Capernaum the Romans maintained a military garrison, and the government operated one of the largest and most important custom houses for collecting import duties on vast volumes of incoming merchandise. Matthew sat at customs here and was widely known as a government official.

Along this artery of trade and travel came merchants, diplomats, scholars, and camel-men who passed from Persia and Mesopotamia to the Nile Valley and Africa. Rich crops of grain, nuts, and fruit were grown locally; sheep, goats, and camels were raised; important fishing companies operated boats and nets, and men worked with them about the sea.

A variety of industries such as had to do with metals, leather, dyeing, weaving, and fish processing were carried on here. In the marketplaces buying and bartering were brisk and went on almost continuously. The population of Capernaum was the largest of all cities beside the sea, and for variety was representative of various cross sections of life.

In this weltering mass of mankind—Greek, Jew, and Roman—sat Matthew in the customs house, and here came Christ to speak as man never spoke, and work as no man ever worked. Here on these beaches, and elsewhere about these shores of

Ruins of a second-century synagogue built at Capernaum

Galilee, Christ, the Saviour and the greatest Teacher of all time, spoke to the people many times—at least once from a flat-bottomed boat that was "thrust out a little from the land, lest the multitude should throng him." On an eminent point not far away He gave the Sermon on the Mount, in which He imparted to man the secret of a happy life. Little wonder that this sermon has been called "the greatest thing ever spoken," for in it was divine wisdom transcending everything which had gone before or was to come afterward.

Bethsaida, the "Fisherman's Village," was located some three and a half miles from Capernaum, on the east side of the Jordan, near the point where it enters the Sea of Galilee. Bethsaida was built somewhat like Paneas, having had the same architect. Josephus says: "When Philip . . . had built Paneas . . . at the fountains of Jordan, he named it Caesarea. He also advanced the village Bethsaida, situated at the lake of Gennesaret, unto the dignity of a city, both by the number of inhabitants it contained, and its other grandeur, and called it by the name of Julius, the same name with Caesar's [Augustus] daughter."[3] It was to Bethsaida that Jesus withdrew upon hearing of the beheading of John the Baptist by Herod Antipas. Near Bethsaida is the desert place where Christ fed the 5,000 (Luke 9:10-17).

Today the Sea of Galilee has pleasant shores fairly well lined with the greenery of gardens, fruit orchards, eucalyptus, and palms. There are some good hotels, many Christian hospices, and a score of Jewish colonies adjacent to the sea—some directly on its shores. To the south of the lake is *Degania,* founded in 1909 by Russian pioneers. It is now a well established kibbutz with large trees, massive barns, gardens, orchards, groves of date palm, and well tended fields. Degania B, a more recently founded colony, "exudes a fresh-built flavor" along with colorful gardens, semitropical plants, and towering palm trees.[4]

The colony of *Nof Ginossar,* on the plain of Genessaret, has a 64-room, air-conditioned guest house with a quiet, unhurried atmosphere and a second-floor dining room with a fine view of the Sea of Galilee and the colorful orange and banana groves.[5]

En Gev is a Jewish colony across the sea from Tiberias, on a

226

small peninsula between the Golan Heights and the lakefront. It is a green and pleasant place, with fishing boats, vineyards, groves of bananas and dates, and a seaside cafe where you may purchase a platter of St. Peter's fish with chips and salad and eat either inside the modern, air-conditioned restaurant or outside on the patio on the lakefront. Out there you can throw a piece of bread into the water and see schools of fish by the hundreds put on impressive spectacles.[6]

The Sea of Galilee supports a thriving fishing industry, excursion boats sail across its waters, and those with maladies bathe in its celebrated mineral springs. Literally millions of pilgrims visit the scenes of Christ's ministry, stroll along the shores of this sea, sense the lingering atmosphere of the sacred past, and with Longfellow say:

> *And Him evermore I behold*
> *Walking in Galilee,*
> *Through cornfields waving gold,*
> *In hamlet, in wood, and in wold,*
> *By the shores of the Beautiful Sea.*
>
> *He toucheth the sightless eyes;*
> *Before Him the demons flee;*
> *To the dead He saith: Arise!*
> *To the living: Follow Me!*
>
> *And that voice still soundeth on*
> *From the centuries that are gone,*
> *To the centuries that shall be.*

CHAPTER 22

The Jordan River and Its Rift Valley

There is no river in the world like the Jordan—none so remarkable in its physical geography, none so wonderful in its historic memories, none so hallowed in its associations, none so revered by millions whether they have seen it or not. Yet it is not a large river and is quite paradoxical in its nature. It rises in Mount Hermon—the highest mountain in Palestine—and after a short run of only about 150 air miles, it ends in the Dead Sea—1,292 feet below sea level—the lowest body of water in the world.

228

The river has never been navigable, has never been a waterway of commerce, has never had a prominent city on its banks. Nor has it possessed a factory, a foundry, or even a fishery of any importance. Yet it is so strangely and so vitally connected with so much of the march of civilization and with so many divine events that it has a fame among civilized nations not accorded any other river on earth. "Surely," says Magregor, "the Jordan is by far the most wonderful stream on the face of the earth, and the memories of its history will not be forgotten in Heaven."[1]

The Jordan River winds its way down the great rift valley, actually travelling more than 200 miles to cover the 65 miles from the Sea of Galilee to the Dead Sea.

The way of the river, from beginning to end, is through the Great Rift Valley, which is the greatest earth fracture and the deepest rift valley known. The most unusual portion of this rift is between the Sea of Galilee and the Dead Sea. Here it is known as the *Ghor,* or "sunken valley." Just south of the Sea of Galilee the valley is only 4 miles wide, while in the vicinity of Jericho it is 14 miles wide. Everywhere it is wholly below the level of the sea, yet on both sides the mountains rise up to elevations from 2,000 to 3,500 feet.

Within this Ghor is the *Zor,* which is a basin or inner gorge lying from 100 to 150 feet lower than the main valley, and is from 600 feet to two miles wide. Then within the Zor is the 90- to 200-foot-wide channel or bed in which runs the river itself.

From a small bay in the southern extremity of the Sea of Galilee, the Jordan makes its exit, running westward for about a mile; then, making a sharp curve to the south, it hurries along on its serpentine course to the Dead Sea. From sea to sea the river would measure only 65 miles in a straight line, but as it descends on its countless meanderings through the Zor valley, it actually travels more than 200 miles. When it leaves Galilee, the river moves in a deep, gorgelike channel 50 to 100 feet wide. Along its way, it varies in width from 60 to 240 feet and is usually from 4 to 12 feet deep. Where it enters the Dead Sea, it is 540 feet wide and about 3 feet deep.[2]

There are many quite high waterfalls on the Jordan, and more than 100 rapids, 29 of which are quite dangerous. South of the Sea of Galilee the Palestine survey party found and tabulated about 40 fording places, the most of which are available for passage only in summer and early autumn. Others have counted as many as 57 fords. These differences are explained by the fact that during the annual overflow of Jordan, some of these crossings may be changed or even washed away or afterwards left as part of an oxbow where the river has changed its course. During Roman times, and since, there have been eight or more bridges, four of which span the Jordan today.

The Zor begins about eight miles south of the Sea of Galilee and is often rimmed in by an irregular line of eroded gray marl

230

cliffs 100 to 150 feet high. The floor of the Zor is usually covered with an almost impenetrable jungle of oleanders, willows, poplars, lofty cane, tangled bushes, creeping vines, and fernlike tamarisk. Here, in this junglelike growth, lurks the jackal, the wild boar, the hyena, and other forms of wildlife. Once the lion was here, but none have been seen since the time of the Crusades. A great many birds remain here the year around, while literally millions of the migratory variety—ducks, geese, brants, cranes, etc.—come and go with the seasons, on their way from the continent of Asia to Africa, or the reverse. At these seasons they sometimes spread out over the fields in such numbers that farmers' families have to drive them away by various means such as white flags on poles.

In the springtime, when the rains are heavy and the snows melt on Mount Hermon, the Jordan then overflows its slippery banks and spreads out over the Zor basin, driving the wild beasts from their lairs in the jungle, and making the river in some places more than two miles wide and very deep. In the Bible the Chronicler spoke of the Jordan "when it had overflown all his banks" (1 Chron. 12:15). Jeremiah said, "He shall come up like a lion from the swelling of Jordan" (Jer. 12:5). The children of Israel crossed the Jordan in the time of overflowing—the difficult, if not impossible, time—that they might "know that the living God" was among them (Josh. 3:10, 14).

There are many tributaries that enter the Jordan, the most of which are small; but there are four which are perennial and fairly large and quite important. Two of these enter from the east and two from the west. The two which enter from the east are the *Yarmuk* and the *Jabbok*. The two which enter from the west are the *Nahr Jalud* and the *Wadi Farah*.

The **Yarmuk River** was never mentioned in the Bible, even though it is almost as large as the Jordan. It drains the great Hauran Basin and is fed by a number of streams coming from southern Bashan and northern Gilead. It enters the Jordan five miles below Galilee, where the waters of both rivers flow into a large and beautiful lakelike reservoir over whose dam the water plunges some 90 feet. This reservoir feeds the Palestine Electric Corporation plant, which for many years produced electric power sufficient to serve the needs of most of Palestine. (This extensive plant has since been partially destroyed by acts of war.) The used but unconsumed waters of both rivers reach the main bed of the Jordan through a new channel. Since the mid-1960s water has been diverted from the Yarmuk River into the East Ghor Canal, which irrigates the north half of the east (Jordanian) side of the valley where live some 64,000 farmers and animal herders.

Some seven or eight miles below the power plant, the **Nahr Jalud** (river Jalud) flows into the Jordan from the west. This small and little-known river has its principal source two miles east of Jezreel, in the large spring of *Ain Jalud* (now called *Ain Harod*). It begins at a wide-mouth cave just under the northern cliffs of Mount Gilboa. At first it flows into a large pool, then makes its way down the Valley of Jezreel, past Beth-shan, and empties into the Jordan River just below the ancient ford which is now called *Abar'ah*. Here the men of Jabesh Gilead crossed when "they went all night" to take the bodies of Saul and Jonathan from the walls of Beth-shan.

The **river Jabbok** (now called *Zerka*) enters the Jordan Valley from the east, just below Succoth (now called *Tell Deir'alla*), where Jacob settled for a time after his night of wrestling with the angel of the Lord. Farther down, well within the rich bottom land of the Zor, and 20 miles above Jericho, the Jabbok empties its waters into the Jordan just above the small but impressive mound of Tell el-Damieh, the ancient city of Adam. About a mile west of Tell el-Damieh there are the remains of a Roman bridge and a new bridge over which passes the highway from Samaria to Gilead.

It was here at Adam (Adamah), that the waters were held back while 20 miles below this point Joshua and the Israelites crossed the Jordan on dry land. It being in the time of harvest when the "Jordan overfloweth all his banks . . . the waters which came down from above stood and rose up upon an heap" (Josh. 3:15-16). The water not only covered the entire Zor from bank to bank, but reached some 12 miles upstream, from Adam as far as the fortress of Zaretan.

An Arab historian states that about A.D. 1265 an earthquake caused a landslide of the chalky marl cliffs in this area which blocked the flow of the Jordan for some hours. A somewhat similar phenomenon took place during the severe earthquake of 1927. These two occurrences have caused some to assert that the Israelites chanced upon just such an occasion which enabled them to cross the Jordan dry-shod.

After examining this area, Dr. Nelson Glueck restates the historic fact "that landslides have at times blocked the normal channel of the Jordan, forcing it to chart a new course." As one who knows the Bible and the Jordan, Glueck then very wisely states that "the first contact of Israel with the Jordan had in it the elements of a miracle" which caused the river to "remain strangely entwined with their subsequent history." And so it is that an unusual phenomenon such as a severe earthquake may block the "normal channel" of the Jordan, but the blocking of the river for the Israelites to cross could and did have in it "the element of a miracle," seeing they crossed at the time of harvest when the river was in flood. At such a time, a cave-in of these high marl embankments would have had little effect.

This entire district hummed with industrial activity during the middle of the 10th century before Christ, when Hiram, Solomon's "master coppersmith," formed earthen molds "in the clay ground between Succoth and Zarthan" (1 Kings 7:46). Day after day, the long caravans of donkeys filed down into the valley from the eastern hills, bringing partly "roasted" copper and iron ore mined in the Arabah and the Ajlun areas, and charcoal from the forest of Gilead. Solomon and Hiram, with the aid of their workmen, turned out many extremely beautiful gold and copper objects such as the altar, the table, the pillars, the pots and pans, the candlesticks, the pomegranates, and many other things which furnished and adorned the new Temple of the Lord at Jerusalem (1 Kings 7:46; 2 Chron. 4:17).[3]

233

About two miles immediately west of Damieh Bridge is *Kurn Sur'tabeh,* a sharp, conical peak which rises more than 2,000 feet above the valley floor, and commands a view of much of the length of the Jordan Valley. A mass of ruins on its summit is a vivid reminder of the towering fortress of Alexandrium, built here by the Hasmonaeans and later rebuilt by Herod the Great to guard the road coming down from Neapolis (Shechem) and the Wadi Farah. The Talmud suggests that it was for a long time used as an observatory, on which beacon fires were kindled to announce the appearance of the new moon.

The *Wadi Farah*, which rises north of Mount Ebal and in the area of the ancient cities of Thebes and Tirzah, hurries down the eastern declivities of Samaria and, passing below Hurn Sur'tabeh, enters the Jordan River some four miles below Adam. Somewhere in this area Naaman dipped seven times, at the word of Elisha, and was cured of his leprosy.

Flowing on for some 16 miles, through fascinating desert landscapes often formed of ashen-gray marl buttes, mesas, and plateaus, the Jordan reaches Nimrin ford, which is usually called "the upper ford." Nearby is a ruined site, called *Tell Nimrin,* whose name is derived from Beth-Nimrah, the more ancient city site located almost a mile eastward. The Septuagint calls it Beth-abra (the house of the ford), which leads many to believe this to be the "Beth-abara beyond Jordan," where John proclaimed the coming of the Messiah King and His kingdom, preached repentance, and baptized thousands. It is where Jesus was baptized and later preached, "and many believed on him there" (John 1:28; 10:40, 42). This place is the scene of the annual immersion of many pilgrims from many parts of the world today.

The main thoroughfare from Jericho to Gilead has been by the way of this ford; therefore we may safely say that it has afforded passage for famous people from time immemorial—probably for the majority of the biblical characters who crossed the lower Jordan.

Just below the ford, on the site of an old wooden bridge which the Turks destroyed, the British military authorities constructed a substantial steel bridge in 1919, and named it Allenby Bridge. It is 1,200 feet below sea level, and until recent years was known as "the lowest bridge in the world." (Now, however,

234

the Abdullah Bridge spans the Jordan just about a mile above the Dead Sea and so rates that unusual honor.)

Just below the Allenby Bridge there is a waterfall, after which the distinctive features of the Jordan rapidly change. Its channel widens, its banks flatten out, the undergrowth along its edge becomes less dense, and its waters flow more smoothly.

About four or five miles farther down is the "lower ford," known as the Pilgrims Bathing Place. This, according to the Greek church, is the traditional site of the baptism of our Lord. Since the sixth century thousands of pilgrims have visited Jerusalem every spring during Holy Week and have come down to this place on Monday after Easter to immerse themselves, in the belief that they are at the very place where Christ was baptized. In this they could possibly be mistaken, yet it was one of the "fords toward Moab" which Ehud took when he delivered Israel from the oppression of the Moabites (Judg. 3:28), and it was almost certainly the crossing place of Naomi and Ruth on their journey to Bethlehem (Ruth 1).

From the "lower ford," the Jordan moves along for four miles on the last lap of its journey. After an unparalleled descent of some 3,000 feet in its course of 150 miles, it emerges from its unique channel and quietly flows into the deep and lifeless Dead Sea.

CHAPTER **23**

The Plain of Jericho

_____

The Plain of Jericho, often likened to "a garden in the wilderness," or even "a little paradise in the desert," lies between the river Jordan and the Judean mountains. It is 5 miles wide by 18 miles long and lies 700 to 900 feet below sea level. It is famed for its climate, its fertility, and its semitropical luxuriance. Sheltered as it is from cold winds and stormy weather, and having balsam and palm groves and almost every manner of fruits and flowers, it has long been known as the ideal country in which to winter. These favorable features

236

have been made possible because of the presence of four strong springs, and a number of wadis or streambeds which at the proper season carry considerable water.

Wadi Kelt (identified with the Valley of Achor) is fed by two large springs higher up, and the other streambeds come from the mountains on the northwest which run with considerable water during the rainy season. By the ancient mound of Jericho is *Elisha's Fountain* that pours forth a strong, wide stream which furnished drinking water for ancient Jericho. It now is used to irrigate several square miles of the plain extending eastward toward the Jordan. Four miles northwest of ancient Jericho are three springs known as the springs of *Ain-ed Duk.* Below the springs is a beautiful waterfall which, in medieval times, turned sugar mills. After propelling the mills, the water was conveyed to the plain by a network of aqueducts and canals.

Jericho, once "The City of Palm Trees," was a Canaanite town of considerable importance. It was the first city taken by the children of Israel as they entered the Promised Land. Joshua laid a curse of most unusual nature upon the man who should rebuild the city, saying: "Cursed be the man before the Lord that riseth up and buildeth this city Jericho: he shall lay the foundation thereof in his firstborn, and in his youngest son shall he set up the gates of it." This prophecy was fulfilled in the days of King Ahab, when Hiel the Bethelite, an apostate Jew, rebuilt Jericho. He actually "laid the foundation thereof in Abiram his firstborn," and set up the gates thereof in his youngest son Segub (1 Kings 16:34).

This city, along with its nearby village of Gilgal, later had a school for the prophets and was visited by Elijah and Elisha just before Elijah's translation on the other side of the Jordan. On returning to Jericho, Elisha turned the brackish waters of the spring into good water, and became head of the school of prophets (2 Kings 2:19-22). The school grew so rapidly that it had to be enlarged.

It was here that Naaman came to Elisha, seeking a cure for his leprosy—which he received after going, in obedience, to the

237

nearby Jordan where he dipped seven times. Other notable characters visited the city from time to time.

Lying as it did in a semitropical clime in one of the world's richest areas, the plain was so developed by the Maccabean rulers that when the Romans took over under Pompey in 63 B.C., its vast date palm industry, its world-famous balsam groves, and its well-cultivated fruit orchards, along with its splendid climate, made it a coveted winter resort. Like a rich pawn in international politics, it passed from one royal person to another. Mark Antony gave Jericho and its plain to Cleopatra, and Cleopatra farmed its revenues to Herod. And it was under Herod the Great that the region enjoyed its greatest prosperity during the last few decades before the birth of Christ.[1]

In the northern section, where grew 49 varieties of dates and "extremely sweet" wine grapes, two important villages named *Archelais* and *Phasaelis* were built. The first was built by Archelaus, son of Herod, and the other was erected by Herod the Great as one of the impressive memorials for his older brother. Outlines of the central buildings remain—the palace, a temple, a marketplace, and the remains of small shops. Water for these two villages was brought in an aqueduct from *Ain Fusail,* five and one-half miles up the Jordan Valley.

238

Looking across the verdant Plain of Jericho

Other important improvements in the way of buildings and roads, along with aqueducts and canals and farming projects, were carried out in the central portion of the plain and in the area of Elisha's Spring. But the most phenomenal of all undertakings was Herod's Jericho, south of Wadi Kelt, which he transformed into a magnificent Roman city.

Here, in what we now call "Roman Jericho," Herod built for himself a magnificent winter palace, fully equipped "with the conveniences and luxuries of swimming pools, baths, etc., that made it both a suitable place to entertain his friends and a place which he could show off with some pride to his political guests such as Cleopatra of Egypt."[2]

On his journey to Jerusalem a few days before the Passover, Jesus came into Roman Jericho where Zacchaeus, the small but wealthy tax collector, climbed a sycamore tree to see the Messiah. When the two met, Zacchaeus repented of the evil in his life, and his entire being was changed and illumined by the transforming power of the Christ who took lodging that night in the elegant home of the "rich little tax collector" (Luke 9:1-10). Likewise the blind man, Bartimaeus, met the Master in Jericho, and by persistent faith "received his sight, and followed Jesus in the way" (Mark 10:51).

Gilgal, where Israel set up their camp after crossing the Jordan and arranged 12 stones from the riverbed for a memorial, where they also renewed the rite of circumcision, and where the Tabernacle remained for a time, is thought by many to have been at *Tell en Nitleh.* It is on a slight elevation some three miles east of Jericho. In this area stone pottery and flint knives have been reported found. Dr. Kelso's excavations have revealed the remains of five Byzantine churches, which would indicate that the Early Church supposed this to be Gilgal.

Today, on the Jericho Plain, there are gardens and groves, fruits and nuts, grapes, melons, bananas, oranges, lemons, and Siamese pumelo, which not only grow unusually well here, but possess a flavor that is superior. Jericho oranges, for example, are larger, and bring a third more on the Jerusalem market. 239

However, only a small fraction of the plain is now in production. Here are some 60,000 acres that with the proper planning and development could well become one of the world's foremost garden spots and furnish food for multiplied thousands of people.

CHAPTER 24

The Dead Sea

The Dead Sea is the strangest and most unusual body of water known to man. To the Jew it is the "Salt Sea"; to the Arab it is *Bahr Lut,* "Sea of Lot." It lies 1,292 feet below sea level and forms the lowest point in the Great Rift Valley. The sea measures 47 miles long, has an average width of 9½ miles, and a maximum water depth near the north end of another 1,308 feet—making the bottom of the sea 2,600 feet below sea level. Its great depth is further enhanced by the mountains of Moab and Judea which rise steeply from the water line, on either side, to a maximum height of 3,000 to 4,000 feet. On the Moab side red sandstone and hard limestone rise abruptly and precipitously, while on the Judean side chalky marl, salt and gypsum cliffs somewhat more terraced and receding jut out near the water's edge.

Into this inland sea the Jordan, the Arnon, and other smaller streams dump an average of 6 million tons of chemical-laden water a day. There is no outlet, except by evaporation. Thus through many millennia the waters that these streams have emptied into this abyss of a sea have evaporated into the air, leaving the mass of chemicals which they had held in solution to accumulate. The chemical stock now constitutes about 26 per cent of its liquid contents. This means that the solution is so dense and buoyant that a man can lie on its waters and not sink. It has a peculiar, bitter taste.

The color of the water is a deep blue, tending toward the leaden. At times the surface is flecked with white wave crests as the wind rises and laboriously whips up a light foam which floats on the surface. During the summer, when evaporation is most rapid, there is a thin, almost transparent vapor which rises from

242

Looking north along the western shore of the Dead Sea

the sea. "When seen from a distance," says Lynch, "its purple tinge blends with the leaden color of the waters and gives it the appearance of smoke from burning sulphur. At times this is so accentuated as to give the sea the appearance of a vast cauldron of metal fused but motionless."[1]

In the rather distant past the Dead Sea was often described as a place of deep and fearful gloom, "where death reigned supreme, where no life might exist, where no beauty ever appeared, and where the body of Mrs. Lot stood encased in a pillar of salt."

However, for many centuries travelers have visited there, and 10 or more special expeditions have studied the various aspects of the sea. The first modern attempt seems to have been made in 1835 by Mr. Costigan, an American, who descended the Jordan in an open boat and traversed the sea to its extreme southern point. He crossed and recrossed it several times, only to be overcome by hunger, heat, and fatigue. He was carried back to Jerusalem, where he died and was buried in the Christian cemetery there.

A second attempt was fitted out by the British Admiralty in 1837 and led by G. H. Moore and W. G. Beke. They spent 19 days exploring the shoreline. In 1841, another British expedition under Major Scott and Lieutenant Symonds was sent. They sounded the maximum depth of the sea. Lieutenant Molyneux led an expedition in 1847, which added much to our knowledge of the sea; but soon after returning to his ship, he was overcome by fatigue and passed away.

A fifth expedition was equipped by the United States government in 1848, and commanded by Lieutenant Lynch. Their researches were of the highest scientific value. In 1924, another expedition (mostly by land) was led by Dr. Albright, Dr. Kyle, Mr. Day, and Mr. Densmore—archaeologists, geologist, and botanist. Meanwhile the commerical possibilities of the Dead Sea had been investigated in 1911 and 1920-21 by Mr. M. A. Novomeysky, a well-known British chemist.

243

The accrued knowledge gained by these and other studies have shown the Dead Sea, and the landscape of the surrounding area to be, in many respects, a place of rare beauty, endless variety, and one of health and fabulous wealth.

Contrary to popular supposition, however, there is more than salt in the waters of the Dead Sea. This had long been suspected and had been shown in part by an analysis made as early as 1854; but when, in 1911, Mr. Novomeysky began official tests by which the waters were carefully analyzed, he found that the greater the depth, the heavier the waters were with chemicals.

An official estimate, based on these and other analyses furnished to the British Parliament, gives a reasonable idea of the amount and value of chemicals in the Dead Sea:

Potash	1,300,000,000 tons	$ 70,000,000,000
Salt	11,900,000,000 tons	27,500,000,000
Bromine	853,000,000 tons	260,000,000,000
Gypsum	81,000,000 tons	120,000,000
Calcium Chloride	6,000,000,000 tons	85,000,000,000
Magnesium Chloride	22,000,000,000 tons	825,000,000,000
	42,134,000,000 tons	$1,267,620,000,000

This incredible valuation may now be even much greater with inflated world prices. Also, there is asphalt or bitumen of an undetermined amount. The chemicals are now being extracted, yet with the incoming waters they are increasing faster than they can be taken out.

From dawn to dark, illusions of color appear on the water and in the nearby cliffs which nature has piled about the depression. One has called it "the most imposing and beautiful lake which exists on the earth." Yet another has declared its beauty to be "the beauty of death. For," says he, "no vegetable life is found along its dazzling white shores, except heaps of driftwood carried down by the river, which are stripped and bleached like bones and incrustated with a layer of salt. No flocks graze beside it, no wild beasts come hither to drink, no fish swim in its depths."[2]

All of this is quite true, yet a few rods back from the beach are plants such as the Spina Christa, a thornbush which bears

Cave Four near Qumran where some of the first Dead Sea Scrolls were found.

piercing thorns and small fruit similar to scrawny crab apples. There is also the Osher, or "Apples of Sodom," a tropical-looking plant which bears a large, smooth apple or orangelike fruit which hangs in clusters of three or four together. When completely ripe, its fruit is yellow and looks very attractive; but if pressed, it bursts with a crack and crumbles away in the hand like soot and ashes. Then there is the oleander, the acacia, the castor bean, and a few wild palms which grow or did grow in the small oases on the east shores of the sea.

For a trip about the Dead Sea, one may leave Kallia, at the northwest end, and, either by motorboat on the water or by car on the splendid new highway, travel safely along the west coast. The rugged cliffs of the Judean Wilderness run alongside the sea in some places as much as a half mile back and in other places very near the sea.

Only three miles south, on a spur of land some 250 feet above the level of the Dead Sea, lie the ruins of *Qumran* where, during the middle of the second century B.C., a group of Essenes "retired from the evils of the world" to pursue a simple way of religious life and teaching. They built their center partly on the foundations of a seventh-century B.C. fort, but extended their buildings considerably on the south and west. They installed an elaborate water supply system, built potters' quarters and kilns, a bakery, a confectionary, a dining hall, an assembly room, and a Scriptorium where they made multiplied thousands of copies of the Scriptures—all of the Old Testament books except the Book of Esther.

When Rome's 10th Legion came in A.D. 68, Qumran was sacked and burned, and the inhabitants massacred or scattered. But they left behind them hundreds or even thousands of scrolls of the Scriptures hidden away, as if by intent, in nearby caves, to be discovered nearly 2,000 years later (1947) and publicized to the world as the Dead Sea Scrolls.

246 The excavated village, along with its cemetery, may now be visited, and the caves inspected. But not all the caves are in the immediate vicinity, for scrolls were found in caves as far south as Ain Jidy, where lived other Essenes.

Two miles south of the Qumran monastery, just near the sea-side, is *Ain Feshkha,* an abundant, freshwater spring and stream which forms a fine oasis around which reeds, marsh grasses, and other vegetation now grow in abundance. Here the Essenes had an irrigation system and grew such fruits, vegetables, and other produce as they needed. Nearby were found the ruins of farm buildings, stables, toolsheds, and what appeared to be rooms for preparing leather for its various uses—including the parchment on which they were to write the scrolls.[3]

Some eight miles farther south are two important springs—*'Ain el-Ghuweir* and *'Ain et-Turaba*—which form another oasis in an otherwise barren landscape.[4] Ten miles farther on is a hot sulphur spring near the coast, and three miles beyond that is En-Gedi, previously described. Ten miles farther down the shore is mighty Masada, "the Gibraltar of the Dead Sea," also referred to earlier.

Four miles south of Masada the tracks of an ancient Roman road approach the narrow point of the Dead Sea and reappear on the eastern side at the southwestern tip of El Lisan. This means that 2,000 years ago the waters of the sea were much lower than they are today.

The eastern shores of the Dead Sea are vastly different from the western side. The rugged sandstone, basalt, and limestone cliffs approach the water's edge so near that no highway may be built there, so a trip along the upper eastern shore means taking a motorboat. For nine miles south of the Jordan, along the Moab coastline, red sandstone, black basalt, and gray limestone cliffs rise abruptly 900 to 1,000 feet and recede steeply eastward to a plateau 4,000 feet above the sea.

The first break in the towering coastline comes with **Wadi Zerka-Ma'in** (by some called the river Callirrhoe), a broad moun-tain stream rushing into the sea through a picturesque mountain gorge 122 feet wide with wild palms, tamarisks, and a jungle of cane and other vegetation on either side. Here one's eyes feast on the red, gray, and black stratified stone cliffs 900 feet high, rising perpendicularly on either side and sometimes seeming to meet.[6] About seven miles eastward, up through the gorge in the highlands, this torrent receives much of its waters from the 10 mineral-laden hot springs of *Callirrhoe,* where during the last year of his life, Herod the Great, at the advice of his physician, sought relief from his fatal malady.

Three miles south of Wadi Zerka-Ma'in are the scant ruins of **Zira,** the ancient Hebrew town of *Zareth-shahar,* where there are strange tropical shrubs, tall grass, canebrakes, and warm sulphur springs. Some suppose Herod bathed here, and he may have done so, for in seeking a cure for his sickness he visited most of the known mineral springs.

Ten miles farther south, along one of the world's most color-ful and charming coastlines, one comes to the **river Arnon,** now known as *Wadi el Mojib,* where the 82-feet-wide and four-feet-deep stream flows into the sea through an impressive gorge of red sandstone cliffs which, on either side, rise sheer and steep some 400 feet and form a scene so romantic as to be called "Arnon's Rock Gate." The color of the cliffs is the same as in the rose-red city of Petra and forms a striking contrast with the silvery stream of the river, the leaden blue waters of the sea, and the patch of green vegetation in the miniature delta at the estuary. A unique experience awaits all who wade up this clear, cool, rock-shaded stream a few hundred yards to the waterfall, and return in the late afternoon to see the entrance of the gorge shot through by the gorgeous shafts of sunlight—a scene which one never cares to forget.

Motoring on some 10 miles southward from the Arnon gorge, one soon comes to a bold, broad peninsula called **El Lisan** ("The Tongue"). From the east shore this strange, tonguelike peninsula extends more than halfway across the sea, then breaks off in a towering, wall-like shoreline 40 to 60 feet high and 9 miles long, with a steep white ridge 20 feet higher running like a spine down the center. Most of the peninsula is bordered by this gray white, wall-like, chalky-marl formation that looms up white and dazzling in the sun, presenting "the appearance of a wall of sawn ice or newcut carbonate of lime" rising out from the leaden blue waters. At one place near the south end, this peninsula rises out, tier upon tier, to a height of some 300 feet. At the foot of the surrounding cliff is a beach of washed-up sand, which varies in length and breadth according to the season—wider in summer than in winter. The northern point of this tonguelike promontory is called Point Costigan, and the southernmost is called Point Molyneux, after the two explorers who lost their lives about the middle of the 19th century while leading expeditions to study the sea.

South of El Lisan is a baylike area, irregular in shape, but some 16 miles long and 8 miles wide, where the water is exceedingly shallow—3 to 17 feet deep.

Almost all who have made a serious study of this baylike area have been led to believe that it now covers the well-watered and fertile "land of the plain," where in Abraham's and Lot's day was located *Sodom and Gomorrah,* on which "the Lord rained brimstone and fire out of heaven, and overthrew those cities, and that which grew upon the ground" (Gen. 19:24-25).

The picture given in the Bible seems to favor a location at the southern end of the sea for the "vale of Siddim" where the "cities of the plain" were located (Gen. 13:10-12; 14:1-3, 10; 19:20-23). The late Greek and Latin writers—Diodoros, Strabo, Josephus, and Tacitus—agree on the southern location.[7] And it seems natural to come to this conclusion when the surrounding physical features of this shallow southern bay of the Dead Sea are examined. Note the indications:

1. Stretching for miles along the east shore of this embayment and extending up along the east side of El Lisan is the *Ghor Safieh,* a broad, luxuriant plain which in ancient and medieval times was a fertile oasis where orchards, dates, wheat, barley, indigo, cotton, sugarcane, and vines grew. Today it is cultivated in places. Five clear streams course down from the mountains of Moab and flow through this long, narrow, fertile area into this very Dead Sea basin. Some of these streams are sizeable, have gravelly beds, and are tapped by little conduits, so that the whole area can be turned into a watered garden or meadow. In some places even now there are patches of corn, barley, millet, and indigo growing. In other places there are trees, shrubs, cane, date palm, and swampland. Much of this area swarms with wild-

life, including the wild boar. Apparently there was a mountain stream for each of the five "cities of the plain." The city sites are thought to be now buried under the shallow water, but the outer fringes of the oasis of Ghor Safieh remain.

2. Higher up in the foothills above the remaining portion of this oasis Drs. Albright and Kyle discovered extensive ruins of a well-fortified "open air settlement with enclosures, and hearths for individual family units." East of the fortified camp was a group of fallen monoliths *(mazzeboth)* or sacred cult pillars, "at which the religious rites of the community of *Bab edh-Dhra* were performed." The absence of debris indicated that it was not continuously inhabited, but "a place of pilgrimage, where annual feasts were celebrated, and to which people came, living in booths and merry-making for several days of the year." The pottery indicated that the place began to be used about 2,300 B.C., and ceased to be occupied around 1,900 B.C., which accords with the Bible narrative and chronology as to when the "cities of the plain" were destroyed.[8]

3. Alongside this shallow, southern end of the Dead Sea area, on its west, is *Jebel Usdum* (Mount Sodom)—a mountain of salt five miles long, three miles wide, and rising 742 feet above the water. The mountain is underlaid by a solid mass of greenish-white, crystalized rock salt 50 to 200 feet thick. Above this salt stratum the mountain has a crust of salt, marl, and clay, topped with a limestone cap-rock. Within this mountain are caves in which are beautiful, cavernlike rooms with stalagmites and stalactites, all composed of pure, crystalline salt.

On the east slope of Mount Sodom, about 40 to 60 feet above the water, rises a lofty, round pillar of salt, capped with carbonate of lime. Tour guides point this out as the "pillar of salt" into which Mrs. Lot was turned for her disobedience. Josephus, Clement, Irenaeus, and some modern historians and explorers mention such a pillar as having been there when they visited this area. Perhaps not the same one, for climatic and geologic factors seem, at times, to change these pillar formations. At least some think that the ancient pillar has been washed into the sea and replaced by the present pillar. Others think the same pillar

250

stands. An occasional salty mist arises in this area and encrustates every object on which it settles.

New potash works have been established on land near Jebel Usdum. Here they pump Dead Sea water into huge earthern "pans" and extract the chemicals by evaporation. It is then purified in the mills and sent out to the world markets. These are now being expanded at a cost of $100 million. Significantly, the new city which serves as a center for these activities is named Sodom. It is rated as "the lowest post office in the world."

Two modern Jewish colonies—new *Zohar* and *En Bokek*—lie just north of Jebel Usdum. Then a bit farther north, we return to the now submerged Roman road which once led across to El Lisan.

Divers have searched many parts of this southern embayment of the sea for ruins of the cities of Sodom and Gomorrah, but none have yet been located, either here or elsewhere. Probably they were so thoroughly destroyed that they will never be found.

CHAPTER **25**

The Arabah or "Valley of the Desert"

Beginning at the southern
end of the Dead Sea, and extending southward for 110 miles to
the eastern arm of the Red Sea, is a depression—the continuation
of the Great Rift Valley. From ancient Bible times it has been
known as the *Wadi el Arabah,* or "Valley of the Desert." This
remarkable valley or depression begins at 1,292 feet below sea
252 level at the Dead Sea and gradually ascends as it goes southward
for 62 miles to reach its highest point of 650 feet above sea level
near *Jebel er-Rishe.* From here it quickly descends until 48 miles

farther southward it reaches the Gulf of Aqabah (the arm of the Red Sea) at Ezion-Geber. The Arabah is from 6 to 12 miles wide and is bordered on either side by towering and forbidding mountains, especially on the east by the mountains of Edom.

An ancient caravan route entered this "Valley of the Desert" at Ezion-Geber and passed along northward to a point south of the Dead Sea, then one road branched northwest toward Palestine and another northeast toward the Jordanian countries. Where parts of this arterial highway now run, the children of Israel once "passed . . . from Elath, and from Ezion-gaber" on their way to the Promised Land (Deut. 2:8). Along this same way came the queen of Sheba on her way to Jerusalem to know more of Solomon's wisdom, and Solomon's men travelled to his mines in the Arabah and to his southern seaport at Ezion-Geber. Here also the Romans established fortified stations to protect their trade.

Surface explorations along with minor digs, carried on by Dr. Nelson Glueck and others, have revealed ancient caravan stations and fortresses at intervals along the valley. There are also ruined villages, mining camps, slag heaps, and remains of copper and silver mines from which ore was dug in the time of Solomon (1000-900 B.C.) and during the time of the Nabateans (300 B.C. to A.D. 200).[1] All of which gives substance to the words of Scripture which spoke of a "land whose stones are iron, and out of whose hills you can dig copper" (Deut. 8:9).

These remnants of ancient mining operations stimulated an interest on the part of the Jews; and when their mining engineers made tests, they were convinced that the mineral deposits in the Wadi Arabah were "far from exhausted," despite the intensive mining by Solomon and the Nabateans. Considerable money and equipment would be necessary in order to carry out modern mining operations, but the Jews met the challenge sufficiently that by 1965, the output from the mines at Timna, near Solomon's mines, was 23 million tons of copper and manganese. The operations have continued, with few interruptions, from year to year. 253

The major portion of the Arabah is made up of shifting sands and salty, brackish soils and gravel, and is extremely hot and dry during much of the year. Rainfall is less than two inches annually. A few spring-fed oases, such as the more famous one at *Ain Ghudyan* in the southwest part of the valley, furnish an abundance of water, both from a strong spring and from a subterranean flow of water which is easily reached with wells. In other places there are swamps with dark loam which cracks into uprolled scales when drying. Also there are small areas where freshwater brooks come down, creating habitable lands, where there were small towns in ancient times. For long centuries, however, it has been mostly wasteland occupied at intervals by only a few Bedouin Arabs.[2]

With the magnificent obsession of salvaging the desert, the Jews, in 1948, began their first farming efforts in the Arabah by founding the colony of *Yotvatah* at the *Ain Ghudyan* oasis. After extensive landscaping, drainage, and reducing the salt and alkaline content of the soil, fertilizing the land, planting shelterbelt avenues of trees around the fields, building access roads and homes, they began to plant crops. Through the years there have been many complicated battles with the soil, and with harnessing the water resources; yet by patient toil and unceasing effort they have shown that fruits, vegetables, melons, and flowers may be grown here the year around. These can be exported to Europe at a time when they are in short supply, thus creating an important source of foreign currency.

Other colonies have settled in the valley—*Ein-Yahav,* near the central part of the valley, and *Hatzeva* farther north toward the Dead Sea, and five more at strategic points. Thus, today, rising out of the desert like mirages, are eight oases of life. Neat houses come into view, surrounded by green gardens; date plantations heavy with fruit; fields ready for crops; sprinklers stilling the thirst of the soil. Eight man-made miracles. Eight new names on the map. Eight villages on land wrested from desolation. The hum of the tractor is broken by the laughter of children, the voices of men, and the singing of women. The caravan route of old is being turned into a highway of progress.

Natural sculptures abound in the southern Arabah, among which are the two delicately formed, yet huge mineral-encrusted rock formations known as the Pillars of Solomon which stand guard over Solomon's Mines at Timna, 16 miles north of Elat. Seldom is there found such variation, delicacy, and beauty combined with massiveness; yet in the nearby mountain passes of Edom eastward and the Paran plateau on the west are corresponding types of rock formations with a delicate blending of rich reds, light browns, and pale yellows.

Elat (Elath) and **Ezion-Geber,** at the southern tip of the Arabah, on the shores of the Red Sea, were stations on the route of the Exodus of Israel from Egypt (Deut. 2:8; Num. 33:35). Here ancient Israel later had its southern port—her gateway to Arabia, Africa, and India. Here King Solomon maintained a navy and sent and received his ships from Ophir, laden with gold, silver, ivory, apes, peacocks, and other exotic treasures (1 Kings 9:26-28; 10:11, 22). Here the queen of Sheba and her retinue are said to have landed when she came to Jerusalem to see Solomon and "commune with him all that was in her heart," and here Jehoshaphat's navy was destroyed (1 Kings 22:48). This was one of the main ports

255

The Jordanian city of Aqaba on the Red Sea at the southern end of the Arabah.

in the Nabataean and Arabian spice trade; from here Roman ships set sail for the east, and now since 1967, Elat has been built into a first-class port city—a veritable "Gateway to Africa and Asia." Phosphates, potash, copper ore, salt, cement, and other commodities are exported from here. Oil tankers dock farther south at the terminal of the oil pipeline.

The smooth, blue waters of the Red Sea (Gulf of Aqaba), the Coral Beach, the glass-bottom boat to the coral reefs, the deep-sea fishing and the maritime museum, along with the all-but-rainless days and pleasant nights throughout the year make Elat one of the finest winter resorts in the Near East.[3] There are many ultramodern hotels and 15,000 permanent residents, most of whom are there to serve the state, the shipping companies, and the needs of tourists. Across the bay on a curve of perfect beach is the Jordanian port city of Aqaba dazzling white "in a blaze of desert sand and partly shaded by rings of date palm trees." Biblical Elath was near where Aqaba now stands. The Crusaders built a castle there, and Col. T. E. Lawrence had a base of supplies at Aqaba. Here three countries meet—Saudi Arabia, Jordan, and Israel. The whole area is heavy with history—especially that history which is tinged with sacredness.[4]

While excavating the ruins of ancient Ezion-Geber, Dr. Glueck was deeply moved by the significance of the geographic and historic setting as represented by the "mighty past" which again "rode supreme" at Ezion-Geber and its environs. He says:

> On days of storm in springtime I have seen enormous clouds hurtling across from Sinai to Arabia. I have heard the thunder roar and have almost felt the ground shake beneath my feet. At such moments it seemed as if I could almost see Moses and his weary people emerging from the wilderness on their way to the Promised Land.
>
> Above them hovered the God of Sinai, who in the midst of such thunder and lightning had spoken to Moses with the sound of a loud trumpet and to Elijah with a still small voice that was stronger than wind, earthquake or fire.
>
> At such thrilling moments a glow of the mighty past lay upon the parched and barren land.[5]

The Eastern Tableland

CHAPTER 26

Mount Hermon

Mount Hermon, the finest and one of the most venerated mountains of Bible lands, forms the southern extremity of the Anti-Lebanon Mountain Range, and is separated from the Anti-Lebanons only by the deep gorge of the river Barada (Abana) which flows eastward to Damascus. It is a gigantic mountain, 5 miles wide and almost 20 miles long, which culminates in three peaks about a quarter of a mile from each other. The tallest of these peaks is in the center and is made up of a small plateau about 435 yards in diameter and is 9,166 feet above the Mediterranean Sea, which is only 30 to 40 miles away. Its noble majesty filled the ancients with veneration and awe, as it rose high above the sources of the Jordan, the city of Damascus, and the Valley of Lebanon. It could be seen from most all parts of Palestine, Syria, and Trans-Jordan.

The Sidonians called it Sirion, the "glittering breastplate"; the Amorites called it Shenir; while the Baal worshipers considered it the very abode of the god Baal-Hermon—the Quibla or focal point of all Baal worship. Today the Arabs call it *Jebel esh Sheik,* the "Chief of the Mountains," or "the mountain of the white-haired."

The geological formation of Mount Hermon is limestone and Nubian sandstone, with occasional veins of black basalt. Nearer the base it is strewn for miles with large boulders of traprock. The lower slopes are well wooded partly with fir, partly with fruit, and here and there stretches of oak and shrubs. On its northern slopes groves of olives and mulberry trees can be found as far up as 5,000 feet. Above this are found only a few scattered oaks, almonds, and dwarf juniper trees.

259

Snow-crowned Mount Hermon, elevation 9,166 feet

One of the striking things about Hermon is the "shadow mountain" effect which on clear days is seen morning and evening. On rising in the morning, the sun casts Hermon's shadow far out across the Lebanons into the Mediterranean Sea. The evening shadow is impressively thrown back eastward across Damascus and the desert beyond.

The winter snowline begins at an elevation of about 3,250 feet, and piles higher and higher to the very summit which causes Hermon to stand out against the skyline like a great white ghost. The summer sun melts most of the snow away, except in the coves and deep clefts with here and there long, deep drifts on the northern slopes. Three-fourths of this water finds its way down the deep gorges of the Great Rift Valley of the Jordan. The other one-fourth drains through the Abana and Pharpar rivers which slake the thirst of Damascus and its great surrounding basin. All these rivers rise and fall according to the amount of snow and rain which falls on Mount Hermon.

Some years ago the writer took Rev. Bud Robinson all the way around Mount Hermon, taking care to point out the drainage. When we had completed the circle, his cryptic reply was, "Well, Mount Hermon is the waterworks of Palestine."

During summer months, when no rain falls, most vegetation throughout Palestine depends on dew for moisture, and Mount Hermon with its high, cold elevations enhances the supply of distilled dew. In Ps. 133:3 the happiness of brotherly love is compared to the "dew of Hermon which descendeth upon Mount Zion." In no other known place in the world is the dew as heavy. It is a natural phenomenon caused by the moisture from the Mediterranean Sea coming in contact with the cold atmosphere of the mountain. The evaporating dew of the morning produces a heavy cloud of mist, which drifts along, forming ribbons of filmy white on a background of green. These dews and mists plus other advantages of Mount Hermon make it the source of many blessings to the land over which it so proudly lifts its form.

260   The height of Hermon along with its isolation and location makes it a promontory second to none from which to view the Holy Land. From its summit a great part of Palestine and Syria can

be seen. To the east lies Damascus, one of the oldest cities in the world, a paradise in the midst of the desert. To the southeast the plain of Bashan is visible, dotted everywhere with ruins. The Huleh Basin, where were the "waters of Merom" of Bible times, lies almost at the foot of Hermon. Further south is the Sea of Galilee, while 95 miles below is the Dead Sea. Between these is the length of the Jordan River in its vast chasm from 6 to 12 miles wide. West of Jordan, one can see peak after peak and many of the sacred sites of western Palestine, such as Nazareth, the Mount of Olives, Mount Carmel, and other notable points; while the expanse of the Mediterranean, which stretches away to the sky, seems almost boundless.[1]

No one point in Palestine acquaints one with the country and with the old forms of worship as does Mount Hermon. It seems to have been the chief of the high places dedicated to Baal before Abraham passed this way preaching the doctrine of one God.

The great confession of Peter, when he boldly acknowledged that Jesus was "the Christ, the Son of the living God," was made at Caesarea Philippi just before the Transfiguration, and the healing of the afflicted child was just after "they came down from the mountain" (Matt. 16:16). Therefore it follows that the "high mountain" must have been Mount Hermon. It also seems reasonable, as many suppose, that Christ would go to this mountain to be transfigured. It is believed that He went to the southernmost peak of the mountain rather than the highest one because of the pagan temple then occupying that most eminent peak. At the transfiguration of Christ there were five representatives with Him: Moses, Elijah, Peter, James, and John. Moses represented the law; Elijah, the prophets; Peter represented persistence; James, administration; and John, love. What a place for such an event! What a company to be present when the Eternal broke through in revelation, attestation, and encouragement.

The Greeks dedicated Mount Hermon to their god Pan, and the village of Caesarea Philippi was called *Panias;* later the Arabs changed it to *Banias.* Jerome, who lived from A.D. 340 to 420, tells us that in his time there was a remarkable temple on the summit of Mount Hermon in which the heathen from the region of

Panias and Lebanon met for worship. In A.D. 420, when suffering from the ravages of wild beasts, the inhabitants about Mount Hermon summoned Simeon Stylites to aid them. He counselled them to give up their idolatry. Soon after this, Theodosius the Younger made a law enjoining the destruction of all heathen temples in default of their being turned into Christian churches. In the 10th century Hermon became a center of the Druse religion when its founder retired there from Egypt, but we have no record of their ever having worshiped on the summit of Mount Hermon.

During the summer of 1934, Dr. J. Stewart Crawford and the present writer led a small expedition in which we studied the ancient Baal shrines surrounding Mount Hermon. We located many ruined shrines, and in each case they were so oriented that, when officiating at the altar, the priests faced the chief Baal sanctuary, or *Quibla,* on the highest of the three peaks of Hermon. We then ascended the mountain and found the ruined temple of Baal, constructed of Herodian masonry, which dated its construction just previous to and during the early Christian era. In a low place near the northwest corner of the temple, we dug up literally loads of ashes and burnt bone which had been dumped there as the refuse from the sacrifices of the Baal temple, which was in full use while Jesus Christ was transfigured on the summit to the south.

CHAPTER **27**

Damascus,
"Pearl of the East"

Damascus, the paradise of the Arab world, and the "Pearl of the East," lies on the Plain of Damascus (known as Al-Ghutah), two miles east of the foothills of Mount Hermon, and 133 miles northeast of Jerusalem. Modern Damascus, with its surrounding villages, is a city of over 1 million people. Its white buildings, broad domes, and towering minarets shine with an iridescent sheen under the oriental sun. The plain on which it is located is a dark, islandlike mass of green, 2,000 feet above sea level, more than 150 square miles in extent, and 30 miles in circumference. Shaped and nourished by the life-giving waters of the Abana and Pharpar of Scripture, it has been a garden oasis of marvelous beauty and fertility for 5,000 years.[1]

The Abana River, now known as the *Barada,* is a cold, swift stream which springs from the northern foothills of Mount Hermon and the Anti-Lebanon. After hurrying through its tree-lined gorge and over its cascades, it enters the plain just west of the city and soon divides fanlike into seven branches. These in turn divide and subdivide into literally hundreds of canals which carry water everywhere until every garden, orchard, grove, public park and quiet, retired nook is irrigated. Every mosque, khan, hotel, restaurant, home, and court has its fountain or fountains.

Almost any place you go in Damascus you will see a stream of running water or hear a gurgling fountain—even in the restaurants and dining rooms where you eat. Orchards, gardens, groves, meadows, and plantations about the city and on the nearby plain receive an abundance of water for irrigation, after which the remains of the Abana flow across a vast meadowland, and at last sink into the desert sands of Lake Atebeh, east of the city.

The Pharpar River, now called the *Awaj,* rises among the eastern foothills of Mount Hermon in three forks which soon merge and flow eastward into the plain some seven miles south of Damascus. After irrigating miles of fields, gardens, and groves of the southern part of the plain, it reforms into two small streams which wind their way into Lake Hijaneh.

Thus the waters of the Abana (Barada) and Pharpar (Awaj), which are so pure, clear, and cool, have given this desert plain its groves of apricot and olive and lime and lemon and orange trees; along with its grape arbors, its date palms, its pomegranates, and its gardens of vegetables and flowers and fruits. It is quite understandable that Naaman, before his healing in the Jordan, regarded these rivers as "better than all the waters of Israel" (2 Kings 15:12).[2]

264   It is little wonder that when seen from afar, the misty white and gold and blue city of Damascus, sitting among all this "gorgeous grove and garden tapestries of purple and green," is

regarded by the Orientals as one of the most beautiful and luxuriant regions in the world. This is especially true when the almonds and plum and apricot orchards are in bloom, and a cloud of pink and white blossoms brood over the oasis. It then appears as a veritable "paradise on earth." When seen at close range, however, it appears more earthy.[3]

Damascus is known for the charm of its winding narrow streets, yet the street called Straight, where Saul of Tarsus received back his sight (Acts 9:11-18), runs in a fairly straight line across the city to the Eastern Gate. It has its long, covered arcade with little windows in the roof, high above the street, dimly lighting the ornate, oriental bazaars and shops below. But it is narrow and can hardly be said to resemble the mile-long 100-foot-wide, arcaded Roman street called Straight which in Paul's day lay 15 feet below the present street level. Here, and in al-Hamidiyah, most famous of the Damascus bazaar streets, you may purchase silks, swords, sandals, saddles, fine oriental rugs, inlaid woodwork, glass and silver ware, brass, copper engravings with gold and silver inlaying. The design may be ancient or traditional, yet it will be the finest of Old World craftmanship. Or you may purchase your trophy in a factory shop where the ancient art of brass and copper engraving, and gold and silver inlaying is completed before your eyes. In the produce market there is almost every kind of fruits, vegetables, and nuts that grow, and they are almost all produced locally. Here is a city that comes as near to being self-sustaining as any city on the face of the earth.[4]

In the very center of Damascus stands the famous *Grand Mosque*, one of the most interesting buildings of the Near East. It has been in turn a heathen temple, a Christian church, and a Mohammedan mosque. Now it is the fourth most holy sanctuary of Islam. The building is 429 feet long and 125 feet wide, has a spacious court, and is surmounted by three lofty towers and a dome 50 feet in diameter and 120 feet high. Its gorgeous interior is very impressive with its many arched colonnades, richly colored mosaics, ornate carvings, and its thousands of waxed candles. The marble floors are covered with expensive carpets and small prayer rugs, some of which are beautiful while others are quite ordinary. In worshiping here, the people kneel wher-everly they wish. The imam, or leader of the mosque, raises his face to heaven and cries, *"Allahu akbar"* ("God is great"), and 1,000 voices echo the affirmation, "God is great."[5]

In the courtyard is the tomb of Saladin, which bears the inscription: "O God, receive this soul, and open to him the doors of paradise, that last conquest for which he hoped."

One of the three minarets towering above this mosque is the minaret of Jesus, who, it is said, will descend upon this min-aret, and with Mohammed and John, judge the world at the last day. Over one of the portals of the Great Mosque, (once a Chris-tian cathedral), may still be seen the significant, prophetic words: "Thy kingdom, O Christ, is an everlasting kingdom, and thy dominion endureth to all generations."[6]

CHAPTER 28

The Land of Bashan

Bashan, "the Land of Giants," has from the earliest times had something of mystery and of "strange wild interest" connected with it. It was known for its oaks, its fruits, its sheep, its cattle, its giants, its rich men and their pampered wives. The oaks of Bashan were used by the Phoenicians of Tyre in building their ships in early Bible times, while the rams and "bulls of Bashan" were sought for as the sires of the choice herds throughout the Middle East. The vine and fig flourished here in luxuriant fashion in the days of Bashan's glory as the

267

winter and spring streams irrigated and enriched the slopes and filled the great cisterns and reservoirs in every city and in the countryside.

The whole country was praised by the Hebrew poet-prophets for the strength and grandeur of its oaks, the beauty of its mountain scenery, the unrivaled luxuriance of its pastures, the fertility of its wide-spreading plains, and the excellence of its cattle (Ps. 68:15; Jer. 50:19; Ezek. 27:6; Mic. 7:14).

Bashan is that broad upland *east* of the Sea of Galilee and the Lake Huleh Basin. Its southern boundary line is formed by the deep gorge of the river Yarmuk, and it extends to the foothills of Mount Hermon on the north. Eastwards, it extends to *Selkhad* in the Druze Mountains. Its elevation ranges between 1,600 and 3,000 feet above sea level.

The land of Bashan is divided into four fairly well defined districts, each having a description peculiar to itself. These districts are: *Jedur, Golan,* the *Hauran,* and *El Leja.* El Leja is so unusual that we will describe it separately.

Jedur extends from the foothills of Mount Hermon and the Pharpar River southward to the latitude of the northern end of Lake Huleh area, and eastward to the Hauran.

The district is thought to have derived its name from Jetur, one of the 12 sons of Ishmael, whose descendants appear to have inhabited that region. During the period of the monarchy of Israel, King David married Maachah, the daughter of Talmai, king of Geshur (Jedur), of whom Absalom was born. It was to Geshur that Absalom fled and remained seven years following the slaying of his brother Amnon. In Greek and Roman times this district was called Iturea (2 Sam. 13:37-39).

Owing to its high elevation and rough terrain, the northern portion is often covered with snow in the winter, which melts and provides moisture for pastures in spring and summer. In the south it spreads out into a broad plain and is a rich pastoral region where many camels, cattle, sheep, and donkeys feed most of the year. There are ruins of 30 or more ancient towns and deserted villages. Less than a dozen are inhabited.

Golan district takes its name from the city of Golan, one of the three "cities of refuge" east of the Jordan (Deut. 4:43). Researches have not found the certain location of that city, but the district of Golan is that broad strip of rich plateau in the central and western portion of Bashan. The western border is made up of the rugged hills and narrow, fertile valleys overlooking the lower Huleh Basin, and the Sea of Galilee. These hills of conflict have been widely publicized in recent years as the *Golan Heights,* where Syria and Israel are occasionally in conflict. In elevation it rises northward by a series of terraces 1,000 to 3,000 feet above sea level, and its plains stretch eastward to *Nahar Allan.*

The topography of Golan, in general, is made up of wide stretches of lava, sandy plains, grazing lands, and black basalt twisted into fantastic shapes and rimmed with limestone. There are some conelike peaks of extinct volcanoes, and a few oak trees grow here and there. The soil is rich, and flourishing wheatfields cover most of the plain. Olives grow well in the hollows, and camels, cattle, and sheep thrive throughout the region.

The many ruined towns and villages found in the district indicate that it was once thickly populated. One of these largest ruins was Golan itself—a strong fortress for defense and a welcome refuge for the oppressed.

It was down the western slopes of Golan's high tableland that demons, expelled by Jesus from the poor man, chased the herd of swine into the Sea of Galilee. It was on the grassy slopes of Golan's lower plains near the sea that the multitudes were twice miraculously fed by the Master. *Kunetra* is now the largest city of this district. A number of new Jewish colonies have recently been located here.

The Hauran, or "hollow," is the name given to the great, all but treeless area between Golan and the Leja, and southeastward to the Jebel Druse Range. The south central and southern portions of Bashan deepen slightly, in basinlike fashion, with the curving downward of the Yarmuk valley. It was called *Auranitis* by the Greeks, and is a great plain about 50 miles long and 20 miles broad in its central area; and about 50 miles wide in the south where it begins northwest of Edrei and extends eastward to Selkhad in the Druze Mountains.

The surface of the district forms a prairielike plain of rich, red soil, broken in a few places by shallow watercourses, and an occasional outcropping of basalt. Springs are rare in the Hauran, but cisterns of enormous dimensions are seen in every village. Where springs are found, there are aqueducts to direct the water to the cities. Most of the oaks of Bashan, for which the district was once famous, have long since perished, but "the bulls of Bashan" and "rams of Bashan" are easily recalled in the herds of cattle and flocks of sheep which graze in the lush grass which grows in the unplowed portions of the plain.

The great plain owes its extraordinary fertility to the fact that its soil is composed of disintegrated lava, which makes it some of the richest of the whole country. Selah Merrill says, "Hauran is like the richest prairie of the west. . . . The natural wealth of the soil here is a constant surprise to me. I have seen men on this plain turning furrows which are nearly one mile in length, and as straight as one could draw a line. The finest wheat in all Syria comes from these old plains of Bashan."[1] Wheat is now the chief crop, and it often yields 80-fold, and barley is said to yield 100-fold. The semitransparent "hard wheat" is very highly valued, and during the season thousands of camel loads of grain are exported to other sections of the country.[2]

The basaltic stones of the district of the Hauran are some of the hardest and best in Near Eastern countries and are ideal for the forming of handmills for the grinding of grain. A handmill is usually from 18 to 24 inches in diameter and is made up of an "upper" and "nether millstone." The top of the "nether millstone" is slightly convex, and the lower portion of the "upper" stone—called "the rider" or "chariot"—is formed so as to fit directly onto the convex or dome-shaped top of the "nether" or lower stone. The "nether millstone" is usually formed of a denser or harder kind of stone than the upper one. The basaltic stone, found in such abundance in parts of the Hauran, possesses the extreme hardness and durability necessary for the manufacturing of these stones. Mills made from them are in such great demand that they are transported by camel and mule caravan to various parts of the Near East.

270

There are a number of strange, ancient cities built of black basalt. Some of these old cities have homes, temples, and churches kept so well that they appear ready to be occupied—and have been at intervals through the centuries. The majority of these date from the Graeco-Roman period, but some partly buried cyclopean structures date much farther back—perhaps to the time of King Og. Once the writer sat on an eminent point for a long while watching one of these cities with walls, towers, and gates of stone. All this time no sentry moved on its walls, no one came or went from its gates—the city was completely abandoned.

The habits and state in which the people of Hauran live are much the same as in the days of Abraham and Joshua. Dr. Porter says:

> I could scarcely get over the feeling, as I rode across the plains of Bashan and climbed the wooded hills through the oak forest, and saw the primitive ploughs and yokes of oxen and goads, and heard the old Bible salutations given by every passer-by, and received the urgent invitations to rest and eat at every village and hamlet, and witnessed the killing of the kid or lamb, and the almost incredible dispatch with which it is cooked and served to the guests . . . that I had been somehow spirited away back thousands of years, and set down in the land of Nod, or by the patriarch's tents at Beersheba. Common life in Bashan I found to be a constant enacting of early Bible stories. . . . Away in this old kingdom one meets with nothing in dress, language, or manners, save the stately and instructive simplicity of patriarchal times.[3]

Sheikh Meskin is usually thought of as the present capital of all the Hauran, being the central city and residence of the chief of the sheikhs. Yet *Edrei* (now called Der'a)—famous for its ancient underground city, with streets, complete with shops, houses, and marketplaces—is a busy center. It will ever be thought of as the chief city because of the Battle of Edrei. It pitted Og and Moses against each other. Og was the king of Bashan and a giant—the only one of the big fellows left among the rulers. His kingdom stretched from Mount Hermon in the northwest to Salkhad, high in the Druze Mountains in the southeast. The prosperous twin cities of *Ashtaroth* and *Edrei* he doted on, for

Ashtaroth was his capital and Edrei his far-famed underground fortification with its network of streets and avenues. Og's name inspired fear more than almost any ruler of his time. His reputation and the strength of his cities reached the Israelites. Yet after destroying Sihon of Heshbon, Moses turned and went marching to Bashan—straight toward Edrei.

Giant Og was so confident that he left his almost impregnable city of Edrei and with his army went out on the broad plain to meet Moses to whom the Lord had said, "Fear him not: for I have delivered him into thine hand, and all his people." Just when the battle was in the process of being joined, a strange, wild, confused consternation entered all the ranks of Og. Hornets swarmed in and stung the big soldiers and drove them wildly about in dismay, while Moses' forces "smote him, and his sons," routed his army, pillaged his cities, and carried away his huge iron bedstead to Rabbath-Ammon as a trophy of war (Num. 21:33-35; Deut. 3:11; Josh. 24:12).

Bozrah, 25 miles to the east and somewhat south of Der'a, was the strongest center of Bashan during both the Greek and Roman rule in Syria. It is not known when the city was established, although its fine natural springs would indicate a very ancient date for a city in this location—perhaps as early as, or earlier than, the time of Joshua. One tradition pushes it back to the time of Job. One strong spring, named Gahier, at Bozrah, has above it a sign in Aramaic which says, "This spring was used 2,000 years before Christ." A splendid underground street runs from this spring directly to the old capital building. Considerable Early Bronze I and II band-slip pottery has been found throughout this area, which means that it was inhabited during the early part of the third millennium B.C.—3000 to 2600 B.C.

In pronouncing the doom of cities across the Jordan, the prophet Jeremiah (ca. 590-80 B.C.) seems to mention Bozrah —associating it with *Beth-Gamul* (probably the present Ummal al-Jamual) and Keiroth, which were only a few miles in either direction (Jer. 48:15-24). However, our earliest certain records extant show it as a Greek military center. (The Bozrah of biblical fame was in Edom.)

In A.D. 105, the Romans made Bozrah a colony, and thereafter for many centuries it ranked as one of the most important commercial, political, and religious cities of the Near East. It attained a population of 100,000, and Christianity became its leading religion. At one time it was the seat of an archbishop, to whom 33 bishops were subject. One or more councils were held here, over which Origen presided. There are now 13 Christian church buildings in Bozrah, one of which bears the date of A.D. 512. Others are much older. Two of these are now used as mosques. The population of Bozrah is now estimated at 100,000.

Tradition says that Mohammed, when a young man, visited Bozrah while directing a commercial caravan for Khadijah (who afterwards became his wife). While there he became acquainted with John Boheira, a Christian monk of the Nestorian faith, who not only taught Mohammed of Christianity but, it is said, accompanied him back to Mecca and became his instructor while writing much of the Koran. The traditional home of Boheira is now shown in Bozrah.

Bozrah instituted a new system of reckoning time, dating from the Bostrian era, which commenced A.D. 105. It was used for some time in a large portion of the country east of the Jordan, but gave way to the Christian date.

The castle fortress is of great size and strength. In its basements were immense reservoirs and numerous cisterns—enough to last a garrison, it is said, for 10 years. One reservoir alone is 390 feet square and 15 feet deep. Bozrah was once a great caravan city, from which radiated great highways connecting it with Damascus, Beirut, Amman, and the port city of Acre. One went eastward, straight as an arrow to the Castle of Salkhad, 12 miles away, then on across the desert to Baghdad.

Salkhad, one of the most remarkable cities east of the Jordan, was known in Bible times as "Salcah," and was the farthest east of all the cities of Bashan—"All Bashan unto Salcah" (Josh. 13:11). Located on a graceful, conical hill, 500 feet in elevation, near the very highest and most striking summit in the beautiful Druze Mountains, its fine old castle fortress rises over intervening peaks until the watchman on the wall could on a clear day view scores

(Above) The remote fortress of Salkhad in Bashan, and (below) some of
the ancient dwellings as well as modern structures on the southeastern
slopes of the hill.

of surrounding cities, villages, and distant places—some as much as 40 and 50 miles away.

On the north lay the black basaltic district of El Leja, "the Refuge"; eastward was Philippopolis, built by Emperor Philip, and beyond was the road leading on through the desert to Baghdad. Southward were mountains and plains and ruined cities, and the road that led to Azraq at the head of Wadi Sirhan, a main route into Arabia. To the west an old Roman road led straight to Bozrah; and northwestward, the eye could sweep across the vast plains of Bashan, even to Mount Hermon.

Immediately below the great old fortress of Salkhad, on its eastern and southern slopes, are a large number of ancient dwellings with their massive stone walls, stone roofs, stone doors, and stone windows—some 800 houses, or enough homes for ample accommodation of hundreds of families.

The city was impressive enough in appearance and in its strategic location to gain the attention of the planning commission in Joshua's day, and the present huge towering fortress and massive private dwellings could have, from all appearances, stood there then, but probably the majority of the structures we now see were built later. Nabatean inscriptions indicate that the place was captured by their King Milik in A.D. 17. Numerous inscriptions from Greek and Roman times have been found, and one of Saladin, the great Arab leader of Crusader times.

There were two ancient moats for defense, and through the centuries the city has had an ample water supply, as attested by the large reservoirs on the east side of the castle, and the many cisterns in connection with the ancient stone homes. New homes have been built during the past few decades, and they are constructed of the same black basalt blocks and slabs.

At present some 3,000 to 4,000 people live in Salkhad, most of whom are the tall, stalwart, hardy mountaineers known as Druse. Their origin and the exact nature of their religion is unknown, yet they believe in the unity of God, and that He was manifest in Jesus, Mohammed, and Hakim. Hakim, the sixth Fatimite caliph of Egypt (who lived in the 11th century), proclaimed himself an incarnation of God, but disappeared while walking in the vicinity of Cairo. His followers believe he will return to this earth to reign and propagate his faith. Druzi, one of his most notable missionaries, proclaimed Hakim's tenets with such zeal in Lebanon that his followers came to be called "Druse." Sultan Atratsh, the president of all the Druse of Lebanon, Mount Hermon, southern Syria, and Palestine, lives in the small town of Kraie, eight miles south of Soueida. The Druse have three chapels of worship.

A hundred or more evangelical Christians live in Salkhad. They have their own pastor and hold church services each Sunday. The few Roman Catholics are visited on occasion by a priest who says mass for the group. There are no Moslems in Salkhad, but many Bedouin Arabs live in tents surrounding the city, and have the entire care of the camels, cattle, donkeys, sheep, and goats belonging to the Druse and Christians who live in Salkhad.

When the Druse took possession of this mountain area in 1860, it appeared barren and unproductive. But the tribesmen with infinite pains laid out terraces on the slopes, carried up fertile earth from the valleys below, set out vineyards, and planted mulberry, lime, pomegranate, apricot, fig, and other fruit-bearing trees. They founded a silk industry and made of the area a practical and profitable place to live.

Being on the rim of the desert, Salkhad has long been a marketplace to which Arab tribes come from the desert, bringing for sale horses, donkeys, lambs, hides, and wool. In turn they purchase clothing, saddles, bridles, dried olives, figs, dates, onions, potatoes, and other supplies. Few market scenes are quite so picturesque, and they are much the same as in ancient times.

CHAPTER **29**

El Leja or "The Refuge"

The Leja, which makes up the fourth section of Bashan, is a most unique land. It is a vast 350-square-mile, oval-shaped lava plateau, 22 miles long and 14 miles wide, located some 20 miles south of the city of Damascus. Its elevation is 20 to 40 feet above the surrounding plains, rising up sheer, like a black wall.

Being made up of vast fields of wavy, congealed lava, often twisted into fantastic shapes, with a labyrinth of passages through its volcanic vastness, this area was known as Argob to the Greeks,

Trachonitis to the Romans, and El Leja, "the Refuge," to the Arabs. It is rough, stony, and inaccessible—so wild and out of the way that it is little known to the outside world.

Almost the entire area is made up of a strange basalt lava, so black or dark brown, as to appear more like steel than stone. Like an island, whose irregular edge rises out like a rocky coast, it occasionally sends out long arms of black basalt into the surrounding plains. Through this irregular shoreline there are a few openings into the interior, but for the most part there are no roads except those which have been excavated to the towns within the Leja.

This great, rough, jagged island of basalt has the appearance of a sea when it is in heavy motion beneath a dark, cloudy sky. But its large waves have no white crests of foam—all is of a dull black cast and motionless. In the process of cooling, this lava often cracked and left great layers of black basalt, between which there are countless fissures and chasms which cannot be crossed. In other sections the lava has the appearance of a great, black, rolling prairie, and between the hillocks of lava there are small intervals of surprisingly fertile soil.

At many points in this strange area there are splendid springs of cool water, a few small lakes, and some fields. At strategic places there are ruins of round watchtowers, especially near the ancient roadways. And, most interesting of all, there are ancient cities, towns, and villages. A list of 71 city names was collected by Professor Ewing in 1895. On one city wall you can stand and see as many as 18 to 20 other cities, some of which are as much as three miles in circumference and have massive black walls and heavy square towers. Their gates, including the hinges on which they swing, are made of the same black stone. Within are temples, houses, and marketplaces. All these, too, are made of stone. Their walls, their floors, and their roofs are blocks of well-hewn stone, the latter being formed of slabs, closely joined, and resting on corbels, or supported in the interior of the rooms by means of arches. In most cases, the doors and windows, including the hinges, are intricately carved and show the amazing skill of the architects and artisans.

These are the "Black Cities" of the *Arabian Nights,* which hung so heavy with weirdness and mystery—because of their black massiveness, the absence of men, and the awful silence that filled the sable ruins; and because "there was never a face, nor a flower, nor a flutter of a robe" in the streets, nor a sentry to walk these city walls, nor guard to keep the gate, and no one to live in these impressive homes. Once people lived there and children played in those streets, but now, in most instances, the entire environs are deserted, standing just as the former occupants left them.[1]

In giving the description of one fine old home, Dr. Porter said:

> It seemed to have undergone little change from the time its old master had left it, and yet the thick nitrous crust on the floor showed that it had been deserted for long ages. The walls were perfect, nearly five feet thick, built of large blocks of hewn stones, without lime or cement of any kind. The roof was formed of large slabs of the same black basalt lying as regularly, and jointed as closely as if the workman had only just completed it. They measured twelve feet in length, eighteen inches in breadth, and six inches in thickness. The ends rest on a plain stone cornice, projecting about a foot from each side of the wall. The room was twenty feet long, twelve wide, and ten high. The outer door was a slab of stone four and a half feet high, four wide, and eight inches thick. It hung upon pivots formed of projecting parts of the slab, working in sockets in the lintel and the threshold, and though so massive, I was able to open and shut it with ease. At one end of the room was a small window with a stone shutter. An inner door, also of stone, was of fine workmanship, and not quite so heavy as the other. It admitted us to a room of the same size and appearance as the other. From it a much larger door communicated with a third room, to which there was a descent by a flight of stone steps. This was a spacious hall, equal in width to the two rooms and about twenty-five feet long by twenty wide. A semicircular arch was thrown across it, supporting the stone roof, and a gate so large that camels could pass in and out, opened on the street, the gate being of stone and in its place. Such were the internal arrangements of this strange old mansion. It had only one story; and its simple, massive style of architecture gave evidence of very remote antiquity.[2]

279

Ancient stone door entrance to a castle in the forbidding Leja region

Whence came this vast lava district, these black stone cities, these massively designed homes, this dread silence? Complete and altogether satisfactory answers cannot be given. When the curtain lifts, however, and we get our first general view, this *Argob* ("rocky district") was being wrested away from Og, the last of the great monarchs (Deut. 3:4-6). It was assigned by Moses to the tribe of Manasseh, and was conquered by Jair the son of Manasseh (Deut. 3:13-14), including all 60 of its cities.

El Leja, "the Refuge," is just what the place seems to have been in the beginning of the first century before Christ—a sanctuary for political outcasts, a refuge for the oppressed, and a rendezvous for robbers. Josephus speaks of the place as habitually inhabited by robbers: "The inhabitants of those places lived in a mad way and pillaged the country of the Damascenes. . . . It was not an easy thing to restrain them since this way of robbery had been their usual practice."[3] For whatever purpose they came here, however, they found a ready-built home of stone awaiting them, and a safe retreat in its rocky recesses. They were jealous of strangers, so much so that no guide will to this day take travelers into the area.[4]

Once the Nabateans occupied the district, but with the coming of Rome, in 64 B.C., one Zenodorus ruled the district. When he failed to sufficiently control the lawless element, Augustus Caesar ordered the area given to Herod the Great, who established a garrison of 3,000 Idumeans in Trachonitis to keep the peace.[5]

While Christ was on earth, the Leja prospered, and afterwards for many decades. New buildings such as temples, churches, homes, and theaters were constructed in the older cities. New cities and villages were established until the Arab invasion of A.D. 634-638. Then the curtains were drawn and little more is known until this last century when intrepid explorers like Burckhardt, Porter, Merrill, and Ewing began to tell of this mysterious region.

Inscriptions cut in the indestructible basalt of the Leja (and throughout Bashan) are numerous and in many cases remarkable. A few are in Hebrew, more in Nabataean, some in Aramaic and

Latin, but the majority are in Greek which was the written language used throughout the Roman and Byzantine periods. The majority of the buildings seem to date from 100 B.C. to A.D. 600, but there are other half-covered buildings, along with underground caves and cellars which are much older—perhaps many go back to the time of Moses and Joshua. Excavations are yet to be carried out here.

CHAPTER 30

The Land of Gilead

Gilead, that great upland cattle country, which played such a large part in the lives of so many biblical characters, was located between the Yarmuk River on its north, and the Wadi Heshbon on the south—50 miles from north to south. It had Ammon on its east.

Gilead seems to have always been thought of as *two* regions: the northern half and the southern half. This division was occasioned by its being cut through just a bit south of its center by the main stream of the Jabbok River (now called Zerka, or Blue

River). Each of these regions had its center—its focal point of interest. Those centers were not necessarily the same as at the present, but today they are Ajlun in the north and Es Salt in the south. Each place is built near the top of the highest mountain in its district.

It is a pleasant country with piled-up mountains, spread-out plains, lush valleys, and wadis that run down to the Yarmuk and Jordan. It appealed to the tribes of Gad and Reuben so well that they said to Moses, "The country is a land for cattle, and thy servants have cattle. Wherefore let this land be given unto thy servants for a possession. . . . Our little ones, our flocks, and our cattle shall be there in the cities of Gilead" (see Num. 32:1-22).

The name "Gilead," however, comes from the occasion when Jacob and Laban "made an heap" of stones to seal their covenant, and Jacob called it Gal-haed, the heap of witness, and from this came the name *Gilead.* Then came the "Mizpah," for Laban graciously said, "The Lord watch between me and thee, when we are absent one from another."

Here Jacob took his last farewell of Laban, the father-in-law; and as he went on his way, "the angels of God met him"; and when Jacob saw them, he said, "This is God's host." The place was ever afterward called *Mahanaim.*

On the brink of the Jabbok River one of the angels focused Jacob's attention on his inner self, and his relation to God and man. All night long Jacob wrestled with the angel of God. At the break of day the climax came, and the sun rose on a changed man. No longer was he to be Jacob "the schemer, the trickster," but "Israel"—a prince, who had spiritual power with God and with man (Gen. 32:24-30).

There was a wild grandeur about Gilead, for it was a rugged, fertile country; famed for its plains so well suited for cattle ranges, for its grain, its noble forests of oaks and pine, its olive yards, its grape vineyards, its palms, its glades with oleanders, and its widely sought-for "balm of Gilead." As for its men, there was a
284   hardiness, a dash, a daring, and a dependableness such as one would think of as characterizing the Texas Rangers of the last generation. For example, there was *Jair,* the judge and ruler of

Israel for 22 years, who had 30 sons who rode 30 donkeys and had the oversight of 30 cities. There was *Jepthah,* who was a general, a judge, and a man who made a vow and implicitly trusted God; and *Jehu,* that speedy driver who stamped out Baalism by beginning at the top with Queen Jezebel. And, of course there was *Elijah,* that sun-bronzed, untutored prophet who wore "a girdle of leather about his loins," burned with indignation at religious compromise, challenged the king and the people to a test between Baal and God on Mount Carmel, rode in a chariot of fire as he was translated to heaven in a whirlwind, and appeared with Moses on the Mount of Transfiguration representing that dynamic breed ·of men known as "the prophets of God." O Gilead, what men, under God, thou didst produce!

Gilead has played a historic role as a place of refuge. Being far removed from the central orbit of men who specialized in politics, in religion, and in war, it has opened wide its arms of welcome to individuals, families, and political or religious groups who, in emergencies, needed a place of retreat where they could continue normal life undisturbed by the pressures which had beset them.

Ishbosheth, the son of Saul, took shelter here when he sought to reestablish the rule of his father's house (2 Sam. 2:8).

David found sanctuary here when he was forced to flee from his rebellious son Absalom. And when he arrived at Mahanaim, the people brought him all manner of supplies: beds to sleep on, utensils with which to eat, along with "wheat and barley, and flour, and parched corn, and beans, and lentils, and parched pulse, and honey, and butter, and sheep, and cheese." For, said they, "The people are hungry and weary, and thirsty" (2 Sam. 17:24-29).

It was here in the thick woods that Absalom lost the battle and, when fleeing upon a mule, went "under the thick boughs of a great oak, and his head caught" in the forks of a limb; and Joab "took three darts and thrust them through the heart of Absalom" and slew him. He then "cast him in a great pit in the wood, and piled a very great heap of stones upon him." 285

It was here at Mahanaim that David sat on the tower of the

city gate and heard the tragic news of Absalom's death and took up the sad lament: "O my son Absalom, my son, my son Absalom: would God I had died for thee, O Absalom, my son, my son" (2 Sam. 18:33).

It became a refuge for Jesus when the high authorities of Judaism sought to stone Him because He said, "I am the Son of God" (see John 10:32-42; 11:1-16).

In the beginning of his ministry, John the Baptist wore a camel's hair coat and a leather belt, and "preached repentance in the wilderness of Judea"—on the Judean side of the Jordan River. But the ruling Jews sent priests and Levites from Jerusalem, asking him, "Who are you?" He merely replied that he was but a voice crying in the wilderness. He then moved those enormous mass meetings across the river on the Perean or Gilead side—the territory where Herod Antipas was the ruler. Therefore, John the evangelist says, "These things were done in Bethabara beyond Jordan, where John was preaching" (John 1:28). John had come "in the spirit and power of Elijah," and the major portion of his ministry was near the place where Elijah had been caught up by a whirlwind into heaven.

It was from the Perean or Gilead side that Jesus entered Jordan to be baptized. And after John had finished his rugged ministry, Jesus returned here and spoke as man never spoke. Here He gave the parable of the great supper, the rich man and Lazarus, the Pharisee and the publican, the lost coin, the lost sheep, the prodigal son, and other such illustrations.

It was here that they "brought young children to [Jesus], that he should touch them . . . And he took them up in his arms, put his hands upon them, and blessed them" (Mark 10:13, 16). And it was here that the rich young man ran and kneeled to him and said, "Good Master, what good thing shall I do, that I may have eternal life?" Jesus gave him his answer but "he went away sorrowful," not willing to pay the price. Jesus then said to His disciples, "How hard is it for them that trust in riches to enter into the kingdom of God!" (cf. Matt. 19:16-23; Mark 10:17-24). So the rich young man did not follow Jesus, but thousands of others did, and the countries of Gilead and Bashan became a great stronghold for Christianity, as attested by church history and archaeology. Most of the cities had one or more Christian churches. Eight have been found standing bold among the ruins of Beth Gemal, and 13 in the city of Bazra.

Gilead had many cities, towns, and villages—Arab, Greek, Roman, Israelite—and stone-circled tenting places of shepherds of an even earlier time. The names of many of these towns we know, and somewhat of the roles they played in making the histories of their day. Yet the uncertainty with regard to so many of their sites make it difficult to be altogether certain about their positions on the map, or to discuss them with exactness. A few of the more famous cities have, with some degree of certainty, been located:

Gadara (now called *Um Quais*) was the capital of "the country of the Gadarenes," and at one time the capital of Perea. It was located three miles south of the Yarmuk, and five miles east of the Jordan River. Its ruins are over two miles in circuit, through which there runs a well-paved Roman street with the bases of colonnades on either side, and ruts worn by chariot wheels in the center. The rich ornamental work in marble, granite, and basalt scattered over the mound, along with the remains of an amphitheater, a theater, a marketplace, and a Christian cathedral, indicate the existence of a city of great wealth and magnificence.

People have often been left to wonder when they read authorities who said, "In the immediate vicinity of this town, the scene of the healing of the fierce demoniac and the destruction of the herd of swine took place" (cf. Matt. 8:28; Luke 8:26). On studying this section of the country more carefully, however, one discovers Gadara to be a member of the Decapolis and the capital of "the country of the Gadarenes." In the north its territory extended beyond the Yarmuk River to the east side of the Sea of Galilee. It was here that the miracle took place—some eight miles north of the city proper where a small mountain ridge rises up in "the country of the Gadarenes, which is over against Galilee" (Luke 8:26).

Jabesh-gilead, is identified with the twin sites of *Tell el-Maqbereh* and *Tell Abu Kharaz,* located on a hilltop overlooking the Wadi Yabis (River Jabesh) just across the Jordan Valley east of Beth-Shan.

This is the city which an Israelitish army of 12,000 attacked because they would not join their brethren in the war against Benjamin, and took maidens to become wives of the Benjamite men who were left without companions (Judg. 21:8-15). Afterwards Saul went to the rescue of Jabesh-Gilead with an army of 330,000 when the men of the place were about to lose their right eyes in a capitulation to the Ammonites (1 Sam. 11:1-11). The men of Jabesh-gilead afterwards showed their gratitude for King Saul's timely relief by traveling all night and taking down the bodies of the king and his sons from the walls of Beth-Shan, where they had been placed by the Philistines after the fatal battle of Gilboa.

It is probable that Jabesh-gilead was the home of the prophet Elijah.[1]

Abel-Meholah, the home of the prophet Elisha, who succeeded Elijah, has been identified with *Tell el-Maqlub,* on the river Jabesh, some five miles east of Jabesh-gilead. If these identifications are correct, then Elijah and Elisha would likely have known each other for years before either of them became prophets.

Ramoth-gilead, one of the six cities of refuge, has been identified with *Tell er-Rumeith,* located some 10 miles southwest of Edrei. Here Jehu, the swift charioteer, was anointed to be king. He rid Israel of the idolatrous Queen Jezebel and gathered in baskets the heads of 70 of the king's sons.

Ahab came here to fight against Ben-Hadad and to recapture Ramoth-gilead, but, in harmony with the prophecy of Micaiah, "a certain man drew a bow at a venture" and smote Ahab so that the blood ran down in the chariot, and the king died with the going down of the sun. They carried him to Samaria where they removed his body, washed the bloody chariot, whereupon "the dogs licked the blood of Ahab" in keeping with Elijah's prophecy (1 Kings 22:37-38).

288   **Pella** is identified with *Tabaqat Fahil,* two miles north of Jabesh-gilead. It is now a great fortress mound, high up in the hills, situated like an eagle's nest on a ledge overlooking the Jor-

dan Valley. "It occupies a unique position with regard to the Jordan Valley, being neither a part of it nor completely separated from it." Pella abounds in clear springs "and a track winds past it, once good enough to carry chariot traffic and donkey trains. . . . It was inevitable that men should settle by this gathering of waters and build houses and temples and strong fortifications."[2]

It was to Pella that the Christians of Jerusalem withdrew just before the destruction of the city by Titus in A.D. 70. The place became a great Christian center and prospered until it was destroyed by the Saracens during the Crusades.

Peniel, or Penuel, is located on the banks of the Jabbok at a place now called *Tell edh-Dhahab* (the "Hill of Gold"). The river bends around the base of this mound on three sides, and in flood season cuts it off altogether from the mainland as if to say, "This is a particularly important place, not to be associated with the ordinary, mundane world." Dr. Glueck says, "My Arab companions were very loath to have me sleep there alone, but would on no condition accompany me there to spend the night. They made their camp at the foot of the hill, warning me that if I persisted in my intention to sleep on top of it, a spirit (jinni) would seize me during the night, and that if indeed I did survive the ordeal I would wake up in the morning *majnun,* that is, possessed by the spirit. But here Jacob had wrestled during the night, . . . being left alone until the break of dawn. And here I would sleep or sit out the night, with the living past breathing its vivid tale into my ears. What would happen to me before I crossed the Jordan again?"[3]

Succoth, to which Jacob journeyed after leaving Esau, and where he "built him a house, and made booths for his cattle," is identified with the imposing ancient mound known as *Tell Deir'alla.* It is in a very rich section, located in the edge of the Jordan Valley just where the Jabbok River enters the valley. A pleasant place for Jacob and his family to live for a while after his inner change and his forgiveness by Esau.[4]

Jerash (or Gerasa), one of the 10 cities of the Decapolis which sprang up across the Jordan after the conquest of Alexander, was located in the heart of the mountains of Gilead, on

the west banks of one of the northern tributaries of the Jabbok. Its ruins, which include a columned street that runs the city's length, arches, gateways, massive walls, theaters, amphitheaters, churches, a temple, a forum, and villas that rise like a dream attest that it is probably the most perfect Roman city left above ground. Destruction came first from the Persians, then the Arabs, then earthquakes. There is nothing visible now that dates before the Christian era. The ruins of Jerash were rediscovered to the west by the German traveler Seetzen in 1806, and since that time the numbers of visitors, scholars, and travelers have steadily increased.[5]

Ajlun, 20 miles north of Jerash, is not a known biblical site, but has a very fine specimen of a medieval Arab castle which the natives call *Kalat al Rabadh.* It is located on a prominence of north Gilead's highest mountain range—a rocky cliff 3,400 feet above sea level, and overlooking the Jordan Valley 4,300 feet below. Its lofty position made it an ideal *beacon station* and *pigeon post* by which news could be sent along a line of message stations extending from Egypt to the Euphrates.

The castle was built in 1184-85 by Azz al Din Ausama, a cousin of Saladin. Its chief purpose was to hold in check the Christian barons of Belvoir Castle (across the Jordan), and Karak Castle (east of the Dead Sea), and to maintain communications with Damascus. The nearby town of Ajlun evidently grew up with the castle, for it was spoken of in 1300 by Dimisishqi, an Arab writer, who found "fruits of all kinds and provisions in plenty." In 1355, Ibn Batuta described it as "a fine town with good markets and a strong castle; a stream runs through the town and its waters are sweet and good."[6]

Jebel Osha (the "mountain of Hoshea") is the most prominent peak of the Gilead mountain range. It is on the southern side of the Jabbok River, and rises 3,597 feet above sea level—one of the highest mountains in Palestine, aside from Mount Hermon. Far up toward the peak is the traditional tomb of the prophet Hosea which the Arab guides show with great respect and veneration.

Standing on top of this peak, one enjoys a commanding view

The Roman theater at Jerash, one of the best preserved of all ancient Roman cities.

all the way from Mount Hermon to the south end of the Dead Sea. The view is so astounding that some verily believed it to be "the mountain . . . over against Jericho," from which Moses viewed the Promised Land (Deut. 34:1-3). A more natural vantage point from which to view the land could not be found east of the Jordan. Yet the topography hardly fits the place where God took Moses for his last earthly look.

Es Salt, with its white buildings and contented people, rises tier upon tier on its hill terraces at the southern base of Mount Osha. It is one of the most highly populated centers of Gilead, and is famous for its olives, figs, apricots, pomegranates, and its enormous crops of choice grapes and raisins which it furnishes for the markets of the Middle East. Native life is seen here at its best, especially on market days.

The "balm of Gilead" is proverbial with the land of Gilead. The Ishmaelites, to whom Joseph was sold, came from Gilead "with their camels bearing spicery and balm and myrrh" (Gen. 37:25). This balm, with its wonderful medicinal properties, was one of the "choice fruits of the land" which Jacob sent down to Egypt as a present to Joseph, who was then the governor of the land of the Pharaohs (Gen. 43:11).

The tree from which came the balm was only a small evergreen with scant foliage and small white blossoms.[7] Its value was in the balsam resin or juice which was drained out through a cut in the bark or obtained from the reddish black berries which, when thoroughly ripe, take the form of a nut with a pulpy case and fragrant yellow seed. An inferior quality of balsam is also obtained from the young wood by a bruising and boiling process. The rare and almost priceless balm was mixed with other ingredients and used internally as a medicine and externally for wounds and certain skin eruptions. It is now used in perfumery. The tree seems to have had its original home on the east coast of Africa, yet it has been found in a few other places, especially at Mecca.

292   There is a tradition that the queen of Sheba presented some of the young balm trees to King Solomon, who planted them at Jericho and En-Gedi. Cleopatra sent to Jericho for some of the

plants for her garden at Heliopolis. Twice this balm tree was paraded in the triumphal processions at Rome: once in 65 B.C. when Pompey returned from his trip to the East and his conquest of Judea, and a second time after the destruction of Jerusalem by Titus in A.D. 70, when the balm tree was taken together with the golden candlestick and the other treasures of the Temple.[8]

Jeremiah said, "For the hurt of the daughter of my people am I hurt: I mourn; dismay hath taken hold on me. Is there no balm in Gilead; is there no physician there? Why then is not the health of the daughter of my people recovered?" (Jer. 8:21-22). The balm tree has been carefully sought for throughout modern Gilead, but none has been found there.

CHAPTER **31**

The Land of Ammon

The Ammonites, descendants
of *Ben-Ammi,* the son of Lot, by conquest displaced the southern
branch of the ancient race of giants called Zamzummims—"The
Lord destroyed them; and they succeeded them, and dwelt in
their stead" (Deut. 2:20). This involved the territory from the
Arnon to the Jabbok, and from the Jordan River eastward into the
294   edge of the Arabian desert.

As their "royal city" and chief trading center, the Ammonites
built or rebuilt Rabbath-Ammon, which came to be called "the

City of Waters," for it had a strong living spring, and was located on a conspicuous "Citadel Hill" in a narrow valley through which ran the main south-north tributary of the river Jabbok (Wadi Zerka). Its walls were high, its gates secure, and its markets enticing to desert men and managers of caravans who came from the desert and the south.

Later they were dispossessed of the western part of their territory by Sihon, king of the Amorites. Then during the Israelite conquest, Moses destroyed Sihon and took all his territory, but heard the word of the Lord, saying, "When thou comest near over against the children of Ammon, distress them not nor meddle with them: for I will not give thee of the land of the children of Ammon any possession; because I have given it unto the children of Lot for a possession" (Deut. 2:19).

The Ammonite kingdom, in its reduced form, was located around the headwaters of the Jabbok. Its exact boundary lines are somewhat uncertain, yet the western boundary line ran to the west of, or with, the south-north tributary of the Jabbok which arose near Rabbath-Ammon and flowed northward to the main

295

A Roman fort at Azrak, a military outpost of the kingdom of Jordan east-west Jabbok (Josh. 12:2). Eastward it extended far out into the edge of the Arabian desert, including the unusual oasis town of *Azrak*, 60 miles southeast of Amman, where Lawrence of Arabia had his headquarters during the latter part of the Arab war against the Turks.[1]

Thus, the kingdom of the Ammonites was only moderately extensive, yet it was prosperous and pleasant—an ideal range for vast herds of camels, cattle, donkeys, sheep, and goats. Gazelle, bustard, partridge, and other game were in plentiful supply, and there were vast stretches of land along the various tributaries of the river Jabbok for gardens, grains, and olive groves.

The Ammonites might have exploited all these resources and been a contented and happy people, but they were not. They lost the territory to Sihon, and later Moses took it from him. They always looked on it as "our land" and blamed their neighbors for being in possession of what they themselves had lost to Sihon. This inordinate claim fed a hostile attitude and prompted them to go to war many times in the coming generations. Always they lost, grew steadily weaker, and settled back with less incentive.

In the time of Jephthah, the Ammonites made war against Gilead with the intent of regaining a great part of the country which had formerly been theirs before the Amorites under Sihon had possessed it. But Jephthah sent messengers to the king of Ammon, assuring them that Gilead had not taken their lands from them, and urged them to be content with what Chemosh, their god, had given them to possess. Instead they resisted all overtures of peace and marched their army against Gilead. The "Spirit of the Lord came upon Jephthah, he vowed a vow unto the Lord," and mightily led the Gileadites as they defeated the Ammonites and forced them back east of the encircling Jabbok (Judg. 11:1-33).

In the beginning of Saul's reign, Nahash, king of the Ammonites, attacked Jabesh-gilead, forcing it to capitulate; but he would accept no conditions other than that the inhabitants submit to having every man's right eye plucked out. This would disqualify them as soldiers and "lay it for a reproach upon all Isreal." The leaders at Jabesh asked for seven days in which to consider the matter. Before those seven days were up, Saul gathered his forces and came with an army of 330,000 and delivered the people from the intended barbarity and scattered the Ammonite army "so that two of them were not left together" (1 Sam. 11: 1-11).

On coming to the throne, David lived on friendly terms with Nahash, king of Ammon, and endeavored to continue the friendship with Hanun, Nahash's son and successor. But Hanun grossly insulted David's messengers when he "shaved off the one half of their beards, and cut off their garments in the middle . . . and sent them away" in shame and disgrace as though they had been spies. The next spring the Ammonites attacked, but David's army under Joab laid siege to Rabbath-Ammon, took over their water supply, and forced their capitulation. It was during this siege engagement that David suffered the shameful spiritual downfall with Bath-sheba. When unable to longer conceal it, he had Uriah, her husband, sent to "the forefront of the hottest battle," where he lost his life under the very walls of Rabbath-Ammon (2 Sam. 11:1-21).

Bands of the Ammonites joined Nebuchadnezzar in the destruction of Jerusalem in 586 B.C., and afterward Baalis, king of Ammon, sent Ismael, an Ammonite, to assassinate Gedaliah, the new governor of Judea appointed by Nebuchadnezzar (Jer. 40: 14—41:10). Judas Maccabaeus broke almost the last semblance of Ammonite power in fulfillment of Ezekiel's prophecy, as the Nabataeans overran their country. It is not known what became of King Og's iron bedstead (size 6 by 13 feet)—the first "king-size" bed of which we have a record—but the Ammonites became extinct as a nation and were gradually blended with the Arabs.

Rabbath-Ammon was rebuilt in grand style by Ptolemy Philadelphus of Egypt, in the third century B.C., and named Philadelphia. It became one of the cities of the Decapolis (the 10 important Greek cities, mostly east of the Jordan which were linked together for defense, trade, and culture). During early Christian times it was a near-desert outpost of the Roman Empire. Its remains of antiquity are now represented by the well-pre-

Amman, Jordan's capital city, has many beautiful modern buildings but also this well-preserved Roman theater.

served ruins of the Graeco-Roman theater in the valley east of the acropolis which was cut in the hillside and built to accommodate about 4,000 people.

Amman, now the modern capital city of the kingdom of Jordan, was only a small village when it became capital of Transjordan in 1921; now a third of a million people live here. It retains its splendid springs of water and is an important marketplace. It has interesting ancient ruins, but also has many beautiful modern buildings and is the home of King Hussein, ruler of the kingdom of Jordan. Yet it is not old Rabbath-Ammon, but Philadelphia, the Graeco-Roman city among whose prostrate ruins you grope your way.

Zerka, built on the site of the Roman town of Gadda, is about 15 miles northwest of Amman. Traces of an ancient roadway have been found coming from Amman through Zerka. In recent years the city has had a rapid growth.

The country of Jordan in general, however, is unlike most

other countries on the face of the earth. In most areas it appears sterile, yet it is amazingly fruitful; in appearance it is inhospitably wild, yet it is one of the quietest, most homelike of lands. The way of life is much as it was in ancient times, in color, in content, and in dress. No Jews live here, only Arabs and Carisians, with a sprinkling here and there of Crusader blood cropping out in those native to the land. Here the Bedouin, the camel, the horse, the donkey, cattle of all kinds, and wildlife in great variety are all at home. Here the Arab has a country and an atmosphere in a setting to his tastes, emotions, and manner of life. Yet hard by is Israel with its metropolitan, agricultural, and industrial stride.

This, then, has long been Jordan. Now a new nation with a solid future is being built upon the ancient heritage of an old country—a new irrigation system, increased agriculture and industry. Of that future, His Majesty King Hussein has said:

> We have given ourselves the goal of economic self-sufficiency. That is a difficult assignment. I am well aware. But with the determination that inspires our people, we will achieve it.
>
> Along with economic independence, we have parallel goals in health, education, and social welfare. While it will take time to reach complete maturity in these areas, steady progress is being made with each passing year. Within a decade I am confident that Jordan will have become with the help of God, a strong, resourceful, and still reverent nation.

CHAPTER **32**

The Land of Moab

The mention of *Moab* stimulates thoughts of Moses, Elimelech, Naomi, and Ruth; and of David, who in time of trouble, trusted his aged parents to the king of Moab (1 Sam. 22:3-4). Also, it starts visions of camel trains, Bedouin tents; of flowing robes and white turbans, and everything that is usually supposed to make up a patriarchal retinue.

300

As a land primitive in its ways, it was famous for its upland pasturelands, its vineyards, its grainfields, its threshing floors, its wildlife, its medicinal hot springs, its inaccessible mountains, and its deep, dark chasms through which its streams rushed to the Dead Sea. It was sufficiently prominent to be mentioned 158 times in the Old Testament.

Moab lay east of the Dead Sea, with boundary lines shifting with the growth of its people, and with the ebb and flow of conquest. Yet during its major history it began in the south with the brook Zered (Wadi Hesa), and extended northward to the river Heshbon. Its known history is mainly related to Israel, to the Nabataeans, and to the Crusades.

Moab is, for the most part, a broad, almost treeless plateau, averaging some 3,000 feet above the sea level and 4,300 feet above the Dead Sea. The crest or ridge is formed by the Abirim mountain wall which towers above the Dead Sea, then gently slopes away eastward to the Arabian desert. This wall-like mountain range is cleft almost to its base by the two deep, narrow gorges of the Callirrhoe *(Wadi Zerka Ma'in)* and the river Arnon *(Wadi Mujib)*. *Wadi Heidan* cuts diagonally through central Moab and joins the Arnon near its mouth, and *Wadi Kerak* in the south augments its drainage. The streams in each of these impassable gorges flow westward into the Dead Sea.[1]

The Moab Plateau is higher than the Judean hills and receives more or less reliable winter rainfall, which makes grain, fruit, farming, and grazing superior to many other sections. In the Book of Ruth the family of Naomi migrated from Bethlehem to Moab, which had not suffered from the drought as much as Judea. On going to Bethlehem, Ruth was experienced in working in the harvest fields. Moab's uplands were so famous for their variety of wild game, for cattle, and for the countless thousands of sheep which grazed its ranges, that even Mesha, the king of Moab, "was a sheepmaster," and at one time rendered an annual tribute to Israel of "an hundred thousand lambs, and an hundred thousand rams with wool" (2 Kings 3:4).

The Plains of Moab, which merge with the southern plain of Gilead, lie below sea level and are about 15 miles in length and 8 in breadth. They are now known as "the Meadow of the Aca-

301

cias." Four streams traverse the plain, and a number of towns and villages were there in biblical times. "And they [the Israelites] pitched by Jordan, from Beth-jesimoth even unto Abel-shittim in the plains of Moab" (Num. 33:49).

The Moabites called for help from the armies of the Amalekites, yet fear prevailed to the extent that Balak, king of Moab, attempted to have the prophet Baalim to curse the Bene-Israel encamped below in the Plains of Moab. But alas, for while the savory odors ascended from the sacrifices on the seven rock-hewn altars on Moab's mountain heights, the venerable old prophet broke forth in those exceedingly significant words:

> How shall I curse, whom God hath not cursed? or how shall I defy, whom the Lord hath not defied? For from the top of the rocks I see him, and from the hills I behold him: lo, the people shall dwell alone, and shall not be reckoned among the nations. Who can count the dust of Jacob, and the number of the fourth part of Israel? Let me die the death of the righteous, and let my last end be like his! . . . How goodly are thy tents, O Jacob, and thy tabernacles, O Israel! *(Num. 23:8-10; 24:5).*

While encamped here on this plain, Moses, the man of God who had marvelously led them for 40 years, heard God calling time on him. With a brave heart the mighty leader committed the people to God and to Joshua, "made an end of writing the words of this law in a book," gave his valedictory address, then, bidding farewell to the people, "went up from the plains of Moab unto the mountain of Nebo, to the top of Pisgah, that is over against Jericho." There the Lord showed him the Promised Land across the Jordan but told him, "Thou shalt not go over thither." So, with this glorious vision fresh in mind, "Moses the servant of the Lord died there in the land of Moab, according to the word of the Lord," and the Lord "buried him in a valley in the land of Moab, over against Beth-peor: but no man knoweth of his sepulchre unto this day" (Deut. 34:1-6).

This was the bravest warrior
That ever buckled sword;
This was the most gifted poet
That ever breathed a word;

And never earth's philosopher
Traced with his golden pen
On deathless page, truths half so sage
As he wrote down for men.

No intelligent clue has been advanced as to which of the nearby deep, wild gorges might be graced by Moses' mortal remains. However, tradition and the most careful of researches have persisted in pointing out a nearby, round mountaintop as being Pisgah, a prominent point on Mount Nebo, as the place from which he obtained his last view. It juts westward from the Moab Plateau, 3,930 feet above the Dead Sea, and commands a most unusual view of the Jordan Valley, the Dead Sea, and the Judean mountains. Even Bethlehem and the towers on the Mount of Olives may be seen on a clear day. Nearby are the excavated ruins of a small church and monastery, the accounts of which may be traced by pilgrim reports as far back as A.D. 394.

In a valley just to the northeast are a group of very fine springs, long known as *Ain Musa* (Moses' Springs). And, four miles east is Heshbon, now called Hasban, the capital of the Amorite king, Sihon, who lost it to Israel. Later it came into the possession of the Moabites.

Five miles south is the city of Madeba, famous as the traditional home of Ruth, and for its large mosaic pictorial map, the oldest original map known. Some think it to be a fitting memorial to Moses' last view of the Promised Land. In ancient times Madeba was a well-known center for northern Moab (Num. 21:30; Josh. 13:16), and it flourished during the early Christina centuries. In more modern times, however, Madeba became only a city mound "on the plain of Madeba." Albeit, the mound contained the ruins of many buildings, including 12 Christian churches.

In 1880, a group of Christians from Kerak founded a new colony about the mound. The Latins and others followed, each building its place of Christian worship. In 1884 the Greek Orthodox people chose for their church site the ruins of an old basilica to the northwest of the mound. While cleaning the foundations, 303

A large, mosaic pictorial map at Madeba, possibly the oldest original map known.

they discovered a most interesting mosaic pavement comprising the entire floor of the ancient Byzantine church.

A Greek monk living east of the Jordan wrote a letter to the Greek patriarch of Jerusalem, telling him of the mosaic pavement covered with names of cities such as Jerusalem, Gaza, Neapolis, etc. Patriarch Nicodemus made no reply. Six years later, after he was exiled, the new patriarch found the monk's letter and sent a master mason with orders to save the mosaic for the new church, if the mosaic seemed worthwhile.

In building on the foundation of the ancient church, the master mason drove a pilaster through the map, and damaged or destroyed other parts of it—all with the trivial explanation that the mosaic did not possess the importance which had been attributed to it. In January of 1897, Father Cleopas, librarian of the Greek Patriarchate, went to Madeba and made notes and sketches of the 65- by 26-foot mosaic map with its "amazingly

304

exact and impressive rendering of landscape features" such as hills, rocks, trees, watercourses, flora, fauna, etc., along with villages, towns, and cities of the Holy Land—all based on the invaluable list of place-names compiled earlier by Eusebius in his *Onomastikon.*

What a surprise and a delight was the news to the outside world! Draftsmen, photographers, and archaeologists hastened to rescue the mosaic. Now thousands journey to Madeba to view the remnant of the map in deep admiration, yet they wonder why such an invaluable geographic and historic treasure should not have been preserved complete.

From Madeba a road runs southwest to the hot springs of *Callirrhoe,* within the wild gorge of the *Wadi Zerka Ma'in,* known in ancient times as "the Valley of God," by Beth-peor, where the body of Moses was said to have been buried. All along its seven miles to the Dead Sea, this deep, narrow gorge is bordered by palm trees and cane, and passes by peaks and through walls of sandstone, limestone, and black basalt. In many places they are almost perpendicular, and as much as 1,000 to 1,700 feet high.

The 8 or 10 springs of Callirrhoe burst from the north cliffs of sandstone and limestone and dash down the sulphur-deposited precipice in numerous cascades and rapids to join the main stream of cool water which flows along the bed of the chasm. The two principal springs are about a half a mile apart, and each sends forth a volume of water sufficient to run a mill. The springs vary in temperature, the one farthest west having a temperature of 143° and the other 130°.

Above the springs and some distance to the south, on an almost inaccessible mountaintop, are the ruins of the ancient fortress-castle of *Machaerus,* built by Alexander Jannaeus. It was destroyed by the Roman general Gabinius and rebuilt on a larger scale and fortified with massive walls and towers by Herod the Great. Here lived Herod, at brief intervals, during the latter part of his life, and, as Josephus says, "bathed himself in the warm baths of Callirrhoe" in the vain attempt to cure himself of his loathsome disease.[2]

Sometime after Herod had died, his son, Herod Antipas,

moved south to Machaerus, bringing his new wife, Herodias, and her daughter Salome. John the Baptist was conducting revival meetings and baptizing farther north along the Jordan. Thousands from Judea "and all the region round about Jordan" heard those weighty words "Repent ye: for the kingdom of heaven is at hand," and "were baptized of him in Jordan, confessing their sins" (Matt. 3:2-6). King Herod attended the meetings and became so deeply interested that "he did many things, and heard him gladly," but never qualified for baptism, for John "reproved . . . him for [having] Herodias his brother Philip's wife, and for all the evils which Herod had done" (Mark 6:18-20; Luke 3: 18-20).

For this reason Herodias chalked up a grudge against John and wanted to kill him, "but she could not." However, she had Herod arrest John and put him in prison in the dungeon at Machaerus. On Herod's birthday, when the party was gay with drink, Salome came in and danced to the great delight of Herod and his guests. He was so pleased that he promised her anything she asked, to half his kingdom. At her mother's instigation Salome "came in with haste to the king" and asked that he would give her on a charger the head of John the Baptist. Herod was aghast, yet because of his oath and the presence of his guests, he sent one of his palace guardsmen, who beheaded John in the prison beneath the castle and brought back his head on a broad dish and gave it to Salome, who handed it to her mother.

"Thus," says George Adam Smith, "Moses and John, the first and the last of the prophets, thirteen centuries between them, closed their lives almost on the same spot. Within sight is the scene of the translation of Elijah."[3] The homegoing of three of the greatest men of all time—all near the same area, and each brought here for that purpose. What a land, and what a Providence!

Twelve miles below Callirrhoe is the *Arnon* (Wadi Mojib)— the deepest gorge and largest river on the east side of the Jordan Rift. The channel of this river is never more than 60 to 100 feet wide, but runs through a narrow valley of rich verdure, whose multicolored sandstone cliffs frequently tower 2,000 feet.

Dibon, the capital city of Mesha, king of Moab, is located on the west side of the highway three miles north of the river Arnon, and 13 miles east of the Dead Sea. It was here that the famous stele of Mesha, known as "the Moabite Stone," was discovered by Rev. F. A. Klein in 1868. It is a black basalt slab three feet 10 inches high, two feet in breadth, and 14 inches thick. The inscription is dated about 850 B.C., and consists of 34 lines of alphabetical script which in dialect, style, and content resembles and supplements the account in 2 Kings 3 of Mesha's revolt against Israel's oppression.

The American School of Oriental Research conducted annual excavations here between 1950 and 1956, and discovered many things of interest, among which was "one of the most impressive pieces of ancient city walling to be seen anywhere in Jordan."[4]

Kerak, the biblical city known as Kir of Moab, is perched high on a rocky plateau 4,407 feet above the Dead Sea, 17 miles south of the Arnon. The general character of the country in which it is located is wild and grand, and the city is separated from the surrounding hills by chasmlike ravines from 800 to 1,000 feet deep. An ancient road led from Kerak down to the Dead Sea.

Arranged in triangular form, and measuring a half mile on each of its three sides, the city occupies the entire summit, with a high, well-built wall surrounding the brow of the precipice on every side. The ancient entrances to the city were by four rock-hewn tunnels, two of which are yet preserved. The one on the west is still used, and is approached by a zigzag path along a very steep, rugged slope of some 1,500 feet. When near the top, the path abruptly turns into an 80-yard-long rock tunnel which leads to the gate and into the marketplace. Here, guarding this entrance, is the "castle of Bibars," while behind and above the complex arises the 27-foot-thick walls of the great Castle of Kerak, one of the strongest castles of the Near East. The chapel within the castle is 90 feet long.

This immense castle, and other fortifications as we now know them, were built by the Crusaders about 1131-36, but they were constructed on Roman and Nabataean ruins, and are "on the wreckage of the Moabite fortress."[5]

Many interesting and some tragic events have taken place at Kerak. It was here that Mesha, king of Moab, retired with the remnant of his army when he was being attacked by Israel and Judah (2 Kings 3). In his extreme circumstance, Mesha offered his eldest son as a sacrifice on the wall. Israel and Judah withdrew in horror, and Mesha carved his version of the war, and his praise of Chemosh, on the "Moabite Stone."

The most famous of Kerak's Crusader rulers was Reginald of Chatillon, who married the lady of Kerak and thus became lord of Kerak. He was handsome and venturesome, yet his rashness frequently prejudiced the cause of the Crusades. Eventually he broke the truce between the Moslems and Christians when he intercepted and plundered a rich caravan on its way from Damascus to Mecca. The treasures were seized and many attendants and pilgrims slain.

Saladin, with due regard for the existing treaty, sent a message to the king of Jerusalem, demanding redress for the outrages committed by Reginald. When nothing was done about the matter, Saladin proclaimed *Jihad,* or holy war, which had its climax in the decisive Battle of Hattin, on July 3, 1187, after which Reginald was slain and Kerak passed into Moslem hands.

The houses in Kerak are close-built, and the city is well populated with many people of both Moslem and Christian faiths—even a strong Protestant group.

The view from Kerak westward is sublime. Far below, only a few miles away, lies the deep cleft of the Arabah, and the waters of the Dead Sea; then tier upon tier is the gray Judean Wilderness; and 50 miles away, on a clear day, one can see Jerusalem and the buildings on the Mount of Olives.

CHAPTER **33**

Colorful Edom and Petra

Edom denotes the land ocu-
pied by Esau's descendants, formerly the land of Seir which was
originally occupied by the Horites (Gen. 14:6; Deut. 2:12-22).
Esau and his descendants intermarried with the Horites and eventually gained the ascendancy so that the country came to be
known as Edom (red). Apparently the term "red" derived from
Esau's being "red all over like a hairy garment" and the singular
harmony of the red sandstone cliffs which are so characteristic
of the country.

309

The land of Edom stretched from the Brook Zered (Wadi el Hasa) to the Gulf of Aqaba, about 100 miles south. The Zered is 35 miles long and has a fall of 3,900 feet, which gives an idea of the wild, rugged, mountainous terrain of the country. Some areas, however, are suitable for cultivation, and for the grazing of cattle and camels. Edom is known as "the Land of Passage," due chiefly to the fact that in Bible times the "king's highway" passed along its central plateau (Num. 20:14-18)—much as the highway passes now. Long stretches of the fine Roman road of Trajan can be seen beside the modern road. It is part of the great paved highway which ran from Damascus to Aqaba. Viewing some of these sections of ancient roadways suddenly jerks us up, and time stands still—momentarily. Eastward is the north-south "desert road," which in part the children of Israel traveled as they "went around Edom." It comes up from Aqaba to Maan, then continues northward past the headwaters of the brook Zered (Wadi el Hasa) and of the river Arnon (Wadi Mojeb).[1]

The places of particular interest in Edom are: Khirbet al Tannur, Bozrah, Shobak, Teman, and Petra.

Kirbet al Tannur is the ruined remains of an impressive Nabataean temple complex which stands on a high plateau on the southern edge of brook Zered 40 miles north of Petra. It was in use 150 years (from 25 B.C. to A.D. 125) and was one of the chief attractions of the Nabataeans. Excavations by the American School of Oriental Research in conjunction with the Jordan Department of Antiquities revealed the plan of the temple. They unearthed considerable fine painted, eggshell-thin pottery, much carved sculpture and a whole pantheon of hitherto unknown Nabataean deities, of which Dushara and Allat seemed to be the chief. The nature of the ruins and the position of the fallen stones led the excavators to believe that the temple was destroyed by an earthquake.[2]

Bozrah, the capital of ancient Edom, is identified with modern Buseirah, 20 miles southeast of the Dead Sea and 25 miles north of Petra on the west of the high road to Petra. Built on a high, flat mountain spur, and shut in by wild canyons, it was considered practically impregnable. The reference "Who is this that

310

cometh from Edom, with dyed garments from Bozrah?" (Isa. 63:1), has been usually considered a Messianic scripture, and also indicative of the grape and sheep industries of ancient Bozrah. Its full import, however, is yet to be fully understood.

Shobak, an important Crusader stronghold, known as Mont Reale, was built by Baldwin I in 1115 to control the road from Damascus to Egypt. It was captured by Saladin in 1189, and restored by the Mamelukes in the 14th century. A village occupies the site today. The only worthwhile ancient remains is a great rock-cut well shaft with 375 steps leading down to an underground water supply.[3]

Teman, the district and town in Edom, was named after the grandson of Esau (Gen. 36:11). Amos names it along with Bozrah, and Eusebius in his *Onomastikon* mentions a Roman garrison by this name 15 miles from Petra. Job and Jeremiah leave us to believe that wise men lived in Teman, and that it was an important center of Edom (Job 2:11; Jer. 49:7).

With these and other bits of information in mind, Dr. Nelson Glueck made extensive researches and eventually located a city mound between *Ain Musa* and the Siq leading to Petra which he considered to be Teman. It is now called *Tawilan,* and is situated a few miles east of Petra, in the heart of a fertile, well-watered area. Here was the meeting point of important trade routes where there could be the benefits of the caravan trade without the caravans passing through.

Petra, "the rose-red city, half as old as time," was known in Bible times as Sela ("the Rock"). As ancient Edom's place of safe refuge, the Nabataeans' formidable commercial and administrative center, and Jordan's most magnificent tourist attraction, Petra has long been known as a unique place, the like of which cannot be found anywhere else in the world. It has been quite correctly designated as one of the greatest wonders ever wrought by nature and man.

Located 50 miles south of the Dead Sea, and 180 miles south 311 of Amman, the city is built within a high mountain basin, surrounded on every side by brilliantly colored granite and

The "Treasury of Pharaoh" sculptured out of the solid cliff walls at Petra

sandstone cliffs—a veritable amphitheaterlike city. Its chief allurement lies in its color, its isolation, and its unique structure.

The only entrance to the city is from the east, by a mile-long waterworn cleft known as "the Siq"—a narrow, winding gorge with high, forbidding, red sandstone walls and mysterious side canyons. On entering the "Gate of the Siq" from the blinding light of the desert sun, one very soon acquires a sense of detachment and is struck with awe as the shadows deepen into a perpetual twilight and the sky becomes a thin blue line above the towering cliffs. The scenery gets wilder and more unlike anything else on earth as on and on the ancient gorge-road meanders between 100- to 300-foot cliffs which overhang to such a degree that in places the sky is completely shut out for brief intervals. The gorge road averages 12 feet wide, but in places the steep side walls are so close that you can almost touch them with your outstretched hands. Yet, you instinctively ride on and on until, as you round a turn in the ravine, suddenly the Siq ends (momentarily). One can hardly believe his eyes as there stands before him in dazzling sunlight the magnificent *Khazneh al Faraun,* or "Treasury of Pharaoh."

It is a 90-foot-high and 60-foot-wide royal temple-tomb, artistically carved from the face of the rose-colored mountain. Its two stories are adorned with gorgeous sculpture, and 12 or more beautifully carved columns of the Corinthian order. On its very apex, high above its attic story, is a massive, yet artistically carved urn which carries the marks of many bullets fired at it in the hope of shattering it and releasing the treasure which local tradition says is hidden there. Within the temple is a moderate size twin-loculi tomb-room which is without ornamentation.

The "Treasury of Pharaoh" is the most perfectly preserved monument of this area, and in its purity and refinement probably the best Petra possessed in the zenith of her power. But its architectural style is so unique, and it is so detached with respect to adjacent monuments, that no one knows exactly when it was carved or to whom it belonged. Archaeologically it is generally regarded as the tomb of a Nabataean king of the late Hellenistic period—perhaps King Aretas the Philhellene (87-62 B.C.). "Aretas" was the Hellenized form of Harith.

Continuing for a time in the Siq, one comes next to a large, rock-hewn Roman theater, with 33 rows of seats, accommodating approximately 3,000 spectators. In the background can be seen fronts of early tombs, partly cut away in making the theater, and leaving the inner chambers now open to the sunlight.

When inside the city, one's eyes may turn almost any direction for a mile and see columned streets, paved roadways, arches, forums, theaters, temples, palaces, dwellings, a banqueting hall, a high place of worship, and hundreds of tombs carved with meticulous care from multicolored Nubian sandstone cliffs towering 200 to 300 feet in the air. In all parts of Petra it seems almost every available rock surface has been sculptured as the front of a temple, a shrine, a palace, or a dwelling.[4] Engrained in these sandstones are surprising shades of reds, pinks, violet, blue, yellow, ivory, raspberry, crimson, and coral—each adding a fresh brightness.

One tomb near the entrance has four pyramidal obelisks towering high above its entrance. The so-called Palace Tomb, with a facade imitating a Roman palace of three stories, contains enormous mausoleums and vaults in which were buried many of the kings of Petra. Nearby, there is the tomb of the Roman governor, Sextus Florentinus, whose name is given in Latin inscription above the portico.

Ed-Deir, one of the largest of all the monuments, is a huge two-story temple of reddish-brown stone 130 feet high and 150 feet wide. It has an altar set in a niche at the back of its one room. Some think it could have been a very fine tomb which was reworked and subsequently used as a monastery and place of worship. It stands at the extreme west portico of the city.

Petra has a 20-foot-wide colonnaded street which runs along the southern bank of the wadi and divides the city into two parts. At the end of the street is a triple monumental gateway, which some regard as a Triumphal Arch. To the west of the triple gateway is the *Kasr al Bint Faraun* (the Palace of Pharaoh's Daughter),

314

which is one of Petra's most beautiful and best preserved monuments.

Just a little north of the citadel, on a leveled-off crag or tableland which rises high above the city, is a *High Place* which is about 47 feet long by 24 feet wide. It is approached by a flight of steps cut in the rock. At the top of the steps, on the high place is an altar 9 feet long, 6 feet wide, and 3 feet high. On top of the altar is a hollow, panlike area for the fire, and just south of the altar is where the animal victims were slain for sacrifice. Here the Nabataeans worshiped the god Dushares, whose emblem was a black stone. In 1934, this great High Place was excavated by the Melchett Expedition in collaboration with Dr. Albright.

In recent years surveys and excavations have been going on in Petra, and it is gradually giving up its secrets and treasures. It is now estimated that there are 800 to 1,000 temples, tombs, shrines, and monuments in Petra. In describing the place, writers use such terms as "rugged beauty," "fantastic," "awe-inspiring."

A city of importance must have long existed here. And Petra almost came into the dim twilight when "Chedorlaomer and the kings that were with him . . . smote the Horites in their Mount Seir" (Gen. 14:5-6). Again it seemed to be in the dim historical background when "Esau took his wives, and his sons, and his daughters, and all the persons of his house, and his cattle, and all his beasts, and all his substance, . . . and went" and "dwelt . . . in mount Seir" (Gen. 36:6, 8). And in the time of the Exodus, when the city was the evident stronghold of the biblical Edomites, they refused to permit the Hebrews to pass through their country on the way to Canaan.

Its known history begins in 312 B.C., when the forces of Antigonus I unsuccessfully attacked the city. In the second century B.C., the Nabataeans, a remarkable Arab tribe (identified with Nabioth of the Old Testament), moved in from Arabia and not only occupied Petra, but soon dominated the great caravan routes that stretched from the Red Sea to Damascus. They planted their outposts throughout this region and amassed a fortune by collecting tolls from the caravans in exchange for a guarantee of safe conduct. This wealth they lavished on their capital, which to them was always a place of safe retreat. Among Petra's citizenry were princes, elders, horsemen, architects, doctors, and bards.

The city reached its height between 100 B.C. and A.D. 100 while the Nabataean Arabs ruled the country as far north as Damascus. In A.D. 106 the Nabataean Kingdom was incorporated into the Roman Empire, but Petra continued to flourish as the Romans built the colonnaded street, the Triple Gate, and carved the theater, the forum, and countless temples in the crimson walls of the sandstone canyons. In the fifth century Christianity penetrated Petra and had a bishop stationed there. The Crusaders under Baldwin I took it over at the beginning of the 12th century, and Baybars visited it between 1260 and 1277; then it was lost to history and the Western world until John L. Burckhardt rediscovered it in 1812.

It is only since about 1925, however, that any except the very intrepid and wealthy have visited Petra—and they under heavy guard. It is now very safe, and many thousands go each year to see the strange city. Some come by train, most by car, and a few fly, yet all must walk or ride a horse the last mile or two. But to visit the mountain fastness of Petra is such an unusual experience that anyone who has been there is quick to say, "I have been to Petra." Of Petra, Dr. Nelson Glueck says, "Even in its present condition of dilapidated elegance, Petra continues to be an unforgettable monument" to the "creative abilities" of the ancient Edomites, and later to the Nabataeans.

Some are anxious to return for a second trip, because of the endless sights and the grandly rewarding spell it casts over the whole self. Mr. G. Lankester Harding, former director of the Jordan Department of Antiquities, says:

> I have visited Petra many times, but always that first breathtaking vision remains in my mind. Nor does familiarity breed contempt here, for at every visit one has to rein up the horse or stop in one's tracks and gaze astonished, as if seeing it again for the first time, at the sharpness and purity of line, of the carving and the glowing brilliance of the rock. . . . Petra is astonishing and fantastic. . . . Before one is a vast panorama of rugged sandstone peaks, white, brown and red in color,

while in the distance to the west can be seen the blue haze of Sinai. Trees cling to the slopes of the crags wherever they can find a foothold and sufficient water to keep them alive, and the whole effect is strangely like looking at a Chinese landscape painting.[5]

> It seems no work of man's creative hand,
> By labour wrought or wavering fancy planned;
> But from the rock, as if by magic, grown
> Eternal, silent, beautiful, alone.
>
> Match me such marvel save in Eastern clime:
> A rose-red city half as old as time.

Reference Notes

(Complete bibliographical data will be found in the bibliography.)

Chapter 1

1. Excavations at Byblos (Gebal), Ras Shamra (Ugarit), and Megiddo attest these early civilizations. The families or tribes were known as the Hittites, the Jebusites, the Amorites, the Girgashites, the Hivites, the Arkites, the Sinites, the Arvadites, the Zemarites (Zerarvites), and the Hamathites. Some failed to become famous, but five or six of them were frequently mentioned as inhabiting Palesine and Syria.

Other tribes lived in Palestine and were occasionally referred to as "Canaanites," but were not of that stock. Among these were the Giants, the Philistines, the Perizzites, and the Moabites. They were not descendants of Canaan, but were called "Canaanites" because they lived in the land of Canaan.

2. Gen. 10:15-20; Herodotus, *The Histories,* Book One, 1:2.

3. In the Tell El Amarna correspondence of the 14th century B.C., the land of "Kanahhn" is referred to as the northern portion of the Mediterranean coast, and from a technical point of view that is usually considered correct.

Even during Augustine's day, he says that if the Carthaginian peasants were asked of what race they were, they would answer, "Canaanites." Greek literature and the Nuzi documents refer to the purple dye obtained from certain species of shellfish found on the Eastern Mediterranean coast.

4. George Adam Smith, *Historical Geography of the Holy Land,* p. 75.

5. Heusser, *The Land of the Prophets,* pp. 32-35.

6. 1 Kings 5:6.

7. *Iliad,* 23:741.

8. Acts 27:3.

9. Matt. 15:21-28.

10. Isa. 23:7.

11. Josh. 19:29.

12. Tyre is now called *Sur,* which in Arabic means "rock." The Hebrews called it *Tzor,* which also meant "rock."

13. Ezek. 27:3.

14. Ezek. 27:12-24.

15. Ezek. 26:2.

16. Ezek. 29:18.
17. Ezek. 26:12.
18. Acts 21:2-6.
19. Ezek. 26:13-14.

Chapter 2

1. Gen. 49:13.
2. *Palestine Annual,* 3:90.
3. Acts 21:7.
4. Bentwich, *A Wanderer in the Promised Land,* p. 74.
5. Gen. 49:13.
6. 1 Macc. 13:12-30

Chapter 3

1. Smith, *Historical Geography of the Holy Land,* p. 338.
2. Song of Sol. 7:5.
3. 1 Kings 17:1.
4. 1 Kings 18:22-24.
5. 1 Kings 18:46.

Chapter 4

1. Some geographers call this narrow, 20-mile-long plain "The Coasts of Dor," and do not begin the Plain of Sharon until the Crocodile River is reached.

2. This bowl is now preserved in the Cathedral of Saint Lorenzo in Genoa, Italy.

3. *Mikveh Israel,* the first agricultural school in Palestine, was established by French Jews in 1870, on land granted by the Turkish Government. Through the school gates you see red-roofed buildings, tall palm trees, and fruit orchards. Better yet to go inside and see what may be done with the fertile acres of the Plain of Sharon. The writer can never forget a day and a half spent here in 1934 while making a survey of the educational institutions of Palestine.

Chapter 5

1. Gen. 10:14; Amos 9:7; *Quarterly of the Palestine Department of Antiquities,* vol. I, no. 4, p. 156.
2. Deut. 2:23.
3. Stewart, *The Land of Israel,* p. 88.
4. Judg. 1:18-19.
5. Amos 9:7.
6. Breasted, *Ancient Records of Egypt,* 4:38, 64.
7. McGarvey, *Lands of the Bible,* p. 22.
8. *Dagon* seems to have at one time been the national god of the Philistines. The image had the face and hands of a man, and the body and tail of a fish. Some are wont to say that it was the "fish-god" which the people were led to believe had risen from the sea.

9. Amos 1:8.
10. Isa. 20:1.
11. Sachar, *A History of the Jews,* p. 56.
12. Duff, *Palestine Picture,* p. 34.
13. 1 Macc. 5:68; 10:83-84.
14. Acts 8:40.
15. Duff, *Palestine Picture,* p. 33; 1 Sam. 6:4.
16. 2 Sam. 1:20.
17. Marston, *New Bible Evidence,* p. 117.

Chapter 6

1. Josh. 10:40.
2. Smith, *Historical Geography of the Holy Land,* pp. 197-99.
3. 1 Chron. 27:28; 2 Chron. 26:10.
4. Smith, *Historical Geography of the Holy Land,* p. 202.
5. Josh. 10:8-14.
6. 1 Sam. 6:1-18.
7. 1 Sam. 17:12-54.
8. Judg. 13:15-20.
9. Judg. 18:1-2.
10. Judg. 14:5-18.
11. Mic. 7:19.

Chapter 7

1. Wilson, *Picturesque Palestine,* 2:18.
2. Song of Sol. 3:9; Hos. 14:5; 2 Kings 14:9; 2 Chron. 2:16.
3. *National Geographic,* Dec., 1946, p. 736.
4. Isa. 2:13; Ps. 92:12.
5. The notation of the exact location of this quotation has been misplaced.

Chapter 8

1. Stewart, *The Land of Israel,* p. 111.
2. Josephus, *War,* 3:3.
3. Hamilton, *Put Off Thy Shoes,* p. 73.
4. *Ibid.,* p. 72.

Chapter 9

1. Payne, *The Splendor of Israel,* pp. 133-34.
2. See our article "Mt. Tabor," in Zondervan's *Biblical Encyclopedia.*
3. Owen, *Abraham to Allenby,* pp. 250-52.

Chapter 10

1. Comay, *Israel: An Uncommon Guide,* p. 283.
2. Rev. 16:16.

3. Smith, *Historical Geography of the Holy Land,* pp. 393-95.
4. Judg. 5:19-21.
5. I first inspected Nahalal in the spring of 1934. Then it was prosperous. The improvements in the past 40 years are all but startling.

Chapter 12

1. Stewart, *The Land of Israel,* pp. 148-50.
2. Wilson, *Picturesque Palestine,* 1:234.
3. Owen, *Abraham to Allenby,* pp. 38-39.
4. *Ibid.,* p. 77.
5. Smith, *Historical Geography of the Holy Land,* p. 214.
6. *Ibid.,* p. 54.
7. *The Story of the Bible,* 1:369.

Chapter 13

1. This book is published jointly by the Beacon Hill Press of Kansas City, Mo., and Baker Book House, Grand Rapids, Mich.
2. The holy family spent about two months in Bethlehem. The presentation in the Temple, which took place 40 days after the birth, and the adoration of the Magi who probably arrived soon afterwards, must have occurred before the flight to Egypt, where they remained till the death of Herod, and then returned directly to Nazareth, their proper home (Matt. 2:22-23).
3. Wilson, *Picturesque Palestine,* 1:139.
4. Josephus, *Antiquities,* 8. 7. 3.
5. Vilnay, *Guide to Israel,* p. 188; McGarvey, *Lands of the Bible,* p. 240.
6. Smith, *Historical Geography of the Holy Land,* pp. 240-41.

Chapter 15

1. Wilson, *Picturesque Palestine,* 1:142.
2. Josephus, *Wars of the Jews,* 8. 9. 1.
3. Erskin, *The Vanished Cities of Arabia,* pp. 126-27.

Chapter 16

1. See Glueck's *Rivers in the Desert* for extensive research on the Negeb.
2. Lowdermilk, *Palestine: Land of Promise,* pp. 49-50, 180-200.

Chapter 17

1. Stanley, *Sinai and Palestine,* p. 3.
2. *Palestine Exploration Fund Quarterly Statement for 1886,* pp. 41-46.
3. Glueck, *Rivers in the Desert,* pp. 283-84.

Chapter 19

1. Wilson, *Picturesque Palestine,* 1:357.

Chapter 21

1. Comay, *Israel: An Uncommon Guide,* p. 295.
2. Glueck, *The River Jordan,* pp. 53-54.
3. Josephus, *The Jewish Antiquities,* 17. 2. 1.
4. Fromer, *Israel and Its Holy Land,* pp. 242-43.
5. *Ibid.,* p. 242.
6. *Ibid.,* p. 237.

Chapter 22

1. Magregor, *Rob Roy on the Jordan,* p. 406.
2. The writer has studied the Jordan River from three of its sources at the foot of Mount Hermon down through the Rift Valley to the Dead Sea, but only from its banks. However, I have received considerable information directly from Mr. John D. Whiting, who with Rev. R. J. E. Boggis, Mr. Spafford Whiting (23), and Mr. John Vester (21), went down the river in rubber boats. Also, have read his article in the *National Geographic,* "Canoeing Down the River Jordan."
3. Glueck, *The River Jordan,* p. 156.

Chapter 23

1. "Settlements in the Jericho Valley During the Roman Periods," by Lucetta Mowry, *Biblical Archaeologist,* vol. 15, May, 1952.
2. *Ibid.,* p. 34.

Chapter 24

1. Lynch, *United States Exploring Expedition,* p. 324.
2. Leary, *The Real Palestine,* p. 138.
3. Trever, *The Untold Story of Qumran,* p. 151.
4. Baly, *The Geography of the Bible,* p. 203.
5. *World of the Bible Library,* vol. 5.
6. McGarvey, *Lands of the Bible,* pp. 370-71; Tristram, *Land of Moab,* p. 300.
7. Harland, *The Biblical Archaeologist,* May, 1942.
8. *Ibid.,* p. 27.

Chapter 25

1. Glueck, *The River Jordan,* p. 146.
2. Kroeling, *Rand-McNally Bible Atlas,* p. 27.
3. Comay, *Israel: An Uncommon Guide,* pp. 203-6.
4. Hamilton, *Put Off Thy Shoes,* pp. 47-50.
5. Glueck, "On the Trail of King Solomon's Mines," *National Geographic,* Feb., 1944, pp. 234-35.

Chapter 26

1. Tristram, *The Land of Israel: A Journal of Travels in Palestine,* p. 614.

Chapter 27

1. Porter, *Five Years in Damascus,* p. 10.
2. *Ibid.,* pp. 96-97, 119.
3. Hamilton, *Both Sides of the Jordan,* pp. 248-50.
4. *Ibid.,* p. 12.
5. *National Geographic,* April, 1974, p. 516.
6. Porter, *Five Years in Damascus,* pp. 22-25.

Chapter 28

1. Merrill, *East of the Jordan,* p. 333.
2. Wilson, *Picturesque Palestine,* 1:82.
3. Porter, *Bashan and Its Giant Cities,* p. 18.

Chapter 29

1. Smith, *Historical Geography of the Holy Land,* p. 644.
2. Porter, *Bashan and Its Giant Cities,* pp. 26-28.
3. Josephus, *Antiquities,* 15. 10. 1; 17. 2. 1-2.
4. Porter, *Giant Cities of Bashan,* pp. 92-93.
5. Josephus, *Antiquities,* 15. 10. 1; 16. 9. 1; 17. 2. 1.

Chapter 30

1. Glueck, *The River Jordan,* p. 170.
2. *Ibid.,* p. 175.
3. *Ibid.,* pp. 112, 117.
4. *Ibid.,* pp. 147, 151.
5. Harding, *The Antiquities of Jordan,* pp. 63-89.
6. *Ibid.,* pp. 42-43.
7. Its botanical name is "Balsamodendrois Gileadensa"—Balsam Mecca.
8. Wild, *Geographic Influences on Old Testament Masterpieces,* pp. 102-3.

Chapter 31

1. Glueck, *The Other Side of the Jordan,* p. 139.

Chapter 32

1. Orni and Efrat, *Geography of Israel,* p. 111.
2. Josephus, *Antiquities,* 17. 6. 4.
3. Smith, *Historical Geography of the Holy Land,* p. 600.

4. Harding, *Antiquities of Jordan*, p. 921; Owen, *Archaeology and the Bible*, pp. 261-63.
5. Glueck, *The River Jordan*, p. 35.

Chapter 33
1. Harding, *Antiquities of Jordan*, p. 19.
2. Glueck, *The Other Side of the Jordan*, pp. 178-98.
3. Harding, *Antiquities of Jordan*, p. 98.
4. Cottrell, *The Past*, p. 366.
5. Harding, *Antiquities of Jordan*, p. 100.

Bibliography

Balmforth, H., et al. *The Story of the Bible,* 4 vols. New York: Wm. H. Wise and Co., 1952.

Baly, Denis. *The Geography of the Bible.* New York: Harper and Brothers Publishers, 1957.

Bannister, J. T. *Pictorial Geography of the Holy Land.* Bath, England: Binns and Goodwin, n.d.

Breasted, James H. *Ancient Records of Egypt.* 4 vols.

Burckhardt, John Lewis. *Travels in Syria and the Holy Land.* London: John Murray, 1822.

Comay, Joan. *Israel: An Uncommon Guide.* New York: Random House, 1969.

Conder, C. R. *Tent Work in Palestine.* London: Richard Bentley & Son, 1878.

Cottrell, Leonard, ed. *The Past A Concise Encyclopedia of Archaeology.* New York: Hawthorn Books, Inc., 1960.

Erskin, Mrs. Steuart. *The Vanished Cities of Arabia.* New York: E. P. Dutton and Co., 1925.

Fodor, Eugene. *Fodor's Israel, 1972.* New York: David McKay Co., Inc., 1972.

Fulton, John. *Palestine, the Holy Land.* Philadelphia: Henry T. Coates and Co., 1900.

Geikie, Cunningham. *The Holy Land and the Bible.* 2 vols. New York: James Pott and Co., 1888.

Glueck, Nelson. "King Solomon's Copper Mines," *Illustrated London News.* July 7, 1934.

———. *Rivers in the Desert.* New York: Farrar, Straus and Cudahy, 1959.

———. *The Other Side of Jordan.* New Haven, Conn.: American School of Oriental Research, 1949.

Graham, William C., and May, Herbert G. *Culture and Conscience.* Chicago: The University of Chicago Press, 1936.

Hamilton, Elizabeth. *Put Off Thy Shoes.* New York: Charles Scribner's Sons, 1957.

Hamilton, Norah Rowan. *Both Sides of the Jordan.* New York: Dodd, Mead and Co., n.d.

Harding, G. Lankester. *Antiquities of Jordan.* New York: Thomas Y. Crowell Co., 1959.

Harland, J. Penrose. *The Biblical Archaeologist.* May, 1942.

Herodotus. *The Histories.* Baltimore: Penguin Books, 1955.

Josephus, Flavius. *The Works of Flavius Josephus.* Philadelphia: David McKay Publishers, n.d.

Leary, Lewis Gaston. *Syria: The Land of Lebanon.* New York: McBride, Nast and Co., 1913.

Libbey, William, and Hoskins, Franklin E. *The Jordan Valley and Petra.* 2 vols. New York and London: G. P. Putnam's Sons, 1905.

Lieber, Joel. *Israel and the Holy Land on $5 and $10 a Day.* New York: Arthur Frommer, Inc., 1972.

Lowdermilk, Walter Clay. *Palestine: Land of Promise.* New York: Harper and Brothers Publishers, 1944.

Lynch, W. F. *Expedition to the River Jordan and the Dead Sea.* Philadelphia: Lea and Blanchard, 1850.

MacCoun, Townsend. *The Holy Land in Geography and in History.* New York: Townsend MacCoun, 1897.

MacGregor, John. *Rob Roy on the Jordan.* New York: Harper and Brothers, 1875.

Marston, Sir Charles. *New Bible Evidence.* New York: Fleming H. Revell Co., 1934.

McGarvey, J. W. *Lands of the Bible.* London: J. B. Lippincott and Co., 1882.

Merrill, Selah. *East of the Jordan.* New York: Charles Scribner's Sons, 1883.

Mowry, Lucetta. *Biblical Archaeologist,* vol. 15, May, 1952.

Owen, G. Frederick. *Abraham to Allenby.* Grand Rapids, Mich.: Wm. B. Eerdmans Publishing Co., 1943.

———. *Archaeology and the Bible.* Westwood, N.J.: Fleming H. Revell Co., 1961.

———. *Jerusalem.* Kansas City: Beacon Hill Press of Kansas City, 1972.

Palestine Annual, vol. 3.

Palestine Exploration Fund Annual, London, 1927.

Palestine Exploration Fund Quarterly Statement for 1886.

Payne, Robert. *The Splendor of Israel.* New York: Harper and Row, 1963.

Porter, J. L. *Five Years in Damascus.* London: John Murray, 1870.

———. *Giant Cities of Bashan.* New York: Thomas Nelson and Sons, 1884.

Sachar, Abram Leon. *A History of the Jews.* New York: Alfred A. Knopf, 1930.

Smith, George Adam. *Historical Geography of the Holy Land.* Magnolia, Mass.: Peter Smith, Publisher, Inc., n.d.

Smith, William Walter. *Students' Historical Geography of the Holy Land.* New York: George H. Doran Co., 1924.

Survey of Western Palestine. London: Palestine Exploration Fund, 1881.

The City and the Land. London: Palestine Exploration Fund, 1892.

Thompson, W. M. *The Land and the Book.* London: Thomas Nelson and Sons, 1910.

Thornbeck, Ellen. *Promised Land.* New York: Harper and Brothers, 1947.

Trever, John C. *The Untold Story of Qumran.* Westwood, N.J.: Fleming H. Revell Co., 1965.

Tristram, H. B. *The Land of Israel: A Journal of Travels in Palestine.* London: Society for Promoting Christian Knowledge, 1886.

Trumbull, H. Clay. *Kadesh-Barnea.* Philadelphia: John D. Wattles and Co., 1895.

Trumper, Victor L. *Historical Sites of Palestine.* Cairo: Nile Mission Press, 1921.

Vilnay, Zev. *Guide to Israel.* Jerusalem: Hamakor Press, 1970.

Vincent, John H. *Earthly Footsteps of the Man of Galilee.* New York: N. D. Thompson Publishing Co., n.d.

Wild, Laura H. *Geographic Influences on Old Testament Masterpieces.* Boston: Ginn and Co., 1915.

Wilson, Colonel. *Picturesque Palestine.* 2 vols. New York: D. Appleton and Co., 1883.

Wolf, Betty Hartman. *Journey Through the Holy Land.* Garden City, N.Y.: Doubleday and Co., 1967.

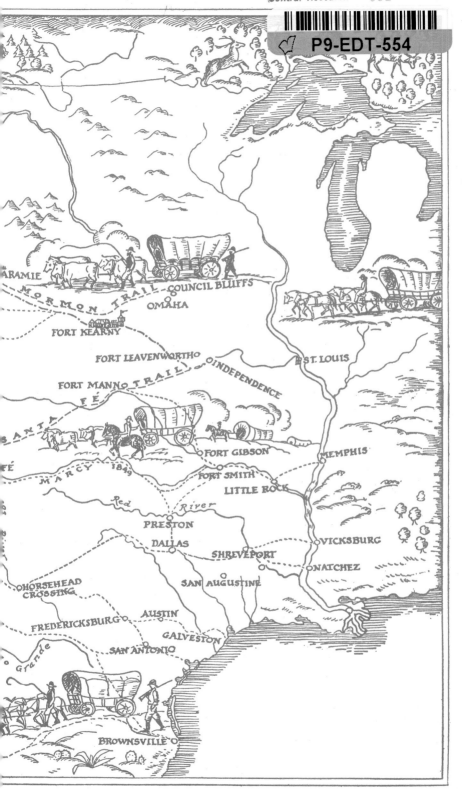

ARAMIE

MORMON TRAIL COUNCIL BLUFFS
OMAHA
FORT KEARNY

FORT LEAVENWORTH O
FORT MANN O TRAIL O INDEPENDENCE
SANTA FÉ
FÉ
MARCY 1849
FORT GIBSON
FORT SMITH
LITTLE ROCK
Red River
PRESTON
DALLAS
SHREVEPORT
HORSEHEAD CROSSING
SAN AUGUSTINE
AUSTIN
FREDERICKSBURG O
GALVESTON
SAN ANTONIO
o Grande

ST. LOUIS

MEMPHIS

VICKSBURG
NATCHEZ

BROWNSVILLE O

WESTWARD

By E. DOUGLAS BRANCH

WESTWARD: THE ROMANCE OF
THE AMERICAN FRONTIER

THE HUNTING OF THE BUFFALO

THE COWBOY AND HIS INTERPRETERS

WARD

The Romance of the American Frontier

By E. DOUGLAS BRANCH

WOODCUTS BY

LUCINA SMITH WAKEFIELD

A Marandell Book

New York

COOPER SQUARE PUBLISHERS, INC.

1969

Originally Published 1930
Published by Cooper Square Publishers, Inc.
59 Fourth Avenue, New York, N. Y. 10003
Standard Book Number 8154-0311-9
Library of Congress Catalog Card No. 76-92485

Printed in the United States of America

INTRODUCTION

THE heart of the Dakota mining country was Deadwood, where the houses clung precariously to perpendicular streets, and the brown and green of the pine trees crowned the unpainted shacks in the little valleys. In Deadwood Mike Russell kept bar, a little Irishman with long, unserried whiskers. Youngsters and women were not allowed in his place. Calamity Jane was the only one of her sex who could get a drink at Russell's bar; she, he said, was the exception that proved the rule.

Such exceptions—Calamity Jane, Simon Girty, Kit Carson, Sam Bass—make good melodrama. Billy the Kid is now in the photoplays, where, so far as I am concerned, he belongs. But in following the history of the American frontier, let us put these noise-makers off by themselves, just as Mike Russell made a separate compartment in his philosophy for Calamity Jane. And without questioning the importance of the West in our national economic history, or the inestimable influence of western votes upon national politics, we may follow in outline the history of the march of pioneers across the American continent. Mr. Claude G. Bowers is welcome to Andrew Jackson if I am allowed to sketch the invasion of the pioneers who made Jackson's election possible.

"Invasion" is not the wrong word: throughout the history of the American frontier is an electric suggestion of advance against opposition, of slugging and shooting, and a grim, merciless conquest. There was opposition indeed —Indians, Frenchmen, and Spaniards. But each of these barriers was bowled over so inevitably and so completely that in retrospect, as the panorama of the American Conquest is being rolled to its last few pictures, the battles with

[v]

the Indians and the conflicts with New France and New Spain dwindle in importance. The battle with Nature, the wilderness; the taming of the land—that is the essential conflict.

It was a battle fought and won by Plain Men; with them this narrative deals. If there is a moral to the history of the westward movement, it is this: the transcendent importance of small things and of "unimportant" people.

There is another overtone in this history, the heavy sound of a huge wheel, revolving slowly but never quiet; a beginning and a progression, a beginning again, and round through a similar progression. Frontier history continually repeats itself. Into a primitive region come men to gain a livelihood; and to grapple with this wilderness they become primitive themselves. As they develop the region, they themselves develop, taking up the folkways and institutions that characterize the district whence they had come. But to the west of them is another region, still primitive; and into it go pioneers who must start at the beginning again.

Sometimes the cycle was repeated in the same region. Pioneers pushed westward, retreated as the menace of Indian wars drove them to more settled regions (or perhaps, as in the Great Plains, it was the stubbornness of the land that drove them back), and pushed forward again. Improvements abandoned by one group of pioneers were relocated by a later group of settlers, for actual occupation was the only sure right to land and cabin.

An instance in the settlement of the Valley of Virginia may be used to point this process, costly in human lives and in wasted labor, but ultimately successful in pushing back the wilderness. John Robinson was an older son in the large family of James Robinson, pioneer farmer in western Pennsylvania. John built his own cabin on Roanoke River, in the Valley of Virginia, in 1743. He was killed by Indians in 1746. Thomas, his brother, took his family still farther, to the western slope of the Cumberland Mountain; he and all his family were killed by Indians. But none the less there came a flock of Robinsons, with friends and relatives whose names were Crockett, Love, Patterson, Calhoun, Patton, Montgomery—plain names, most of them of English origin, the rest Scotch; plain names that dot the frontier. These people bought lands southwest of the Roanoke, built cabins, cleared fields, and stayed. As early as 1746 four roads were ordered to be built connecting the Roanoke settlements in the Valley of Virginia to waterways, or to that "state" highway which crossed the Blue Ridge and led to Richmond.

In 1747 Valentine Sevier, living on the upper waters of the Shenandoah, petitioned the General Assembly that he be licensed to keep a tavern and saloon at his house, since he was "very much infested with travelers." By 1750 settlements on Wood's River were sufficiently thick to afford the luxury of a constable and a justice of the peace. Pioneers moved on, to the banks of the Clinch, the Holston, and the Powell. New roads, farther into the West, were built. In 1754 the war cloud broke upon these far-western settlements, and the community on the Holston River was almost annihilated. A judicial order of 1755 was returned to the court "not executed by reason of the murder done on New River by the Indians." But the French and Indian War was hardly over when the cycle had begun again; and this time the wheel did not slip.

"Westward" is not accurate as a direction. The frontier was not slavishly wedded to parallels. To mention two instances of many, from Massachusetts and New York frontier currents moved toward Vermont, and from south-central Pennsylvania the advance of settlement followed the Appalachian valleys into the south. "West" finds its greater meaning as a transitional phase in American life.

INTRODUCTION

There is not a region in the United States that overleapt this phase; this common experience of a frontier stage in society has given American life and politics the distinctive tropisms that have baffled European understanding.

E. D. B.

CONTENTS

[ix]

CONTENTS

MAPS

PART I
THE BRITISH FRONTIER IN AMERICA

There's no land in America now left y'ts worth anything, but what's on the Mesisipi.
—PRICE HUGHES, 1713

CHAPTER I

WHEN MASSACHUSETTS WAS WEST

NEXT church-meeting's sermon was written, and his womenfolk were ahum with work, brewing the beer according to his own excellent directions; and Cotton Mather, having nothing else to try his temper, took up his quill and turned to his unfinished manuscript, *Wonderful Passages which have Occurred, First in the Protections and then in the Afflictions of New England.* The setting is tecla, but these sentences are genuine: "Do our *Old* People, any of them *Go Out* from the institutions of God, Swarming into New Settlements, where they and their untaught families are like to *Perish for Lack of Vision?* They that have done so heretofore, have to their Cost found, that they were got unto the *Wrong Side of the Hedge,* in their doing so. Think, here *Should this be done any more?*"

Mr. Mather was not the last gentleman to ask that question, nor the first; but the westward movement of the Americans stood not upon the order of "should." This swarming into new settlements, and swarming on past the new settlements, is a brave tale—the greatest conquest of the greatest wilderness. Many forces impelled and shaped that advance of the American frontier, but the logic of comfortable people was not one of them; and Cotton Mather's "hedge" metaphor counted for as little as Elbridge Gerry's awful lamentations eleven decades later, when the Congress of the United States was being asked to approve the purchase of Louisiana. Youth was one of the forces that did count; and the insatiable restlessness which was engrafted into Anglo-Saxon stock by the happy, ephemeral blend of races called the Norman, and which reburgeoned in the era of Elizabeth. And poverty, a proprietor's foreclosure or a government's confiscation, or the death of an old dream of comfort. A man's intense desire to show himself as big as any other man, and to have as many privileges. The staleness of too-familiar societies. The cheapness of new lands. Ambition and speculative enterprise, looking toward the unexploited West for magnificent opportunities and a magnificent rate of profit.

In the vague dawn of the Commercial Revolution, this panorama is mistily adumbrated along the American shore: barques and brigantines from European ports; invariably brought in these ships, "Hookes, Knives, Sizzers, Hammers, Nailes, Chissels, Fish-hookes, Bels, Beades, Bugles, Looking-glasses, Thimbles, Pinnes, Needles, Threed, and such like" (as Purchas inventoried the trading stuffs carried on Martin Pring's voyage in 1603); and, awaiting the landing of the European adventurers, Indians with stores of furs. Go back as far as one may into the records of the earliest voyages to the Atlantic shore, one finds that the Indians had collected furs in anticipation of the voyagers.

Colonel William Byrd of Westover recorded the beginnings, as a well-read gentleman of eighteenth-century Virginia understood them: the history of Virginia properly begins with Sir Walter Raleigh, blessed be Queen Bess; just so the history of the fur trade begins with Captains Amidas and Barlow, commanding the ships which Raleigh despatched. They lowered anchor not far from Roanoke inlet. "They ventured ashore near that place upon an island now called Colleton Island, where they set up the arms of England, and claimed the adjacent country in right of their sovereign lady, the queen; and this ceremony being duly performed, they kindly invited the neighboring Indians to traffick with them. These poor people at first approached the English with great caution, having heard much of the treachery of the Spaniards, and not knowing but these strangers might be as treacherous as they. But, at length, discovering a kind of good nature in their looks, they ventured to draw near, and barter their skins and furs for the bawbles and trinkets of the English."

The mercantile altruism of the adventurers and the naïveté of the Indians are both fictions of the delightful Virginian; but the fur trade was a substantial reality, and the portrait of the fur trader is the largest upon the great canvas of the colonial American frontier. The traders were first to encounter the Indian tribes of the interior, and, penetrating to the westward, successively brought the tribes within the scope of the white man's policy, economic, political, and—so far as distilled beverages and gunpowder were representative—cultural. Beyond its economic significance, the fur trade with the Indians was a means of political alliance, and a factor in international diplomacy. Through the history of the entrenchment of the British from the Atlantic seaboard to the Mississippi, and thereafter until the division of the Pacific Northwest between the United States and Great Britain in 1846, the frontier fur trade retained its importance in international politics.

Captain John Smith related having seen some four thousand deerskins "pyled up in one wardrobe of *Powhaton*";

[5]

such a collection could have been for no other purpose but trade with Europeans. Commerce between Virginians and Indians quickly developed; after the London Company was dissolved in 1624 and the colonists enjoyed a greater measure of personal freedom, there appears a class of professional fur traders. Curiosity, rather than enterprise in this commerce, led the first Virginians on their occasional explorations; while the Virginians clung to the navigable rivers, the Indians brought stores of furs within their reach. Leonard Calvert wrote from Maryland in May, 1634: "Whilst we were a-doing these things [necessary to settlement] our pinnace by our directions followed the trade of beaver through all parts of this province. But by reason of our so late arrivall here we came too late for the first part of the trade for this year: which is the reason I have sent home so few furs (they being dealt for by those of Virginia before our coming)—the second part of our trade is now in hand, and is like to prove very beneficiall. The nation we trade withal at this time a-year is called the Massawomeckes. This nation cometh seven, eight, and ten days journey to us. . . . We have lost by our late coming 3000 skins, which others of Virginia have traded for."

In 1623 John White and the Dorchester Company in England sent out a fishing and trading expedition, which settled at Cape Ann and removed to Salem three years later. That group of fur traders and fishermen laid the foundation of the first Puritan settlement; and the charter of that company, made over to the "Governor and Company of Massachusetts Bay," gave the Massachusetts Bay Colony its legal authorization. Meanwhile, the first settlement in New England, the colony of Pilgrims at Plymouth Bay, was active in the fur trade. In 1625 Edward Winslow and other men of Plymouth took a boatload of corn to the Kennebec River, bartered with the Indians

[6]

there, and returned with seven hundred pounds of beaver. From that beginning developed an extensive trade between the Pilgrims and the tribes along the Kennebec and the Penobscot, a trade which successfully challenged the French adventurers who came into Maine. The commercial ventures of the Plymouth colony also extended to the Connecticut River, where Dutch traders had gained a footing. The history of the foreign relations of the New England colonies begins with these incursions of the fur traders into stretches of wilderness claimed by other nations.

Concord, west of the Cambridge farms, was the first inland settlement in New England. In September, 1635, the General Court of Massachusetts authorized the settlement ("there shalbe 6 myles of land square to belong to it"), and several families moved to this frontier site that same autumn. Captain Edward Johnson, Puritan historian, described their first homes: "They burrow themselves in the earth for their first shelter under some hill-side, casting the earth aloft upon timber, they make a smoaky fire against the earth at the highest side. . . . In these poor wigwams they sing psalms, pray and praise their God, till they can provide them houses, which ordinarily was not to be with many till the earth, by the Lord's blessing, brought forth bread to feed them, their wives and little ones, which with sore labors they attain."

A minister was directly concerned in the founding, as was typical of the first New England towns, but equally important was a merchant, Simon Willard. Willard had become acquainted with the site in his pursuit of the fur trade; it was he who arranged the purchase of the title to the lands from the Indians; in the practical affairs of Concord he was consistently the leader. He laid out the bounds of the town to include six valuable mill sites and a maximum of water frontage. The meadows of Concord village were bordered by tracts of uplands that had been cleared by fire

[7]

and brought under cultivation by the Indians. Besides his house lot, each man in the original company of settlers received his due proportion of planting ground and meadow lying near by; the remainder of the township, woodland and grazing fields was undivided and held in common. By order of the General Court no dwelling house could be built more than half a mile from the meetinghouse without the Court's special permission.

Natural clearings, such as those of the Concord uplands, simplified the tasks of the first pioneers of the New England interior. As an anonymous pamphleteer in 1630 described the country, "The Land affords void ground enough to receive more people then this State can spare, and that not onely wood grounds, and others, which are unfit for present use; but in many places, much cleared ground for tillage, and large marshes for hay and feeding of cattle, which comes to passe by the desolation hapning through a three yeeres Plague, about twelve or sixteen yeeres past, which swept away most of the Inhabitants all along the Sea coast, and in some places utterly consumed man, woman, & childe, so that there is no person left to lay claime to the soyle which they possessed." Where there still were Indians, as at Concord, a dole of presents, not at all lavish, sufficed to remove the Indians. But when the westward pressure of settlement demanded that the Indians move a second time—then active resentment and open hostility began.

Concord was not ten years old when glowing accounts of better things to be attained farther into the wilderness prompted an appreciable group of the inhabitants to leave in a body to a new settlement on Long Island Sound. But two years before this emigration the frontiersmen of New England had served the Indians dreadful notice of what they might expect if they attempted to block the westward movement. That notice was the Pequot War of 1642.

John Mason and John Underhill, two men whose sadism had been unyoked by the wilderness, led the New Englanders in the capture of the walled village of the Pequot nation; five Indians out of the seven hundred in the village got away with their lives, and the whole bloody business was begun and completed in less than an hour.

After the establishing of Concord—the first nibble into the wilderness—home-makers made bold to follow the fur traders. Ministers who resented the political hegemony of certain entrenched theologians, and congregations whose common pasture lands and private farming lands were being overtaxed, demanded leave of the General Court to establish new homes in the West. John Oldham, of the Plymouth Trading Company, returned from the company's fur post on the Connecticut River a prophet of agricultural successes in the valley; and little parties of pioneers, bringing with them their cattle and goods, trudged to new homes beside the Connecticut River. Thomas Hooker, pastor at Cambridge, led his congregation on the pilgrimage to Hartford in June, 1636. Emigrants from England arrived at the coastal towns in mounting numbers—more fuel for the westward movement. By May, 1637, eight hundred people were living in three towns on the Connecticut; exactly one year later Thomas Hooker was proclaiming that "the foundation of authority is laid in the free consent of the people," and in another eight months the freemen of Connecticut were agreed upon a document which had nothing at all to say of His Gracious Majesty, the King of England, Scotland, Wales, and Newcastle-upon-Tyne, nor of the government of Massachusetts Bay Colony—the Fundamental Orders of Connecticut, first of a long series of constitutions devised by frontiersmen who had no legal authority to erect their own government, no authority but the necessity and the inclination.

In May, 1636, an agreement for the founding of Spring-

[9]

field was signed by eight men—"the first adventurers and subscribers for the plantation." The most notable of these men was William Pynchon; the prospect of large returns in the fur trade was the magnet which had brought him and many another from England to the new country, and which brought Pynchon into far-western Massachusetts. The little streams flowing into the Connecticut were yet abundant with beaver; the open spaces along the river bank, promising excellent farming, attracted emigrants from the eastern towns. In July, 1636, Pynchon and two associates bought off the Indian title to the Springfield lands; "and the said Pynchon hath paid in hand," runs the deed, "the said eighteen fatham of wampam, eighteen coates, 18 hatchets, 18 howes, 18 knifes." The other five proprietors abandoned the enterprise; and thereby Springfield was spared the bitter quarrels that thread through the history of many a New England settlement—a division of interest between the absentee proprietors and the common people who were the actual inhabitants.

Traditional institutions had to prove themselves by the standard of the frontier—a test according to convenience and necessity. "Wee intend by Gods grace," the selectmen of Springfield went on record, "as soone as wee can w'th all convenient speed to p'cure some Godly and faithfull minister." But these westerners had other foundation blocks to lay: they proceeded to the surveying and assigning of house lots and pasture lots, and agreed, "We intend that our towne shall be composed of forty familys, or if we thinke meete after to alter our purpose yet not to exceede the number of fifty familys, rich and poore"; "that all rates that shal arise upon the towne be layed upon lands accordinge to every ones proportion aker for aker of house lots and aker for aker of meddowe." The West was reworking tradition, like must put into thin wine; one of the things that happened was that these transplanted

Puritans of Springfield waited two years before they secured a minister.

The idea that property rights were contingent upon use came naturally to this first generation of westerners. In their first meeting, the Springfield selectmen resolved that "if any man fell any tymber out of his lot in any common ground, if he let it ly above three months before he worke it out, it shall be lawfull for any other man to take it that hath p'sent use of it"; and later they agreed that any man might fell any "canoe tree" for his own use.

"Ontogeny recapitulates phylogeny," children learn by rote in high school science classes. One generation of wilderness breakers relived a social development that had taken the race hundreds of years to accomplish—beginning with a throwback to a primitive society practically without division of labor, taking on complexities bit by bit. One may follow this process in the history of Springfield or of any other town which was begun under frontier conditions. "The sealed peck which Mr Pynchon hath" was agreed upon as the standard of measurement; neighbors were ordered to share equally the costs of fencing, and all dwellers upon the highway were admonished to keep the ditches "well scoured for the ready passage of ye water yt it may not be pent up to flowe the meddowe"; all men had to meet for military drill one day in the month; exact wages were fixed for carpenters, mowers, "alsoe for husbandry or any ordinary labor"; official surveyors were named and their fees provided; one man was appointed "to see ye high ways cleerd and kept in repair of all stubs sawpitts or tymbr & if any man shall not amende on sufficient warnynge what is amiss all things yt are Judged offensive betwixt this & michaelstide shall forfeite 12d for every such default."

At the meeting point between Indians' hunting grounds and pioneers' farm lands, pioneers had to be ready to fight. In the town records of Springfield are these requirements:

[11]

that every man should keep a gun in readiness for use, with a pound of powder and twenty bullets laid beside it; that certain appointees should be vigilant in restraining the Indians from planting corn near the limits of Springfield; and that "no P'son in ye Plantation shall trade give or lend to any Indian any quantity of powder, little or great, under ye penalty of 40s for any tyme yt any P'son shall be found a transgressor in this kind."

By order of the General Court of Massachusetts in 1645, the inhabitants of Concord, Sudbury, and Dedham—"being inland townes & but thinly peopled"—were forbidden to move from these frontier settlements without the special consent of the Court. From time to time in the early years of the Virginia settlements, the General Assembly of that colony found it necessary to order that every residence be enclosed in a strong palisade. After the Indian massacre of 1622 the order went forth, and again in 1626. But by 1645 the frontier of Indian danger had retreated from the tidewater plain. In that year the General Assembly authorized the building of three blockhouses along the frontier north of the James, these stockades to be erected by a public levy and manned by the local militia. Next March the Assembly provided for a fourth post, Fort Henry, at the falls of the Appomattox; the fort and six hundred acres about it were presented to Abraham Wood, "Provided that he the said Capt. Wood do maintayne and keepe ten men constantly upon the said place for the term of three years, during which time he, the said Capt. Wood, is exempted from all publique taxes for himself and the said tenn persons."

This post was the Fort Leavenworth of its day; from it soldiery rode out against Indians who had breached the peace, squads of Rangers set out from the fort on regular patrols, and at its warehouses the pack trains of the Indian traders were outfitted with the barter stuffs. Fort Henry was the home of Abraham Wood for thirty years or more; many of the traders were his own agents, and from England Wood imported the goods traders needed—"Guns, Powder, Shot, Hatchets (which the Indians call Tomahawks), Kettles, red and blue Planes, Duffields, Stroud-water blankets, and some Cutlary Wares, Brass Rings and other Trinkets."

Important as the fur trade was in the early years of New England settlement, that importance did not last, because the native supply of beaver was not large, and because, in a day when rivers were the highways of commerce, New Englanders were cut off from direct access to the westward sources of supply. The rivers of New England lie north and south; and the greatest fur region south of Hudson Bay was the region about the Great Lakes. The St. Lawrence River tapped this rich country, but that stream was in the hands of France; the Hudson, by way of its tributary, the Mohawk, tapped it, but the Dutch were in possession of that river system.

Sir Fernando Gorges and Captain John Mason, having title to the territory between the Merrimac River and the Kennebec, expected to make their fortunes from the fur trade. There had existed from the days when Captain John Smith coasted along the New England shore a tradition that most of the furs came from certain great lakes in the interior; Gorges and Mason identified these lakes with Lake Champlain—"the Great Lake of Erocoise," as Thomas Morton called it; and they secured from the Council for New England an extension of their grant to include all the region "commonly called or known by the name of the River and Lake or Rivers and Lakes of the Irroquois." They made an attempt to reach this western country by ascending the Piscataqua River; but the obstinacy of that river in taking its course from the north, rather than from the west, defeated the attempt. Thomas Morton, founder of the lively little village of Merrymount, which the Puritans suppressed for motives commercial as well as moral, became greatly interested in the westward expansion of the New England trade, and was responsible for another expedition which attempted to find a water highway to the Great Lake of Erocoise. "There are also more abundance of Beavers, Deare and Turkies breed about the parts of that lake then in any place in all the country of New England," wrote Morton; "and also such multitudes of fish (which is a great part of the foode that the Beavers live upon), that it is a thing to be admired at: so that about this Lake is the principallst place for a plantation in all New Canaan, both for pleasure and profit."

The question of the control of the beaver trade of the Connecticut Valley quickly became answered, for the migration of entire congregations into the valley advanced the cycle from the fur traders' frontier to the farmers' frontier. Could not the Dutch be as summarily expelled from the Hudson Valley? It irked Morton, and many another adventurous Englishman, that this luxuriant region, this New Canaan, should be in the control of the Dutch. "It would be adjudged an irreparable oversight to protract time, and suffer the Dutch (who are but intruders upon his Majesties most hopefull country of New England,) to possess themselves of that so pleasant and commodious country of Erocoise before us."

A mariner-merchant of New Haven discovered that there was a profitable fur trade on the Delaware being exploited by the Dutch and Swedes, each too weak to drive out the other. A Delaware Company, of the leading men of Connecticut, was formed to venture into this trade; and in the spring of 1641 the Company sent agents to the Delaware to purchase lands of the Indians, paving the way for a settlement. But this possibility of westward extension was blocked: the trading post built by Connecticut men near the mouth of the Schuylkill was destroyed by the Dutch and

Swedes, who could unite at least for the work of driving out the English. With the opportunism of true frontiersmen, several of the Connecticut men stranded in the Delaware Valley preferred to submit to Swedish rule rather than abandon the fur trade.

In 1644 "divers of the merchants of Boston," recorded John Winthrop, "being desirous to discover the great lake Champlain or Ontario [they were one and the same to Thomas Morton, and probably so to Winthrop], supposing it to lie to the northwest of our patent, and finding that the great trade of beaver, which came to all the eastern and southern parts, came from thence, petitioned the court to be a company for that design, and to have the trade which they should discover, for 21 years." In the spring of 1644 this company sent a pinnace to the Delaware, William Aspinwall captain. The plan was that Aspinwall should sail up the Delaware as far as he could, and continue up the river in a boat or canoe—doubtless in the hope of finding that the Delaware issued from this Great Lake to the west of Massachusetts. Governor Kieft of New Amsterdam, however, had ordered that no Englishmen be allowed to ascend the river, under any pretense; and a cannonball from the Dutch fort on the Delaware effectively stopped that attempt at exploration.

Another attempt to extend the Connecticut fur trade to the Delaware region, new attempts to reach the West by direct overland expeditions from Massachusetts—no avail. In 1657 the General Court of Massachusetts ordered that "the trade of furs with the Indians in this jurisdiccon doth properly belong to the commonwealth," and appointed a committee to regulate the enterprises. Thereafter, fur traders were licensed by localities, paying for their franchise according to the value of the trade in the particular locality. The highest license was for the Merrimac region, where the privilege of monopolizing the Indian trade cost £25.

Coincidentally a trading company made up of the most influential merchants of Salem and Boston was organized for a flyer in this frontier enterprise. The General Court granted the company ten square miles of land, to be located forty or fifty miles west of Springfield. Governor Peter Stuyvesant, in New Amsterdam, thundered when the news reached him; and the company appealed to the Confederation of New England and the General Court of Massachusetts for official support. The General Court responded handsomely, granting the company a monopoly of the fur trade within fifteen miles of the Hudson for twelve years, and sent emissaries to Stuyvesant with a joint letter from the merchant company and the General Court—as if Stuyvesant cared—asking free passage up the Hudson for the New Englanders. The document was emphatic about the weakness of the Dutch title to the upper Hudson, and explained, "Being now increased and wanting convenient places to settle our people, wee conceive no reason can be imagined why we should not improve and make use of our just rights in all the lands granted us, especially those upon Hudson's river not being actually possessed by your nation, which is the only thing that at present we intend."

So quickly was the farmers' frontier following upon the fur traders'. It is that quick succession that most distinguishes the English frontier from the French; it was the absence of a farming population which might have followed the westward extension of the fur trade that spelled ruin for New France.

CHAPTER II

THE OTHER SIDE OF THE MOUNTAINS

INDIAN rumors, wonderfully mangled, concerning the lands beyond the Appalachians were common in Virginia as Sir William Berkeley began his governorship. "And the Indians have of late acquainted our Governour," wrote a pamphleteer in 1649, "that within five dayes journey to the westward and by South, there is a great high mountaine, and at the foot thereof, great Rivers that run into a great Sea; and that there men who come hither in ships, (but not the same as ours be) they weare apparrell and have reed Caps on their heads, and ride on Beasts like our Horses, but have much longer eares and other circumstances they declare for the certainty of these things." And on the twenty-seventh of August, 1650, seven men set out from Fort Henry to discover the truth of these relations.

Captain Abraham Wood and one Edward Bland, merchant, led the little party. They crossed the rolling slopes of the Piedmont, that were to be occupied in the westward advance of the plantations, and on the last day of the month reached the falls of the Roanoke, close to the present North Carolina line. They had come, they thought, to a westward-flowing river; the region was christened New Brittaine, the explorers speculated on the probability of gold and silver deposits within their discovery, and began the return journey. But the Indian villages of "New Brittaine" were already known to a few fur traders.

There seem to have been other expeditions of "diverse gentlemen" with "a voluntaire desire to discover the Mountains" within the next few years; but no authentic evidence survives. By 1660 Virginia traders were familiar with the Piedmont, and were buying furs from the tribes at the eastern slope of the mountains. England had a throne again, gorgeous and merry; exploration and land speculation were newly invigorated, and the American frontier leapt westward under the impulse. The Hudson's Bay Company was organized; Charles II, taking no notice of the rights of Spain to the south Atlantic, granted Carolina to a group of his courtiers; New Netherland was seized from the Dutch; and from England the group of court favorites and commercial adventurers directed the penetration of the frontier beyond the Piedmont. Dryden may have been the bard who gave these adventurers a salute in 1672:

> Friend, once 'twas Fame that led thee forth
> To brave the Tropic Heat, the Frozen North,
> Late it was Gold, then Beauty was the Spur;
> But now our Gallants venture but for Furs.

The possibility of finding precious metals, however, still gleamed over the western horizon; there was still hope of finding a water passage to Asia. And the advertisements of Carolina reveal that the Lords Proprietors expected profits from land speculation. In 1669 Lord Ashley took over the promotion of Carolina from his agents, and in April of the next year some one hundred fifty colonists arrived at the mouth of the Ashley River—the first permanent settlers of South Carolina. "If the Porch be so beautifull, what must the Temple be?" Carolinians were not long in learning. Henry Woodward for fifteen years led

[18]

them in the exploration of the interior and in establishing trade with the Indians. Meanwhile Sir William Berkeley—one of the Lords Proprietors of Carolina, as well as governor of Virginia—was promoting a series of explorations into the Virginia hinterland.

Two hundred gentlemen of Virginia were ready, Berkeley wrote to his patron, Lord Arlington, "to goe along with me to find out the East India sea, and we had hopes that in our Journy we should have found some Mines of silver; for certaine it is that the spaniard in the same degrees of latitude has found many." But in this spring of 1668 "unusual and continued Raynes" dampened every one's ardor, and the expedition was never assembled. In the spring of 1669 Berkeley despatched an agent into the West—John Lederer, a German adventurer. Berkeley had made a poor choice for explorer-general: Lederer was a romancer, and something of a liar.

On the ninth of March, 1669, Lederer with three Indians set out from the Indian village at the falls of the Pamunkey. After four days he had passed its head springs; and the Blue Ridge Mountains clung like low clouds to the horizon. In a few days the little party was at the face of the mountains; and, related Lederer, "The eighteenth of March, after I had in vain assayed to ride up, I alighted, and left my horse with one of the Indians, whilst with the other two I climbed up the rocks, which were so incumbred with bushes and brambles, that the ascent proved very difficult: besides the first precipice was so steep, that if I lookt down I was immediately taken with a swimming in my head; though afterwards the way was more easie. The height of this mountain was very extraordinary: for notwithstanding I set out with the first appearance of light, it was late in the evening before I gained the top, from whence the next morning I had a beautiful prospect of the Atlantick-Ocean washing the Virginia-shore." Mr. Lederer was dizzy.

For several days he fumbled about for a passage through the mountains, but found none; the cold was becoming unendurable, and the retreat began. In the late spring of 1670 Berkeley sent out Lederer again, this time with one Major William Harris and "twenty Christian horse, and five Indians." The party left the falls of the James on May 22, 1670; three days later they passed through the village of the Manakin tribe, and asked the way to the mountains. An ancient Indian described two paths, one northwest and one southwest; these strenuous Englishmen had no patience with tangents, and rode due west. It was very bad going. After four or five days of blunt encounter with the rough and rocky hills, they struck the James again. Harris did not recognize the river, but he was sure that it was impassable; and the discouraged major with his "twenty Christian horse" turned homeward. Lederer, with just one Indian, kept on into the wilderness, traveling southwest by south to avoid mountains. He passed through several Indian villages; on June the twenty-first he rested in the village of the Saura tribe, on a northern tributary of the Yadkin. He may have gone a bit farther into the southwest; it is more likely that he asked the Sauras about the tribes beyond, and embroidered upon their relations. His tale is of silver tomahawks, squaws with a mania for peacocks' feathers, a lake ten leagues broad, and a barren sandy plain two weeks' journey in width—all this in the Carolina Piedmont.

Lederer made a third attempt to find a way across the mountain barrier, in company with one Colonel Catlett, nine colonists and five Indians. On August 21, 1670, they left the falls of the Rappahannock, following the north fork. "The sixth and twentieth of August we came to the mountains, where finding no horseway up, we alighted, and left our horses with two or three Indians below, whilst we went up afoot. The ascent was so steep, the cold so intense, and we so tired, that having with much ado gained the top of one of the highest, we drank the kings health in brandy, gave the mountain his name, and agreed to return back again."

He had, at least, learned quite a bit about the Indian tribes of the Piedmont; and, unlike the traders who knew this frontier better than did Lederer, he made that information available. Make your journeys, he advised, in small companies, six or ten men, and most of these Indians; "for the nations in your way are prone to jealousie and mischief towards Christians in a considerable body, and as courteous and hearty to a few, from whom they apprehend no danger." And, travelers, notch your trees when you pass through level country; if you don't blaze your trail, you will probably lose your way on your return. The Indians nearest the settlements, so Lederer advised Virginians who were becoming alert to the profits of the fur trade, wanted useful articles, cloths, guns and ammunition, hatchets and knives. "Sometimes you may with brandy or strong liquor dispose them to an humour of giving you ten times the value of your commodity; and at other times they are so hide-bound, that they will not offer half the market-price, especially if they are aware that you have a designe to circumvent them with drink, or that they think you have a desire to their goods, which you must seem to slight and disparage." The Indians farther in the wilderness were still to be fetched of their furs and wampum with mirrors, beads and bracelets of glass, and like "gaudy toys and knacks of children."

Governor Berkeley was an imperialist and a speculator, a capitalist as well as an officer of the Crown; following both interests with a splendid persistence, he laid plans for yet another expedition, one that should be equipped to pass the river that had stopped Harris and Lederer. He consulted the right man, Abraham Wood, now major general of militia, and from the Appomattox Indian village across the river from Fort Henry five men set out on the first of September, 1671. Three of them were gentlemen: Captain Thomas Batts, Robert Fallam, and Thomas Wood. They bore a commission from Abraham Wood "for the finding out the ebbing and flowing of the Waters on the other side of the Mountaines in order to the discovery of the South Sea."

They followed a traders' path due west for the first few days; they crossed the Staunton into the wilderness, traveling "sometimes southerly, sometimes westerly as the path went over several high mountains and steep Vallies crossing several branches and the River Roanoke several times all exceedingly stony ground"; and they were beneath the main range of the Alleghenies. Mountains and hills seemed piled up in a forbidding mass; but an Indian guided the party over the divide into the valley of the New River. In their way through the mountains they passed three trees that bore man-markings, M A N I decipherable on two and the other cut with M A "and several other scratchments." This company, then, was not the first to surmount the eastern continental divide; but Batts and Fallam are the first who made a narrative of the journey. The fact that Wood had commissioned them simply to find out about the tidal waters west of the mountains is further evidence that the mountain passes were already known.

On the seventeenth of September these Virginians found four trees arow that had been half stripped of bark; and here they proclaimed the sovereignty of the Crown. First the cry, "Long Live Charles the Second, by the grace of God King of England . . . Defender of the faith"; then the salute by guns; then, with a pair of marking irons, the graving of the legends on the trees—a conventional symbol for the Crown, initials for Sir William Berkeley, Major General Abraham Wood, and the Englishmen of the party.

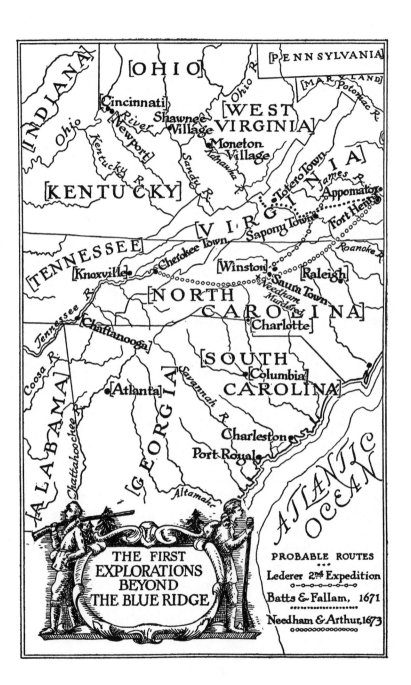

THE FIRST
EXPLORATIONS
BEYOND
THE BLUE RIDGE

PROBABLE ROUTES
• • •
Lederer 2ⁿᵈ Expedition
∘–∘–∘–∘–∘–∘–∘
Batts & Fallam, 1671
••••••••••••••••••
Needham & Arthur, 1673
∘∘∘∘∘∘∘∘∘∘∘∘∘∘∘∘

"It was ebbing Water when we were here. We set up a stock by the Water side but found it to ebb very slowly. Our Indians kept such a hollowing that we durst not stay any longer to make further tryal. Immediately upon coming to our quarters we returned homewards and when we were on the top of a Hill we turned about and saw over against us, westerly, over a certain delightful hill a fog arise and a glimmering light as from water. We supposed there to be a great Bay." Always, as travelers turn homeward, this brief, beautiful vision glimpsed from a height— a silvered arm of the South Sea!

At the confluence of the Mohawk and the Hudson was Fort Orange, relic of the Dutch West India Company. Great estates were the common form of land tenure in the colony of New Netherland; the Hudson was lined with these manorial holdings, "a discouragement to the settling and improving the lands in the neighborhood of them." The proprietors favored the leasing rather than the sale of the lands; settlers preferred to go to other frontiers where the land policy was more liberal, and the trading community at the mouth of the Mohawk, exempt from the pressure of an agricultural population ever reaching out for more and more land, remained primarily a fur-trading community until the beginning of the French and Indian War.

The Iroquois tribes remained staunch allies of the nation that controlled this post, whether Holland or England, not out of undying hatred for the race of which Champlain was a member—that myth should have died out with Peter Parley's textbooks—but because of the soundest of business reasons. From the Dutch traders at Fort Orange the Iroquois got the guns and ammunition wherewith they extended their hegemony over far western tribes not yet in contact with white men; and they acted as middlemen in the fur trade between the western tribes and the Dutch traders. The French built trading posts along the Great Lakes; but the Iroquois, jealous of their commercial position, succeeded in preventing the Dutch or English from doing likewise.

In 1664 Fort Orange, with the rest of New Netherland, passed into the possession of the English; and an English garrison supplemented the Dutchmen in the fort. Thereafter this frontier post, now called Albany, was the focus of the three great conflicting interests in the struggle for the continent—the English, the French, and the Indians. Albany stood as a rival to Montreal in the fur trade, and as the barrier to a French passage down the Hudson to the sea. The Iroquois depended upon the Albany traders for their firearms, wherewith they had attained and held mastery over all the Indian nations of the Old Northwest. But the community remained predominantly Dutch; and few flashes of political imagination interrupted the traders' preoccupation with the art of gaining the largest number of furs for the smallest amount of merchandise. The trade at Albany, in the hands of such aggressive frontiersmen as the Carolinians, could well have been the means of supplanting French influence by English throughout the interior of the continent.

In this transitional period Colbert, the genius of the Commercial Revolution in France, aggressively restated French colonial policy. France was to occupy the whole of the Mississippi Valley and the Great Lakes region, actually and effectively; French merchants were to monopolize the American fur trade. When a force of several hundred French and Indian allies appeared near Schenectady to overawe the Mohawk Iroquois, and when later in that same year, 1666, war broke out between France and England, the way was open for Governor Nicolls to convince the Dutch traders that France plotted the destruction of Albany and its commerce. Within the next generation the French did extend their occupation of the American West, but they failed to subdue the Iroquois, and the Stuart kings were not quite complaisant enough: they could not be persuaded to cede New York to the French crown.

As early as 1671 lawless *coureurs de bois* began to carry their furs to Albany; and the Iroquois bought furs from tribes in the upper Lakes region, passing along their purchases to the Albany traders. Largely to circumvent this loss of trade from Montreal, in 1672 Fort Frontenac was built near the northeast shore of Lake Ontario. In November, 1679, Governor Frontenac wrote to his superiors in Versailles that he feared French trade with the Ottawas and other tribes of the Lake region would be impaired by British influence among the Indians; and that Governor Andros had cordially received several *coureurs* "who have been debauched from Sieur de la Salle."

In 1683 Colonel Thomas Dongan, an imperialist and a vigorous executive, became governor of New York; the Albany trade was to his hand as a weapon of western expansion, and he used it. "Acting rather the part of a trader than a governor," was the tag affixed to Dongan by a caste-conscious official. He pressed the British claims to the Great Lakes region in an extraordinary correspondence with Governor Denonville of New France wherein both gentlemen made belligerent statements in the most polite of phrases. He attempted to persuade the Iroquois to allow English traders an open route to the western Indians. To the community of Albany he gave a charter confirming its old monopoly—"the Privilidge Preheminence & Advantage of haveing within their owne Walls the Sole Managmt of the Trade with all the Indians Liveing within & to the Eastward Northward and Westward of the said County of Albany within the Compasse of his said Majestyes Dominion." In the autumn of 1685 he licensed Captain Johannes Rooseboom to make a trading expedition to the western Indians; and with ten canoes loaded with trading stuffs, Rooseboom's party, guided by a renegade Canadian, followed the chain of the Great Lakes through Lake Huron into the region of the Ottawa and Huron Indians, where they were welcomed.

Denonville was overwhelmed at the news of the expedition; he wept to the French ministry, "Missilimakinac is theirs. They have taken its latitude, have been to trade there with our Ottawa and Huron Indians, who received them cordially on account of the bargains they gave. . . . Unfortunately we had but very few Frenchmen at Missilimakinac at that time." Then he took up an irate pen to demand of Dongan what meant this incursion into French domain. Dongan in replying enjoyed himself thoroughly. This place with the polysyllabic title (the French post on the strait between Lake Huron and Lake Michigan) he pretended was utterly unfamiliar, even by name. "I have only permitted severall of Albany to trade amongst the remotest Indians with strict orders not to meddle with any of your people, and I hope they will finde the same civillity from you—It being so farr from pillageing that I believe it as lawful for the English as French nations to trade there, we being nearer by many leagues than you are . . . certainly our Rum doth as little hurt as your Brandy and in the opinion of Christians is much more wholesome; however, to keep the Indians temperate and sober is a very good and Christian performance but to prohibit them all strong liquors seems a little hard and very turkish."

In the winter of 1686-1687 Dongan decided to clinch his invasion of the Great Lakes fur country. Rooseboom was sent out again, with a company of fifty people to manage twenty canoes laden mostly with rum; in September, 1686, he left Albany, to winter with the Senecas and proceed to Michilimackinac in the spring. A second company of thirty men left Albany when the spring season opened. But Denonville, meanwhile, was planning an expedition to crush the Iroquois; the commandants of the French posts on the Lakes had been ordered to concentrate their men at Niagara. In this movement toward Niagara, the French troops encountered Rooseboom's canoes in Lake Huron, and counted coup; the second company of Englishmen were discovered in Lake Erie, and likewise captured.

With the downfall of James II, British foreign policy sharply veered. War was declared upon France. Louis XIV made an astute move to protect his American possessions: the Comte de Frontenac was returned as governor of New France, and the Hudson Valley was soon made aware of the change. In 1690 a band of French and Indians swept into New York and burned the town of Schenectady.

To contest for the beaver of the Great Lakes was now too hazardous a business; and the Albany traders sought another outlet westward. The Shawnee nation made peace with the British; and the Ohio Valley was open. Arnout Cornelius Viele, onetime official Indian interpreter for the province of New York, was no stranger to the wilderness; he had lived for several years among the Indians, and had been one of the Albany adventurers captured in Lake Huron in 1687. In the autumn of 1692 Viele, with a few Delaware and Shawnee Indians, set out to break the way for the colonial traders of the north. His course was south to New Jersey, across Pennsylvania to the Allegheny, and down that tributary into the Ohio. Viele explored the Ohio waters as far west as the Wabash, and made a fifteen months' sojourn in the home of the Shawnee, between the Ohio and the Cumberland. In the summer of 1694 he headed back into Pennsylvania, bringing hundreds of Shawnees ready to enter the covenant chain with the British.

In the spring of 1673 General Abraham Wood equipped James Needham, Gentleman, and Gabriel Arthur for a three months' journey across the mountains. Needham

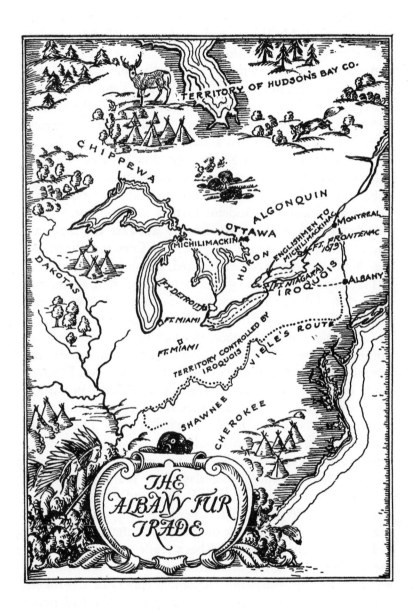

TERRITORY OF HUDSON'S BAY CO.

CHIPPEWA

ALGONQUIN

OTTAWA

MICHILIMACKINAC

HURON

ENGLISHMEN TO MICHILIMACKINAC

MONTREAL

FT. FRONTENAC 1673

DAKOTAS

FT. DETROIT

FT. NIAGARA

IROQUOIS

ALBANY

FT. MIAMI

FT. MIAMI

TERRITORY CONTROLLED BY IROQUOIS

VIELE'S ROUTE

SHAWNEE

CHEROKEE

THE ALBANY FUR TRADE

was a freeholder of South Carolina, Arthur was a youngster who was probably indentured to General Wood's service; both were acclimated to the wilderness, and had the stamina and courage to carry through Wood's bold project of a trade with the Cherokee Indians on the Tennessee River. The greatest obstacle was the "unwillingness of the Indians before the mountaines, that any should discover beyond them," as Wood wrote to a friend in London. These Indians, the Occaneechi tribe, attempted to preserve an enviable position: they were the medium between trans-Allegheny tribes and the Virginia fur traders, and they possessed English firearms while the Indians farther west did not. Their fortified island in the Roanoke was athwart the highway, known as the Trading Path, into the Carolina Piedmont. Needham and Arthur were blocked, but not for long; later in that same spring the two adventurers started again, had the luck to fall in with some far-wandering Cherokees, and in their company traversed the Blue Ridge of Carolina.

Across the forested slopes, through the luxuriantly black gorges, the party of Indians and white men gained the summit. "Ye ridge upon ye topp is not above two hundred paces over; ye decent better then on this side. in halfe a day they came to ye foot, and then levell ground all ye way, many slashes upon ye heads of small runs. The slashes are full of very great canes and ye water runes to ye north west . . . turkes, deere, ellkes, beare, woolfe and other vermin very tame"—and, fifteen days' fast journeying beyond the last village on the Trading Path, Needham and Arthur were at the village of their Cherokee companions, beside the Tennessee River or one of its larger tributaries.

For many years there had been trade relations between the Cherokees and the Spaniards of Florida, concluding— naturally enough—in a thoroughgoing enmity of Cherokees towards Spaniards. But men of English stock had never been among these Indians. Needham and Arthur were

handsomely received, "even to addoration in their cerri-
monies of courtesies and a stake was sett up in ye middle
of ye towne to fasten ye horse to, and abundance of corne
and all matter of pulse with fish, flesh and beares oyle for
ye horse to feed upon and a scaffold sett up before day for
my two men . . . that their people might stand and gaze
at them and not offend them by their throng."

After a short rest at the Cherokee village, James Needham determined upon returning to Fort Henry with a delegation of the Cherokees, leaving Arthur behind to learn
the language. Needham completed the journey, and took
leave of the elated General Wood to go to the Cherokee
village again, to spend part of the winter trapping season
among the Indians and to bring Arthur back with him in
the spring.

Late in January, 1674, a flying rumor reached Abraham
Wood that Needham had been killed; and in a few days an
independent trader arrived from the Carolina Piedmont to
confirm the story that the discoverer of Tennessee had been
murdered by an Occaneechi Indian. Gabriel Arthur, the
wilderness cub who had remained with the Cherokee,
traveled with them on several forays toward Florida and
toward the Ohio. In a skirmish with the Shawnee Arthur
was wounded and captured; these Indians, as yet entirely
untouched by the fur trade and unacquainted with firearms
or iron artifacts, made much of their white captive, and
ultimately gave him provisions and freedom. He hunted
with the Cherokee again, and in May, 1674, led nineteen
Indians laden with furs toward Fort Henry. The Occaneechi waylaid the party; but the young man escaped,
and came safely into Fort Henry on the eighteenth of
June, 1674.

"Thus endes ye tragedy," wrote Abraham Wood to his
friend in London, "I hope yette to write cominically of ye
buisness. If I could have ye countenance of some person

[31]

of honor in England to curb and bridle ye obstructers here
for here is no incouragement att all to be had for him that
is Sir Youre humble servant   AB WOOD."

In the last quarter of the seventeenth century the agricultural frontier attempted to barricade itself against the
Indians. In 1675-1676 Virginia adopted a plan to establish a chain of forts along the frontier line. At the same
time delegates to the General Court of Massachusetts were
proposing that a fence of logs or stone eight feet high be
erected along the western fringe of settlement, hemming
in the entire colony. That project failed because frontiersmen had no liking for such a literal barrier; in Virginia
seven forts were built, but because of the expense of maintaining garrisons the posts were allowed to fall into ruin.
The frontier was in truth a fighting community, that preferred to meet Indian danger quickly and decisively when
the danger arose, and then to go back to its business. Yet
until the accession of George III the presence of a common
danger along their frontiers was the greatest single factor
toward a union of the colonies. Because that factor was
not uniform nor constant, none of the colonial attempts at
union, not even the New England Confederation, exhibited
any real strength.

A democratic, self-sufficing society, a distinct class of
frontiersmen, was already formed. In New England the
frontier towns were too near the coastal towns, and woven
into too close a political net, to gain this full distinctiveness;
but in Virginia the social division between the older districts
and the back country becomes startlingly vivid in its angry
manifestation of 1676. Bacon's Rebellion was provoked
chiefly because Governor Berkeley would not allow the
frontier settlements to place the command of their militia
in men of their own choosing, nor authorize the militia to
carry on a fight which the Indians had begun. Berkeley

[32]

and his influential friends were interested in the fur trade; and warfare would have injured that trade. But the legislation passed by the General Assembly when Governor Berkeley had fled from the capital and Nathaniel Bacon's presence gave the assemblymen courage, is highly significant: it is a series of attacks against an established order, a property-holding and office-holding class. No man could serve as sheriff for two consecutive terms; surveyors, escheators, clerks of the court, and sheriffs could hold only one office at a time; councilors were no longer to be exempt from taxation; self-perpetuating vestries, which had long controlled the parishes and levied church taxes, were to give way to bodies elected by the freemen; the people were to elect representatives equal in number with the county justices, to have a voice "in laying the countie assessments, and of making wholesome lawes"; the franchise in colonial elections was extended to all freemen. These bills were quashed when the rebellion had collapsed and Berkeley's iron fist was beating out revenge; but a frontier society had spoken, shouting the first changes it would make when it had the power.

In this turmoil was lost the impetus to further achievements in western exploration. In England an aristocracy of Whiggery, with none of the flash and fire of the Cavalier aristocracy represented by the Lords Proprietors of Carolina, was shortly to thrust the Stuart line from its crown and install a substitute to its own liking; there were no more Lord Ashleys to impel the westward extension of the American frontier. But, following Needham's trail, traders from Virginia were reaping the profits of the Cherokee trade; other Virginia traders were following the New River toward the Ohio. And lone frontiersmen were establishing themselves beyond the Blue Ridge—men who lived by the gun and the beaver trap, men who liked very little company, and that little preferably feminine and Indian.

[33]

CHAPTER III

THE SOUTHERN FRONTIER

WILLIAM TALBOT, in dedicating his edition of *The Discoveries of William Lederer*, fairly scraped his plumes on the ground in compliment to Lord Ashley, most noteworthy of the proprietors of Carolina. Lederer's journals, stated Talbot, clearly foreshadowed the long-hoped for discovery of the South Sea; "and Carolina out of her happy experience of your Lordship's success in great undertakings, presumes that the accomplishment of this glorious Designe is reserved for her. In order to which, the Apalataean Mountains (though like the prodigious Wall that divides China from Tartary, they deny Virginia passage into the West Continent) stoop to your lordships Dominions, and lay open a Prospect into unlimited Empires." And, taking full advantage of the absence of a mountain barrier, Carolinians in the last decade of the seventeenth century were penetrating far into the wilderness. After the period of General Abraham Wood's vigorous leadership on the Virginia frontier, the Carolina traders far outmatched the Virginians in initiative. Only the French-Canadian traders, the *coureurs de bois*, ventured as audaciously into the wilderness.

The same magnet drew Frenchmen and Carolinians to far-distant places: peltries. The explorations of New France were for the most part induced by the fur trade, and almost always the fur trade made the explorations profitable. When St. Lusson and Nicholas Perrot took official possession of the American Northwest for France at the Sault Ste Marie in 1671, the cost of that expedition was defrayed by trade in beaver. Joliet was an experienced and successful fur trader. La Salle's ambition was to make the Mississippi a French highway for the transportation of buffalo hides and beaver skins from the Northwest.

Because of the strength of the Iroquois between the Great Lakes and the Ohio, the French knew little of the central Ohio Valley. French explorers in the Mississippi Valley eked out their scanty acquaintance with the country to the east by the information given them by the Shawnees, who were being dislodged from their home in the Cumberland-Tennessee region by the incessant battering of their enemy, the Iroquois. On French maps after the period of La Salle's explorations the Tennessee River was depicted in its approximate course, and the route which the Cherokee and the Shawnee followed from the Tennessee country to the Spanish trading towns of Florida was laid down. Tonti, a privileged trader in the Illinois country, in 1694 warned his fellow-French that Carolinian traders were already among the Cherokee Indians on the upper waters of the Tennessee; La Salle himself feared that the Carolina traders penetrating beyond the Appalachians would encroach upon French plans to encompass the Indian trade of the heart of the continent.

[35]

Jean Couture, a *coureur de bois* of Canada, had been one of those who followed Tonti down the Mississippi, in 1686, in the unsuccessful attempt to join the Sieur de la Salle; shortly afterwards he and others of Tonti's *coureurs* had built a stockaded post at the mouth of the Arkansas, in an attempt of the French to maintain a military and commercial alliance with the Arkansas Indians. Several years later he was a renegade from Tonti's service, living among the English on the western fringe of South Carolina; out of the obscurity that darkens the movement of fur traders he emerges with this reputation, "the greatest Trader and Traveler amongst the Indians for more than Twenty years." He became involved in a characteristic scheme of English gentlemen-adventurers, to discover gold and pearls known to Indians "above a hundred leagues beyond the Appalatean Mountains"; but the seventeenth century was almost at an end, and the enterprise died of its own triteness. In 1700 his real talents were requisitioned; he was the guide of a party of English traders, whose high-flung intention was to divert the fur trade of the Mississippi Valley from New France to South Carolina.

General Francis Nicholson, who became governor of Virginia in 1699, did not know much about the West; but, like most governors of the oldest colony, the fur trade was to him a personal interest, and its protection an official responsibility. He recommended to the Lords of the Board of Trade that adventurers be encouraged to seek commerce with the far-inland tribes, and by underbidding to drive the French from the competition for furs. With better hope of results, he conducted active correspondence with the governors of New York and South Carolina, who faced similar responsibilities. Governor Joseph Blake of South Carolina, one of the principal traders of his own province, entered fully into Nicholson's spirit: the colonial frontier must be on the move again, must make its greatest advance into the

[36]

wilderness. And from South Carolina, as the new year began, Jean Couture led a group of traders toward the Mississippi.

The traders carried with them presents of ammunition and merchandise wherewith to introduce themselves to the Mississippi tribes, and papers from Governor Blake claiming the Mississippi country as a part of the English empire: Following a natural highway, the Tennessee River, the Ohio, the Mississippi, the party arrived at the mouth of the Arkansas in February, 1700.

Among the French of Louisiana the news of this expedition created a profound sensation—an apparition of a tide of immigration rushing over the Appalachians in the wake of these traders and peopling the Mississippi Valley with Englishmen. It seemed that the road was open for lawless *coureurs de bois* to carry furs directly into Carolina, and for the Carolina traders to extend their commerce to the farthest Indian tribes. Since there was as yet no official depot for their peltry in the Mississippi Valley, the *coureurs* above the mouth of the Ohio were forbidden to bring their beaver down the Mississippi. In partial response to Iberville's recommendations transmitted with his report of the coming of the Carolina traders to the Arkansas, the French ministry conceded that, for the present, furs from the upper Mississippi could be purchased in Louisiana by an agent of the deputies of Canada; but already several Canadian *coureurs,* following Couture's route, had come to the Cherokee villages in the Tennessee country, and, discovering a convenient portage to the Savannah River, had presented themselves to the governor of South Carolina at his plantation near Charleston. Governor James Moore, like his predecessor, Governor Blake, had interests of his own in the Indian trade; the Canadians negotiated with him for the opening of a trade for themselves and several fellow renegades who had remained on the Mississippi, and

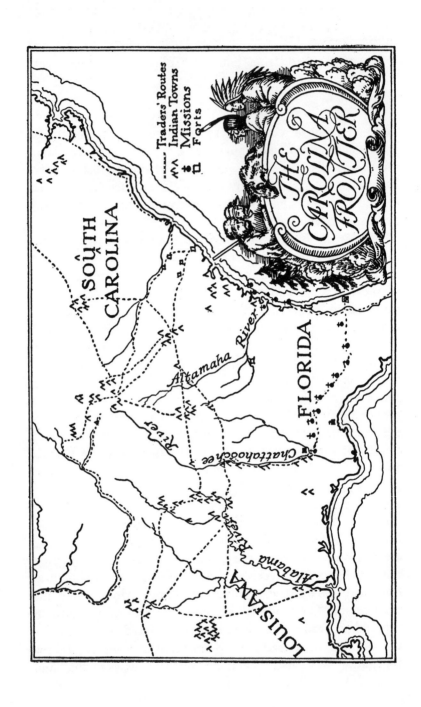

THE CAROLINA FRONTIER

Traders' Routes ----
Indian Towns ʌʌ
Missions ✝
Forts ☐

SOUTH CAROLINA

FLORIDA

LOUISIANA

Altamaha River

Chattahoochee River

Alabama River

although the Carolina assembly was unwilling to license these foreigners, it seems likely that Moore made a private arrangement with them. The tradition in New France was that the *coureurs,* returning to the upper Mississippi, brought English merchandise back with them.

Yet, during the sixty years of conflict between France and England in Europe and America which now began, this highway into the Mississippi Valley which the Carolina traders had opened never assumed its possible importance. The young colony which Iberville had established near the mouth of the Mississippi took firm root; French missionaries among the tribes of the lower Mississippi Valley successfully persuaded the Indians to give preference to French traders; and the emotions of war time prevented the *coureurs de bois* from bringing their furs to Carolina.

Beaver pelts from the southern streams were in quality inferior to those taken in northern waters; but the Carolinians had a compensating advantage, in the vast numbers of deer in the southern woodlands. "There is such infinite Herds," wrote Thomas Ashe in 1682, "that the whole Country seems but one continued Park." London, unlike Paris, was an eager market for heavy buckskins. From 1699 to 1715 an average of fifty-four thousand deerskins was annually exported from Carolina to England. The fortunes of the Indian hunters, the flaring-up and subsiding of Indian hostility, the number of traders licensed, and other factors, accounted for great vicissitudes in the trade; it was a speculative pursuit, this bartering for furs, never lifted above the uncertain level of frontier conditions until John Jacob Astor brought the talents of a Wall Street "pirate" into the business. And by that time the fur traders' frontier had vanished from the South.

The explorations of the Carolinians were not paralleled by the fur traders of the northern colonies. Charleston traders ranged the forests from the Savannah River northwest to the Tennessee and west to the Yazoo. They had commerce with tribes close to the outposts of France and Spain, and among the more distant tribes upon the frontiers of Florida and Louisiana pushed their disreputable side business in Indian captives. That business had begun very early in the history of Carolina, when audacious traders raided the Indian towns near the Spanish missions in Florida, and bought the captives of tribes allied with the Carolinians; but this traffic was moribund after the first quarter of the eighteenth century, when negro slavery had been demonstrated a much better investment.

"Charles Town Trades near 1,000 miles into the Continent," boasted the governor of Carolina in 1707. The traders of Albany could match that claim, but in their case the trade normally ran through Indian channels down to the very confluence of the Mohawk and the Hudson.

In these years at the turn of the century the farmers' frontier made appreciable strides to the westward. The proprietary colonies were the most active in promoting immigration. These colonies were, in intention at least, great private estates; they were of no use to the owners unless they were peopled. In New Jersey, the "Concessions and Agreements of the Lords Proprietors" in 1664 set forth that every freeman who left ship before January, 1665, provided with a musket, ammunition, and six months' provisions, should receive a hundred and fifty acres of land, and an additional amount for every able-bodied manservant whom the freeman brought with him; after five years the land should be subject to a yearly quitrent of one halfpenny per acre to the lords proprietors. The proprietors of the Jerseys offered similar concessions in the succeeding years, and William Penn followed suit. There was little uniformity in the size of the grants in the proprietary colonies; but there was some uniformity in the difficulty in collecting quitrent. One of the first fruits of the frontier was the settler's sincere feeling that he ought not to pay for his land, since it was virgin wilderness before he labored upon it.

Along the southern frontier servants who had worked out their indenture, and other poor folk, were following a lazy business in cattle-raising. The scrawny, half-wild kine roamed the unfenced woods. "The Keepers live chiefly upon Milk," recorded a British officer who was sent into the frontier, "for out of their vast Herds, they do condescend to tame Cows enough to keep their Family in Milk, Whey, Curds, Cheese and Butter; they also have Flesh in Abundance such as it is, for they eat the old Cows and lean Calves that are like to die. The Cow-Men are hardy people, are almost continually on Horseback, being obliged to know the Haunts of their Cattle." As Charleston, Williamsburg, and other towns exhibited the first twinges of urbanity, cattle-droving developed on a modest scale; in the autumn the cattlemen culled out their fattest steers, and urged these herds along the trails eastward. About the regular garrisons on the frontier cattlemen sometimes built cabins and made a rail-fence enclosure for the calves; when the militia were called into service for some foray against the Indians, the cattlemen found their largest market in supplying the army on the march.

The extension of the frontier into the uplands of the southern colonies was haphazard and disorganized in contrast to New England, where the General Court had held the leash. An anonymous narrator, in Virginia in 1695, exclaimed at the "ignorance and knavery of surveyors, who often gave out draughts of surveys without ever actually surveying, or even coming on the lands. Only they gave description by some natural bounds, and were sure to allow large measure, that so the persons for whom they surveyed might enjoy much larger tracts of lands than they were to pay quit-rent for. Then all courts were very lavish in allowing certificates for rights." One who took out a patent for a tract of the King's land in Virginia was obligated to settle upon it within three years; the building of a house was accepted as sufficient evidence of settlement, or the planting and tending of as little as one acre.

The fur trade of Virginia was thrown open to unrestricted competition by an act of the Assembly in 1705, with the proviso that any one who should begin trade with an Indian nation "situated or inhabiting to the westward of or between the Appalatian Mountains," should enjoy a monopoly of that trade for fourteen years.

In 1710 Alexander Spotswood, colonel in the British army, came to Williamsburg to begin his new career of statesman. He brought a fighter's ardor to the governor-ship of Virginia: France, he was convinced, was planning to join its far-scattered posts in America into an unbroken chain of settlements and fortresses which should restrict the British colonies to the seaboard; and Spotswood intended that his defense should be an attack. As he explained to the Lords of the Board of Trade, "To prevent the dangers w'ch Threaten his Maj'ty's Dominions here from the grow-ing power of these Neighbors, nothing seems to me of more consequence than that now while the Nations are at peace, and while the French are yet incapable of possessing all that vast tract which lies at the back of these Plantations, we should attempt to make some Settlements on ye Lakes, and at the same time possess our selves of those passes of the great Mountains, w'ch are necessary to preserve a Com-munication w'th such Settlements." In his first year in Virginia the governor led a gay reconnaissance to the crest of the first range of mountains; and, in common with many another gentleman in the colony, he speculated a bit in the fur trade.

After six years of wrangling with the House of Burgesses, Spotswood was again free to return to western exploration; and on the morning of August 20, 1716, several gentlemen, with their horses and the necessary baggage and servants, waited upon the governor at Williamsburg. They breakfasted at the governor's mansion, and set out upon the grandiose junket of the Order of the Golden Horseshoe.

Spotswood's chief aim, he wrote the Board of Trade, was "to satisfy my Self whether it was practicable to come at the Lakes"—whether a highway could not be opened between Virginia and the Great Lakes. There were reports, too, that a colony of Germans on the Rappahannock River were mining silver; and the languishing fortunes of Spotswood's Indian Company needed some bold stroke for their rehabilitation. Spotswood's excursion of 1716 is not an important episode in the westward extension of the British colonies, particularly since a squad of Virginia Rangers had crossed the Blue Ridge into the Shenandoah Valley earlier that same spring—a fact which Spotswood, protecting his own glory, seems not to have cared to report to the Lords of the Board of Trade. But it is a handsome pageant.

Four days' ride from Williamsburg, Spotswood and his gentlemen arrived at the German settlement at the forks of the Rappahannock, where, wrote John Fontaine in his diary, they had "bad beds and indifferent entertainment."

This westernmost settlement had been planted in 1714; Spotswood himself was responsible for its location. An order of the executive council of Virginia, April 28, 1714, reveals the circumstances: "The Governor acquainting the Council that Sundry Germans to the number of forty two men women & children who were invited hither by the Baron de Graffinreid are now arrived, but that the said Baron not being here to take care of this Settlement, the Governor therefore proposed to settle them above the falls of Rappahannock River to serve as a Barrier to the Inhabitants of that part of the Country against the Incursions of the Indians and desiring the opinion of the Council whether in consideration of their usefulness for that purpose the Charge of building them a Fort, clearing a road to their settlement & carrying thither two pieces of Canon & some ammunition may not properly be defrayed by the publick." The Council acceded unanimously; the emigrants had been moved to the far frontier, and the settlement had taken root.

Here Spotswood's party was reinforced by two companies of Rangers, thirteen men in all, and four Indian guides. The gentlemen idled, shooting at targets for diversion; and after three days the party crossed the Rappahannock. The way to the west was laced with brambles; much the worse for thorns, the company squirmed through thickets to the headwaters of the James. Trudging up the slope, most of the way too steep for the gentlemen to use their horses, on the afternoon of the fifth of September the expedition gained the crest of the Blue Ridge. "We came to the very head spring of the James River," recorded John Fontaine, "where it runs no bigger than a man's arm, from under a large stone. We drank King George's health, and all the Royal Family's, at the very top of the Appalachian mountains. About a musket-shot from the spring there is another, which rises and runs down the other side; it goes westward, and we thought we could go down that way, but we met with such prodigious precipices, that we were obliged to return to the top again. We found some trees which had been formerly marked, I suppose, by the Northern Indians"—most likely by traders or Rangers who had anticipated Spotswood's expedition—"and following those trees we made a good, safe descent. Several of the Company were for returning; but the Governor persuaded them to continue on. About five, we were down on the other side, and continued our way for about seven miles further."

These seven miles brought the party to the river now known as the Shenandoah. Spotswood's zeal for exploration was satisfied; and he proceeded to leave permanent memorials of his "discovery." He had graving irons; but the hard stones baffled him. Fontaine graved his own name upon a tree beside the river; and the governor buried a bottle containing a written statement of the discovery, and announcing possession in the name of his Majesty, George I of England. After the company had assembled for a dinner, toasts and salvos were in order. The king's health in champagne, followed by a volley; for the heir apparent, a toast of burgundy, then a volley; the health of the rest of the royal family drunk in claret, then another salvo from

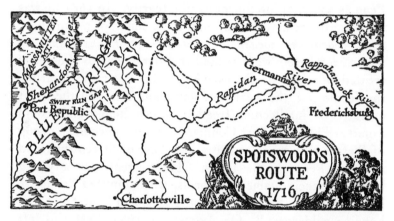

the muskets. And thereafter the governor's health, and much quaffing in self-gratulation. The expedition was well equipped for these ceremonies, having brought red and white Rapidan wine, Irish usquebaugh, brandy, shrub, champagne, canary wine, cider, two varieties of rum and a few odd bottles.

For this expedition the gentlemen had been required to have their horses shod; in the soft turf of tidewater Virginia there were few stones, and shoeing was not necessary. Spotswood, returned to Williamsburg, presented each of his companies with a golden horseshoe bearing the amiable inscription, *Sic juvat transcendere montes.* As the Reverend Hugh Jones explained, "This he instituted to encourage gentlemen to venture backwards, and make discoveries and new settlements; any gentleman being entitled to wear this Golden Shoe that can prove his having drunk *his Majestys health* upon MOUNT GEORGE"—the highest mountain which Spotswood's expedition had scaled.

In 1677 William Penn was in Germany, pleading the cause of the Society of Friends. Groups listened to him with respect and admiration; the Society did not gain many members, but German Protestants became acquainted with Penn as a man of intelligence and integrity. In 1681 he was speaking to them again, through the medium of a pamphlet, *Eine Nachricht wegen de Landschaft Pennsylvania in Amerika,* wherein were recited the attractions of the newly created province of Pennsylvania: the favorable location, the fertile soil, the wealth of game and fish, and the great measure of intellectual freedom which immigrants could expect. The Frankfort Company was the outcome, a group of Pietists who made an initial purchase of fifteen thousand acres of Pennsylvania lands. Their agent was a young lawyer, Francis Daniel Pastorius, who admitted "a desire in my soul . . . to lead a quiet, godly, and honest life in a howling wilderness." On August 20, 1683, Pastorius left ship at Philadelphia with the first contingent of the immigrants, all Mennonites; in October arrived the *Concord,* with the first shipload of Germans. A tract about six miles above Philadelphia became the site of the first permanent German settlement, Germantown, in America. Philadelphia itself had been laid out only two years before.

Devastation of their homelands by war, the persecution which Protestant sects endured, and the tyranny of the princes of small domains, throughout the eighteenth century induced German folk to follow the pioneers of Germantown across the Atlantic. Letters from American friends were favorable to the new country; shipping facilities were increasing, and shipowners were employing immigration

[46]

agents to good effect. A heavy current of German immigration had swept into the American frontier before the battle
of Lexington marked a moment's halt.

The first influx was concentrated upon New York. The
valley of the Schoharie River, "to which," said Governor
Robert Hunter, "the Indians have no pretence," was
sprinkled with German villages in 1710. In the next decade
German immigrants newly arrived, reënforced by Johann
Conrad Weiser and many of his followers from the
Schoharie settlements, invaded the Mohawk Valley. The
greater part of the German immigration in the eighteenth
century landed at the port of Philadelphia, pushed beyond
the Quaker settlements near the Delaware, and claimed the
wilderness midway between the Delaware and the Susquehanna.

These Germans gravitated naturally to the frontier.
They were poor, and had to go where land was cheap. They
sought out wooded areas, in the knowledge that good soil
was to be found underneath rich forest growth; and they
had the doggedness to undertake any task of forest-clearing.
They husbanded their cattle well, they worked their fields
tenaciously, their wives and daughters cared for truck gardens and were willing to work in the grainfields when the
men needed help. Confronted with Indian hostility, these
colonists tenaciously extended the farmers' frontier farther
into the wilderness; when they suffered—and the Mohawk
Valley Germans endured Indian ravages as frequently as
any pioneers on the American frontier—they returned for
the disheartening work of rebuilding, as soon as the savage
menace had recoiled again. When the choice was left to the
Germans, they maintained friendly relations with the
Indians. The settlers in the Schoharie Valley were called
to account by Governor Robert Hunter, suspicious of their
amiable contacts with the Indians; they answered candidly
that it was good policy, that if they chose to be harsh and

belligerent they would be constantly exposed to attacks by both the Indians and the French.

But pushing beyond the Germans' clearings in many areas, extending the frontier line of settlement yet farther west, another European element found itself at home in America. In the seventeenth century the seaboard colonies had received several "congregations" of emigrants from Ulster, and other Presbyterians from Scotland. In the next century the Scotch settlements in northern Ireland poured out their increase, and a goodly portion of their principal, into the American colonies. After the Crown had in 1704 approved a bill of Parliament that all public officers in Ireland must take the Sacrament according to the rites of the Established Church, and there had been begun a long series of laws penalizing the very protestant sects, emigration became desirable to the Scotch-Irish; when the woolen manufactures were suppressed, and a succession of famine years followed upon the ruinous economic measures of Parliament, emigration became necessary. "Both ministers and people going off," the records repeat. The seaboard region assimilated a very few of these emigrants; their place was on the frontier, and they were hardy enough and primitive enough to fit.

Most of the passenger ships sailing from Ireland during the eighteenth century were bound for ports in Pennsylvania—Lewes, Newcastle, Philadelphia. The keystone province became the center of Scotch-Irish settlement in America. Before 1720 Scotch-Irish pioneers were clearing lands near the mouth of the Susquehanna, and in the next decade were claiming the lands along the eastern bank of the river. Because the Scotch-Irish moved readily toward the frontier, becoming a buffer between the Indians and the pacifistic Quakers, the proprietors of the province exempted them from quitrents; and the Scotch-Irish made other exemptions in their own favor. A letter from James Logan, secretary of the province, to John Penn, written in November, 1727, expresses the discomfort of an official whose jurisdiction was growing all too rapidly for him: "We have many thousands of foreigners, mostly Palatines so-called [the Germans]. . . . We have from the North of Ireland great numbers yearly. Eight or nine ships this fall discharged at Newcastle. Both these sets frequently sit down on any spot of vacant land they can find, without asking questions. The last Palatines say there will be twice the number next year; and the Irish say the same of their people. Last week, one of the latter applied to me in the name of four hundred, as he said, who depended on me for directions where they should settle. They say the Proprietor invited people to come and settle his country; they came for that end, and must live. Both they and the Palatines pretend that they will buy, but not one in twenty has anything to pay with."

Two years later, in 1729, Logan surmised one important effect of the rush of Scotch-Irish into the frontier: "The Indians themselves are alarmed at the swarms of strangers, and we are afraid of a breach between them—the Irish are very rough to them." He was right. The eagerness for free lands led the Scotch-Irish farther into the Indian country, settling upon lands to which the Indian title had not been quieted. As part of their quick adaptation to the American frontier, these pioneers treated the Indians with sometimes unquenchable savagery. The Scotch-Irish and the Indians understood one another.

The rising scale of Pennsylvania lands, changing from £10 for one hundred acres and two shillings quitrent to £15½ for the same quantity of land and quitrent of one halfpenny per acre in 1732, soon turned the current of settlement southward, in search of new and cheaper lands. In Maryland in 1738 lands were being offered at £5 for one hundred acres; simultaneously in the Valley of Virginia, the Executive Council was making free grants of a thousand acres for each family, asking only an annual quitrent of one shilling for every fifty acres; and in the piedmont region of North Carolina ample tracts of land were being sold to settlers for a few shillings.

In 1720 the Virginia Assembly recognized the growing importance of the frontier by establishing two western counties, Spotsylvania and Brunswick. Each was huge; Brunswick County extended to the Blue Ridge Mountains, including within its limits the "Southern Pass," the water gap of the Roanoke; Spotsylvania County included Swift Run Gap, through which Spotswood had passed in 1716, and extended well beyond the Blue Ridge. The act establishing these counties appropriated one thousand pounds from the public treasury to equip the "christian titheables" who settled in the West with muskets and ammunition. Three years later settlement was so well advanced that the inhabitants of these counties were able to present an impressive petition voicing a characteristic plaint of the frontier, and to get results; for, "Whereas their Excellencies the Lords Justices have by their Order in Council bearing date the 6th day of August, 1723, signified their Excell'cies pleasure upon an Humble Address made to his Majesty by the Council and Burgesses of this Colony for exempting the Inhabitants of the new erected Countys of Brunswick and Spotsylvania from the purchase of Rights and payment of the Quitt Rents, and the said Order of the Lords Justices being this day laid before the Board, it is the opinion of the Council and accordingly Ordered, that their Excellencys pleasure for granting a Remission of pay'mt of Quitt Rents for 7 years to be reckoned from the 1st day of May, 1721, be notifyed to the Surveyors of the said Countys to the end such as desire to take up Land in those Countys may be inform'd of the Encouragement thereby granted them."

In 1730 the settlement of the Valley of Virginia was

officially begun, when the Executive Council made four grants of land beyond the Blue Ridge; but it need hardly be said that squatters were already in the valley, living out their truculent independence in little cabins erected without benefit of law.

CHAPTER IV

MILLIONS OF ACRES FOR GENTLEMEN

THE adventure-hunger of frontiersmen on the western slope of the Blue Ridge, and the grand speculations of gentlemen in the inner circle of Virginia aristocracy, alike turned to the West. John Howard must have been among the first Scotch-Irish to follow the passage between the Blue Ridge and the North mountains into the Valley of Virginia; but in 1737, three years before the migration of Pennsylvania farmers into the Valley began in earnest, he was restless and ready to move. The Virginia Council liked his proposal of a far-western exploration: the governor wanted adequate maps of Virginia "from sea to sea," and the gentlemen of the Council very likely hoped for ten-thousand-acre estates marked out of the wilderness. The Council secretary recorded: "John Howard, by his Petition setting forth that he, together with divers other Inhabitants on Sherrando River, are willing at their own charge to go upon discoveries on the Lakes & River of Mississippi, and praying a Commission for that purpose, it is accordingly Ordered that a Commission be granted the said Howard to Command such men as shall be willing to accompany him on such discovery, but with this caution that he don't offer any Hostility to any Indians or others he may happen to meet with nor go to any ffort or Garrison possess'd by the ffrench on the said Lakes or River." And, by way of good will, the Council ordered that Howard be furnished out of His Majesty's stores with forty pounds of powder, a proportionate quantity of bullets, and four iron kettles.

Five years lapse, unaccountably, in the brave tale of John Howard; all that is certain is that he did not go a-discovering into the West. Meanwhile he did obtain an Order of Council for ten thousand acres of land, to be divided equally among himself and his fellow adventurers. In March, 1742, Howard reappears upon written record, in the narrative of a Swiss emigrant, John Peter Salley, who had followed the vanguard of Scotch-Irish settlers in the Valley of Virginia in 1740. John Howard came to Salley's cabin, on a fork of the James River close against the western slope of the Blue Ridge, in March, 1742, and spun his project. Salley and two other listeners were ready and willing. These three men, with Howard's son, entered into a written covenant with John Howard; and on the sixteenth of March the five pioneers set out for the West.

They knew, vaguely, that a few outposts of New France were in the Ohio Valley, near the Mississippi, and that since the turn of the century Frenchmen, in numbers and resources unknown to Virginians, had occupied the lower Mississippi Valley. There were folk-recollections of the explorations of Colonel Abraham Wood, and the bare knowledge that traders from North Carolina had traversed the wilderness as far as the Mississippi; it is doubtful if these explorers knew much else.

On the bank of Wood's River the party killed five buffaloes, and with their hides made a bull-boat large enough to carry all the company and their provisions; when waterfalls became frequent and mountains hemmed in the little stream, they struck out overland. At a fork of Coal River they built a boat, and embarked again. "Where we came to this River the Country is mountainous, but the farther down the plainer, in those Mountains we found great plenty of Coals, for which we named it Coal River." Drifting down this tributary of the Great Kanawha and into the parent stream, on the sixth of May the five explorers reached the Ohio.

Salley was pleased with the "large Spacious open Country on each side of the River," as the craft was borne down the Ohio. "At this Time we found the Clover to be as high as the middle of a man's leg. In general all the Woods over the Land is Ridgey, but plain, well timbered and hath plenty of all kind of Wood." Water, fertile soil, timber-land—these three, within one plot, were the stuff of pioneers' dreams.

The Falls of the Ohio they passed safely, and on the seventh of June swung into the Mississippi. Then came drama: "We held on our passage down the River Mississippi until the second day of July, and about nine o' the Clock in the Morning we went on Shore to cook our Breakfast. But we were suddenly surprised by a Company of Men, Vizt. to the Number of Ninety, Consisting of French men Negroes, & Indians, who took us prisoners and carried us to the Town of New Orleans, which was about one Hundred Leagues from us when we were taken, and after being examined upon Oath before the Governor first separately one by One, and then All together, we were committed to close Prison." The French convoy had discovered the adventurers only by chance; the soldiers were returning from an expedition against the Choctaws.

New Orleans was genuinely alarmed; the appearance of these five Englishmen on the Mississippi conjured up the bogey of an English invasion of Louisiana. Governor

Bienville examined the prisoners diligently, and reported to Versailles, "They had been sent on their perilous journey for the purpose of exploring the rivers flowing from Virginia into the Mississippi, and to reconnoiter the terrain looking to establish a settlement, for the English pretend that their boundaries extend as far as the bank of the Mississippi. I have thought fit to have this affair investigated by a mixed council of civil and military officers to obviate misunderstandings among our own people and to allay the alarm excited by an enterprise which, though bold, after all was foolhardy." It was clearly important to Bienville that the adventurers should not be allowed to return to Virginia, to bear witness of the actual condition of Louisiana. The commanders of the forlorn settlement had no wish that the English should know its weaknesses.

Eventless days dragged wearily—a pound and a half of bread each day, ten pounds of pork a month, for each prisoner. Bienville sailed for France, and a new governor, Vaudreuil, presided in New Orleans; the only difference to the five Englishmen was that their pork was taken away, and rice and bear's oil were given them instead. Salley spent profitable hours in drawing from French prisoners information about Louisiana, its government, the temper of its military strength; he spent profitless hours in revolving means of escape. He had been confined for over two years when the opportunity came.

One Baudran, a prisoner who had escaped and been recaptured, was kept fast in irons. "With this Miserable French Man I became intimate and familiar," runs Salley's narrative, "and as he was an active man, and knew the Country, he promised, if I could help him off with his Irons, and we all got clear of the Prison, he would conduct us safe untill we were out of Danger. We then got a small file from a Soldier wherewith to cut the Irons and on the 25th day of October, 1744 we put our Design in Practice. While the French man was very busie in the Dungeon in cutting the Irons, we were as industrious without in breaking the Door of the Dungeon, and Each of us finished our Jobb at one instant of time, which had held us for about six hours; by three of the Clock in the Morning with the help of a Rope which I had provided beforehand, we let our Selves down over the Prison Walls, and made our Escape Two Miles from the Town that night, where we lay close for two days." Only one of the Virginians was able to escape with Salley and Baudran; the other three Governor Vaudreuil, harassed by the fear that they too might escape, sent to France in December.

A good friar (who belongs in any romantic chronicle, true or fictitious) sheltered Salley and his companion fugitives for four days, while they regained strength; and from him they probably got a gun and ammunition. At the edge of Lake Pontchartrain they shot two buffaloes, made a bull-boat of the hides, and to make their oars tied the shoulder blades to sticks. They pushed out into the lake at night, and "passed a point, where there were thirteen men lay in wait for us, but Thro' Mercy we escaped from them undiscovered. After we had gone by Water sixty miles we went on Shore, we left our Boat as a Witness of our Escape to the French."

They made their way to the Pearl River, in Choctaw country. Baudran, in Vaudreuil's own words, was "a brave and enterprising man, much beloved by the Indians"; the Choctaws were friendly, and kept the adventurers concealed for seventy days, while French soldiers with orders to shoot at sight scoured the woods about.

Late in January the fugitives entered the Gulf of Mexico in a pirogue, and skirted the coast to Choctawhatchee Bay, east of Pensacola. They had avoided the French garrisons at Mobile and Montgomery; a short distance overland was the country of Lower Creek Indians, to whom Carolinians came for trade.

Following a trading path, Salley traveled toward Charleston; on the first of April he paid his respects to the governor of South Carolina. After a few days of detention and inquiry, the governor allowed him to take passage for Virginia.

There is one more adventure in this Elizabethan tale. "On the Thirteenth of April, the same Day about two of the Clock we were taken by the French in Cape Roman and kept Prisoners till eleven of the Clock next day, at which time the French after having robbed us of all the Provisions we had for our Voyage or Journey, put us into a Boat we being twelve in number, and so left us to the Mercy of the Seas and Winds." The luckless voyagers were at sea two days, and on the fifteenth brought their little boat into Charleston harbor. As soon as he could obtain another pass, and a gentleman had given him a gun, Salley followed a footpath to Virginia; and on the seventeenth of May, 1745, he was at his home in the Blue Ridge.

"Marco Polo" Salley was a flame to the imagination; and to his descendants, who were still living in the Blue Ridge a century and a half later, he became somewhat a folk-hero, who had been captured by the Illinois Indians, adopted by a squaw, purchased from her by the Spaniards for three strands of beads and a calumet, and ultimately redeemed by the governor of Canada; or, as another mountaineer would have recited as the family tradition, sent from New Orleans in a vessel bound for Spain, there to be tried as a British spy, but that providentially the Spanish vessel was captured by an English one, which landed Salley at Charleston.

Before Salley's return the expansion of Virginia into the West had already begun. Benjamin Borden, who began his life on the Virginia frontier as a fur trader, and later became land agent for Lord Fairfax, who could measure the royal favor bestowed upon him in terms of thousands of acres, himself became infected with the fever for overlordship, and secured several valuable tracts of land from Governor Gooch. One of these was a grant of one hundred thousand acres at the head of the James River, on condition that he locate within two years a hundred families upon his tract. At the end of the contingent period he had induced ninety-two families to settle there, and a patent was granted him, in November, 1739, for all but about ten thousand acres of the tract. Borden died three years later, before he could further develop his estate. But a beginning had been made in the farmers' conquest of the land west of the Blue Ridge.

John Lewis, of the County Donegal, Ireland, had a price upon his head; like many another fugitive, he sought the frontier. When Salley returned to the Blue Ridge, Lewis and his family were living in the Valley of Virginia, near the present site of Staunton. Lewis and John Mackey, one of the many adventurers who had come into Virginia with the wave of English emigration, then at full swell, listened attentively to Salley's description of the handsomeness and fertility of the western slope of the Blue Ridge, and prevailed on Salley to accompany them in a quest for home sites. With the pick of the country before them, they all were careful to settle along water—Lewis a few miles beyond Staunton, on the creek which now bears his name; Mackey on the middle branch of the Shenandoah; and Salley in the forks of the James River, beyond the Natural Bridge.

In the meager accounts which have survived, Lewis and Mackey seem to epitomize two types of men to whom the frontier was a lodestone. Lewis obtained authority from Governor Gooch to locate one hundred thousand acres of land in separate parcels on the Shenandoah and James

Rivers. On his surveying tours Mackey accompanied him —to hunt buffalo. Lewis accumulated a large estate; Mackey died leaving no greater wealth than the field of free land on which he had built his cabin.

Between 1745 and 1754 the Governor and Council of Virginia made thirty-four grants of land, as the clerk of the Council informed the House of Burgesses, "between the Allegheny Mountains and a Line that may be run from the Western Boundary of North Carolina to the Confluence of the River Ohio with the Mississippi." After most of these grants, in the clerk's list, is the notation, "Nothing done"; but the number itself is indicative of the enlivened ambition of Virginians rich and poor, of the attractiveness of western lands, for speculation and for private domain, to the optimistic Americans who were still, in name, Englishmen.

These grants were bountiful, careless of geography. To Bernard Moore and associates, for instance, there was granted in July, 1749, "100,000 acres on the waters of the Mississippi River. Beginning at the two trees marked P. T. G. standing in the fork of a Branch of the said River known by the name of New River and so down the said River and the waters of the said Mississippi River." And on June 5, 1750, there was granted to Adam Hannan and associates "7000 acres lying in Augusta on both sides of Bluestone Creek beginning about 3 miles from where the said creek runs into said Wood's River at a marked Tree standing upon the No. side thereof, thence up the same Including the several branches on both sides to compleat the compliment."

At the half-century mark, dreams of western empire flowered into two generous enterprises, the Ohio Company and the Loyal Land Company. Quickened by indications that France intended to make good its claim to the Ohio Valley, the English government readily encouraged by royal charter these two companies—enterprises promoted by prominent Virginians, with a smattering of speculative Englishmen in their membership.

The Loyal Land Company was organized in 1749, with a grant of eight hundred thousand acres of land to be located north of the dividing line between the western domains of North Carolina and Virginia. Thomas Walker, surveyor, wanderer, and occasional practitioner of medicine, had a modest fame for his judgment in locating surveys. The Loyal Land Company made an offer; and Walker was persuaded "to go to the Westward in order to discover a proper Place for a Settlement."

March 6, 1750, Walker and five companions began the journey, from the eastern slope of the Blue Ridge. Each man had a horse; there were two pack ponies in addition. Skirting the rise of the hills, they rode southwest, lingering in hospitable cabins on the way. On the thirteenth "we went early to William Calloway's and supplied ourselves with Rum, Thread and other necessaries & from thence took the main Waggon Road leading to Wood's or the New River. It is not well clear'd or beaten yet, but will be a very good one with proper management." The next day they crossed the Blue Ridge at the easy ascent of Buford's Gap.

The party stopped on the fifteenth at a well-known salt lick on a creek of the Staunton. Already, Walker found, frontiersmen had made waste of the natural abundance: "This Lick has been one of the best places for Game in these parts and would have been of much greater advantage to the Inhabitants than it has been if the Hunters had not killed the Buffaloes for diversion, and the Elks and Deer for their skins."

Leaving a Dunkard settlement on the upper waters of the New River, the party rode on past scattered cabins to the Holston River, where Walker found a hunter and

Indian trader, Samuel Stalnaker, who had just decided to curb his restlessness, and to have a quiet house of his own—the farthest cabin to the west. The explorers helped Stalnaker to build his cabin; and Walker received information as to his route and the localities beyond.

The Cumberland Mountains were to the northwest; the ridges guarding the Clinch River had first to be crossed. The divides were troublesome until the last, when they found the trail of the first pathfinder in the West, the buffalo: "We kept down the Creek [the big Sycamore] 2 miles further, where it meets with a large Branch coming from the South West, and thence runs through the East Ridge making a very good Pass; and a large Buffaloe Road goes from that Fork to the Creek over the West Ridge, which we took and found the Ascent and Descent tollerably easie."

On the thirteenth of April the party passed through Cumberland Gap. Beyond was Kentucky. In the next few days the party crossed nameless streams; and the zestful explorer who led the party was generous with christenings. The great gap through the mountains itself came to be known by the name Walker later gave it, Cumberland Gap.

Following a creek, Walker came upon a river which he called Cumberland, after that ruthless duke who slaughtered the Highland forces at Culloden (whom Walker conceivably admired out of a hearty dislike for the Scotch-Irish on the frontier). On the nineteenth "we left the river but in four miles we came on it again at the Mouth of Licking Creek, which we went up. . . . In the Fork of Licking Creek is a Lick much used by Buffaloes and many large Roads lead to it. This afternoon Ambrose Powell was bit by a bear in his Knee."

Three days later one of the horses was found badly crippled; and Walker proposed that he proceed with two of the company, while the rest should linger "to provide and salt some Bear, build an house, and plant some Peach Stones and Corn." All five wanted to go on; so the men drew lots.

Walker and his two companions kept on to the west, following the valley of the Cumberland. The country was little to Walker's liking; on the twenty-fourth he writes, "We kept on Westerly 18 miles, got Clear of the Mountains and found the Land poor and the woods very Thick beyond them, and Laurel & Ivy in and near the Branches. Our Horses suffered very much here for want of food." He went only five miles farther on the following day, "the Land continuing much Same, the Laurel rather growing worse, and the food scarcer. I got up a tree on a Ridge and saw the Growth of the Land much the same as Far as my Sight could reach. I then concluded to return to the rest of my Company."

On the twenty-eighth of April Walker was back at the spot where the three men had been left. They had built a house—the first, probably, that white men built in Kentucky—made a clearing, and planted a crop. On the last day of the month Walker blazed a way from the cabin to the Cumberland River; and, leaving this solid evidence of the claim of the Loyal Land Company, the party resumed the journey. Going to the north, they passed a succession of little streams, tributaries of Rockcastle River, each of which Walker named for one of his five companions. The explorers reached the Kentucky River on the twenty-second of May. They had to build a canoe to cross it.

Henceforth, the party traveled eastward, across numerous creeks swollen by rain, following a buffalo path choked with timber blown down by a recent storm—a storm which blew down the explorers' tent, crashed trees about them, and dispersed them, thoroughly frightened, in different directions for shelter. They found the Big Sandy almost impassable. Walker's entry for June the thirteenth discloses the trials of this soggy return: "We are much hindered by the Gust & a shower of Rain about Noon. Game is very scarce here, and the mountains very bad, the tops of the Ridges being covered with Ivy and the sides so steep and stony, that we were obliged to cut our way through with our Tomohawks."

Following the Greenbriar River to the mountains, the party crossed the Allegheny Divide on the eighth of July. They were again at the extreme western edge of settlement —a group of cabins on Jackson's River, a branch of the James. "Having Shaved, Shifted, & made new Shoes we left our useless Raggs at ye Camp & got to Walker Johnston's about noon. We moved over to Robert Armstrong's in the afternoon & staid there all night. The People here are very hospitable and would be better able to support Travellers was it not for the great number of Indian Warriers, that frequently take what they want from them, much to their prejudice." In three days more the party was at Staunton; and the expedition was over.

The Ohio Company was organized in 1748, with an influential membership including John Banbury, merchant of London; Thomas Lee, president of the Council of Virginia; and Lawrence Washington. Its royal charter bestowed "a grant or Grants of Two hundred thousand Acres of Land between Romanetto and Buffaloe Creeks, on the south side of the Ohio; and betwixt the two creeks and Yellow Creek on the North side thereof, or in such part to the Westward of the Great Mountains as the Company should think proper for making settlements and extending their trade with the Indians." A fort had to be erected, a garrison maintained, and within seven years a hundred families must have been settled within the tract, if the grant were to become valid. A grant of another three hundred thousand acres awaited the successful completion of the terms of the first grant.

The Company purchased land at Wills Creek, on the upper Potomac, and there erected storehouses; they had a large cargo of goods sent from England, and engaged Thomas Cresap to open a wagon road to the three forks of the Youghioghany, eighty miles away. Most important, they made Christopher Gist a payment of £150, promised him more, and sent him westward to mark out the most desirable tracts of their domain.

Christopher Gist, native Marylander, was one of those men of education who, in every decade, found the rigor and activeness of life on the frontier more stimulating than any professional career. Like Walker, he had become known as a surveyor of western lands; but when the Ohio Company sought him out, he had returned to become a frontier farmer, and lived on the Yadkin River near the home of Daniel Boone.

Gist started out from Thomas Cresap's house on the upper Potomac on the last day of October, 1750. On the nineteenth of November he was resting at Shannopin's Town, the Delaware village at the forks of the Ohio. He concealed his compass: if the Indians were to be loyal to the English in the imminent struggle with the French for the overlordship of the Ohio Valley, they must not be convinced that the Virginians intended to settle upon their lands. Gist was accepted by the Indians whom he met in the course of his expedition as a representative of the governor of Virginia, sent out to reassure them of the friendship of the English.

On the twenty-fourth Gist's party swam their horses across the Ohio. Following the north bank of the river, occasionally meeting Pennsylvania traders, they held to their westward course and struck out for the forks of the Muskingum. At the Wyandot village there they found a surprising spectacle—the British colors flying from the chief's lodge and from the trading house of George Croghan. Gist was informed that the French had lately taken some English traders and their goods, and that

Croghan had sent messengers to warn the traders in more western towns to retreat to his refuge.

On Christmas Day Gist was still at the Wyandot village. "I intended to read prayers," he writes, "but after inviting some of the White Men, they informed each other of my Intentions, and being of several different Persuasions, and few of them inclined to hear any Good, they refused to come. But one Thomas Burney a Black Smith who is settled there went about and talked to them, & several of them came, and Andrew Montour invited several of the well disposed Indians, who came freely," and Gist satisfied his conscience.

The Indian council, for which Gist was waiting, had been postponed until distant chieftains should arrive. On the twelfth of January all seemed ready; but "some of the King's Council being a little disordered with Liquor, no Business could be done, but We were desired to come next Day." On the thirteenth Croghan and Montour, with speeches and presents, practiced successfully their minor trade of diplomacy.

Gist was away again on the fifteenth, still traveling westward, every day faithfully noting in his journal the quality of the land, and the plants and trees he found. By the close of January the party was at Shawneetown, an Indian settlement of one hundred lodges, on the west bank of the Scioto. Here, and at a little Delaware village they passed on the way, George Croghan—whose mission from the governor of Pennsylvania was too well timed with Gist's journey to have been simply a coincidence—made speeches of conciliation, and presented the chiefs with wampum.

The party traveled on to an Indian village on the upper waters of the Great Miami, and here met all three tribes of the Miami Indians in a heartening, friendly council. The danger of war with the French had made that part of his instructions which dealt with the Indians most important to Gist; and indeed settlement in the Ohio Valley, by the Ohio Company or by any other, had to wait until the overhanging war cloud should burst.

On the third of March Gist parted with the Pennsylvania traders and retraced his way to Shawneetown. Here he met a Mingo chief who informed him that a party of Indians friendly to the French were hunting at the Falls of the Ohio, and that if Gist went ahead he certainly would be killed or taken prisoner. Gist changed his plans. He crossed the Ohio, and traveled along the south bank of the river as far as he dared venture, then turned his horse to the southwest. He was within a day's march of the Kentucky River, when, on the twenty-first of March, he turned his course eastward.

His return journey was somewhat more southerly than Walker's had been; like Walker, he encountered swollen creeks, matted patches of laurels, and continual rain. His path was the more troublesome, across the foothills of the Cumberland Range. On the eighth of May he crossed Wood's River on a log raft of his own making; and in ten days more he was at his own house on the Yadkin River. He had a barren welcome: "I found all my family gone, for the Indians had killed five People in the Winter near that Place, which frightened my Wife and Family away to Roanoke," thirty-five miles eastward.

The Ohio Company found his report cheerless, and sent Gist out again, from November, 1751, to the following March, to discover the best lands of their grant between the Monongahela and Wood's rivers. The grantees were discovering that the West was not to be settled in the grand manner, by fiat of organized enterprises. The Ohio and the Loyal Land Company anticipated conditions they never found—coöperation from the government of Virginia, willingness on the part of the Indians. The Ohio Company appealed futilely to the King: "The Governor and Council having not thought fit to comply with the prayer of the said Petition, to allow your Petitioners to survey their Lands in different Tracts as would best accomodate the settlers and secure their frontiers from attacks, the President and Masters of the College [William and Mary] also refusing to give out a Commission to a Surveyor; and the late Governor and Council having made out large Grants to private persons, Land-jobbers, to the amount of near 1,400,000 Acres . . . your Petitioners apprehend . . . the Company may be prevented from fulfilling their Covenant of settling the Lands and Compleating their Fort in the time specified"—and, indeed, they were.

In 1748 fur traders from Pennsylvania and Virginia established a post at Pickawillany, on the Big Miami. *La Belle Riviere* was, from the Monongahela to the Mississippi, within French domain; the furs taken in the country between the Ohio and the Great Lakes by right followed the channels of trade to the French outpost of Detroit. That was the credo at Quebec and at Versailles; and in the summer of 1749, Celeron de Blainville, with his leaden plates, came to the Ohio River to emphasize that belief. English traders were in every Indian village he passed on his route from Lake Erie; he drove them out. The plates, graven with a declaration of the sovereignty of France, he buried in the river bank. In 1752, Charles de Langlade with his Chippewa Indians swept down upon the post that the English upstarts had built at Pickawillany, and burned the place; the Chippewas killed, boiled and devoured the Miami chief who had permitted the post to be built. Mohawk warriors who came to Albany to visit Sir William Johnson, the King's agent in Indian affairs, brought alarming reports: canoes bearing French soldiers were breasting Lake Ontario, pushing to the west. In 1753 there were fifteen hundred French soldiers in the Ohio country. The challenge was simple and direct.

[67]

Virginia, the oldest of the colonies, the one with the most ambitious claim to the disputed wilderness, picked up the glove and flung it back. When the second session of the Virginia Assembly under Governor Robert Dinwiddie convened on November 1, 1753, it faced a request from the King "to grant such Supplies, as the Exigency of the present Affairs requires . . . for defeating the designs of our Enemies." But because Dinwiddie was attempting to exact a personal fee upon land patents, the governor and the assembly were hopelessly at odds. In the deadlock Dinwiddie took it upon himself to send a young major in the Virginia militia, George Washington, to the commander of the French forces in the Ohio country.

Between the upper waters of the Ohio and Lake Erie was a chain of French posts; one of them, at Venango, they had seized from the Pennsylvania traders. At Fort Le Boeuf, twenty miles south of Lake Erie, was Legardeur de Saint-Pierre, commander-in-chief of these garrisons. Through the rigor of early winter in 1753 Washington, with Christopher Gist and four other men, made his way to Fort Le Boeuf. Mr. Dinwiddie to Monsieur de Saint-Pierre, greetings: "The lands upon the River Ohio, in the western parts of the Colony of Virginia, are so notoriously known to be the property of the Crown of Great Britain that it is a matter of equal concern and surprise to me, to hear that a body of French forces are erecting fortresses and making settlements upon that river, within his Majesty's Dominions . . . in violation of the law of nations, and the treaties now subsisting between the two Crowns." Saint-Pierre received the messenger and the message with studied courtesy. Washington carried on his return journey a message from commander to governor affirming that the troops were in the western country by order of the Marquis Duquesne, governor of Canada, and that Saint-Pierre would carry out with energy the instructions he had received. Washington also brought to Dinwiddie reports of things said by younger French officers, who spoke more freely: "it was their absolute design to take possession of the Ohio" and "by God they would do it."

The gateway to the Ohio Valley, the confluence of the Monongahela and the Allegheny, was as yet unoccupied, save by occasional Pennsylvania traders. It was logical that Duquesne should order a fortress built there, and logical that Washington should have made the same recommendation to Governor Dinwiddie. The Ohio Company was also interested; and in coöperation with this company Dinwiddie despatched Captain William Trent with a body of militia to build a fort at this key location. Trent was commissioned to enlist an additional hundred men from among the traders on the border. Dinwiddie wrote to his patron, Lord Fairfax: "I therefore, with advice of the Council, think proper to send immediately out 200 men to protect those already sent by the Ohio Comp' to build a Fort, and to resist any Attempts on them." The command of these reserves was given to that efficient young officer who had visited Fort Le Boeuf thirteen months before.

When this reserve expedition reached Wills Creek, where Cumberland, Maryland, now stands, Washington encountered the volunteers who had gone out with Trent. The fort-builders had come to the Forks of the Ohio too late; a French force of five hundred men had arrived while the stockade was yet unfinished, the Virginians had been compelled to leave, and the French troops were completing the stockade. Thus were raised the walls of Fort Duquesne, center of French power on the Ohio during the next five years.

Washington's commission read, "You are to act on the Defensive, but in Case any Attempts are made to obstruct the Works or interrupt our Settlem'ts by any Persons whatsoever You are to restrain all such Offenders, and in Case

[69]

of resistance to make Prisoners of or kill and destroy them"; and Washington kept on. About sixty miles short of Fort Duquesne he became aware that a party of French were marching toward him. At a bare plain known as the Great Meadows he halted. When one evening a runner brought definite information of the location of the French scouting party, Washington marched his company over the tangled route through the night. The next day the little armies encountered each other, and without parley began firing. The young officer, Jumonville, commanding the French parties, was killed; and Washington's Indian allies left the battleground with the scalps of ten Frenchmen. Two years before a state of war was formally professed at Versailles and London, on the Virginia-Pennsylvania frontier the French and Indian War had been begun.

Washington's company was bulwarked behind a makeshift stockade at Great Meadows when the French counterattack swept down; their commander felt compelled to accept terms of surrender, and the Virginians were allowed to march out with the honors of war. From tribe to tribe the news passed; on all the frontiers from Pennsylvania to Georgia the Indians thought that the British cause was lost. War parties ravaged the isolated settlements in the back country. Even the Iroquois were restive; a spokesman for the Mohawks appeared at the congress of seven colonies at Albany in 1754 with the taunt, "You English are all like women, and the French may come and turn you out."

These were crucial years in the back country. In answer to the persistent calls from Governor Dinwiddie, the British ministry was aroused; General Edward Braddock with two regular regiments was sent to America, with orders to make Virginia his base. In June, 1755, Braddock advanced with some twenty-two hundred men from Wills Creek to the Forks of the Ohio; this well-intentioned martinet was marching to his death. After the smashing defeat of the

[70]

British regulars the frontier was again harried with scalping parties. Three years passed before the Indians had cause to fear retaliation. In 1758 Brigadier General John Forbes, having organized his expedition in Philadelphia, followed the traders' roads across Pennsylvania to the Ohio; the French at Fort Duquesne, outnumbered, burned their buildings and departed for Canada. The Ohio Valley was abandoned to the British; and in 1760 the military conquest of all New France was completed.

In time, a petition was addressed to the Governor and Council of Virginia, by "George Washington, Adam Stephen and Andrew Lewis Esquires in behalf of themselves and the rest of the surviving officers and soldiers who enlisted in the service in 1754, for 200,000 acres on the Ohio River or near it in consequence of Governor Dinwiddie's proclamation the 19th of February 1754." After the French and Indian War had been formally ended, in 1763, officers and soldiers of Virginia were riding into the western valleys, scanning the wilderness to find likely lands to claim under their warrants. Washington himself, as leader of the expedition of 1754 to which the governor had promised land bounties, became possessed of extensive tracts, purchased the warrants of other soldiers, and began his policy of investing a large part of his money in western lands. By 1784 four hundred thousand dollars, the greater part of his wealth, lay in holdings in the wilderness. And he wrote to a friend: "Would to God we may have wisdom enough to improve the opportunity!"

PART II

INDEPENDENCE: PERSONAL AND NATIONAL

. . . In this character of the Americans, a love of freedom is the predominating feature which marks and distinguishes the whole: and as an ardent is always a jealous affection, your colonies become suspicious, restive, and untractable, whenever they see the least attempt to wrest from them by force, or shuffle from them by chicane, what they think the only advantage worth living for.

—Edmund Burke

CHAPTER V

LIFE AND LABOR IN THE BACKWOODS

FROM Chester and Lancaster counties the overflow of Scotch-Irish settlement lapped into the frontier. By 1748 the Kittochtinny Valley was pretty well settled. Beyond was the valley of the Juniata, lands not yet purchased from the Indians. The Scotch-Irish, augmented in their occupation of western Pennsylvania by an ever increasing number of English, pursued the dream of free lands and easy crops up the Juniata.

Particularly as long as the French menace overhung the western border of the province, the proprietors of Pennsylvania were anxious to preserve their alliance with the Delawares and the Iroquois. These nations complained of the advance of clearings and cabins into their territory; and in 1750 Governor Hamilton gave orders to Secretary Richard Peters and Conrad Weiser to hale to justice all the obstreperous settlers on the unpurchased lands.

With George Croghan and the justices of Cumberland County, Peters and Weiser followed the trail of settlement up the valley. At the Big Juniata the army of the law found five cabins. Peters ordered two of the cabins burned. Most of the men surrendered; two, George and William Galloway, resisted. "Having got at some distance from the sheriff," Secretary Peters reported, "they called to us, 'You may take our lands and houses, and do what you please with them; we deliver them to you with all our hearts, but we will not be sent to jail!'" At the Little Juniata, and farther to the west, was many another cluster of unlawful cabins. The Secretary's party followed the Tuscarora Path, "through which the way to Allegheny lies"; the settlers were bound to appear in court, and to remove from the valley with all their effects. "Having voluntarily given possession of their houses to me," Peters advised the governor, "some ordinary log-houses, to the number of eleven, were burnt to the ground; the trespassers, most of them cheerfully, and a very few of them with reluctance, carrying out their goods. Some had been deserted before, and lay waste. . . . It may be proper to add that the cabins or log-houses which were burnt were of no considerable value; being such as the country people erect in a day or two, and cost only the price of an entertainment."

The provincial government was strong enough to drive the pioneers back from the Juniata Valley, but immeasurably too weak to keep them out. The Penns did the graceful thing: at Albany in 1754 they bought the Indian title to a large area which embraced the valley of the Juniata for the trifling consideration of £400, divided among a few sachems. The Penns' reputation for peace was intact—but not for fair dealing. The dissatisfaction of the great number of Pennsylvania Iroquois with this treaty forced the Penns to relinquish title to all the land lying north and west of the Allegheny Mountains within the province; but the restoration came too late to check the steady filtering in of emigrants.

[76]

Captain James Patterson, to pick one settler from many, stoutly represents the tough fiber of these Scotch-Irish on the frontier. He came into the Juniata Valley in 1751 with five companions, from Cumberland County, having probably sold his field and cabin there to some emigrant newly arrived from Ulster. Patterson and his companions cleared away a field on either side of the river and built two large log houses pierced with loopholes. He did not condescend to make a private purchase from the Indians, nor did he build a stockade for the protection of his little colony. Announcing that Providence had designed the land "for the use of Christian people to raise food upon, and not for Indian war-dances," Patterson staked off a claim far larger than he cared to cultivate.

This anecdote lingered on the frontier: "Patterson used to keep a target, the center of which was riddled with bullets, leaning against a tree. Whenever he found a party of friendly Indians approaching, he used to stand under his door and blaze away at the target, but always stop when the Indians were near the house. The Indians would invariably examine the target, measure the distance—about four hundred feet—with the eye—and conclude among themselves that Patterson would be an exceedingly tough customer in a fight!"

In 1755 Patterson became alarmed at the prowling about of Indians in war paint, and with his companions took refuge in Sherman's Valley, across the Tuscarora Mountains. After a few years he left his clearing in Sherman's Valley and returned to the Juniata; but he found his lands occupied by other settlers, who held deeds of purchase from the proprietary government. Nothing daunted, he staked out another field in the wilderness, and commenced cultivation, without the bother of taking title. If it was not morally wrong of the Penns to wheedle the Indians out of millions of acres of land for a paltry £400, Mr. Patterson wanted to know, why should he not cheat the Penn family out of a farm?

During the Indian wars of 1762 and 1763, most of the inhabitants of the Juniata Valley fled to more densely settled districts for safety. There were many of these rebuffs in the history of the West, interludes in the advance of the frontier when Indians thrust back the cabin-building invaders; but after each local Indian danger had subsided there were, it seemed, twice as many emigrants ready to creep in under the lifting shadow.

By proclamation of George III on October 7, 1763, "all the lands and territories lying to the westward of the sources of the rivers which fall into the sea from the west and northwest" were reserved under the protection of the king. Colonial officials were forbidden to make grants of land west of this proclamation line. To this prohibition were added the proclamations of several colonial governors forbidding settlement in the Indian country. Grants for military bounties were practically the only authorized exceptions. The policy of the Crown was to attempt to maintain a neutral ground between the settlements and the Indian tribes. But all these proclamations were insignificant obstructions to the westward push of settlement. Both the frontier folk hungry for new settlements and the moneyed gentlemen eager to speculate in western lands were alienated from the Crown by this policy.

In 1770 the acting governor of Virginia, writing of the frontier settlements, was forced to remark, "Very little if any Quit Rents have been received for his Majesty's use from that quarter for some time past; for they say, that as His Majesty hath been pleased to withdraw his protection from them since 1763, they think themselves bound not to pay Quit Rents." Colonel Henry Bouquet, commandant at Fort Pitt, made another of those futile attempts to clear the Indian country of pioneer settlers by the use of force. Virginia land speculators tried to bribe Bouquet by inviting him to become a member of the Ohio Company, and thus share their claim to twenty-five thousand acres beyond the Proclamation Line; when this very unusual colonial officer refused, his existence was made so unpleasant that he asked to be transferred.

In the five years of little-interrupted peace from 1765 to 1770, thousands of emigrants found their way into the Pennsylvania wilderness. Settlements extended into the upper lands of the Juniata Valley, and into the vicinity of the dreaded Kittaning Path, highway of Iroquois warriors. To the southwest, settlements followed "the way to the Alleghenies," again an Indian trail. In 1767 a few families were established in the vicinity of Fort Redstone, on the Monongahela; from their settlement, called Brownsville, flatboats and keelboats not many years later were to make the months-long voyage to New Orleans.

In 1761 two men, John and Samuel Pringle, deserted Fort Pitt, and made their way up the Buckhannon River. At the mouth of a small branch they took up their abode in the hollow of a giant sycamore; and not until they were reduced to only two loads of powder would these defiant individualists seek out the company of other men. In the autumn of 1767, then, John left his brother and headed for a trading post on the Shenandoah. Samuel, left alone, wasted one of the powder-loads in a fruitless attempt to shoot a buck; with his remaining load he brought down a buffalo, and feasted until his brother's return. John had news of a new world: the French had been vanquished, and peace had been made with the Indians. The lone huntsmen were excited into wishing themselves done with solitude; and they went to the settled country on the south branch of the Potomac, to bring emigrants into their game-rich valley. Land was no longer dirt cheap on the south branch; and many discontented settlers were ready to follow the Pringles.

In the spring of 1769 a group of pioneers followed Samuel Pringle to the Buckhannon, and planted corn, enough to provide for their families through the following winter. When cabins were built and the corn well advanced, these men went back to the south branch to bring their families. Returned to the new clearing, they found their crops entirely destroyed. Herds of buffalo had trampled over the rail fences, and eaten the corn to the ground.

But the settlement was successfully established in 1770. Soon after other settlements were made on the upper branches of the Monongahela; and below Fort Pitt a thick stockade of cabins and cornfields was lining the Ohio.

Alexander Scott Withers, of the succeeding generation, passed kindly judgment on these pioneers: "With a capability to sustain fatigue, not to be subdued by toil; and with a cheerfulness, not easy to be depressed; a patience which could mock at suffering and a daring which nothing could daunt, every difficulty which intervened, every obstacle which was imposed between them and the accomplishment of the objects of their pursuit, was surmounted or removed; and in a comparatively brief space of time, they rose to the enjoyment of many of those gratifications, which are experienced in earlier and more populous settlements. That their morals should, for a while, have suffered deterioration, and their manners and habits, instead of approximating those of refined society, should have become, perhaps, more barbarous and incouth, was inevitable."

A "settlement" was of necessity a fort, a stockaded group of cabins and blockhouses. The blockhouses were built at the corners of the stockade, two-story affairs, projecting two or three feet beyond the outer walls of the cabins and the log walls which connected the cabins. The thick-slabbed double gate which closed the fort was built to face the settlements' water supply, spring or creek.

The fort to which John Doddridge "belonged" was about

three-fourths of a mile from his farm. "The family were sometimes waked up in the dead of night with a report that the Indians were at hand," his boy Joseph remembered. "This was easily done, as an habitual fear made us ever watchful and sensible to the slightest alarm. The whole family were instantly in motion. My father seized his gun and other implements of war. My stepmother waked up and dressed the children as well as she could, and being myself the oldest of the children I had to take my share of the burdens to be carried to the fort. There was no possibility of getting a horse in the night to aid us in removing to the fort. Besides the little children, we caught up what articles of clothing and provision we could get hold of in the dark, for we durst not light a candle or even stir the fire. All this was done with the utmost dispatch and the silence of death. The greatest care was taken not to awaken the youngest child. To the rest it was enough to say *Indian* and not a whimper was heard afterwards. Thus it often happened that the whole number of families belonging to a fort who were in the evening at their homes were all in their little fortress before the dawn of the next morning. In the course of the succeeding day their household furniture was brought in by parties of men under arms."

People married young, of course. Young men need not wait until they had money; labor was commodity enough to start an establishment. Frontier economy offered nothing to spinster daughters but a protracted share in the household drudgery.

From his father's house the groom led his friends in a caravan to the bride's house, arriving in time to dispose of the marital ceremony before noon. A feast followed, a glorified table of as large a variety of meats and vegetables as the backwoods afforded. After dinner the dancing commenced. The first figure was a "square four" set, closed when one of the couples was singled out for a jig; and with reels, square sets, and jigs, the dancing lasted till sun-up. Ladies could rest and gentlemen could drink, while other ladies and gentlemen kept the fiddler at his almost incessant sawing; but if any weary ones attempted to snatch a little sleep, they were hunted up, paraded on the floor, and the fiddler ordered to play "Hang on till to-morrow morning." If boisterousness was not real, it had to be courted.

About ten in the evening the bride and groom were smuggled away from the company into a precarious solitude, likely to be broken whenever the company decided that the pair would like some whisky or some food. The company consumed enormous quantities of whisky, answering the double demand of general sociability and of compliments to the bride and groom. "Health to the groom, not forgetting myself; and here's to the bride, thumping luck and big children": that was a very proper and friendly toast.

The building of a cabin for the young couple was again a neighborhood enterprise. Logs, clapboards, and puncheons were made ready in one day; on the next friends collected for the raising. Four corner men were elected, whose business was to place and notch the logs. The rest of the company furnished them with the timbers. The wall of logs mounted fast; and sometimes the roof and floor were finished on this same day. In another day the floor was leveled, a door and table built, the interior of the cabin "dressed up" a bit, and a chimney constructed. Another all-night dancing bout dedicated the cabin; and on the day following the young couple took possession.

Then the young frontiersman had to begin the clearing of his field. With his mattock he grubbed out the underbrush and saplings, making progress at the rate of a quarter-acre a day if the forest was of oak or some other hardwood; if his field was in a section of dense pine, hemlock, poplar, or ash, work was slower and much more tedious. The cut brush had to be stacked, and, if there was any need for fencing, the best pieces culled out for rails. The Marquis de Chastellux described the next step in the process: the pioneer "boldly attacks those immense oaks, or pines, which one would take for the ancient lords of the territory he is usurping; he strips them of their bark, or lays them open all around with his ax. These trees mortally wounded, are the next spring robbed of their honors. . . . The flames consume what the iron was unable to destroy." The dead timber was cut into twelve or fifteen-foot lengths. The work with ax and saw carried through the winter.

In the springtime, after the piles of brush had become thoroughly dry, this débris was burned up. The cut logs were still lying in the field when the pioneer sowed his first crop. Wooden plows were becoming antiquated; the improvement lay in the addition of iron plates at the colter and along the shoe. A triangular harrow was used as a drag in the process of seeding the ground.

The sickle, of immemorial use in harvesting grain, was being supplanted by the cradle, a broad scythe, with a light frame of four wooden fingers of a length nearly equal with the blade. With the cradle grain could be cut and gathered in one operation; by a dexterous turn to the right the reaper could throw the grain in a swath, ready to be raked and bound into sheaves.

Grain was usually threshed by a flail. Itinerant workers were sometimes available at harvest time; the price of their labor was one bushel of every ten, and board. Ten bushels of wheat or twenty bushels of oats was a good day's flailing. Some pioneers used horse power for the threshing. The sheaves were laid in a circle, the farmer stood in the middle of the circle to turn over the straw occasionally; and, with a boy riding one horse and leading another, the tramping-out

[83]

process commenced. Two hand-riddles, one coarse and one fine, were used for cleaning the grain. These riddles were made entirely of wood; the bottom was a network of woven splints.

After the harvesting, usually, the pioneer turned to the work of logging. This was a coöperative enterprise; five men and a team of oxen were needed. And, of course, one or two gallon jugs of whisky. Neighbors brought their own handspikes, long hardwood poles, to control the roll of the logs over the skids into the pile. The log piles were burned; and the harrow scattered the ashes over the field. This was the one occasion in the pioneer's tenure of a field when some attention was given to fertilization.

At house raisings and harvesting parties every man was expected to do his share; failure to take up arms against the Indians, when occasion demanded, was a serious offense. General indignation, general scorn, was a weapon no man in a frontier community could stand against. The victim was, as the folk put it, "hated out." Idleness or flagrant dishonesty met that punishment. Its result was usually reformation or exile.

When, in the absence of public law (as in the long-disputed region between Virginia and Pennsylvania), volunteer juries held malefactors to account, whipping was an approved punishment. "A thief must be whipped": that was the maxim of the Allegheny frontier. Thirty-nine stripes was a frequent penalty for the theft of something of value. Petty thieves received "the flag of the United States"—curt humor to signify thirteen stripes. For many years in western Virginia the legally constituted magistrates were in the habit of giving small offenders the choice of a jail sentence or a whipping.

"Private" fights, for all their brutality—biting, kicking, gouging—were no concern of the courts. Some rudeness in customs was demanded by frontier conditions. Aggressive equality, frontier equality, meant open hospitality, cordial harmony, warm and constant friendships; it meant also vengeful resentments, and sometimes a license to coarseness.

Confronted with the demands of this western life, tradition in clothing lost half its force. Hunters and fighters found it best to dress somewhat like the Indians.

A wide-sleeved hunting shirt, made of linsey-woolsey generally, of linen or deerskin less often, was a storeroom that supplanted pockets. Mittens, bullet-bag, tomahawk, and the scalping knife with its sheath, were held by the belt. Breeches and leggings were in one piece, reaching down to deerskin moccasins.

The women wore linsey-woolsey dresses. Their only furbelow, usually, was a handkerchief around the neck. A wardrobe was also an art gallery: petticoats, bedgowns, and shirts were hung on wooden pegs in full display on the cabin walls.

This linsey-woolsey was a fabric of spun flax and wool made by the women themselves. "When wool became more plentiful and flannels were manufactured," recollected a pioneer of western Pennsylvania, "there were no fulling-mills such as existed in later years. Necessity was the mother of invention more frequently in early days than now; and one of the methods of fulling flannels was sufficiently primitive; while, at the same time, it was intensely exhilarating. . . . The woolen web was saturated with soap and water and thrown down in an emulsient mass upon a clean space in the center of the cabin floor. The men of the neighborhood,—especially the young men,—rolled their pantaloons up to their knees, and with bare feet sat in a circle on the floor about the woolen web in the center. At a given signal each one commenced kicking vigorously upon the web, and his kicks were met with equal ones by the opposite operator. It became a matter of muscular endeavor

[85]

by each one not to be kicked back on the floor by his antagonist; hence quick, prolonged, and spasmodic kicking was paid out upon the web, which was occasionally plied by the laughing house-women with additional soap and warm water. The result was that the flannel was thoroughly fulled, the operators thoroughly saturated with sweat, soap and water." The "kicking frolic" closed, in the honorable tradition of folk-gatherings, with a full meal and its complement of drams.

Wooden bowls spaced about the table marked places for the members of the family, quite a few wooden bowls, most likely, for, as Fortescue Cuming said, "Wherever you see a cabin, you see a swarm of children." Beside each bowl was a wooden noggin or a flattened gourd, ready for water or milk. Into the wooden trenchers in the center of the table the housewife, or the oldest girl, dished up the contents of the iron pots and pans—game, fish, or fried pork, or "hog and hominy," or mush sweetened with molasses, sugar-and-water, bear's oil, or gravy; johnnycake, buckwheat "souens," or cornpone; and something or other out of the truck patch—"roastin' ears," pumpkins, squashes, beans, or potatoes. And with iron knives and forks, supplemented by fingers, the family attacked the spread. Pewter dishes and spoons after a while replaced the wooden things, sometime when the head of the house had been east for salt and iron, and had some extra money. The backwoods people did not like glazed pottery, "delft ware." It was too easily broken, and clasp knives were dulled as, in carving meat, they hit against the plates. Tea ware was too small for *men;* tea and coffee, for that matter, were "slops."

In most kitchens was a block and pestle, a "hominy block," which did very well in making meal for johnnycakes and mush, before the corn became too hard in the autumn. Hand mills of two circular stones were common; to the upper stone, the runner, was attached a handle, permitting two people to work together in grinding the hard corn. Large sweeps and mortars were sometimes used to lessen the toil of grinding the grain. Neighbors brought their corn to a house whose enterprising owner had built a sweep; they were welcome to its use. For bolters women used sifters made of deerskins stretched over a hoop and perforated with a hot wire.

Almost every house contained a loom. Each family tanned its own leather, made its own shoes. In the recollection of Joseph Doddridge, "There was, in almost every neighborhood, some one whose natural ingenuity enabled him to do many things for himself and his neighbors, far above what could have been reasonably expected. With the few tools which they brought with them into the country they certainly performed wonders. Their plows, harrows with their wooden teeth, and sleds, were in many instances well made. Their cooper ware, which comprehended everything for holding milk and water, was generally pretty well executed. The cedar ware, by having alternately a red and a white stave, was then thought beautiful. Many of their puncheon floors were very neat, their joints close and the top even and smooth. Those who could not exercise these mechanic arts were under the necessity of giving labor, or barter, to their neighbors in exchange for the use of them, so far as their necessities required."

For two essentials, salt and iron, and for whatever "luxuries" they felt they could afford their households, the backwoodsmen had to recross the mountains. And in the fall of the year, after seeding time, caravans of pack horses set out from each settlement, carrying pelts and furs and ginseng, snakeroot, and bear's grease, for the bartering.

The pack horses followed the trail in single file, usually in divisions of twelve or fifteen horses, with one man on horseback to lead the division, and another rider in the rear to look after the safety of the packs. The horse collars, often made of woven corn husks, were made gay with bells. The bags that were to bring back salt were filled with feed for the horses; on the journey a part of this feed was left at convenient places, to support the return of the caravan.

Whenever possible, emigrants into newly settled country joined an experienced caravan, and followed after the pack horses burdened with crooked bars of iron and dangling bags of salt. Twenty days or more, according to the weather and the condition of the trail, were necessary to cross to the headwaters of the Ohio by the best road through the mountains, the wagon-trace left by General Braddock in his disastrous campaign against the French outposts.

After 1755 Conestoga wagons were following Braddock's Road, foretelling the end, within forty years, of the pack-horse era. In the valley of the Conestoga River, Lancaster County, a breed of very heavy horses had been developed; perhaps the huge, heavy wagon took its name from its draft horses. No sooner was a road made fit for wagons than a Conestoga appeared on it—one single wagon bearing a family and its household stuff into the West, or a caravan of emigrants. And for generation after generation, until the westward march of empire had halted in the valleys of the Pacific West, the Conestoga wagon was in the van of the march. These first Conestogas, in western Pennsylvania, were vividly decorated by their proud owners, risen above the status of pack-horse drivers. "It was, indeed, an animated sight," wrote one chronicler, "to see five or six highly fed horses, half covered with heavy bear skins, or decorated with gaudily fringed housings, surmounted with a set of finely toned bells, their bridles adorned with loops of red trimming."

Farthest into the Indian country went pioneers whose only interest was in hunting. Some of these men dreaded the bondage of a cabin and clearing, and built makeshift cabins that could be lightly deserted if game receded or Indians approached. Under the responsibilities of matrimony many true-born hunters attempted to be husbandmen, with varying success. Joseph Doddridge knew these hunters: "As soon as the leaves were pretty well down and the weather became rainy . . . they became uneasy at home. Everything about them became disagreeable. The house was too warm. The feather bed too soft, and even the good wife was not thought for the time being a proper companion. The mind of the hunter was wholly occupied with the camp and chase. I have often seen them get up early in the morning at this season, walk hastily out and look anxiously to the woods and snuff the autumnal winds with the highest rapture, then return into the house and cast a quick and attentive look at the rifle." All backwoodsmen hunted at times; pelts could be transported across the mountains, and exchanged for products nature could not provide. For venison and for skins frontiersmen sought deer, from June until early spring.

From June until October the most successful method of hunting deer was the fire hunt. Philip Tome, venerable hunter of western Pennsylvania, thus described the art:

"The deer would come to the river after dark to eat the moss which grew on the bottom, and collect together about the ripples, in groups from three to ten. The hunters would build a fire of yellow pitch pine in the middle of a canoe and station a man in the stern to steer, and one or two more in front to fire at the deer. When there was no deer in sight they could push and paddle the canoe along. When they came within sight of the deer the canoe was allowed to float down with the current, and the steersman laid it in a position the most advantageous for those who were in the bow with guns. The deer would generally raise their heads and stand looking at the fire until the canoe came within a few yards of them. The hunters could judge by their movements whether they would make a break or stand still until they came near them, and fired or not according to the movements of the deer. When the deer attempted to run out of the water where the bank was bluff and steep, they would see their own shadows, and thinking it was a dog or a wolf, would utter a cry and spring back into the water, sometimes coming near enough to the canoe to give the hunters two or three more shots at them. In this manner they would kill from one to four deer in one place. Having dressed and laid out the meat on the shore, they would proceed down the river in search of another group. If the night was favorable, from three to ten deer were killed in this manner."

Deer, elk, bear, and fox were most valuable. Boys who grew up in the backwoods quickly learned naturecraft, and added their share to the bales of peltry which represented the negotiable wealth of the frontier.

The erratic path of the true-born hunter, who did not write and hated to plow, defies a careful tracing. In 1769 forty hunters reached Kentucky, and hunted the game along the Green and Lower Cumberland rivers; they were so long absent from the frontier settlements that they became known as the Long Hunters. But even they, once in the hunting grounds, had broken up into groups of three or four who did not meet for months. The aged Major John Redd wrote to some one, probably Lyman Draper, who had inquired about a particular hunter: "Walden settled on the holston about 18 miles above where knoxville now stands. I know not how long he lived there. In the year 1776, I called by to see him, he was not at home, his wife informed me that he had gone on a hunt and had been absent a month. A few years after this he moved to Powel's valley, remained there a short time, removed from there to Missoura and settled in the vary extreme settlement up the Missoura river. I suppose his object in going to Missoura was to get where game was more plentiful; he followed up hunting as long as he was able to follow the chase; he died on the fronteers of Missoura at a very advanced age; he performed no military duty during the war."

CHAPTER VI

THE BATTLE OF ALAMANCE

DOWN the Appalachian valleys moved the back-Virginia creepers into North Carolina. The vanguard, which was resting on the headwaters of the Yadkin in 1740, was of that tenacious Pennsylvania-Ulster stock, still belligerent, still poverty-stricken, still reaching out for free farm land. Little colonies of Welsh, Germans, Moravians, Quakers, came after. In these western valleys this migration met a countercurrent, the sifting in of "poor whites" from the eastern slope, who were finding the cultivation of small farms, with few slaves or none, precarious and uncomfortable. Large plantations, with owners who were of the Established Church and whose cultural outlook was toward the seaboard and beyond, plantations with great gangs of slaves, were coming near the pine belt; the result was that another group of small-clearing farmers was forced into the mountain valleys, to reënforce the English influence in the assortment of races in the back country. The southerly trend of the pioneer migration was checked; families and congregations scattered into the many grassy valleys of the Blue Ridge, more hospitable than the Pennsylvania mountains.

Between the two sections, the planters' North Carolina and the pioneers', was a monotonous pine forest stretching from the Roanoke Valley to Cape Fear. This natural barrier supplemented cultural differences. Fayetteville, not far below the falls line on the Cape Fear River, was the commercial mart of western Carolina; its merchants were Pennsylvanians or Scotch. The first Presbyterian ministers in western Carolina were sent by the synods of New York and Philadelphia; when the region produced its own ministerial talent, these students were sent to Princeton. The only constant communication across the pines was governmental; and the channels of government flowed always from the east.

The political institutions of provincial North Carolina were bureaucratic. The governor was not paid by the people's assembly and was accordingly independent of their influence, a chief executive, in fact. The governor in council appointed the county justices; the governor alone appointed the officers of the militia, and selected the sheriff from three freeholders whose names were submitted by the county court. The county and parish taxes were levied by the county court and collected by the sheriff. The clerkships of the county court were under the control of one state officer, a clerk of pleas, who appointed to the county positions those applicants who paid him most. The westerners in Carolina were not overliterate, had no broad political information, had no communication with the predominant groups in provincial politics. But they were exponents of a homely democracy, and expected a share in their own government. Local grievances accumulated, and there was no constitutional voice of redress.

Officers in North Carolina counties were paid by the fee system. As soon as western counties were organized there came sheriffs, clerks, lawyers, and other bureaucrats, whose only interest in the community was in their perquisite fees, legal and extralegal. Lawyers and court officials seemed to be in collusion to postpone cases in order that they might get more fees; in one county in 1766 nearly a thousand cases cluttered the docket.

"The sheriffs have embezzled more than one-half of the public money ordered to be raised and collected by them," declared Governor Tryon in 1767. A dishonest sheriff did not fear prosecution; the treasurer usually feared to sue for the arrears lest he lose the support of the "court-house gang" necessary for his own reëlection. Tryon made several attempts to secure a statement of the condition of the public accounts. In 1770 he secured his report: the several sheriffs had turned over £49,000 less than they had collected. By order of the assembly of 1771 this report was distributed in the counties, and the treasurers were ordered to prosecute the delinquents. A fair proportion of the arrears drifted back into the treasuries; but in the six western counties the delinquent sheriffs, in most instances, had no securities worth attaching or had run away.

Extortionate fees, dishonest sheriffs—there were other grievances on the frontier. The taxes themselves seemed ill-apportioned, resting too heavily upon the poor man; a new residence was built for the governor, taking five years to erect, 1765 to 1770, and costing £15,000 (a monstrous extravagance to one who had built his cabin with his own hands). Lord Granville, who had extensive lands in the West, had no agent in the colony who would give deeds for his lands. Settlers had taken possession, but refused to pay taxes upon their farms, and were in constant trouble with the sheriffs. Encouraging the discontent was the scarcity of money. The English colonial policy was draining the colonies of specie and of patience; the shortsighted policy of the provincial government of North Carolina in redeeming its paper money—issued during the French and Indian War—at that very time when the current of immigration was rushing rapidly down the Appalachian sluices, aggravated the situation. As always in times of a contracting currency, the distress fell hardest upon the frontier.

The first protests of the frontier had no hint of warfare upon government. Hermon Husband, expatriate Quaker, industrious, intelligent, who reprinted and circulated republican political pamphlets, set about effecting reform by stirring up public sentiment. There were others who talked a great deal. Rednap Howell set the country-side to singing lampoons of the most prominent malefactors. When the protest had brought the Westerners upon the battlefield at Alamance, James Hunter was asked to take command. His answer put the strength and the weakness of the frontier into one terse capsule: "We are all freemen, and every one must command himself." The tolerance of the frontier has generally cloaked a few who held a preference for private law as against organized government; at Alamance these men who wanted literal self-command, and the democrats who were exasperated beyond their endurance, fought side by side.

At a county court in Orange County, late in August, 1766, a call was read for each neighborhood to send delegates to a meeting "at some place where there is no liquor," where it should be asked "whether the free men of the county labor under any abuses of power or not, and let the same be notified in writing if any is found, and the matter freely conversed upon, and proper measures used for amendment." The officers present acknowledged that the call was reasonable, and promised to attend. When the delegates met, on October 10, the officers were not there. These delegates agreed upon a statement which suggested an annual meeting wherein the people might investigate the actions of their representatives. This claim that officeholders were responsible to their constituents was heresy to the officers; and Colonel Edmund Fanning, the chief among them, read a formal statement branding the

[95]

suggested measures as insurrectionary. The agitators, laboring under threats of legal reprisals, collected £50 to prosecute the offending officers; but the only lawyer in the county whom they thought honest was afraid to take the case. And the forecast of the Regulation, this agitation of Sandy Creek men, dwindled to private mutterings.

A year and a half later Orange County was ready for organized resistance. Immediate fuel was a notice posted by the sheriff, in the spring of 1768, that he would receive taxes at five specified places, and for all not paid there he would levy a distress of two shillings eightpence. The settlers were aware of no legal authority for this innovation; there probably was none. The "Mob" held two meetings (the name was their own first choice; the quieter color of the name "Regulation" was an afterthought), the first productive of a violent manifesto, the second of a better-ordered statement: "We, the subscribers, do voluntarily agree to form ourselves into an association, to assemble ourselves for conference for regulating public grievances and abuses of power, in the following particulars, with others of a like nature that may occur: (1) We will pay no more taxes until we are satisfied they are agreeable to law, and applied to the purposes therein mentioned, unless we can not help it, or are forced. (2) We will pay no officer any more fees than the law allows, unless we are forced to do it, and then to show our dislike and bear open testimony against it. . . . (3) In case of difference in judgment we will submit to the judgment of the majority of our body."

These resolutions Edmund Fanning and the lesser officers flailed down with shouts of insurrection. But they did not know the literal-mindedness of the Westerners. Soon after, in early April, a Regulator's horse, with saddle and bridle, was seized and sold to meet one levy. A party of the compact-makers rode into Hillsboro and reclaimed the horse. As they passed Fanning's house—by the Regulators' account—some one came to the door, brandished a pistol, and threatened to fire. The Regulators anticipated his fire, and left several bullet holes in the roof.

"Militia!" called Fanning, and warrants were issued for the arrest of four leaders of the raiding party. He reported to Governor Tryon: the Regulators had sworn to pay no taxes, intended to kill all officers who attempted to collect taxes, planned to arraign all officers before "the bar of their shallow understanding," desired to become "the sovereign arbiters of all right and wrong." On the third of May the insurgents intended to surround Hillsboro and, if their demands were not met, burn the town. So Fanning reported, probably misled by some fiery "private papers" in surreptitious circulation among the Regulators. There is no evidence at all that the leaders and rank and file had decided upon the torch. Their actions indicated no plot: on April thirtieth, obedient to a promise given the parish clergymen, they met and elected thirteen delegates to present their cause in Hillsboro on May eleventh. These thirteen delegates, some of them not of the "Mob," were men in whom the community placed confidence; they were given generous powers, and bound by oath "to do justice between the officers and the people."

With Tryon's cordial consent Colonel Fanning, expecting the aid of the militia of seven counties besides his own, followed his preconceived plan to nip in the bud the supposed incendiary plot. On the second of May he arrested William Butler, a Regulator, and Hermon Husband, no Regulator, "whose only crime [in Husband's own words] was in being active in trying to bring on the intended settlement." The charge was inciting to rebellion.

Seven hundred men were on their way to Hillsboro in the morning. The frightened officers forthwith released the prisoners. The governor's secretary, one Edwards, was in Hillsboro; he addressed the crowd, promising that if the Regulators would petition the governor for redress, and preserve the peace, Tryon would see that justice was done them. Justice was what they wanted; and they appointed a committee who should lay before the governor and council all the papers of the Association, with a statement of the history of the movement, together with a request for pardon for anything they had done contrary to the King's peace and government. And they sent the governor affidavits to support their charges against the sheriff, clerk, and register, in twenty cases of illegal fees.

Tryon had no sympathy with the westerners. He denied that he had authorized his secretary to pledge his interference; he hinted at treason, and directed the Regulators to desist from all further meetings and submit to the tax-collecting. He did promise a proclamation against abuses, and gave assurance that he should order the attorney-general to prosecute all cases presented against those who were taking illegal fees. But he also called Fanning into the council chamber, where the council formally expressed its thanks to the colonel and his men "for their prudent and splendid behavior." To Regulators elsewhere Tryon was more conciliatory, apparently to keep them aloof from their suspect fellows in Orange County.

A proclamation against illegal fees was duly set up in Hillsboro; no fees were lowered. Confidence in the disinterestedness of the governor had been destroyed. Rumors were about that the province had collected £30,000 more than was needed to retire its outstanding currency. Meetings of the Association had been forbidden; but there was no way—not even with Tryon himself at Hillsboro—to silence private mutterings.

On the first of August the malcontents met to consider an answer to the governor's pronouncement. The sheriff of Orange County read a letter from the governor, reiterating the demand that the Regulators submit quietly to the collection of taxes; but they shoved aside the document and the gentleman. To Tryon they sent a statement that the officers had paid no attention to the proclamation against illegal fees, adding, "Seeing that these sons of Zeruiah are like to prove too hard for your excellency, as well as for us . . . we have come to the resolution to petition the lower house, as the other branch of the legislature, in order to strengthen your excellency's hands."

Demands and protests countered rapidly. Demand: the trial of Butler and Husband on the charge of inciting to rebellion must proceed without any interference. Protest: the Regulators had not intended to rescue the prisoners. Demand: twelve leaders of the Regulators must present themselves to the governor and become surety in a bond of £1,000. Protest: these leaders could govern the men and prevent outrages, whereas if they entered into such a bond their influence would be destroyed.

Tryon moved swiftly and relentlessly, coming into the western counties, and there cajoling the Presbyterian and the Baptist ministers, distributing patronage to the neighborhood leaders, providing entertainment for the men and officers of the militia, to raise a force against the Regulators.

He assembled a force of almost fifteen hundred men. Over three hundred of these were officers. Most of these officers, be it noted, also held political positions; many of them were in the provincial assembly, that body to which the Regulators had decided to appeal. Tryon brought his army into Hillsboro just before the September term of the superior court, at which Butler and Husband were to be tried.

The back-country farmers were not prepared to make a stand before such an array. They assembled, on September twenty-second, a gathering of thirty-seven hundred, and made overtures of submission. The council of officers demanded the surrender of five leaders from Orange County, two from Anson, and two from Rowan; that the people lay down their arms before the militia, and promise to pay taxes in future. Pardon at the price of betrayal of some of their number was too dear; and the folk-army dispersed without making submission.

A body of troops was sent to arrest those whom Tryon especially wanted; but these prisoners were soon released, because a true bill could not be found against them. Overt hostility to "law and order" sharply subsided. The Reverend George Micklejohn, the parish priest, preached to the militia, assuring them that the rebels could not hope to escape hell; the troops were disbanded; and on the third of October Tryon proclaimed a general pardon of the insurgents, excepting thirteen leaders.

Meanwhile the wheels of justice began turning, to no very mechanistic conclusion. Husband was acquitted. Butler and two others were fined, and sentenced to three or six months' imprisonment; but Tryon released them. Other true bills were quashed; Tryon's policy was now to be lenient, to bring the malcontents back to submission. Colonel Fanning, the register of Orange County, was found guilty on five counts, and fined five pennies. At the March, 1769, meeting of the Superior Court in Hillsboro, other officers were tried, with small success for the people. In Rowan County, when the Regulators attempted to prosecute the officers for extortion, they found that at least nine men on the grand jury were officers.

The issue had been sharply defined now. The Regulators had at first directed their protests to the local officers; they had been told to apply to the courts, and complied; they had found that the laws favored the officers. They now determined to attack the provincial lawmaking body, the general assembly.

The election of 1769 reflected a strong feeling against the office-holding oligarchy. Of the seventy-eight members of the assembly, forty-three were newly elected. The issue of the Regulators was not raised in all counties, of course, for it was purely a western issue; but in the four counties where Regulators were strongest, the change of delegates was complete.

Anticipating fair treatment from the reconstituted assembly, the Regulators prepared statements of their political hardships and suggestions of redress. The petition drawn up by the Regulators of Anson County indicates significantly the political demands of the frontier—demands of a far larger area than western North Carolina, vigorously carried forward in the transition era when Provinces were becoming States: at all elections the vote should be given by ballot; taxation should be apportioned on a property basis and not per capita; people should have the privilege of paying their taxes in commodities; paper money should be issued and loaned on land; the chief justice should have no fees, but should be given a salary; the fees of the clerks should be restricted. They asked for reforms in the quitrent system, the issuing of land warrants, and the valuing of improvements on land. And among their other requests was one that all denominations have liberty to conduct the marriage ceremony according to their own rites.

The course of constitutional redress was suddenly cut off by a premonitory tremor of the imperial conflict. The assembly had been in session only ten days when the lower house passed unanimously some defiant resolutions directed against the Royal government; and on November sixth the governor ordered the assembly dissolved.

Months had passed without sign of relief; from the Regulators of Orange County an ominous rumble swelled in volume. Another fruitless petition to the officers of the superior court, in the summer of 1770, asked for unprejudiced juries, fair trials of extortionate officers, and a proper settlement of the public accounts; but there was little humility to this petition: "Our only crime with which they can charge us is vertue in the very highest degree, namely, to risque all to save our country from rapine and slavery in our detecting of practices which the law allows to be worse than open robbery. . . . As we are serious and in good earnest, and the cause respects the whole body of the people, it would be a loss of time to enter into argument on particular points, for although there is a few men who have the gift or art of reasoning, yet every man has a feeling and knows when he has justice done him as well as the most learned."

They did not wait to see what reforms, if any, the assembly of 1770 might accomplish. When the superior court met at Hillsboro, in late September, a crowd of a hundred and fifty Regulators milled about the courthouse. Too many bludgeons were carried by too many turbulent men. Somehow the violence began. Fanning got the worst of it: he was seized and clubbed until (as the justice of the court reported) he "by a manly exertion miraculously broke holt and fortunately jumped into a door that saved him from immediate dissolution." In the morning, the twenty-fifth, the mob promised no further harm to Fanning if he took to the road and kept running until he was out of sight; and he complied at once. They stormed and destroyed his home.

A small gathering had pushed the whole body of Regulators into outlawry. Friends in the provincial assembly were alienated by fear. Wild rumors circulated of marauding marches planned by the Regulators, of a plan to overawe the assembly by force. On a November night the dwelling of Justice Henderson of the superior court was burned. When the Presbyterian ministry was won over to the officeholders by promise of a college in Mecklenburg

County and the right to perform the marriage ceremony, an important moderating influence was lost to the malcontents.

As the year 1770 ended, the Regulators themselves precipitated the drastic force of the law. Rumors that a mob planned to march upon Newbern, where the assembly was in session, gained sudden substantiation; and an emergency riot bill was rushed to the governor.

The legislature then went on to pass bills correcting abuses in the fee system, and a bill to erect four additional counties in the under-represented western part of the province. But Tryon did not wait to see how far these long-wanted laws might restore law and order; he had a drastic riot act as weapon, and at once ordered the arrest of the leaders in the outrages at Hillsboro. A special grand jury was impaneled, and the case against Hermon Husband pressed; the jury returned "no bill," and Tryon discharged the jury. His second jury was shamelessly packed: select only "gentlemen of the first rank, property, and probity," Tryon directed the sheriffs. Witnesses were carefully selected; and all sixty-two indictments presented were returned "true bills." By the terms of the riot act, these defendants would be considered outlaws, and as such liable to be killed with impunity, if they did not present themselves for trial within two months.

Meanwhile energetic preparations were made for a military expedition against Orange County. Tryon had just been appointed governor of New York; and he was anxious to have his tenure in North Carolina end in a blaze of glory. Scraps of provocative utterance against the peace of the province were in his hands—for instance, a letter from Rednap Howell to another leading Regulator, which said, "I give out here that the Regulators are determined to whip every one that goes to law, or will not pay his just debts . . . that they will choose representatives, but not send them to be put in jail; in short, to stand in defiance, and as to thieves, to drive them out of the country."

Over the Regulators' protest that Tryon's driving tactics would produce greater commotion, the governor continued to levy troops. In May his army, in two columns, marched upon Hillsboro. The western column, about two hundred and fifty men and fifty officers, was beleaguered in Salisbury; Tryon, with a thousand men and officers, marched from Hillsboro to relieve the smaller division.

Five miles west of the Alamance River two thousand Regulators had assembled. No more than half the farmers, probably, had arms. There was no concerted intention, no military organization. They had resolved, the Regulators had told the governor, that every man should take his horse from the plow and meet the governor "to know for certain whether you are really determined to suppress all the disturbers of the public peace and to punish according to their deserts the original offenders in government." But once in camp, the turbulent element could not be kept in restraint.

Dr. David Caldwell and Hermon Husband were there as peacemakers. Caldwell twice interviewed Tryon in an attempt to find some basis for agreement; he came back to report failure and advise the farmers to return to their homes. Stolidly they stood their ground—"Our civil liberties are certainly more dear to us than the good opinion of a ruler"—and Caldwell and Husband rode away.

So little did the people realize what a battle might be that several of the men were engaged in wrestling matches when an old soldier among them advised them to look out for a volley. In a few minutes the firing began.

The battle did not take very long. There was no higher officer than captain among the Regulators; each little company tried to form itself and hold its lone position, while independent fighters crouched behind rocks and trees and returned the only effective fire. Tryon's army lost its artillery, but the insurgents abandoned the pieces when the troops rallied against them. Long before this most of the Regulators had taken to flight. Nine men on each side had been killed, and a great number wounded. The Regulation was crushed; and to strike the note of finality Colonel Fanning ordered the summary execution of a half-insane visionary, James Few, who had been taken prisoner.

On the next day, May seventeenth, Tryon pardoned by proclamation all those who should submit themselves to the government and take the oath of allegiance, except those who had recently been outlawed and those who were taken prisoners at Alamance. On June nineteenth the army, still lingering in the west, was drawn up to witness the execution of six of the prisoners.

When the new governor, Josiah Martin, arrived in the colony, he found a quieted West. Six thousand four hundred and nine persons had taken the oath of allegiance by July 4, 1771. In the next year the outlawed leaders surrendered themselves. Their trials hung fire; and when the American Revolution was imminent the King, as a matter of policy, had the governor issue a proclamation of pardon for all, except the fugitive Husband, who had been concerned in the Regulation.

Elsewhere in the western counties of the provinces—in Pennsylvania, Massachusetts, Virginia—news of the drastic suppression of the Regulation taught dissatisfied people caution. But in each of these frontier areas, it may be noticed, discontent ultimately became explosive—in Pennsylvania, the Whisky Insurrection; in Massachusetts, Shay's Rebellion; and in Virginia, the long offensive against the state constitution which culminated in the creation of West Virginia in 1863. If truculence of spirit, distrust of the leisured gentlemen in politics and distrust of older cultures seem to mark Americans in their westward march, one may find in these conflicts in the old-west regions the grim experiences that hardened the pioneer mind.

In western Virginia, spared the flagrant abuse of the fee system, there was no Regulation; the other grievances of the Carolina back country were common. In Virginia, as in North Carolina, huge western counties, growing in population, were given no greater representation in the assembly than small, thinning counties of the older east. Here, too, governors and others of the office-holding oligarchy had engrossed large estates, often taking far more water front than was necessary. Petitions from the Virginia country beyond the falls line for the construction of roads and bridges, for improved navigation of the rivers, and for more adequate military protection, were passed over by an unconcerned legislature. Quitrents were often diverted from their legal destinies. Occasionally there were more homely grievances, as that one which Governor Spotswood reported in 1715, "relating to the ringing of Hoggs, which, however trifling in themselves, may serve to show how great an Alteration there is in the temper of ye People, since even, in my time, it was enough to loose a man's election as Burgess, that he had shew'd the least inclination towards the ringing of hoggs."

To explain why John Finley, Daniel Boone, James Harrod, John Sevier, and James Robertson sought out the transmontane lanes into Kentucky and Tennessee, it may not be necessary to remember the unanswered demands, political, military, economic, of the Appalachian valleys. But it was from these valleys that men of the vagrant spark recruited their followers; they were back-country folk from Carolina, Virginia, and Pennsylvania who trudged across the mountains to some eye-satisfying place where they traced their own boundaries, drove their own stakes.

CHAPTER VII

THE WILDERNESS ROAD

FROM the upper waters of the rivers of lower Virginia and Carolina across the Great Smoky or the Unaka Range into the lush-forested region of many valleys that is now eastern Tennessee was but a short step; and many a family of Carolina hill folk crossed directly westward, while families of Virginians followed the southerly course of the Alleghenies, to the headwaters of the Clinch, the Holston, the Watauga, or another of those little rivers whose waters ultimately unite to form the Tennessee River. And in this far-western refuge there probably was more than the usual sprinkling of scoundrels upon a frontier—Scotch-Irish whose mentality was atavistic of the semisavage clans of the Highlands and the Hebrides; English whose ancestry had been degenerate in England and had a smell of prisons and convict-ships; fugitives from provincial justice.

On the Watauga the first settlement was a natural extension of the group of Virginia frontiersmen on the headwaters of the Holston. In 1770 James Robertson came here; two years later came John Sevier. Robertson, thoroughly a backwoodsman, was then laboriously learning from his young wife how to write and to spell; Sevier, a Huguenot and a gentleman by birth, was a polished correspondent of Madison, Franklin, and others high in continental prestige. To these two men, because of some indefinable distinction they possessed in common, gravitated the leadership of the Watauga settlement, and, when war came, the leadership of fighting Tennessee.

The frontiersmen on the Watauga assumed that they were within Virginian domain; they had taken it for granted that Virginia's treaties with the Indians protected them, and that Virginia law governed them. But in 1771 an archetype of scientific skepticism, Anthony Bledsoe, a newcomer who knew something of surveying, ran out the boundary line of Virginia some distance to the westward; the Watauga settlement was below it, within the limits of North Carolina. After the battle of the Alamance in this same year, hundreds of the back-country people of North Carolina turned westward for new courage and new opportunity; many of them settled among the pioneers of the Watauga at this time when the western colony found itself estray from government, and in Cherokee domain.

Under Robertson's leadership the independent community of Watauga formally took shape in the spring of 1772. Isolated in the wilderness, instinctively these frontiersmen conned the covenants and constitutions they or their fathers had cherished, and evoked the Articles of the Watauga Association. There is hardly a characteristic of the American frontier stronger than the passion for democratic organization, a fondness for constructing documents in which the words "delegates," "representatives," "majority," figure prominently.

The settlers met in a general convention; and then, or soon after, elected a representative assembly. Apparently the men of each little palisaded village elected one of their number to this legislature. The thirteen men so elected chose five of their number, among them Sevier and Robertson, who should carry on the actual business of government. The form of constitutional democracy had been satisfied; the burden of administration had been passed on to the men who wanted to assume it; and the settlers, in general, were content with their creation, the Commonwealth of Watauga. The little government happened to be democratic in fact because of the fiery democratic passion of its five Commissioners.

Taking the laws of Virginia as their guide, the commissioners met in court session at stated intervals, supervised the recording of debts and wills, issued marriage licenses, prosecuted horse thieves, and adjudicated all "legal" differences between the settlers. They took measures for the common safety; and they had one sovereign power which they were never called upon to exercise, the power to purchase lands by treaty with the Indians. The Cherokees had agreed upon "articles of accommodation and friendship," and in considerations of merchandise and muskets consented to lease the country on the waters of the Watauga, but would not sell.

Something of the background of this experiment lies in the story of the first church in the Watauga country, a Presbyterian meetinghouse built in 1777. Following the practice of back-country Presbyterians, the settlers appointed a committee to choose the ground, direct the building of the church, and to collect the minister's fee and all church expenses by exacting proportionate taxes from the congregation. Twice a year the congregation was to meet in a business session at which the committee should give a full account of church affairs.

The commonwealth found rather rough going; and in the spring of 1776 John Sevier, in the name of the Wataugans, petitioned the Council of North Carolina, not fɔr the first time: "We . . . trust we shall be considered as

[109]

we deserve, and not as we have (no doubt) been many times represented, as a lawless mob. It is for this very reason we can assure you that we petition; we now again repeat it, that it is for want of proper authority to try and punish felons, we can only mention to you murderers, horse-thieves and robbers, and are sorry to say that some of them have escaped us for want of proper authority. . . . That you may . . . delay no time in annexing us to your Province, in such a manner as your wisdom shall direct, is the hearty prayer." And, belatedly, the Council admitted the Watauga settlement, under the name of "District of Washington," into the provincial congress of North Carolina.

And at about the same time Richard Henderson, governor of the independent commonwealth of Transylvania, was making a losing fight to prevent this other republic in the wilderness from becoming simply a county of Virginia.

Richard Henderson, Virginia-born, was inducted in adolescence into the office-holding oligarchy of North Carolina. He enjoyed himself, and made the most of the machine; constable, then undersheriff, then—after a twelve months' reading—a barrister, he became an associate chief justice of the province. The Regulators had no fancy for him; in 1770, when he was presiding at the Hillsboro court, his courtroom was invaded by a mob, and Henderson mounted a fast horse and galloped out of town.

Lewis Collins, early historian of Kentucky, has garlanded Henderson with five adjectives: "of great ambition and somewhat ostentatious," he became involved in speculations, and his fortune was ravaged; "bold, ardent, and adventurous," a greater speculation, the founding of a western barony, excited his imagination.

His plan was to purchase from the Cherokees the expansive territory between the Kentucky River and the Cumberland—one-half the present state of Kentucky. The

Shawnees had recently been defeated in war and had obligated themselves to hunt no more on the Kentucky side
of the Ohio. The claims of the other great Indian nation,
the Iroquois, to the "dark and bloudy ground" had been
relinquished in 1768, by the Treaty of Fort Stanwix. The
King's Proclamation of 1763 was twelve years old, and
long on Virginia statute books had been an act forbidding
the private purchase of lands from the Indians; these
checks to his enterprise received Henderson's imperial
disregard.

In March, 1775, at the Sycamore Shoals of the Watauga
River, twelve hundred Indians met Henderson and the
several land-hungry men whom he had enlisted in his "Transylvania Company." A shadowy title to twenty million
acres changed hands. "An infamous company of land
pirates," fumed the governors of Virginia and North Carolina; but preparations went ahead.

The talent of Daniel Boone had been solicited; Henderson needed a skillful woodsman, well acquainted with the
wilderness of Kentucky, to cleave a road into the heart of
Transylvania.

Daniel Boone was twenty years old when his father, in
1752, led the caravan of a great many descendants and
a very little household stuff to the forks of the Yadkin
River. In this region of "rank Grass and prodigiously
large Trees . . . plenty of Fish, Fowl and Venison,"
Boone had rare play for his uncommon skill at hunting.
As a wagoner and mechanic he had followed Braddock in
that march of 1755 when the English troops, silhouetted
against the sky, had been mowed down by the French and
Indians. He was one of those hunters who had edged westward into new mountain fastnesses when the close of the
French and Indian War relaxed the Indian menace. John
Finley, peddler and Indian trader, had fired his imagination
with accounts of the abundant herds of great game animals

[111]

in Kentucky; and in 1769 Boone, Finley, and four companions had undertaken a long and adventurous exploration of the wilderness below the Ohio. There was no white man in 1772 who knew Kentucky better.

Felix Walker, one of Henderson's associates at Sycamore Shoals, recorded: "The purchase made, we proceeded on our journey to meet Col. Daniel Boon, with other adventurers, bound for the same country; accordingly we met and rendezvoused at the Long Island on Holsteen river, united our small force with Colonel Boon and his associates, his brother, Squire Boon, and Col. Richard Callaway, of Virginia. Our company, when united, amounted to thirty persons. We then, by general consent, put ourselves under the management and control of Col. Boon, who was to be our pilot and conductor through the wilderness, to the promised land."

Boone's party left the Holston on the tenth of March, heading for the Cumberland Gap on as direct a line as possible, by way of Clinch River and Powell's River. He avoided abrupt descents and arduous upgrades as best he could in the mountainous country. For those who followed, Boone's hatchets blazed the way and hacked at the hampering underbrush.

Henderson with his party left ten days later. Hard on his heels was a little group of emigrants from Prince William County, Virginia, among whom was William Calk, diarist, whose faithful journal in hazardous English chronicles the labor and endurance of these pioneers.

On April the first Calk writes, "this morning there is ice at our camp half inch thick we start early and travel this Day along a verey Bad hilley way across one creek whear the horses almost got mired some fell in and all wet their loads we cross Clinch River and travell till late in the Night and camp on Cove Creek having two men with us that wair pilates."

Three days later, on the western slope of Powell's Valley, the Virginians overtook Henderson. Thereafter they traveled together. Boone's path-blazers had passed through the underbrush country into thirty miles of canebrake, and on to discover "the pleasing and rapturous appearance of the plains of Kentucky." Early on the twenty-fifth of March the little party, asleep in camp, was fired upon by Indians. Two men were killed and the company dispersed. They regathered, in gloom; "high calculations of long life and happy days in our newly-discovered country were prostrated; hope vanished for the most of us, and left us suspended in the tumult of uncertainty and conjecture," wrote Walker. The firmness of Boone and the other experienced woodsmen of the party pushed the company on; but on the seventh "comes a letter from Capt. Boone at caintuck of the indians doing mischief" to Henderson's company, "and some turns back."

Boone and his company of thirty reached their destination the sixth of April, in the heart of the blue-grass country near the confluence of Otter Creek and the Kentucky River, a spot Boone had chosen years before as an ideal place for settlement.

The spot was in a sheltered hollow, made important by two lively springs. One, a sulphur spring, had incrustations of salt about it; and the rich soil of the hollow was almost cleared of undergrowth by the tread of buffalo and deer who had haunted this salt lick. The other furnished abundant drinking-water.

This was journey's end. Boone and his woodsmen, after a good rest, began to build several log huts; these the company named "Fort Boone." But the work lagged as the men became engrossed in hunting and fur-collecting.

Back on the Wilderness Road trudged the larger company of emigrants. They were bringing their cattle with them, and so made slower marches. On the eleventh Calk

writes: "this is a loury morning and like for Rain
but we all agree to start Early and we cross Cumberland
River and travel Down it about 10 miles through some tur-
rabel cainbrakes as we went down abrams mair Ran into
the River with her load and swam over he followed her and
got on her and made her swim back agin it is a very raney

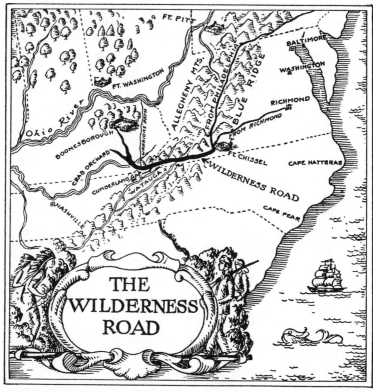

THE
WILDERNESS
ROAD

Eavening we take up Camp near Richland Creek they kill
a beef Mr. Drake Bakes Bread without washing his hands
we Keep Sentry this Night for fear of the indians." Rainy
days, miry roads, flooded creeks; then, on the twentieth,
"We start early and git Down to caintuck to Boons foart
about 12 o'clock where we stop they come out to meet us &
welcom us in with a voley of guns." The army of occupa-

tion had come—forty mounted riflemen, and slaves, and a drove of beeves, forty pack horses, and a wagon train of provisions, ammunition, household stuff, and seed.

Henderson saw at once that his men and the wagon stuffs would require more substantial shelter than his tents or Boone's little cabins. He selected a site above the hollow for his station. In a week of preliminary work the ground was cleared, trees were felled and logs shaped and notched, clapboards were made; and on the twenty-ninth the fort was begun. Boone directed the work. A powder magazine, a storehouse, a blockhouse for Henderson's residence, other cabins, rose up on the plateau. "Boonesborough," completed, consisted of about thirty-one cabins arranged in a hollow square and linked by a log stockade joining their outer walls, with a two-story blockhouse at each corner of the square. It was a typical palisaded village of the early frontier.

While the woodsmen were busy on the banks of the Kentucky, representatives of the Transylvania Company yet in North Carolina were seeking to secure for their enterprise the support of Thomas Jefferson and Patrick Henry, already conspicuous in the preliminary fanfare of the Revolution. But these men were busy with other, more sharply defined problems of self-assertion; as Jefferson said later, when in the Continental Congress, it was his wish to see a free government established in the back country, but he "would consent to no congressional acknowledgment of the colony until it was approved by the Virginia Convention."

Henderson had a predecessor in Transylvania, James Harrod, who with some forty men had left the Monongahela Valley for Kentucky, by way of the Ohio River, in May, 1774. Near the center of the state, on a plateau eight miles from the Kentucky River, he laid out the village of Harrodstown. Indian title or Virginia title was no bother to Harrod. James T. Morehead, once Senator from Kentucky, paid elegant compliment to this pioneer: "If he received information that a party of hunters had been surprised by the savages, 'let us go and beat the red rascals,' was his instantaneous order; and the command and its execution were synonymous with him. If a plow horse were missing—having strayed from the station,—and its owner, unaccustomed to the range, or unwilling to encounter the risk of making search for him, was idle in consequence, Harrod would disappear, and it would not be long before the horse would be driven to the owner's premises. Of a restless and active temperament, the dull routine of life in a station was unsuited to him. He loved, like Boone, the free and unrestrained occupation of a hunter. While others were standing still for want of employment, disdaining repose, he would range through the forest, hunt the wild game, or attach himself to expeditions into the Indian country or exploring parties on the frontier." A month after the founding of the settlement, Boone had come with the word that the Shawnees were on the warpath; and Harrodstown had been deserted for the season, to be permanently settled about a month before the founding of Boonesborough.

But Harrod expressed willingness to take title from the Transylvania Company; and a group of Virginians under Captain John Floyd, official surveyor for Virginia, quite recently come to central Kentucky, voiced similar recognition of Henderson's purchase of the Indian title. One difficulty of the Transylvania Company—protection of its title—seemed on its way to a favorable answer. Another problem faced Henderson, the safeguarding of the proprietors' interest in Transylvania against the instinctive desire of its settlers for self-government.

In May, 1775, elections were held at the four little settlements south of the Kentucky River—Boonesborough, Harrodstown, Floyd's settlement, and Boiling Spring, lately founded by Harrod; and on the twenty-third the chosen representatives rode up to the log dwelling of the Chief Proprietor, Richard Henderson. A huge elm in the hollow was selected as the temporary forum of the assembly. On the next day (let a Kentuckian speak) "under the spreading dome that the Immortal Architect himself had fashioned, and which overshadowed what an eyewitness called 'a heavenly green' of fine white native clover, was attempted for the first time in the vast region west of the Alleghenies the founding of an independent State which proclaimed that sublime axiom that 'all power is originally in the people.'"

Judge Henderson in his formal opening of the House of Delegates asserted, "We have the right to make laws for the regulation of our conduct without giving offense to Great Britain or any of the American colonies." And the delegates set at the task of legislation, making august use of all parliamentary procedure that they knew. The fruits of this first session included acts establishing civil and criminal courts and procedure, an act for establishing a militia, "an act to prevent profane swearing, and Sabbath breaking," and one—Kentucky being Kentucky—"for improving the breed of horses." Daniel Boone was chairman of the committee which framed a law for the preservation of game, in answer to Henderson's recommendation: "the wanton destruction of our game, the only support of life amongst many of us . . . together with the practice of many foreigners, who make a business of hunting in our country, killing, driving off, and lessening the number of wild cattle and other game, whilst the value of the skins and furs is appropriated to the benefit of persons not concerned or interested in our settlement: these are evils, I say, that I am convinced can not escape your notice and attention." Henderson's "wild cattle" were the buffalo, then fast being exterminated on the western slope of the Alleghenies. Already hunters from Boonesborough had to ride twenty or thirty miles from the settlement to find elk or buffalo.

The delegates agreed upon a compact "between the proprietors and the people," the constitution of Transylvania. The document bears evidence to the fine hand of Richard Henderson: the power of taxation was the sole office of real importance in the province of the delegates; otherwise there was little check on the proprietors. Henderson must have hoped for a reproduction of that oligarchic system under which his political fortune had flourished in North Carolina.

On the last day of the session there was enacted the ancient feudal ceremonial, "livery of seisin," by which the transfer of Transylvania from the Cherokees to the company was formally concluded. Under the great elm John Farrar, the attorney employed by the Indians, cut a piece of the luxuriant turf and extended it to Henderson. So a long obsolete ceremony emphasized the colonial simplicity of this occupation of the wilderness. And on the following day, Sunday, prayers were publicly recited for the King and royal family of England, for the first and the last time on the soil of Kentucky.

News, long on the road, reached Transylvania: in Massachusetts blood had been shed in conflict between colonial and British troops. The sympathies of the Kentuckians instinctively were with the Rebels. Reports of Lord Dunmore's efforts to incite the Indians brought home the fact that they might have a part in the war; and Henderson and Boone seized the chance to impel the woodsmen to complete the log fort.

In mid-June Boone set out for his family, still in the stockaded home of a friend in western Virginia. In September he was back at Boonesborough, with a score of emigrants besides his family. His wife and daughter were the first women in the little settlement; and the presence of these two made Boonesborough more livable. "An ash-hopper, soap kettle, and clothes line were set up. Hickory brooms and home-made wash-boards multiplied. The sound of the spinning-wheel was heard in the land, and an occasional sight could be had of a little looking-glass, a patch-work quilt, knitting-needles, and a turkey-tail fan."

A proprietary government, no matter how many trappings of a republic it adopted, could not flourish on the frontier, nor find favor in the philosophical democracy of the Continental Congress. James Hogg, a shrewd Scot, was sent to Philadelphia by the proprietors in hope of securing recognition of Transylvania as the fourteenth colony. The great spirits were interested, very interested. Silas Deane's Yankee constituents were becoming restless; two thousand of them, it is said, were debating the prospects of existence in Transylvania. And Deane documented an outline scheme of government for Transylvania, based upon the procedure of his own Connecticut. "There ought to be some terms on which a man becomes free of the community," he added. And: "The General Assembly must be the supreme fountain of power in such a state, in constituting which, every free man ought to have his voice. The elections should be frequent, at least annually; and to this body every officer ought to be amenable for his conduct. Every impediment in the way of increase of people should be removed, of course marriage must be made easy." John Adams pointed out that Congress would be greatly handicapped in any effort at conciliation with the Crown if it received into the union a colony established in violation of the King's Proclamation of 1763. And to Transylvania was left the hopeless task of guiding its own destiny.

The people in Kentucky ominously let the month of September pass without holding the scheduled meeting of the Assembly. A constant stream of immigration had followed the Wilderness Road through Cumberland Gap into the blue-grass region—among the newcomers, George Rogers Clark, who was to conquer the British posts in the Ohio Valley; Jesse Benton, the father of Thomas Hart Benton; and many another aggressive personality. John Williams, uncle of Richard Henderson, and newly appointed general agent of the Transylvania Company, arrived at Boonesborough on the first of December, and opened a land office; the price of land was at once increased from twenty to fifty shillings for one hundred acres, the company retained half the mineral rights, and assessed fees which totaled two pounds before a purchase was completed. A formal remonstrance delivered to Williams brought out no satisfactory reply. There were other exasperations: the proprietors had reserved for themselves and a few friends nearly seventy thousand acres at the Falls of the Ohio, the most likely site for a commercial town; the company's store at Boonesborough was charging exorbitant prices. The settlers were done with overlordship; and a determined movement was under way, by the spring of 1776, to break the power of the company.

After that—what? Freedom in the Indian-infested wilderness, with the danger of war daily drawing closer about them? Recognition by Virginia that the Kentucky settlements were a part of her own territory, a part needing military protection, was the safer alternative. The people threw off the name of Transylvania, announced their region "West Fincastle of the Colony of Virginia, being on the North and South Sides of the River Kentucke," and hastened George Rogers Clark and John Gabriel Jones to the Virginia Convention with a petition. This was a pert document, stressing the desirability to Virginia of a loyal outpost in the Indian country: "We cannot but observe how impolitical it would be to Suffer such a Respectable Body of Prime Rifle Men to remain in a state of Neutrality . . . the Tyrannick Ministry will not stop at any means to reduce the loyal americans to their detestable ends and that if these pretended Proprietors have leave to continue to act in their arbitrary manner out the controul of this Colony the end must be evident to every well wisher to American Liberty."

The Virginia Convention, though pressed for time, ordered an investigation into illegal purchases of land from the Indians, and an inquiry to determine accurately Virginia's chartered interests in Kentucky—two measures bringing the long-dreaded day of battle to the Transylvania Company. Henderson fought desperately; but under the new order of things, after July 2, 1776, any proprietary government was an outcast in America. On the seventh of December the just-created state legislature of Virginia created the county of Kentucky on its western frontier—the domain which was destined to become the state of Kentucky. Transylvania was swallowed up; and Boonesborough now found itself a wilderness outpost of Virginia.

In opening a continuous road across the Alleghenies to the banks of the Kentucky River, in its inspiriting occupation of virgin soil, in planting the strongest far-western barrier against the Indian, Richard Henderson and company had taken a proud part in the permanent conquest of the West. Fittingly, the Virginia house of delegates voted the proprietors of Transylvania a grant of two hundred thousand acres of Kentucky land, and the assembly of North Carolina later made similar acknowledgment. But ill luck dogged the company; when the western lands of the states were ceded to the national government, their title all but vanished.

Following the everyday life of the frontier, the people of Boonesborough were fast accumulating in the mountain valleys the little "conveniences" of their old homes—soft soap and maple sugar, whisky jugs and inkpots, the Bible and almanacs, bundles of medicine herbs, and bunches of tobacco leaf. At Boonesborough now were sheds for corn and fodder, and for peltry; stock troughs made from hollow logs; a blacksmith shop; iron plows brought from the east, and wooden plows made in the wilderness.

In April, 1777, this existence of farming and hunting, hammering iron and fashioning wood, was interrupted by the first drive of the Indians against Boonesborough. The Revolution had found out the frontier. Thereafter Indian danger was incessant, fighting was frequent. Often the danger was such that hunters did not dare venture far, and the sole dependence of the settlement was the little amount of corn, potatoes, and turnips raised just outside the stockade. In September, 1778, Boonesborough had to withstand a nine days' siege, one of the longest the restless North American Indian ever attempted; the fort's simple defenses were proven amply effective. Other settlements in Kentucky were deserted or ravaged in this trying year; but before spring of 1779 was over settlers had planted themselves once more on the north side of the Kentucky River, and new blockhouses and stockaded cabins rose up between Boonesborough and the Ohio River.

As the spectacular work of George Rogers Clark in holding the Old Northwest became known, the stream of immigration increased; and Boonesborough became the busiest spot in Virginia's remotest county. It was a stopping place of the many companies of settlers, traders, and land speculators, who came over the Wilderness Road; and those whom business or family called eastward passed through Boonesborough, since the floating craft that came down the Ohio could not make the return journey. The inhabitants of Boonesborough, strengthened and encouraged, laid off additional lots, named contemplated streets, and petitioned the Virginia assembly to incorporate their settlement as a town, and grant it a ferry. In October, 1779, Boonesborough attained its double dignity.

In the spring of 1778 Richard Henderson appeared once

more in Boonesborough. The old Company had promoted a settlement, French Lick, the future Nashville, in its lands on the Cumberland River. The little stockaded village in Tennessee was half starving; and Henderson came for grain. The corn he bought cost two hundred dollars a bushel, in Continental currency; it was loaded in log pirogues, which made their tortuous way down the Kentucky into the Ohio, on to the mouth of the Cumberland, and up that river to its destination. Boonesborough had seen its last of the governor of Transylvania.

CHAPTER VIII

THE FRINGE OF THE REVOLUTION

FORTY-SEVEN Indians, making their noiseless way through pathless forest, heard the crunch of ax against wood; deploying to the sound, they saw three men working on a clearing. They rushed, and fired; in a moment one man was dead, one a prisoner, but the other was speeding away toward Harrodstown, five miles away. Fleet Indians were outdistanced by this remarkably swift lad, James Ray, who brought the alarm of war to Harrodstown in March, 1777. The militia was organized, ammunition prepared, and water and grain were brought inside the fort.

"From this period [George Rogers Clark is fairly launched in his *Memoir*] we may date the commencement of that bloody war in Kentucky which has continued with savage fury ever since. Upwards of two thousand souls have perished on our side, in a moderate calculation, and the war has been most severely felt by the most active Indian nations. It is impossible to enumerate all the little actions that took place. They were continual, and frequently severe when compared to our small forces. The forts were frequently attacked. Good policy would seem to have required that the whole force be embodied in one place, but our dependence upon hunting for the greatest portion of our provisions forbade this. No people could be in a more alarming position. Detached at least two hundred miles from the nearest settlement of the states, we were surrounded by numerous Indian nations, each one far superior to ourselves in numbers and spurred on by the British government to destroy us, as appeared from many instruments of writing left us on the breasts of persons killed by them."

John Connolly, who had been the western agent of Virginia's land-grabbing, Indian-hounding governor, Lord Dunmore, was the first loyal Britisher to realize the possibilities of a battering campaign against the frontier settlements. His own vehemence, already manifested in his militant occupation of Pittsburgh when the Pennsylvania-Virginia boundary was in dispute, might have successfully carried through his plan to capture Pittsburgh and ultimately to unite the troops marching from Detroit with the troops of Lord Dunmore, but he was taken prisoner; and so it was that an ineffectual, amiable person, Major Henry Hamilton, lieutenant governor of New France, stationed at Detroit, directed the war against the frontier.

Hamilton courted Indian allies. Many loyal Englishmen abhorred the plan, among them Governor Abbott of Vincennes, who thrust his protest at Hamilton: "It is not people in arms that Indians will ever daringly attack, but the poor inoffensive families who fly to the deserts to be out of trouble, & who are inhumanly butchered sparing neither women or children." But Hamilton believed that Indian barbarity would be restrained by British rectitude. Gifts were presented to the Indians, he asserted, "on every proof of obedience that they shew, if sparing the lives of such as are incapable of defending themselves." Hamilton

[125]

lingered unenviably in frontier memory as the "hair-buyer," for the common impression was that he paid Indians for the American scalps they brought in. Fighting was nastiest on the frontier; the "Long Knives" of Kentucky adopted the barbarities of Indian warfare in bloody retaliation.

The pioneers were making homesteads in the Kentucky hunting grounds; from the British posts in the northwest no settlers were invading Indian domain. George Morgan, agent of the Continental Congress, was at Pittsburgh, making promises to the Indians that American traders were coming with excellent, underpriced trading stuffs, and that the congress was sending presents; but British traders were already among them with full-loaded packs ready for generous barter, and Hamilton was making lavish presents to the tribes. Finally, a bloody outrage destroyed whatever chance there was that American commissioners might persuade the Indians to remain neutral, and flung them into friendship with the British: frontiersmen of Pennsylvania wantonly murdered the friendly chief, Cornstalk, and three of his tribe, in the autumn of 1777. Thereafter Cornstalk's tribe, the Shawnee, was committed to a series of vicious attacks on the settlements of Kentucky and western Virginia.

In the summer and autumn of 1777 lone Indians and small skulking bands haunted the forests about Boonesborough; the planting season passed, then the harvest season, but the pent-up settlers had only a pitiful crop to show for the year. Salt became distressingly low; in December there was none at all, in any of the settlements in Kentucky. Cornbread, turnips, and venison had become the monotonous ration; and sickness threatened.

The pioneers determined to make their own salt at an ancient spring, the Blue Licks, where in their first season in Kentucky the hunters had killed buffalo. On the first of January, 1778, Daniel Boone led a party of thirty men from the several stockaded villages on the cold ride to the salt springs. Their pack horses carried the largest iron kettles in the settlements. These kitchen kettles were the best makeshifts they had; but salt-making was a painfully tedious business. Five hundred to eight hundred gallons of salt-spring water had to be boiled to produce one bushel of salt. This one bushel, not surprisingly, was worth a cow and a calf in barter.

Three of the men took back a little salt to the settlements, while the rest stayed at the Licks to carry the work into February. On the seventh of the month a band of a hundred Indians, with two of Major Hamilton's French employees, suddenly ended the salt-making. The Kentuckians, numb from cold and cramped by the work, were easily captured. The Indians could have taken Boonesborough had they kept on; but Boone, playing the game of loyal Englishman, convinced them that Boonesborough was too strongly garrisoned. They withdrew to the north side of the Ohio; and with them perforce went twenty-seven Kentuckians. The loss of these men, especially the loss of Boone, was the greatest calamity that had yet overtaken the little settlements in the Kentucky wilderness. Spring passed without a word of the prisoners; and savages still skulked about Boonesborough, waiting to waylay any one who went out to hunt.

George Morgan would have had the Continental Congress marshal an army at Pittsburgh, and attempt the capture of Detroit, center of British influence in the Northwest. But there was no money to spare for such a difficult and distant offensive. When the Indians began the ravaging of the borderlands, General Edward Hand was sent to Pittsburgh as commander, relieving Captain John Neville and his garrison of one hundred men at Fort Pitt, the sole defense of the Forks of the Ohio. But the General had few men and fewer supplies; the Indians grew bolder in their devastations. In the spring of 1778 Hand, over-burdened with his difficulties, was relieved of the post at his own request, and a more vigorous soldier, General Lachlan McIntosh, took command. He had visions of leading an army to the fortifications of Detroit; but he could raise only five hundred men, and could not get horses and provisions enough for them. His plan was abandoned, and McIntosh contented himself with building small forts a short distance into the wilderness.

The agent of the British government in the Mississippi region, the Chevalier de Rocheblave, was stationed in Kaskaskia; but here also was Thomas Bentley, English merchant married to the daughter of a rich and important English family, a man financially and socially eminent in the Illinois country. First attempting to play off the Americans against the British for his own profit, he became the enemy of Rocheblave; and, from the enemy of the British agent, he became the enemy of the British government.

Information constantly seeped into Kaskaskia of the progress of the Revolution in the East; Bentley, other English-speaking merchants, and their associates talked openly among themselves of the revolutionary movement, and crammed their French fellow-citizens with new ideas. This quiet propaganda continued until Kaskaskia and the neighboring settlement of Cahokia were amiably awaiting the approach of an American army which should dislodge the remnant of British soldiery and raise a new flag over the Illinois country. In the spring of 1777—so Rocheblave charged—Bentley sent boats to the Ohio River to sell supplies to a crew of Americans returning with munitions from New Orleans; to these Americans Bentley's agent gave full information of the conditions in the Illinois villages, and urged that an American army be sent to seize them. Bentley was made prisoner and taken to Quebec for confinement; but Rocheblave was in a hopeless position, and could not stay the danger. George Morgan promised the representatives of the rebels that troops would be sent from Pittsburgh, and set the date, vainly, in the winter of 1777-1778. Rocheblave sent to Detroit useless letter after useless letter, beseeching troops to meet the expected attack. "We are upon the eve of seeing here a numerous band of brigands," he wrote; and a little army of backwoodsmen was pounding its muskets against his door.

In making Major George Rogers Clark chief commander of the militia, the Kentuckians knew they had chosen a man of vigor and military ability; his ambitious imagination was yet to be demonstrated in its boldest attainment. If he could oust the British officers and traders from the French-founded towns in the lower Ohio Valley, he would then have removed an agency that encouraged the Indians in their hostility; and Clark saw larger implications in such a triumph, which, he tersely said, "might probably open a field for further action."

Two young hunters, Samuel Moore and Benjamin Linn, he sent as spies into the Illinois country. Late in June, 1777, they returned. They did not know of what use these facts were to Clark; but they brought the information he needed to set aside his caution. "I found by them that the Illinois people had but little expectation of a visit from us. Things were kept in good order, however, the militia trained, etc., that they might be prepared in case of a visit. I learned that the greatest pains were taken to inflame the minds of the French inhabitants against the Americans, notwithstanding which the spies had discovered traces of affection for us on the part of some of the inhabitants; and that the Indians from that region were generally engaged in the war upon us."

In January, 1778, Governor Patrick Henry, after many a private council, gave Major Clark all the authority he wished. He had three resources to draw upon: £1,200

[129]

in Virginia paper money; an order upon the commander at Pittsburgh for boats and ammunition; and the fighting ability of the frontier. The officers at Pittsburgh, knowing nothing of Clark's destination and being told nothing, discouraged men who would have enlisted; and Clark resolved to push on with about one hundred and fifty men, most of them frontiersmen from Virginia. His friend Major William Smith was to join him at the Falls of the Ohio with two hundred fighters from the Holston settlements. But Major Smith was not there. The secrecy of Clark's plans had defeated his expectation of drawing upon the southern valleys of the Alleghenies for fighters. Why enlist for the unknowable when the Holston settlements themselves were in danger of attack? Augmented by only one company from the Holston Valley, and another company from the Kentucky settlements, who could ill spare one fighting man, Clark's militia set out to make history for pageantry and romance. On the twenty-fourth of June, 1778, "we shot the Falls at the very moment the sun was under a great eclipse, which caused various conjectures on the part of the superstitious among us."

Opportunely, Clark received a letter from Colonel John Campbell at Pittsburgh, with news worth two companies of militia: France had taken up the cause of the colonies. Clark set principles for himself: remembering that the Indians were more amicable to the French than to any other race, always to do what might tend to bind the French and the Indians to the American interest.

On the Ohio, Clark met a party of hunters who had recently been at Kaskaskia. They were eagerly accepted as guides; and they brought appreciated information. The inhabitants of Kaskaskia and Vincennes had been taught, they reported, that the Virginia frontiersmen were more barbarous than the Indians. The opportunist was pleased: "I resolved to make capital of this should I be fortunate enough to gain control over them, since I considered that the greater the shock I could give them in the beginning the more appreciative would they be later of my lenity, and the more valuable as friends. This I conceived to accord with human nature as I had observed it in many instances." The alarm in the British settlements at the savage ferocity of their foes had some foundation in fact; for Captain James Willing, Philadelphian, had a short while ago secured a vessel at New Orleans, surprised and captured several British vessels on the river, and had ravaged, plundered and burned British settlements on the Mississippi.

After three days' march overland, on the fourth of July Clark's militia were within a few miles of Kaskaskia. Apparently no reports of his advance had reached the town, and that night he crossed the Kaskaskia River, setting out for the fort with a third of his militia while the other two-thirds proceeded to different quarters of the town. The surprise was complete; the fort was an easy capture, and those of Clark's men who could speak French ran through the streets warning the inhabitants to remain in their houses on pain of being shot down, while the troops with vociferous noises evoked the illusion of great numbers. Once the populace had recovered from its fear of these half-naked, briar-scratched barbarians, "every appearance of extravagant joy was manifested"; and when Clark proposed to send a detachment of his militia to surprise the neighboring town of Cahokia, the inhabitants of Kaskaskia offered to accompany his militia and accomplish an amiable surrender.

The other villages in the Illinois country quickly capitulated, if that is the word for so cordial an adjustment. Clark wisely made no strict inquiry to discover those who had been engaged in inciting the Indians; he commenced a friendly correspondence with the Spanish officers on the farther side of the Mississippi; he awed the Indian tribes, and apparently won them over; "within a few days the country appeared to be in a state of perfect harmony." But Clark had before him the serious, difficult business of capturing Vincennes. While Lieutenant-Governor Abbott was away from Vincennes to visit his superior officer at Detroit, the French inhabitants were easily persuaded by their Kaskaskia friends to take the oath of allegiance to the American cause, and took possession of the fort; but Governor Hamilton came down from Detroit with as many Indians as his lavish inducements could persuade to accompany him, and the American flag was soon cut down.

In January, 1779, "we now saw that we were in a very critical situation, cut off as we were from all intercourse with the home government. We perceived that Governor Hamilton, by the junction of his northern and southern Indians, would be at the head of such a force in the spring that nothing in this quarter could withstand him. Kentucky must fall immediately and it would be fortunate if the disaster ended here. Even if we should immediately make good our retreat to Kentucky we were convinced that it would be too late even to raise a force sufficient to save that colony, as all the men in it, united to the troops we had, would not suffice, and to get succor in time from the Virginia and Pennsylvania frontiers was out of the question. We saw but one alternative, which was to attack the enemy in his stronghold."

A Mississippi bateau was refitted into a war galley by Clark's Virginians in two days' time. On the fourth of February the galley set off with forty men; the captain's orders were to force his way up the Wabash and wait near Vincennes. The French inhabitants of Kaskaskia raised a company of volunteers among themselves; and with a force of one hundred and thirty men Clark began the cross-country march against Vincennes, in "rainy and drisly weather."

Across the network of flooded streams, through mud and water in the wilderness traces, across soggy plains, the men picked their heartbreaking way. After eight days' floundering forward, on the thirteenth of February the army reached the two Little Wabash rivers; "although three miles asunder they now make but one," Clark wrote, "the flowed water between them being at least three feet deep and in many places four, being near five miles to the opposite hills. The shallowest place, except about one hundred yards, was three feet. This would have been enough to have stopped any set of men that were not in the same temper we were, but in three days we contrived to cross."

The flooded Wabash halted the march when Vincennes was almost within reach; but by great good luck a boat bearing five French hunters from Vincennes was decoyed ashore, and following these hunters' directions Clark's men located another boat, adrift.

After many a ferrying of the two small boats, all the men were across; they confronted another expanse of drowned lands. Led by Clark, they plunged into the backwash. "I intended to have them ferried across the deepest part of the water but when we continued out about waist deep one of the men told me he thought he felt a path. We found it to be so and concluded it kept to the highest ground." So, with luck and ability favoring them, and fatigue the worst enemy they had to meet until they confronted Vincennes, they attained a copse of timber not two miles from the fort. "We were within full view of a town which contained upward of six hundred men, counting soldiers, inhabitants and Indians, with no possibility of retreat open to us in case of defeat. The crew of the galley, although numbering less than fifty men, would have constituted a reënforcement of great importance to our little army. But we would not permit ourselves to dwell on this." But this reënforcement did not arrive; the galley was fighting the flood waters, and did not reach Vincennes until the show was over.

By a captive Frenchman Clark sent a proclamation into Vincennes, announcing his determination to take the fort that night, and warning the inhabitants: "Those that are true friends of Liberty may expect to be well treated as such. I once more request that they may keep out of the streets, for every person found under arms on my arrival will be treated as an enemy." He watched for activity in the garrison once this audacious announcement of his intentions became known; there was none. The garrison had retired into the fort for roll call; the proclamation was circulated among the inhabitants, and, amazingly, not one of the Frenchmen cared to notify the British soldiers. Powder and ball were actually brought from Vincennes to supply the invaders. The town was taken easily; "firing was now commenced on the fort, but they did not believe it was an enemy, until one of their men was shot down through a port as he was lighting his match."

Irregular hot fires, casual scattering shots, the sound of companies of men shaken with laughter, the proven certainty that snipers had the exact range to bring down a soldier who approached the fort's cannon—the bewildered garrison had no idea of the numbers of the enemy; and on the evening of the twenty-fourth, after a night and a day of "eternal alarm," Governor Hamilton sent proposals of a three days' truce and conference. Clark accepted the conference but not the truce; the outcome was that, in Hamilton's account, "Our little Garrison surrendered Prisoners of War the 25th of Feby. and marched out with Colors flying, lighted match, & fixed bayonets."

Daniel Boone was a privileged prisoner of the Shawnee, taken with them in their aimless or malevolent excursions. Once these Indians went to Detroit, to wheedle gifts from Governor Hamilton and to dispose of some of their prisoners. Hamilton curiously became fond of Boone, and wished to ransom him, but the Indians had no wish to part with the Long Knife they had adopted into the tribe.

In mid-June the Shawnee were sulking at their ignominious failure to raid a little stockade on the Virginia frontier, and decided to avenge their honor by an immediate surprise and capture of Boonesborough. Boone could not have lingered with the Indians to find a more dramatic moment for his escape. On a horse that Hamilton gave him he fled that night from the Indian camp in the interior of Ohio; his huntsman's instinct pointed the way through the wilderness of leaf and cane, and only five days later the exhausted and half-starved fugitive rode through the gates of Boonesborough.

The bastions of the stockade were strengthened, and the fort put in hasty preparation for siege; but no Indians came. News trickled into the backwoods of the arrival of the French fleet to coöperate with the American army; a messenger brought the encouraging word that Kaskaskia had fallen; then came the news that the settlement hoped it would not hear. Stephen Hancock, another of those whom the Shawnee had captured at the Salt Springs reached Boonesborough with the information that the Indian attack, delayed because of Boone's escape, was likely to occur at any time. In August scouts reported that the war parties of the Shawnee were again gathering in Ohio. Vincennes became American domain; and Hamilton, ashamed and exasperated, urged on the savages to retaliate against the Kentucky settlements.

And in September almost four hundred and fifty Indians, the largest expedition that had yet threatened the Kentucky settlements, with twelve Frenchmen, moved swiftly to the Ohio, and from the south bank followed an ancient warpath into the heart of Kentucky. On the morning of the seventh they were opposite Boonesborough, in a thicket of trees and underbrush within rifle shot of the fort. The whole fighting force within the stronghold was but thirty men and twenty boys.

An overwhelming show of strength, Hamilton and the Indian chiefs had agreed, would probably be sufficient to bring Boonesborough tumbling down; and before a shot was fired the Indians proposed a conference. Three Kentuckians and three Indians met in the open space between the thicket and the fort. Black Fish, Shawnee Chief, spoke benignly: he had come "to take people away easily"; he had brought along "forty horses for the old folks, the women, and the children to ride." The pioneers were intent on delay, in the hope that reënforcements had been sent by Colonel Arthur Campbell from the Holston Valley; they asked for two days' consideration of these amiable terms of surrender. The complacent savages consented, and the meeting closed.

The answer was put by Boone: the garrison had "determined to defend the fort while a man was living." The Indians were astonished and disappointed; they had hoped for better things of this adopted son of Black Fish. But they had no wish for an arduous siege (that was no way for Indians to fight), and talked peace again. The garrison selected eight peace commissioners; and on the morning of the ninth they walked out of the gates of Boonesborough to meet Black Fish, the other chiefs, their interpreters and attendants, in the hollow at the Lick Spring. Under the sycamores the pioneers were invited to seat themselves on deerskins and panther skins beside the chiefs, while pipes and whisky were passed about. By sunset, after a day of protracted powwows and protracted feasting, a compact was agreed upon, to be signed the next morning.

After sunup the treaty was signed, when Black Fish put in a word for an old Indian custom: a handshake all around, two braves to each white man. The braves approached in high good humor; but something supertense in the atmosphere gave the game away. The Kentuckians broke loose; and in a moment rifles were blazing away from the pickets in the blockhouse and from the ambuscaded warriors in the thicket. Bullets from two hundred guns thudded into the logs of the stockade, but only one hit a Kentuckian, and that not mortally. Suddenly totally different sounds, a bustle of loading packs and gearing-up ponies, succeeded the whine of bullets from the camp of the Indians. The savages meant it to be known that they were disgusted with the failure of their trick, and were preparing to leave. That night their horses were heard splashing their way across the Kentucky River, and the calls of the Frenchmen's bugle resounded fainter in the distance.

Somehow the pioneers detected this second stratagem; the gates of the fort were not opened, and the warriors who had noiselessly retraced their way to the dark thicket waited in disgust. By the late morning they were all about Boonesborough again; from behind logs, stumps, and hillocks they kept a day-long rifle fire directed against the cracks and portholes of the stockade. They made every effort short of direct assault to bring down the fort; they exaggerated the number of sharpshooters within the walls, and had no intention of presenting themselves in the cleared space just before the fort.

The next day the Kentuckians discovered that dirt was being loosened from the river bank. A new, unexpected danger threatened them. Some one solved the riddle: DeQuindre, chief of the Frenchmen accompanying the Indians, was having a cave burrowed, to place a mine under the fort. Day after day from the watchtower riflemen watched the progress of this underground digging, and the pioneers began the digging of a countermine which would cut off the enemy's tunnel. At each dawn sharpshooters on either side were waiting to pick off the unwary, and to exchange shots with enemy snipers; and each day one side or the other added to its list of casualties.

On the thirteenth of the month the beleaguers again did the unexpected: they hurled lighted torches against the side of the stockade, and shot blazing arrows into the roofs of the cabins. There was far too little water to fight fire with; Boonesborough was saved by sheer luck. The wood had been watersoaked by recent drizzles; and the blazes sputtered out.

By the fifteenth the Indians had pushed their mine so close to the fort that the guards in the countertrench could hear the sound of their implements. The crisis was at hand. The pioneers had reached the starvation point; the incessant strain had frittered nerves, and the leading officers were quarreling among themselves. Rain fell throughout that dark and gloomy day; and in the thick darkness of that night the watchers could learn nothing of the imminent danger.

In the rainless morning the Kentuckians were surprised, bewildered, and delighted. No sounds came from the mine or from the thicket. Slowly the truth dawned that the savages had abandoned the siege; and wary scouts went out to find that the Indian army was in leisurely retreat. The rain had caused a cave-in in the tunnel; and the savages were too disgusted with the prospect of further manual labor to continue. A collection of huge torches which they had abandoned suggested that their plan was to emerge from the tunnel just outside the back wall of the fort and burn a passage through the stockade. So ended one of the longest sieges that the high-strung Indians ever attempted, a curious war of unexpected devices and overlooked opportunities. The Indians wandered to the other Kentucky stations, destroying and pillaging, and soon followed the warriors' trace to the north.

In a snappy, decisive border war in 1776, the towns of
the Cherokee had been laid waste by armies of Carolinians,
Virginians, and Georgians; the general assembly of South
Carolina offered a bounty for fresh Indian scalps, and many
a frontiersman collected. The Cherokee remained cowed
during the first few years of the Revolution; and Richard
Henderson, bloody but unbowed after his fight to retain
Transylvania, set about colonizing that part of his purchase which lay below the Virginia boundary. The British
offensive against the southern states was yet to come, and
there were many people of various shades of indifference
to the Revolutionary conflict who were willing enough to
work at field-clearing and home-building in 1779. James
Robertson was induced to leave the Watauga settlement
to head the march into the valley of the Cumberland; on
Christmas Day, 1779, the colonists under his leadership,
most of them Wataugans who were ready for another westward trek, arrived at the Great French Lick. A week later
they crossed the frozen Cumberland, obedient to the traditional attractiveness of the other side of the river, and
made their settlement on the present site of Nashville.
Another party, setting out from Fort Patrick Henry on the
Holston in a flotilla of some thirty flatboats, dugouts, and
canoes, ran the gamut of the hostile Chickamauga villages
along the Tennessee, and reached the Cumberland settlement in April, 1780.

Its remarkably democratic articles drafted by Judge Henderson, the Cumberland Compact served the settlements on
the Cumberland—there were eight of them, all closely associated, within a few months—until the constitution of
North Carolina could catch up with the state's westernmost
county. James Robertson was chosen presiding officer of
the court of twelve commissioners created by the Compact,
and was also elected commander-in-chief of the military
forces. Here for the next two years the Tennessee fron-

[139]

tiersmen successfully held their lands against the occasional forays of the savages.

Meanwhile the British army and navy had begun, with the successful attack upon Charleston in May, 1780, its vigorous offensive against the southern colonies. When Cornwallis invaded North Carolina, the war between the Redcoats and the Continental Army became a reality to the backwoods, and armed frontiersmen turned eastward. Colonel Patrick Ferguson, leading thousands of South Carolina loyalists, threatened to march his army over the mountains and lay waste the backwoods with fire and sword. Sevier talked with another fighting man of Tennessee, Colonel Isaac Shelby; they decided to stake their fortunes upon a surprise attack, and to take the trail for Spanish Louisiana if Ferguson defeated them.

At the Sycamore Shoals of the Watauga the mountain men gathered, on September 25, 1780. At various places along their eastward march they were joined by detachments of other frontiersmen. Ferguson was soon apprised that an army of about a thousand men, nearly all of them mounted, was coming from the West to hunt him down. He stood his ground, making camp on King's Mountain, just south of the borderline between the Carolinas.

His pickets were taken prisoner before one of them could give the alarm; and between the hours of three and four in the afternoon of October the seventh, the vicious battle was fought. "Every man for himself" against drilled, organized lines of soldiery; the frontiersmen decisively won, and the British invasion of North Carolina was checkmated.

Another frontier received the full brunt of the Revolution—the frontier of western New York. These frontier settlements might have been saved from destruction; warning after warning was sent to the military commanders. "It is much to be lamented," wrote General Schuyler to

Governor Clinton, "that the finest grain country in this state is on the point of being entirely ruined for want of a body of Continental troops"; reënforcements for the local militia, however, did not come. General Horatio Gates, lamentably, was in command of the Northern Department; timorous as he was with his whole body of men about to face Burgoyne, he was equally timorous when the Hudson Valley had been made secure, and he still kept his soldiery clustered about him.

Joseph Brant, Mohawk chief, led in the efficient desolation of the Susquehanna Valley, although, because his enmity was directed against the New York frontier where Mohawk lands had passed into the possession of the whites, he would not lead the destroying army below the New York border into Pennsylvania. It was there in the Susquehanna Valley that the town of Wyoming had been founded by emigrants from Connecticut; on July 3, 1778, the "home guard" of old men and young boys—for the ablebodied men had enlisted in the Continental Army—was easily overwhelmed. Captives were tomahawked and scalped, houses and barns were burned, and throughout the Wyoming Valley howling savages left slaughter and desolation.

The thriving settlement of German Flatts in the Mohawk Valley, the farthest advance westward on the Mohawk, was converted to smoldering logs, hot ashes, and blackened fields, in view of the inhabitants huddled into their forts. Later in 1778 Continental troops came belatedly into western New York, pursued the Indians, and burned their two largest villages. In retaliation the Indians again took to their war paint, and were planning a raid upon Cherry Valley at the same time that General Edward Hand, promoted to the command of the Northern Department, was contemplating the withdrawal of the small remnant of troops not yet returned from western New York. On the eleventh of November the attack was made, one of the most vicious episodes in the ugly story of frontier war. Families were wiped out, bodies mangled; "such a shocking sight my eyes never beheld before of savage and brutal barbarity," wrote war-hardened Captain William Warren of the desolation of Cherry Valley. Surviving families in western New York abandoned their homesteads and hastened to the east; and the region was given over into a battleground, where ultimately the Iroquois were utterly beaten and left destitute, their lodges and fields ruined.

PART III

TWENTY YEARS FROM YORKTOWN

. . . A character in Washington County, Pennsylvania, of the name of Foreman, who is at this time *ninety-eight* years of age. I had about two years ago [1808] called on him. . . . Among other things he observed that "The fashions of the day had injured society, and had led astray the minds of young men and women from the paths of simple and rustick honesty they used to walk in fifty or sixty years ago. That there was much hypocrisy in the shew of so much religion as appeared at present. That people were too fond of lying in their beds late in the morning, and drinking too much whisky."

—ZADOC CRAMER, 1810

CHAPTER IX

THE OLD NORTHWEST

FROM Detroit in 1780, British forces set out to reclaim the Ohio Valley. They took to the Mississippi at Prairie du Chien; they got no farther than St. Louis, for their attack upon the capital of upper Louisiana was humiliatingly unsuccessful. For once, the Spanish proved useful allies to the Americans. In the same year six hundred Indians and Canadians (the Indians subvened by scalping knives, vermilion, looking-glasses, and ear-bobs, at the expense of the British Indian Department) came down from the Northwest, and captured two outlying stockades on the Kentucky frontier. Then the commander's courage oozed out; and the expedition returned. In October, 1781, the British army in Virginia marched disconsolately through the files of French and American troops, and the Revolution in the East was at an end; but in the West the Indians, fending off the time when land-grasping Americans would overrun their hunting grounds, continued their savage warfare as long as the British at Detroit supplied them with ammunition and ornament.

While the Continental Congress was shaping the Articles of Confederation, a delegate from Maryland introduced the resolution: "That the United States in Congress assembled shall have the sole and exclusive power to ascertain and fix the western boundary of such states as claim to the Mississippi or the South Sea, and lay out the land beyond the boundary so ascertained into separate and independent states, from time to time, as the numbers and circumstances of the people thereof may require." That resolution received no votes but Maryland's; but the issue of the control of the unoccupied lands had been raised, even before Clark had ousted the British from their posts below Detroit. Every one assumed that the western lands, when sold for settlement, would enrich the owners—the states, or the nation. Fearful of being overshadowed by states battening in wealth and political power on the proceeds of the sale of their western lands, the states whose royal charters gave no claim to the territory beyond the Alleghenies balked at the prospect of confederation until the western lands were made the property of the nation; and they won out. Maryland took up the brunt of the attack; satisfied by February, 1781, that the Old Northwest was to be national territory, the legislature instructed its delegates in Congress to sign the Articles of Confederation. On the first of March the official scribe of Congress made note that "the Confederation of the United States of America was completed, each and every of the Thirteen United States, from New Hampshire to Georgia, both included, having ratified and confirmed, and by their delegates in Congress ratified the same."

After Clark's victories in the Old Northwest, Great Britain had left only thirty-five hundred white subjects in the West; all of these were along the Great Lakes, and most of them were French Canadians of indifferent allegiance. Clark's victories had won over two thousand subjects, and had made possible the great tide of immigration that did not wait for the Revolution to be over before it swept into the West. But the sovereignty of the western lands was not yet definitely won; the last battle was fought in Paris, and the contest began with John Jay against the field.

When in 1778 Vergennes, France's minister of foreign affairs, sent his confidential secretary, Gerard, to submit the treaty of alliance between France and the American States to the Continental Congress, Gerard carried also secret instructions to induce Congress to acknowledge the Spanish claim to a large part of the lands east of the Mississippi. Gerard was baffled; sick and disappointed, he returned to Europe, and with him went John Jay. Jay's mission was to get Spain to make an alliance with the American states, and to lend Congress several million pounds. Spanish demands for western lands and for the exclusive right to the navigation of the Mississippi stood in the way, and Jay's mission was a failure; but the envoy had learned more than any other American knew of the subterranean ramifications of European diplomacy.

Vergennes had found John Adams, appointed as peace-treaty commissioner for the United States, unbending and unmanageable; the French government demanded that Congress "draw a line of conduct to that minister," and Congress obeisantly appointed Jay, Franklin, and Henry Laurens as joint commissioners with Adams. Their instructions included a humiliating admonition to make "the most candid and confidential communications upon all subjects to the ministers of our most generous ally, the King of France, to undertake nothing in the negotiations . . . without their knowledge and concurrence, and ultimately to govern yourselves by their advice and opinion." Jay was convinced that obedience to these instructions would leave the United States little or none of the territory west of the Alleghenies. He sounded out Lord Shelburne, the prime minister of Great Britain, who had been called to power to end the wearisome and expensive war; and shortly two British agents were in Paris to treat secretly for a

separate peace with the United States. Adams unhesitat-
ingly approved Jay's course; Franklin, who had long been
fawned upon by French nobles and savants and liked it,
was offended, but gave a sulking consent.

"We had much contestation," Franklin wrote of the
negotiations, "about the boundaries and other articles. . . .
They wanted to bring their boundary down to the Ohio,

THE UNITED STATES
September 3, 1783

ⱧⱧⱧⱧⱧ [Northern Boundary of New Spain, fixed by treaty in 1819]

and to settle their loyalists in the Illinois country." Demanding the whole of the trans-Allegheny region, the
American commissioners were immovable, up to the last
minute of the negotiations; Shelburne's commissioners
yielded, and signed Jay's draft of the preliminary treaty
making the center of the Mississippi the western boundary
of the United States.

During the formative years of the Confederation, the
states whose royal charters gave them claim to some part
of the lands above the Ohio relinquished title to the federal

government. As early as September 6, 1780, the Continental Congress had urged such a cession of the western lands; and, anticipating the generosity of the states, the Congress had promised bounty lands in the West to encourage enlistment. The formal treaty of peace had not been concluded before the officers of the Revolutionary Army were demanding fulfillment of that promise.

On May 7, 1783, "His Excellency the president and Honorable Delegates of the United States in Congress" were petitioned by the officers of the Continental Line, for a grant of the Ohio lands between the Pennsylvania border and a meridian twenty-four miles west of the mouth of the Scioto: "that this country is of sufficient extent the lands of such a qualety and its Sittuation such as may induce Congress to asigne and mark it out as a tract or teritory sutable to form a distinct goverment (or Colloney of the United States)—in time to be admitted, *one* of the *Confedirated States of America.*" Congress did not act upon the petition.

But a more ponderous concern than the redemption of land warrants troubled the Congress of the Confederation. The Articles of Confederation gave Congress no power to tax, simply conferring the privilege of recommending to the states that they contribute to its expenses. But financial obligations could not be paid off in polite requests. While the national domain was in process of creation, a congressional committee had reported that the western lands should provide an important fund for the discharge of the national debt. That idea that the national domain, the Old Northwest, was an important financial resource for the nation thus early became a public policy.

But the Crown had followed no such policy when the Atlantic seaboard had been a frontier region. The colonial provinces had attempted no such exploitation of their western lands. The Crown had imposed a small quitrent; but it had rarely been paid. Virginia had required two cents an acre to be paid before the locating of a tract; but that sum could hardly have covered the expenses of a land office. West Virginia, Kentucky, and western Tennessee were "taken up" in the most casual manner; surveys were not made by the province, private surveys were not carefully scrutinized by the land office, and overlappings and discrepancies in landtitles were common. Lawyers profited by this *laissez-faire* policy of frontier settlement; the parent colonies certainly did not.

The West was later to turn savagely upon the idea that the public domain should be a source of national revenue; that policy was to be hammered at, and modified, and modified again, until the ultimate, complete victory of the West —the Homestead Act of 1862, making homesites free to settlers upon the public domain. But, to the very good fortune of Americans, the Congress of the Confederation believed that it was possible to obtain a great deal of revenue by the selling of lands in the Old Northwest. Without that conviction, the national land system would have derived much less from New England precision, and would have reflected the haphazard Southern ways. Such efficient programs as the Land Act of 1785 and the Ordinance of 1787 are not devised out of pure altruism.

In March, 1783, the general assembly of Pennsylvania set aside certain lands lying west of the Allegheny and north of the Ohio River to be sold to redeem depreciation certificates given officers and soldiers of Pennsylvania, and also to give land bounties to its veterans of the Revolution. These lands, about a fourth of the state's area, were still held by the Iroquois; this triviality did not disturb the legislators. In February, 1784, commissioners were chosen to treat with the war-humbled Indians. The general assembly authorized the buying of nine thousand dollars' worth of "such goods, merchandise, and trinkets" as might be pabulum to the Indians for the loss of their Pennsylvania domain. At Fort Stanwix in October the chiefs of the several Iroquois tribes were assembled, and perforce agreed to the extinguishing of their title to the soil of Pennsylvania. Three months later, at Fort McIntosh on the Ohio, the state's commissioners appeased the western Indians, Wyandots and Delawares, who had claims to the same lands.

With these agents of Pennsylvania at Fort Stanwix and at Fort McIntosh were three commissioners delegated by Congress to begin the task of extinguishing the Indian claims in the Old Northwest. Congress could not hold the dykes against the onrush of emigrants into the West; the one solution was to attempt to remove the probability of more Indian wars before belligerent frontiersmen swarmed upon Indian lands. "Such is the rage for speculating in, and forestalling of lands on the No. West of the Ohio," George Washington wrote in the autumn of 1784, "that scarce a valuable spot, within any tolerable distance of it, is left without a claimant. Men in these times talk with as much facility of fifty, an hundred, and even five hundred thousand acres, as a gentleman formerly would of one thousand. In defiance of the proclamation of Congress, they roam over the Indian side of the Ohio, mark out Lands, survey and even settle on them." At Fort Stanwix the Iroquois surrendered their claims to the lands north and west of the Ohio; at Fort McIntosh the western Indians, reserving occupation of northwest Ohio, ceded thirty million acres to the United States. Only the Shawnee, most warlike of the Ohio tribes, had not been sufficiently humbled in the war to listen to treaty talk.

With that abstract problem of sovereignty apparently settled, with the precedent established that the Indian title must be extinguished before any part of the national domain should be opened for settlement, Congress proceeded to the problems of survey and administration. In March,

1784, a committee whose chairman was Thomas Jefferson brought in proposals that were elaborated into the Ordinance of April 23, 1784. The states that were to emerge from the western domain (Jefferson proposed ten such states in the Old Northwest, boxed out with ruler's edge severity, and given sadly polysyllabic titles) were forever to remain a part of the United States; to be subject to the Congress and the Articles of the Confederation; to maintain governments republican in form; and to pay their share of the Revolutionary debts. All surveys had to be made before the land was sold, and all grants carefully recorded, by surveyors and registers appointed by Congress. But beyond that bit of wisdom borrowed from New England, the laxness of Jefferson's scheme reflected his Virginian environment. The land was to be sold in exchange for warrants, by square-mile "lots" or ten-square-mile "hundreds," to be located wherever the settler chose. No reservations were made for educational or religious purposes, and the price of the land was not mentioned.

In 1785 the year-old ordinance was read twice in Congress, and referred to a grand committee. The outcome was the Ordinance of May 20, 1785, definitely fixing the principle of rectangular surveys in the national land system. "Compact and progressive settling," wrote Washington to a friend, "will give strength to the Union. . . . Sparse settlement in several new states, or a large territory for one, will have the directly contrary effects; and, whilst it opens a large field to land jobbers and speculators, who are prowling about like wolves in many shapes, will injure the occupiers and useful citizens, and consequently the public interest." The Ordinance of 1785 conscientiously tried to avoid those possibilities which Washington deprecated. Surveyors were to mark out townships six miles square, subdivided into thirty-six sections. Alternate townships were to be sold as a whole, the others in sections of six hundred

[152]

and forty acres. One-seventh of the land as surveyed was to be reserved to redeem the warrants held by the men of the Continental Army. Forthwith, Captain Thomas Hutchins, official geographer of the United States, took his corps of surveyors into the Old Northwest, and began the running of the lines.

General Benjamin Tupper had been one of the signers of the officers' petition of 1783; in 1785 he was one of Hutchins' surveyors. By 1786 he was again in New England, exchanging narratives with his old friend and fellow-soldier, Rufus Putnam. Putnam had been up to Maine, and was heartily damning the soil and the climate; Tupper was fresh from Ohio, with a stock of pleasant impressions. The outcome was a broadside entitled "Information," issued by these two men at Rutland, Vermont, on the tenth of January. "The subscribers take this method to inform all officers and soldiers, who have served in the late war, and who are by a late ordinance of the honorable Congress to receive certain tracts of land in the Ohio country, and also all other good citizens who wish to become adventurers in that delightful region, that from personal inspection, together with other incontestible evidences, they are fully satisfied that the lands in that quarter are of a much better quality than any other known to New England people; that the climate, seasons, product, etc., are in fact equal to the most flattering accounts that have ever been published of them; that being determined to become purchasers, and to prosecute a settlement in this country, and desirous of forming a general association with those who entertain the same ideas, they beg leave to propose the following plan, viz.: That an association by the name of *The Ohio Company* be formed."

As the call had provided, on the first of March the pioneers-to-be met under the genial sign of the Bunch of Grapes tavern in Boston, and discussed the formation of a

land company to be financed with the reams of continental
currency that Congress had forced upon them in payment
of Army salaries. The money was worthless in everyday
use; but Congress had issued it with a "promise to pay,"
and could not well refuse it. Winthrop Sargent, Samuel
Parsons, Manasseh Cutler, many another officer of the
Revolutionary Army and member of the Society of the
Cincinnati became interested, Articles of Agreement were
drawn up, and subscription books circulated. The promoters were buoyant and aggressive; they made light reference to "two or three other petty companies" planning to
found settlements in the West, suggesting a merger of interests; Manasseh Cutler proposed to be one of the first
emigrants, bringing with him the seeds of "the Indian tea,
the Japanese varnish tree, and European grapes" among
other foreign plants; more to the point, Putnam, Cutler,
and Parsons were appointed the agents of the Ohio Company and despatched to New York. Capable lobbying was
a necessity. Since the Ordinance of 1785 provided no
method for the sale of more than one township to a purchaser, Congress had to provide a way. There was as yet
no scheme of government for the West; Congress had to
provide that.

On July 6, 1787, the tenuous Congress of the Confederation, having succeeded in gathering a quorum, took up the
"Ordinance for the Government of the Territory of the
United States northwest of the River Ohio" for its third
reading. The directors of the Ohio Company were on the
lookout for this moment; Manasseh Cutler was on the spot,
armed with many letters of introduction, and at once in-
gratiated himself into the midst of the congressional circle.
New ideas came to the front, a new committee was appointed; on the eleventh this committee reported back
Nathan Dane's drafting of the ordinance. Some members
of the Congress were declared "in" on the purchase; and

[154]

promptly, on the thirteenth of July, the Ordinance of 1787 became law.

It included a scheme for the partition of the Northwest into states, a plan of successive provisional governments graduating into full statehood, a law regarding title to property by descent (aimed against the old tidewater custom of primogeniture), and a bill of rights. This statement of unalterable rights has given the Ordinance its greatest importance; there is a healthy spiritual strength to these downright axioms that has outlived the territorial status of the most distant section of the Old Northwest. That axiom which is frescoed above the assembly stage of a great middle western university—"Religion, morality, and knowledge, being necessary to good government and the happiness of mankind, schools and the means of education shall forever be encouraged"—was not put there as meaningless ornament. A fruit of this declaration was the practice, begun in 1802, of granting section sixteen of each township to the inhabitants of the township "for the use of schools." Slavery was prohibited; and the promise was made, "No person demeaning himself in an acceptable or orderly manner shall ever be molested on account of his mode of worship or religious sentiments in the said territory." Additional guarantees of individual liberty were directly derivative from older constitutions. The Congress of the Confederation, having enacted the Land Ordinance of 1785 and the Ordinance of 1787, had done its important work; already the Constitutional Convention was in closed session at Philadelphia, well upon its work of framing a new compact.

In the first stage of government provided by the Ordinance, a governor and three judges, all appointed by Congress, were autocratically to "adopt and publish in the district such laws of the original States, criminal and civil, as may be necessary and best suited to the circumstances"

[155]

—but when the district had attained a population of five thousand adult men, a general assembly, with lawmaking control subject to the governor's veto, was to be elected. When the total population should have reached sixty thousand, the district was ready to hold a constitutional convention, frame its own basic law, and enter the Union. That framework, substantially, marks the course by which western states have been created out of the public domain.

On July 27, 1787, Congress authorized the transfer of nearly seven million acres of the Ohio lands to the Ohio Company and the kindred—but less savory—enterprise, the Scioto Associates. The price was identical for all lands: one dollar an acre, payable in continental money, with a discount of one-third on account of the swampy or otherwise useless lands that might be scattered through the tract. Almost two million acres were contracted for by the Ohio Company. The Scioto enterprise, most of the members New Yorkers, headed by Colonel William Duer, took an option on almost five million acres, and divided the option into thirty shares which were allotted among the members. In June, 1788, these enterprising gentlemen of New York despatched Joel Barlow to Europe to dispose of their lands. Advertisements and maps of a utopian colony, having charms of climate, health, and scenery rivaling the Isles of the Blessed, were circulated. The upshot was the arrival, in the spring of 1790, of some six hundred French peasants and artisans. There were no agents to meet them, nor lands awaiting them: the Scioto Associates for devious reasons had never exercised their options. Duer hastily arranged to quarter them on the Ohio Company's lands, and in October, 1790, the exotic settlement of Gallipolis was founded opposite the mouth of the Great Kanawha, to lead a miserable, starved existence for a few years, and to leave in its wake tales of suffering and fraud for Congress to attempt to adjust.

The Ohio Company, once Congress had approved the purchase and the first half-million dollars had been paid in Continental currency, was ready to begin the permanent occupation of the Old Northwest. The vanguard of frontiersmen, the squatters, was driven out of Ohio, as nearly as Congress could accomplish that difficult eviction. On October 3, 1787, Congress enacted a resolution "to raise seven hundred troops to protect the settlers on the public lands from the depredations of the Indians, to facilitate the surveying and settling of said lands, in order to reduce the public debt, and to prevent all unwarrantable intrusions thereon." The troops found pioneer settlements near the present Steubenville and along the Ohio just below the Falls. The squatters were driven out, and their cabins and cornfields burned.

Under the leadership of Rufus Putnam, forty-eight men despatched by the Ohio Company in the winter of 1787-1788—carpenters, shipbuilders, blacksmiths, farmers—followed the road from Philadelphia across the mountains, and paused on the banks of the Youghiogheny. There they built boats, christening one of them, sentimentally, the *Mayflower*. That spring the advance guard arrived at the Muskingum, landing on the eastern bank. Opposite was Fort Harmar, built by federal troops in 1786. More emigrants came in the summer; and at the first meeting of the directors held on the Ohio Company's lands, on the second of July, the settlement was christened Marietta, in compliment to Her Majesty, Marie Antoinette.

Putnam was the energetic John Smith of the settlement; his fellows were of far better pioneering caliber than the London adventurers. Surveying, felling, and grubbing soon subdued a hundred and thirty acres of land; cabins emerged in the clearings; and a stockade was built to surmount an ancient fortification of the mound builders. Town lots were laid out and distributed; new accessions of emigrants brought dignity and talent into the community; and Marietta signalized its importance with a pageant on the Fourth of July—a procession of the citizens and the soldiery from across the river, an eloquent oration, and a barbecue. General Arthur St. Clair arrived in July to take up the governorship of the Northwest Territory.

In the spring of 1788 John Cleve Symmes, influential citizen of New Jersey, purchased from Congress, for himself and associates, another huge tract of Ohio lands—a tract bounded by the Great and Little Miami rivers, and extending north into the Indian country. John Filson, the first historian of Kentucky and biographer of Daniel Boone, was concerned in this transaction. Working as a surveyor in the Indian-infested wilderness, he met his death—an end immortalized by a melancholy poet:

> In the vigor of life, with a spirit
> That shrank from no duty imposed,
> John Filson's career as surveyor
> Between the Miamis closed.

As early as November, 1787, Symmes issued a prospectus describing his tract, and inviting first comers to take the choice of lands at cost price, two-thirds of a dollar per acre. He reserved for himself the township at the mouth of the Big Miami; and there, in 1788, a little community of pioneers laid the beginnings of Cincinnati.

Most of the important Indian villages in the Ohio Valley were located along the Wabash and the Maumee; but certain tribes, the Shawnee, the most powerful among them, hunted freely over Indiana and Ohio. These tribes had not been represented in the conferences at Fort Stanwix and Fort McIntosh; they, and not the treaty-signing tribes, were the actual occupants of the north bank of the Ohio. Governor St. Clair plunged into the thankless situation; and after a long succession of conferences at Fort

Harmar, from September, 1788, into January, 1789, he had secured a treaty that seemed at last to clear the Indian title to Ohio. But the tribes had only a hazy idea of just what a cession meant; braves who had not personally signed a treaty felt themselves at liberty to ignore it; and the Indians were well aware that the upper regions of the Old Northwest were still in possession of British garrisons. Still, annually, Indian hunters were bringing their furs to Detroit or other British posts, there dealing with British traders.

In July, 1783, General von Steuben had been sent by Washington to Canada, to request the transfer of the British posts in the Northwest. Governor Haldimand had refused, claiming that he had received no orders. Haldimand retailed the interview to Lord North, adding that the longer withdrawal was delayed, the more time would be given the fur traders to deal with the Indians. Lord North's answer, dated April 8, 1784, was comforting: "You are certainly justified in every part of your proceedings, even if you had been in possession of the Definitive Treaty of Peace. The seventh article stipulates that they should be evacuated with all convenient speed, but no time is fixed, and as America has not on her part complied with even one article of the treaty, I think we may reconcile it in the present instance to delay the evacuation of these posts."

Canadians, whose interests were closely bound up in the fur trade, were indignant that the Old Northwest should have been conceded to the independent colonies. The Canadian fur trade in 1785 was worth one hundred and eighty thousand pounds; five-ninths of the trade was from the limits of the United States. Doubtless, under such circumstances, British traders in the upper Northwest posts kept the Indians reminded that extensions of American settlement would destroy the hunting, and force the tribes to seek new homes.

[159]

It was not war between the Americans and the Indians that the British traders wanted, although certainly when war began they gave aid to the Indians. The ideal situation for the British was that the Northwest be left fairly in the hands of the Indians, as a neutral ground between the American settlements and Canada; in that contingency English presents and English courtesy, balanced against the inevitable occasional aggressions of American frontiersmen, would have retained the Indian trade in British hands.

"The Americans send us nothing but speeches, and no two are alike": that was the Indians' summation of the series of parleys. And in the spring of 1790 Indian ambuscades were never more fierce. General Harmar led an expedition against the Maumee villages, the first of a long series of demonstrations designed to overawe the tribes. In the spring of 1790 St. Clair himself was in the field. He set about building a chain of forts from the mouth of the Big Miami north to the Maumee, from which garrisons would be able to quiet insurgent tribes at short notice; but the Indians drove him back to cover.

Washington, exercising his own judgment, appointed General Anthony Wayne to succeed St. Clair in command of the army in the West. Wayne went about his job painstakingly and thoroughly. In 1793 he marched his legion along St. Clair's cordon of forts, and wintered on the border of the Indian country. In the summer of 1794 he took to the open. Moving down the Maumee, he found his way blocked by Indian lines, extending nearly two miles from the bank of the river, behind thickets of trees a tornado had torn down. There, on August 20, 1794, the picked warriors of the Ohio Valley were demoralized and thoroughly defeated. The Treaty of Greenville followed in due order upon that defeat, thrusting the limits of the Indian country much farther westward; and while the generation of Indians that had fought Wayne was respected at the council fires, the expansion of the American settlement in the Old Northwest met no challenge.

Two tracts in Ohio had been reserved in the general cession of the western lands. One, the Virginia Military Reserve, had been held back by Virginia to meet the land-bounty warrants that the legislature had given to the state troops. These warrants had been bought and sold freely; and when surveyors from Virginia came into the Scioto Valley in 1790 to mark out the lands, the settlers who followed them into the valley were, most of them, from Kentucky. Chillicothe became their principal town, as aggressively republican as the first government of the Old Northwest was inflexibly Federalist.

The other tract reserved was Connecticut's—the Western Reserve, along the Lake Erie shore. At the mouth of the Cuyahoga River, Moses Cleaveland and his staff of surveyors laid out the nucleus of Cleveland. In 1800 settlements had been begun in thirty-five of the one hundred three townships east of the Cuyahoga; a thousand people, predominantly from Connecticut, had begun the occupation of northern Ohio. Each year a large emigration from the New England states came into the Ohio Company's lands. By 1800 over fifty thousand Americans were in the Northwest Territory.

By the authority of the Ordinance of 1787 and by his own temperament, Governor St. Clair was an autocrat; in 1798, when the Northwest Territory passed into the second stage of provisional government and an elected legislature was created, there began a bitter conflict between the gelid Federalist, with his party colleagues, and the Jeffersonian Democrats who had come into their first taste of authority. The end of such a conflict was evident in 1801, when Jefferson, who mustered a tie vote with Aaron Burr in the national election, was awarded the presidency by the House of Representatives. But St. Clair's first loyalty was to his principles; and he held back the frontier democracy as long as he could. Every important statute that the first territorial legislators had enacted he vetoed. But in May, 1800, the Northwest Territory was partitioned; and, thereby, the eastern division was started towards statehood. St. Clair

was allowed to linger in his post for more than a year after Jefferson became president; but to his acute humiliation the seat of government was shifted from Cincinnati, where the governor was among friends, to bitterly partisan Chillicothe.

The great increase of emigration to Ohio in the first two years of the new century brought the Eastern Division of the Northwest Territory to the legitimate demand of full statehood. St. Clair tried to block the way; and late in 1802 Jefferson dismissed him from office. The inflexible Federalist retired into lonely years of silence and neglect.

Among the papers of General Ephraim Douglass, pioneer of western Pennsylvania, was found this note:

> Uniontown, 13th February, 1809.
>
> Received of General Ephraim Douglass, one hundred dollars, which I promise to pay on demand, or at the furthest by the sixth day of June next.
>
> Signed,
> AR. ST. CLAIR.

Underneath, in Douglass' handwriting, was a postscript: "Never to be demanded. To save the feelings of an old friend I accept this receipt, after refusing to take an obligation."

CHAPTER X

THE INDEPENDENT STATE OF FRANKLIN

TO care for its own westward-trekking citizens and
for the constant filtering down of Virginians
through the Appalachian trough into the West,
the State of North Carolina created three counties in the
Tennessee Valley. Delegates from these counties, and
from the one other western county, which included the
Cumberland Valley, duly went east to the state legislature
at Hillsboro, there to be duly outvoted. North Carolina parried against the pressure upon it to cede its western
lands to the Confederation. Governor Alexander Martin,
writing in December, 1783, explained the value of delay
to the state's delegates in Congress: "We have made provision for our continental line [the soldiers in the Army
of the Revolution] on Cumberland, and a territory reserved for the purpose is erected into a county by the name
of Davidson; the residue of the lands . . . is opened for
entry of any citizen of this or the United States, who will
pay to the entry taker ten pounds per hundred in specie,

specie certificate of this State, or currency at 800 for one, restricted however to 5000 acres. . . . I can venture to say there will be no cession of any land worthy of acceptance, as the principal lands will be entered before this reaches you." As a part of the domain-looting enterprise even the Chickasaw lands west of the Tennessee to the Mississippi, in sovereign disregard of the Indian title, were opened for settlement. In the rush to the entry-taker's office, three million acres of the choicest lands in west Tennessee were taken up. Settlement lagged behind entry-taking, of course; but in the three counties of the Tennessee Valley there were in 1788 from twenty-five to thirty thousand people.

In April, 1784, North Carolina tendered its domain west of the Appalachian Divide to the Confederation of the United States. Returning delegates from the western counties brought the unexpected news, with tart details of the attitude epitomized in one remark: "The inhabitants of the western counties are the off-scourings of the earth, fugitives from justice and we will be rid of them at any rate." Congress had been allowed a year to accept the cession; that contingent period would doubtless be extended until the infant federal government gained enough vigor to take up the proffered responsibility. Meanwhile, no protection of the border settlements from the Indian forays, no extension of the machinery of civil and criminal law to keep apace with the growing West, could be expected of North Carolina. Remembering the Watauga that was, settlers talked of an independent state.

On August 23, 1784, delegates from each militia company of the three counties in the Tennessee Valley in convention, listened to just one speech, and unanimously declared the three western counties independent of North Carolina. With equal dispatch they resolved: "As the welfare of our common country depends so much on the

[165]

friendly disposition of Congress, and their rightful understanding of our situation we do therefore unanimously agree, speedily to furnish a person with a reasonable support, to present our memorial, and negotiate our business with Congress." Because their commonwealth-to-be needed numbers, they urged the southwestern settlements of Virginia to join with them.

That October the situation was complicated: the legislature of North Carolina discovered that among the conditions imposed in the cession of its western lands was no provision that the federal government assume the unpaid expenses of the several expeditions of the state militia against the Indians; and, by way of giving the debt-ridden state a chance to drive better terms, the legislature repealed the cession. But before the news of this gybing course reached the West, the frontiersmen were again in convention at Jonesborough.

"To remove the doubts of the scrupulous; to encourage the timid, and to induce all, harmoniously and speedily, to enter into a firm association, let the following particulars be considered. If we should be so happy as to have a separate government, vast numbers from different quarters, with a little encouragement from the public, would fill up our frontier, which would strengthen us, improve agriculture, perfect manufactures, encourage literature and every thing truly laudable. The seat of government being among ourselves, would evidently tend, not only to keep a circulating medium in gold and silver among us, but draw it from many individuals in other states, who claim large quantities of lands that would lie in the bounds of the new state." What (the rhetorical question resounded at this meeting on December 14, 1784) was there to gain in protracted connection with the old counties of North Carolina? "They are the most numerous, and consequently will always be able to make us subservient to them; that our interest must be generally neglected, and sometimes sacrificed, to promote theirs, as was instanced in a late taxation act, in which, notwithstanding our local situation and improvement being so evidently inferior, that it is unjust to tax our lands equally, yet they have expressly done it; and our lands, at the same time, not of one fourth of the same value." And twenty-eight of the forty delegates resolved that the best time to form a separate state was the present.

William Cocke and David Campbell devised a constitution, making a startling beginning with a paraphrase of the Declaration of Independence, which out of a "decent respect to the opinions of mankind" made "manifest to the world" a hearty animus against North Carolina. There followed a listing of no less than twenty-five Rights of Man, and thereafter came forty-six resolutions embracing the whole frame of government, after the model of the North Carolina constitution of 1776.

The first legislature of the State of Franklin met at Jonesborough the following March. The leader perforce followed the mob: John Sevier was elected governor, probably without opposition. He was thus borne to the crest of the movement for autonomy simply by the people's faith in his ability; Indian-fighting, speculation in lands, playing hands-under-the-table with Spanish emissaries, were far more to his liking than this thankless political struggle. But, henceforward, the cause of Franklin was identified with Sevier.

These pioneer legislators in that first session demonstrated how the West had sharpened the capacity of the plain man in things political. Their enactments validated the land titles derived from North Carolina; reincorporated the one institution of "higher learning" in Franklin, Martin's Academy (founded in 1780 by a Presbyterian minister, Samuel Doak); established a militia; established a judicial system; fixed salaries; and, in view of the scarcity of currency on the frontier, fixed a scale for payment of taxes in kind. Linen, linsey-woolsey, woolen cloths, beaver, otter, raccoon, fox, and deerskins, tallow, beeswax, peach or apple brandy, "good distilled rye whiskey," "good country made sugar," and "good, neat and well managed tobacco, fit to be prized," were acceptable. These things were the wealth of the backwoods.

Governor Martin of North Carolina, too clever to become violent, gave Sevier the unsolicited title of brigadier general of militia, and sent a private agent, Samuel Henderson, a veteran of Indian wars, to discover all things, public and private, about the State of Franklin. Henderson brought Sevier a conciliatory letter from Martin. Sevier flung it into the assembly; and the legislators were pleased to advise Martin, "It is our duty and inalienable right to form ourselves into a new independent State," and ungently to remind him of slights put upon the western counties when they were a dutiful part of North Carolina: the inequality of the land tax, the failure to send state judges into the West, "the frequent murders committed by the Indians on our frontiers": "How far North Carolina has been accessory to those murders we will not pretend to say. We only know that she took the land the Indians claimed, promised to pay them for it and again resolved not to do it; and that in consequence of the resolve, the goods were stopped."

Benjamin Franklin had been an involuntary godfather to the christening of the new state, and he proved to be a graceless one. He declined to use his influence in behalf of the western commonwealth; and William Cocke, at New York where Congress was in session, saw his cause fail by the vote of a single state. Seven states voted to disregard North Carolina's repeal of its cession act, and to accept the western territory as a part of the United States—an action almost equivalent to greeting Franklin as a fellow-state. But the delegates from South Carolina were paired off; and the votes of Virginia and Maryland were in the negative. Perhaps the luckless westerners had selected the wrong godfather; a state christened "Jefferson" might have found the votes of Virginia's delegates manipulated in its favor. Jefferson was, in many ways, one of the Westerners; and he was quite as vain as most men. He had once been connected with a land speculation in Tennessee, but out of his lifelong fear of "ill intended observation" he had withdrawn. Yet he was frank enough in writing, in 1786, "the people of Kentucky think of separating from Virginia, in which they are right." From his minister's post in France he wrote frequently to inquire after the current of events in the West; but somehow the amateur statesmen of Franklin let slip their opportunity to make of Jefferson an active partisan.

In November, 1785, delegates met for the adoption of a permanent constitution for Franklin. It was easy to imagine from the political-mindedness of frontiersmen that there were in frontier conditions the seeds of doctrinaire radicalism, and in the next four decades many community-builders with a bizarre variety of dreams turned to the frontier as their natural experimental field. But the true political constructiveness of frontiersmen was of a more conservative sort; commonly state-building on the frontier consisted of the taking over of the constitution of that eastern state which most of the builders had known, with a few modifications toward limiting the prerogative or the tenure of executives, and toward bringing the ultimate control of legislation closer to the people.

In 1785 the utopianists were Presbyterians, graduates of Liberty Hall, the citadel of Presbyterian education in the Valley of Virginia—among them the Reverends Samuel Houston and Samuel Doak, and several influential laymen of Franklin. Houston was the proponent and advocate of their constitution at the November meeting. By provisions in the fundamental law the vicious part of society should be excluded from political power: the franchise was to be extended only to virtuous believers, for all that full religious liberty and the rights of conscience were not to be molested; no person was to be eligible to political office "who is of an immoral character, or guilty of such flagrant enormities as drunkenness, gaming, profane swearing, lewdness, Sabbath-breaking, or such like." The legislature (to be unicameral) was hemmed in jealously; all bills of public nature were to be printed and submitted to the people "for debate and amendment" before being read in the Assembly for a third time and voted upon. But the delegates would have none of this despumation of Franklin by the Reverend William Graham, president of Liberty Hall, and his baccalaureates; and, with the common sense that lends logic to this spontaneous construction of a state, adopted that provisional constitution which William Cocke and David Campbell had devised in 1784.

But the heat of the controversy over Houston's constitution welded together the malcontents who, for one reason or another, hoped to break down the authority of Franklin. And Richard Caswell, the new governor of North Carolina, aimed at the dissolution of Franklin by promising that the North Carolina assembly would welcome delegates from the western counties, and by sending state judges into the West. Within Franklin, Colonel John Tipton was in open hostility, personal and public, to Sevier, and under commission from North Carolina held court sessions ten miles above Jonesborough, in which town the superior court of the state of Franklin met twice annually.

There was bitter confusion in Franklin in 1786 and 1787, as rival jurisdictions clashed in tax assessments, in court warrants, and in fisticuffs. Proponents of each authority raided its rival's courts. Sevier and Tipton came to blows, as an early historian of Tennessee related: "He and Tipton met in Jonesborough, where as usual a violent verbal altercation was maintained between them for some time, when Sevier, no longer able to bear the provocations which were given him, struck Tipton with a cane. Instantly the latter began to annoy him with his hands clenched. Each exchanged blows for some time in the same way with great violence and in a convulsion of rage. Those who happened to be present interfered and parted them before victory had been declared for either."

In the fall of 1786 David Cocke appeared before the general assembly of North Carolina; he spoke for several hours, in an eloquent appeal for recognition of the separation. The danger of Indian war was inspiration for pathetic passages: "It is the well-known disposition of the savages to take every advantage of an unpreparedness to receive them, and of a sudden to raise the shrieking cry of exultation over the fallen inhabitants. The hearts of the people of North Carolina should not be hardened against their brethren, who have stood by their sides in perilous times, and never heard their cry of distress when they did not instantly rise and march to their aid. Those brethren have bled in profusion to save you from bondage, and from the sanguinary hands of a relentless enemy, whose mildest laws for the punishment of rebellion, is beheading and quartering."

But the assembly was determined that North Carolina's sovereignty should be vigorously asserted, and brushed aside the protest of Franklin and the protest of the Congress of the Confederation ("Consider with candor and liberality," that body had asked, "the expectations of sister states, and the earnest and repeated applications made by Congress" for the cession of the western lands.) To influence the people of Franklin to renew allegiance to North Carolina, taxes due and unpaid since 1784 were waived. Another enactment, however, to eject the frontiersmen who had pushed beyond the original borders of Franklin into the Cherokee hunting grounds, could not fail to fan the irritation. The legislature also made clear that the men who had resigned state offices to become leaders in Franklin could expect short shift if the western country came again under the authority of North Carolina.

Added to the other sparks of unrest were the efforts of errant soldiers of fortune to foment an attack upon the Spanish at New Orleans. Captain John Sullivan, his tusks whetted by the War of the Revolution, was typical of these fire-eaters; it was probably Sullivan who wrote from Nashville, in May, 1787, to a friend in Georgia, that within ten years "we shall have mustered at least 60,000 men capable of bearing arms. Is it probable that we shall suffer our lands to lie without cultivation or our produce to perish on our hands from want of a river by which our products may be carried to a market? Is it probable that we shall suffer a few Spanish soldiers to seize our boats? I think not!"

The election of the fall of 1787 made the future history of Franklin an opaque muddle. Two sets of sheriffs attempted to open the polls; North Carolinian officials attempted to bar all voters who had not paid taxes to North Carolina; the officers of Franklin suddenly announced their candidates for election to the North Carolina assembly; ballots were torn up, blocks of "voters" ranged into counties where they did not belong, and every group legitimately charged the other groups with foul play. Benjamin Franklin's paternal admonition to Sevier, "There are only two things that humanity induces me to wish you may succeed in: your accommodating your misunderstanding with the government of North Carolina by amicable means, and the avoiding [of] an Indian war by preventing encroachments on their land," was a futile splash of oil upon a rough sea.

The Constitutional Convention sealed one avenue to

[172]

Franklin, in making the admission of a new state contingent upon the consent of the old state which claimed sovereignty over it. It was especially because of this article in the Constitution—the seventeenth—that Luther Martin, the venerable defender of small democracies, retired to Maryland to roar defiance at the coming order of things. "Should this constitution be adopted . . . ," Martin addressed the legislature that had despatched him to Philadelphia, "the State of Maryland may, and probably will, be called upon to assist with her wealth and her blood in subduing the inhabitants of Franklin, Kentucky, and Vermont . . . in compelling them to continue in subjection to the States which respectively claim jurisdiction over them." Statesmen of that day were not commonly given to overt recognition of economic motives, and it is not surprising that Martin missed the point: the real interest of North Carolina was not in permanent hegemony over the western country, but in the exploitation of the western lands to the last continental dollar.

Colonel John Tipton, leading the opposition against Sevier for personal reasons, determined that the most effective thrust against the State of Franklin would be to stop the functioning of its courts. At the February, 1788, term of the Carolina court of Washington County, an order was entered "that Johnathan Pugh, Esq., sheriff take into custody the court docket of said county, supposed to be in the possession of John Sevier, Esq." Tiptonites and Franklinites made raids and counter-raids. Driven from Jonesborough, the Franklinites fell back upon Greenville. Sevier determined to suppress all opposition to the courts of Franklin at one blow; and late in February one hundred fifty men were gathered at the banks of the French Broad. Marching toward Tipton's home on Sinking Creek (a mile and a half from the present Johnson City), gathering other frontiersmen as it went, the little army drew up before Tipton's fortified home. Not venturing a quick attack, they waited too long; when battle began, the besieged Carolinians had ample reënforcements. It was not a bloody battle. In the opposing force were many of Sevier's former friends; and Sevier was a silent, morose commander. There is testimony that many men of both parties purposely aimed too high to hit any one.

General Joseph Martin, commanding the brigade of North Carolina militia west of the mountains, was absent at the time of the skirmish. Promptly he wrote a close friend of Sevier's: "I am greatly distressed and alarmed at the late proceedings of our countrymen and friends, and must beg your friendly interposition, in order to bring about a reconciliation, which, you well know, was my object in accepting a brigadier's commission." The probability of further skirmishes was diverted as the frontiersmen were involved in a desperate Indian war. In January, 1789, Sevier fought his last battle under the flag of Franklin; and wrote to the "Privy Council" of the western state, "It is with the utmost pleasure I inform your honors, that the arms of Franklin gained a complete victory over the combined forces of the Creeks and Cherokees, on the 10th inst."

But Sevier had in the summer of 1788 given up his residence in Jonesborough, and was living on the Cherokee lands between the French Broad and the Little Tennessee rivers. The State of North Carolina, notwithstanding many instances wherein it had granted lands and taken the purchase money from the settlers, periodically threatened the removal of the fifteen hundred families upon the Cherokee Reservation. These hard-pressed pioneers hoped that Sevier and Franklin would save for them their little holdings; so these people were the last subjects of the crumbling State.

John Sevier "should keep the command of the inhabitants of the frontier, or any that may come to their assistance," a convention of the border people agreed, in January, 1789. The title of Franklin had become too inflaming a word, but, to give substance to their petition to the Assembly of North Carolina that the territories west of the mountains be ceded to Congress, they adopted articles of association. "We, the subscribers, inhabiting south of Holston, French Broad and Big Pigeon Rivers," as they described themselves, united in another voluntary compact. "Said articles," the document concluded, "shall be the temporary form of government until we are received into the protection of North Carolina, and no longer." And at the February term of the nearest North Carolina court, John Sevier and his officer-colleagues "came into court and took the oath of allegiance, agreeable to the Act of the Assembly in such cases made and provided." The last thread that gave existence to the State of Franklin had been broken.

Sevier was elected to the state senate of North Carolina in 1789, despite the statute barring officers of Franklin from "enjoyment of any office of profit or trust" in the parent state; he was sworn in and seated several weeks before the legislature repealed the act of disbarment. And in that session North Carolina finally ceded its western domain to the United States. There were then no vacant lands that North Carolina had left unsold.

In the next year Congress extended a government to the ceded domain, under the ample title "Territory of the United States of America, South of the River Ohio." In the wide umbrage of that title there were, in addition to the area of Tennessee, the thin ribbon of land from the Appalachians to the Mississippi ceded by South Carolina to the United States, and the Yazoo strip. This last tract, fronting the Mississippi between the thirty-first parallel and the parallel of the little Yazoo River, a hundred miles to the north, had been bandied about in international treaties until Spain, the United States, Georgia, and South Carolina each claimed it in good faith. In 1790 Spain was still in actual possession.

The census of 1790 rather generously gave Tennessee about twenty-five thousand inhabitants. In Kentucky, by the same census, there were 61,133 white persons and 12,430 slaves.

Kentucky had attained that population by steady, uninterrupted emigration, an annual influx of pioneers that had started in the dark times of the Revolution and had mounted with each year. The end of the Revolution and its promise of a diminution of Indian raids in Kentucky brought eight thousand emigrants into the region in 1783.

Emigrants who came down the Ohio most likely disembarked at Limestone (later called Maysville), a settlement east of the Licking River, the key to the interior lands. They found in 1783—if they cared—that the diminution of Indian dangers in Kentucky was only a promise, and that the voyage itself was arduous and dangerous. J. B. Taylor's account of his voyage, late in the season of 1783, from Brownsville on the Monongahela to a Kentucky settlement, is a dismal paragraph: "We took water at Redstone, and from want of a better opening, I paid for a passage in a lonely, ill-fixed boat of strangers. The river being low, this lonesome boat was about seven weeks before she landed at Beargrass. Not a soul was then settled on the Ohio between Wheeling and Louisville, a space of five hundred or six hundred miles, and not one hour, day or night, in safety; though it was now winter, not a soul in all Beargrass settlement was in safety but by being in a fort." So much for the experiences of pioneers if one isn't a pioneer at heart!

The overland gateway into Kentucky, the Wilderness Road through the Cumberland Gap, was also the first road of emigrants into Tennessee whose particular star hovered over the Cumberland River region west of Franklin. These emigrants followed the Wilderness Road as far as the Rock-castle Hills, and there turned southward to follow an old trace leading to the Bluffs on Cumberland River, the location of Nashville. But in 1783 a road that wagons could use was opened from the Clinch River directly into middle Tennessee. Many a pioneer settler in southwestern Kentucky used that road, traveling on it as far as Gallatin before striking out to the northwest. Western Tennessee was in the possession of the Chickasaw Indians long after Tennessee became a state.

In 1784 ten thousand emigrants came into Kentucky. The beginnings of the state had been secured by the pioneers themselves; their ability had been tested, and their confidence in the results was justified by each year's mounting emigration. Naturally they demanded the control of the commonwealth they were building. The first of the conventions called to voice the demand for separation from Virginia was held on December 27, 1784, at Danville. That convention was made up of delegates from every militia company in Kentucky; conservatively, it limited itself to the suggestion that the citizens at large elect a convention of twenty-five delegates to carry forward the movement. That second convention, meeting in May, 1785, behaved with diffidence and discretion strange in frontiersmen, but accounted for by the fact that the dramatic history of Franklin, being acted before Kentuckians' eyes, awakened sympathy but restrained emulation. A third convention, in the following August, was as vigorous as Kentuckians traditionally should be; and the General Assembly of the State of Virginia promptly passed an act for the separation of Kentucky.

But there were conditions attached. A convention composed of five representatives from each county must determine if an actual majority of the Kentuckians really wished separation. And the federal Congress must, before June 1,

1787, assent to the admission of Kentucky into the Union. The people of Kentucky wanted immediate liberty of action, primarily to organize an Indian-hunting army that should carry on the work of extermination much, much better than federal troops could be expected to do; and they wanted immediately to be in a position to assert vigorously their interest in the free navigation of the Mississippi to its mouth, Spanish New Orleans or no Spanish New Orleans. These were the months when politicians high in Kentucky were susceptible to whispers of Spanish assistance, and intrigue was most devious.

Three times within the next four years the General Assembly of Virginia reworded its offer of political liberty to Kentucky. Meanwhile, the Constitution superseded the Articles of Confederation; and whereas the Articles had demanded the consent of nine states for the admission of a new one, under the Constitution admission was based simply upon act of Congress, with the added condition—in such cases as Kentucky—of the consent of the parent state. In February, 1791, Congress passed an act for the admission of Kentucky in June of the year following; and in April, 1792, the tenth of the Kentucky conventions met at Danville, this time for the drafting of a constitution.

In the course of the debates at Philadelphia that shaped the national constitution, Gouverneur Morris laid down an axiom: "The busy haunts of men, not the remote wilderness, was the proper school of political Talents. If the Western people get the power in their hands they will ruin the Atlantic interests. The Back members are always most averse to the best measures." As a product of the established order, Morris did well to deplore the political articles of faith that were being written in the backwoods. The constitution of Kentucky was a long stride forward in the direction of political democracy; in 1792 it was an expression of the political ideas that the frontier had asserted,

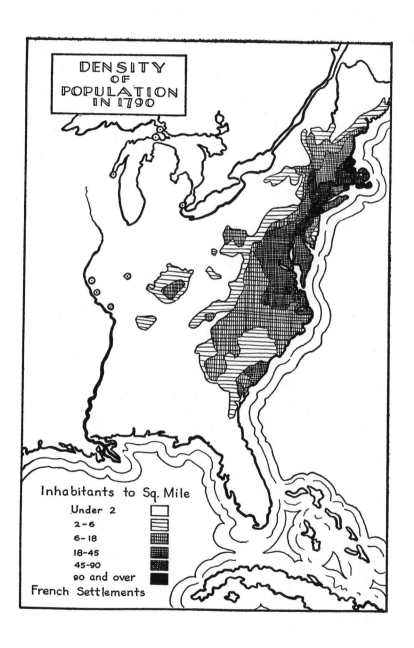

DENSITY
OF
POPULATION
IN 1790

Inhabitants to Sq. Mile
  Under 2
  2-6
  6-18
  18-45
  45-90
  90 and over
French Settlements

that the experience of frontiersmen had approved. The franchise was given to all male citizens, except convicted felons. Ministers were not eligible candidates for legislative positions. To remove questions of land title beyond the effect of local prejudice, in all such cases involving Virginia patents the supreme court of the state was to be the court of first instance. And the heavy hand of the South had not yet smothered frontiersmen's uneasiness about slavery: slaves were not to be brought into Kentucky as merchandise, none were to be brought into the state that were imported into America after 1789, and it was recommended that the legislature pass laws permitting the emancipation of slaves under the limitation that they should not become a charge upon the county in which they resided. George Nicholas, who probably drafted the constitution, showed his strong belief in direct representation by resigning his seat in the Danville convention and resubmitting himself as a candidate, to gain an expression of the will of the people on a particular point, the jurisdiction of the Supreme Court in land title cases, which he had not discussed at the time of his election.

At Danville—where Transylvania Seminary, endowed by the Virginia legislature, was opened in 1789—was a capital forum for up-and-coming Kentucky politicians. It was called "The Political Club," and existed from 1786 until 1790; nearly all of its members took part in the series of constitutional conventions in Kentucky, and its minutes show the gravity and earnestness of men who were self-consciously commonwealth-builders, and felt their responsibility. Major Beatty, paymaster in the United States Army, was in Danville on the night of August 29, 1786: "Very much disturbed by a Political Club which met in the next house where we slept and kept us awake till 12 or 1 o'clock. This club is very commendable in a new country. It is composed of members of the most respectable people in and near

Danville, who meet every Saturday night to discuss politics. Some pretty good speeches and some tolerable arguments made last night. The dispute was: one side insisted that an Act of Assembly was not law when it did not perfectly agree with the Constitution of the State. It was opposed by the other party, and a very long debate took place."

The club was organized under a written constitution and rules of order. Every Saturday evening the members met to debate upon one of the immense variety of topics that were before politically minded Westerners: "Whether the immediate navigation of the Mississippi River will contribute to the interest of this district or not," "Whether an immediate separation of this district from Virginia will tend to its benefit," "Whether annual or other elections are to be preferred," "Has a member of any government the right to expatriate himself without leave," "Whether the emission of paper currency would be an advantage to the inhabitants of this District." The Political Club of Danville was an evidence of the intense interest of the West in current politics, a positiveness which expressed itself most fully in the rabid opposition to all not-Jeffersonian projects introduced into Congress.

On the first of June, 1792, the day on which Kentucky was to become a state, the state government had already been installed, and the first senators and representatives of Kentucky were in Philadelphia awaiting the moment of their admission to Congress. They had perhaps a hundred thousand constituents. In 1795, Governor Blount conducted a census in Tennessee; 77,262 persons were listed. Four years after the admission of Kentucky, Congress ushered Tennessee into the Union.

And still the emigrants came. In December, 1796, Moses Austin left southwestern Tennessee to go to a far-flung frontier, the western bank of the Mississippi, where he was to become a Spanish citizen and work the lead mines of

[181]

Missouri. To this inveterate pioneer other pioneers, doing much the same thing, seemed very strange creatures. He was following the same road with hundreds of families going westward—"women and children in the Month of Decemb^r Travelling a Wilderness Through Ice and Snow, passing large rivers and Creeks, without Shoe or Stocking, and barely as maney raggs as covers their Nakedness, without money or provisions except what the Wilderness affords. . . . Can any thing be more Absurd than the Conduct of man, here is hundreds Travelling hundreds of Miles, they Know not what for Nor Whither, except its to Kentucky, passing land almost as good and easy obtained, the Proprietors of which would gladly give on any terms, but it will not do, its not Kentucky, its not the Promis'd land, its not the goodly inheratence, the Land of Milk and Honey."

CHAPTER XI

GENESEE COUNTY AND COOPERSTOWN

FROM the disbanded regiments of the Revolutionary Army, surviving frontiersmen returned with new courage to their desolated homesteads; from the blockhouses and from eastern refuges their women and children came to meet them. Each type of migrant—the hunter and the cabin-and-garden-patch pioneer, who moved just beyond the reach of surveyors and landlords; the surface-grubbing, half-shiftless farmer, whose wife was annually concerned with childbirth and biennially concerned with packing the household stuffs into the wagon for another trek; the just-married ambitious man and the grim hard-working older man who made the actual conquest of the land—seems to have taken the establishing of a new nation as signal for the establishing of a new home.

From the more thickly settled parts of New England, emigrants came into the new lands of Maine, New Hampshire, and Vermont; drawing almost altogether upon older New England, Maine alone gained fifty thousand settlers between 1790 and 1800. Settlers from Connecticut reclaimed their lands in the Wyoming Valley, and elsewhere in northern Pennsylvania trees were being girdled or felled, Yankee emigrants were building cabins.

In New York the greatest opportunities for expansion lay beyond the Hudson. The older towns on the river felt the influence of the incoming New Englanders; but in the central and western portions of the state most of these pioneering sons of pioneers found homes. There were many tracts forfeited to the state when the Tory landlords had taken up arms against the colonies, and into these tracts and many others New Englanders came until the older pioneers, the Germans and Scotch-Irish, were numerically and politically plowed under.

Gentlemen of New York were quick to take advantage of this interest in the forested wilderness of their state. Men who had been officers in the Revolution were given bounty lands; they used these grants as the basis for a larger business in land speculation. Alexander Hamilton invested all his surplus funds in lands about Oswego. The Roosevelts purchased largely in what is now Oneida County. James Watson, Federalist senator from New York, owned sixty thousand acres in central New York. Gouverneur Morris, General Henry Knox, John Delafield, Stephen Van Rensselaer—the list of those who held large tracts of western land is almost a list of the "first names" of Federalist New York. They sent promising young friends into their western lands as agents in opening up settlement; later they sent their younger sons, to build stately houses wherefrom to radiate the ancestral prestige, and ultimately, alas, to marry commoners.

Settlers in the Green Mountain valleys, in the northeastern corner of New York, were irked, just as were frontiersmen elsewhere on the fringes of great states, by the overlordship of a government committed to the desires of regions more conservative, regions geographically and economically different from the frontier. In 1777 the inhabitants of the two northeastern counties solemnly declared themselves independent of the State of New York, as well as of Great Britain; and they seemed in a fair way to preserve that independence. Certain gentlemen of ambition—John Livingston, Caleb Benton, Peter Ryckman, and others—read their own lesson into the happenings in northeastern New York, and determined upon creating a western state of their own.

In 1787 several chiefs of the Iroquois signed a contract with John Livingston and his associates, leasing all of the lands of the Six Nations in western New York, except such tracts as the chiefs should reserve for their own habitations, for "a yearly rent of two thousand Spanish milled dollars, payable on the 4th of July in each year of the 999 for which the lease was drawn." Governor George Clinton warned the legislature of this private treaty; and in March, 1778, former enactments against intruders on Indian lands were strengthened. Clinton threatened fire and sword; and another flamboyant enterprise was dissolved. In 1793, by dint of constant lobbying, they carried off a consolation prize of ten square miles of land.

The authorities were especially vigilant just then because the ancient conflict between New York and Massachusetts over the title to six million acres of western lands had been amicably settled only two years before. The preëmptive right, the right to purchase title to the soil from the Indians, was conceded to Massachusetts, while the ultimate sovereignty was vested in New York.

In 1787 the legislature of Massachusetts sold these six million acres of western New York to two gentlemen of capital, Oliver Phelps and Nathaniel Gorham, for one million dollars, a third of the sum in cash at hand.

In the next summer, accordingly, Oliver Phelps left Granville, Massachusetts, to go into the West. At Canandaigua Lake, a hundred and thirty miles beyond the German settlements on the fringe of the frontier, Phelps met the Iroquois chiefs; and the Indian title to more than two million acres was there yielded. The area was, roughly, from a point eighty miles from the northeast corner of Pennsylvania westward along the Pennsylvania boundary, until the Genesee River had been passed; then northward to Lake Ontario, and from the eastern tip of the lake east and south to the point of beginning.

After the treaty, Phelps directed the surveying of the lands, after the proven system which the United States was to use in the cutting up of its public lands: townships six miles square, designated by numbers. In 1789 he opened a land office in Canandaigua, selling his townships by "articles," a device that was irresistible to so many gentlemen-proprietors after Phelps; for by it the possession, but not the fee simple, of the land was conveyed. Somewhat under a third of the tract was sold.

But Phelps and Gorham quickly found that their enthusiasm had carried them too far beyond their credit for land sales in the wilderness to make up the difference immediately. The commonwealth of Massachusetts wanted that other two-thirds of the purchase money; in March, 1790, the legislature consented, in lieu of the purchase money, to take back the preëmptive right to four million acres—all that Phelps and Gorham had not secured from the Indians, and the needed fraction of the lands which they had secured. Eight months later the tamed capitalists sold their holdings to Robert Morris of New York. And the untamed Mr. Morris bought the remaining four million acres of the "Genesee lands" from Massachusetts.

Pieter Stadniski and Son, bankers of Amsterdam, had turned a nice profit in securities of the American government, and had reason for high hopes of the United States as a field for investment. In 1789 the Stadniskis, with three other Dutch banking houses, sent a representative to America—Theophile Cazenove, expansive, jovial, infinitely affable and optimistic. By the summer of 1791 Cazenove had become enthusiastic about the possibilities of speculation in western lands. His acquaintances were talking of enormous profits awaiting men who could buy up large

[186]

tracts of the wilderness. Robert Morris demonstrated to him how easily a million acres bought in 1791 could produce one million, five hundred thousand dollars, by 1801. No less than fifty thousand young people would be looking for new homes every year; American wealth, to speak conservatively, would double every twenty years; there were unlimited resources to be tapped, potash, maple sugar, whisky: such was current talk of office building and street corner financiers in 1791.

There were quite a few huge areas of wilderness land then on the market. The Connecticut Reserve, more than two million acres on the south shore of Lake Erie, was at the disposal of the Connecticut legislature. Alexander Macomb bought a tract of four million acres in northern New York from the state in 1791, and was willing to sell at an immediate profit. John Duer, who had bought two million acres of Maine lands in 1790, was already in financial straits and eager to liquidate.

Cazenove was most attracted by the western two-fifths, eight hundred thousand acres, of Robert Morris' purchase from the State of Massachusetts. These lands extended to the western border of New York state; they were near the better known lands of northwest Pennsylvania, which were certain to settle very rapidly. On Christmas Eve, 1792, he purchased these lands from Morris. Meanwhile Robert Morris, Jr., had gone to Amsterdam and battered his way into the vaults of the Dutch banking firms; Cazenove's employers had bought an additional one million, eight hundred thousand acres of Morris' lands. That amazing international enterprise, the Holland Land Company, had begun. On the first of January, 1793, the first Dutch flotation upon landholdings in the American West was opened for public subscription; and within a few days all the shares had been sold. Cazenove was directed to keep on with his land purchasing; and when in February, 1796, the *Hollandsche Land Compagnie* was formally organized, it owned one million, three hundred thousand acres east of the Allegheny River, and five hundred thousand to the west. All of western New York, except a small reserved strip along the Niagara River, passed through the hands of Dutch bankers.

The company went directly into the business of settlement. Their experiment ground was in central New York, where the lands were already surveyed into township units and the title was entirely cleared. The town of Cazenovia was the fruit, planned on a handsomely paternal scale. A handbill of April, 1793, announced that the company's American agent "is forming a settlement in the Road Township, at the outlet of a beautiful lake about three and a half miles long and one mile wide, where he is laying out a town for the accommodation of mechanics; building mills, erecting a well assorted store, potash works, and opening different roads to Whitestown, the Salt-Springs, Chenango river and Catskill." Handbills and maps were distributed among the churches of Massachusetts and Connecticut. By 1797 there were a thousand residents in the settlement, very few of them in Cazenovia itself; by 1800, six hundred more. "Most of the settlers in these parts are Yankees, the rest Low Dutch," the agent wrote to the bankers.

But the capitalists were becoming restive under the increased burden of expense; and the agent was urged to busy himself about back payments and interest on the homestead sales. The settlers made it plain that they could not pay; typical of emigrants in their first few years anywhere in the West, that was true. The agent tried various expedients: he promoted the growth of the just-born village of Utica, to improve marketing conditions; he experimented with accepting payment in produce; he ejected a few of the settlers; ultimately the Dutch learned to abate a part of the interest due, as a means of collecting the rest.

[188]

There was an unheeded lesson for the Holland Land Company in the fate that overtook Robert Morris between 1796 and 1799, when his finances toppled about him, and, his holdings transferred by civil judgments to other hands, the wreck of that brilliant mind became daily more evident.

General St. Clair's defeat by the Ohio Indians in 1791 was exulting news to the Iroquois, as to all other Indians; and until Anthony Wayne chastened the Ohio tribes, and penned them down with the Treaty of Greenville in 1795, the Holland Company had to wait with what patience it could for the Iroquois to be in a mood amenable to the extinguishing of their title to the Genesee lands.

In August and September, 1797, the Big Tree Treaty was drawn up, and, except for tracts reserved by the Indians for their own habitation, title to the four million acres passed to the Holland Company. It was not easily gained; these Iroquois chiefs were no fools, and each had his price. Cazenove wrote to his principals of the happy termination of the conference: "Mr. Thomas Morris had conditioned a gratification of $4000 to be divided between the three interpreters, Johnston, Jones and Parish, but your agents perceiving that it was necessary to animate them further, promised an extraordinary gratification on the part of the Holland Company of $1000 to each of the three above named interpreters and one of $2000 to Captain Chapin, agent of the federal government to the Six Nations, gratifications which were not to be paid if the Indians reserved to themselves more than 200,000 acres. This stimulus had a great effect." In addition, twenty-five hundred dollars was distributed among the chiefs, and five of them were promised further annuities; and accordingly they bargained away their tribal heritage.

One other hindrance was removed, after years of earnest lobbying, in April, 1798. Pennsylvania was the only state in the Union which specifically allowed foreigners to hold lands within its borders. The Holland Company discovered that its millions of acres in New York were in danger of being confiscated by a truculent, provincial, patriotic legislature; ultimately, after the Holland Company had bought the logrolling abilities of Philip Schuyler by promising financial support to his Western Inland Lock Navigation scheme, an act was passed permitting aliens to hold land. Agents for English land speculators had assisted; and probably the crowning agent in securing the legislative concession was Aaron Burr, who hoped to find English purchasers for his burdensome holdings in western lands. There was one restriction in the enactment: aliens could only sell their lands, they could not lease them.

Joseph Ellicott, chief surveyor for the company, entered the forested country in the spring of 1798 with a crew of a hundred and thirty men; it was two full seasons before the entire Holland tract was subdivided into townships and the complete record of the survey submitted to the company. But a permanent job was done; one with field notes so carefully detailed that the company could fairly visualize every section of its lands.

In 1796 speculation in extensive tracts of western lands had abruptly fallen away, when bankruptcy overtook many speculators, and did not gather momentum again for several years; the Genesee lands accordingly had to be sold in small farm sites to actual settlers, or at the most in divisions no larger than three thousand acres. The Holland Company had a strong negative example in its expensive Cazenovia, and sought carefully for the right man, trustworthy and conservative, to manage the sales. They found their man in Joseph Ellicott, who had passed almost all his life in the American backwoods.

A few main roads, an office for the agent, a tavern for prospective buyers, Ellicott listed as necessary expenditures. He recommended some others if the money could be spared;

but he envisioned no such expensive inducements as had Cazenove. He foresaw that sales would be easy but collections difficult, and therefore proposed that the proprietors accept payment in live stock and grain, clearing a pasture and building a gristmill to care for these payments. One essential of his scheme demanded that every tract purchased be actually settled within a short time. The company acquiesced to most of his suggestions, fixed a minimum price of $1.25 an acre, made appropriations for a shop for a blacksmith and a loan to a storekeeper, overruled the idea of payment in produce; and in November, 1800, sales were opened.

The proprietors' stipulations called for an advance payment. It was all very well to agree among themselves that some cash payment was necessary to keep out the shiftless and the stray debtors from other settlements; but honest-intentioned men who wanted land had little cash in hand, and needed that for the first year's costs of living and sowing. They were accepted; in December, 1801, Ellicott wrote: "I have made no actual sales this fall where the stipulated advance has been paid." Many of the applicants were admitted upon their agreement to give their labor to the company, in road building, in construction work of some sort, to the amount of the advance. The legal rate of interest on land debts, 7 per cent, was charged by the Holland Company; almost all landholding enterprises levied as much.

Under Ellicott's direction, a road was built from Genesee on the Genesee River to Batavia, and soon extended southwest to the Allegheny River at Olean. A second road began at Batavia and ran northward, opening a communication to Lake Ontario. Later, narrower roads were interwoven about the farm sites. Yankee labor performed the work, part in credit on the purchase-debts and part in cash. The company opened a trail to Buffalo, and a road

[191]

from the shore of Lake Erie into northwest Pennsylvania invited emigrants northward. A sawmill was built to provide the flooring needed for the settlers' cabins; and in time, the company fondly hoped, the settlers would build houses of sawn boards to replace their log cabins. A gristmill was built later, between 1803 and 1805. Ellicott frequently advanced small sums, up to a thousand dollars, to trustworthy men; the company does not seem to have lost a cent of these accounts.

In March, 1802, the legislature created the County of Genesee, on Ellicott's assurance that the Holland Company would construct the public buildings; and shortly after the sawmill was ready to turn out the timbers, he built an amazing box that compartmented a jail, a courthouse, and a tavern under one roof. The company donated lots for churches, and when the frontiersmen were belated in beginning schools encouraged them out of its own pocket. A policy of indulgence to its many remiss settlers generally characterized the Holland Land Company; this method seemed in the end to promise the best returns. In its thirty-five years of active management of the Genesee lands the company was only very rarely in the courts to collect its debts or to expel its debtors. Physically the settlement thrived, and western New York entered upon its stable existence as an area of diversified agriculture. The Holland Land Company trod a rocky road in business and in politics and was happy to take advantage of the revived speculative spirit in 1834 to sell its remaining lands to American capitalists.

Those holdings which Phelps and Gorham sold to Robert Morris in 1790, twelve hundred thousand acres, did not remain long in his hands; an English gentleman of title, Sir William Pulteney, bought the lands, and through his agent, Charles Williamson, seriously attempted his purchased rôle of paternal overlord. Settlers purchased their lands of Williamson for three dollars an acre, on long-term payments. No interest was charged on the indebtedness for the first five years. He gave each family a cow, and supplied them with wheat for the first year, to be repaid in kind. The town of Geneva developed encouragingly; in 1800 it had seventy-five families, with at least three lawyers in its population. Williamson had built an inn there, occupied a suite himself, and saw to it that provisions, liquors, beds, and stabling were satisfactory to travelers and prospective buyers. By 1795 the scattered community was self-supporting; and a traveler in 1800 ornately wrote, "So suddenly has plenty burst forth where there was famine, and so quick the change of scene from dark-tangled forests (whose deathlike silence yielded but to the growl of bears, the howl of wolves, and yell of savages) to smiling fields, to flocks and herds, and to the busy hum of men, that, instead of being indebted to others for their support, they will henceforth annually supply the low country, Baltimore especially, with many hundred barrels of flour and heads of cattle." The Pulteney Estate was indeed well-settled and thriving, and Sir William Pulteney was taking a profit—alas, a paper profit.

Of the many other wilderness-land enterprises in New York, "minor" enterprises only beside the Holland Company and the Pulteney Estate, William Cooper's land-proprietorship best shows the step-by-step development of a western community.

In compensation for far-western lands he lost in the Treaty of Fort Stanwix, George Croghan secured a generous estate about Otsego Lake, the largest of the sources of the Susquehanna. William Franklin, son of Benjamin, took a mortgage on the lands, and in due time foreclosed. The title to the estate was shuffled about until in 1785 most of it was owned by William Cooper, Gentleman, of Burlington, New Jersey.

[193]

In the autumn Cooper visited his tract, riding three hundred miles from Burlington into a rough and hilly country where there was not an inhabitant or a trace of a road. Living on the brook trout, the benevolent Federalist leisurely explored his domain and shaped his plans for establishing a settlement.

In May, 1786, forty thousand acres were placed on sale in small farm tracts; and in half a month all the tracts were taken up, "by the poorest order of men." They paid forty shillings an acre for their holdings. Many families came in before the snow had melted, and in the spring of 1787 more emigrants appeared. Cooper began to think more seriously of his rôle of overlord; he extended his possessions in the adjacent patents, and began the building of his manor. Early in 1788 it was ready—a two-story affair, with two wings; the siding was of large boards, beaded but not planed. There was only one other board house in Cooper's domain; the rest were log cabins.

Then the proprietor platted Cooperstown. With judicial precision he laid out a rectangle, broken only by his Manor House in the middle, and named the streets: Front Street along the lake, Water Street along the river, most of the rest conservatively named by number. There was a Main Street, of course.

In the winter of 1789-1790 there were seven frame houses with thirty-five inhabitants in Cooperstown; log cabins were scattered about the estate, outside the village plot. In the tract there were about two hundred families in all. Cooper had a stock of goods brought into the village, and brought in a storekeeper; now he began to do his conscientious best to abide by the tradition of an English squire. The Manor House that winter established its reputation for handsome hospitality. The narrative of Monsieur Ebbal is like an eighteenth-century print of Tories on holiday.

Cooper and a party of guests had a large lumber sleigh fitted out for a sally on the ice. On the western bank of the lake lived one Monsieur Ebbal, once an officer in the French army. As the sleigh and four approached his house, he went out to make the proper greetings. Cooper invited Monsieur Ebbal to join the party, promising him a feast of game and madeira; but the Monsieur, ordinarily a good table companion, was reticent. He could not be persuaded; wherefore the well-wined gentlemen abducted him. He took his captivity in good part; but he refused to lay aside his long-skirted surtout, even when he took his seat at table. Warmed with the plentiful food, the heavy potations, and the blazing fire, at last he unbuttoned his coat; and the delighted gentlemen discovered that, by the exigencies of life on the frontier without a servant and without a regular washday, Monsieur Ebbal had perforce come abroad without a shirt. He was uncoated on the spot, and Cooper gave him a linen shirt with ruffled wristbands.

But, residing among his settlers, Cooper was unpleasantly aware of their poverty, and did what a benevolent proprietor could to tide them over the first few years. "I erected a storehouse, and during each winter filled it with large quantities of grain, purchased in distant places. I procured from my friend Henry Drinker a credit for a large quantity of sugar kettles; he also lent me some potash kettles, which we conveyed as best we could, sometimes by partial roads on sleighs, and sometimes over the ice. By this means I established potash works among the settlers, and made them debtor for their bread and laboring utensils. I also gave them credit for their maple sugar and potash, at a price that would bear transportation, and the first year after the adoption of this plan I collected in one mass forty-three hogsheads of sugar, and three hundred barrels of pot and pearl ash, worth about nine thousand dollars. This kept the people together and at home, and the country soon assumed a new face." In seasons of slack farmwork he assembled the settlers for road-making and for building bridges over streams that were too deep to ford.

Judge Cooper brought his family, fifteen persons, including the servants, from Burlington in 1790. In February, 1791, the County of Otsego was formed, with Cooperstown its county seat. In keeping with the tradition, William Cooper wished to be a judge; and the inhabitants duly elected him. A courthouse was built, a framework room over a squared-log jail. The jury rooms were in a tavern occupied by the jailer, on the same lot. During the summer a hostelry, bravely named the Red Lion, was erected; the population of Cooperstown gained its first two lawyers and its first physician. This physician, incidentally, was not long welcome; he mixed an emetic with the punch drunk at a ball in the Red Lion Inn, was tried and convicted, put in the stocks, and banished.

By the end of 1791 there were at least twenty houses and stores, and one hundred inhabitants, in the village; and the land about was dotted with farms. Their market was at Baltimore, for the easiest transportation was the Susquehanna River; each year flatboats laden with wheat, and a few with lumber, were floated down the river to the mart in Maryland, or to Harrisburg or another of the Pennsylvania trading towns on the Susquehanna.

The soil and climate were favorable in the western counties of New York; the face of the country was then overshadowed by immense trees wherever the land was unreclaimed by the settler; the bears, wolves, and panthers of the region were fast being exterminated for the bounties. "The reward is paid by the County Treasurer," Cooper explained, "under a law passed by a majority of the people in open town-meeting. The farmers are always disposed to vote for a high bounty in revenge for the sheep they have

lost, and the hunters because they have hope of the reward."

During the first ten years of the existence of Cooperstown, the inhabitants depended entirely upon chance for the
little religious instruction they received. The Presbyterians
were the most numerous sect in the community; they were
also the poorest. Occasionally a traveling Baptist or a
Methodist preached in the schoolhouse or in the tavern;
in 1791 the Presbyterians engaged a minister to settle
among them, in six months repented of their extravagance,
and the minister went his way. Typical of the frontier
was this setting-aside of religious organization until the
first few years, the hardest years, of frontier life were
done; typical then was the noisy emotionalism of the belated recognition of this negligence, the hectic scramble to
get aboard some Protestant sect and float into the respectability proper to an established settlement.

But there was a public school very early in the history
of Cooperstown; classes were held in the courthouse until
pedagogy had its own square-log temple. Plans for an
Academy were under way as early as 1795, when subscription pledges were circulated at town meeting, and forty-two
signatories pledged $1,441.25; Judge Cooper's donation
was $725 of this. In September one hundred men assem-
bled for the "raising," and the Academy was built in a day.
James Fenimore Cooper wrote of the Academy, "It was
one of those tasteless buildings that afflict all new countries, and contained two school rooms below, a passage
and the stairs; while the upper story was a simple room.
Nothing superior to a common English education was ever
taught in this house, all attempts at classical instruction
failing. This must be ascribed to the general want of means
in the population, at the time; the few who gave their
children classical educations usually sending them abroad
for that purpose."

A state road was laid out between Albany and Coopers-town in 1794. In the next February arrived Elihu Phinney, from Connecticut, with type cases and a tiny press; on the third of April, 1795, appeared Volume One, Number One, of *The Otsego Herald, or Western Advertiser*. Judge Cooper's court was crowded with petty litigation. The young settlement was taking on its permanent colors. In 1799 it had so outgrown its overlordship that one James Cochran almost defeated William Cooper in a congressional campaign, notwithstanding that Judge Cooper caused this broadside to be freely circulated:

"Otsego County, ss.

"Personally appeared Stephen Ingalls, one of the con-stables of the town of Otsego, and being duly sworn, de-poseth and saith, that he was present at the close of a bruising match between James Cochran, Esq. and William Cooper, Esq. on or about the sixteenth of October last, when the said James Cochran confessed to the said William Cooper these words: 'I acknowledge you are too much of a buffer for me,' at which time it was understood, as this deponent conceives, that Cochran was confessedly beaten.

"Stephen Ingalls.

"Sworn to me this sixth day of November, 1799. Joshua Dewey, Justice of the Peace."

In 1795, Cooper decided that the Manor House had become inadequate, and let the contracts for a grand stone residence, Otsego Hall, which was not finished until 1799. For many years it was the largest private residence in west-ern New York, and one of the very few not built of wood. In 1800 Cooperstown had some three hundred fifty inhabitants. About this time a public library was opened, and the Presbyterians acquired a resident minister. In 1802 lightning struck Otsego Hall, and very shortly after the first lightning rod in Cooperstown was erected; with that lightning rod, let us say, Cooperstown was halfway through the chapter of its frontier years.

Judge Cooper, who could recall in his old age that "there are forty thousand souls now holding land, directly or indirectly, under me," in his years of management of land and management of men, accumulated a set of precepts upon proprietorship, precepts whose successful working out in Cooperstown suggests that the failure of most great gentlemen's enterprises in western lands failed not because squatter settlement or small independent homesteads was the best technic of frontier development, but because the gentlemen were not Judge Coopers.

He denounced "the impolicy of reserving certain tracts in a new settlement on the speculation of their future rise in value. This mistake, where trade is the object, is still more pernicious, for as liberty is in my apprehension the very child of commerce, so the one will not remain where the other cannot be." He wrote: "I hold it essential to the progress of a trading town, that it should be settled quickly and compactly, and the only point in which I would thwart the wishes of the settler, whether merchant or mechanic, would be in the desire which most entertain of possessing a large lot. It is for his own advantage that this should be resisted, for if he be half tradesman and half farmer he will neither prosper as one or the other."

Other gentry with large western domains fell into the errors Cooper could have warned them against, if a Federalist had been willing to listen even to another Federalist. They reserved favorite tracts, and retained mill sites in their own hands; they insisted too soon and with overmuch rigor upon full payment for their lands, and were too ready to have recourse in foreclosure; they played the overlord too grandly, and built costly roads and bridges at their own charge. Cooper, reaching into his own experience, wrote, "My advice is to fill the land with people, whether rich or

poor; call them together when occasion requires to undertake some general work, where every one feels his own
particular interest, and a few quarts of liquor cheerfully
bestowed, will open a road or build a bridge, which would
cost if done by contract, hundreds of dollars." The most
grievous error of the gentlemen-proprietors in western
New York was to refuse to sell in fee, to attempt to create
a system of landholding based on perpetual leases binding
the tenants to the payment of perpetual rent. This system
toppled about the heads of the sons of these landlords, and
the social history of New York was burdened by the "Anti-
Rent War" and occasional outbursts of mob rule.

With thousands of its residents whose land tenure and
whose finances reflected frontier conditions two decades
after the actual frontier of settlement had moved far to
the westward, the state's politics were hotly factional, and
enlivened by contests between conservative property owners
and democratic debtors. In 1792 an anti-Federalist legislature attempted to impeach William Cooper, then in Congress. One witness testified that Cooper "had been round
to the people and told them that they owed him, and that
unless they voted for Mr. Jay, he would ruin them"; and
another stated, "Judge Cooper then said to me, what, then,
young man, you will not vote as I would have you—you
are a fool, young man, for you cannot know how to vote
as well as I can direct you, for I am in public office."

Another event in frontier times was portent of the political storm: the election of 1807 in Genesee County. The
majority of the settlers were from Vermont, and were
Democrats. In Vermont there had been no property restrictions of the right to ballot; and they had been accustomed to go to the polls just as if their installment-payment
contracts made them freeholders. In the election of 1807
the Federalists placed qualified challengers at the voting
places in Genesee County. The Vermonters came into the

villages, had their several bracers at the taverns, and proceeded to the polls, only to be met by the challengers and ordered to produce evidence of their status as freeholders. Joseph Ellicott ended his relation: "The Consequence was that quarreling and Blows passed which occasioned more bloody Noses and black Eyes than has been done ever since the Commencement of the Sale of the Company's Lands."

CHAPTER XII

REPENTANCE, SALVATION, AND THE JERKS

AGAINST the opposition of the plantation counties, the back-country delegates in 1785 wrote Jefferson's ideal into the fundamental law of Virginia: "no man shall be compelled to frequent or support any religious worship, place or ministry whatever; or shall be enforced, restrained, molested, or burthened in his body or goods, nor shall otherwise suffer on account of his religious opinions or belief; but that all men shall be free to profess, and by argument to maintain their opinions in matters of religion, and that the same shall in no wise diminish, enlarge or effect their civil capacities." And, a rare stroke of fortune for succeeding generations, deism (a polite agnosticism burning its tiny candles before images which turn out to be mirrors) was in that decade strong enough to wedge into the Constitution, without many murmurs, a guarantee of religious liberty.

"Reconstruction," in the fifteen years following the Revolution, was a reconstruction of substantial things—of private business, of state politics, and the rebuilding, along untried lines, of a central overlordship. Beyond the Alleghenies the reconstruction was comprehensive and energy-devouring: a simple thing, a kitchen table; a complex thing, the constitution of a state; and many things between, had to be remade.   While memory and custom, conscious and subconscious, were being called upon for the building of Jared Goodyear's house, the Ohio Company's *Mayflower,* the town of Cincinnati, Transylvania University, and the state of Kentucky, the Church and the soul were not much spoken of; these topics were provocative of too heated dissensions, and as palliatives to the great American appetite for informal debate they had not the solid beauty of politics and cerebral philosophy.

A toppling over of the Episcopal Church was a consequence of the Revolution in the states where Western influence was strong.   Forced into silence and compromise by the war, Episcopalian sermons had become (in Bishop Meade's phrase) "brief and most unimpressive"—lifeless discursions upon natural religion and morality.   In the north, outside the charmed region east of the Connecticut River, which was consecrated to the Congregationalists, the Episcopal Church made healthy progress; but in Virginia, where in 1776 there were ninety-one Episcopal clergymen, there were only fifteen with parishes in 1783.   When, two years later, the Protestant Episcopal Church was organized, the Reverend David Griffith was selected to be made a bishop; but he could not go to London for consecration because the Virginia churches could not raise money enough to pay his traveling expenses.

The Episcopal Church had long neglected the frontier, and had been cordially neglected by frontiersmen in return. Its diminishing influence made room for the expansion of more zealous denominations.   In 1784 there were 20,940 Baptists in the states of Virginia, North Carolina, South Carolina, Georgia, Kentucky, and Tennessee; in 1792 there were 39,319.   In 1784 the Methodist Church definitely struck out for itself as an organized church; there were then about fifteen thousand members, over four-fifths of them in the south and west. In 1790 the church had a total membership of 57,631.

In this shift of denominational allegiance and the increase in church membership on the frontier, women must have been largely responsible; certainly they could not have swaggered in irreligion like Ohio River roustabouts, nor discoursed abstract morality like Kentucky lawyers. And they must have been influential in the organization of the praying societies, the first hint of the storm of spiritual energy that was to sweep over the West. These societies were composed of "persons who were distinguished in some things from all denominations, though blended with them in their outward communion. These professed to be in search of the truth and power of religion, and ready to embrace it wherever it would appear, but did not believe it was among any denominations, in purity." Ladies and gentlemen who attended the praying societies read from the Scriptures, without commenting; prayed for the Divine Spirit to descend, for the accomplishing of the wonders promised to precede the millennium; lamented the deplorable state of mankind in general, and the deplorable laxities of the gelid, corrupt professors of Christianity in particular.

Meanwhile introspective ministers were feebly lamenting the pall that clouded their own souls. "I have this winter past preached with difficulty, my heart but little engaged. I know I am not as I ought to be, yet cannot be affected with my sad case," wrote a western minister to a friend in 1798. A minister in Lexington answered a correspondent: "Yesterday I received your kind letter, and I undertake now to answer it. The dead state of religion is truly discouraging here, as well as elsewhere. . . . When I look into my wretched heart, and consider how much I have dishonored God by a dead and careless life, I have reason to cover my head in the dust. If some are spotted with sin, I am spot all over."

In 1794, most likely, the first camp meeting was held; a Methodist church in Lincoln County, North Carolina, sponsored a meeting of men, women and children in the neighboring forest, while several ministers coöperated or contested in the saving of souls. Camp meetings were an annual affair after that, among Methodists of North and South Carolina. In New England, Timothy Dwight, president of Yale College, was manfully breasting the tide of infidelity. Edward Dorr Griffin began preaching at New Salem, Massachusetts, in 1793, where there had been no church meeting for forty years, and promptly garnered a hundred converts. But while there was a general quickening of religious feeling in the Puritan colonies, there was no rabid evangelism. In 1795 the new settlements north of Pittsburgh were suddenly religion-struck; in 1798 Presbyterians became evangelical in western New York. Late in 1799, in southwestern Kentucky, came the first gusts of the storm.

Kentucky's population of seventy-five thousand in 1790 had become almost two hundred and twenty-five thousand in 1800—an inflow of about four hundred people on every day of the decade. But the Methodist Church, with eighteen hundred members in 1790, had not gained at all by 1800. Three thousand Kentuckians in 1790 were Baptist communicants; by 1800, only two thousand names had been added to the church rolls. There were about fourteen hundred communicants of the Presbyterian Church in Kentucky in 1790; that sect, like the Methodist, did not gain enough members in the decade to offset the number of withdrawing schismatics.

James McGready was the son of Scotch-Irish frontier folk in Pennsylvania. In August, 1788, he was licensed to preach by the presbytery of Redstone, on the Monongahela, and soon he left for a "gospel tramp" through Carolina. In Orange County, North Carolina, he was most successful in his revival-making. "His gestures were *sui generis,*" another minister described him. "Everything appeared by him forgotten but the salvation of souls. Such earnestness, such zeal, such powerful persuasion. . . ." But in South Carolina McGready was snagged; his pulpit was burned, and people averse to pulpit-burning thought McGready a pernicious distraction. He admitted the force of the opposition by turning west. From eastern Tennessee he was called, by some of his former hearers who had settled in southwestern Kentucky, to become the pastor of three churches, one on each of the little streams in Logan County. His fervent tactics were successful; 1797 was a year of quickened religious interest in his section, and a covenant of McGready's composing was signed by many who agreed to offer special prayer every Saturday evening, Sunday morning, and the third Saturday of each month for one year for the outpouring of the Holy Spirit in Logan County and the rest of the world.

"A sense of the total depravity of human nature, and the entire separation of the soul from God," explained a Kentuckian and philosopher in 1807, "is the first thing necessary to prepare the way for the entrance of spiritual life. Therefore, such as honestly confessed their lost and deplorable state, and intensely groaned for deliverance from it, were not in so dangerous a condition, as those who made a high-sounding profession and glorified in some plan of salvation, that still left them in bondage to corruption. But a conviction of being lost never saved any one; though many have made conviction a great evidence of their election, and vainly rested upon that light, which searches out the evil and wickedness of the heart, without going any further. But such as were honest before God could not stop here; they must be at the *truth* and the *substance.*

Therefore, it was necessary that the channel, through which the quickening power of God has access to the soul, should be opened; namely, the everlasting covenant of redemption." McGready flung the channel gates wide open; and preachers of his evangelical stamp in other Kentucky churches suddenly found that multitudes were listening. John McGee, Methodist; his brother William, Presbyterian as his father in North Carolina had been; William Hodge, a Presbyterian from North Carolina; William McKendree and William Burke, both prominent in western Methodism throughout their lives; Louis and Elijah Craig, successful "exhorters" from Baptist churches in Virginia—these ministers and lesser colleagues were swept to hypnotic heights by the storm.

These men were much alike in method; their manner was fervid, without dignity but with cumulative blazes of intensity. Demagoguery became them, glovelike: education displayed was a detriment, for it separated them from their congregations; the homelier the thought and the phrase, the more unresisting was the audience. It was written of the Reverend William McGee: "he would sometimes exhort after the sermon, standing on the floor, or sitting, or lying in the dust, his eyes streaming, and his heart so full that he could only ejaculate, 'Jesus, Jesus!' "

In July, 1799, McGready administered the sacrament of the Lord's Supper at his Red River church; sinners wept during the sermon, and after dismissal the congregation lingered about, returning to the meetinghouse for voluntary prayer. In August McGready was at the church on Gaspar River; after he had spoken sinners felt their bodily strength oozing away, and they fell to the ground and groaned. McGready made note of the young people, who "could not behave with common decency," but writhed and cried for salvation. During the summer of 1800 the Great Revival became so inescapable a fact that McGready likened the

work of 1799 to the scattering drops that precede a mighty
rain.

In June, 1800, several Presbyterian ministers of the Kentucky Cumberland region joined forces with McGready in
a revival at Red River. The sobbing of sin-burdened hearers was a constant, mournful accompaniment to the preaching; and on the last day of the "religion-feast" a woman
lost self-control, and shouted in victorious competition with
the Reverend William Hodge. The congregation lingered
after the sermon, tearful and distraught. The Reverend
William McGee sank unconscious upon the floor of the pulpit; John McGee attempted to preach, but a paroxysm of
trembling shivered his words. The shouting woman was
at it again; and John McGee, too, was in a moment shouting and exhorting. Nerves snapped; people writhed between the benches, and moaned for mercy.

That religion-feast was followed in quick succession by
meetings at Gaspar River, Muddy River, and elsewhere
on the Cumberland frontier. Francis Asbury, at the
Methodist General Conference at Baltimore in 1800, took
up the firebrand and despatched numbers of his under-
shepherds to evangelize the blue-grass country of central
Kentucky. In western Tennessee the Great Revival flared
into dozens of camp meetings; by the autumn of 1801,
Kentucky, Tennessee, the Carolinas, western Pennsylvania,
western Virginia, and the new settlements upon the north
bank of the Ohio River were shaken and exalted alike by
repentance and exhortation.

Ministers coöperated regardless of denominations; predestination, regeneration, universal salvation, were jumbled
in one theological scramble in which "the sweetness of
redeeming love," "the overflowing fountain of grace,"
seemed uppermost. This Arminianism was a strange garment for Presbyterians; when the excitement of the Great
Revival had begun to subside, and denominational lines

became once more evident, Methodism gained members as the presbyteries lost them.

Churches were deserted for the open field; families drove to the camp meeting in wagons, bringing provisions and bedding with them, from thirty, fifty, a hundred miles away. Meetings began on Thursday or Friday, and lasted through the following Tuesday, while soul-saving went on night and day. Confession and exhortation became a delirious orgy. Richard M'Nemar's *Short History of the Late Extraordinary Outpouring of the Spirit of God in the Western States of America* admirably brings the ebullitions of a religion-excited throng into one focus: "How striking, to see hundreds, who never saw each other in the face before, moving uniformly into action, without any preconcerted plan, and each, without intruding upon another, taking that part assigned him by a conscious feeling, and in this manner, dividing into bands, over a large extent of ground, interspersed with tents and wagons; some uniting their voices in the most melodious songs; others in solemn and affecting accents of prayer: some lamenting, with streaming eyes, their lost situation, or that of a wicked world; others lying, apparently, in the cold embrace of death: some instructing the ignorant and directing the doubtful, and urging them, in the day of God's visitation, to make sure work for eternity; others, from some eminence, sounding the general trump of a free salvation, and warning sinners from the wrath to come; the surrounding forest, at the same time, vocal with the cries of the distressed—sometimes to the distance of half a mile or a mile. . . . How persons, so different in their education, manners and natural dispositions, without any visible commander, could enter upon such a scene, and continue in it for days and nights, in perfect harmony, has been one of the greatest wonders that ever the world beheld."

In June, 1801, four thousand people were present at a

rousing revival in Concord, Kentucky. At Cane Ridge in August there were fifteen or twenty thousand. Evangelists rose to the occasion; they learned how to handle such huge crowds. A tract of ground two or three hundred yards square was lined with tents; behind the tents was cleared space for the wagons and horses. A speakers' stage was built, usually one at either end of the enclosure, and benches were huddled in. A day's religion-feast began at dawn, when a trumpeter blared as he strode in front of the tents; ten minutes later a single long blare called the people to pray at their tent doors. Breakfast was a punctuation between sermons, one at sunrise and one at ten. Dinner at one and supper at sunset; preaching at three in the afternoon, and an orgy of preaching at night. The cook-fires in front of the tents were rekindled, candles fixed to the stages and to the trees were lighted, making blotches and dots of yellow and amber light against the aphrodisiac night.

The rut of whisky drinking had been frontiersmen's only emotional debauch, and that had not given an answer to the uneasiness, the unspoken awareness of the hopeless conflict between the pioneer's search for power and his search for personal freedom. And whisky drinking, of course, was a way open to few women; prejudices of the coastal plains society died harder with them, and the interminable grind of working and childbearing left their constitutions precious little strength for any bodily debauchery. The Great Revival, the surging up of emotions so strong that they burst the body's control, with its invitation, "Whosoever will, let him come and take of the water of life freely," was an opportunity for them all, adolescents, women, huskies. "To see a bold Kentuckian (undaunted by the horrors of war) turn pale and tremble at the reproof of a woman, a little boy, or a mean African," wrote a chronicler of these times; "to see him sink down in deep remorse, roll and toss, and gnash his teeth, till black in the face; entreat the prayers of those he came to devour [presumably his womenfolk, first to follow the "New Light"]; and, through their fervent intercessions and kind instructions, obtain deliverance; and return in the possession of the meek and gentle spirit he set out to oppose: who would say the change was not supernatural and miraculous?"

Frenzies were contagious. Confronted with something that fascinated them, evangelical religion—"Make me, Saviour, what thou art; live thyself within my heart"; "Then the world shall always see Christ the holy child in me,"—camp-meeting crowds were receptive, nerves in a sympathetic tremor. Then some overwrought soul began it: falling in a stupor, rolling on the ground, jerking and twisting, or barking like a dog. These exercises were faintly mortifying, before and after camp meetings, to victims and friends; but scoffers at a camp meeting, once their self-satisfaction wavered, were caught up in the emotional vortex as easily as twelve-year-old girls. M'Nemar plead the case of the orgiasts: "In spite of all the efforts of nature, both men and women would be forced to personate that animal, whose name, appropriated to a human creature is counted the most vulgar stigma—forced I say, for no argument but force, could induce any one of polite breeding in a public company, to take the position of a canine beast, move about on all-fours, growl, snap the teeth, and bark in so personating a manner, as to set the eyes and ears of the spectator at variance. It was commonly acknowledged by the subjects of these exercises, that they were laid upon them, as a chastisement for disobedience, or a stimulus to incite them to some duty or exercise, to which they felt opposed."

At the Cane Ridge camp meeting in August, 1801, Jesse Crawford, an older minister, remained aloof and counted the devastation: three thousand people fallen to the ground.

Some had early symptoms, they afterwards described—a throbbing of the arteries, a rush of blood to the heart; others collapsed suddenly, and recollected nothing. An evangelist in western Pennsylvania wrote the *Massachusetts Missionary Magazine* of the wonder-workings: "The persons who are struck are generally first observed to pay close attention to the preaching; then to weep and shed tears plentifully for a while; after this a twitching or jerking seizes them, and they fall to the ground helpless, and convulsed through their whole frame as if in the agonies of death. In the beginning of this awakening, it was common for those who fell after they had been lying for a while to speak in an astonishing manner as to length of time, matter, and loudness of voice. Some of the most powerful sermons I have heard from mortals came from the mouths of persons of the above description, unable to help themselves. Some have spoken almost without cessation for the space of five hours, and some parts of the time so loud that they might be heard at a distance of a mile."

When the superhuman energies of the Great Revival were spent, the West had left its permanent imprint on American religions. The "Great Awakening" of New England, from 1734 to 1742, left no such train of consequences, for all Whitefield's thundering about the absolute necessity of supernatural grace and all Edwards' lurid daubing of hell. There were then no protracted staging of revivals, very few meetings outside the ordinary routine of the churches, no "inquiry meetings," no "anxious seats." The churches were spiritually quickened, newer denominations in the provinces—Baptists and Presbyterians particularly—expanded, and out of the rivalry of Christian sects a broader civil toleration emerged; but beyond that, the religious effervescence of the 1740's was an agonized return to the old simplicities of Calvinism.

The stimulating force of the frontier upon doctrinaire religion, and upon the manners of the faithful, is most vivid in the "left wing" of the Great Revival—the self-constituted presbytery of Springfield. In the autumn of 1803 Richard M'Nemar (whom the Reverend John Lyle described as "lively in desultory exhortation and speaks and sings with all his power and in address much like a Methodist") was haled before the synod of Kentucky for preaching anti-Calvinistic doctrines. Knowing that their fate was interwoven with his, four other Presbyterian ministers who had become whole-hearted revival workers joined M'Nemar in a document denouncing the action of the synod, declaring their withdrawal from its jurisdiction and their continued communion with the Presbyterian church at large. Having resigned, they were fired: the synod of Kentucky suspended them. And the five revivalists constituted themselves into the presbytery of Springfield.

In April, 1804, the independent presbytery decided to scuttle the Presbyterian Confession of Faith, adopting the Scriptures as the only standard of doctrine and discipline. In June a further simplification was achieved, the dissolving of the presbytery of Springfield. And nowhere but in the American West could there have been such a document as the Last Will and Testament of Springfield Presbytery:

THE PRESBYTERY OF SPRINGFIELD, sitting at Cane-ridge, in the county of Bourbon, being through a gracious Providence in more than ordinary health, growing in strength and size daily; and in perfect soundness and composure of mind; but knowing that it is appointed for all delegated bodies once to die, and considering that the life of every such body is very uncertain, do make, and ordain this our last Will and Testament, in manner and form following, viz.:

Imprimis. We *will,* that this body die, be dissolved, and sink into union with the body of Christ at large; for there is but one body and one Spirit, even as we are called in the hope of our calling.

Item. We *will,* that our name of distinction, with its reverend title, be forgotten. . . .

Item. We *will,* that each particular Church, as a body, actuated by the same Spirit, choose her own preacher, and support him by a free will offering, without written *call* or *subscription*—admit members—remove offences—and never henceforth *delegate* her right of government to any man or set of men whatever.

Item. We *will,* that the people henceforth take the Bible as the only sure guide to heaven; and as many as are offended with other books which stand in competition with it, may cast them into the fire if they choose; for it is better to enter into life having one book, than having many to be cast into hell.

Item. We *will,* that preachers and people, cultivate a spirit of mutual forbearance; pray more and dispute less. . . .

Item. We *will,* that our weak brethren, who may have been wishing to make the Presbytery of Springfield their King, and wot not what is now become of it, betake themselves to the Rock of Ages, and follow Jesus for the future.

Item. We *will,* that the Synod of Kentucky examine every member, who may be *suspected* of having departed from the Confession of Faith, and suspend every such suspected heretic immediately, in order that the oppressed may go free, and taste the sweets of gospel liberty.

There follow the names of the "witnesses"—the insurgent ministers. And the Last Will was probated in the court of final judgment.

In 1805 three men from the Shaker community in Canaan, New York, came to Kentucky with the message that the Shaker doctrine was the natural culmination of the Great Revival; within a year several Shaker communities had been established in Kentucky and Ohio. Two of the five ministers who had erected and destroyed the presbytery of Springfield joined the Shakers. Two others returned to the Presbyterian fold; one in time found his way, as did many who had received the "New Light" in the Great Revival, into the Christian Church. That church, its dynamics the constant study of the Scriptures and the endeavor to apply them as the rules of daily life, was itself a creation of the Great Revival—the outgrowth of the Christian Association of Washington, Pennsylvania, organized in 1807 by Thomas Campbell.

The Presbyterian sect suffered other losses as a consequence of the Revival. The Cumberland Presbyterian Church became a definitely independent body in 1810, recognizing the wreckage that had been made of the orthodox doctrine of predestination. In 1803 the National Assembly Reports of the condition of the church show thirty-one presbyteries and 322 ministers; in 1804 four presbyteries had been lost, and there were but 130 ministers.

The Methodist sect and the Baptist sect became the frontier religions. In the vernacular they have come to be known as such, rightly; in enthusiasm, emotionality, and procedure they took to themselves the color of the frontier; as the West demanded it, attitudes were shaped and the boundaries of religious feeling and religious activity were enlarged. In 1800 the Methodist churches in the West had reported about twenty-seven hundred communicants; in 1805 they reported twelve thousand. There were one hundred and six Baptist churches in Kentucky in 1800, with five thousand communicants; three years later the number had already increased to two hundred nineteen churches, with over fifteen thousand members.

The West's most distinctive contribution to religious procedure, the camp meeting, was taken up for all that it was worth by the Methodists; in 1811 Bishop Francis Asbury noted that "Our camp-meetings, I think, amount to between four hundred and five hundred annually, some of which continue for eight days. . . . Backsliders are restored, and the union of both preacher and people is greatly increased." Geniuses at revival preaching were ferreted out in theological schools and at ministers' annual conferences, and their abilities nurtured. Confession of sin, "coming forward" to be saved, the milling of a congregation's elect ones about the doubtful and repentant in their midst, the synchronous overlapping of exhortative phrases and hymn music, were written into both denominations, most emphatically into the Methodist sect. The camp meeting idea developed into several emotion-coddling forms, including the elaborate summer encampments of southern Baptists.

Itinerant Methodist ministers, "circuit riders," had traveled in the West beyond the Alleghenies since 1785. They preached in stockades and cabins, slept on straw or on buffalo skins wherever hospitality was offered them, rode through all sorts of weather from frontier post to frontier post, received sixty-four dollars a year, and later eighty (in either case the traveling preacher had to "find his own horse and fixin's"); under the direction of Francis Ashbury, most zealous of circuit riders, these itinerants of single purpose entrenched Methodism on the frontier. More, they had described a technique that was to expand as the West expanded, keeping militant protestantism—"frontier religion"—well abreast in the first waves of the westward movement. With the Great Revival, older denominations caught the infection, and followed after the Methodists in reclaiming the lost sheep of the frontier.

In 1800 interest in the far-flung frontiers of missionary work called forth the first publication of its kind, the *New York Missionary Magazine and Repository of Religious Intelligence,* seizing upon the moment to justify itself: "Were the present a period of ordinary aspect, perhaps there would not be so much reason to lament the want of such a channel of public intelligence a journal to transmit religious information. But it is far otherwise. . . . We learn from the most respectable and authentic sources that a spirit of awakening and sanctification is poured out from on high, in copious measures, in several parts of the United States—that the number of converts to the cross of Christ seems to be increasing—and that additions are daily making to the Church (in some instances from those who were lately her bitterest enemies), of such as there is reason to hope, in a judgment of charity, will be saved." Five years later the work was done: religion had banged its way into the West, and the West had banged its way into religion.

CHAPTER XIII

INSURRECTION: LITTLE, MIDDLE-SIZED, AND BIG

FRONTIERSMEN of the Juniata Valley felt it incumbent upon them to demonstrate the temper of the West. James Bryson, brigade inspector of the Pennsylvania militia, refused to commission two colonels elected by their regiments, and—as he had a legal right to do—appointed two men of his own selection. Soon, thereafter, the governor elevated him to a judgeship; and the militiamen resolved that he should not enjoy his office.

On the twelfth of September, 1791, court session at Lewistown was opened; and at David Jordan's tavern on the Narrows of the Juniata a mob gathered. Soon the three judges heard a fife and the firing of guns; the mob was marching upon the courthouse. The sheriff was seized; and the judges ordered John Clark, district attorney, to meet the rioters, remonstrate with them, and warn them of the revenging hand of the law. "But all endeavor was in vain," Clark related, "the mob was crying out, 'March on! draw your sword on him! ride over him!' I seized the reins of the bridle that the principal commander held, viz., William Wilson, brother of the sheriff aforesaid, who was well mounted and well dressed, with a sword, and, I think, two pistols belted around him; a cocked hat, and one or two feathers in it. He said he would not desist, but at all events, proceed and take Judge Bryson off the bench, and march him down to the Narrows, to the judge's farm, and make him sign a written paper that he would never sit there as a judge again."

Probably to the amazement of the rioters, the judges showed fight; one of them announced, most unjudgelike, "You damned rascals, come on; we will defend the court and ourselves; and before you shall take Judge Bryson you may kill me and many others, which seems to be your intention, and which you may do!" The mob withdrew, while its committee of three agreed to present a petition of their grievances to the legislature, on condition that until their petition was acted upon Bryson was not to exercise his judgeship.

But the fife was soon playing again, and the turbulent crowd surrounded the courthouse—too late; Judge Bryson had gone. The mob had documented its demands, and signed the sheet "The People." They presented it to John Clark; "they went off swearing, and said that they were outgeneralled."

On the next day the sheriff assaulted Judge Bryson. "Judge Armstrong seized the sheriff, and commanded the peace, and took the sheriff's rod from him; the coroner took his place, and the sheriff was brought up before the court. I moved he might be committed to gaol; and his mittimus being written and signed . . . he submitted. The court adjourned. After night the drum beat, and Holt collected about seventy men, who repeatedly huzzaed, crying out 'Liberty or death.'" The sheriff became penitent; and a mob of three hundred men that had gathered at the Narrows dispersed when they were told that the sheriff had been released on his own recognizance. John Clark wrote an account of the affair for the governor's information; and added an ominous footnote, "The excise law is execrated by the banditti; and, from every information, I expect the collection of the revenue will be opposed."

From the affairs of mankind, Mr. Alexander Hamilton had derived a small but select stock of maxims, one of which was, "The People is a great beast." And so it was—particularly in its kinship with a dignified beast of the frontier who had lifted his fangs above the phrase, "Don't tread on me." Resentment of an excise had figured in the late unpleasantness; the Congress of 1774 had tagged excise "the horror of all free states." The Secretary of the Treasury, nonetheless, recommended and obtained from the first national congress the enactment of a levy of from ten to twenty-five cents upon every gallon of domestic distilled liquor, and a correlative tax upon stills, graduated according to capacity. The People was a backwoodsman of western Pennsylvania, where a man's distillery was his castle. Since the People was a frontiersman, as yet unscrubbed and unruffed, the beast could still strike.

Excises upon whisky were not new in Pennsylvania. In 1756, as a part of the program to check the wastrels who were just cultivating a taste for luxuries, the provincial legislature had placed a tax upon imported spirits. In the dark years just preceding the Revolution the tax was revived, and extended to spirits distilled within the province beyond the amount the owner himself intended to use. This excise leapt at once into complete desuetude. Probably all that was distilled from domestic grain was assumed to be for the use of the owner; and in those years that assumption was fairly near the truth. The people of the sparsely settled West took their rye and malt to the still, and paid for the distillation in kind or in money—just such a domestic transaction as that which converted the wheat harvest into flour and brought it back to the farm. The troops at Fort

Pitt and the emigrants who, despite or because of the war, were scattering through the backwoods, accounted for the surplus of flour and whisky.

After the Revolution the increased settlement in the West augmented the surplus of whisky and flour, just as the army quartermasters with their great stacks of Continental currency, such currency as it was, departed. The natural highway to the market, the course that brought the waters of the Monongahela to the Gulf of Mexico, was sealed by the Spanish death grip at its mouth. The long pack trails to the East offered no profits to grain sellers; a pack horse could carry only four bushels.

And in every neighborhood in the four western counties of Pennsylvania there was soon a distillery. Every sixth man, probably, owned a still—not for profit, but as a necessity. His neighbors brought their grain to his still, and paid the owner for his work, or perhaps directed the alchemy themselves.

Each horse of a pack train could carry two eight-gallon kegs of whisky, worth about a dollar a gallon "on the other side of the mountains," and half that in the West; and the caravan returning brought some salt, worth five dollars a bushel in Pittsburgh, and a little iron, worth fifteen or twenty cents a pound in the little town at the forks of the Ohio that had not yet discovered its underground wealth.

As the Confederation stumbled into its last years, the states were seeking ways to ease the weight of their own debts. Pennsylvania was reminded of its excise on domestic spirits. One Graham, ex-tavern-keeper, obtained a commission for collecting the excise in all the western counties; and he set about making his fortune. He acknowledged to William Findley that his racket was rewarding his expectations.

When "protection" became a nuisance, the Westerners disposed of the collector. "At the court of Westmoreland,"

Findley recorded, "in the evening a man in disguise, supported by several others, called him to the door of his chamber, and attempted to pull him out, telling him that he was Beelzebub, and would deliver him to a number of other devils who waited for him without. But the collector being armed with pistols stood on his defence." A later assault upon his happiness, in Washington County, was successful in forcing the collector to resign his commission, but the horseplay had romped past decency, and the circuit court awarded him high damages against twelve of the mob whom he identified.

It must be remembered that state law, then national law, came to these Westerners as a new breeze from an unexpected quarter, and because the breeze was fresh to them, they recognized the taints. Every one in western Pennsylvania knew that the state law was not being enforced east of the mountains. And Hamilton's national whisky tax of 1791 had the taint of inequality. The duty, levied by quantity, was to be paid on the liquors before they were removed from the distilleries; but whisky in the West could not be sold for more than half the eastern price. It had the taint of officiousness: the law provided for the creation of inspection districts, with a host of petty officers whose duty was to examine all distilleries, the capacity of the stills, to gauge their barrels, brand their casks—to be, a defender of the insurrection put it, "spies on the industry of the people, and practically authorized at almost any moment to inflict domiciliary visits upon them, to make arbitrary seizures, and commit other vexatious acts." And the law had, it must be admitted, the foul smell of confiscation. That flavor was not intentional; its presence was simply one of several blunders of a government of planters and lawyers not too well informed of conditions in the backland, and no more altruistic than governments are wont to be. Furthermore, the revenue from the tax was to be used for objects dear to Federalists but gangrene in the West—for the redemption of Continental securities in the hands of speculators, toward "the unreasonable interest" of the public debt, and toward the payment of official salaries which seemed exorbitant to the small farmers of the back-land.

Meetings were held at Brownsville and at Washington, Pennsylvania, in 1791, and at Pittsburgh in August, 1792. The people in convention exercised the right of petition, and the inalienable right of passing a plethora of resolutions; they came no nearer unlawful resistance. But the vigor of this very youthful and very serious resolution, passed at the last of these meetings, prompts one to half expect the signature "Sons of Liberty":

"That whereas, Some men may be found among us, so far lost to every sense of virtue and all feeling for the distresses of their country as to accept the office of collector, therefore,

"*Resolved,* That in future we shall consider such persons as unworthy of our friendship, have no intercourse or dealing with them, withdraw from them every assistance, withhold all the comforts of life which depend on those duties that as men and fellow-citizens we owe to each other, and upon all occasions treat them with the contempt they deserve, and that it be, and is hereby most earnestly recommended to the people at large to hold the same line of conduct towards them."

Under cover, without the approval of the petitioners, without being known for certain in the communities which they disrupted, there were, of course, the boys who threw the tea into the harbor. In September, 1791, Robert Johnson, collector for Washington and Allegheny counties, was waylaid, tarred and feathered, his head shaved, and he was required not to show his face again in the mountains. Occasionally in the next three years there was a clandestine assault, an attack upon a collector or upon a distiller who had

[223]

paid his tax, a barn burned or a still dismantled—an outbreak no one knew anything about, nor could any one identify the participants. With the modification of the duties in 1792 and the government's concession that payments be monthly, the confiscatory features of the law had been removed. The demand for whisky for the supply of the army offered distillers a source of cash wherewith to meet the excise; and commissary officers induced respect for law and order by buying whisky only from distillers who complied with the law.

But, as on every occasion when the West flung off the thin rein of tradition and established "frontier law," ultimately the vigilance committee became the gang. "Tom the Tinker" was the figurehead, as mythical and as saintly as St. Golias; Tom presided over whisky and whisky stills. Under his signature rallying notices and threats were posted —such fanfare as this, from the *Pittsburgh Gazette* of August 31, 1794: "Four or five men below has scared a great many, but few is killed yet, but I hope none of those are any that ever pretended to be a friend to Poor Tom, as I would have all my friends keep up their spirits and stand to their integrity for their rights and liberty, and you will find Poor Tom to be your friend. This is fair warning."

In December, 1793, the collectors published in each of the five counties public notice that suits were to be brought and seizures made against those who did not enter their stills in the tax lists. And in due time the federal marshal was in western Pennsylvania with a bulky bag of warrants. On his way into Pittsburgh he served thirty-nine writs; there was a fortieth, which stayed in the marshal's bag that day. On the day following, the fifteenth of July, 1794, he returned to the outskirts of the town to serve that warrant; with him was General John Neville, chief inspector of the western district of Pennsylvania. Neville had been in the state legislature when the law was passed. In the Brackenridge view (and the Brackenridges represent ably the attitude of the protesting farmers), "His acceptance of an odious office, merely for the sake of the emolument, as it was believed, when he was already the wealthiest man in the West, had not only deprived him of his former popularity, but rendered him an object of hatred." Some one fired a shot, not intended, most likely, to hit Neville, because it did not—and these backwoodsmen could strike off the head of a squirrel almost at pleasure—but fired to see the squirrel scamper. And the warrant was not served that evening.

That was the shot heard 'round southwest Pennsylvania. General Neville, once "the People's Candidate," was piloting the marshal to the People's door; and more important than personal resentment was the fact that the warrants demanded appearance at Philadelphia. The expense of the slow journey across the mountains was burdensome enough without the inevitable fine. The slightest breath of precept was enough. The Tom-the-Tinkers were busy overnight. In the morning there was a pitched battle about Neville's house, and five or six of the insurgents were wounded. Neville's house and its outbuildings were burned.

David Bradford, loudest and most lawless of the insurgents, made the grave mistake of robbing the mails; in the packet from Pittsburgh he found what he wanted, letters from prominent people denouncing the late outrages, letters that could be used to inflame the backwoods folk against their overlords. Heading a self-created junto, he sent out a call to the officers of the militia in the western counties: "Having had suspicions that the Pittsburgh post would carry with him the sentiments of some of the people in the country, respecting our present situation; and the letters of the post being now in our possession, *by which certain secrets are discovered,* hostile to our interests, it is, therefore, now come to that crisis, that every citizen must express his sentiments, not by his words, but by his actions. You are then called upon as a citizen of the western country, to render your personal service, with as many volunteers as you can raise, to rendezvous at . . . Braddock's Field, on the Monongahela, on Friday, the first day of August next 1794, to be there at two o'clock in the afternoon, with arms and accouterments in good order. If any volunteers shall want arms and ammunition, bring them forward, and they shall be supplied as well as possible."

There seems to have been no well-defined intention beyond presenting a formidable front, a pathetic faith in a show of force. Pittsburghians adroitly saved themselves from any rioting the city might have suffered because it harbored conservative, propertied citizens who had no patience with the insurrectionists, by resolving in town meeting "that the inhabitants of the town shall march out and join the people on Braddock's Field, as brethren, to carry into effect with them any measure that may seem to them advisable for the common cause." And the offensive conservatives were persuaded to absent themselves.

It was a curious assemblage that moiled about Braddock's Field that Friday: David Bradford, power-drunk Demos, in the full martial trappings of a major-general, with plumes and sword; battalions of western Pennsylvanians, on the field because, having once adopted violence, they were in the forlorn position of being committed to violence; the two hundred and fifty militiamen from Pittsburgh, and a committee· of unarmed citizens. There were in all about six thousand men on the field.

Hugh Henry Brackenridge was there: "The ground where Braddock fought is on the east side of the Monongahela, and on the same side with the town of Pittsburgh. The militia from Washington County had therefore to cross the river in order to come upon the ground. They had crossed in great numbers, at the same ford where Braddock did, and were now on the ground. They were dressed in what we call hunting shirts, many of them with handkerchiefs on their heads; it is in this dress they equip themselves against the Indians. They were amusing themselves with shooting with balls at marks, and firing in the air at random with powder only. There was a continual discharge of guns, and constant smoke in the woods and along the bank of the river. There appeared great wantonness of mind, and a disposition to do anything extravagant." Every man was afraid of the opinions of the others, Brackenridge soon ferreted; but he could not guess how many were there from choice, how many from fear of being thought too spineless to defend their cause. Certainly, the dangerous vehemence and the expansive sentiments that democrats had learned from the French Revolution were generally in evidence.

The next morning Bradford held open court, reading the irritating letters, demanding some sort of reprisal against the younger Neville, Major Butler, Neville Craig, and three letter-writers. "The people came out to do something, and something they must do": insurgency got no nearer a program of action. They decided upon marching through Pittsburgh. While the hotheads who had assembled the mob were fumbling for words, Brackenridge put in the order of the day: "We will just march through, and making a turn come out on the Monongahela bank, and taking a little whisky with the inhabitants of the town, the troops will embark and cross the river." So, half drunk and half amiable, the mob left Pittsburgh.

A few days had elapsed when a group with unsatisfied energies burned the residence of the revenue collector for Fayette and Westmoreland counties, and compelled him to resign his commission. Liberty poles were raised everywhere in the western valleys, with brave inscriptions—"An equal tax, and no excise," "United we stand, divided we fall"—and a device that had seen a better cause, a snake divided. The general impression seemed to be that the excise laws had been suspended by the will of the people; in other respects, there was no disregard of the authority of the local magistrates.

Edmund Randolph, Secretary of State, wrote to the President: "A radical and universal dissatisfaction with the excise pervades the four transmontane counties of Pennsylvania, having more than sixty-three thousand souls in the whole. . . . Several counties of Virginia, having a strong militia, participate in these feelings." He was excited over rumors that British aid had been offered the insurgent counties. He italicized for Washington's attention: *"There is another enemy in the heart of the Southern States, who would not sleep with such an opportunity of advantage.* It is a fact well known, that the parties in the United States are highly inflamed against each other; and that there is but one character who keeps them both in awe. As soon as the sword shall be drawn, who shall be able to restrain them?" And the Secretary's advice that every power of conciliation and judicial persuasion be first used before the military power should be invoked, fell upon acquiescent ears.

State and federal commissioners hastened toward Pittsburgh while delegates from each turbulent township, meeting at Parkinson's Ferry on the Monongahela, appointed a committee to meet them. Frontiersmen could not simulate the "perfect and entire acquiescence" that the commissioners demanded as the price of amnesty; the oath which the commissioners demanded of every man in the insurgent counties—"I do solemnly promise henceforth to submit to the laws of the United States; that I will not, directly nor indirectly, oppose the execution of the acts for raising a revenue on distilled spirits and stills; and that I will support, as far as the law requires, the civil authority in affording the protection due to all officers and other citizens"—people were reluctant to sign. The word "solemnly" distressed Presbyterians, as equivalent to bringing God into the affair; "henceforth" was an insult to conscientious persons: the commissioners in consequence gave notice in the *Pittsburgh Gazette,* the only newspaper in western Pennsylvania, that those words might be omitted, but copies of the *Gazette* reached few of the backwoods districts before September eleventh, the day set for the avowals of submission. Most men believed that the signing of the oath would involve some sort of dangerous confession. Many settlers, having had nothing to do with the turbulence, took offense at the idea of being called upon to sign a paper of submission.

"Out of about forty different places of meeting," wrote William Findley, to whom Alexander Hamilton attempted to assign a Jack Cade's part in the insurrection, "at only two of them were the papers destroyed by a desperate banditti. . . . At one place in Allegheny county, the signing was prevented by violence, or terror, where it was the interest of many to subscribe; at a few other places the subscribing was accomplished with difficulty. Nevertheless, those who had been deeply engaged in the excesses, signed, with the exception of a few of the most ignorant and obstinate. There were some, indeed, who had dared to engage in the greatest outrages, who had not courage to subscribe from fear of their own safety, lest they should be considered as deserters."

Late in September the inhabitants of Pittsburgh, in town meeting, unanimously resolved that the men whose letters Bradford had seized "were unjustly expelled, and the said proscriptions are no longer regarded by the inhabitants of Pittsburgh, and that this resolution be published for the purpose of communicating these sentiments to those who were the subjects of the said proscriptions." The district

courts were opened, and the civil authority met no resistance. Indictments were made out against a group who
had insulted Washington's commissioners by raising a liberty
pole in front of their lodgings in Pittsburgh. Sheriff Hamilton, of Washington County, offered with twenty men to
arrest any man or set of men in the western counties for
whom the district court issued summonses. The Whisky
Rebellion was already moribund, a dying cause, when on
the twenty-fifth of September the President declared a
state of insurrection to exist, and fifteen thousand militiamen made ready to march into western Pennsylvania.

Jackson's Battle of New Orleans was not the only folly
that bad communication between West and East made possible. If there had been a Baltimore & Ohio in 1794, or
even a Cumberland Road, the guardians of the nation would
have had later information than the report of the baffled
and indignant peace commissioners, a report of the western
temper as unfriendly observers found it on the eleventh of
September, submitted to Washington on the twenty-fourth.

It was a thwarted army that was sent into the West with
no ragged backwoodsmen in battle line to shoot at, no
summary examples of the folly of resistance to leave
pendant from tree limbs. There was nothing for it to do,
except by its glowering to support that curious judiciary
composed of the Secretary of the Treasury, military officers,
and civil authorities.

During the night of November the thirteenth, some three
hundred arrests were made; it was the "Dreadful Night"
that made western Pennsylvania safe for the Democrats.
Taken into Pittsburgh by squads of soldiers who made the
most of this rare opportunity to be offensive, most were
kept a few days, in barns or in whatever jails could be im-
provised, then examined and discharged. The government
discovered that its prosecutions were not worth pursuing.

There happened to be a Whisky Rebellion in western

Pennsylvania not simply because of the whisky excise and the issuing of warrants returnable across the mountains at Philadelphia, but because the common stock of discontent throughout the West needed only a local spark to kindle a local flame. A committee of three Westerners, Edward Cook, Albert Gallatin, and Hugh Henry Brackenridge, had met the state and federal commissioners with a documentation of the grievances of the four rioting counties, and they had a great deal to say of other matters than excises and judicial districts: decisions of the state courts which set aside squatters' "improvement rights" in favor of paper titles; laxity of the government in driving back the Indians, and too frequent calls for militia service to repel Indian incursions that the army should have prevented; failure to force the British from their western posts; the apparent indifference of the government to the free navigation of the Mississippi. "The forcible opposition which had been made to the law," the committee protested, "was produced by the pressure of grievances, and not by hostility to the government; but if there was any prospect of redress, no people would more readily show themselves good citizens, and cease their opposition to the obnoxious measures of government."

For three years after the Treaty of 1783 the frontiersmen of the Old Southwest were almost nationalists: liberty, equality, the vocabulary of republicanism, they used honestly and optimistically, and sought to have their western regions brought into the federation of states upon terms of full equality. The rights of mankind seemed to impel them to a separation from their parent states, Virginia and North Carolina; the Confederation of the United States was an honorable body, and the sum of dignity was to have full-fledged representatives in its Congress. But in August, 1786, that same Congress passed a secret resolution authorizing a treaty with Spain that would, if Spain demanded the concession, close the Mississippi to American shipping for twenty years. By December this secret resolution was common knowledge throughout Kentucky, and soon the autonomy of which pioneers were talking was not autonomous membership in a confederation.

The far-western counties of Virginia joined in a remonstrance to the Virginia assembly, which the clerk summarized: "Their prosperity must principally depend on the navigation of this river the Mississippi . . . it will be impossible for their products to find a market through any other channel; this project, therefore, presents to them the melancholy prospect of ruin to themselves and families. . . . With the same process might Congress barter away their right to the trial by jury, or aliene a county, or a state, for advantages in trade, as occlude the Mississippi. . . . Never have they before heard of a project being proposed —much less a treaty formed—which shut the door of commerce to one part of the community, and deprived it of its natural rights, for the benefit of the other."

This treaty, which would have given the seaboard states privilege in Spanish trade as a reward for recognizing a Spanish monopoly in Mississippi navigation, was frightened into death by the thunder from the West. John Jay, in charge of foreign affairs, hesitated in his negotiations with Don Diego de Gardoqui, representative of Spain; paused when alarming fictions reached him that George Rogers Clark was about to descend the Mississippi with a great army to drive the Spaniards from Louisiana; and on April 12, 1787, he reported to Congress: "From the temper visible in some of the papers sent from the western country, as well as from the intelligence they convey, your secretary apprehends that the period is not far distant when the United States must decide either to wage war with Spain, or settle all differences with her by treaty, on the best terms in their power." He had unloaded upon Congress the full responsibility of choosing between a commercial treaty with Spain and the likelihood of war with Spain; conscientious to that tradition of inefficiency by which it was to be remembered in schoolbooks, the Congress of the Confederation chose to neglect the issue.

General James Wilkinson, bankrupt after the Revolutionary War, but pretending to be "the leader of a large commercial company in Philadelphia," was fully embarked in his audacious career on the western border. Those accounts of Clark's mythical army which frightened Jay into dropping his treaty negotiations were of Wilkinson's invention, designed to remove Clark from the many-forked road of his ambitions. Playing upon the Spaniards' fear that American frontiersmen would invade Louisiana, he induced Governor Miro at New Orleans to permit him, and him alone of all the Americans, to bring wheat and other back-country produce down the Mississippi to the Spanish markets; in return he was to use his influence in Kentucky in behalf of Spain, and to send to the Spanish authorities secret advices of insurgent tendencies in the West.

From 1786 to 1796 there were portentous undercurrents of separatism in Kentucky and Tennessee. The Spanish-controlled Mississippi seemed to Westerners to offer the only cheap means of transporting their produce, a matter of increasing importance as thousands of emigrants annually took up virgin farm lands; and merchants were eager to cultivate trade with Spain, especially because in those days of uncertain currency Spanish milled dollars were highly prized: but political dependence upon Spain was never the western idea. Even Wilkinson, protesting over and over again his own devotion to Spain, warned Governor Miro that the Kentucky separatists would not tolerate a proposal to come into the Spanish Empire, and that the best Spain could hope for would be an alliance with the independent nation of Kentucky.

[233]

In a convention of Kentuckians in July, 1788, Wilkinson and two other Kentuckians of high standing, Harry Innes and Benjamin Sebastian, openly urged the convention, it seems, to declare Kentucky independent of the United States. But the convention decided to await the hopeful reconstruction of the federal government, trusting that the experiment of the Constitution might vindicate the proud syllables of republicanism. Indications that the new government intended to respect and protect the interests of the West were soon evident, and prospects of an independent Kentucky dwindled away.

The truth was that the Federalist government was anxious to placate every possible friend, New York financier or Kentucky frontiersman. Thomas Jefferson's appointment as Secretary of State was assuring to the West, for frontiersmen were almost as much indoctrinated in philosophical democracy as was Jefferson, and he had taken the lead in opposing Jay's recommendation that Spain be allowed exclusive navigation of the Mississippi. Alexander Hamilton, for all that he represented their creditors, let the Westerners know that he regarded American shipping on the Mississippi as indispensable to national prosperity. William Blount, land speculator, a man of influence among the frontiersmen, was appointed Governor of the Southwest Territory and superintendent of Indian affairs in the South; John Sevier and James Robertson were appointed brigadier generals under him. Wilkinson had been promoted to brigadier generalship by March, 1792; Sebastian was appointed United States attorney-general and Henry Innes, district judge for Kentucky. To the delight of frontiersmen, preparations were made for an active campaign against the intransigeant Indians north of the Ohio; and tribes in the Southwest were forced into new land cessions.

But until the Louisiana Purchase removed the threat of interference by foreign nations with the passage of American commerce down the Mississippi, and that river was bordered throughout its length by American domain, the intrigues of Wilkinson and a few other money-hungry Kentuckians followed devious underground paths. Their greatest importance lay in the dribbles from the Spanish treasury into the pockets of these men who raised the wolf cry of a frontiersmen's invasion of Louisiana. After the Purchase, Aaron Burr's hegira was an anticlimax of these intrigues; and that—as every student of Texas history knows—was by no means the last of the unchartable story of frontiersmen's "understandings" with the Spanish Empire. What Burr intended when in 1806-1807 he led his flotilla of musketed followers down the Mississippi, many historians have attempted to explain. When Fortescue Cuming stopped at an inn in western Pennsylvania, "Col. Burr's present situation and intentions were discussed, when our host gave it as his decided opinion, that he had secured the friendship and assistance of a warlike and powerful nation of Indians, inhabiting a country on the banks of the Missouri about 1500 miles in circumference, where is the celebrated mountain of salt. That they fought on horseback and were armed with short Spanish carabines; and that with their aid he meant to conquer Mexico, and erect an empire independent of both Spaniards and Americans." That is probably as good an explanation as any.

CHAPTER XIV

DOWN THE O-HI-O

FORT DUQUESNE was put to the torch on November 23, 1758, and the French troops took to their canoes. The British army arrived at the Forks of the Ohio to find that victory was already theirs. Colonel Henry Bouquet and a small company were assigned to remain; beside the ashes of the French stockade Fort Pitt came into existence. On Thanksgiving Day Bouquet wrote to a friend in Philadelphia that he needed "A Number of Cows and Bulls, Mares and Stallions, Garden seeds, etc. every moment is precious and the Land so rich, and the pastures so abundant that everything would thrive and the Garrison would be able to support itself." The Indian traders quickly made this post their headquarters; and pioneers took up lands about the stockade, to furnish the garrison and the traders with grain, vegetables, and beef. In 1760 Pittsburgh, exclusive of the garrison, had a population of one hundred fifty. Within another year the population had almost doubled. There were taverns, sawmills, kilns and tanyards; traders, farmers, and stockmen shared the streets and the bars with inebriated Indians.

Colonel George Croghan, the greatest of the Pennsylvania traders, was the leading citizen of infant Pittsburgh. He owned extensive tracts of land in the vicinity, which he had bought from the Indians in 1749; he was too im-

portant a man for the military authorities to remind him
that such private purchases were unlawful. Along the
Allegheny River just northeast of Fort Pitt he built a house
and trading buildings. In an Indian foray in 1763, the
year of Pontiac's Conspiracy, these houses were burned.
Croghan built his new residence on a nobler plan, named
it Croghan Hall, and kept a luxurious establishment with
several servants. Colonial travelers and Indian chiefs were
entertained here; missionaries from the East brought letters
of introduction to Croghan, and had cause to thank him for
much practical assistance. He was deputy superintendent
of Indian relations under Sir William Johnson, an appointment culminating years of invaluable service as Indian agent
for the Pennsylvania proprietors.

After the general uprising of the Indian tribes in 1763,
the little settlement about Fort Pitt was only partially rebuilt. The uncertainties of Indian relations and the difficulties between Virginia and Pennsylvania over title to the
Forks of the Ohio delayed the advancement of the town.
Its fortress, however, was one of the posts slated for aban-
donment, in the gradual reduction of the British army in the
West. There were no echoes of Indian alarums in western
Pennsylvania in the autumn of 1772; and the commandant
of Fort Pitt marched his men away. In Pittsburgh there
was consternation; and a petition was sent to Governor Penn
urging that the troops be retained. General Gage, commander-in-chief of the British forces in America, answered
the retailed petition: "No government can undertake to
erect forts for the advantage of forty or fifty people."

Nor was Pittsburgh much of a town. George Washington, on the way to his landholdings farther west, had visited
the settlement two years earlier: "We lodged in what is
called the town, distant about three hundred yards from
the Fort, at one Mr. Semple's, who keeps a very good house
of public entertainment. . . . These houses, which are built

of logs, and ranged into streets, are on the Monongahela and I suppose may be about twenty in number, and inhabited by Indian traders, etc."

The beginning of civil government for Pittsburgh and western Pennsylvania was the appointment in 1771, by Governor Penn, of four magistrates for Westmoreland County, which then included almost all of western Pennsylvania. But—in the dispute over colony boundaries—Virginia militia, then Pennsylvania troops again, restrained the progress of civil government and civil affairs; and the War of the Revolution emphasized that as yet Pittsburgh was characteristically a military post.

After the Revolution, interest in western expansion looked past Pittsburgh, toward the wilderness of the Northwest Territory; and it was as a commercial point, a way station where emigrants must stop, that Pittsburgh began its substantial progress. "The people here do not become rich through industry and frugal habits," wrote a disgruntled traveler; "they prefer to replenish their houses by extorting money from strangers and travellers."

The paper beginning of settlement on the neglected fork of the Ohio, the Allegheny, was in 1783, when an act of the general assembly of Pennsylvania reserved a tract of three thousand acres "opposite Pittsburgh" to provide for the redemption of the certificates issued to the officers and soldiers of the Pennsylvania line, and to fulfill the state's promise to donate lands to its soldiers; but the land was not laid out in lots until 1788. In January of 1784 the Penns, who had been allowed to retain title to the "manor" of Pittsburgh despite the Revolution, sold to Isaac Craig and Stephen Bayard the ground, about three acres, from Fort Pitt to the Allegheny and Grant's Hill. This estate was surveyed into a townsite that same year. Even before the lots were laid out on paper, the proprietors were making deeds to eager purchasers. Craig and Bayard themselves carried on a mercantile business, set up a distillery, and erected a sawmill up the Allegheny.

Arthur Lee, Virginian, in Pittsburgh in 1784, noticed that the town was making use of its great resources of coal, but found no hints that Pittsburgh was to be the first metropolis of the West. "The town," he wrote, "is inhabited almost entirely by Scots and Irish, who live in paltry log houses, and are as dirty as in the north of Ireland, or even Scotland. There is a great deal of small trade carried on, the goods being brought at the vast expense of forty-five shillings per cwt. from Philadelphia and Baltimore. They take in the shops, money, wheat, flour and skins. There are in the town four attorneys, two doctors and not a priest of any persuasion, nor church, nor chapel; so that they are likely to be damned without the *benefit of clergy.*"

First brick-making for the local military works, then boat-building for the traders, had pushed Pittsburgh upon its industrial career. By 1786 the population of the town was approaching five hundred; and John Scull and Joseph Hall, on the twenty-ninth of July, published the first number of the *Pittsburgh Gazette,* the first newspaper west of the Allegheny Mountains. Curiously, this little four-page pioneer sheet was a supporter of Washington and the Federalist party; it stumbled its uneven way, printed sometimes on cartridge paper borrowed from the garrison, often plaintively appealing for the payment of subscriptions ("in cash or produce"); and ultimately it prospered.

The *Gazette* did yeoman service in advertising Pittsburgh and the West. In its first summer there appeared a series of "Observations on the Country at the Head of the Ohio River, with Digressions on Various Subjects," by Hugh Henry Brackenridge, lawyer in Pittsburgh since 1781. "Of mechanics and laborers there is still a great want," he made known; "masons and carpenters are especially wanted,

indeed from this circumstance the improvement of the town
and buildings is greatly retarded. This town in future
time will be a place of great manufactory. Indeed the
greatest on the continent, or perhaps in the world. The
present carriage from Philadelphia is six pence for each
pound weight and however improved the conveyance may
be, and by whatever channel, yet such is our distance from
either of the oceans that the importation of heavy articles
will still be expensive. The manufacturing them will therefore become more an object here than elsewhere."

Abreast with the Ordinance of 1787, Pittsburgh discovered its responsibilities as gateway of the West. Its first
regular mail communication was established, by postrider
to Alexandria, Virginia, "weekly from May first to November first, and once a fortnight the remainder of the
year"; a market house was erected; and by act of the state
assembly the Pittsburgh Academy reached the chrysalis
of incorporation. In 1791 the courthouse of Allegheny
County was definitely located at Pittsburgh.

At the end of the thirty-four years, from 1758 to 1792,
that Pittsburgh had been under English and American control, there were "130 families" and "36 Mechanics" in the
town, by an account of August, 1792: "1 Clock and Watch
Maker, 2 Coopers, 1 Skin Dresser and Breeches Maker,
2 Tanners and Curriers, 4 Cabinet Makers, 2 Hatters,
2 Weavers, 5 Blacksmiths, 5 Shoemakers, 3 Saddlers, 1
Maltster and Brewer, 2 Tinners, 3 Wheelwrights, 1 Stock-
ing-weaver, 1 Ropemaker, 2 Whitesmiths." (A whitesmith
is one who finishes and polishes ironwork; the iron, be it
noticed, was bar iron transported from the eastern side of
the mountains.) There were, besides, boat-builders, brick-
makers, vintners, distillers, and hat-manufacturers. The
barrier of mountains to the east of Pittsburgh demanded
the beginnings of diverse manufactures. By the close of
the century Pittsburgh was the focus of seven wagon roads,

such as they were; but freight rates on the goods brought from the east by pack horses or by Conestoga wagons were still five or six dollars for a hundred pounds.

In November, 1790, the first iron-ore furnace in western Pennsylvania began operation—the Alliance Iron Works, on Jacob's Creek of the Youghiogheny River. Thereafter, from the Alliance works and others that soon were established in the neighboring counties, Pittsburgh was supplied with quantities of iron—bar iron, kettles, dutch ovens—that had not the burden of the high transporting charges.

With all Pittsburgh's advantages, natural and acquired, the town grew rapidly, and in the spring of 1794 was duly incorporated as a borough; "whereas," the Act of Assembly read, "it may contribute to the advantage of the Inhabitants of the said town as also to those who trade and Resort there, and to the Public utility that nuisances, encroachments of all sorts, contentions, annoyances and inconveniences in the said town should be prevented, and for promoting rule, order and government in the said town."

By this year post offices had been established at several towns on the Ohio; and since an overland post still took the chance of Indian dangers, a line of mail boats was established from Wheeling, whither postriders brought the mail from Pittsburgh. Regular communication by water with Cincinnati was inaugurated, also in 1794; soon passengers could depart weekly from Cincinnati upon well-cannoned boats with bullet-proof cabins.

In 1796 General James O'Hara (who supplied Pittsburgh with salt, brought five hundred miles from Onondaga, trans-shipped from wagons to boats, to wagons and boats again) and Major Isaac Craig persuaded a skilled glassworker to leave Philadelphia and take charge of the erection and operation of a glass manufactory in Pittsburgh. Green glass was being made in 1797. "To-day," reads a memorandum of the General's, "we made the first bottle at a cost of $30,000." In 1800 a second glass works was erected near Pittsburgh; and thereafter the industry multiplied and prospered.

Boat building prospered, too. In 1797 Congress, fearful of French influence in the lower Mississippi, ordered two vessels to be built in Pittsburgh. Ships, brigs, and schooners were built in great number following the establishment of the shipyards of Tarascon Brothers, James Berthoud and Company, in 1800. In 1798 the city held a lottery to raise $12,000 for the building of piers to protect the banks of the Allegheny and the Monongahela from the encroachments of the currents. Flatboats, barges, keelboats—carpenters were busy men.

There were some sixteen hundred residents in 1800. The city had its waterworks and its fire engine. In 1802 the burgesses ordained "That foot ways of brick, stone or gravel, bounded by curb stones, or by squared pieces of timber, shall be made." Judge Brackenridge established the second newspaper of Pittsburgh, *The Tree of Liberty,* fire-eating, democratic. Mail came twice a week now. Manufacturing increased, new industries were established. "The merchants, manufacturers and citizens of Western Pennsylvania and Virginia turned their earnest attention to building up trade with the west and south," writes the city's historian, Miss Killikelly. "The aim of the Western Pennsylvanian of this period was to make Pittsburgh the manufacturing and trade center of all the great west, to make it independent of the east as far as possible."

In 1804 the first iron foundry in Pittsburgh was partly finished; the first textile factory was established, largely by public subscription; and Pittsburgh's first banking house, a branch of the Bank of Pennsylvania, was opened. On the Fourth of July a regular line of stages, on a weekly-departure schedule, brought Pittsburgh and Philadelphia together.

Let two or three merchants of bustling Pittsburgh in 1805 cry their wares:

JAMES ADAMS has lately opened in the house formerly occupied by Mr. William Steel, corner of Market Street in the Diamond. A NEW and SELECT ASSORTMENT OF Fashionable Split Straw and Leghorn BONNETS, Laced and Cambrick Muslins, Laced Muslin Shawls, Cambric and Common Dimities, Cotton Cassimeres, A variety of Chintzes and Cassimers, Cloths, Coatings— Callicoes, IRISH LINENS, and Swansdowns, Madeira and Sherry Wines, Fourth proof Cogniac Brandy, Jamaica Spirits, Holland Gin, Tannets' Oil, A quantity of old Whiskey by the Barrel or Gallon. All of which he intends selling on the lowest terms, for cash or country produce.

NOTICE. THE SUBSCRIBER takes the liberty to inform the public, that he has commenced the manufacture of WHITE, BROWN and PERFUMED SOAP, in partnership with a person from England, which they will sell at Philadelphia prices—the quality inferior to none heretofore brought to this place, and where country stores, and gentlemen descending the Ohio can be supplied at the shortest notice. NATHANIEL RICHARDSON.

Now preparing for the Press, THE PITTSBURGH MAGAZINE ALMANACK For 1806, With which, as well as common ones, merchants may depend on getting a supply. German Almanacks also may be had. Orders handed in early will prevent disappointments. Zadok Cramer hopes the friends to the publication of Brown's Dictionary of the Bible, and Anderson against Bellamy, are using their exertions in obtaining subscriptions for said works. Catalogues of Books and Stationary will shortly be published.

West from the hills of Pittsburgh the transparent waters of the Allegheny softened the yellow, muddy stream from the southeast: westward flowed the Ohio River, highway to the distant wilderness.

In the spring season, from the breaking-up of the ice in mid-February to the midsummer subsidence of the waters, and in the fall season, from October to the advent of win-

ter, multitudes of water craft bore emigrants and trade
stuffs to the West. The current of the Ohio was a kindly
guide. Zadok Cramer, Pittsburgh printer and crony of
boatmen, advised: "Much exertion with the oars is . . .
generally speaking of no manner of use; indeed it is rather
detrimental than otherwise, as such exertion frequently
throws you out of the current which you ought to continue
in, as it will carry you along with more rapidity, and at
the same time always takes you right. By trusting to the
current there is no danger to be feared in passing the
islands as it will carry you past them in safety. On the
other hand, if you row, and by so doing happen to be in
the middle of the river when approaching an island, there
is great danger of being thrown on the upper point of it
before you are aware, or have time to regain the current."

Each year hundreds of newly built flatboats made their
one-way journey down the Ohio. They were the standard
craft of westward-bound emigrants; like them, the flatboats never came back. These boats were built of green
oak plank fastened by wooden pins to a frame of timber,
and calked with tow. Never less than twenty feet long
and ten feet in width, its timber hull rose three or four
feet above the surface of the river, an oaken fort to skim
past Indian dangers. The average flatboat was about forty
feet long, with six oars. "New Orleans" flatboats were
the strongest, and were entirely roofed over; "Kentucky"
flatboats, which swung to final bank somewhere on the
Ohio, were not so well finished.

The barges, the common craft of burden on the river,
were huge, pointed hulks carrying forty or fifty tons of
freight, and manned by a large crew. They descended with
the current, accelerated by a wide sail or by the toiling of
four of the crew at the long oars; they returned, upstream,
at a crawling pace, as men with bulging muscles pushed iron-
tipped poles or occasionally used towropes from the shore.

Down the river went an endless variety of freight and provisions; barges that went to New Orleans fought their way back with sugar and molasses.

In 1792, Tarascon, Berthoud and Company, Pittsburgh shipwrights, introduced the use of keelboats on the Ohio; and these now-forgotten craft brought the rich interior lands of the Ohio Valley into communication with Pittsburgh and the newer commercial towns upon the great river. Keelboats were long and narrow, and carried a mast and sails. On either side of the cabin, running boards extended from pointed prow to pointed stern. Along its bottom ran a four-inch timber, to meet the shock of a collision with a snag or some other submerged obstruction. One steersman and two men at the broad sweeps could navigate the craft downstream. Six or ten men besides the steersman must work to force the keelboat upstream: the crew, divided equally on larboard and starboard, "set" their poles at the head of the boat; then, pushing the boat forward, they trod the running boards until the stern was almost under their feet; and at the command of the captain-steersman, they ran quickly to the prow, to "set" and push again.

As pioneer settlements spread up the tributaries of the Ohio, these keelboats, which could ply even in the low water of midsummer, carried their imports and exports.

Arks, galleys, pirogues, ferry-flats, many a sailing vessel, plied the highway into the New West; and truculently original emigrants added to the variety of craft with strange boats of their own devising. Fortescue Cuming, following the Ohio in 1808, encountered a memorable curiosity: "A keel of forty tons came to the landing at the same time we did. She was worked by a horizontal wheel, kept in motion by six horses going round in a circle on a galley above the boat, by which are turned two cog wheels fixed each to an axle which projects over both gunwales of the boat. Eight paddles are fixed on the projecting side of each axle, which impel the boat about five or six miles an hour, so that she can be forced against the current about twenty miles a day. One Brookfield, the owner, who conducts the boat, had her built last year about two miles above Louisville . . . and then went in her to New Orleans, from whence he was now returning, disposing of a cargo of sugar from place to place in his ascent."

The Ohio packet boat was the most ambitious development of the keelboat era. It was from seventy-five to a hundred feet long, and fifteen or twenty feet wide; it had a crew of many polemen, and had a sail or two. A separate cabin was partitioned off for ladies; passengers could be supplied with provisions and liquors of a high quality; the packet services attained even the dignity of a time-table. On a swift packet boat a traveler could go from Pittsburgh to Cincinnati and back again in a month.

To most emigrants navigation on such a broad stream as the Ohio was a new experience. Goods and families had been brought by wagon and by pack horse to the river bank, at Pittsburgh or at one of the five thriving little towns below Pittsburgh on the Monongahela. Here the head of the party could buy a flatboat, or perhaps, outside the towns, make one; but not every landlubber had the confidence to assume command in this unfamiliar travel. He could buy Zadok Cramer's *Navigator,* the handbook of the river pilots; he could arrange to travel with other flatboats, as one of a fleet; often, for his lone flatboat or for a fleet, he sought an experienced navigator. As emigrants' pilot or as freighter, there developed in these pre-steamboat days on the Ohio the professional boatman, "half horse, half alligator" by his own boast. He was vain of his acquaintance with every vagary of the river, vain of his toughness, reckless and belligerent—as vain, and as skilled in his way, as the steamboat pilots of a later day, whose condescension extended to everything but the Mississippi.

Travelers gaped at the iridescent vocabulary, the rich jargon, of these huskies. "You hear of the danger of 'riffles,' meaning, probably, 'ripples,' " Timothy Flint jotted down, "and planters, and sawyers, and points, and bends, and shoots, a corruption, I suppose, of the French 'chute.' You hear the boatmen extolling their prowess in pushing a pole, and you learn the received opinion, that a 'Kentuck' is the best man at a pole, and a Frenchman at the oar. A firm push of the iron-pointed pole on a fixed log, is termed a 'reverend' set. You are told when you embark, to bring your 'plunder' aboard, and you hear about moving 'ferninst' the stream; and you gradually become acquainted with a copious vocabulary of this sort." And the costumes of the boatmen were as characteristic as their argot—nearly always a bright red flannel shirt covered by a loose blue jerkin, and coarse brown trousers of linsey-woolsey.

The work of the riverman was in turn very indolent and very laborious. On the days of indolence, when the current of the river carried his burden, the boatman's dark-tanned face was taciturn, mobile only as he shifted his tobacco-quid; in the moment of hazard that would certainly come, when the current swerved against an island or when a snag announced its ugly presence, his wits and his muscles moved instantaneously; and after the tumult the boatman subsided into his lethargy. The voyage upstream was a different matter, a relentless contest of muscle against current.

Sufficient danger, plenty of whisky, loud words and fists —the life of a boatman was the ambition of youngsters along the river who, working in their fathers' clearings, heard the blatting invitation of the boat horns day after day. Boatmen could spit marvelously, and wagered on their abilities at hitting a knot hole or a fly. There was a fiddle or two aboard every flatboat; fiddle music and whisky went naturally together. There were songs that lingered over the water as the boatmen sat their poles:

Hi-O, away we go,
Floating down the river on the O-hi-o.

When the boatman goes on shore
He spends his money and works for more,
I never saw a girl in all my life,
But what she would be a boatman's wife.

Hi-O, away we go,
Floating down the river on the O-hi-o.

The Paul Bunyan of the boatmen was Mike Fink, who passed quickly from history into legend. He was an arch-rowdy, tough, brutal; superb with his gun, always drinking but never drunk—the swaggering cock that every boatman would have liked to be.

Banditry and river piracy added an uglier color to the panorama of the keelboat era. At Cave-In-Rock, on the northern bank of the lower Ohio, Samuel Mason in 1797 established an inn, whose promise of rest and drink decoyed travelers into a den of shrouded crime. Somewhere on the banks of the river a passing boat heard the hail of a man or a woman, an offer to buy some necessity or a hail for passage; the boat that turned in was seized by a gang of robbers who had been hidden in the brush. A boat was scuttled or wrecked in a surprise attack; boarders appropriated the goods and killed the crew. Many boats loaded with valuable cargoes that left port on the upper Ohio under the guidance of experienced, trustworthy officers were disposed of, with cargo, by different crews; and the officers and crews to whom the boats had been entrusted never returned. In 1794 a packet company whose boats plied between Pittsburgh and Cincinnati pointedly advertised this advantage of its boats: "A large crew, skilful in the use of arms, a plentiful supply of muskets and ammunition, an equipment on each boat of six one-pound cannon, and a loop-hole, rifle-proof cabin for passengers."

[248]

The river pirates, hunted out by volunteer posses, were first to disappear as the day of the keelboat came to its close. The onrush of emigration into the Ohio Valley, which began to be reckoned in thousands in 1788, had been carried to western homes by the clumsy flatboats; other timbered craft, for all their creeping pace, had borne the commerce of the valley.

But in 1811 Cramer's *Navigator* announced a portentous thing: "There is now on foot a new mode of navigating our western waters, particularly on the Ohio and Mississippi rivers. This is with boats propelled by the power of steam. . . . A Mr. Rosewalt, a gentleman of enterprise, and who is acting it is said in conjunction with Messrs. Fulton and Livingston of New York, has a boat of this kind now on the stocks at Pittsburgh, of 138 feet keel, calculated for 300 or 400 tons burden. And there is one building at Frankfort, Kentucky, by citizens who no doubt will push the enterprise. It will be a novel sight, and as pleasing as novel to see a huge boat working her way up the windings of the Ohio, without the appearance of sail, oar, pole, or any manual labor about her—moving within the secrets of her own wonderful mechanism, and propelled by power undiscoverable!"

For the next fifteen years flatboats and keelboats remained the dominant craft. As these years passed, the contest became vicious, boatmen against roustabout and barge against steamboat, the steersman's bugle against the steam whistle. The crews of keelboats and barges had to learn that fact which experience thrust upon the packhorse drivers, then upon the wagon teamsters, then upon the towboat men: that the West could not be prevented from growing up.

PART IV
THE GREATER WEST

Warehouse and its quay besides
Teemed with furs and raw cowhides,
Grain from the tilled land, zinc from the fallow,
Lumber, herbs, and buffalo-tallow,
Wild-bee wax and wild-bee honey,
Western tender for eastern money.

—A. E. TROMBLY

CHAPTER XV

THE GREAT PURCHASE

JAMES WILKINSON, having closed his private bargain with Governor Miro, stowed great quantities of flour, bacon, tobacco, butter, and hams on his flatboats beside the Louisville quays; early in January, 1789, with the Kentucky colors flying on each boat, the flotilla cast off to follow the current to New Orleans. This parade of Ohio Valley produce launched in its logical channel—logical until railroads should transcend the mountain barrier to the east—spurred Kentuckians and certain statesmen to the conclusion that the Mississippi must be kept open for western commerce. Thomas Jefferson, then Secretary of State, wrote to the American *Chargé d'affaires* at the Spanish court: "It is impossible to answer for the forbearance of our western citizens. We endeavor to quiet them with an expectation of an attainment of their ends by peaceable means. But should they, in a moment of impatience, hazard others, there is no saying how far we may be led; for neither themselves nor their rights will ever be abandoned by us." In December, 1791, a Spanish commissioner intimated to Jefferson that his Catholic Majesty might be willing to make some arrangement.

President Washington was favorable; and on January 11, 1792, the American representatives at Madrid and at Paris were authorized to negotiate "with any person or persons who shall be duly authorized by his Catholic Majesty, a convention or treaty concerning the navigation of the river Mississippi by the citizens of the United States." William Carmichael and William Short presented their special credentials to the court at Madrid; they were faced by a skilled veteran, Don Diego de Gardoqui, who was more than their match. (Chess provides the proper metaphors for this diplomatic game: it was tedious, procrastinating, and, as Gardoqui intended it should, ended in checkmate.)

Meanwhile every Ohio River packet which ventured into the Mississippi with goods for an Atlantic port, was sure—if it escaped confiscation—to be stopped at New Madrid, boarded and searched, and the captain compelled to purchase a pass to continue down the river to New Orleans. At the capital the entire cargo had to be unloaded, and a duty paid of 15 per cent of the value. Thereupon the goods had to be reloaded, and suffer an export tax of an additional 6 per cent. Westerners first threatened the Spaniards, indignation at the restrictions on their commerce being coupled with democratic fervor to gouge the eyes out of the reactionary enemies of the French Republic; when that excitement passed, Westerners addressed the national government, but in their demands was still the undertone of a threat. Washington nominated Thomas Pinckney, of South Carolina, envoy extraordinary to Spain, with instructions to make every possible effort for a favorable settlement of navigation rights.

When Carmichael and Short were at Madrid, Spain was openly hostile to the French Republic and in amiable cooperation with England. Two years later, when Pinckney arrived at Madrid, Spain had come out much the worse in the war with the French Republic, and the alliance with England had become intensely unpopular. In July, 1795, Don Manuel Godoy, prime minister of Spain, suddenly broke off both the war and the alliance. He was acclaimed by his delighted countrymen. The rôle of "Prince of Peace" therefore pleased him, and Pinckney's arrival gave him an opportunity for an encore number. He was dilatory, and kept Pinckney in prolonged suspense; but all that was according to the rules of the higher diplomacy. When the American commissioner demanded his passports, Godoy dropped his evasive tactics; the result was the drafting of the treaty of San Lorenzo del Real. The northern boundary of Florida was fixed, extending westward along the thirty-first parallel. While both banks of the Mississippi below that parallel were, therefore, confirmed as Spanish domain, "His Catholic Majesty has likewise agreed that the navigation of the said river, in its whole breadth, from its source to the ocean, shall be free only to his subjects and the citizens of the United States." For the next three years, 1795 to 1798, American citizens were free to use New Orleans as a port and place of deposit, with no other charge than the usual warehouse fees. This treaty was so acceptable that the United States Senate ratified it with hardly a quibble.

By the summer of 1800 the First Consul of the French Republic was well started on his road to imperial supremacy. Ministers were despatched to Madrid to negotiate for the recovery of Louisiana. The inducement to the Spanish royal pair was a promise of an increase of their daughter's titles and dominions, the addition of a territory containing no fewer than one million inhabitants to the Italian duchy of Parma, ruled by his Catholic Majesty's son-in-law. The Emperor's conscience was disturbed: these gains of Italian territory would be at the expense of the Pope. But he yielded to his wife's entreaties, and assented to the trade. In the secret treaty of San Ildefonso, signed on the first of October, Louisiana was returned to France. Spain was to retain actual possession until the promised increase of Parma should actually be realized. Florida was, or was not, included in the cession; that obscurity remained to vex the relations of Spain and the United States long after the possession of Louisiana had been permanently settled.

Rumors of this secret treaty filtered into the United States in the spring and summer of 1801. President Jefferson was alarmed; he asked Dupont de Nemours, just returning to France, to use his influence with Napoleon to prevent a French attempt to possess Louisiana, and he unburdened himself to Robert R. Livingston: "France, placing herself in that door [the mouth of the Mississippi], assumes to us the attitude of defiance. Spain might have retained it quietly for years. Her pacific dispositions, her feeble state, would induce her to increase our facilities there, so that her possession of the place would hardly be felt by us, and it would not, perhaps, be very long before some circumstance might arise which might make the cession of it to us the price of something of more worth to her. Not so can it ever be in the hands of France. . . . They, as well as we, must be blind if they cannot see this; and we must be very improvident if we do not begin to make arrangements on that hypothesis."

Apparently convinced that Napoleon's continental difficulties would stay the French from taking possession of Louisiana, the Spanish intendant at New Orleans, on October 16, 1802, set about the reëstablishing of Spanish exclusiveness: he declared the right of Americans to use New Orleans as a port of deposit, on which nothing had been said since the Treaty of San Lorenzo, at an end. Again that undertone of threats from the West; James Monroe, just retired from the governorship of Virginia, was drafted by Jefferson as the best man for the emergency, and was bidden godspeed to Paris.

His instructions were to purchase New Orleans and

Florida. The resident minister in Paris, Robert R. Livingston, might just as well have been instructed to make overtures; but the sending of a special minister provided obvious evidence to Westerners that the Democratic-Republican party was working in their interest. The issue of free navigation of the Mississippi was highly important in partisan politics. On February 15, 1803, a Federalist senator, Ross of Pennsylvania, introduced a resolution requiring the President to take immediate possession of New Orleans by an armed force; and Monroe, on the eve of his departure for Europe, wrote to Jefferson: "The resolutions of M^r. Ross prove that the federal party will stick at nothing to embarrass the adm^n. and recover its lost power. They nevertheless produce a great effect on the publick mind and I presume more especially in the western country. . . . If the negotiation secures all the objects sought, or a deposit with the sovereignty over it, the federalists will be overwhelmed completely." And so they were.

On April 19, 1803, Jefferson was informed that the Emperor of Spain had repudiated the order of his intendant at New Orleans, and that the right of American shippers to use the port was forthwith restored. But the President and his advisers expected that within a year or two Napoleon would take possession of Louisiana, and did not interrupt the negotiations at Paris.

Napoleon's plans of an American empire had been rudely jolted by the revolt of the natives in Santo Domingo. Within a year fifty thousand French soldiers had perished on that island. To abandon the project without making it evident that defeat forced the move, Napoleon diverted the world's attention: four days after Monroe had departed from New York, the First Consul thundered to the British ambassador that he "must either have Malta or war," and both France and England began promptly to prepare for a renewal of the struggle. In view of his greater undertaking,

Napoleon seems to have reasoned, Louisiana could be disposed of without his losing prestige; retained by France, the province was easy spoil for the British navy.

Monroe and Livingston were staggered by the suggestion that the United States buy the whole of Louisiana; Monroe's instructions had contemplated at most the purchase of Louisiana and Florida. But there was no time to apprise Jefferson and await his further orders; the two commissioners accepted the sudden responsibility. The treaty of cession was signed on the second of May.

The news of the purchase reached the United States on the thirtieth of June. When only the purchase of New Orleans and the Floridas had been contemplated, Jefferson had debated the problem of authority. The Constitution nowhere authorized the national government to acquire territory by purchase; and Jefferson was theoretically bound to a strict interpretation of the Constitution. But when the treaty was at hand, including a clause demanding its official ratification by a certain date, Jefferson realized that there was no time for the laborious process of settling this constitutional nicety. He wrote to John Breckenridge: "The less we say about constitutional difficulties respecting Louisiana, the better. . . . What is necessary for surmounting them must be done *sub silentio.*" The theorist had become as much an opportunist as any frontiersman. Federalists wrangled; but the Senate ratified the treaty, and the House joined it in appropriating the purchase sum of eighty million francs.

With that Purchase the fundamental spirit—opportunism, energy, expansion, conscious virtue and conscious strength—of the frontier became a fundamental influence on the national government; and thereafter, until the close of the Spanish-American War ushered in a new era, Washington was in the shadow of the West.

Napoleon had definite ideas upon the moot subject of the

boundaries of Louisiana, and his written explanation was in Talleyrand's desk when Monroe asked the French minister of foreign affairs a question—just what were the boundaries? Talleyrand answered that he did not know: "I can give you no direction; you have made a noble bargain for yourselves, and I suppose you will make the most of it." The treaty begged the question, referring back to the cession of Louisiana to France in 1800; but the treaty of San Ildefonso had simply transferred "the Colony or Province of Louisiana, with the same extent it now has in the hands of Spain, and that it had when France possessed it." Don Manuel Godoy had been able to withhold the Floridas from the final treaty of San Ildefonso, so that obviously the Floridas were not included. It was commonly understood that Louisiana extended northward to the source of the Mississippi, but no one knew the location of the source. Whether or not lower Louisiana extended to the Rio Grande, including Texas, was a matter for argument; the view that the proper western limit was the Sabine was most tenable.

In 1803 the population of Louisiana—exclusive, of course, of the Indians—was somewhat more than fifty thousand. Three-fourths of the number were below the line of the thirty-third parallel. Along that parallel the province was divided, by act of Congress in March, 1804. The great expanse of territory above that line was attached to Indian Territory, and in 1805 made a separate territory. The area south of the line, under the name of the District of Orleans, was left in the hands of William C. C. Claiborne, who had been appointed to govern the whole of Louisiana when the United States took possession. Pierre Clement Laussat, who had formally surrendered Louisiana in the name of France, scored off Claiborne not very unfairly: "Estimable qualities as a private man, but possessing little intellect, a good deal of awkwardness, and being

[259]

extremely beneath the position in which he was placed." In him were vested all the powers of the Spanish officials whom he replaced; he was charged with the duty of enforcing laws which he could not even read, and local regulations in New Orleans which were thoroughly inconsistent with his own political training. Feeling between Creoles and Americans ran high. The governor's private secretary was killed in one of the many duels on the streets of New Orleans.

On the first of June, 1804, a mass meeting at New Orleans was invoked by the merchants, with the aid of the sugar planters of the vicinity. The convention decided to petition Congress for the immediate admission of Louisiana, with its original boundaries, as a state in the Union. The territorial government launched in October, whereby the governor was to divide his duties with an appointed council, was no salve: four of the original appointees flatly refused to serve. Early in January the petition of the "Merchants, Planters, and Other Inhabitants of Louisiana" was read to the senate. Its main contention was for the early carrying-out of the promise in the treaty that the inhabitants of the ceded territory were to be incorporated into the Union. "What right do we enjoy, what immunity can we boast, except, indeed, the degrading exemption from the cares of legislation and the burden of public affairs?"

The outcome of several weeks' debate was an act, on March 2, 1805, providing for the establishing of a government in the Territory of Orleans similar in all respects to the territorial government of Mississippi—a bicameral legislature, the lower house elected by the people. As soon as the free population should reach sixty thousand, the people were authorized to form a constitution and a state government.

Jefferson's appetite for information was voracious and unlimited. He had a lively interest in scientific attainment, both in data-gathering and law-deducting; and, for reasons which that intricate, far-reaching mind never permitted to be expressed, he had a keen interest in the fur trade. These interests united upon one thing: an expedition up the Missouri and into the far West, to describe the topography and the resources of the little-known expanse, and to report upon the endeavors of other nations to capitalize these resources. With Jefferson in the presidency, there would have been a Lewis and Clark expedition if there had been no Louisiana Purchase.

Meriwether Lewis, captain in the United States Army and private secretary to the President, was ready to begin his traversal of the West before Louisiana was officially transferred to American sovereignty. His second in command was William Clark, brother of the frontiersman who had led the back-country volunteers against the British posts in the Ohio Valley. Jefferson's instructions directed a search for a route across the continent, observations of the topography, of the Indians—everything about them that could be gleaned—records of the flora and fauna of the Great West. It was typical of the philosopher-statesman who was responsible for the expedition that there was not one genuine scientist in the party.

The *Compania de descubridores del Misuri* ("Company of the Explorers of the Missouri") had been organized at St. Louis in October, 1793, for the exploitation of the fur trade, and for objects more grandiose. As a member of the company reported the intentions of Zenon Trudeau, its promoter, "His purpose was, at the same time, to enlighten the age, in regard to that portion of the globe, as yet so little known. To this effect he required that in pursuing this trade, those engaged in it would pay attention to unite to employees they might send to the country, enlightened persons, who would use every exertion to penetrate to the sources of the Missouri, and beyond, if possible, to the Indian Ocean." In 1794 the company despatched a trading

[261]

expedition to the Mandan Indians, near the Great Bend of the Missouri; but Juan Baptista Truteau and his ten companions were waylaid by the Sioux, forced to sacrifice the greater part of their goods as presents, and did not go further up the Missouri. An expedition up the river in the next year was pillaged by the Ponca Indians.

James Mackay, a Scotchman who had become a Spanish subject, and John Evans, a Welsh adventurer, were hired to direct subsequent trading enterprises of the company with the Indians of the upper Missouri. Evans went upstream to the Mandan villages, and even beyond. Mackay was a busy Indian agent for the Spanish capitalists, distributing presents and making promises, hoping to estrange the Indians of the upper Missouri Valley from the British traders with whom they dealt. The transfer of Louisiana ended the contest between Spanish and British fur-trading companies almost before it had begun. But the result of these enterprises was, in the hands of Lewis and Clark, a journal kept by Truteau of one of his expeditions up the Missouri; a map of the river as far as the Mandan villages, made by John Evans; and a map made by James Mackay. Jefferson himself secured and sent to Lewis the Truteau journal and the Evans map. Lewis and Clark had examined the meager available literature of French exploration of the Northwest. Fragmentary and dubious French records; the information set down by the Spanish expeditions, which extended no farther than the Mandan villages—with these for their full stock of foreknowledge, Lewis and Clark, with three boats and forty-two men, began the journey up the Missouri in the late spring of 1804.

Late in October, having taken five and a half months for the arduous ascent, the three boats reached the Mandan villages. Here the company passed the winter, in stockades of their own building. Agents of the North-West Company and other British traders came and went from the

Mandan towns; Lewis had ample opportunity to learn the ramifications of the fur trade, and to observe the amicable relations between British and Indians that sprang out of this commerce.

In April, 1805, the party again took up its line of travel. Following the westward course of the Missouri through the wilderness to the final rill of the headwaters, the expedition crossed the Great Divide, leaving Louisiana to penetrate a country that four nations claimed and none occupied. The Shoshone Indians of the region had never before seen white men. The Indians throughout the journey had been amiable; the Sioux tribes whom the explorers knew were dangerous had been avoided, and the other Indian nations had shared their food with the expedition and lent interpreters. The resources of the company were exhausted as they began the descent of the Snake River into Oregon; but from the Indians they secured food enough—roots, dried salmon, horse meat, dog meat, and fish—to keep them alive. On the seventh of November, sweeping down the Columbia, they came in sight of the Pacific Ocean.

After a winter among the pine groves the adventurers began the return journey, seeking out new ways in their zeal for knowledge. Below the mouth of the Yellowstone the separate parties were united. At St. Louis in September, 1806, the expedition was broken up; and five months later the assiduous chroniclers who had led the company were in Washington. The documents they had to show Jefferson, a voluminous record of informal narrative, things observed and information gleaned from Indian hosts, were the record of the opening wedge of the American frontiersmen's conquest of the Great West. And, glittering with the personalities of the men who wrote them, these records have a yet unappreciated importance as American folk-literature.

In August, 1805, Lieutenant Zebulon Montgomery Pike

was despatched on an expedition to the sources of the Mississippi—an exploration that had long been necessary, for the treaties delineating the British-American boundary line, in tracing the line west of the Great Lakes, had solemnly given legality to geographical absurdities. Pike's exploration was completed with his return to St. Louis at the close of the next April. In mid-July he began a second exploration, a foray across the wilderness toward Santa Fe. The intent of this march is yet inscrutable; extensive researches have uncovered contradictions without resolving them. Pike, Wilkinson, Jefferson—one of these, two, or all three, had devious intentions that Pike's official instructions and the surviving records of the expedition do not reveal.

On a May evening in 1806, General James Wilkinson was talking with his friend, Joseph Daviess, about Pike's exploring expedition up the Mississippi. The general's thoughts seemed rambling on a tangent; he took out a manuscript map of New Mexico, tapped it with his finger, and, said Daviess, "told me in a low and very significant tone and manner, that had Burr been president, we would have had all this country before now." In the previous spring Jefferson had given General Wilkinson verbal permission to make a general exploration of the borders of Louisiana. When Pike had returned from his expedition up the Mississippi, Wilkinson's official instructions were that he should escort a group of Indians to their homes in the Osage and Pawnee villages, and then to proceed to the headwaters of the Arkansas and the Red rivers. Jefferson, late in life, wrote Wilkinson, asking—either to refresh his memory or gain a written admission—if Pike's expedition had not been "an exploration for reconnoitering the Indian and Spanish positions which might be within striking distance." The general's answer was verbose, elegant, and noncommittal.

In July, 1807, after Pike had returned from his quixotic

journey, Judge Timothy Kirby of Missouri made affidavit:
"I also had a conversation with Genl. Wilkinson concerning
Lt. Pikes Expedition to the westward which was nearly as
follows: a few Days previous to the departure of Lt. Pike
I asked the Genl. what was the object of the expedition
and where Mr Pike was going. he smiled and said it was
of a *secret nature* . . . that Lt. Pike was yet ignorant of
the nature of his journey . . . that his route would be by
Land from the Osage Towns in order to treat with several
Nations of Indians by which he would pass. I asked the
Genl. if Mr. Pike was sent by the Government of the
United States. he replied no that it was his own (the Genl.)
Plan and if Mr. Pike succeeded he the Genl. would be
placed out of the reach of his enemies and that in the course
of eighteen months he would be in a situation (if the plan
suckseeded) to call his Damnd foes to an a/c account for
their Deeds."

Lieutenant Pike's party of some twenty soldiers and fifty
Indians began the overland journey, apparently without a
guide and without information—certainly with no equipment to meet the hardships that lay ahead. Spanish agents
in Missouri had sped the word southward; and Spanish
troops were on the march to intercept the American
expedition.

After delivering his Indian charges at their native villages, Pike pushed forward to locate the headwaters of the
Red River. Winter caught the party unprotected by adequate clothing or blankets. The expedition blundered
about the headwaters of the Arkansas, then followed the
valleys southward. Pike had built a stockade on the west
bank of the Rio Grande when there arrived fifty dragoons
and fifty militia, under command of Don Ignaçio Salleto.
Pike's arrest for trespassing on Spanish soil was a delightfully courteous affair; and the governor at Santa Fe was
equally delicate—but he was determined upon securing all

of Pike's papers to send to headquarters at Chihuahua. The papers were confiscated; and Pike and his troops were sent under guard to headquarters for a final judgment. General Nemesio Salcedo spoke of the invasion as "an offense of magnitude," but decided to return the Americans to their own country. By way of San Antonio and Natchitoches the bedraggled company was returned. Pike had lost his records; and the exploration had become an unwritten footnote to a greater puzzle, the history of Aaron Burr.

The news of the purchase of Louisiana was yet fresh when Jefferson forwarded questions about maps and boundaries to William Dunbar, the most noted scientist of the Mississippi Valley; to Daniel Clark, American consul at New Orleans; and to William Claiborne. The information he received was meager and fragmentary, much of it at variance with his own studies; and he determined upon as thorough an exploration of the new frontier as he could arrange. To Meriwether Lewis he wrote, "The object of your mission is single, the direct water communication from sea to sea formed by the bed of the Missouri and perhaps the Oregon"; he planned other explorations to trace the lesser rivers that flow from the west into the Mississippi.

Force of circumstance restricted the great expanse of wilderness which Jefferson wished explored to the Red and Ouachita rivers. In this limited area, about the Louisiana-Texas boundary, William Dunbar, George Hunter, John Sibley, and Thomas Freeman were in turn assigned the task of garnering information. Dunbar and Hunter, at first intending to go as far into the West as the headwaters of the Arkansas, were balked by news of hostile Indians and by the probability that the Spaniards would stop the expedition; in the late fall of 1804 they approached the Texas-Louisiana boundary by way of the Ouachita River. This exploration was hardly through wilderness, but through a cosmopolitan frontier—Indians, French-Canadian settlers,

Spanish and French Creole families, a smattering of American, German, and Irish frontiersmen. Settlement did not extend to the upper courses of the river, but here were hunters' lodges used by Indians and whites in the autumn kill. The reports of this expedition, together with the data gathered by John Sibley, the Indian agent at Natchitoches, gave the national administration its first satisfactory picture of the southern portion of the new Purchase.

Jefferson was prompted to signalize his second term in the presidency by a farther westward exploration. He secured an appropriation adequate to send an expedition into the foothills of the Rockies; but Dunbar concluded not to accept this second invitation, and as sixth choice one Thomas Freeman, astronomer, was selected as the official leader. Months were required to secure scientists in other subjects to accompany the expedition: when scientists were bred in the library, it was hard to find gentlemen who combined the requisite knowledge with the physical stamina for frontier exploration.

Jefferson suggested that William Claiborne, now governor of Orleans Territory, write the Spanish boundary commissioners to secure a passport for the expedition—offering to include a Spanish representaive or two in the party, by way of proving its exclusively scientific nature.

The Marquis of Casa Calvo, who had acted as one of the commissioners for Spain in its transfer of Louisiana to France, had remained in New Orleans in his other capacity as commissioner to mark the limits between Spanish-owned Texas and the domain of the United States. He was a keen watchdog of Spanish interests, a diplomatist in the classic mold. As early as June, 1804, he had written the governor of Texas that he had definite information of Jefferson's intention to send an expedition up the Red River, and had urged immediate measures to hinder or destroy any such expedition; to the Spanish minister of state for foreign affairs he had written much the same thing, with the added recommendation that the progress of Captain "Lewis Merry Whether" up the Missouri be blocked.

When in 1805 Governor Claiborne approached him with a request for a passport for Freeman's expedition, Casa Calvo could not deny the request without, probably, cutting off his stay at New Orleans; but he was convinced that the apparent scientific nature of the expedition was sheer pretext cloaking Jefferson's land-grabbing rapacity. Captain-General Salcedo in Chihuahua, to whom Casa Calvo wrote immediately, agreed with him: this proposed exploration of the Red River, and that of "Mr. Merri" up the Missouri, were in truth attempts to gain military knowledge of the country and to tamper with the allegiance of the Indians. Both these Spaniards in reading Jefferson's intentions were more nearly right than wrong.

Early in January, 1806, Governor Claiborne received an administrative order to require the immediate departure of all Spanish officers still at New Orleans. Casa Calvo left in high resentment; the passport given by him to the expedition lost its value with his departure, and the order of ejection excited the resentment of all the Spanish frontier officials of the vicinity. The governor of Texas ordered a military force to the frontier to intercept Freeman's expedition; and Captain-General Salcedo ordered out a second force from New Mexico, to intercept the expedition if it should slip by the first line of troops.

Meanwhile the long-delayed expedition up the Red River was setting out. Borne in two flat-bottomed barges and a pirogue, the party made its course, rowing and pushing, through the matted drift-brush of the river. On June 7, 1806, the explorers were encamped at the most remote white settlement on the river, forty-five miles above Natchitoches. On the next day an Indian runner despatched by John Sibley, the Indian agent, overtook them with the news that a Spanish force had set out from the Texas outpost of Nacogdoches to intercept them. But they kept ahead. The "Great Raft," a tangle of fallen logs, brush, mud, and swamp land, reticulated by bayous, creeks, and small lakes, delayed them for fourteen days before they were again on the undivided channel of the river. No boat, Indian canoe or French pirogue had penetrated that morass for fifty years.

About twenty miles of up-river travel after they had re-entered the channel brought the explorers to the village of the Coashutta tribe. Freeman was deferential and formal, and a good speech-maker. Among the presents to the Coashutta chief and to the chief of the Caddo village near by were American flags.

On the twenty-sixth of July three Indian runners from the Caddo chief caught up with the expedition: Spanish troops had entered their village, cut down the American flag, and threatened to kill the Americans if they refused to turn back. Freeman had his instructions—to proceed until stopped by a superior force. And the expedition continued its westward course.

Two days later Freeman encountered the overwhelmingly superior force mentioned in his instructions. The Spanish camp overlooked the river; there was no answer but to turn back. Moreover, the low stage of the water promised that not much farther up the river the boats would have had to be abandoned. And the expedition began the retreat. The result to Jefferson was a bitter disappointment; Freeman's distance of six hundred miles up the Red River was barely as far as actual French occupation had extended, and what-ever prestige he had built up with the Indians was offset by the fact of his retreat. Not for thirteen years was another formal expedition sent into any part of Louisiana. But the march of pioneers has never waited upon formal expeditions to precede it.

When in 1808 Napoleon's invasion of Spain brought about the fall of the Spanish monarchy, revolution seethed throughout the Spanish-American colonies. The flame spread to West Florida, where the population was a gallimaufry of Spaniards, Englishmen, and Americans—an unruly frontier, uncertain whether it wanted an independent government, a provisional government in the name of the deposed king of Spain, or annexation to the United States. In the excitement of the summer of 1810 a declaration of independence was issued, a standing army raised, a lone-star flag adopted, and a constitution adopted. An American was president of this volatile republic. The Spanish fort at Baton Rouge was stormed and captured; and the elated republicans formally declared West Florida free and independent, and authorized President John Rhea to treat with that other president, Thomas Jefferson, for the annexation of West Florida to the United States.

Jefferson and his cabinet accepted Rhea's terms: that the province be added to the Territory of Orleans, retaining full possession of its public lands, and receiving a loan of one hundred thousand dollars. Claiborne was ordered to put into effect the presidential proclamation ushering West Florida into American domain; and before the end of the year all of the country west of the Pearl River was organized into civil districts. East of the Pearl River the country remained a renegades' haven, with no governmental organization to oppose the confusion.

Meanwhile, the current of the westward movement had made the Territory of Orleans more homogeneous and more American. The capital city bravely and beautifully resisted the invasion of American settlers, with no little success; but that was a contest of morals and manners, and did not affect the numerical victory of the pioneer. In the session of 1810-1811 the question of state government for the Territory was before Congress. Federalists made a last stand:

the independence of the old states would soon be lost, their control of the government would become a thing of the past, they would be completely overbalanced by the new commonwealths of the West. But the enabling act was passed without difficulty. The name of Louisiana was given to the new state, which was to include the Territory of Orleans and the organized districts of West Florida. The territory north of the thirty-third parallel was henceforth to be known as the Territory of Missouri. On April 30, 1812, Louisiana became a state.

CHAPTER XVI

THE INSATIABLE PIONEER

THE government's land policy was a failure. Resting squarely on the Confederation's Ordinance of 1785 in its provisions for surveying and sale, it required the purchaser of six hundred forty acres, the minimum amount offered, to pay one-twentieth of the price in cash, allowing a credit of thirty days on half the balance, and a year's credit on the remainder. By the time the last payment was due—and the government was prompt to oust settlers in default, confiscating the first payments—the land had not begun to be productive; forty acres, at the utmost, could have been cleared. Less than fifty thousand acres were sold between 1796 and 1800. Home seekers who could have chanced the two dollars an acre, the minimum price for public lands, complained that conspiracy of speculators blocked them from the sales. But even speculators in collusion could not push the price of western lands much above the two-dollar price. The anticipated flow of gold into the national treasury from the land sales had turned out to be, as metallurgists say, a trace. Then William Henry Harrison stalked into Congress.

He was a Virginian, whose father was a plantation owner in the tidewater region. The young man had joined the army when he was nineteen, had served under Wayne in the Indian campaign; a political position kept him in the Northwest Territory, and in 1799 the first territorial legislature elected him delegate to the national Congress. He had become, thoroughly, a frontiersman; and that meant, among other things, a heavy-footed earnestness in the straightforward path of direct action. He took the oath as delegate on December 2, 1799; on the twenty-fourth of the same month he introduced a resolution "that a committee be appointed to inquire . . . what alterations are necessary in the laws authorizing the sale of the lands of the United States northwest of the Ohio." Harrison was chairman of the resultant committee; and three months later a frontiersman's conception of a land law was before the House.

By the land act of 1800, signed by the President on the tenth of May, lands were to be sold in half-sections (three hundred and twenty acres) at local offices in the West. For the first three weeks after the tracts of a district were offered for sale, the half-sections were to be put on auction; thereafter the unsold tracts could be bought at private sale, on credit extending four years or more. At the time of filing his claim the purchaser paid the survey fee of three dollars, and a deposit of ten cents an acre; no other down payment was required. A very little stock of money, a large stock of optimism: these were all that the government asked of the pioneer.

In February, 1803, Ohio came into the Union, with a constitution rabidly democratic, carrying forward the back-country distrust of executive and judiciary that had re-written the constitutions of the older states in the Revolutionary era. In the political theory of the frontier, the legislature was the bulwark of the people's rights; this view maintained itself until 1824, when in response to the personal strength of Andrew Jackson frontier philosophy swung to the idea of a powerful executive to protect the people against the legislature. The governor of Ohio was given no veto nor appointing power; the supreme justices were to be elected by the legislature meeting in general assembly for seven-year terms, "if so long they behave well." The liberality of the franchise, too, is a measure of the frontier's advance from colonial precedent. If a man were on the tax books of county or state, he was a qualified voter; it was not required even that he pay his tax. And the lengthy bill of rights in the constitution began with a confident revision of the Declaration's phrase into "All men are born equally free and independent."

By 1810 the area of settled lands in Ohio was a thick crescent following the Pennsylvania border and the Ohio River, extending well toward the center of the state. The western end of this thick band of settlement overlapped well into Indiana Territory. The census of 1810 revealed a population of 230,760; Indiana had almost twenty-five thousand inhabitants, and Illinois, its French Canadian population swamped by accessions of Kentuckians, had 12,282. The boundaries of Indiana had been reduced to an approximation of their final shape, and separate territorial governments in Michigan and Illinois administered the remaining parts of the old Northwest Territory. Kentuckians and Carolinians from the South and Southeast, New Englanders coming into the Western Reserve and pushing farther toward the northwestern part of the state: these two currents of immigration, nearly always distinct, each keeping its own bounds, pushed into Indian domain. Harrison, now governor of Indiana Territory, steadily pressed upon the Indians for further land cessions. That was the conventional technic of officially beginning the extension of the frontier; but frontiersmen who understood the velocity of that incessant current sweeping them westward meditated a grand coup. In 1812 they were given their opportunity.

The War of 1812 viewed as a "fight for a free sea" is lush in heroics and utterly lacking in plausibility. Henry Adams spiked that pose: "A nation which had submitted to robbery and violence in 1805, in 1809, could not readily lash itself into rage in 1811 when it had no new grievance to allege." The seaboard merchants of New England and New York denied that the war was of their seeking, and were vigorously insistent that the hostilities would mean their economic ruin. Protection of American maritime commerce and protection of American seamen liable to be impressed into British service, ostensible causes of the war, could not have maintained the West in belligerent furor; and it was the West that most hotly desired and supported the War of 1812.

From 1792 to 1816 the electoral vote of the frontier states was multiplied by six, while the electoral vote of the original thirteen states was increased by only one-third. In 1800 the political allegiance of the frontier had been clean-cut, obvious: Jefferson and democracy; and a black-ball for the conservative, aristocratic opposition. But by 1810 the Federalist party had slipped far back in national politics, and political allegiances were not nearly as incisive as in the old days of two-party conflict. If the successors of Jefferson in national control wished to retain power, it was proper that they should listen to the increasingly important West.

Nor were unusually sharp ears necessary. Henry Clay of Kentucky, in the Senate because no one remembered that the constitution prescribed a minimum age for senators, was the spokesman of western self-confidence in 1810: "I trust I shall not be deemed presumptuous when I state that I verily believe that the militia of Kentucky are alone com-

petent to place Montreal and Upper Canada at your feet."
No war in 1810! Clay was outdone and unreconciled:
"When the regular troops of this House . . . are inactive
at their posts, it becomes the duty of the raw militia to step
forth in defense of the honor and independence of the
country."

The conquest of Canada was, unmistakably, a hope of
the West. Vistas of boundless Canadian lands ("agrarian
cupidity," fumed John Randolph), and prospects of ousting
Canadians and British from their highly profitable fur
trade, excited many an ambitious frontiersman. But, although pioneers mistrusted the prairie and much preferred
forested or partly forested land, there were great stretches
of such lands in the Ohio Valley that pioneers had not yet
taken up by 1812. To open up the northern parts of Ohio
and Indiana, to give a sense of security to every settlement
in the Old Northwest: these ambitions looked forward to
the conquest of Canada and the end of British support to
hostile Indians. In the far South, Americans felt the same
greed and the same uneasiness: Florida was owned by
Spain, an ally of England: and the conquest of this territory, giving the southern frontier security and an open
course of expansion, was looked upon as a certain fruit of
war with England.

In 1809 national commissioners met chiefs of four tribes
of the upper Wabash region; title to three million acres
of the best land in the territory of Indiana was relinquished
to the United States. On the crest of Indian opposition
to that treaty Tecumseh, Shawnee chief, came into tremendous influence. By April, 1810, the settlers in the Ohio
Valley were convinced that Tecumseh was organizing an
Indian confederacy, waiting only the most opportune moment for a general outbreak—and that ramifications of
British influence were woven into his confederacy. They
were right.

In the autumn of 1811 the insurrection came—not desired by Tecumseh nor any British official, for Tecumseh had not had time to bring the southern Indians into the confederacy. Early in the year Sir Isaac Brock, administrator of Upper Canada, had invited the chieftains of the northwestern tribes into council. Brock and his colleagues attempted, coldly and formally, to dissuade the Indians from making war; and at the end of the council dismissed the Indians with liberal presents of military stores. Brock wrote afterwards, "I lament to think that the Indians retired from the council, in which they declared their resolution of going to war, with a full conviction that, although they could not look for active coöperation on our part, yet they might rely with confidence upon receiving from us every requisite of war." The hand had not been played very well, and a premature outbreak ruined the chances of conspiracy.

When Indian marauding began in the spring of 1811, General William Henry Harrison was sent into the field, with vague and vacillating instructions that kept him at Vincennes pondering the right thing to do. The pressure of public opinion at Vincennes led him to augment his regiment of regulars with a considerable force of militia, and make a hesitant advance toward Tecumseh's village on the headwaters of the Wabash, at Tippecanoe Creek. Harrison met the Indians, and parleyed; Tecumseh was absent, and rash leaders decided for war. In the early morning of November 7, 1811, hordes of Indians made a sudden onslaught; the regulars and militia were stubborn, and their stamina ultimately won the battle. After the Indians had retreated the army waited, tired and with strained nerves, with jagged holes in the ranks, for the next onslaught. After twenty-four anxious hours, General Harrison was convinced that he had won a victory. By the time the army had marched back to Vincennes, it had become a glorious victory. Twenty-nine years later the Battle of Tippecanoe was to underwrite the General's ticket to the presidency.

Harrison did not have the men and equipment to extend the victory into an adequate military occupation of the Indian country, nor did the national government act vigorously to stop the Indian raids. But the congressional elections of 1811 in the West were days of reckoning for the members who had worked for peace. Nearly one-half of the members of the Eleventh Congress were not re-elected; "submission men" were decisively rejected in the West and lower South, and "warhawks" controlled the Twelfth Congress. With only a skirmish the insurgents seized the speakership for Henry Clay on his first day of service in the House. The leadership of the Senate was likewise captured by a Westerner. Clay placed three vehement insurgents on the Committee on Foreign Relations. News came of the battle of Tippecanoe, and Andrew Jackson demanded that "the blood of our murdered countrymen" be avenged in blood, and addressed Harrison, "I do hope that Government will see that it is necessary to act efficiently and that this hostile band which must be excited to war by the secret agents of Great Britain must be destroyed." On the twenty-ninth of November the Committee on Foreign Relations reported in favor of war and of immediate warlike measures. A great deal was said in Congress about mercantile rights, especially by Westerners whose dignity impelled them to prove some deep interest in the commercial questions involved; there were any number of declamations on the national honor; and the whole problem of Canada, from western eyes, was put forward: Canada's monopoly of the fur trade, its wealth, its intrigues with the Indians, the secret yearning of its population for the free institutions of American republicanism, the absurd ease of the conquest of Canada. A representative from New York drawled a comment: "When a man rises in this House, you may almost tell how ardent he will be by knowing how far distant he lives from the sea."

The nation entered the war in June, 1812, with a high proportion of its best citizens apathetic or openly opposed. The regular army suffered from this opposition, and from the contempt of the Executive for trained military officers. The main reliance of the West in its drive for the conquest of Canada was, therefore, the militia—the untrained, independent, truculent volunteers, like those Amos Kendall saw mustered in Kentucky in 1814: "The soldiers are under no more restraint than a herd of swine. Reasoning, remonstrating, threatening, and ridiculing their officers, they show their sense of equality, and their total want of subordination." The Indian-fighting pioneers were one generation distant in the past; since Wayne's victories seventeen years had elapsed, and in the Ohio Valley that keen fighting sense of the pioneers had been lost through disuse.

The general plan of attack proposed by General Henry Dearborn provided for a main expedition against Detroit using the old war route of Lake Champlain, with synchronous invasions of Canada from three widely separated points on the international boundary. Hull was sent to Detroit to begin the advance from that point; and the general plan, having gone so far, collapsed. Hull, "old, vain, respectable, and incapable," had an obsession: if Lake Erie were not controlled by American vessels, Detroit and the Northwest were at the mercy of the enemy. Lake Erie was not so controlled; and the old general was beset with timidity. He made a few timorous demonstrations on the Canadian shore opposite Detroit, was alarmed by his success, and sent a runner with an order to the commandant of Fort Dearborn, at the southern tip of Lake Michigan, to evacuate that distant post. This order, obeyed by Captain Nathan Heald with military rectitude and against his common sense, exposed the American families clustered about the fort to Indian assault; as the soldiers were marching out the attack came, the grim tragedy that has come to be known as the Fort Dearborn Massacre.

Hull had, brilliantly, despatched his muster rolls and instructions, with his baggage and hospital stores, by schooner to Detroit. The capture of this vessel by the British gave Major-General Isaac Brock, lieutenant-governor of Canada, his first clear knowledge of American intentions. Fort Malden, on the Canadian shore of Lake Erie several miles below Detroit, had taken Detroit's place in British schemes as the depot of Indian trade and amity; from Malden guns, ammunition, and beverages had been lavishly dispensed to the Indians of the Old Northwest. British prestige with the fur-trading savages would crumble with the loss of Malden; and Brock bestirred himself to marshal his army. In numbers his force was distinctly inferior to Hull's; but the American general ordered a retreat from the neighborhood of the British post. He had heard of the British capture of Michilimackinac, the post at the northern tip of Lake Huron; he feared the unleashing of "a vast number of chiefs who led hostile bands" from the northern frontier and from western Michigan, and recrossed his army to Detroit. When Brock followed, frightening the old man who opposed him with suggestions concerning the tomahawks and scalping knives of the British Indian allies, Hull's vanishing courage oozed completely out. To the rage and chagrin of the Americans, and to the utter amazement of the British themselves, a white flag was exhibited, and on August 15, 1812, Detroit with its army was presented to the enemy.

General Harrison succeeded to the command of the American regulars and volunteers in the West. The frontier had confidence in him, and rallied again. But transportation was execrable and the commissariat no better; through the wet autumn and early winter the army floundered through mud in western Ohio, camping in woods and swamps, waiting for the winter freeze-up to make the country passable. Nine hundred troops from Kentucky, detached for a special expedition, were attacked by more than a thousand men on a foray from Malden on January 22, 1813; in this "Raisin River Massacre" five hundred Americans were taken prisoners, four hundred were killed in battle or massacred by the Indians after the withdrawal of the British soldiery, less than forty made their escape. Weakened by this great loss, Harrison was compelled to retreat; in February the terms of the militia enlistments expired, and he was left with a handful of regulars.

He set about the difficult task of gathering another force —difficult, until in mid-September young Oliver Hazard Perry sent word that his ships controlled Lake Erie. Harrison with his rejuvenated army crossed to the Canadian shore, and on the fifth of October overtook the fugitive British troops on the banks of the Thames River, scoring a victory in a sharp, quick battle. The Treaty of Ghent, closing the war on December 14, 1814, provided for a better definition of the boundary between the United States and Canada; but there was no surrender of territory on either side. So ended, save for stray threads which ran through American history for several decades, the epic of the conquest of Canada.

The bounty of western land offered by Congress to stimulate recruiting in the war, the launching of the first steamboats on the Ohio, the smacking impact of western leadership in Congress on Eastern Federalists, all helped to announce the presence of open lands and of equal opportunity for poor but honest men. Every campaign along the western border during the war prepared the way for a new rush of settlers. The commercial distress that the international struggle in Europe had visited upon the Atlantic seaboard did not dispel quickly after the Battle of Waterloo; and New Englanders turned westward.

Connecticut Yankees led the emigration. Newspapers were filled with the advertisements of New York and Ohio land agents, and with buoyant letters from western correspondents. "Ohio fever," the ultraconservatives called it, and rejoiced with President Timothy Dwight of Yale that emigration was a safety valve for the standing order, ridding the state of discontented people within whom was "a consuming fire which made of them potential revolutionists." But men of capital were becoming interested, as investments in western land gave evidence of safety combined with quick upturns. Western lands certainly were much more fertile than the worn-out farms of Connecticut. In the "Gimcrack State" the price of farm lands ranged from fourteen to fifty dollars an acre, taxes were high, and every year saw hundreds of small farms sacrificed under the auctioneer's hammer. In the West better lands could be purchased for three dollars; taxes were at a minimum; transportation was becoming better each year. Land agents, bidding for quick settlement, offered easy terms, payment over a period as long as seven years; they made special inducements in price to actual settlers; they took care of the poor man, willingly selling tracts as small as fifty acres.

The primary appeal of the West was that the small farmer in New England was on the under side of the economic scale. Somehow, one never thought of a mortgage upon a western farm—until one came into the West.

And many a New Englander was discontented with the narrow religious system of the entrenched church, the close scrutiny over private behavior exercised both by church congregations and neighbor busybodies.

By 1817 the established order in the New England states put a less smug interpretation upon the exodus; and the newspapers obligingly shifted emphasis to the privations of pioneer life and the dubiousness of ultimate success. One newspaper, doing its best to abate the westward movement, argued: "When the civil, social, literary and religious institutions of New England are taken into account, it seems the height of madness for men, *who have no extraordinary reasons for removal,* to leave their homes for the wild lands of the West, and their still wilder state of society." It was precisely those New England institutions that constituted the extraordinary reasons impelling many Easterners to follow the westward movement. But such civil institutions as the township and the common-school system they carried with them, to replant in Michigan, Wisconsin, Illinois, and Minnesota. In all the states of the Old Northwest, New Englanders were primarily responsible for the establishing of a free school system.

In these years the emigration from the southern states was even greater. The popular idea that the mountainous districts of the South were populated by poor whites pushed from the bottom lands by encroaching plantations fails to recognize that the vernacular, alone, of the mountain folk reveals that they chose their isolated districts before the plantation system began its ruthless expansion in the southern lowlands and in the Kentucky blue-grass country—and fails to take into account the tremendous emigration from the South into the old Northwest. Nor is mention of the dwindling economic opportunity of the small farmer in the slavery district needed to explain much of the emigration from the southern shore of the Ohio. The Appalachian backwoods, the Kentucky forest, was the breeding ground of the insatiable pioneer. This emigration had by 1820 populated more than half of Ohio, the southern third of Indiana, and the lowlands of southern Illinois.

Government land in Illinois was first offered at public sales in 1814. During the year ending September 30, 1817, about two hundred and fifty thousand acres were sold at the three Illinois land offices, nearly twice as much as in the three preceding years; but the sales in 1818 did not fall far short of six hundred thousand acres. The favored areas of settlement were widely separated tracts: the wedge between the Mississippi and the Kaskaskia rivers, an area of two thousand square miles wherein, in 1818, fifteen thousand people were living; and, on the eastern side of the state, a ribbon of land some fifteen miles wide along the Wabash River. Between these districts, and to the north, was a frontier area of scattered cabins. Most of the population of Indiana, similarly, was settled within the Ohio bottom lands and wedges extending northwest along the Wabash and northeast along the Ohio boundary.

While settlers from New England were moving into western New York, western Pennsylvania, and Ohio, the current of southern emigration was preponderantly responsible for the creation, in 1816, of the state of Indiana, and for the establishment of statehood in Illinois in 1818. Between the census of 1810 and the count of 1820 the population of the Old Northwest was more than doubled. In 1820 Ohio contained 581,295 settlers; Indiana, 147,178; Illinois, 55,162; and the extension of settlement into the Michigan frontier was well under way.

Journeying through Ohio in 1818, William Faux talked with a farmer who raised potatoes—only a hundred bushels to an acre of his rich land, a fourth of an acre's yield in England. " 'I guess,' says he, 'that we Ohio folks do not manage potatoes so well as they do in Ireland and England.'— 'No, sir, if I may judge by your quantity, you do not indeed.' 'No, I guess not.' " That was all; but the Englishman caught the point. These pioneer farmers were at war with the earth, manpower matched against the stubbornness of the wilderness; and the quantity of land subdued was the measure of their success. "The great object," Faux put it, "is to have as many acres as possible cleared, plowed, set, sown, planted, and managed by as few

[284]

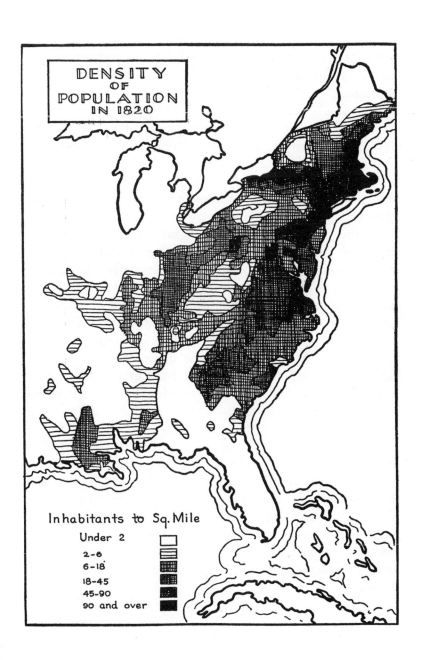

DENSITY
OF
POPULATION
IN 1820

Inhabitants to Sq. Mile

Under 2
2-6
6-18
18-45
45-90
90 and over

hands as possible; there being little capital, and therefore little or none to spare for hired labor. Instead of five acres well-managed, they must have 20 acres badly managed."

Put simply, this outstanding feature of pioneer agriculture is *extensiveness:* the scarce commodities, capital and labor, were spread thinly over large tracts of land—the cheap commodity. The pioneers took no complex equipment into the wilderness: an ax, a gun, some household goods, a yoke of oxen or a horse or two, a little live stock. The bull plow, the wooden cart, the wooden-toothed harrow, the cradle wherewith the grain was harvested, the flail, fan, and sieve for the threshing and cleaning, were all constructed principally of wood, with iron parts hammered out by the village blacksmith. Many a western settler occupied his farm for years before he put up a barn, or any outstructure except a corncrib and a stable for his workhorses. Hay and straw were stacked and foddered without shelter; threshing, even, was often done in the open air, upon a piece of ground made hard by repeated treading. The cows ambled in the woods, foraging for themselves all winter along the streams; where this was not possible, the pioneer found hay ready for cutting in the wild grasses of the prairies. Hogs did not need corn to get fat; they throve on the mast in the woods.

As the swelling tide of the Great Migration bore the frontier farther into the West and Northwest, in the older districts traces became roads, clearings became farms, villages grew into towns; commercial centers developed, affording a home market for the farmers, and canals gave inland regions access to the river highways and the Great Lakes.

There were men who did not wait to be caught up in this increasing stabilization, "genuine" frontiersmen who became restive as homes thickened about them, and farms were being cultivated only two or four miles away from their own clearings. Burke Williams, backwoodsman in the New Spoon River district, Illinois, in the early eighteen-forties, can speak for these men.

John Regan, traveler, drew up his buggy beside a stout-built little man, who was making sap troughs for the maple sugar season. Burke Williams, his name was.

"Good evenin' sir," said Burke, "how are you?"

"Pretty well. You're busy, I see."

"I'm bound to be, sir."

"Do you live near this?" (Mr. Regan had his own idioms. We must depend on him, however, for the transcribing of Mr. Williams' speech.)

"About a hundred rods off, right over thar."

"Have you been long settled here, sir?"

"Not a great while; I only came in last spring."

"And you have settled in the heart of the forest—I should think you might prefer to purchase cleared land."

"Wal, I guess I hain't purchased any. I've settled right down hyar till the owner comes along. I did live in Ohio before I came out hyar, but I got my house thar burnt up, an' every stock and rag I hed went up in smoke. . . .

"I brought the old 'oman an' the children along in a Pennsylvaney wagon, an' except that an' a span o' horses, I was clear-handed enough for a western country. Wal, I had been *raised* in the woods, and I didn't much like the bare prairies, so I pulled upon a stump in this forest, in the month o' May last. I knocked up a few sticks, an' whittled away with my ax, till I got this house put together. I've cleared five acres down thar, and got me in some wheat. This winter I'm calc'latin' to clear ten more, or maybe fifteen, and I guess that'll about do."

"What," the traveler inquired, "if an owner to the lands should present himself?"

"If the owner *should* come along in a year or two, maybe

[287]

I'll be able to make a trade with him. I don't trouble myself about that. If thar's work to be done, I go at it, an' that's all there is about it."

So much for the influence of the passing years, even upon the congenital pioneer. Burke Williams' grandfather, in a similar situation, would have demanded full pay for his improvements, and failing that would have stood off the owner with a shotgun until the provincial militia burned his cabin and drove him off.

Many of these whose lives and feelings were inseparable from the frontier actually owned their lands, of course; but when the time had come for them to move, they did not have to wait long for a buyer. And the frontier seeker chucked the household stuffs into his wagon, hung the bucket beneath and the feed box behind, harnessed up his horses, and commenced the journey westward. He walked, keeping his herd of ambling live stock to the road. His oldest boy sat astride the right-hand wheel horse, holding the reins in one hand. As the wagon rumbled over the long grass and through the open sunlight of the prairie, the frontier seeker knew comfort in his soul. His womenfolk did the cooking over the camp fire, and when the family did not stop overnight in a cabin by the wayside, they slept in the wagon-bed or on the ground. If the jolting of the wagon became tedious, they walked awhile, and took a turn at driving the cows. "I have met many hundreds of these moving caravans," Eliza Farnham wrote, "and scarcely ever saw an unhappy or anxious face among them." These women were an American product; one's involuntary tribute is, they are amazing.

A study of the nativity of the pioneers of the Illinois of 1818, tracing the former residence of over seven hundred settlers, has suggested these conclusions: from the Old South had come 53 per cent of the pioneers; from other states in the Ohio Valley, 18 per cent; from New England and the

Middle Atlantic states, 18 per cent; and from abroad, 11 per cent. About half the heads of families in Illinois in 1818 had been born in Maryland, Virginia, North or South Carolina, or Georgia; and approximately the same proportion had come into Illinois from homes in Kentucky, Tennessee, Ohio, and Indiana. Two-thirds of the state's population at this time were of southern stock. Precious few of these Southerners, however, were from the plantation area; they were from the uplands and the Appalachian valleys—the backwoods. They were Westerners rather than Southerners, lovers of the frontier, people who were happiest on the fringe of settlement.

In the population were "enterprising men," as Elias Fordham called them—"Young Doctors, Lawyers, Storekeepers, farmers, mechanics, etc., who found towns, trade, speculate in land, and begin the fabric of Society"—the men who were to lead Illinois out of its frontier status. "Enterprising men" deplored two economic handicaps of the frontier state, the lack of adequate transportation facilities and the lack of a laboring class. Backwoodsmen were little concerned with these characteristic deficiencies of the frontier. They were economically independent; they had little or no ready money, but they could obtain most of what they wanted by bartering. But for all the amiability of life in the back country, the pioneer was particularly vulnerable to two annoyances: one, financial burdens incident to the land—purchase-price, taxes, and the like; and crop failures. Either was a reflection upon the community in which he had settled; and either turned the pioneer's mind to thoughts of emigration.

The backwoods pioneer carried the elements of discontent within him, wherever he went; and his escape, therefore, never quite came off. His life was one of alternate enthusiasm and apathy, alternate energy and laziness. He drank too heavily; he knew the taste of good whisky but he had no objection to "rotgut." In his zest to be "natural," he was careless of personal comfort and cleanliness, dosed himself too heavily with perhaps the wrong things whenever he became downright sick, and never learned that swamp land bred miasma. Acute travelers noted "the great stimulus and excitement of the mental passions, which adventurers and first settlers are, by the situation, subject to." There was little contentedness in the religion he demanded; there was, instead, a great deal of loud hallooing and violent action.

Individuals were rare that were so desirous of elbow-room that they did not want company. Pioneers' institutions, therefore, manifest a truculent sociability—in religion, play, even in work. It was this quality that gave western hospitality its individuality and its satisfying fullness.

That hospitality was aptly described by a traveler among the Boone's Lick pioneers of Missouri: "Enter his door and tell him you are benighted, and wish the shelter of his cabin for the night. The welcome is, indeed, seemingly ungracious: 'I reckon you can stay,' or, 'I suppose we must let you stay.' But this apparent ungraciousness is the harbinger of every kindness that he can bestow, and every comfort that his cabin affords. Good coffee, corn bread and butter, venison, pork, wild and tame fowls, are set before you. His wife, timid, silent, reserved, but constantly attentive to your comfort, does not sit at the table with you, but like the wives of the patriarchs, stands and attends on you. You are shown the best bed that the house can afford. When this kind of hospitality has been extended to you as long as you choose to stay, and when you depart and speak about your bill, you are most commonly told, with some slight mark of resentment, that they do not keep tavern. Even the flaxen-haired urchins will run away from your money."

CHAPTER XVII

THE HEART OF THE WEST

CIVILIZATION was tightening its first grasp on Kentucky; land sharpers, shyster lawyers, and its other emissaries were making themselves at home in the blue-grass country. Daniel Boone was heartsick; and he moved into the valley of the Kanawha, in western Virginia, where the westbound emigrants stopped only to trade. A son of Boone's, a chip off the old block, ventured into the Spanish dominion west of the Mississippi, to hunt and to trap beaver. He came back with glowing accounts of the warmth of his welcome by the authorities at St. Louis, the plentifulness of game, the abundance of fertile wilderness; the old pioneer listened, and pulled stakes again. In the spring of 1795 he bundled his family and their goods on pack horses, and led the way on foot—Boone was sixty-one then—through the trailless bottom lands of the Ohio to St. Louis.

In his day Boone had come to be accepted as the arch-Pioneer, the wilderness-breaker; the Spanish officials treated the migrant and his family as distinguished guests. The garrison at St. Louis was paraded in his honor; and the Spanish and American flags were displayed side by side. The lieutenant-governor of Louisiana presented Boone with a warrant for one thousand arpents of land, to be located wherever he pleased within the "District of the Femme Osage," which embraced all of Louisiana north of St. Louis. In the rich bottom lands of the Missouri, close by the banks of the shifting stream that was ultimately to lave over the site, Boone built his cabin.

The lieutenant-governor at St. Louis offered Boone a grant of ten thousand arpents of Missouri lands, conditional upon his bringing in one hundred American families. But the old pioneer, who never grasped the technicalities of contracts, lost his land by neglecting to have the grant confirmed by the governor at New Orleans. Meanwhile he had made known the attractions of the Missouri frontier to his friends, and Kentuckians and Carolinians dribbled into the Femme Osage Valley. Some of them, like Boone, had acquired a few slaves; others were backwoodsmen with no wealth besides their families; others were the rough and tough men who inevitably sifted to the farthest frontier. In the summer of 1800 the Femme Osage district was given local organization, with Daniel Boone commandant. The arrangement would not have been possible in Kentucky: Boone's judgment, his assignment of penalty, was final.

The old pioneer was getting a bit lazy; it was about this time that he built himself another cabin, within fifty or sixty feet of a spring—not only a supply of drinking water for the pioneers, but also a magnet for the game. Boone could sit in the door of his cabin, and lay in a winter's supply of meat; he had his choice of deer, elk, buffalo, or bear. Wild turkeys roosted in Boone's shade trees and even on the roof of his cabin; hollow trees nearby were crammed with honey.

The first murder within Boone's palatinate was committed in December, 1804. Commandant Boone remanded the offender to the action of a grand jury. Eleven of the twelve members could not write their names; the scholar among them was chosen foreman, drafted the indictment, and the others affixed their X-marks. This document was the first indictment drawn in Louisiana Territory under American government:

"That one James Davis, late of the District of St. Charles, in the Territory of Louisiana, Laborer, not having the fear of God before his eyes, but being moved and seduced by the instigation of the Devil, on the 13th day of December, in the year of our Lord one thousand eight hundred and four (1804), at a place called Femme Osage, in the said district of St. Charles, with force of arms, in and upon William Hays, in the peace of God and the United States, then and there Feloniously, willfully and with malice aforethought, did make an assault, and that the said James Davis, with a certain rifle gun, four feet long, and of the value of five dollars, then and there charged with gun powder and one leaden bullet, with the said gun the said James Davis, then and there in his hands had and held, fired and killed William Hays." At the subsequent trial Mr. Davis was cleared.

Concerning this James Davis, hunter and trapper, relative and companion of Daniel Boone, a sober historian relates a tale of frontier hardship and frontier resourcefulness. Davis was hunting alone in western Missouri, in the winter of 1813. A party of Otoe Indians captured him, stripped him of everything he possessed, even his clothing, leaving him to perish in the cold. Having a sense of humor, they presented their naked victim with an antiquated musket containing a single charge. Davis, separated by more than a hundred miles of wilderness from a settlement, began the impossible journey; he trudged all day, and toward evening looked for some shelving ledge that might offer him some little protection through the night. He found such a sheltered place, and in it a hibernating bear. Davis crawled up until the muzzle of the old musket almost

[293]

grazed the animal's shaggy forehead; his superlative will steadied his frostbitten fingers: one shot, one tremor, and the bear was dead. Taking the flint from the musket lock, he stripped off the hide, and drew it over his own body. That night he slept beside the skinless carcass, and at daylight he resumed his march. Three days after, late in the evening, he walked into Jonathan Bryan's cabin in the Boone settlement.

In the summer of 1807 two sons of the old pioneer were in a party of five that traveled up the Missouri to some salt springs near the bend of the river, and manufactured salt. That fall the salt was shipped down the river in hollowed-out sycamore logs, the ends made waterproof by clay daubing. They returned to the Femme Osage; but the salt-makers left to the district about Cedar Creek the name, "Boone's Lick."

As settlement in the Femme Osage district developed apace, the Indians became increasingly restive; Tecumseh's insurrection flared up in the Ohio Valley, its embers were scattered, yet the Indians in Missouri were not overtly hostile. When in the summer of 1812 the Femme Osage settlements learned that war had been declared against Great Britain, they constructed stockades and organized companies of rangers. These men in buckskin, patrolling the fringe of the wilderness, were as sanguinary as any Indians; each ranger carried a tomahawk and scalping knife besides his rifle. When the war fever reached the Sauk and Foxes, isolated cabins were burned and their occupants murdered, horses were stolen and crops destroyed; yet of the several score little battles fought along the Missouri during the War of 1812, it seems fair to credit the rangers with starting their half.

Each winter the Femme Osage settlers employed some itinerant "professor" to impart book learning to the youth of the community. As a coöperative enterprise they had built a schoolhouse, and made split log seats and puncheon writing desks. Eight, ten, or twelve children in a family was a not unusual crop; if the number expanded to eighteen or twenty, the likely explanation was that the pioneer had buried one wife and had married again—or twice again.

The settlers went to St. Louis for the few shop-goods they wanted; they took thence furs and pelts, which brought Spanish silver dollars in exchange. In St. Louis and in the settlements these dollars were for convenience in change-making cut into quarters and eighths, and Missourians talked of "six-bits," "four-bits," "two-bits." For salt men from all the settlements north of the Missouri went to Boone's Lick; and the Boone's Lick Road was opened, an emigrants' thoroughfare for half a century.

In 1813 Boone and his son "General" Nathan, with their slaves, completed a several years' labor, a stone mansion, built with hammer and chisel—thick blocks of blue limestone encased in plaster that had been "ripened" by being buried through the winter. Here the old patriarch spent his last days. Pipe, dinner plate, rifle, dogs, past dangers to recall and present esteem to bask in. Even after his eightieth birthday was past he could not put away his love for the hunt; and twice a year, accompanied by a negro man to attend the camp and skin the game, he tramped off into some remote hunting ground. On the twenty-sixth of September, 1820, he died. His residence in Missouri spanned that district's history from the first approach of American pioneers, when Louisiana was Spanish domain, to the first session of the legislature of the sovereign American state of Missouri.

In 1820 fifty-six thousand American settlers were in Missouri, with about ten thousand slaves. The majority of slaves were personal servants, or were used in general agricultural work under the owner's direct supervision. Cotton was not a favored crop in Missouri; tobacco-growing had been begun on a small scale, and hemp, "the nearest thing to a staple crop ever developed in Missouri," was little produced until the mid-thirties. Slaves in Missouri were not the basis of a plantation system, but were, rather, a mark of wealth and social position. Accordingly the number of slaves was small in the newly settled districts, and largest in St. Louis and the Femme Osage region. The area of settlement was a wide band along the Mississippi, with a vigorous thrust into the west along both banks of the Missouri. Northeastern Missouri and the Boone's Lick country were receiving the majority of the emigration as Missouri entered its travail of statehood.

By 1820 every little settlement had its church, Baptist or Methodist, most likely, spokes in the wheel of the circuit riders. In almost every town was some one with a little learning who had not adjusted himself to the frontier, and advertised for pupils in English and classical subjects. Not even in St. Louis was there a regular school system in operation. St. Louis, with its numbers of young lawyers, was the repository of liberal arts in Missouri.

At least six-sevenths of the settlers were farmers, raising corn and wheat, owning cattle. These pioneers were self-sustaining, but the exportation of foodstuffs was a very incidental concern—largely because there was a very incidental market available. The bulk of the exports was in lead and furs. In St. Louis, with a population of about four thousand, the old French merchants had adjusted themselves to the new order, and retained their eminence in the city's commerce; the *Gazette* still printed some of its advertisements in French. St. Genevieve, the oldest settlement in Missouri, was the one other town on the Mississippi with more than a thousand people; its priority and its sustained settlement St. Genevieve owed to the lead mines. Beyond the Mississippi was only one town of consequence, Franklin. This ambitious city, laid off with streets eighty-seven feet wide, grew rapidly, becoming the center of wealth and fashion for the Boone's Lick country. It was the outfitting point for the farther West, the metropolis of the caravan trade to New Mexico and the Indian trade of the Great Plains. The *Missouri Intelligencer,* first newspaper established west of St. Louis, printed its first issue in Franklin in April, 1819. In May the town received the first evidence of a greater glory, the steamboat *Independence,* first steamship on the Missouri. The *Intelligencer* bustled into print: "With no ordinary sensations of pride and pleasure, we announce the arrival, this morning, at this place, of the elegant steam boat Independence, Captain Nelson, in seven sailing days (but thirteen from the time of her departure) from St. Louis, with passengers, and a cargo of flour, whiskey, sugar, iron castings, &c., *being the first steam boat that ever attempted ascending the Missouri.* She was joyfully met by the inhabitants of Franklin, and saluted by the firing of cannon, which was returned by the Independence. The grand *desideratum,* the important *fact* is now ascertained, *that steam boats can safely navigate the Missouri river."*

In the fall of 1817 leading men in the Missouri settlements were circulating petitions; the drive for statehood was on. It was timely. Across the river Illinois, somewhat less in population, was on the brink of admission to the Union. Emigration was seeking out the western country. John Mason Peck recorded, "The 'new comers,' like a mountain torrent, poured into the country faster than it was possible to provide corn for bread stuff. Some families came in the spring of 1815; but in the winter, spring, summer and autumn of 1816, they came like an avalanche. It seemed as though Kentucky and Tennessee were breaking up and moving to the 'Far West.' Caravan after caravan passed over the prairies of Illinois, crossing the 'great river' at St. Louis, all bound for Boone's Lick. The

stream of immigration had not lessened in 1817. Many
families came from Virginia, the Carolinas and Georgia,
and not a few from the Middle States, while a sprinkling
found their way to the extreme West from Yankeedom and
Yorkdom. Following in the wake of this exodus to the
middle section was a terrific excitement about getting land.
My first visit in 1818 was at this crisis; and I could not call
at a cabin in the country without being accosted: 'Got a New
Madrid claim?' 'Are you one of these land speculators,
stranger?' "

Illinois became a state, and Alabama followed a year
later; but Missouri waited. Its slightly dark complexion
was against it; northern congressmen would not allow another slave state to upset the precarious balance between
the political weight of the sections. Missourians were
lividly resentful: "gross and barefaced usurpation," "unprecedented restriction," and many an unquotable phrase
rang a variation upon Duff Green's toast at a banquet in
Franklin in 1819, "The Union—it is dear to us but liberty
is dearer."

"From the battle of Bunker Hill to the treaty of Paris,"
wrote Jefferson to John Adams, "we have never had so
ominous a question." The grand jury of each of the seven
counties of Missouri went on record in formal protest
against the exclusion. From April to December of 1819,
wherever Missourians met they tilted their glasses in unison
—a toast in defiance of the attempts of Congress to dictate
what the sovereign state of Missouri should have in its
constitution. The St. Louis *Enquirer* chronicled in the
late autumn of 1819: "Probably from thirty to fifty wagons
daily cross the Mississippi at the different ferries, and bring
in an average of four to five hundred souls a day. The
emigrants are principally from Kentucky, Tennessee, Virginia and the states further south. They bring great numbers of slaves, knowing that Congress has no power to

impose the agitated restriction, and that the people of Missouri will never adopt it."

In July, 1819, Missouri Territory was sliced along the parallel of 36°30', and the Territory of Arkansas was created—a region of a few small clearings, and one trading post near the mouth of the Arkansas River. When Congress reassembled in December, the District of Maine was a candidate for statehood. It was never a territory of the United States, but a detached part of Massachusetts, admitted to the Union with the consent of the parent state. The free-state majority in the House welcomed this far-northern state; but its fortunes became bound up with Missouri's.

Henry Clay put forward his Compromise, so called; it was more in the nature of a club. "Equality is equality, and if it is right to make the restriction of slavery the condition for the admission of Missouri, it is equally just to make the admission of Missouri the condition for that of Maine." The House, on March 2, 1820, yielded its opposition to Missouri by a vote of ninety to eighty-seven. The Compromise was completed by a later resolution that slavery should be permitted in no other part of the Louisiana Purchase north of Arkansas Territory.

The enabling act, signed by President Monroe four days later, authorized the inhabitants of Missouri to adopt a state constitution. That document, completed and signed on the nineteenth of July, opened sturdily: "We, the people of Missouri, inhabiting the limits hereinafter designated, by our representatives in convention assembled at St. Louis on Monday, the 12th day of June, 1820, do mutually agree to form and establish a free and independent republick, by the name of the State of Missouri." That, to Missourians, was the last step in the process of attaining statehood. State officers were elected; the legislature met in St. Louis in September. (On the twenty-sixth it adjourned for the

[299]

day, as a memorial tribute: Daniel Boone was dead.)
United States senators were elected, and the territorial
delegate from Missouri insisted that his proper title was
now "Representative"; but Congress was reluctant to complete the process of admission by formal resolution.

Through the winter of 1820-1821 the House wrangled.
The situation became comical when House and Senate met
in joint assembly to receive the count of the electoral college. The total was read off: "Were the votes of Missouri
to be counted, the result would be for James Monroe for
President of the United States 231 votes; if not counted,
for James Monroe for President of the United States 228
votes; but in either event James Monroe is elected President of the United States." Several members bounced
simultaneously from their seats; the Speaker declared every
one out of order but John Randolph; as Randolph put the
motion for the inclusion of Missouri's votes in the official
total, some one moved an adjournment, and the august body
broke up. Clay, soon after this debacle, produced a formula
for admitting Missouri: the state must first pass a "solemn
act" that the clause in its constitution excluding free negroes
and mulattoes from settling in the state should not be construed to affect any citizen of any other state. And the
legislature compliantly passed an act of elephantine solemnity, high in the annals of official impudence. Congress
pretended that it was acceptable, and on August 10, 1821,
President Monroe formally proclaimed that Missouri had
been admitted into the Union.

In the period that began with the departure of Manuel
Lisa's keelboat up the Missouri in the spring of 1807 and
closed with the outbreak of war between the United States
and Mexico, all of Louisiana north and west of Missouri
was the theater of the American fur trade. St. Louis was
its *entrepôt:* all lines of trade and travel to the Far West
centered there; all military movements, all freighting to

frontier posts, the enterprises of missionaries and explorers, made use of St. Louis as base of operations. At the mouth of the Missouri, St. Louis was the beginning and the culmination of the trade cycles that used that highway. South, down the Mississippi, was New Orleans; east, up the Ohio, was Pittsburgh. Theorists of the next generation, visualizing an American empire populated to its present density, almost invariably located the future capital of the United States at St. Louis. As long as navigable rivers were the supremely important highways, St. Louis retained that idealistic significance.

The valleys of the Missouri and its tributaries were the fur trader's routes of travel; the posts and Indian camps in which he lived and worked were in these valleys. Beaver were in the streams, buffalo on the near plains. Up these streams traders propelled their keelboats, laden with merchandise to barter for furs; down these streams, in the keelboats and in chains of tublike crafts made of buffalo hides and willow poles, the trappers and traders floated their furs to market. Brigades of supply parties striking overland from the Missouri border toward the Rockies, and caravans of merchandise destined for New Mexico were alike dependent on the Missouri River for their transportation from St. Louis to the outpost of Franklin and its successors, Independence, Westport, Kansas City, and Atchison.

> She glides along by the western plains
> And changes her bed each time it rains;
> Witching as any dark-eyed houri,
> This romping, wild brunette, Missouri.

Incidentally inspiring bad poetry and better humor, the great river was the life stream of the fur trade.

The Spanish régime of forty years in Upper Louisiana, for all its sporadic ambitions, produced but one master of the fur trade. That adventurer, Manuel Lisa, links old Louisiana with the new West. By 1800 he had become prominent enough to secure from the Spanish government the exclusive trade with the Osage Indians on the Osage River. He was first to grasp the importance of the information brought back by Lewis and Clark of the resources of the upper Missouri; and in the spring following their return Lisa was heading an expedition embarked upon the Missouri, its destination the Indian tribes two thousand miles away.

Hiram Martin Chittenden, classic historian of the American fur trade, described the hazard of the early expeditions: "Above the friendly tribe of the Omahas, who dwelt not far from the mouth of the Platte, the navigator had to pass the country of six or seven tribes who might prove hostile or friendly according as circumstances over which he had no control might turn. It was a very rare thing for a keelboat to run the entire gauntlet unmolested, while in many instances disastrous conflicts were precipitated. The channel of the river, so capricious and shifting, often ran close to the shore, and placed a boat party in frequent jeopardy, if not absolutely at the mercy of the Indians. A leader of great experience, full of nerve and tact, and of that scarcely less valuable quality described by the word 'bluff,' was indispensable in these delicate emergencies. The lives of the party frequently hung as upon a thread which the slightest maladroitness or weakness would break. Defects of leadership cost many a life on the hostile shores of the Missouri."

Lisa halted in the heart of the Crow domain at the mouth of the Bighorn, and there built the first American trading post, Fort Lisa, on the upper rivers of the Far West. Again in St. Louis in the summer of 1808, Lisa interested several Westerners of capital, Pierre Chouteau, William Clark, and eight others, in the formation of the

Missouri Fur Company. The American Fur Company, organized by John Jacob Astor in 1808, invaded the Far West in 1817. The Rocky Mountain Fur Company, founded by William Henry Ashley and a remarkable group of young adventurers, was the third of the three great fur companies whose province was the wilderness beyond Missouri. There were many smaller companies which arose and disappeared with the vicissitudes of the fur trade; there were also free trappers, bound to no company, independent and improvident, casually taking up life with the Indians, or preserving their truculent freedom in isolated cabins.

A majority of the fur companies' employees were French Canadians. The streams were their natural element; they cordelled the keelboats up the long course of the Missouri, and their strokes pushed canoes up the small streams to the beaver lodges. They were nearly all illiterate; these voyageurs were a distinct class of frontier dwellers, volatile in temper, sentimental and contented, inured to hardship and indifferent to it. In them colonial France was acclimated to the American frontier.

Americans were the best trappers in the wilderness beyond the rivers. These mountaineers were hard, robustly free from restraints, proud as lords. "No court or jury is called to adjudicate upon his disputes and abuses save his own conscience," wrote Josiah Gregg; "and no powers are invoked to redress them save those with which the God of nature has endowed him." The mountaineer dressed much like the Indians, and like them limited his "fixings" to the minimum. He had two pack animals besides the horse he rode; the smaller his personal equipment, the greater the number of furs they could carry. Rifle and ammunition, traps, knives, hatchets; some iron pans to cook in, and a coffeepot; coffee, sugar, and salt; a blanket or two; some alcohol and some tobacco—that was enough. He got low wages, and he was committed to the doctrine that money should be spent as quickly as it was earned. His language became a medley of English, French, and Spanish, amazingly remote from grammar and beautifully profane. He had a fierce attachment for his few friends, and a closer tie to the rugged country in which he lived. These fur traders were the genuine pathfinders of the West; official explorers, John C. Frémont and the others, who made the wilderness known to Americans in "the States," depended greatly upon trappers to guide them, and bereft of that guidance displayed an irrepressible talent for getting lost.

The American Fur Company, by virtue of greater capital, imperialistic methods, and covert alliances with gentlemen of national influence, came to dominate the fur trade. But preceding the organization of the Western Department, Astor had made a spectacular venture in the far-western field. This was the Astoria enterprise, from one aspect a brave chapter in the annals of American exploration, from another aspect a fragment of a great scheme to undermine British-American relations and sweep the fur trade of the entire Northwest into the hands of one man.

A trading station was to be established near the mouth of the Columbia, a central supply post from which the fur trade would radiate far into the interior. The trading stuffs were to be sent annually from New York by sea; the ship would receive the returns of the trade, dispose of the furs in China, and return to New York with oriental goods. Other plans, other ships . . . and trappers coming and going from St. Louis.

Early in the spring of 1811 the overland expedition, which was to pick sites for trading posts along the Missouri and undertake the beginnings of the commerce with the Indians of Oregon, left the thriving city at the mouth of the Missouri. William Price Hunt, Donald McKenzie, and Ramsay Crooks were among the notable party.

At the village of the Aricaras, Hunt was impressed with

[304]

the great danger of attempting to pass the country of the Blackfeet, bordering the upper Missouri; and he decided to make the rest of the journey by land. The company bought horses from the Aricaras and from Manuel Lisa— who had pursued the Astorians up the Missouri in anxiety to protect his own interests—and took up the long and uncertain journey to the westward. With the aid of Crow guides they surmounted the mountain barrier, and in September were on the western slope of the Rockies. Down the Wind River into the Bighorn, across the range into the Green River Valley, across the divide between the Green and the Snake rivers, the expedition pressed through the tortuous country. On the banks of the Snake the trappers in the party were urgent in their desire to abandon the horses and take to the river. Hunt acquiesced; and the company spent ten days in making a flotilla of canoes. On the nineteenth of October the fifteen boats were launched upon the swift river. The descent was rapid and exhilarating; but the course became a torrent, the canoes swirled into treacherous places, and on the twenty-eighth a canoe was wrecked and one of the voyageurs drowned.

Wreckages and losses had reduced their provisions until the party fairly confronted starvation. They had a large quantity of goods, and no means of transporting them. Reconnoitering groups tramped about, bewildered, while another group cached the goods. An advance party returned with the information that the river was absolutely unnavigable; and the party attempted the rest of the journey afoot. They marched in two detachments under Hunt and Crooks, one descending each bank of the river. Mountains on either bank seemed to bar each party after a few days, and the want of provisions became desperate. A retrograde march was necessary to reach an Indian camp where the expedition could get food. Crooks, ill through most of the journey, and several others decided to remain among the Snake Indians rather than undertake the hardships of a winter journey across the Blue Mountains; the majority of the party pushed ahead, with the invaluable guidance of a Snake Indian; and on January 21, 1812, the main body of the expedition reached the banks of the Columbia. From the Indians along the river Hunt learned that the expedition sent by sea had arrived safely in the preceding spring, and had built the trading post, "Astoria," on Columbia Bay. An advance contingent of the overland expedition, separated at the time when the navigation of the Snake was abandoned, came into Astoria on the eighteenth of January; almost a month later Hunt and the main party arrived at Astoria.

The outcome of the War of 1812 scotched Astor's plans; and the lonely outpost on the Pacific was sold, as the best way out of the situation, to the Northwest Company.

The disheartening conclusion of the Astoria enterprise, the evidence of British influence with the Missouri tribes and the waning fortunes of American traders against the competition of the Hudson's Bay Company—these considerations persuaded the national administration to make a formidable show of its authority to the Indians of the Northwest. The parade of military pomp was to include naturalists, geologists, topographers, and an artist. Major Stephen H. Long was given the baton. Advance notices roused high expectations in Missouri. The St. Louis *Enquirer* declared, "The Northwest and Hudson Bay Companies will be shut out from the commerce of the Missouri and Mississippi Indians; the American traders will penetrate in safety the recesses of the Rocky Mountains in search of its rich furs; a commerce yielding a million per annum will descend the Missouri, and the Indians, finding their wants supplied by American traders, their domestic wars restrained by American policy, will learn to respect the American name."

In the fall of 1818 troops from Plattsburg, Philadelphia, Detroit, and Bellefontaine were ordered to assemble at the mouth of the Kansas. The War Department did not seem to care how many troops were detached for this expedition; gentlemen in Washington apparently believed that the movement would save the military establishment several thousand dollars, owing to the diminished cost of subsistence in a region where game was abundant.

Fur traders ascended the Missouri with their trading stuffs in keelboats; but for this great enterprise nothing but steamboats possessed sufficient elegance. No steamboat had yet entered the Missouri River; and the five vessels which a contractor provided for the expedition, ready just after the *Independence* had entered the river, were woefully unfitted for the unique stream. Two of the five, apparently, were not able to enter the Missouri at all; one abandoned the trip thirty miles below Franklin; and the other two succeeded in reaching the mouth of the Kansas. The troops spent the whole summer of 1819 in attempting to negotiate the distance between St. Louis and the northward bend of the Missouri. Late in September they reached the Council Bluffs, abandoned all thought of going farther that year, and made camp for the winter. By spring three hundred of the men had taken scurvy; one hundred of them died.

For the use of Major Long and his colleagues in science a special boat was built—the *Western Engineer*, probably the first of the stern-wheel steamboats. "The *Western Engineer* is well armed," reported the *Missouri Gazette*, "and carries an elegant flag representing a white man and an Indian shaking hands, the calumet of peace and the sword. The boat is 75 feet long, 13 feet beam and draws 19 inches of water. The steam passes off through the mouth of a large figure-head (a serpent)." This ornate craft, built by Pittsburgh shipwrights, performed worthily:

[307]

it was the only steamboat of the six that made the distance to the Council Bluffs. The log of the *Western Engineer* bore the notation, "Average running time five hours per day. Average leisure time for examining the country ten hours per day."

In cantonment for the winter near Manuel Lisa's residence, the scientists passed the winter pleasantly, making short excursions into the wilderness and stuffing their notebooks with data, and exchanging hospitalities with the officials of the Missouri Fur Company and the two ladies at Fort Lisa. But Congress, confronting the wastage of its appropriation and having to settle the scandal about the contract for the five steamboats, was not in a pleasant mood when Long's expedition was mentioned, and declined to appropriate any further funds.

Major Long and a small party were diverted to an exploration of the source of the Platte. The party was so reduced from the previous year's standard of stateliness that when, on June 11, 1820, Long reached the Pawnee villages on the Loup River and requested a council, the chiefs declined on the ground that they were rather busy. In July the expedition was within the foothills of the Rockies. The headwaters of the Platte were located, but not followed to the source. For the return journey the party was divided, one group following the Arkansas and the other, under Major Long, following the Canadian under the misconception that it was upon the banks of the Red River.

The published narrative of the expedition of 1818-1820 was a very interesting botanical and geological disquisition, with side-discursions upon the Indian tribes; but the public, interested in the wealth of the Rocky Mountains and in the possibilities of travel overland to the Pacific, was disappointed. And, by way of belying completely the intended purpose of the expedition—a flying wedge to cleave a way for civilization—Major Long added in his report: "Although tracts of fertile land, considerably extensive, are occasionally to be met with, yet the scarcity of wood and water, almost universally prevalent, will prove an insuperable obstacle in the way of settling the country. This objection rests not only against the immediate section under consideration, but applies with equal propriety to a much larger portion of the country. . . . This region, however, viewed as a frontier, may prove of infinite importance to the United States, inasmuch as it is calculated to serve as a barrier to prevent too great an extension of our population westward."

This irrepressible legend of the Great American Desert, nourished by Major Long and a score of others who described the West, never did any great harm. Fur traders knew the far frontier infinitely better than government explorers; and they loved the country. The soldiers in the frontier posts were not deterred by the legend from cultivating vegetable gardens near the stockade walls, nor did the vegetables seem to suffer. And Missourians were not disposed to take any one's advice. "They have no motive to build with old Cato, 'for posterity and the immortal gods,' " reported Timothy Flint. "Next to hunting, Indian wars, and the wonderful exuberance of Missouri, the favorite topic is new countries."

CHAPTER XVIII

THREE HIGHWAYS

THE freedom of the Mississippi had been guaranteed, and the ugly word of treason had been invoked to save Mr. Burr from his friends. All very well: these were two sizable strides toward congeniality between East and West. But other exertions were being expected of the national government.

The West was clamoring to be brought out of the backwoods. The way to commercial unity had been blazed in 1802; it awaited the national ax to clear it. Exactly a year before the drafting of the Louisiana Purchase in Paris, Congress approved an act enabling the people of Ohio to form a state. Among the provisions were: "That one-twentieth of the net proceeds of the lands lying within said State sold by Congress shall be applied to the laying out and making public roads leading from the navigable waters emptying in the Atlantic, to the Ohio, to the said state, and through the same, such roads to be laid out under authority of Congress, with the consent of the several states through which the roads shall pass." In the ultimate adjustment three-fifths of this sum was to be spent by the state legislature on road-building within Ohio; and the remaining 2 per cent of the proceeds of public land sales in Ohio was reserved until Congress should fulfill its promise of a national road.

This "2 per cent fund" was intrinsically a tiny thing; it would have been a blinding beam to the fathers of the constitution. Franklin and James Wilson had attempted to include among the powers of Congress the privilege of making canals when necessary, and had been summarily voted down. "No state shall without the consent of Congress lay any duty of tonnage"; that in the Constitution is the only actual nibble at the question of internal improvements. Maryland in 1790 commenced the policy of state tonnage duties with the consent of Congress, and other states followed suit; inland states had no such recourse for funds to build canals and roads. Jefferson hoped for a constitutional amendment that would allow the national government to open and improve ways of communication within the states.

The West was not to be fed constitutional niceties when it wanted bread and butter. Every Congress was besieged with letters and petitions for a road; and in 1806 the weight of reiterated demands had its way. In the previous December a senate committee reported upon the route that National Road could best follow to the advantage of the citizens of Ohio, outlining a route from Cumberland to Wheeling. "Politicians have generally agreed that rivers unite the interests and promote the friendship of those who inhabit their banks; while mountains, on the contrary, tend to the disunion and estrangement of those who are separated by their intervention. In the present case, to make the crooked ways straight, and the rough ways smooth, will, in effect, remove the intervening mountains, and by facilitating the intercourse of our Western brethren with those on the Atlantic, substantially unite them *in interest,* which, the committee believe, is the most effectual cement of union applicable to the human race." In March the recommendations of the committee were enacted virtually unchanged into law.

Three eastern cities were striving for the trade of the Ohio Valley—Philadelphia, Baltimore, and Richmond. Richmond's interest was more an ambition than a commerce; and from that city, "from the hilly and rough condition of the country, no roads are, or can be, conveniently made leading to the principal population of the State of Ohio." The prospect of a road from Philadelphia, on the other hand, needed no government encouragement; Philadelphians were so greatly interested in facilitating trade with western Pennsylvania that, the committee was assured, "they will of course surmount the difficulties presented by the Allegheny Mountain, Chestnut Ridge, and Laurel Hill." In Maryland roads were already being built to radiate from Baltimore through the state; the Potomac Company, evidently, would soon clear the Potomac River of all obstructions. Cumberland, on the north bank, at the eastern foot of the Allegheny Mountains, seemed aptly located for the starting point of the National Road. The route would meet the roads leading from Baltimore and Washington, would cross the Monongahela at Brownsville, whence goods might be carried to Pittsburgh by boat, and would lead into the southeast corner of Ohio, the most peopled part of the state.

Constitutional cavils were to be sidestepped by obtaining the consent of the states crossed by the National Road. Pennsylvanians were jealous of the commerce of Baltimore, and withheld consent until Jefferson should agree to a more circuitous route swinging up into western Pennsylvania. The President resented this attempt of the state to dictate the route; but Albert Gallatin advised him, "The county of Washington, with which I am well acquainted, having represented it six years in Congress, gives a uniform majority of about two thousand votes *in our favor,* and if this be thrown by *reason* of *this Road* in a wrong scale, we will infallibly lose the state of Penn'." Jefferson, after consideration, agreed that if deflections would benefit certain towns and better accommodate travelers, he should authorize them.

This byplay was not finished until 1811. Meanwhile the road had been surveyed; estimates of the expense of construction had been made; and in April, 1811, contracts were let for building the first ten miles west of Cumberland. In the next few years contracts were let for section after section; and in 1818 United States Mail coaches were running over the National Road from the Potomac to Wheeling on the Ohio.

"The road shall be raised in the middle of the carriageway with stone, earth, or gravel and sand, or a combination of some or all of them," ran the commissioners' orders; and contractors were enjoined carefully to provide for watercourses on either side of the roadway. The roadbed was rough, substantial, honestly made, a "metal" road, with sturdy stone bridges. A flood of traffic swept over the great highway once it was completed to Wheeling, huge-wheeled wagons with huge loads. As the freighters scrunched over the stones and cut into the gravel, naturally swells and transverse fissures developed in the turnpike; naturally, after the habit of well-traveled roads, the Cumberland Road needed repairs.

The Constitution, law and order, quaked. Could President James Monroe conscientiously approve the use of national funds to replace one unturned stone or deepen one ditch along the Road? Not, certainly, if the funds were to be raised by tollgates along the pike; and in 1822 he rejected an act authorizing the President to establish tollgates for the support of the road, squarely upon the ground that

Congress was not constitutionally competent to exercise jurisdiction over internal improvements.

In the next year Monroe approved an act appropriating $25,000 from the general revenues for the repair of the Cumberland Road. But the western congressmen were introducing resolutions for new, almost unlimited projects at national expense, the constitutionality of these projects was still a touchy question, and the whole issue of internal improvements was a dirty and much-abused political football. Monroe hoped that by some arrangement responsibility for keeping the Cumberland Road in fit condition for traffic would be assumed by the states it traversed; but in his last official act he approved the extension of the Road west of the Ohio.

The repairs on the Road were almost a rebuilding. The War Department instructed its engineers to use Mr. Macadam's system; and as no one knew much about it, selections from *Macadam on Roads* were reprinted and distributed. The old roadbed was to be torn up, and a nine-inch bed of stone put in; stone for the lower three-inch layer was to be so broken up that pieces would pass through a seven-inch ring, and the bits for the upper six inches must not be too large to pass through a three-inch ring. Old contractors actually provided these measuring rings, and enforced a strict compliance. As the work progressed common sense relaxed the requirements, and where the old bed had withstood the fatigue of its yeoman service, it was allowed to become the base of the new. Stone-breakers pounded upon granite and limestone with a one-pound hammer, a round ball of iron; sometimes heavy stone was thrown into a hole and crushed with a heavier hammer. In midsummer these huskies sometimes made canvas sunshades, and under them pounded away from sunrise to sunset. In the late forties somebody invented a stone-crushing machine operated by horsepower; it balked at Pennsylvania limestone, and was laid aside on Laurel Hill to rot. So perish all schemes to deprive honest men of their livelihood—and the men at the stone pile took another slug of whisky. The national enterprise was now a national benefit; from Wheeling the swinging stretches of the Ohio protracted the highway into old Louisiana.

Yet the pike had been completed to less than half its proposed extent. The "2 per cent fund" from the sale of public lands in Ohio had been the nest egg of the Cumberland Road; *"to* and *through* the State," the compact had read. The same reservation had been written into the enabling acts of Indiana and Illinois, and was to be repeated with the admission of Missouri. After years of caviling and delay, in 1825 Congress approved the building of the Road to Zanesville, Ohio, and authorized the extension of surveys into Missouri, through the capitals of Ohio, Indiana and Illinois.

In this same year a more ambitious enterprise, the Erie Canal, was completed, another highway opened into the west. De Witt Clinton in 1816 had exhorted the New York state legislature, "The improvement of the means of intercourse between different parts of the same country, has always been considered the first duty and most noble employment of government. If it be important that the inhabitants of the same country should be bound together by a community of interests, and a reciprocation of benefits; that agriculture should find a sale for its productions, manufacturers a vent for their fabrics; and commerce a market for its commodities; it is your incumbent duty. . . ." The impending completion of the Cumberland Road to Wheeling, with its promise of Western commerce to Philadelphia and Baltimore, was a spur to the pride of New York; Clinton was swept into the governorship, and in 1817 the building of the canal began. There was no American precedent for this gigantic project of an artificial waterway from the Hudson River to Lake Erie; only the credit of the state could raise the funds, how immense no estimates presaged; elementary matters of construction had to be learned by experience. But in eight years the canal was opened from river to lake; on October 26, 1825, the canal boat *Seneca Chief* left the little construction town of Buffalo, carrying the news to the seaboard that an old route of fur traders was now remade for national commerce and national travel. A floodgate for emigration, the Erie Canal opened the upper half of the Old Northwest for rapid settlement; and its freight traffic far overshadowed that of the Cumberland Road.

In 1825 New Englanders had not settled in influential numbers in the Old Northwest, except in the Western Reserve and in six other districts—the Muskingum Valley, the upper valleys of the two Miamis, and three tiny tracts in Indiana. Virginians and Carolinians had been crowding into Ohio ever since the Virginia Military Tract was opened; Indiana and Illinois at that date were almost wholly southern, the lower lands only being occupied, and those mostly held by Southerners who had crossed the Ohio from the Kentucky shore. The completion of the Erie Canal, first quickening the settlement of the remaining wilderness lands in western New York and northwestern Pennsylvania, and building cities all along its route, hastened and multiplied the emigration of New Englanders into the West. New Englanders and New Yorkers poured into Indiana and Illinois in numbers that dismayed the pioneers in the lower halves of the states. Michigan and Wisconsin began to come out of the wilderness; emigrants were singing in 1837, to the overtone of a Connecticut twang,

Then there's the State of New York, where some are very rich;
Themselves and a few others have dug a mighty ditch,
To render it more easy for us to find the way,
And sail upon the waters to Michigania,
     Yea, yea, yea, to Michigania.

But the Cumberland Road poured into the Old Northwest its thousands of emigrants, thousands of wagonloads of factory stuff; back over it came the flour, whisky, hemp, bacon, wool, live stock of the West, western merchants and stockmen to Philadelphia and Baltimore, western politicians to Washington. "How do you do, General Jackson, Sir?" The General was highly popular with tavern keepers and all the "boys" of the Road. General Harrison, James Polk, Zachary Taylor, each passed over the Road on his

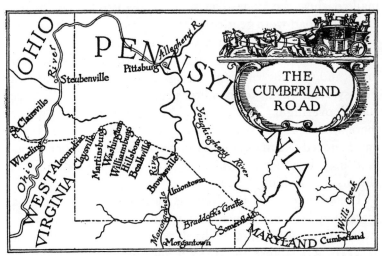

way to his inauguration, each in a splendid coach built and gilded for the occasion. Jennie Lind, P. T. Barnum and troupe, passed over the Road in chartered coaches of the Stockton Line. Henry Clay traveled the Road often, greeting stage drivers and tavern keepers by name; and being in a coach that overturned, spoke that elephantine *bon mot*, "This, sir, is mixing the Clay of Kentucky with the limestone of Pennsylvania." These travelers were merely the beads in the bottle; the real body was the stuff under the canvas of the many Conestoga wagons.

"The wagons were so numerous," said a traveler, "that

the leaders of one wagon had their noses in the trough at the end of the next wagon ahead." In 1822 one of five commission houses in Wheeling unloaded almost 3,800,000 pounds of freight from 1,081 wagons; in the next decade the population of the river town, battening on the increasing trade, had almost doubled.

During the prosperous era of the Road, it was not uncommon to see on left or right as many as fifteen stagecoaches in continuous procession; besides the passenger and mail coaches, the Conestoga wagons, the private equipages, along the road were gentlemen traveling singly in the saddle, with all their accouterments in the saddlebags; Yankee peddlers with wagonloads of gewgaws for farmhouse parlors; and droves of hogs being driven from back-track Pennsylvania farms to slaughter pens in Baltimore. "I have stayed overnight . . . ," an old wagoner writes, "where there would be thirty-six horse teams on the wagon yard, one hundred Kentucky mules in an adjacent lot, one thousand hogs in other enclosures, and as many fat cattle from Illinois in adjoining fields."

The commerce of the Road is succinctly illustrated in a freighting trip of Daniel Barcus in 1838. A Baltimore merchant engaged him to haul a load, 3,800 pounds, of general merchandise to Mt. Vernon, Ohio. The wagoner was to receive $4.25 for each hundred pounds. Barcus put in two days with a gallon of whisky by way of conditioning himself, and started out. He delivered the merchandise in thirty days, having driven about four hundred miles. At Mt. Vernon he loaded his wagon with Ohio tobacco, seven thousand two hundred pounds packed in hogsheads, for which he received $2.75 a hundred pounds. Mt. Vernon was thirty-two miles in the "back country"; and Barcus has left the statement that when he reached the National Road again, at Jacktown, he "felt at home again."

It is no wonder that when in 1832, after the Road had

again been neglected for years, Congress made a substantial appropriation for repairs and rebuilding, the citizens of Cumberland were exuberant; that the hotels were illuminated, and an illuminated stagecoach was driven about the city, with "upon the top of the vehicle several gentlemen who played on various instruments, which contributed very much to the amusement of the citizens and gave a zest to everything that inspired delight or created feelings of patriotism."

There were two classes of wagoners, the "regular" and the "sharpshooter." The regular was on the road constantly with his team and wagon; freighting was his sole occupation. Sharpshooters were farmers, who put their farm teams on the road when prices were high, and went back to the plow when the gravy was thinned. The Road was a pleasantly provincial institution: regular wagoners hated sharpshooters; back-country boys were jealous of Pike boys; on rival stages even the passengers became noisy partisans of the line by which they traveled.

Regular wagoners were the real "Pike boys"—their own phrase. Like every western coterie, theirs was a diverse group united by devotion to their profession. Among them, Robert Allison, a fighting man, who bit off the nose of a stage driver; David Harr, fiddler, and William Keefer, jigs and buck-and-wing, who together warmed the barroom of many a tavern. And "there was an old wagoner whose name was Hill, and he lived at Triadelphia," who never drove his team of a Sunday, and after his many years on the Road became a rich man. There was another, Michael Teeters, a sputtering old wagoner, famed for his careless and continual profanity; the biographer of the Pike boys ends this wagoner's story, "When age and infirmity came upon him, he exchanged the tramp over the hills of the old pike for a walk 'over the hills to the poor house,' and died in the county home." Most of the wagoners hoped to keep a tavern beside the Pike in their old age; and a few achieved that ambition.

The wagons, genuine Conestogas, invariably with the blue underbody and the bright red upper work, were usually drawn by six horses. The "gears" were of immense proportions; it required a strong man to throw the chain-iron traces over the back of a big horse. The Cumberland Road had stayed out of the muck, following the hill crests; but descents easy for pack ponies were menacing to heavy wagons. The wagoners, as an old Pike boy tells, "would cut a small pole about ten or eleven feet long and tie it to the bed with the lock chain and then bend it against the hind wheel and tie it to the feed trough, or the hind part of the wagon bed, just tight enough to let the wheel turn slow. Sometimes one driver would wear out from fifteen to twenty poles between Baltimore and Wheeling." There were no bridges then across the Monongahela or the Ohio; wagons were ferried across on flatboats. In winter, if the river was frozen over, all was well; if not, the wagoner simply had to wait for the ice to behave.

Stagecoaches drawn by superb, showy horses raced along the Road in intense competition for passenger traffic and mail contracts. "Make this time or we'll find some one who will," read the drivers' waybills. The "little fellows" could not last, but comfortable coaches, companionable drivers, fast horses, quick schedules became a tradition that lasted as long as the Road.

The National Road Stage Company, headquarters at Uniontown, was the largest of them all. Its manager was Lucius Stockton, with a zest for competition and a love for horses. When in 1830 the Baltimore and Ohio Railroad began the use of locomotives, it was Stockton who took up the challenge on behalf of the stagecoaches; it was a horse of Stockton's, driven by Stockton, that raced against the *Tom Thumb,* and won. It is typical of the man's worship

[320]

of energy that his two favorite horses ("whom he drove frequently from Uniontown to Wheeling between breakfast and tea time, tarrying two or three hours at Washington") were taught to demand a little whisky in their water buckets. His chief competitor was James Reeside, owner of most of the stage lines running out of Philadelphia and the holder of more mail contracts than any other man. In 1810 a wagoner, in 1830 he was christened by the newspapers the "Land Admiral." He was a staunch Democrat, but the waywardness of fortune in making Amos Kendall Postmaster-General was too much for him; after his contracts under Kendall expired Reeside's lines carried no more mail. A splotch of red on the Cumberland Road meant Reeside—a red stage, the Good Intent Line; a red vest and a red necktie, the man himself.

A through fare from Baltimore to Wheeling was $17.25; from Cumberland to Wheeling, $8.25. The coaches ran night and day alike. Relays of fresh horses were spaced about twelve miles apart. The coach sped up to the station; a jarring halt, and the driver threw down the reins; almost instantly the panting team was detached, and an already-harnessed fresh pair was backed into place; the reins were thrown up to the driver, the coach was speeding away again, and the little group of village loafers dispersed.

Stage drivers were paid twelve dollars a month, with board and lodging at the stagehouses. Perhaps the smallness of the compensation, perhaps the prominence of the Scotch-Irish element among the Pike boys, accounts for the invention and the popularity of that cigarlike curiosity first called the Conestoga cigar, later the Pittsburgh stogie.

"Stage drivers as a class"—this is a wagoner's verdict— "did not rank as high morally as wagoners, but despite this there were among them men of good sense, honest intentions, and steady habits." Preëminent among them, and as flashing a figure as the Old Pike produced, was Redding

Bunting, Stockton's favorite driver. Six feet six he was, affable and companionable; his faithful biographer wrote, "His voice was of the baritone order, deep and sonorous, but he was not loquacious and had the habit of munching." In 1846 Redding Bunting drove the great mail coach from Cumberland to Wheeling which carried Polk's proclamation that a state of war existed between the United States and Mexico. Leaving Cumberland at two in the morning, he was in Uniontown at eight, breakfasted there with his passengers, sped the coach on into Washington at eleven, and jumped off the coach at Wheeling three hours later. As his biographer remembered Bunting, "Despondency and depression of spirits seemed to have encompassed him, when business ceased on the road, and he appeared as one longing for the return of other and better days."

James Burr and David Gordon, the two heavy-fisted drivers who defeated all comers but were afraid of each other; Peter Payne, who got rich playing poker; Montgomery Dennings, 465 pounds in weight ("Old Mount in the front boot of a coach balances all the trunks that can be put in the rear boot")—these were a few of the drivers who carried the tang of the Road from tidewater to the Ohio.

The taverns, stagehouses and wagon houses, were not a mile apart between Cumberland and Wheeling. They were good taverns. The defense needs only one witness, T. B. Searight, the first historian of the Road: "Surprise is often expressed that there were so many good taverns in the mountains, remote from fertile fields and needed markets. That they were equal to the best on the road is conceded; and that the old taverns of the National Road have never been surpassed for bounteous entertainment and good cheer, is likewise conceded; in fact, has never been disputed." And some one has left a redolent, reminiscent paragraph: "The white façade was checkered by the leaves of a sheltering chestnut or elm, and the fragrance of the locust mingled with the air. The glittering and gilded sign swung out from one of the branches, and a moss-grown trough over-flowed and trickled melodiously before the porch. . . . An hour before the coach was due the landlord was to be found in a little alcove of the taproom, transferring his liquors from demijohns to bottles . . . bidding his servants make haste with the supper."

The floors were usually sanded, the beams were usually uncovered; a great fireplace dominated the main room, and a little bar, perhaps ornamented with fancy lattice work, was a lesser lodestone on one side of the room. There were no "temperance" drivers; whisky sold at five cents for one or two glasses.

During the winters the fireplaces were kept constantly alight. In many instances the grates were seven feet across; and while the landlord might not care if a Pike boy wandered behind the bar, stoking the fire, with a poker six or eight feet long, was the landlord's exclusive privilege. Boss Rush, "the prince of landlords," kept his poker under lock and key. About the roaring fire the Pike boys drank, exchanged the gossip of the fraternity, and wrangled over national politics. If the landlord or one of the company was a fiddler, the wagoners "limbered up" after the day's ride with a hoe-down. And about the roaring fire they slept on the floor in a semicircle, their feet toward the blaze.

The most important official service of the National Road was in carrying the mails. When the system reached its highest perfection, two great mail lines, with hundreds of connecting mails, passed daily over the Road—the Great Eastern mail out of Washington, and the Great Western mail from St. Louis. The express mail stages made remarkable time. In 1833 the Great Eastern mail left Washington at seven in the evening and Baltimore at nine, and arrived at Wheeling in fifty-five hours. Leaving Wheeling at 4:30 in the morning, the coach was in Columbus at five the following morning, and arrived at Cincinnati exactly twenty-four hours later. In the mid-thirties a Pony Express was introduced, to speed the transmission of light mails; but these fleet couriers did not remain long on the Road.

Congress appropriated one hundred and fifty thousand dollars, in March, 1825, for the building of the Road to Zanesville, on the Scioto, and extending the survey "to pass by the seats of government of Ohio, Indiana, and Illinois," into Missouri. Appropriations in 1827 and 1829 furthered the ambitious undertaking. Going west in literally the straightest line to Columbus, construction was completed to the Ohio capital in 1833. Work had already begun on the extension west. Posters such as this were in Ohio post offices in the thirties:

NATIONAL ROAD IN OHIO.—Notice to contractors.—Proposals will be received by the undersigned, until the 19th of August inst., for clearing and grubbing eight miles of the line of the National Road west of this place. . . .

The trees and growth to be entirely cleared away to the distance of 40 feet on each side of the central axis of the road, and all trees impending over that space to be cut down; all stumps and roots to be carefully grubbed out to the distance of 20 feet on each side of the axis, and where occasional high embankments, or spacious side drains, may be required, the grubbing is to extend to the distance of 30 feet on each side of the same axis. All the timber, brush, stumps and roots to be entirely removed from the above space of 80 feet in width and the earth excavated in grubbing, to be thrown back into the hollows formed by removing the stumps and roots. . . .

Notice is hereby given to the proprietors of the land . . . to remove all fences and other barriers now across the line, a reasonable time being allowed them to secure that portion of their present crops which may lie upon the location of the road.

From Indianapolis the Road was built both eastward and westward, and grading was carried forward as far as Vandalia, capital of of the pioneers' Illinois. Work went no farther. Construction of the National Road could not keep abreast of the changing times; progress overtook it, subtly fought it after 1832, and within a decade halted it.

In 1836 the House Committee on Roads and Canals seriously considered substituting a railway for the Cumberland Road past Columbus. In 1838 Congress shrugged its shoulders of the whole matter, granting the last appropriation that the Cumberland Road received. And title to the Road passed to the states through which it ran.

The great highway into the farther West, the Ohio River, had more than maintained its prestige against the work of the road-builders; and the canals that in the eighteen-thirties were being planned in dozens of districts in the Old Northwest were all to be, in a sense, tributaries of the Ohio. In 1811 Nicholas Roosevelt brought shipwrights and machinists from New York to Pittsburgh, to build the *New Orleans,* the deep-drafted, round-bellied steamship which was launched into the water on the seventeenth of March. Five years later Captain Henry M. Shreve, a "river man" to his marrow, built the first double-deck steamboat, a flat-hulled, high-pressure boat, the true progenitor of the steam craft that by 1834 dominated the Ohio and the Mississippi.

Pittsburgh in 1834 had won its by-phrase, "the Birmingham of America." Its banks of coal and iron were being exploited; cutlery, iron-castings and ironmongery of many descriptions, engines, nails, glass, paper, wire, were its industrial products. The rich lands in the valley below the city were well settled, and properly renowned for their corn, wheat, and fruit. Each year great quantities of whisky, cider, and apples were sent downstream.

Samuel Cummings' *Western Pilot* took many a navigator safely down the Ohio and into the Mississippi. Like Cramer's *Navigator,* it was reissued annually; the shifting

[325]

channel took no account of the expense of revised editions. An amateur pilot setting out from Pittsburgh in 1834 turned to the first page of his *Western Pilot:* "From the landing at Pittsburgh, on the Monongahela side, keep near the right shore, and, at high water, pull directly out into the Allegheny current, which sets strong over to the left shore. At low water, when nearly up to the point, keep over to the left, towards O'Hara's glassworks, which will carry you clear of the bar at the point, and of the Monongahela bar on the left." Seventeen miles from Pittsburgh, past Dead Man's Island; eighteen miles, past Economy, the "ideal" town which the utopianist George Rapp had lately founded; on, fifty-two miles farther, to the up-and-coming town of Steubenville. This little city on the high prairie of the north bank, Samuel Cummings informed the pilot, "exports large quantities of whisky, flour, grain, etc. It contains . . . about 3,000 inhabitants . . . three flour mills, a very large and justly celebrated woollen factory, at which 60,000 pounds of wool are annually manufactured into cloth. . . . There are, besides, two cotton factories of 3,000 spindles, [and] a large paper mill, belonging to Mr. Holdship, of Pittsburgh, which manufactures the finest and best paper made in the western country."

Eighteen miles down the river the voyager came to Wheeling, the vanquished rival of Pittsburgh. Here the National Road crossed from Virginia into Ohio, and stagecoach routes radiated into the interior country. Wheeling, advised the useful Mr. Cummings, "contains above 5,000 inhabitants, has about 600 dwelling houses, a court house, a jail, a bank, two churches, a book store, a printing office, library, academy, a large number of stores and commission ware houses, and several inns, some of which are highly respectable. Flat-boats and keel boats are built here; and, of late, a number of steam boats."

Beyond Wheeling lay Marietta, whose inhabitants were still renowned for sobriety, industry, and civil deportment; but the town had been left behind in the rising tide of emigration. Forty miles farther boats negotiated the tortuous, log-glutted channel past Buffington's Island. Maysville, four hundred miles from Pittsburgh, was still the supply depot of eastern Kentucky. Fifty-five miles farther, on the north bank, glittered the Queen City of the West. The *Western Pilot* crammed the navigator with statistical facts about Cincinnati, whose population of thirty thousand outdistanced that of any city in the West except New Orleans. "Steamboats, many of which are owned here, arrive and depart almost every hour in the day. There already are a great number of wholesale stores, which supply the merchants of the interior at a small advance upon the eastern prices. They have, at great expense, constructed one of the finest river landings in the world. There are two very respectable museums, and a gallery of paintings." And much else besides—strides forward in "wealth, enterprise, population, manufactures, taste, literature, and improvements of every description" that made Cincinnati a unique entity, neither western nor eastern, a thing of rare flavor not simply explained by the presence of hundreds of well-to-do Germans. English travelers whose published journals were grievous barbs to American pride, always wrote of Cincinnati as of an oasis.

Farther downstream, beside the most dangerous stretch of the river—the Falls—was Louisville, its three principal streets gangling parallel to the stream. The city had some ten thousand inhabitants in 1834; it thrived, comfortably but not to gorging, on the market needs of interior Kentucky, and the consignments of upward-bound cargoes.

Beyond the Falls, passing the lowlands of the Indiana and Illinois bottoms, the navigator had little hazard until he reached the Grand Chain of Rocks, four miles long, that zigzagged boats fairly from one bank to the other. And, nine hundred fifty-nine miles from Pittsburgh, the rush of the current carried the ship into the full southward swing of the Mississippi.

CHAPTER XIX

THE SANTA FE TRAIL

THE friars were disappointed: their flails beat fruit-
lessly against pagan chaff. The gentlemen of
fortune, governors and captains, were disappointed: there were lean pickings in this barren, pueblo-
mottled plateau. And in September, 1608, the Council
of the Indies recommended that the province of New
Mexico be abandoned. In December arrived one Father
Ximenez, reporting great accessions of pueblo-dwellers to
Christianity, bringing samples of ore to ask if these were
silver. The order to abandon was suspended, and New
Mexico was saved for Spain.

A startlingly sensible policy of gradual development of
New Mexico at royal expense was begun. Royal orders
outlined the establishment of a new city designed expressly
to be the capital; in 1609 this city, Santa Fe, was built.
The military were not to enter hostile pueblos except as
escorts to the friars; Spaniards' cattle were to be kept out
of Indian cornfields.

The serious dangers of Indian hostility and Spanish
rascality faded within a hundred years. Sheep herders and
farmers found a place in northern Mexico, about Santa Fe,
or Taos, or another of the little settlements. New
Mexicans cultivated the knack of barter. Once a year, in

July or August, a grand fair week was held at Taos. The Comanches and other Plains Indians came here, smack into a beautiful system of imaginary currency, smack into guile; but they went away with the blankets, the iron tools, and the gew-gaws that they wanted. The one important link of this isolated commerce with Mexico itself was the January fair at Chihuahua, five hundred miles to the south from Santa Fe. The departure and return of this annual caravan were the great events of the year; but the system left the traders quite at the mercy of the Chihuahua merchants. In time the King of France deeded his white elephant, Louisiana, to Spain; but St. Louis was an unconscionable distance from Santa Fe, and had then but little trade of its own.

Pedro Vial was one of those Westerners who lived with Indians as easily as with their own people; Fernando de la Concha, becoming governor of New Mexico in the year of Washington's inaugural, decided that communication through the Indian country to the Missouri River would stimulate the commerce of his province, and in 1792 summoned Vial for the commission. The governor gave him detailed instructions "to open communication with our settlements . . . which are located on the shores of the Misuri River," how to use a compass, how to trace his route, to note distances: "he shall endeavor to keep a diary, as exact as possible, noting therein the directions which he takes; the daily distances; the rivers which he finds, their flow, and the quantity of their waters; the mountains and tablelands which present themselves to him, explaining their configuration, and supplying to them names analogous to it; the tribes whom he finds, their customs and what he may find out from them; and whatever else he believes can be of use for new information and clearness." And, lest these instructions be too levelheaded: "Whatever unforeseen accident occurs during his march, he shall overcome it, and

[330]

remove it according as his prudence and his knowledge assist him, in the manner that he believes most useful to the service of the King, and the honor of his Province."

With this auspicious commission, Vial set out with two companions—sixty pesos in silver for these two to divide, if they came back alive! Their horses plodded along steadily, to the Pecos, then northeast, then east, crossing strange rivers which Vial futilely christened. At first each day's march was about twenty miles; but on the fifth day out, "We met seven Comanches with their wives, among whom was a Spanish interpreter. . . . They made us return to the Pecos River in joy at having met me, for it was a long time since they had seen me. Consequently we lost the march of that day." After twelve days, bad weather and rough table-lands sometimes slowed the march. On the twenty-eighth of June, the forty-eighth day out, "We kept quiet all day in order to rest our horses." The next morning there occurred that "unforeseen accident" that Concha's opaque advice had presaged. The party found some slain buffaloes on the prairie; this was "Indian sign," and they followed. In the afternoon they met with the Indians, a Kansas tribe. Every one, runs Vial's narrative, shook hands cordially; then the Indians took possession of the party's horses and goods, and debated the several merits of dispatch by arrows or by hatchets. Ultimately, perhaps because Vial was recognized by one Indian, there was no butchery. "But the one called Vicente Villanueva had his horse cut and a dagger thrust in the abdomen which would have proved fatal had he not shrunk away when the blow was delivered. An Indian, who wished to save him, received all the force of the blow on his arm and was quite badly wounded. They kept us naked among them in the said camp until the fifteenth of August."

On the sixteenth the tribe returned to its village, ten days' march away, on the banks of the Kansas. About mid-

September a French lone trapper came with his pirogue of trading stuff. He staked the three prisoners to clothes, a gun and ammunition, and tobacco. Brother trappers, passing with an empty pirogue, gave them a lift. On the sixth of October, 1792, Vial presented himself to the commandant at St. Louis.

It would have been an epochal expedition—if anything had come of it.

As it was, incursions above the borderlands were left for private initiative. The years dragged away. *Ciboleros* wandered through the buffalo plains, killing game, carrying on desultory trade with the Indians. These hardy Mexicans, with their betasseled lances and guns, sallied sometimes an amazing distance from their New Mexican villages. But the *cibolero* who went to Indian camps was usually a lone wolf; there was no organized trade to the northeast, and the "road" of Pedro Vial was rubbed out by the gritty sands.

Then, while Lewis and Clark were engaged in their magnificent field trip, the "insatiable pioneer" looked beyond the hazy border line of the Louisiana Purchase toward Santa Fe, stroked his chin bristles, and began his attempt to capture the profits of New Mexican commerce. Some mines were being worked now; Santa Fe had some bullion and specie to export, and there were horses, burros, beaver skins and buffalo robes available for exchange. Chihuahua was too far removed from the seacoast to be a first-rate mart for New Mexican traders; after the long haul from Vera Cruz, goods were astoundingly high. The obvious answer was American enterprise and American goods: American caravans from the Missouri River to Santa Fe. That answer was obvious to every one but Spanish officials.

The Spanish Empire was a beggar in velvet; its commercial laws reaffirmed a national exclusiveness long after that exclusiveness had fairly choked the commerce it meant to protect. Baptiste La Lande, a French Creole, was sent to Santa Fe by William Morrison, a merchant of southern Illinois, to try his luck with a small stock of goods and report on the wants of that market. The government of New Mexico had no wish to have La Lande's information available to American merchants; the amiable scoundrel yielded to the first courteous "suggestion," pocketed Morrison's profits, and made himself at home in Santa Fe. A year later, in 1805, James Purcell, Kentuckian, after some curious experiences in Indian trade arrived in Santa Fe. Zebulon Pike found him there in 1807, making a comfortable living as carpenter, but kept under close surveillance by the Spaniards. "He entertained me with numerous interesting anecdotes of his adventures with the Indians, and of the jealousy of the Spanish government," writes the American lieutenant. "He was once near being hanged for making a few pounds of gunpowder, which he innocently did as he had been accustomed to in Kentucky, but which is a capital crime in these provinces. . . . He still retained the gun which he had with him his whole tour, and said confidently that if he had two hours' start not all the province could take him." Some parties of American traders who ventured to Santa Fe in the next few years were treated as alien smugglers, and their goods confiscated. There must have been some trading parties who found Spanish officials amenable to reason and to bribes, but no record, no memory, remains. Mexico flared into revolution in 1821, and the prohibition upon American trade was one of the old fiats that crackled away. Traders who had been in prison for nine years were set free, and as the news of the successful revolution filtered into Santa Fe, the trade began in earnest.

The husky days of the Santa Fe Trail began with the expeditions of William Becknell, Missourian, whose horses clumped along the route that quickly became the standard one from the Missouri River to Santa Fe. Not that there was one standard, immutable trail; there was no such thing in this early West. Standardization waited the coming of the stagecoaches and the railroads. On level, grassy ground, ruts and paths spread, diverge, from horizon to horizon: but when water is scarce, when mountains athwart the course of the trail are broken only by one or two passes, when arroyos and creek beds crack up the surface of a prairie, the haphazard threads of the trail are drawn into one.

Becknell's first journey, 1821, began curiously late in the season; it was the twenty-fourth of September before his company reached the Arkansas. Innumerable buffaloes were on either side of the wide, shallow stream; prairie dogs, rabbits, and later wild horses appeared abundantly on the incessant prairie.

> Onward where Campania's plain, forsaken, lies
> A weary waste extending to the skies—

Becknell could not forbear quoting Goldsmith, despite the immense number of animals who fed upon this "weary waste."

The Arkansas River was followed to the mountains: "We now had some cliffs to ascend, which presented difficulties almost insurmountable, and we were laboriously engaged nearly two days in rolling away large rocks, before we attempted to get our horses up, and even then one fell and was bruised to death." Again, in crossing the rugged cliffs of the Canadian River, this travail was necessary. Lack of wood, lack of water, little food for the overworked horses, a storm of wind and snow, added to the difficulties of this semi-final stretch. In mid-November the company reached San Miguel, the little cluster of mud-wall huts about the Pecos River which was the gateway to Santa Fe.

[334]

The capital was two days away, over unformidable ridges and table-lands.

The company was received with excited pleasure; the Governor invited Becknell to visit him. "His demeanor was courteous and friendly. He asked many questions concerning my country, its people, their manner of living, etc.; expressed a desire that the Americans would keep up an intercourse with that country, and said that if any of them wished to emigrate, it would give him pleasure to afford every facility." And Becknell kept his eyes open, learning a great deal.

"Those who visit the country for the purpose of vending merchandise will do well to take goods of excellent quality and unfaded colors," he summed up for his fellow-Missourians. "A very great advance is obtained on goods, and the trade is very profitable; money and mules are plentiful, and they do not hesitate to pay the price demanded for an article if it suits their purpose, or their fancy."

Becknell, four years later, casually referred to 1822 as "When I opened the road to Santa Fe." In his expedition of that year Becknell made an effective revision of his march of 1821: instead of following the Arkansas to the tenacious mountain barriers of its upper reaches, he cut southeast to the Cimarron.

In 1825 Senator Benton, bolstered by a meaty letter from Augustus Storrs, citizen of Franklin, wrested from Congress an appropriation of twenty thousand dollars to placate the Indians just beyond Missouri, and ten thousand dollars for the building of a road to the Mexican border in the direction of the Santa Fe. Commissioners accordingly salved the Osage and Kaw Indians for the invasion of their domain, and secured their promise not to molest the traders. A field engineer surveyed the road, made neat compilations of the distance in miles and chains, and a few stakes were driven. That was all well enough. More important to the traders than these works of Government was the good will these works seemed to manifest; and the trade boomed.

Franklin, until it found a watery grave, and thereafter Independence, farther westward yet, only twenty miles from the western border of Missouri, was the most favored spot for outfitting the wagon trains. Here, about the first of May, the traders assembled to buy their provisions and trading stuff. Flour, bacon, coffee, sugar, and salt, had to be bought, to supplement the real staple of meals on the Trail—buffalo. Pack animals were seldom used once the Trail had become familiar; Pittsburgh wagons, brought by steamboat down the Ohio and up to the docks of Independence, were the schooners of these Santa Fe flotillas. Four brace or more of mules or oxen hauled a load of about five thousand pounds—"dry goods and notions," as the Franklin storekeepers probably announced.

Trader Josiah Gregg was alive to the romance of the departure: "The charioteer, as he smacks his whip, feels a bounding elasticity of soul within him, which he finds it impossible to restrain;—even the mules prick up their ears with a peculiarly conceited air, as if in anticipation of that change of scene which will presently follow. Harmony and good feeling prevail everywhere. The hilarious song, the *bon mot* and the witty repartee, go round in quick succession; and before people have leisure to take cognizance of the fact, the lovely village of Independence, with its multitude of associations, is already lost to the eye."

One morning out from Independence, the Trail crossed Big Blue Creek, and the western prairie began. The last frontier enclosure, the last cabin, was passed that same day. Behind the caravan, up-and-coming Missouri; before it, "treeless plains of green, as they had been since the flood," wrote traveler Thomas Farnham, "beautiful, unbroken by bush or rock; unsoiled by plow or spade; sweetly scented with the first blossomings of the spring. They had been, since time commenced, the theater of the Indian's prowess —of his hopes, joys, and sorrows." All very well; but the Indians' hopes and joys would certainly run to thoughts of theft, not inconceivably to a vision of butchery. An organization of the caravan, in military fashion, was its best protection against Indians; its greatest danger was the pioneer's talent for kicking over the traces.

Council Grove, a hundred and forty-five miles from Independence, offered irresistible arguments to be lazy awhile; and the traders usually deferred the necessity of organizing until they reached this spot.

The prairie was at its handsomest in May, with many varieties of young flowers gemming the green plains, and bands of elm, willow and hickory trees tracing the banks of the many little creeks. But Council Grove Creek was luxuriously timbered with a hundred and fifty acres of shaded land. The contrast to the hot, shadeless march prompted open admiration from reticent men. "A beautiful lawn of the wilderness," one traveler called it; others invented an idyllic past for it as a peace sanctuary of warring Indian tribes; and the Grove fanned the expansion-fever of other Westerners: "All who have traversed these delightful regions, look forward to the day when the Indian title to the land shall be extinguished."

Aspirants for the captaincy of the caravan were pushed forward, and the traders in assembly debated and bickered, defended and denounced, until balloting settled the question. "There may be some honor in it," jotted a just-elected captain in his diary, "but not much profit." The captain could direct the course of march, select the night's camp ground, and handle other matters of routine, expectant of being obeyed; but in emergencies any or many of the sovereign members of this social compact was apt to renege.

A check-up of the company's strength came next. Major

Wetmore's company of 1824 offers a fair picture: "We this evening ascertained the whole strength of our company to be 81 persons and two servants; we also had 2 road waggons, 20 dearborns, 2 carts and one small piece of cannon. The amount of goods taken with us is supposed to be about $30,000. We have with us about 200 horses and mules." Tragedy on the Trail in 1828 emphasized the possibility of Indian attacks, and larger caravans became the rule. Josiah Gregg's company of 1831 mustered nearly a hundred wagons, carrying merchandise worth about $200,000, and had two cannon upon carriages.

The caravan was generally divided into two or four divisions, each division forming a column in the march; for each division a lieutenant was appointed, who was to keep in advance of his column, select the best water-crossings, and keep his eye alert. "After this guard," as Farnham described his party of 1839, "the head teams of each column lead off about thirty feet apart, and the others follow in regular line, rising and dipping gloriously; two hundred men, one hundred waggons, eight hundred mules; shoutings and whipping, and whistlings and cheerings, are all there; and, amidst them all, the hardy Yankees move happily onward to the siege of the mines of Montezuma."

Beyond the clear-watered branches of the Neosho, over swelling meadows whose waves became more gentle as the days passed, the caravan moved toward the Arkansas. At evening the wagons maneuvered into a rough quadrangle, within which the most valuable horses and oxen were put, and the rest of the stock staked or "hobbled" just outside. Among these animals a night watch was kept; the guard crouched motionless for his two hours, vigilant for any moving shadow against the line of light around the lower edge of the horizon.

About two hundred and seventy miles from Independence, the caravan reached the valley of the Arkansas. "An imposing and majestic appearance," it presented to Josiah Gregg: "Beneath a ledge of wave-like yellow sandy ridges and hillocks spreading far beyond, descends the majestic river . . . bespeckled with verdant islets, thickly set with cottonwood timber." But several days' march along the valley wore away the picturesqueness with desolate monotony—only here and there a tree, an occasional little grove of stunted cottonwoods; flat, grassy islands dividing the wide, shallow river; high sandy hills at the edge of the valley. Meals were cooked over buffalo-chip fires now; hunters deployed into buffalo herds; the riders in the vanguard kept popping away at rattlesnakes.

The safest course was to follow the valley as far as Chouteau's Island, three hundred miles from Taos. Twenty miles above the island the banks of the Arkansas were very low on either side; and here the caravan made its crossing, a long oblique march over unstable sands. Fuel was plentiful, and travelers baked bread enough to last them for the next hundred miles.

But the safest course did not happen to be the shortest course; and wherever the Arkansas was crossed, the "waterscrape" began soon after. As the traders became richer in experience, the caravans usually struck across the Arkansas about a hundred miles east of Chouteau's Island, heading boldly into the "desert" between the Arkansas and the Cimarron, fifty miles away. The plain was hard, unmarked by ruts, destitute of water; every keg was filled before the wagons left the Arkansas, and the caravan tried to push through the distance in two days. And there was a chance that the Cimarron would be dry.

The rigors of this "water-scrape" were met by M. M. Marmaduke's caravan of 1824. "Traveled 30 miles," reads his journal for June the twenty-ninth, the first day out from the Arkansas; "left our encampment at 4 o'clock, A.M., and traveled without making any halt until about 4 o'clock, P.M.,

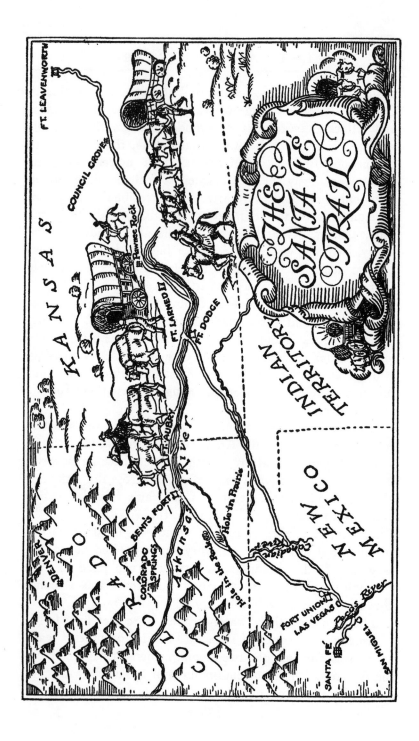

without a drop of water for our horses or mules, by which time many of them were nearly exhausted, as well as a number of the men; a dog which had traveled with us during our journey, this day fell down and expired, such was the extreme heat and suffering. Fortunately for us all at about 4 o'clock a small ravine was discovered and pursued for a few miles, and after digging in the sand at the bottom of it, water was procured in sufficient quantity to satisfy both man and horse, but not until after five or six wells were sunk." And up the Cimarron, it was the same story; "water remarkably bad and scarce, having to dig for it at every place we stopped."

Past the Cimarron, nature offered no serious hazards; but only a little water, and that filthy, was to be had, and the way was arduously rugged. On the summit of the ridge between the Cimarron and the Canadian, the traveler came into view of the Rockies. The march pricked up now; and a party of "runners" pushed forward in advance of the caravan for Santa Fe. These emissaries were to buy and send back a supply of provisions, and to arrange for warehouse space in Santa Fe; most important, they were to learn what imposts confronted the trading stuffs, and grease a few swarthy palms if need be. Mexican tariffs and Mexican laws had retained the old Spanish grace of convenient alteration, and were supple, inflexible, venal, arbitrary, or reasonable, patterning after their administrators.

"*Los Americanos!*"—"*La entrada de la caravana!*"; there was parade in the streets of Santa Fe. But the traders attended at once to the serious business of their visit; the goods were discharged in the warerooms of the custom-house, and were soon on the market.

Prices were tilted handsomely, of course; but for ready exchange and an early return from Santa Fe traders often sliced their possible profits and disposed of their entire stock at wholesale. Thus a letter from Ceran St. Vrain to his employers in Missouri explains: "It is with pleasure that I inform you of my last arrival at Santafe which was the 4th of August 1830. We were met at Red river by General Biscusa the customhouse officer and a few soldiers, the object in coming out so far was to prevent smuggling and it had the desired effeck, there was a guard placed around our wagons until we entered Santafe, we had all to pay full dutys which amounts to about 60 percent on cost. I was the first that put goods in the Customhouse and I opened immediately, but goods sold very slow, so slow that it was discouraging. I found that it was impossible to meet my payments if I continued retaling. I there fore thought it was best to hole Saile & I have done so. I send you by Mr. Andru Carson and Lavoise Ruel one wagon eleven mules, one horse and 653 skins of Beaver . . . which you will have sold for my account."

Traders who set up store for themselves drifted with the domestic current of Santa Fe until the goods were disposed of, and perhaps lingered into the following spring for better passage into the States. These American residents must have enjoyed themselves hugely; for nearly all who afterwards put their impressions of Santa Fe in writing found an extensive variety of vices and indecencies to denounce. "Men and women will indiscriminately and freely converse together on the most indecent gross and vulgar subjects that can possibly be conceived, without the least embarrassment or confusion," reported Marmaduke; and he and many another credit the Santa Feans with every vice that their poor means would permit them. The unquestioning religious enthusiasm of the people was an affront to these frontiersmen, and the evils and poverty of New Mexican society were readily blamed upon the priests. While Mexican and American were learning to coöperate amiably in commerce, these social contacts stiffened the definitely Protestant bias of the West.

The threat of Indian molestation constantly overshadowed the caravans on the Trail between Council Grove and the foothills of the Rockies; but tragedies were curiously few. Many of the Missourians who freighted to Santa Fe had grown up in the Old Southwest between the Alleghenies and the Mississippi, and vigilance had become second nature; too, Plains Indians without excuse for blood revenge usually preferred to steal than to kill. Tribes followed in the wake of the prairie schooners like dolphins, eager for any scrap that might be tossed to them—and eager to steal horses. In any caravan, apparently, there was always one frontiersman ready casually to kill any Indian discovered alone. Certainly the little detached groups of traders who were the first to follow the Santa Fe trail ran the gamut without loss of life; it was not until 1828, the era of hundred-wagon caravans, that any traders were killed on the trail.

In that year two young men, with a caravan returning to Franklin, were surprised asleep and killed. Two days later, at the Cimarron, the caravan encountered a few Comanches. Perhaps these were of the group who had murdered McNees and Monroe, perhaps not: that was a quibble. The Missourians blazed into the group, killing all but one Indian. And the miserable cycle revolved. The Comanche tribe pursued that caravan to the Arkansas, making away with nearly a thousand mules and horses; unsatisfied, these Indians waylaid the next party on the return trail, daring first a running fight, then skirmishing in the true Indian style. "When night came on," as an old frontiersman recounted the story, "the Indians resumed their attacks, endeavoring to stampede the horses so that they could chase them off and capture them. Their attempts were almost successful several times during the night and they were only kept from accomplishing their purpose by tying the bell mare to one of the wagons and jingling the bell every time the Indians charged. The next day the Comanches resumed the attack as vigorously as ever. Forming a circle, they galloped round and round the ill-fated caravan, shouting their demoniacal war whoops in a most fiendish manner. So fierce were the harassing tactics which they used that the little line of prairie schooners succeeded in advancing only five miles during the day. The annoyance was kept up night and day for a week until the travelers were almost exhausted from loss of sleep." The Indians ultimately made off with all the party's live stock, and killed one of the traders.

Frontiersmen were done now with orderly, documented appeals to the national government for military protection along the Trail. The importance of the Santa Fe trade was axiomatic to Missourians by 1828 (one hundred wagons had carried $100,000 worth of merchandise to New Mexico that year), and the Indian outrages of this year were added indictments of Washington's indifference. There was a curt, truly western color to the words of Missouri's governor to Missouri's legislature that fall: "The General Government has been applied to for protection—for *even* the establishment of a military post on the Arkansas. It has not been granted. Protection to our maritime trade is extended by the Government, to our merchants and other adventurers, in all parts of the world; and we have a right to expect and demand it for our inland trade to Mexico." And the exasperated legislature memorialized Congress: "Savages are restrained by nothing but *force.* . . . If the post on the Arkansas be established, and the escort as hereinbefore mentioned be furnished, we shall have full security for our traders and others within our territory; and if the Mexican government could be prevailed upon to afford protection within their territory, this important and heretofore flourishing branch of trade would be amply secured. Your memorialists . . . confidently expect that some relief

[344]

be afforded them." But for all that Senator Benton could do, Congress adjourned without providing relief.

In March a Westerner became President; and before the first of May Missourians learned that Andrew Jackson's Secretary of War had ordered four companies of infantry to accompany the caravan of 1829 as far as the international boundary line on the Arkansas. And, delightfully, the *Missouri Intelligencer* hooted at the idea, labeling the escort "an electioneering maneuvre of the Government for popularity."

Four companies, under Major Bennett Riley, met the traders at Round Grove, about thirty-five miles on the Trail from Independence. The march was at first exhilarating to the dragoonsmen fresh from Jefferson Barracks; but fatigue and monotony had dulled the experience before they reached Chouteau's Island, the end of the convoy's journey. "Weary and athirst, on the sandy hills, under a scorching sun," wrote a lieutenant of the company, "we beheld, amid the waves of the broad river, this beautiful island; its green carpet of grass and umbrageous groves, inviting us to the cool shade and pleasant breezes." The traders continued towards Santa Fe. There was no pastoral poetry for them; they had hardly advanced six or seven hours, when from a pass between the sand hills Indians fired upon a little vanguard group, killing one man. Horsemen hurried back to Chouteau's Island with the news; Major Riley at once gave the word to strike tents, and led his battalion into Mexican territory. The reinforcement reached the caravan at night probably unseen by the Indians; and the traders believed that if reveille had not been sounded, the unsuspecting Indians would have attacked the party in the morning. The escort marched with the caravan for several days; but there was no further molestation on the route. Back at the Arkansas, Indians scurried about the encampment of the dragoons for a few days; in a succession of attacks four soldiers were killed and most of the horses and oxen were driven off.

In mid-October the traders arrived from Santa Fe, escorted by a strong detachment of Mexican troops. The officers exchanged compliments, and the battalion was reviewed and drilled for the edification of the Mexican officers. When the American officers were extending the courtesies, Lieutenant Cooke recorded, "Seated cross-legged around a green blanket in the bottom of the tent, we partook of bread, buffalo meat, and, as an extraordinary rarity, some salt pork; but to crown all, were several large raw onions, for which we were indebted to the arrival of our guests; a tin cup of whiskey, which, like the pork, had been reserved for an unusual occasion, was passed around, followed by another of water."

Early in November the caravan, with its escort, was back in Missouri, with reports of unusually high profits, and let it be known that the military escort had been essential to the success of the expedition. President Jackson had done what he could; it remained for Congress to grant an appropriation to mount and properly equip these troops.

Petitions from Missouri carried on the agitation for military protection, for all that an escort which could go no further than the Mexican border was about as serviceable as a ferry which should offer accommodations to midstream. Again Senator Benton made a speech that lasted for hours, and again Congress did nothing.

A caravan twice as large as the preceding year's company set out in May of 1830, "without waiting longer on our dilatory and speech-making Congress, for the long-expected escort." The caravan returned without having been once molested. Missouri felt its muscle, and the brawny giant let it be known, "Were Missouri to consult the chivalrous feelings of her sons, she would stand by her own means of defence, and would scorn to ask for succor from any quarter; but it behooves her, in following the strict line of her duty under the law, to pursue a different course and to look to the general government whose province it is to provide for the general defence."

The activities of Missouri and its own Benton brought fruit of a sort in 1832, in a voluminous report from the Secretary of War. It was made up largely of the letters of traders and Indian agents, all tending toward the conclusion pointed by Lewis Cass, "It is quite time that the United States should interpose, efficaciously, to put a stop . . . to the depredations of the Indians against our own citizens." Enlivened also by an Indian outbreak, the Black Hawk War, on the northwestern frontier, Congress authorized the President to raise a mounted force for the protection of the frontier.

In 1834 and again in 1843 a body of dragoons was diverted from post duty to escort the Santa Fe caravan; and that, it seems, was all. The legislature of Missouri left off its memorializing ways; the Santa Fe traders had learned that their best protection was in a well-knit organization and in vigilance. After 1832 there was no loss of American life in Trail warfare.

The bulk of a caravan's goods nearly always was cotton fabrics. Josiah Gregg recommended to his fellow-traders that at least half of their trading stuffs be "domestic cottons, both bleached and brown. . . . The demand for calicoes is also considerable, but this kind of goods affords much less profit. The quantity in an assortment should be about equal to half that of the domestics." Part of the cotton goods, and that remaining fourth of the assortment, cutlery, hardware, odds-and-ends, was largely of foreign manufacture. As the movement for military protection sputtered out, the traders iterated demands for relief from "double taxation," the necessity of paying both American and Mexican taxes upon the same article. This demand found insistent voice in General William H. Ashley, a magnate of the fur trade, Representative from Missouri in the eighteen-thirties. Re-exporters from the Atlantic seaboard to the ports of Mexico were allowed drawbacks, he pointed out; barred from this favor, the Santa Fe traders were paying about a fourth again as much for foreign-made goods. Eastern Representatives had no intention of aiding business rivals of their own constituents, and bills to make Independence a port of entry and to provide a system of rebates for the Santa Fe trade were summarily voted down. Memorials from the Missouri legislature trimmed sail to meet all possible winds, one of 1837 evaluating the trade at half a million dollars annually, and one of 1838 representing the commerce to Santa Fe as languishing almost to extinction for want of the rebate. After Josiah Gregg had in 1839 organized a party of Santa Fe traders in Arkansas, the delegation of that state was likewise insistent. But the years rolled by, until on the last day of Tyler's administration, the "double taxation" burden was lifted. The act provided for rebates on imported merchandise and provided for customs inspectors to be stationed at Independence and in Arkansas. On the next day Mr. Polk moved into the White House, and the Mexican War was only an almanac away; the relief had come too late to mean a thing to the Santa Fe trade. But many of the traders meanwhile had achieved sounder finance by ignoring the merchants of Franklin and St. Louis and buying goods directly from the wholesalers of Philadelphia.

In 1831 one hundred thirty men followed the Trail to Santa Fe, with an investment in merchandise of $250,000. The western perspective magnified this sum, and Western optimism foresaw this annual investment multiplied in the next year or so. As a matter of fact, the annual investment sent southwest in the prairie schooners did not reach $200,-000 again until 1839; but the significance of these pioneer caravans striking across eight hundred miles of Indian and alien domain, through the Great American Desert to the Rocky Mountains, was not to be measured in the calicoes these wagons carried.

PART V
NEW STATES, NEW FRONTIERS

Pioneers are half gypsy. The lookout is on hori-
zons from which at any time another and stranger
wandersong may come calling and take the heart,
to love or to kill, with gold or with ashes. . . .
—CARL SANDBURG

CHAPTER XX

THE HISTORY OF A BORDER PROVINCE

SPAIN, inheriting the expansive province of Louisiana in 1763, hoped to build along the western bank of the Mississippi an impassable barrier against foreign aggression. The policy allowed exceptions in such small quantity as not to damage the rule. The hapless Acadians, driven from Nova Scotia by British policy, naturally were welcomed into Louisiana; almost nine hundred of these refugees arrived at New Orleans in 1765 and 1766, and were settled in the parishes of lower Louisiana. In upper Louisiana the trading post of St. Louis was established, and a number of French families were permitted to locate at St. Genevieve; in 1767 two forts were begun at the mouth of the Missouri, to hold back the English trappers from the fur country to the west. By a royal order of April 5, 1786, Louisiana was offered as a temporary haven to Americans bitter against their own government and to the British loyalists who had fled across the Mississippi to escape Revolutionary vigilance committees; as a result, a large number of English and American families settled at Natchez and in the adjacent farm lands. Irish emigrants were made welcome; but few made the trip.

In 1788 the Spanish minister at Philadelphia, Don Diego de Gardoqui, in a moment of aberration arranged with Colonel George Morgan of New Jersey to select a location on the west bank of the Mississippi for a colony of sober, industrious farmers and mechanics; and Morgan, trooping through Pennsylvania and Kentucky with the enthusiastic promise of religious freedom and commercial advantages "such as they had never dreamed of before," settled a number of families opposite the mouth of the Ohio. The settlement was christened New Madrid. A Spanish military commandant was stationed there, and Governor Estevan Miro placed many embarrassments in Morgan's way: but the stream of American immigration into the Spanish dominions had been begun. To bring friends of Spain into Louisiana in the likely event that trouble with the United States should arise, the barriers were let down occasionally to European emigrants; but Spanish policy was fairly consistently antipathetic to foreign traders and to non-Catholics.

When Louisiana was secretly returned to France by the treaty of San Ildefonso, in October, 1800, "ambitious and too adjacent neighbors"—Americans—were already crowding the eastern bank of the Mississippi, particularly along the shore opposite lower Louisiana. American traders were established, by devious influences, in Natchitoches, and even in the Texas outpost of Nacogdoches. When, against the fuming impotence of the Spanish monarchy, Napoleon sold the province of Louisiana to the United States, there was only one thing a Catholic Majesty could do, and that was done: former Spanish vassals in Louisiana were encouraged to enter Texas, and by royal decree of September 24, 1803, were permitted to move their effects free of duty. So the door into Texas was opened. No newcomers were allowed to remain near Nacogdoches; it was thought better to keep this post a village, lest it become a den of renegade Americans busy by night in contraband trade with the towns across the Sabine.

In the summer of 1804 Nemesio Salcedo, assigned to duty in the interior provinces for the particular purpose of guarding against foreign attack, made a serious mistake: he ruled that, owing to conditions in Louisiana which often made it impossible for the would-be emigrant to secure documents proving his identity, good character, and orthodox faith, the frontier officials might accept undocumented assertions instead. Americans not greatly troubled by false oaths, and easily bribed Spanish officials at Nacogdoches, enjoyed a brief period of coöperation.

Antonio Cordero, governor of Coahuila, was in 1805 given the additional duties of the governorship of Texas. He was something of a theorist, and wished to see settlements along the arterial routes, land and water, of Texas. Thereby he hoped to have channels for communication and for supplies in case of attack, to increase the commerce in furs, and give the Indians an additional motive for behaving themselves. Cordero succeeded in establishing two *villas,* one, Santissima Trinidad de Salcedo, on the Trinity River, and the other, San Marcos de Neve, upon the San Marcos River. The Trinity River settlement contained only thirty-seven inhabitants at the outset, but within three years had increased almost threefold. Its origins were cosmopolitan, but no Americans were among the settlers. The colony upon the San Marcos was settled entirely by Mexicans; it contained less than a hundred inhabitants in the beginning, and after the invariable habit of settlements formed by native Mexicans, never grew at all.

Out of fear of Napoleon's apparently boundless schemes of aggrandizement, a fear supplemented by the ingrained mistrust of the Americans, the commandant-general Salcedo in June, 1809, ordered all immigration into Texas from Louisiana stopped. "You will find nothing touching Span-

[355]

ish emigrants from Louisiana except wholly prejudicial
things," Salcedo railed at the governor of Texas. "They
believe, with good foundation, that they will not be denied
anything they want and become each time more troublesome
and dangerous. I can do nothing less than to set this matter
frankly before you in order that you may strictly carry out
my orders . . . for, in the end, they [the emigrants] are
not and will not be anything but crows to pick out our
eyes." There were then, by his estimate, 3,112 settlers
in Texas; and the population was completed by somewhat
more than a thousand soldiers. That was the high-water
mark of colonization for the next decade—a turbulent ten
years for the province, when active enemies, headstrong
subordinates, and rebellious vassals crumbled the buffer
which Spanish policy had built up against foreign aggression, and all but tore the jewel of Texas from the diadem
of the Empire.

In 1820 an insurrection of his troops forced the king of
Spain to announce his willingness to follow a "constitutional" course again; and it became possible for the provincial assemblies, charged with the duty of developing
agriculture and commerce, to take measures for extending
settlements in the dominion. The *ayuntamiento* of Bexar,
the capital of Texas, openly favored a revival of colonization in Texas. And in December of that liberal year Moses
Austin presented his compliments to the governor at Bexar,
announced that he represented three hundred families, and
submitted a proposal for a colony.

It is of no more than incidental interest that when Austin
first presented himself he was peremptorily ordered to leave
the province, and was granted an audience only after a personal acquaintance, the Baron de Bastrop, interceded in his
behalf; Austin had simply failed to exhibit the necessary
calling card, documentary evidence that he was a subject of
the king of Spain. Nor was it any mysterious change of

[356]

policy that led the Spanish officials to consider his colonization project favorably. The current crop of Spanish officials was conscientiously following a "liberal" star. Despite the ten-year lapse when plans for the colonizing of Texas had been decidedly out of fashion, the precedents were there; and the officials in 1820, by the very atmosphere of the times, had discarded that traditional cynicism, founded on experience, which had cut short similar proposals. And Austin worded his petition very discreetly: the heads of the families now wishing to enter Texas were nearly all men of means, and were all industrious; they promised to bring sworn testimonials of good character, and to bind themselves to defend their adopted country against Indians, filibusters, and other aggressors; they promised to obey all existing laws. His petition, Austin represented, was in accordance with the royal intention at the time of the sale of Louisiana to allow Spanish subjects in Louisiana to move elsewhere in the king's dominion. The Spanish officials elaborated one point: all the emigrants must be Catholics, or must become such. And the petition, so far from being an affront to Spanish principles, was an amenity.

When in 1821 Mexico won its independence from Spain, that official attitude of liberality was not affected; and without much quibbling the Republic of Mexico reconfirmed the Austin grant.

Austin's presence in Bexar was the fruit of a life of pioneering. He was born in Durham, Connecticut, in 1761. A tradesman in New Haven, he became a merchant in Philadelphia and in Richmond. In 1789 he secured title to some lead mines on Wood's River, and in 1791 moved into southwestern Virginia. Five years later he was on his way to the lead mines in Missouri; he made the journey overland, for he set out too late in the winter of 1796 to find open water in the Ohio. Early in spring he was back in Virginia, assured that his negotiations with the Spanish authorities would be successful. On June 8, 1798, "Moses Austin and family"—Austin, like Cæsar, preferred the third person when writing about himself—"consisting of Maria his wife, Stephen F. Austin his son, and Emily M. B. Austin his daughter together with Moses Bates and family and Other Whites and Blacks to the number of Forty persons, and Nine Loaded Wagons and a Coach and four Horses, all left Austin Ville and took the Road for Morrises Boat Yard on the Great Kanawha." Seventeen of the twenty who boarded ship survived the tedious, enervating trip; in September Austin with his group was in Missouri.

The transfer of the territory to the United States brought in its wake taxation, militia duty, and a rigid land system; but Austin's mining interest survived until the War of 1812 paralyzed industry. His other interests—merchandising, banking, slave labor—were equally unlucky. Stephen, his son, struck out for Arkansas in the first year, 1819, of its territorial existence; on another frontier the family fortunes might be improved. In October Stephen and his father were in conference at Little Rock, and in November Moses Austin set out for Bexar, with a horse, a mule, a negro man, and fifty dollars in cash.

His interest in the colonization of Texas was primarily financial. As he wrote his son James, in school at Lexington, "I found nothing I could do would bring back my property again, and to remain in a country where I had enjoyed wealth in a state of poverty I could not submit to." Before his petition for a land grant was finally allowed, Moses Austin held applications for homesteads in his grant which he expected would bring him eighteen thousand dollars in fees.

When in the summer of 1821 the old pioneer was "blistered and bled most copiously" and died, his son Stephen took up the financial enterprise. Beginning as a business executive, Stephen Fuller Austin became a statesman. The work of pioneering became far more important than the profits; the ambition that illuminates his leadership of Texas was, in his own floreate definition, "a mild and gentle one, consisting more of the wish to build up the fortunes and happiness of others and to realize my dreams of good will to my fellow men than of the overbearing spirit of military fame or domineering power. . . . I took upon myself the task of getting secure and valid titles for their land, and to furnish each emigrant with solid grounds on which to build the hopes of his family, and his humble 'forest home.' Avarice was as incompatible with such views as I trust it has ever been foreign to my heart."

Hundreds of American families were ready to follow Austin. Texas was all the more attractive to many pioneers in 1821 because it was not a part of the United States. After July 1, 1820, the system of selling public lands on credit was abolished; while under the new enactment the minimum unit of sale was reduced to eighty acres, the price ($1.25 an acre) had to be in cash at hand. The credit system had been a gigantic failure: by the reckoning at the close of 1820, payments to the United States by individual purchasers of public lands were twenty-one million dollars in arrears. But congressmen from the border states of Indiana, Illinois, and Mississippi voted, significantly, against the abandonment of the credit system. The reaction of Westerners to the change in the public land policy is simply put: in 1819 the United States had sold over five million acres of public lands; in 1820 not quite eleven hundred thousand acres were sold, and in 1821 less than eight hundred thousand acres. Coincidentally with the establishing of the cash-in-full system, the panic of 1819 carried distress and bankruptcy throughout the West; and the forced curtailment of wildcat banking and cheap paper money, as the federal government and the states tried to put their shaky financial institutions in order, increased the distress in the debtor communities of the West.

Under such circumstances, the sudden opening-up of Texas to American colonists was admirably timed. The *Missouri Advocate* of St. Louis, weighing the easy terms of Austin's grant against the new land policy of the United States, said what hundreds of pioneers had already deduced for themselves: "The difference is too great not to produce its effect between a republic which gives first rate land gratis, and a republic which will not sell inferior land for what it was worth."

And Texas was in the direct line of slave-labor expansion. Slave labor to be at all economical demanded large plantations; and no group of land barons except the tobacco planters was ever so successful in exhausting the soil as the owners of the cotton plantations. From Virginia the tobacco growers had perforce gone into Kentucky; and, plantation by plantation, the cotton growers had encroached westward from Georgia. Between 1811 and 1821 the cotton raised west of Georgia became nearly a third of the total crop. When in 1817 Mississippi Territory was divided and the Territory of Alabama was created out of it, Mississippi was forthwith made a state, and Alabama had to wait for only two years. Meanwhile the process of pushing the small farmers who had cleared the rich lands into the hills or farther to the west gathered momentum, as the planters with money to buy cleared lands came into the lower valleys. In 1820 the population of the two new southern states was over two hundred thousand; by 1830 their population had risen to 446,148.

Mexico was congenitally opposed to slavery; but, in 1823, Austin obtained from the federal congress at Mexico City permission for the three hundred families of his first colony to bring in slaves. When in 1827 the Coahuila-Texas constitution prohibited slavery he induced the legislature to enact a law recognizing contracts with indentured servants —a patent subterfuge. The way into Texas was opened for independent pioneers and slave owners alike.

"I had an ignorant, whimsical, selfish and suspicious set of rulers over me to keep good natured"—Austin, writing in April, 1829, was unburdening his soul to William H. Wharton—"a perplexed, confused colonization law to execute, and an unruly set of North American frontier republicans to controul who felt that they were sovereigns, for they knew that they were beyond the arm of the Govt. or of law, unless it pleased them to be controuled." Complying with the terms of his concession, Austin could not make Texas a fair cross section of the American frontier. The oath by which settlers vowed adherence to the Catholic Church barred families whose Methodist or Presbyterian allegiance was an ingrained pride. Since only Roman Catholic churches were available, very few Texan colonists gave Sunday any other observance than "visitin' around" or breaking in mustangs. W. B. Dewees wrote from Austin's colony in November, 1831, "I have not heard a sermon since I left Kentucky, except at a camp-meeting in Arkansas." But Dewees embroidered the truth to impress his Kentucky friends when he added, "It is nothing uncommon for us to inquire of a man why he ran away from the States! but few people feel insulted by such a question. They generally answer for some crime or other which they have committed; if they deny having committed any crime, and say they did not run away, they are generally looked upon rather suspiciously."

The Mexican grant particularly favored the settling of families only; but Austin was besieged by numbers of single men, who were allowed to obtain the most generously sized homesteads by banding together in groups of two or more as a "family." Austin did make an honest attempt to examine the credentials of each applicant; and the result was that he could write, "When you come here, you will be astonished to see all our houses with no other fastening than a wooden pin or door latch, even stores are left in this state—there is no such thing in the colony as a stable to lock up horses nor pens to guard them in." A burglary in August, 1830, was the first to occur in Austin's colony. Texas had its full share of dangers, however—highwaymen, occasional bands of Mexican outlaws, and inevitably and incessantly on the fringes of settlement, the Indians.

The concession to Moses Austin had been the signal for numerous applications to the Mexican government for other land grants. Without the slightest judiciousness, without waiting to discover how truly the Austin colony might become an integral part of Mexico, several of these applications were favored. The colonization law passed by the Coahuila-Texas legislature in March, 1825, set the terms and conditions. Certificates attesting the proper religious faith were required, of course; otherwise the conditions were generous and even lax.

Thousands of Americans had come into Texas before the belligerent outburst of Hayden Edwards, the "Fredonian War," revealed to Mexican officials the outcome of their liberal policy. Edwards, who had obtained in 1825 a concession for the colonizing of an extensive tract about Nacogdoches, was a genuine American jingoist: a cardinal article of his faith was that the Mexicans were the real intruders north of the Rio Grande, and that destiny and history alike had bestowed Texas upon the Americans. When he found land titles in his grant to be hopelessly involved, he raised an army of two hundred men, created the Republic of Fredonia—no less—which forthwith adopted a complete constitution and made an alliance with another sovereign power, the Cherokee Indians. The revolt was a short-lived affair; but even a Mexican official whose life was all *comida* and *siesta* could not sleep through that alarm.

[362]

Forthwith the attitude of the government toward its American colonists was drastically changed.

Mexican misrule, petty official annoyances, the nerve-racking flux and vacillation of Mexican political institutions, hastened the assembling of that convention of Americans in Texas which met on the first of March, 1836, at Washington on the Brazos. The public opinion of thwarted and harassed Americans dictated the declaration of independence which that convention unanimously adopted on the second of March.

There were twenty thousand American colonists in Texas; and independence was not difficult to achieve. The Texas militia and the Mexican army were already engaged in civil war when the declaration of independence was being drafted. Seven weeks later the main body of Mexican troops, under General Santa Anna, was put to rout; and the General, under duress, signed a treaty in his fleeting capacity of president of Mexico recognizing the independence of Texas. As a matter of course the hero of the war, General Sam Houston, was elected the first president of the Republic of Texas, defeating a reluctant and tired candidate, Stephen F. Austin, who had only a short while to live.

Emissaries were immediately sent to Washington to demand the annexation of Texas to the United States. The best they could secure was the formal recognition of the Republic of Texas and the exchange of diplomatic agents. The issue he had himself created, the dissolution of the National Bank of the United States, was hounding Jackson in his last days in the presidency, concentrating his time and interest; and his successor, Martin Van Buren, was not the man to affront the northern Democrats by advocating the annexation of a slavery state. The greedy cries of expansionists were not often heard in the straitened times that followed the panic of 1837. And the Republic of Texas, left to its own devices, set about exercising the various rights of sovereignty, in particular the right to accumulate an immense national debt.

In 1839 three merchants of Chihuahua pooled their fortunes in an amazing enterprise. On the third of April their caravan set out from the provincial capital—eastward. Seven wagons and five hundred mules carried silver bullion worth nearly a half million dollars. Crossing the Rio Grande at El Paso, the caravan, trusting to chart and compass, struck through a region none of the company knew. In May the bullion train was at Shreveport, and merchants were crowding to get their share of the bonanza. A few days before the arrival of the Chihuahua merchants at Shreveport, a caravan had started from Van Buren on the Arkansas River, bound for Chihuahua. Josiah Gregg was in this company of forty men, whose eighteen wagons carried twenty-five thousand dollars' worth of merchandise.

Inevitably the thought came to Texans, why not divert the whole of the Santa Fe trade from Missouri? Already Texas was building a military road from Red River to the Nueces; and men talked sanguinely of a road from Austin to Santa Fe. Despite the strained relations of Texans and Mexicans, the province of New Mexico might be conciliated. The route of trade would be shortened three or four hundred miles.

Mirabeau Bonaparte Lamar, President of the Republic of Texas, flavored his statesmanship with romance. Trade and territorial expansion seemed twin fruits of a Santa Fe trade with Texas: control of the Santa Fe region would make good the territorial pretensions of the Republic, and would smooth the course of trade over a route already proved feasible. Early in 1840 three agents were in Santa Fe, commissioned by Lamar to care for Texan interests and to prepare the natives for the change of government. And, with brazen magnificence, Lamar instructed the Texan representative at Washington to attempt to make a treaty with Spain for open commerce with Cuba: Texas was to be a torch of commerce whose beams were cast from Chihuahua and Santa Fe to Havana.

In January, 1839, the congress of Texas had presented Lamar with a joint resolution, authorizing him to give every encouragement and support in his power, "compatible with the safety of the country," to the trade between the settlements of the Republic and the Mexican towns on the Rio Grande. Late in 1840 a resolution was introduced into the lower house asking that the committee on finance report on the expediency of "laying off and setting apart so much of the public domain intermediate and equidistant between Austin and Santa Fe, as might be adapted to the establishment of a colony of actual settlers, with a view to the opening, facilitating and securing the trade of the latter place." In other schemes the Santa Fe trade played a lively part in that congress. Lamar and David G. Burnett, acting president during Lamar's illness, wanted authorization to send a military expedition to Santa Fe; when congress adjourned in 1841 they had not received it, nor, actually, had appropriations been made for the support of the regular army.

Lamar's fine plans were not to be ruined. Authorization or no authorization, orders were issued to the quartermaster and commissary-general of the militia to outfit an expedition; and Lamar ordered the comptroller of the Republic to honor the bills.

In May, 1841, groups of volunteers began to assemble at Austin; and late in June the expedition broke camp. A long train of wagons heavily moved forward; on either side rode companies of volunteers in double file, all well mounted and well armed. Love of adventure and love of the unknown had brought congenial men together. Congeniality was promoted by the circumstance that the expedition was outfitted with no breadstuffs, but instead with a

[365]

quantity of tobacco for each man. Supper was a simple, hearty affair—beef roasted on sticks or ramrods before the open fire, a little rice, coffee—and after the meal little groups congregated around the camp fires for an hour's yarn-spinning, of border wars and gun fights, buffalo hunts and Indian forays. At daybreak the reveille was sounded on fifes and drums, blankets were rolled up, breakfast—like supper, but without the rice—was eaten, and the cavalcade was on its march again.

Far into northwest Texas, following the blind surmises of its leaders and the dubious directions of a Mexican named Carlos, a trapper in the Red River country, the expedition found itself in a water-scarce region. The volunteers were not so genial now. Overnight the Mexican guide disappeared. The men drank from springs of bitter water, strongly cathartic; even that was better than no water. The ration of beef was reduced one-half at a time when the beeves had become lean and tough, and the men had become worn down by long and fatiguing marches. Luckily they found a passage through the mountains; and they found a village of prairie dogs, which village they fairly depopulated, and feasted well. Indians murdered a party out hunting for water, and stole some horses.

Fairly into the eastern spurs of Rocky Mountains, the company was oppressed by an acute shortage of food—that, and the consciousness that each day's course through the desolate country was guided by nothing better than guesswork. George Wilkins Kendall described one of these days: "The road we had found and followed some distance in the morning we hunted for in vain in the afternoon: all the old wheel-marks had lost themselves in a barren, gravelly prairie. . . . As the sun gradually sank behind their lofty and ragged summits, a raw, chill breeze sprang up from their neighborhood. It was the first cold weather we had experienced, and in our weak and exhausted condition the biting wind seemed to pierce directly through us.

"We continued our march until we reached the dry bed of a mountain stream, upon the banks of which we camped for the night. A flock of wild turkeys had taken shelter under the banks, running off as we approached their roost. Although contrary to strict orders, nothing could restrain our men from banging and blazing away at the turkeys as they sped across the prairie—fifty rifles and muskets being discharged at them before they were out of sight. Two or three only were killed by the volley and running fire which ensued, and they were but half grown, and so extremely poor that they did not furnish a meal for half-a-dozen men. To go farther without *something* to eat was impossible—the wild and haggard expression, the sunken eyes and sallow, fleshless faces of the men too plainly showed that some means of sustenance must be speedily provided. A horse which in the early part of the campaign had been one of the best animals in the command, was now found to be so poor and badly broken down that it was resolved to shoot him and divide his flesh among the different messes. . . . Poor as it was, however, and hard to swallow, I am confident that many a man in the party ate four or five pounds of it, half cooked and without salt. . . . A buzzard, that sat perched on the dry limb of a cottonwood overhead, appeared to look down at us reproachfully, as he saw us appropriating food that legitimately belonged to him."

Lamar's hopes that the New Mexicans would welcome the extension of Texan sovereignty over their settlements were not entirely fantastic; but reports of conditions in New Mexico were antedated before they were received in mid-Texas. In June, 1840, Manuel Armijo, Governor of New Mexico, wrote to the minister of war at Mexico City in prophecy of the Texan Expedition, and in fear of it: "The people will not defend themselves because they have expressed a desire to join the Texans in order that they

[367]

may secure better conditions, and they are now merely waiting for the proper opportunity." But within another month Armijo was able to write that he had suppressed a revolution in Taos, and that the arrested ringleaders had testified the secret of their strength to be the hope of the lower classes that the Texans would arrive in New Mexico and cancel all debts. The ministry of war was fully aroused: funds were sent to Armijo for defense, customs duties were converted for military purposes, and Armijo was advised to meet the Texan Expedition before it was near enough to gain accessions of discontented natives. While the Texans were stumbling through the desolate table-lands, Armijo was waiting.

On September 18, 1841, Armijo proclaimed that the Texans were near, come to steal, murder, and burn. He called for volunteers to the national standard, to prevent the loss of religion, country, and possessions; and ablaze with the emotional effects of the appeal, the New Mexicans forgot their disaffections and rallied to the defense. No sooner had the Texan volunteers approached the New Mexican settlements than Mexican soldiery captured them. Their arms, their equipment, their personal effects were taken away. Within their hearing Armijo's officers debated: should the *Americanos* be executed forthwith, or should they be sent to the City of Mexico as trophies to the valor of the New Mexicans? And by one vote the officers decided to take their trophies to the capital.

The miseries of that march to Mexico City were almost insupportable. Once at the capital the prisoners were put in dungeons and left there. Those who could prove American or European citizenship were released in the spring of 1842; and on the thirteenth of June, in celebration of his birthday, President Santa Anna opened the gates to the remaining prisoners.

Texas had gained nothing; and in the eyes of Mexican

[368]

officials the Santa Fe trade revealed sinister possibilities of American territorial aggression under the masquerade of American commerce. The Santa Fe Trail had had a banner year in 1839: a quarter-million dollars' worth of merchandise had been brought to Santa Fe, in one hundred thirty wagons. From one extreme the trade oscillated to the other; 1840, 1841, and 1842, were rather lean years. In 1843 two hundred thirty wagons, bearing goods worth $450,000, followed the Trail from Missouri to Sante Fe. Santa Anna was alarmed by this overwhelming volume of trade; and on August 3, 1843, the decree went out: "The frontier custom-houses of Taos, in the department of New Mexico, Paso del Norte and Presidio del Norte in that of Chihuahua, are entirely closed to all commerce. This decree shall take effect within forty-five days after its proclamation in the capital of the Republic."

But the Santa Fe trade had not been without its compensations to the Mexican government. Duties collected annually at Santa Fe on the goods of the caravans were usually from fifty to eighty thousand dollars; and not more than half of that was embezzled by the officers of the customs. For this and for other reasons, the ban was lifted by the beginning of April, 1844; and that summer and fall about ninety wagons loaded with merchandise followed the Trail to Santa Fe. That was the last year of the Missouri-to-Mexico trade.

The overwhelming Whig victory in the national election of 1840 was a triumph of resentment: it was a devastating comment on Jackson's and Van Buren's financial policy, but left the issue of territorial expansion untouched. John Tyler, President by luck when General William H. Harrison died soon after his strenuous inaugural, would have liked to usher Texas into the Union, but he had no personal following in Congress. To the cotton planters, as Calhoun summarized their theory, the annexation of Texas promised the only guarantee of the perpetuity of the Constitution. But the planters were not strong enough alone to bring a slave state into the Union.

Support came from the speculators and business men of the North. In the financial sections of every large community, Texas scrip issued by ambitious colonizing companies was afloat. Stocks underwritten by land claims of doubtful validity had been issued to the gullible public. After the establishing of the Republic of Texas, a huge quantity of bonds and notes issued by that commonwealth was sold in the United States. As the doleful condition of the treasury of the southern Republic became known, holders of Texas securities did not have to be astute to see that the one possibility of redemption in full lay in the annexation of Texas to the United States.

The election of 1844, by which James K. Polk, a Tennessee democrat, was made President, revealed (as Professor Paxson has summarized) that the South, in general, was for both slavery and expansion; the West was for territorial expansion, and not greatly concerned over slavery; the East had a strong minority opposed to both. The victorious forces interpreted the election as a mandate for the annexation of Texas, and northern Democrats, conciliated with the promise of the admission of Oregon, were willing to let that interpretation stand. In March, 1845, Congress enacted a joint resolution providing for the addition of Texas to the Union. Ellis P. Oberholzer, biographer of the financier extraordinary, Jay Cooke, has let the cat out of the bag: "Mr. Cooke always believed that the northern opposition in Congress to the addition of this large slave territory to the national domain was overcome through the selfish exertions in their own interest of the holders of the Texas debt certificates, many of whom were influential northern men."

CHAPTER XXI

THE AMERICAN INVASION OF OREGON

TOWARD the ragged end of the War of 1812 Captain Black of His Majesty's fleet sailed across the bar of the Columbia River, to batter down the fort of Astoria and win glory for himself. To his chagrin the American fur post had already passed, peacefully, into British hands; but Black took possession nonetheless, changed the name of Astoria to Fort George, and sailed out again. In the negotiations of the Treaty of Ghent, Great Britain waived the point of possession, however, and in October, 1818, the little fort on the south bank of the Columbia was formally handed over to an American officer. In that year English and American commissioners gently wrangled over the tracing of the international boundary line west from the Lake of the Woods. They agreed upon the line of the forty-ninth parallel, extending to the Rocky Mountains; as to the boundary from the mountains to the Pacific the commissioners differed, the American suggestion to extend the forty-ninth parallel all that distance being counterchecked by the British intimation that the Columbia River itself was the most convenient boundary that could be adopted. Since in 1818 the extension of a boundary line

across that far-flung region seemed purely an academic matter, no one quarreled, and Article Three of the Convention
of 1818 embodied a casual makeshift, a provision for the
joint occupation of Oregon.

Two other claimants to this key piece of the international
frontier, Spain and Russia, withdrew altogether within the
next few years. When in 1819 the United States purchased
Florida from Spain, the northern boundary of Spanish
North America was set along the Red River to the line
of the hundredth degree of longitude, along the Arkansas
River to its source, along the forty-second degree of latitude
to the Pacific Coast. "His Catholic Majesty cedes to the
United States all his rights, claims, and pretensions to any
territories east and north of the said line": thus the earliest
claimant to the Oregon country was eliminated. Russian
trading posts had intruded within striking distance of San
Francisco Bay; but by conferences in 1824 and 1825 between
Russia and the United States, and Russia and England, the
Imperial Eagle accepted the line of fifty-four degrees,
forty minutes, as the southern boundary of its Alaskan possessions. In 1827 the theoretical owners of Oregon renewed their theoretical occupation, extending the agreement
of 1818 indefinitely, subject to abrogation by either Great
Britain or the United States upon due notice.

Headquarters of the Hudson's Bay Company in the far
West were at Fort Vancouver, on the level slope of the
north bank of the Columbia, six miles above the mouth of
the Willamette. Behind the grapevine trellises of the key
cell in this hive of British enterprise lived Dr. John
McLoughlin, "governor" of Oregon, so called by common
courtesy. Immense and portly, crowned with long white
hair, he easily lived up to his appearance: he was sole commander of the diverse craftsmen at the fort and all British
trappers west of the Rocky Mountains, sole arbiter, a
benevolent despot. On Sundays, he himself read the ser-

[372]

vice of the Church of England to the officers and servants at the post; but he was above the egotism of proselyting. New Englanders and New Yorkers, in the first flush of missionary zeal in the eighteen-thirties, were not. The Missionary Board of the Methodist church called for volunteers to carry the Message to the Indians of Oregon; Jason Lee, and later his nephew David, responded.

Early in March, 1834, Jason Lee left New York for the West, preaching by the way. Late in April the missionary party set out from Independence, the Lees and three Methodist laymen; for guidance and for safety they traveled with a company of fur traders led by Nathaniel Wyeth and William Sublette. Across the Kansas River, along the Platte, past Independence Rock, the missionaries followed the trappers until in late July they had arrived at Green River and the trappers' rendezvous. Thence into Oregon two Englishmen guided the missionaries. They were tired and bedraggled when Dr. John McLoughlin received them, and gave them every hospitality a gentleman could offer them. Their tools and goods had come by ship from New York, with Nathaniel Wyeth's trading stuffs. Jason Lee had a colonizer's heart and a pioneer's shrewdness; his mission, he decided, would be located in the fertile Willamette Valley, open by water route to the sea, and obviously designed by nature to give New England farmers a foretaste of heaven. McLoughlin provided the missionaries with a boat and crew to move their goods to the site; their cattle were driven overland. By the first of November Jason Lee and his party were housed in a log cabin of their own making, and the missionary invasion of Oregon was fairly established.

About them were French Canadians pensioned off by the Hudson's Bay Company, occupying little farms. Untutored savages were not nearly as numerous in the Willamette Valley as in other places Lee might have chosen for his mission. The school for Indian children probably never had more than thirty-five pupils in its best years. Hubert Howe Bancroft in 1886 fried the Lees to a golden brown upon history's griddle: "When," was his rhetorical question, "when will men learn that in the affairs of the savages the benevolence of civilization curdles into a curse, and missionary efforts are like a burst peat-bog sowing its black mud over the land!"

Late in October, while the mission was being built, the Lees had other company, not greatly to their liking: Hall J. Kelley, once a Boston schoolmaster, but in 1834 the first of the American filibusters to reach Oregon. He had come from New Orleans by a circuitous route across Mexico, and in California had picked up an assorted following of American trappers and horse thieves. His object was, in short, to found an American settlement, and bring Oregon under the sovereignty of the United States. Since 1815 the desirability of Oregon had been the driving force of his life; senators and presidents had been influenced by his energetic lobbying. In 1829 a publication of his, *A General Circular to all Persons of Good Character who wish to migrate to the Oregon Territory, embracing some Account of the Character and Advantages of the Country,* set forward his conviction: "The time is near at hand, and advancing in the ordinary course of Providence, when the Oregon country shall be occupied by an enlightened people, skilled in the various improvements of science and art." But once actually in Oregon, Kelley found Dr. John McLoughlin, six feet six inches high, with a large blue coat thrown about him, towering immovably in his way: and in spring, 1835, the lobbyist, sorely disappointed and impotently raging, left Oregon by sea.

But in the next few years the working out of the missionaries' invasion established an American counterpoint to the presence of British fur traders in Oregon. In 1835

Samuel Parker, Presbyterian minister and missionary, made the overland journey to Oregon. In 1836 Marcus Whitman and H. H. Spalding, with their brides, drove across the Great Plains, through the South Pass, to the trappers' camp on the Green River. Whitman made a tenacious attempt to bring his wagon the whole distance; at Fort Hall he had to take off two wheels, reducing the wagon to a cart, and at Fort Boisé the horses had so little strength left that the cart had to be abandoned. William Gray, a layman who had come with Whitman, was despatched to the East the following spring to bring more missionaries. He was successful; three additional Presbyterian missionaries were soon in the field. Reënforcements for the Methodist mission came in September, 1837, by boat from Boston. Activities of Methodists and Presbyterians expanded; and in 1840 the Jesuits sent out their splendid, keen-witted veteran in western service, Father de Smet, to establish a mission in the Bitter Root Valley.

In 1838 Jason Lee was again in the States, talking Oregon wherever he went. Peoria, Illinois, was an unexciting frontier after the War of 1812; when Lee lectured there, nineteen young men discovered that Oregon was the place for them. Only two had reneged when Thomas J. Farnham and the rest set out on horseback from Independence in May, 1839. "Pack mules and horses and pack-saddles were purchased and prepared for service. Bacon and flour, salt and pepper, sufficient for four hundred miles, were secured in sacks; our powder-casks were wrapped in painted canvas, and large oil-cloths were purchased to protect these and our clothing from the rains; our arms were thoroughly repaired; bullets were molded; powder-horns and cap-boxes filled, and all else done that was deemed needful, before we struck our tent for the Indian territory." They were equipped with all the earnestness of pioneers to meet the challenge of the Great Plains and the Rockies; and,

[375]

the events of the journey demonstrated, they had sufficient measure of the tenacious individualism of pioneers to defeat their own purposes. The course they chose, for the greatest security, was west-by-south, along the Santa Fe Trail to Bent's Fort on the headwaters of the Arkansas; there the party broke up, and the property in common was divided among the members of the expedition. Farnham, with "three sound and good men, and one wounded and bad one, strode our animals and took trail again for the mountains and Oregon Territory."

Guided by a trapper, the little company clambered across the mountains to the headwaters of the Platte. They were in Ute hunting grounds; but Farnham found the country honeycombed with French Canadian and American trappers—the "mountain men," who drank alcohol, hunted, trapped beaver, lived indifferently alone or among the Indians, and minded their own business. Past Fort Hall, Farnham was guided by an Indian across the burnt plains of the Snake River into the region of the Bannack Indians; traveling the short distance to Fort Boisé—the Hudson's Bay Company's counterpoise, built in 1832, to Nathaniel J. Wyeth's stronghold for American trappers, Fort Hall— Farnham hastened his way to the Willamette. "We were on our way before the sun rose. The dawn on an Oregon sky, the rich blue embankment of mountains over which the great day-star raised his glowing rim, the blandness of the air, the lively ambling of the caravan towards the neighboring abode of my countrymen, imparted to my mind and body a most agreeable exhilaration."

At Whitman's mission, on the north bank of the Walla Walla, Farnham rested awhile; on the thirtieth of September he lashed his packs again and traveled down the Columbia, stopping at a Hudson's Bay post and at Indian camps, passing several little settlements and isolated houses, keeping record of it all. His Indian guides brought the canoe

[376]

to Vancouver; and Farnham took ship for the States. In 1841 he published the narrative of his four-months' journeying. *Travels in the Great Western Prairies* found ready readers; largely because it contained extensive descriptions of Oregon, it was a successful book. Farnham made mention of the Columbia Valley: "The bottom lands of the river were alternately prairies and woodlands; the former clad with a heavy growth of the wild grasses, dry and brown—the latter, with pine, fir, cottonwood, black ash, and various kinds of shrubs." That was exactly the kind of land that pioneers who had the right of pick-and-choose had always preëmpted; such watered tracts, part timberland and part prairie, had been the preferred lands from western Virginia to the banks of the Mississippi.

Elijah White, Methodist missionary in the Willamette Valley, found Jason Lee's imperiousness in small matters too much for him, and returned to the States in disgust. Lee had written the Administration in 1839 that the setlers and Indians in Oregon sadly needed the protection of the laws of the United States, and asking that some one suitable—modesty forbade a more direct description —be appointed civil magistrate for the territory. The delightful answer to Lee's request was the appointment of Elijah White, in 1842, as sub-Indian-agent for Oregon, to look after the relations between the Indians and citizens of the United States. He was instructed to proceed forthwith to Oregon, overland, and to use his best persuasions to induce emigrants to accompany him. And so he barnstormed by the way; as he records at one stop, "Last night all the other appointments were taken up to hear me lecture on Oregon, and as the weather was fine and travelling good, the noble church was filled, the pulpit lined with ministers of all denominations, and I talked an hour and a half with all my might." On the fourteenth of May, 1842, one hundred and twelve people were at the rendezvous of Elm

[377]

Grove (twenty miles southwest of Independence), ready to follow White to Oregon. Most of them, probably, had decided on their own account to go to Oregon, and were waiting for White to take advantage of his acquaintance with the strange wayfaring; and most of them, it is safe to say, were Missourians.

On the sixteenth they set out, eighteen Conestoga wagons and a procession of horses, pack mules, and cattle. Fifty-two of the company were men—too large a party, the veteran Sublette had told White, too many self-willed frontiersmen to be content with White's captaincy throughout the long journey. And just when the party left the Santa Fe Trail to follow a northwesterly course to the Kansas River, an order of White's began the rumbling. Kill the dogs, White ordered, lest they go mad from lack of water on the arid stretch ahead of the company. Kill a Missourian's dogs! But after a vote most of the men yielded. The caravan was west of the South Pass when White's one-month term as captain expired. The company wanted no more of White, and elected a truculent party, Lansford Hastings, who blustered that he would "govern and not be governed," thereby splitting the company into two factions who marched in separate columns for several hostile days. At Fort Laramie the company was reunited, at the urging of the commandant of the post, to present a solid front to the marauding Indians between Laramie and Fort Hall. At Laramie many emigrants were convinced that it would be impossible to drive their wagons and oxen through to Oregon, and sold them to the residents of the fort at the prices they had paid in the states; in exchange they took coffee, flour, and sugar, at a dollar a pound, and miserable horses that did not survive the climb through the mountains.

Thomas Fitzpatrick, fur trader and companion of Jim Bridger, was hired to guide the company to Fort Hall.

They needed some one like Fitzpatrick; the Sioux were ranging throughout the country hunting buffalo, but anxious to steal emigrants' horses and to raid wagons.

At Fort Hall the emigrants got rid of the last of their wagons. Elijah White and a few others pushed ahead, with some Hudson's Bay trappers to Fort Boisé, thence through Burnt River Canyon and over the Blue Mountains; from the foot of the mountains an Indian guided them to Whitman's mission. Most of the emigrants, captained by Hastings, followed the south bank of the Snake River as far as Fort Boisé; on the fifth of October they were in the Willamette Valley. The farmers' occupation of Oregon had begun. Oregon City was founded by these families that came in 1842. The Methodist mission used many of the emigrants as carpenters and mechanics; John McLoughlin hired workers at fair wages, and gave goods on credit to the most needy pioneers.

Flux, insecurity, discontent, optimism—Oregon was an acephalous thing in 1842, without a government, even without a nationality. The Methodist missionaries had in 1841 attempted to form a government; but too many of the select brethren were bent upon personally enjoying the governorship, the other settlers announced their opposition to any governor from the party of the vineyard workers, and every one was afraid of the numerical strength of the French Canadians in a democracy. Elijah White found himself a pariah among the Methodists; and except in Indian affairs he could exert no authority. A debating society in Oregon City never got far from the question of a government. Hastings was not the only emigrant who liked the idea of Oregon as an independent republic; but vague foreshadowings of the jurisdiction of the United States hung over these discussions.

Organized defense against the Indians might sometime be needed, American settlers argued to the indifferent

French Canadians, and the absence of any land laws, they gave warning, would not long be endurable. Politically-minded frontiersmen chafed at the bonds of anarchy; and at a mass meeting at Champoeg on the second of May, 1843, they carried their point by a narrow majority. A committee of nine was appointed to draw up a constitution. Meeting at an old barn belonging to the Methodist mission at Willamette Falls, they harked back to the Ordinance of 1787 and the laws of the Territory of Iowa, and reported to the reassembled convention on the fifth of July. "We, the people of Oregon Territory," ran the preamble, "for the purposes of mutual protection and to secure peace and prosperity among ourselves, agree to adopt the following laws and regulations, until such time as the United States of America extend their jurisdiction over us." So much for British interests in Oregon! But in the dividing of Oregon into four electoral districts, the constitution of 1843 did not specifically set the northern boundary at the "fifty-four forty," contenting itself with speaking of "the northern boundary of the United States." There were no American settlers in Oregon north of the Columbia nor west of the Cascade Mountains until 1845.

Each district according to its population was to have proportionate representation in a legislative body of nine. "Every free male descendant of a white man of the age of twenty-one years and upward, an inhabitant of this territory at the time of its organization," was a qualified elector. The executive power was to be an elected council of three; the supreme court—the exclusive court, for that matter—was to consist of "a supreme judge and two justices of the peace." Before the convention adjourned the provisional government was completed and in operation. Appearances were satisfied, the pioneers of Oregon had added to their dignity; if the government had no money, no buildings of its own, what of it?

While the vanguard of the farmers' invasion was drawing up a compact for the governing of Oregon, the caravans of the Great Emigration were already rambling through the Great Plains and across the plateaus of the eastern slope of the Rockies. From nine hundred to a thousand people came into Oregon in 1843 by way of the Overland Trail. The discussions in Congress had given Oregon wide publicity, lush, uncritical advertising; pioneers recognized in these descriptions agricultural lands of the sort they had learned to master—but better lands. Farmers in the western valley of the Mississippi were dissatisfied; they were in the position of Kentuckians in 1800, producing commodities without good distribution and with limited markets. New Orleans was glutted with produce; railroads from the East were not to reach into Iowa and Missouri for many years. The agricultural lands of Oregon had the inestimable advantage of the Pacific shore; and in the "fabulous forties" the idea of many-sided commercial relations with China and the islands of the Pacific was a glittering magnet.

Newspaper articles and letters by people who knew something of Oregon were handed about until they were smudged into illegibility. And early in the spring of 1843, not by preconcert but by common impulse, emigrants from every part of Missouri and from the neighboring states pointed their ox-drawn wagons toward Independence. Many of them came in colonies, groups of neighbors or of relatives; their herds of cattle overran the highways. Five companies bound for Oregon shared the Trail with one company headed for California.

Pioneering emigrants usually had little or no money; and when these emigrants of 1843 had reached Oregon they had almost nothing wherewith to face the winter, nothing except an unshakable confidence in the West, and the lean-flanked, travel-weary survivors of the herds. If one is to appreciate the rôle of women in the building of frontiers, one must remember these men, rough, vigorous, in every sense masculine, who brought their wives and children through tedious, arduous weeks across the Overland Trail, a whole summer's journey in wagons that jolted so that walking became a relief—brought them to face an autumn and winter of destitution. Dr. John McLoughlin, without waiting to be asked, offered credit to the emigrants of 1843, furnishing them with their immediate needs and staking them to seeds and farm implements. The missionaries sent some provisions to their personal acquaintances in the emigration who needed help. In general, the vineyard workers rather dulled the glamor of their pioneering achievements in Oregon. In an emigrant's brusque account, "Jason Lee played the devil up at the Dalles. He said the Mission had always ruled the country, and if there were any persons in the immigration who did not like to be ruled by the Mission, they might find a country elsewhere to go to. It got all over the country, of course, very quickly. That made war with the missionaries at once. We came here pretty independent fellows, and did not ask many favors."

When the legislature of Oregon met in June, 1844, at Oregon City, the executive committee submitted a message: "At the time of our organization it was expected that the United States would have taken possession of the country before this time, but a year has rolled around, and there appears little or no prospect of aid from that quarter, consequently we are yet left to our own resources for protection. In view of the present state of affairs, we would recommend to your consideration the adoption of measures for a more thorough organization." The legislature made some slight provisions for revenue, and as a palliative to the pioneer missionaries forbade the manufacture and sale of alcoholic liquors. Missourians who had emigrated to Oregon had come back to an earlier West, and in that western spirit forbade slavery in Oregon; they also voted to spare themselves the sight of a free negro. The organic law was changed: the executive committee was superseded by a single governor.

By the session of 1845, the long strides forward of American settlement had reduced the influence of the missionaries and the French Canadians to the vanishing point. Legal talent had come into Oregon with the migrations of 1843 and 1844; with this leadership the legislators framed a revised compact. The word "constitution" they carefully avoided, to minimize the possibility of an independent Oregon, a republic separate from the United States. The compact was submitted to the Oregonians, and approved. Thereby were secured the fundamental enactments of the first legislature of Oregon, and there came into existence a government "strong without an army or navy, and rich without a treasury." That government existed until February 16, 1849, exercising even the sovereign function of carrying on a war, the Cayuse War, against the Indians who in November, 1847, murdered Marcus Whitman, his wife, and several other people at the Walla Walla mission. All that the United States could have wished to accomplish in securing a strong foothold in the Oregon country had been done, and that without affronting England by the creating of a United States territorial government. The high card of the English— the fur trade—had been covered by the top card of the Americans—settlements. It was the same play by which the English had beaten the French, when the stake was half a continent.

Most of the emigrants of 1844, about fourteen hundred people, followed the route from Green River to Fort Hall opened the year before, by way of Fort Bridger. The spring had been unusually rainy; many days had been lost while the companies waited helplessly on the eastern bank of swollen streams, and dysentery and rheumatism followed on the dank weather. It was a discouraging thing, after that, to learn at Fort Bridger that one was only halfway to the Oregon settlements! Snow began to fall in the mountains while a large part of the emigration was between Fort Boisé and the Dalles. The loss in life was slight, but many a provident emigrant lost a ruinous amount of property in cattle, clothing, and household stuffs. Oregon had not had time to recover from the draft upon its resources in the previous year. Thanks to the fertility of the soil there was food enough for all, yet many preferred to live on short rations rather than run too far into debt. But there was not nearly enough clothing to be had. Pieces of cloth were put together without regard to color or texture, and moccasins became the almost universal foot covering.

The emigration to Oregon in 1845 was larger than in any preceding year; three thousand people traveled overland that year. That summer's journeying began auspiciously, and the companies made good progress to Fort Hall and beyond. But at the hot springs near Fort Boisé some fool persuaded two hundred families to try a cut-off, with the assurance that two hundred miles would be saved by following the Malheur River and traveling cross-country to a pass in the mountains at the head of the Willamette Valley. The route, an abandoned trail of the fur trappers, led the emigrants into a country so stony that wagon wheels left almost no imprints. The cattle's hooves were lacerated; grass was scarce, and where there was grass the water was poisonously alkaline. The company lost the trail, and went on blindly through the mountains. Twenty persons had died before the emigrants reached the Dalles, in mid-October, and another score died soon after from the effects of that journey or from overeating at the Dalles after their starving time. The emigrants who followed the usual trail had their own trials; the supply of boats at the Dalles to bring them down the Columbia was far inadequate, and while they waited their provisions gave out. Some emigrants attempted to continue overland, crossing the Cascade Mountains with their wagons; they had to finish afoot, trudging through snow in the mountains and rain in the valleys.

After Parliament and Congress had ratified the extension of the agreement of 1818, there was no word of Oregon in Congress for nearly ten years. Within those years, from 1827 to 1837, more than three hundred thousand people had crossed the Mississippi and settled in the states of Missouri and Arkansas and the Territory of Iowa. In five years more there were more than three hundred thousand people in Missouri alone; and Missouri was the radial point whence lines of hope and adventure, of trade and liberty, blazed into all sectors of the West. But when in 1837 a congressional resolution called upon the President to furnish any correspondence that had taken place with any foreign power "in relation to our territory west of the Rocky Mountains," the President promptly answered that there had been no such correspondence. Yet the first of the missionary-colonizers had been in Oregon for three years. Senator Linn of Missouri, accepting the part of spokesman for Missourians' insatiable desire to follow those radiating lines into the West, flagged up interest in Oregon through the next few years; but it was a thankless business until 1842. In that year probably only the fear of interfering with the British and American plenipotentiaries, Lord Ashburton and Daniel Webster, prevented the passage of a bill extending the jurisdiction of American courts to citizens in Oregon and promising large grants of land to actual settlers.

The Webster-Ashburton convention assigned a definitive boundary between the United States and Maine. Conspicuous in that document was its omission to describe a boundary line between the United States and Canada from the Rocky Mountains to the Pacific Coast. President Tyler made a vigorous comment: "The tide of population, which has reclaimed what was so lately an unbroken wilderness, in more contiguous regions, is preparing to stretch over those vast districts which stretch from the Rocky Mountains to the Pacific Ocean. In advance of the acquirement of individual rights of those lands, sound policy dictates that every effort should be resorted to by the two Governments to settle their respective claims." In the spring of 1843 Dr. Marcus Whitman was in Washington, conducting a ballyhoo for Oregon. Other influences were at work. Politicians were sniffing for the smell of a sure-fire issue. A compound aroma rewarded them: "the immediate reannexation of Texas" and "the whole Oregon or none." While better men hesitated, James K. Polk exploited that program to its full political value. The Democratic leaders of the Middle West, Lewis Cass of Michigan, Stephen A. Douglas of Illinois, William Allen of Ohio, Edward Allen Hannegan of Indiana, at first opposed to the annexation of Texas, a slavery state, because it was offered without a compensating addition of free soil, worked heartily with the Southerners on behalf of Polk after the addition of Oregon to the Union had been offered to balance matters.

When Congress assembled after the election, the victorious Southern democrats pressed the annexation of Texas; and before Polk was installed in office a messenger was traveling toward Austin with the news that Congress had passed a joint resolution for annexation. But the election of Polk presaged far greater spoliation of Spanish North America than the mere annexation of Texas. It was perhaps more than a coincidence that Polk's inaugural address should have been printed in the New York *Journal of Commerce* directly above an article headed, "California Coming." Henry Clay, the Whig candidate, had insisted that the annexation of Texas would involve war with Mexico; the Administration cheerfully looked forward to the event which Cassandra bewailed.

Now, according to the bargain, Oregon was to be added to the Union. When Congress met in the winter of 1845-1846, resolutions to give notice of the termination of the joint occupancy agreement were introduced. But Calhoun led the Southern Democrats in opposition; and "Fifty-four forty or fight" became an echo of a lost cause. Their betrayed colleagues were bitter; as Hannegan exploded, "Texas and Oregon were born in the same instant, nursed and cradled in the same cradle—the Baltimore convention—and they were at the same instant adopted by the Democracy throughout the land. There was not a moment's hesitation until Texas was admitted; but at the moment she was admitted the peculiar friends of Texas turned and were doing all they could to strangle Oregon."

And the questions raised by the frontier settlements in the Pacific Northwest were subdued while the pageant of the Mexican War held the stage. It was a pageant of neatly trimmed duration, from May 9, 1846, when the city of Washington received the news that a detachment of the United States Army had been attacked by Mexican soldiers on the Texas side of the Rio Grande, and Polk declared on the following Monday, "The cup of forbearance had been exhausted even before the recent information from the frontier," to the signing of the treaty at Guadalupe-Hidalgo on February 2, 1848. There was a great deal of local color, the romantic scenery of desert sands and adobe fortresses, and two heroes emerged, Zachary Taylor and Winfield Scott; but critics of the pageant have complained that the *deus ex machina* is entirely too evident, and that the motivation seems rather tawdry.

In Oregon war feeling was tense, but the hostility was

toward Great Britain. Commissioners were talking compromise, however, while the settlers were talking war; on June 15, 1846, Secretary of State James Buchanan arrived at a convention with the British plenipotentiary whereby the line of the forty-second parallel was extended from the Rockies to the Pacific Ocean. The insatiable pioneers grumbled at the compromise of the boundary line, and at the concessions allowed the Hudson's Bay Company; but the limits of Oregon were at last definitively set.

The emigration of 1846 brought not more than fifteen hundred pioneers into Oregon. Many of the companies on the Trail were following a newer star, California; Joel Palmer, traveling fast with a small company, for two hundred miles continued to meet companies of from six to forty wagons. In all he passed 541 wagons (five emigrants are usually reckoned for one wagon), of which 212 were bound for California. Because of the settlement of the boundary question and the supposition that Congress would donate lands in Oregon to actual settlers, emigration in 1847 was greatly increased. From four to five thousand people came into Oregon that year; the first wagons appeared at the Dalles as early as the twenty-second of August, and emigrants continued to arrive until November. Congress was slow in meeting its responsibility toward Oregon; not even a special message from the President brought a government for Oregon out of the Congressional tangle. Free-Soil senators appealed to their colleagues "not to turn a deaf ear to the cries of our citizens in Oregon, surrounded by hostile Indians"; and when a bill to extend a territorial government to Oregon was the order of the day, Southern senators made an amazing attempt to foist slavery upon Oregon, prolonging the discussion for over six weeks. On Sunday morning, officially "Saturday night," March 13, 1846, the long ordeal was over, and Oregon was a Territory of the United States, on her own terms.

CHAPTER XXII

BOOM YEARS IN THE MISSISSIPPI VALLEY

WHILE the maps of school geographies had the words "Interminable Swamp" stamped across Michigan, Lewis Cass, governor of the Territory from 1813 to 1831, was working valiantly to make the opportunities of that wilderness known to prospective settlers. Many soldiers from the older frontier whom the War of 1812 brought into the region about Detroit remained there as squatters. Before the beginning of public land sales in Michigan in 1818, three counties already were organized. The most populous was Wayne County, harboring Detroit; all three were along the eastern shore, and contained always a larger proportion of French Canadian settlers than any other part of Michigan Territory. The eastern shore received the first American settlers.

Detroit in 1818 contained a few more than a thousand settlers. It was an outpost of a self-sufficient frontier, the center of a flourishing fur trade. The war had made money scarce, and the unit of exchange was a pound of prime beaver skin. A small quantity of leather was tanned by the French Canadians, and marketed at Montreal. The Indians brought Detroit merchants great quantities of maple sugar annually, and odd handicraft articles; but the fur trade so overbalanced all else that the exports of the town were sixfold greater than its imports. Lake Erie was the only channel of commerce; one miserable road ran southward from Detroit, over which mail coaches came and went once a week if the mud permitted.

In 1819, the adroit Governor Cass secured national aid for an expedition to report upon the soil, minerals, and Indian conditions of the upper Great Lakes region; in the next year the exploration was accomplished, with Henry R. Schoolcraft as its smooth-tongued publicist. A decade later John Farmer's maps and gazetteers of Michigan found a demand in eastern cities that the press in Detroit could hardly supply; Jedediah Morse excised the old comments on the interior of Michigan—"stunted trees," "scanty vegetation," substituting bouquets; and newspapers in New York state were calling to emigrants' attention the natural freighting highway of the Great Lakes between Michigan and the Erie Canal.

With the completion of the Erie Canal in 1825, the town took on a new self-consciousness; fifty-eight new buildings were erected in that same year; and in 1826 mail was transported on a tri-weekly schedule. A committee of the common council, reporting on needed improvements, pressed these four desiderata: a sewer, the removal of refuse from the margin of Detroit River, an efficient fire engine, and pavement for the main streets. In 1831 "the demand for stores and houses is unprecedented. We have not been prepared to meet the exigencies arising from so rapid an increase of our numbers, and almost every building that can be made to answer for a shelter is occupied and filled."

The direction of settlement into the interior was from the eastern shore, along the larger rivers and the two roads inland—the Chicago Road, built as a military enterprise to connect the forts at Detroit and Chicago, the great axis of settlement in southern Michigan; and the Territorial Road, through the Kalamazoo Valley, passing through the center of the lower peninsula. From Ohio and Indiana, in the mid-thirties, came another current of settlement into inland Michigan.

In the upper Mississippi Valley was a rich lead region, embracing corners of Wisconsin, Illinois, and Iowa. The mines had been worked by adventurers of New France; they had figured in the far-western skirmishes of the Revolutionary War. In 1825 about one hundred Americans were working the mines; within another year the number had increased fourfold; and in 1827 a general rush of prospectors and miners rocketed the population of the district to about five thousand.

Pioneers on their way to the lead mines passed the great village which for a hundred years had been the headquarters and the burying ground of the Sauk tribe. Here, during the spring and summer, Indian women cultivated the fertile cornfields on the river bank, raised unfailing quantities of pumpkins, squashes, and beans. Rock Island, opposite the fields, was a garden of wild fruits and nuts. Pioneers liked the place, and they took it. The fringe of settlement was fifty miles away; this was the one spot in the wilderness of Illinois that the Indians actually used.

The Sauk and Fox nation had killed no white men since after the War of 1812, its chiefs had signed a peace treaty; it did not fight now. Keokuk, the most important Sauk chief, decided that the tribe had better move to its lands on the western bank of the Mississippi. "Many of our people," as Black Hawk said, "instead of going to their old hunting grounds, where game was plenty, would go near to the settlements to hunt—and, instead of saving their skins to pay the trader for goods furnished them in the fall, would sell them to the settlers for whiskey, and return in the spring with their families, almost naked." But Black Hawk, an old war chief whose sixty years had been turbulent and proud, protested. After months of wrangling between the two factions, Keokuk persuaded the majority of the tribe to follow him into Iowa. Black Hawk and his band remained at the village.

A temporary land act of 1830 allowed settlers to preempt quarter sections of land in advance of the date of public sale; the squatters on the Sauk farm lands took advantage of it, and ordered the Indians to move, not only off the preëmpted lands, but to the west bank of the Mississippi. Black Hawk turned on them indignantly, his braves scowled, and the settlers fled in panic. They memorialized the governor of Illinois: the Indians had "threatened to kill them; that they acted in a most outrageous manner; threw down their fences, turned horses into their cornfields, stole their potatoes, saying the land was theirs and that they had not sold it . . . leveled deadly weapons at the citizens . . . rolled out a barrel of whisky, and destroyed it." The governor proclaimed Illinois to be in a state of invasion, and called for volunteers.

When, late in June of 1831, six hundred volunteers and ten companies of regulars marched into the Sauk village, they found it empty; Black Hawk and his six or eight hundred braves had withdrawn across the Mississippi.

But it was too late to plant crops in Iowa, and the fields on the eastern bank were in the hands of spoilers. That was a winter of famine for the Sauk; and in April, 1832, despite his promise to General Edmund P. Gaines, commander of the expedition of the previous June, never again to cross the Mississippi, Black Hawk and six or eight hundred followers came to the eastern bank. His intentions were peaceful enough, for the moment, and naïve enough: he should raise a crop with his friends, the Winnebago, and perfect his plans for a coalition of Indian tribes, with British aid, to strike back at the Americans.

At the news of Black Hawk's coming, the Illinois frontier was ablaze with excitement. Volunteers were gathered from the fields; they formed themselves into companies, elected their officers, and rushed off to fight the Indians.

Black Hawk, to his amazement, could get no coöperation from the Winnebago or the Potawatami. His hopes of reprisal were dashed. Three braves were sent forward under a flag of truce, while Black Hawk and forty warriors waited not quite a mile away. The volunteers were not to be cheated of their fun; they shot down the Indian carrying the flag of truce, and galloped toward the warriors. Black Hawk formed his line behind a clump of chaparral, with a stirring appeal to sell their lives dearly; and as the raw and rabid volunteers approached, the forty warriors burst from cover in a wild, whooping, explosive dash. Forthwith the pioneers, conceiving the dusk to be thickly peopled with bloody warriors, turned in frantic terror.

Panic swept the state; clearings were deserted, families and whole settlements scuttled to the protection of the forts. The governor issued a levy for a new force of two thousand men, as the militia already raised was disheartened by the single combat and was perforce mustered out of service. Meanwhile an irregular bushwhacking warfare was being carried on, costing the lives of two hundred settlers.

Black Hawk's band fled north into the rough land near the Dells of Wisconsin, desolate country that offered little food for the Indians, who had come not for war, but with their women and children. On the seventh of August General Winfield Scott arrived to take the command of the pursuing army. He was five days too late to prevent the volunteers from bayoneting the Indian women and children, slaughtering all but a hundred and fifty of the starved, exhausted thousand that had followed Black Hawk.

The old chieftain was among the prisoners. In June, 1833, he was released. He had a simple curtain speech: "Rock River was a beautiful country. I loved my towns, my cornfields, and the home of my people. I fought for it. It is now yours. Keep it as we did."

After the Black Hawk War, the Indian title to the upper Mississippi Valley was quickly effaced. What was left of the Sauk and Fox concluded a treaty of submission and cession in September, 1832, whereby they surrendered a fifty-mile strip of their Iowa lands along the Mississippi. The Winnebago were transported across the river in that same year, and in 1833 the Potawatami were removed from Illinois and Wisconsin. With the country between Lake Michigan and the Mississippi cleared of Indians, and the General Land Office ready to run township lines and open new tracts for sale, the upper valley entered upon its boom years of settlement.

By 1836 successive treaties had extinguished the Indian title to the whole of Michigan's lower peninsula. The strong-arm methods of national policy toward the Indians gave renewed assurance to pioneers who would not bring their families into a dangerous frontier. The westward movement burst all leashes in 1835 and 1836. Sales of public lands in Michigan, reaching their previous high mark in 1825 with 92,332 acres, leaped in 1835 to 405,331 acres, and in the next year fairly climbed the perpendicular when nearly one and a half million acres were put under claim.

Early in 1835 the land office at Detroit was thronged with speculators and home seekers; the hotels and lodging houses were overwhelmed, and many newcomers perforce slept on boats in the harbor. The town achieved a population of ten thousand within the next two years; and government surveyors led the tide of settlement into interior Michigan, the Saginaw Valley and the Grand River country. When the effete Miss Martineau visited Detroit in 1836 she found the society "very choice," and was sure that "under its new dignities Detroit will become more and more a desirable place to live." A public library of four thousand volumes, a lyceum and a lecture course, flourishing newspapers, schools and churches, a museum and a public garden, bespoke a new metropolis of the West.

The one interruption of this westward movement, the Panic of 1837, was in large part the product of the over-enthusiastic, overconfident West. New towns appeared without forewarning; property values in villages and cities that appeared to have strategic locations went skyward. Chicago was not the only town whose development began with trumpet blasts from speculators; it was not in the only locale in which even the preëmption rights to a quarter section of land could be sold for several thousand dollars by the lucky squatter. The Chicago area was decidedly unusual in that it afterwards justified the ballyhoo.

"The western country is full of men, wandering from place to place, for the purpose of inspecting public lands and entering them, when found sufficiently fertile and well situated to be tempting to real settlers," narrated the *New Orleans Times* in December, 1836. "The land speculator goes forth with a guide and a pack horse; and for weeks perambulates the uninhabited forests—he pitches his tent every evening, builds his fire, and prepares his frugal meal which has been afforded him by his unerring rifle. When he has selected some tracts of virgin soil, shaded with oaks, interspersed with natural prairies and watered by some deep, broad stream, he returns to the land office and pours his *all* into the coffers of the government. He talks loudly of the unexampled prosperity of the western country, of inexhaustible resources, and finally points out a particular section of the country, which, he says, is selling fast, and is superior to anything *he* knows of. He meets the tide of emigration and endeavors to direct it toward the spot of his predilection. If he succeeds, he realizes in a short time a ten-fold profit, and begins again, with enlarged capital. Hardly ever does it happen that he fails—he may have to wait more or less long, but the spreading sea of emigration finally covers the district in which he made his location—his lands, being choice tracts, command a preference, and are bought at ten or twenty dollars an acre, when government lands alongside are rejected at ten bits."

Interlocking with speculation in lands was the mania for canal-building in the western states after the completion of the Erie Canal. Canals were authorized to be built through unsettled regions, on the ground that population would immediately increase, creating taxable values that would soon warrant the outlay. Here again the West was borrowing overconfidently against the wealth of the future. "By the winter of 1836-1837, every Western state, like every western citizen," so Professor Paxson summarized, "had pledged its future upon the success of speculative ventures, whose mere continuance was contingent upon free access to capital and the perpetuation of good times." The outcome of the war between President Jackson and the second Bank of the United States was a devastating reversion to the hard times of 1819. Financial jugglery, careless banking, too sanguine investments, again brought a period of deflated capital and capsized schemes. The westward movement suffered a momentary lull—then rushed ahead without waiting for prosperity to catch up.

Wisconsin Territory was established in 1836, extending from Lake Michigan to the Missouri. The territorial census of 1838 revealed a population of eighteen thousand in Wisconsin proper. Frontiersmen advancing beyond the lead district had discovered the attractions of the wooded prairies and the hardwood forests. Within the next decade the population bounded upward with an increase of one hundred thousand settlers. In Wisconsin two streams of emigration met, one coming from the east through Chicago, the other ascending the Mississippi from the settlements of Illinois. In Iowa this mixing of two unlike currents, and the slow formation of first an emulsion, then a genuine blend—inviting the label "Western Brand"—was to be an even more pronounced characteristic of the frontier years.

In 1836 Iowa lands were supporting ten thousand settlers; men were exploring the country as far inland as the Iowa River Valley about the present Iowa City in their hunt for most attractive homesteads and for elbowroom. Iowa received most-favored-frontier treatment in the Eastern newspapers, and throughout the next two decades waxed in population under this benign publicity.

Iowa Territory was created in 1838, comprising all that part of the Territory of Wisconsin west of the Mississippi. At that time over twenty thousand settlers were on Iowa lands; yet not an acre of that public domain had been offered for sale. These squatters fully expected Congress to grant them first opportunity to buy the land on which they were settled; that "inalienable right" had long been part of the frontiersman's conception of justice. And until land offices were opened in Iowa, they banded together in claim associations. Over a hundred of these spontaneous protective societies existed in territorial Iowa. Organization made it possible for settlers to take up lands in the public domain, surveyed or unsurveyed tracts, and begin the work of home-making without the immediate expense of paying for the land. The land clubs removed the settlers' fears of being ousted, by government or newcomers or speculators. Custom was preceding statute: the land clubs were as democratic as they were extralegal, and they were effective.

The records of the Claim Association of Johnson County, Iowa, almost unique in their survival to this day, begin on March 9, 1839. The settlers in these rolling prairies had entered into no association until the first territorial legislature assigned the location of the capital to their county; then they immediately busied themselves with an organization to protect first comers' rights. The constitution of the

[397]

Claim Association bears the names of Robert Lucas, governor of Iowa Territory, and S. C. Hastings, later chief justice of Iowa, beside the scrawls and X-marks of unremembered pioneers.

"The officers of this association shall be one President, one Vice President One Clerk or Recorder of claims deeds or transfers of Claims, seven Judges or adjusters of claims or boundrys. One of whom shall be qualifyed to administer the oath or affirmation and whose duty it shall be to attend all judicial courts of the association and two Marshalls." All officers were to be elected annually. The judges and marshals were to be salaried for each day spent in attending to their official duties; the clerk was to receive fees for recording claims and making conveyances, "and Twelve & a half cents for the privalege of examining his Books. . . ." The way in which claims were to be marked out in the field and entered upon the clerk's records was prescribed; a maximum to any one person's holdings was set. Qualifications for membership and for voting were defined, with provisions for the manner of trial in cases of disputed claims. "Any member refusing to be governed by the laws of the association or decission of the court shall no longer be considered a member and his name shall be stricken from the association for the faithfull observance and mantanance of all the foregoing laws we mutually pledge our honours, and subscribe our names here unto."

In only two cases, such was the security given bona fide settlers by the Claim Association, were the landrights of a member defied. In one case the offender received a fair number of lashes well laid on; in the other instance an impromptu committee of sixty men marched to the spot where the claim jumper had built his cabin. It was a substantial log house, with a clapboard roof, and the truculent claim jumper inside it. The vigilantes parleyed. Was he willing to abandon his claim? He was not; and he warned every one in general to molest him at his own peril. Whereupon the vigilantes set about tearing the house down; and in fifteen minutes the truculent one, with ax in hand, was standing amazed in the center of the vacant space once occupied by his cabin.

On August 3, 1840, the land office at Dubuque was opened; and the members of the Claim Association of Johnson County set out to buy the lands they were already occupying. The employees of the land office were furnished with large plats of the two townships to be sold, on which the name of each claimant was written. When the sale was to begin, the crier stepped out on the platform, and called out each eighty-acre subdivision as rapidly as he could rattle off the numbers; when he came to a tract with a claimant's name written across it, the crier's hammer came down, and the name was passed along to the clerk. The two sections were offered in less than thirty minutes; the crowd about the platform had stood in unbroken silence; not a call had answered the crier. The little comedy of a public sale was over, and the members of the Claim Association had acquired legal title to their lands. Outlying townships within the Association's jurisdiction were offered at a public sale in the prairie town of Marion in 1843; and soon after that sale the Claim Association of Johnson County was dissolved.

The case for the squatter was vigorously put in a memorial of 1837 from settlers about Peoria, wherein Congress was warned of the alternative: "either that there will be such violence used in defence of the rights of the settlers as we must seriously deplore, or that many a settler will be driven from his present pleasant and beautiful abode, and his well cultivated fields, by the more opulent capitalist or the greedy and merciless spceulator." Since the heart of the public land policy was the welfare of the common man, and an act of 1807, forced by Southern representatives, prohibiting unauthorized settlement had been practically repealed seven years later, Congress could well consider legislation to recognize the first rights of the squatters. Henry Clay, to whom the squatters were a "lawless horde," was for many years in the way; but in 1841 popular sovereignty had its inning. From Wisconsin to Mississippi the frontier was demanding a revision of the land law; and the Whig Party, having won in the presidential election of 1840 because General William Henry Harrison was tremendously popular in the West, needed to maintain its strength in the new states. Representatives of the original thirteen states were Clay's only sure adherents in opposition; and Senator Benton's "Permanent Prospective Preemption Law" was enacted.

Under the provisions, one hundred sixty acres of public lands could be occupied in lawful preëmption; when the section was put on the market, the squatter could buy his piece of land, free from competitive bids, at the minimum government price. The concession was restricted to settlers on surveyed lands; therein it ran counter to the ancient independence of frontiersmen. The Act of 1841 was only half satisfying to the West; but it would do, until the political strength of the frontier should be strong enough to eradicate the last vestige of the public-lands-for-revenue idea, and make the public domain free to the settlers.

Outright donations of public land were made by Congress in four instances between 1842 and 1853. The first of these was avowedly a military measure: one hundred and sixty acres of certain Florida lands were to be given to each settler on this frontier where there was danger of Indian attacks. Over thirteen hundred entries were made in response to the offer. In 1850, as a reward to the settlers who had won Oregon from the British and the Indians, a half section of land was donated to any man who had settled in Oregon prior to 1850, and to a married woman the same amount, her half section, interestingly, to be patented in her own right and not to be included in her husband's grant. Settlers who should come into Oregon between 1850 and the close of 1853 were to be given quarter sections. When Washington was divided from Oregon in 1853, the act granting land to pioneer settlers was made operative in the new territory; 2,826,972 acres were thus donated to the pioneers of the Pacific Northwest. In 1853, as a military measure, donations of a quarter section each were offered to settlers in New Mexico.

These acts foreshadowed the trend of Congress toward a general plan of donations to homesteaders. Since 1797, when a group of squatters along the Ohio River asked to have the lands they occupied donated to them, on condition of four years' residence, Congress had been presented with many a memorial asking for land donations; and Senator Benton had been a staunch advocate of free lands. "The settler, in a new country, pays the value of the best land in the privations he endures, in the hardships he encounters, and in the labor he performs." So spoke Benton; so spoke the frontier. In 1844 Representative Thomasson of Kentucky proposed a free grant of forty acres to the head of every family settling upon the public domain; and Ficklin of Illinois denounced the practice of one uniform price for all lands, whether fen, bog, marsh, prairie, or wooded upland, adding, "The new states, unlike the old, pay tribute to the federal government for their land . . . the federal land officers are a sort of conduit pipe that convey the bulk of money from the new States to the national treasury." A representative from New York offered a measure providing for the sale of one hundred sixty acres to actual settlers at one tenth of a cent per acre. When Congress convened in March, 1846, four bills for a general donation policy were presented to the House, one of them by Andrew Johnson of Tennessee.

In 1848 the Free Soil Party made its appearance in national politics, with emphatic advocacy of free grants to settlers. The plank of 1848 cited the burden to the settler of the other expenses incurred in breaking the wilderness, and the benefits that accrued to the nation. The platform put forward in the national election of 1852 approached the issue from a more philosophical bias: "That all men have a natural right to a portion of the soil; and that, as the use of the soil is indispensable to life, the right of all men to the soil is as sacred as their right to life itself. . . . The public lands of the United States belong to the people, and should not be sold to individuals nor granted to corporations, but should be held as a sacred trust for the benefit of the people, and should be granted in limited quantities, free of cost, to landless settlers." Thomas Jefferson speaking; speaking in his library as he takes his foxed copy of Montesquieu from the shelf; but speaking with the relentless logic of Lincoln in 1858. If this right to the soil is an inherent right of humanity, what of slaves? The Free Soil Party of 1852, and its lineal descendant, the National Republican Party of 1856, anticipated and gladly accepted the implication; and the Civil War was no more definitely a war against slavery than it was a war for free land.

Free land, more explicitly, means free land desirable for farming. Since 1840 that phrase had acquired a new content.

In 1800 a nearly unbroken forest had extended from the Atlantic coast northwesterly to the far end of Lake Erie and southwesterly to the Mississippi and into Texas. In the settlement of western Pennsylvania and western New York, eastern Ohio, and the lower Ohio Valley, the first task of the pioneer had been to clear his land of brush and trees. It was slow work, the extension of a "patch" into a farm worthy of the name, the work of years. In Ohio and Indiana many of the small prairies near water and timber had been settled. Forested "openings" in the Mississippi Valley states, tracts like those in southern Wisconsin which Hibbard described, "Immense 'orchards' of stately oaks— usually the burr oak—standing well apart, their superb tops spreading over a radius of forty or fifty feet, yet with plenty of room for wind and sunshine between, favoring the presence of prairie grasses or hazel brush," were favored spots for settlement in the decade of the thirties. By 1840 the farmers' frontier had reached the great prairies.

Because of tradition, recollection of the wooded regions whence they came, the miry woefulness of prairie roads in the spring and Indian summer, the difficulty of digging wells, the fact that the squatters in the prairie lands seemed uniformly to have fever and "the shakes," most pioneers were reluctant to enter the prairies when there was other cheap land to be had. And it must be remembered that the cultivation of crops, alone, did not provide a pioneer and his family with all their needs. The pioneer's work was much more diversified than the work of the farmer of a later day; it had to be. Timbered land offered the surest sustenance, the greatest equipment for the needs that the pioneer had to satisfy for himself. Let him produce a handsome surplus of grain or live stock: in the money-tight decade after the panic of 1837 the settler was fortunate to sell his products at his home for any price, and the cost of transportation to a cash market was quite likely equal to the selling price.

But as a result of the Great Emigration, all the available lands on the edge of the large prairies in the older regions had by 1850 passed into the possession of farmers or speculators. To obtain good lands, the pioneer had to go into the far-distant West to find the partly timbered tracts he preferred—Oregon offered such fields—or he had to venture into the prairie.

[403]

Rising admirably to the contingency, the prairies invited the pioneer into their midst, and promised him profits. In the winter of 1845 the price of wheat, corn, cattle, and hogs in western markets took a definite trend for the better. Within the next fifteen years improved agricultural machinery permitted more extensive harvests. And railroads chugged through the prairie region.

At the New York state fair in 1842 more than forty plows of different designs were on exhibit. Special plows were being produced for special soils. Plow-making, in short, was passing from the village smithy to the factory. In 1837 John Deere had made his first steel plow, and within a few years his products had wide celebrity in the Mississippi. Most other agricultural machinery was still in the experimental stage, for all the promises of the manufacturers—with one supremely important exception: the reaper. Obed Hussey made his first reaper in Cincinnati in 1833; in the next year Cyrus H. McCormick, Virginian, patented his instrument. By 1847 the reapers, after much revision, had become genuinely substantial and effective. And by 1850 the rising price of wheat in the West gave settlers new incentive to attain them. The only defense of inertia was the initial capital. He was a fortunate pioneer who could readily find the purchase price of a reaper in his trousers pocket.

By 1850 railroads were no longer local enterprises; trunk lines extending from the seaboard were answering the western farmer's need of marketing facilities, the key to his prosperity and the key to the settlement of the prairies. In 1846 the Erie Railroad was completed to Dunkirk on Lake Erie, the first railroad to bridge the gap between the Atlantic and the Great Lakes. The Baltimore & Ohio, the Grand Trunk, the consolidation of local lines under the title of the New York Central, before 1854 extended from Atlantic terminals into the agricultural West. In Ohio canals

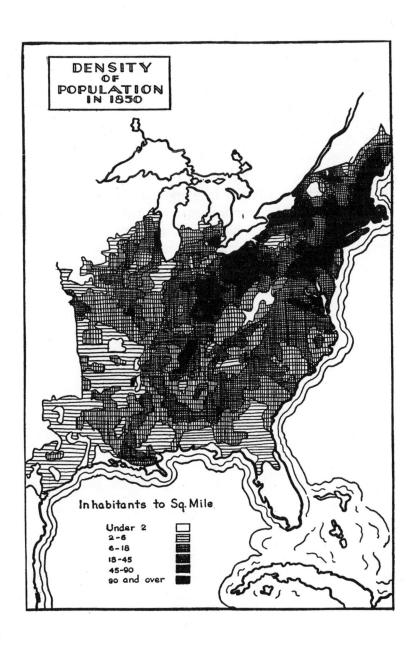

DENSITY
OF
POPULATION
IN 1850

Inhabitants to Sq. Mile

Under 2
2-6
6-18
18-45
45-90
90 and over

traversed the most populated regions and retarded the building of railroads; but Sandusky on Lake Erie, deprived of a canal by political maneuvers, supported the building of the Mad River & Lake Erie railway, which joined at Springfield a railway to Cincinnati. Thereafter the Ohio canals were in the twilight of their usefulness. In the four years after the completion, in 1848, of the Mad River & Lake Erie nearly nineteen hundred miles of track were laid in the Old Northwest. In the spring of 1852 two lines from Michigan entered Illinois, leasing trackage into Chicago. The advance of the frontier was no longer dependent on the natural roads and the navigable rivers; the railroads were catching up with the West.

CHAPTER XXIII

GARDEN IN THE DESERT

INTO the Great Plains, the expanse from the western boundary of Arkansas and Missouri to the border line of Spanish domain, most of the Indian tribes within the settled districts of the United States were to be transferred. That area seemed the permanent hunting grounds of the Indians; the devices of frontiersmen in their fight with nature were blunted there. By 1834 the process of removal was well under way; and a benign committee of Congress on Indian affairs swung a holy censer. "Whatever difference of opinion may heretofore have existed, the policy of the Government, in regard to the future condition of these tribes of Indians, may now be regarded as definitely settled. To induce them to remove west of the Mississippi, to a territory set apart and dedicated to their use and government forever; to secure to them there a final home; to elevate their intellectual, moral, and civil condition and to fit them for the enjoyment of a free government, is that policy. And the further hope is now encouraged, that, whenever their advance in civilization should warrant the measure, and they desire it, that they may be admitted as a state to become a member of the Union."

So much for the social waste of the Great Plains, happily disposed of forever; what lay beyond the hundredth meridian, what was the geography of the country beyond the Rockies, Spanish America or Oregon, was no part of American education. Maps ten years later were not far wrong in tracing the Pacific Coast, but between the coast and the Rockies in Spanish North America delineated these three features: the Colorado River, following a marvelously straight course; a wide stream entitled "Buenaventura River," departing from the western slope of the Rockies at about the fortieth parallel, and flowing westward to its outlet midway between the port of San Francisco and Santa Barbara; and a third stream from "Youtaw Lake" near the Rockies at about the forty-second parallel, flowing into the Bay of San Francisco. Fur traders knew better than all that; but geographers had no traffic with fur traders.

American traders were trapping beaver in the mountain waters of Idaho by 1824. Etienne Provot, heading a small band of independent trappers, worked his leisurely way, garnering beaver skins, to the northwest shoulder of the Uintah Range, and crossed over to the upper reaches of Weber River about due east of the site of Salt Lake City. Descending the Weber River northwesterly, his band emerged from the Wasatch Range into the floor of the Salt Lake Valley, at the present site of Ogden. Hostile Indians attacked them; seven trappers were killed before the Indians were put to retreat. And the dispirited trappers turned north, to make winter quarters, in 1824-1825, in a sheltered alcove of the mountains northeast of the site of Ogden.

In Willow Valley, employees of Major Andrew Henry and William H. Ashley made casual conjecture of the farther course of Bear River. Jim Bridger was sure he was right; some one made a bet with him, Bridger stretched buffalo hides upon a willow frame, and pushed his bullboat out into the stream. He passed down the boisterous water through the canyon, and stopped to reconnoiter. From the rocky shoulder of the canyon, Bear River Valley was spread out before him; and in the distance, some twenty-five miles away, glistened a body of water. Bridger returned to his bull-boat, and kept down the river to its outlet in Bear River Bay of the Great Salt Lake. He tasted the waters beyond the estuary of the bar; the taste was salty. When he was back in winter quarters, the trappers mulled over the information, and decided that Bridger had reached a bay of the Pacific Ocean. But in the spring of 1826 four men, embarked in bull-boats, circumnavigated the lake, to discover if any streams containing beaver emptied into it; and the Great Salt Lake, as such, came into the cognizance of fur traders.

In August, 1826, Jedediah Smith with a party of fifteen left the rendezvous above Great Salt Lake to explore the unknown country to the southwest. Passing down the valley of the Lake, the party traveled southwesterly across the Sevier Valley to the Virgin River, down which they rode into the Colorado. From the Mojave villages Smith followed a western course, across the desolate wastes of southern California. In mid-October the party was at San Diego—heartily unwelcome. Resident Americans there interceded for him, and the explorer was permitted to purchase supplies and depart. The party trapped beaver in several California streams, and lingered about the Sierras, to the exasperation of Mexican officials. In May, 1827, Smith and two companions, with nine pack animals loaded with provisions and forage, triumphed over the soft snow of the mountains, crossing the Sierras in eight days. Twenty days more brought him to the southwestern corner of Great Salt Lake; in mid-June he was at the trappers' rendezvous. He had been first (as far as written record shows) to travel southwest from Great Salt Lake to California, first to cross the Sierra Nevada Mountains, first to cross the deserts of Utah and Nevada.

A month after his return, he set out again for California, with a party of eighteen, to bring back the trappers he had left there. The Mojaves, incited by the Californians to let no American come down the Colorado, attacked his party, killing ten men and capturing all the effects of the expedition. The survivors made their way, through intense privations, to San Gabriel in ten days. Smith was thrown into prison at Monterey; in late autumn he was freed, and ordered to speed himself from Mexican territory. Perverse again, his party spent the winter on the north fork of the Sacramento, thereafter called the American Fork. In April Smith and his company, with huge bundles of furs, set out for Oregon. Indians killed fifteen of the party, and made off with the furs. Smith and his three surviving companions arrived at the Hudson's Bay Company post, Fort Vancouver, destitute. The splendid gentleman who was factor there, Dr. John McLoughlin, sent out a force to trace down the Indians and recover the bales of beaver. McLoughlin purchased the recovered furs, and Smith, in March, 1829, returned to his familiar trapping ground on the Snake River.

While Smith was still in camp on the American River, Sylvester Pattie, Kentuckian, his son, James Ohio Pattie, and a company of six adventurers, had come into California. Sylvester Pattie died in prison in San Diego; most of the others, liberated, became residents of California. After them came other parties of Americans overland into California, wandering along the inland valleys and streams, hunting and trapping—truculent, self-reliant frontiersmen with no regard for Mexican law or Mexican officials, and no great concern as to whether they were followed or not by colonizing Americans.

In May, 1843, John C. Frémont, whose fortunes in the United States army were carefully nurtured by his father-in-law, Senator Benton, was sent out to examine the broad region between the Rocky Mountains and the Pacific, south of the Columbia. Separating himself from all avenues of communication whence quibbling restraints from his superiors might reach him, Frémont followed up the valley of the Kansas River, across the parched country between the Smoky Hill and the Republican to the South Platte, thence east and south to explore the *terra incognita* (except to fur traders) of Colorado. Late in July Frémont traveled west to the Green River, and left that river to follow the emigrant road to Bear River. The country touching Great Salt Lake to the west and north was carefully explored; and the expedition made its way down the Snake and the Columbia to Fort Vancouver. In November, Frémont began the return journey—a journey of intense suffering and privation, across the Sierras through thin-crusted snows. In March, 1844, the party was among American friends on the Sacramento River. The return journey followed a course south through the mountains to the Mojave Desert, thence along Mexican trails.

Frémont, back in Washington and writing his voluminous report, made favorable comment on the country just west of Salt Lake: "I can say of it in general terms that the bottoms of this river [Bear River] and of some of the creeks which I saw form a natural resting and recruiting station for travelers, now and in all time to come. The bottoms are extensive, water excellent, timber sufficient, the soil good and well adapted to the grain and grasses suited to such an elevated region."

Brigham Young was an omnivorous reader; Frémont, surely, did not escape him.

In 1830 the *Book of Mormon* was published: its philosophy of history exacted no more credulity than the cosmogony of Genesis; its faith was the-old-time-religion, brought up to date without being modernized; and Joseph Smith seemed reasonably enough to have acquired the literal mantle of Elijah and Elisha. Within a year there were a thousand converts, and zealous apostles steadily brought in new converts from far afield. From Kirtland, Ohio, their first agricultural community, hemmed in by the intense dislike of "Gentile" neighbors and handicapped in their necessary expansion by land values, the Mormons turned westward, and at Independence, Missouri, began the building of a model theocratic city. The patriarch Enoch had built a great city, over which rolled the waters of the Gulf of Mexico because its inhabitants had become so far advanced that further earthly residence was unnecessary. The new Zion at Independence never invited such inundation; its foundations were hardly begun when the virulent intolerance of frontier farmers shattered the mortar. Missourians were afraid that the Mormons, voting as a solid phalanx, would sometime dictate the politics of the state; they were individualists profoundly suspicious of people who were dominated by group loyalties and group egotism; afraid to strike a balance of the results upon themselves of their war against nature, they were pierced to the quick by that Mormon catchword for outsiders, "Gentiles," with its arrogant suggestion of Mormon superiority.

Since war on the rights of the Mormons was part of the policy of the state administration, the Mormons petitioned that the legislature assign them to some other place of residence, where they might not be an annoyance to the good citizenry of Missouri; and the legislature directed them to a sparsely settled region (the present Caldwell County) north of Independence. Here they bought the claims of most of the inhabitants, took up several sections of government lands, and laid out the town of Far West. On the fourth of July, 1838, they undertook again to lay the cornerstone of a temple of God. "In a day or two . . . ," wrote a Mormon historian, "the thunder rolled in awful majesty over the city of Far West, and the arrows of lightning fell from the clouds, and shivered the liberty pole from top to bottom; thus manifesting to many that there was an end to liberty and law in that state."

The rapid extension of the farmers' frontier in Missouri pressed upon the Mormon settlement. In January, 1839, the community was plainly told that it need expect no redress for spilled blood and destroyed property from the legislature or the courts of Missouri; and in midwinter began another forced march, painful to flesh and spirit. A little above the mouth of the Des Moines River, on the Illinois side of the Mississippi, was the relic of an experimental community—twenty empty houses surrounded by unweeded farm lands. The Mormons purchased the title; and Zion was moved again. It was called Nauvoo this time. The legislature granted the Mormons extensive privileges, because in the hair-trigger balance of Democrats and Whigs in Illinois politics, the Mormon voting phalanx had the aspect of a valuable asset.

A temple of white limestone was built upon the highest spot in the city; a hotel, a college, other spacious buildings, clustered in the center of a town of fifteen thousand people. Lumber came from the pineries of Wisconsin, where Lyman Wight was in charge of the Black River Company, a Mormon enterprise.

Whatever politicians might think of the Mormons, farmers in Illinois were no more tolerant than farmers in Missouri; and again the Mormons felt the cumulative pressure of intolerance. The "Gentiles" now had another grievance, a moral one: polygamy had been openly introduced into the cult. Joseph Smith announced himself a candidate for the presidency of the United States in 1844. Not even Smith could have attained that dizzy height of megalomania alone; he was borne there by the megalomania of the group. The Mormons had been hounded into a conviction of their own superiority. Ultimately, in Utah, they made the conquest of a new kind of landscape, a coun-

[413]

try miserably forested and poorly watered, quite unlike the country east of the Missouri. Experience upon the old frontiers was not enough for that conquest; Utah made new demands. Tenacity and unity were the new elements that pioneer settlers in a subhumid country must possess; the rabid hostility in Missouri and Illinois which sought to break the Mormons succeeded in pressing tenacity and unity into Mormon fiber.

Early in 1844 a Mormon delegation—chosen, apparently, from the members of the Black River Lumber Company—appeared before the legislature of the Republic of Texas, with a proposal to purchase a vast tract between the Colorado River, the Rio Grande, and the Gulf of Mexico. Here the Mormons expected to be recognized as a separate nation, and to help Texas defend itself against Mexico. While the delegates waited for some definite answer, word came that Joseph Smith and his brother had been killed by a mob. The proposal had been little more than a straw flung in the wind; only Lyman Wight saw it fall.

Wight was no friend of Brigham Young, Smith's successor as head of the faith. The Wisconsin lumber mills were sold; and on March 28, 1845, in four homemade boats, a company of one hundred fifty men, women, and children, began the journey down the Mississippi. Early in November the party forded Red River at Preston, Texas, and in a deserted fort waited out the winter. Late in April, 1846, the emigrants broke camp; marching to the southwest, they crossed the Brazos River near the site of Marlin, "swimming their teams and cattle, and ferrying the wagons across by means of small canoes." On the sixth of June they reached their chosen location, near the Colorado River in south-central Texas.

The Mormon colony gained almost immediate renown by the building of the first power-driven gristmill and lumber mill on the south Texas frontier. By the end of July houses and shops had been built, and crops planted; the City of Zodiac had arisen. There was soon a strong stone fort, but there were no Indian troubles. Along the bank of the little Perdinales River stretched a broad road; back from the road stretched a series of irrigated farms, separated by stone fences. In December, 1848, two delegates of Brigham Young's visited the Texas colony, threatening Wight and his followers with disfellowship if they stayed out of the fold. Lyman Wight made a Texas-flavored answer: that "nobody under the light of the sun except Joseph Smith . . . could call him from Texas to go to Salt Lake City."

But, woe betide, Wight had not had the guidance of a revelation in choosing the site of Zodiac; his own judgment had taken no account of freshets. In July, 1850, the mill was swept away and the houses were flooded. A second flood early in 1851 drove the colony to a new location, fifty miles up the Perdinales. Here they encountered the open warfare of the Indians; but new mills were erected, the ground was broken, and as furniture-makers and farmers the colonists were profitably busy. Lyman Wight, however, had become a pioneer first and a Mormon afterwards; he was as restless as any irreligious frontiersman, and in 1853 he sold his rights in the settlement to one Noah Smithwick. The gradual break-up of the Mormon colony began.

Wight and the company of Mormons who preferred to follow him moved westward. Their wanderings in the next few months took them to the Medina River, where, twelve miles below Bandera, they founded the community of Mountain Valley—a pioneer outpost in a country lonelier than they had bargained for, and menaced by Indians. Wight petitioned the state and the national government for troops to give his community a chance to survive. "While Congress is spending six or eight months to find out whether it is best to reinforce the army or not," he wrote, "the Indians are killing men women and children and driving off large quantities of stock and nothing to hender. We make this one more appeal to Government and if this fails we have but one alternative and that is to abandon the frontiers alltogether." And the colony perforce retreated, not to be reassembled; but Wight, the insatiable pioneer, was planning when death overtook him to preach Mormonism through Mexico and Central America.

Mormonism, like any other cult, was constantly sending out offshoots from the main stock; the hardiness, the vigor, of the main stock, so much more important than all the offshoots, was due primarily to Brigham Young's wholehearted concentration upon his rôle as Smith's successor. A Mormon elder was beside Young in his last sickness: "It seemed to me that he was indispensable. What could we do without him? He has been the brain, the eye, the ear, the mouth, and hand for the entire people of the Church of Jesus Christ of Latter-day Saints. From the greatest details connected with the organization of this church down to the smallest minutiæ connected with the work, he has left upon it the impress of his great mind." Smith, fearful of his life, had decided to flee to the Rockies; Young determined to bring the entire Mormon body into the Far West. Frémont's report of his explorations had given Young his cue. At a meeting of the elders in October, 1845, Young put the motion: "That we take all the saints with us, to the extent of our ability, that is, our influence and property"; and the motion was carried unanimously.

On February 10, 1846, flatboats carried the first teams across the Mississippi, and from dawn till solid darkness skiffs took emigrants and baggage to the western shore. The last remnant of the Mormons left Nauvoo on the seventeenth of September. Twenty thousand people had been driven from Nauvoo and the neighboring Mormon settlements; most of them were encamped beside the Missouri, some had scattered through the western states in search of employment, some had joined a battalion of the United States Army and were marching toward Santa Fe.

Early in April the first company of pioneers left winter quarters, a train of seventy wagons, Brigham Young in command. Along the north branch of the Platte, past Fort Laramie, then making a new road a little to the south of the Oregon Trail, the train was at the South Pass in late June, well ahead of the full tide of that year's emigration to Oregon. At five each morning the hundred and fifty emigrants, three women and two children among them, were roused by bugle call for prayer; then they breakfasted, and at seven began the day's journey. At night there was private prayer in each wagon. On Sunday there was little else but prayer—no traveling. But the guns were always loaded, the powderhorns were kept filled. The horses were fed the young shoots and inner bark of the cottonwood trees; when there were no trees, the stock was sustained on the company's grain and biscuit, while the emigrants made shift with buffalo and fish alone.

With the South Pass behind them, they skirted the Colorado Desert, following the Big Sandy; they passed Fort Bridger, and found a rugged way through the Uintah Range. Too many of the party were sick with mountain fever; and at Echo Canyon the train halted, but not for long. Young was too ill to go forward; but he directed Orson Pratt to take the strongest men of the company and cut through the mountains into the Salt Lake Valley. The advance party found a plain road already made for them— the tracks of the Donner company's wagons. On the banks of City Creek, near the only trees in sight, the men staked off lands for crops; through the afternoon of the twenty-third of July three plows and a harrow were at work.

A dam was commenced, and water-conduits cut into the earth. The rest of the company, urged forward by the will of a man too weak to sit up in a wagon, arrived the next noon.

In the next few days lumber-cutting began in the canyons; a city was plotted; log cabins were built, stockade fashion; on the twenty-second of August a conference agreed upon the name, "City of the Great Salt Lake." Wilford Woodruff wrote in his journal: "We have laid out a city two miles square, and built a fort of hewn timber drawn seven miles from the mountains, and of sun-dried bricks or adobes, surrounding ten acres of ground, forty rods of which were covered with block-houses, besides planting about ten acres of corn and vegetables. All this we have done in a single month."

Sixteen hundred emigrants left winter quarters on the Missouri that July. "The word and will of the Lord concerning the camp of Israel" was an admirably explicit revelation received by Brigham Young for their guidance; it was a divine endorsement of the common practices of overland travelers—the method of organization, the disposing of the wagons, corralwise, at night, the using of buffalo chips for fuel, the sending out of advance parties to locate camping grounds. As the new year began, the seventeen hundred Mormons at Salt Lake were adequately housed and clad, and generally contented. Parley Pratt wrote romantically: "Here life was as sweet as the holidays, as merry as in the Christian palaces and mansions of those who had driven us to the mountains." The stockade of log cabins was extended by additional rectangles. Each cabin had its minimum amount of homemade furniture; and its maximum capacity of mice and wood bugs, against which Mormon housewives waged pious and incessant war.

In February, 1848, the Mexican War came to a formal

close. The peace negotiations had been a carnival for the expansionists: the northern boundary of Mexico was pushed down to a line due west from El Paso, along the westward course of the Gila, thence to the Pacific across the peninsula of Lower California. In this vast aggrandizement Utah had become part of the domain of the United States—an outcome that Young had probably foreseen, with no pleasure, from the beginning of the war. But geography was in his favor: the farmers' frontier had been halted at the edge of the Great Plains, unable to go farther, except to establish a separate frontier on the Pacific Coast. Geography gave Mormons the time they needed to build a state, and postponed the inevitable conflict between the Mormon hegemony and the national government until a time when the Mormons should be able to take care of themselves.

Mormon emigrants in 1848 brought with them cattle, pigs, chickens, sheep, dogs, geese, even beehives and cats. The first companies to arrive brought millstones, printing presses, type, paper, and a wool-carding machine. Sawmills, gristmills, a threshing machine, were ready by midsummer. Gardens were flourishing, when black and baleful crickets, a phalanx millions strong, began havoc; posthaste and miraculously, myriads of gulls came from over the lake, and banqueted upon crickets. By the close of the year there were five thousand settlers in Salt Lake City. Wagon boxes and adobe huts were the best habitations many could have; and the winter's store of foodstuffs had to be eked out with sago and thistle roots. Salt Lake was not a communistic community, and prices soared, wheat to five dollars a bushel, and potatoes to twenty; but "those persons who had imparted measurably to those who had not, so that all extremity of suffering from hunger was avoided."

The community was almost moneyless. The Prophet himself had only fifty dollars in his pocket when he first came to Salt Lake, and eighty-four when he returned in 1848. Paper money which Joseph Smith had had the audacity to issue at Kirtland was ordered put into circulation, "thus fulfilling the prophecy of Joseph," the Council added, "that the Kirtland notes would one day be as good as gold." The first use of the printing press in Salt Lake was to strike off paper money, in anticipation of the mining of gold; for already word had come from California of gold in the Rockies. The migration of gold-seekers to California brought far more wealth to the Mormons than their mines, though some gold was coined in Salt Lake City. Two things restrained most of the Mormons from deserting Zion for the California mines: the profits of trading with discouraged and bedraggled travelers who passed through the city, and the invective of the Prophet. "If you elders of Israel want to go to the gold mines," Young said, "go and be damned. If you go, I would not give a picayune to keep you from damnation." The threatened exodus was stayed; about six hundred Mormons left for the mines, and Young's benediction was a hearty request that they never return.

Early in 1849 a convention of "the inhabitants of that portion of Upper California lying east of the Sierra Nevada Mountains" met in Salt Lake City. Since the end of the Mexican War had left the territory permanently in American control, the days of government by the ecclesiastical council were numbered. The name of Deseret—"honeybee" in the Book of Mormon—was adopted for the future state; a provisional government was organized, and a constitution was drawn up, barren of novelties except in its providing for compulsory service in the militia. A general election was held on the twelfth of March; Young was duly elected governor. The legislature met in July; and the State of Deseret, ordained by no power but its own citizens, was fairly launched. Congress had done nothing for the immense domain the United States had just acquired except to extend over it the revenue laws, and to make San Francisco a port of entry. The question of the admission of Deseret and California as states became tangled in the hopeless moils of the slavery question; and when Henry Clay's muddling Compromise of 1850 was effected the self-constituted state of Deseret emerged as the Territory of Utah.

As each succeeding summer brought companies of Mormons into the new Zion, adventurers explored the unknown country, and other settlements were founded. While Salt Lake City was still but a village, the church dignitaries promoted new settlements, ordering the adequate number of mechanics and craftsmen to become part of each colony, dictating the amount of foodstuffs and live stock to be taken. But Salt Lake City dominated the Territory.

From cabins and wagon boxes the settlers were moving into the houses of their own building, filling in the mold of the city that Young had outlined. A tabernacle, a council house, a bowery, a hall of science, a social hall, were built in the next three years. Theatrical performances were given by the blooming Deseret Dramatic Association at the social hall in winter and at the bowery in summer. The church supervised all public entertainment, but it was lavish. The anniversary of the arrival of the pioneers (the twenty-fourth of July), Independence Day, and Christmas were among the officially festive occasions. As Christmas of 1849 drew near, the Council issued regulations: the holidays—dancing, singing, party-going—were to commence on the twentieth, and continue till the Council announced an end; all friends and well-wishers, all who had remembered the poor of the city, were welcome to attend the dances, even if they were not Mormons; but "Woe unto them that dance with guile and malice in their hearts toward their neighbor! Woe unto them that have secretly injured their neighbor or his or her property! Woe unto them that are ministers of disorder and of evil! If these go forth in the dance without confessing and forsaking their guilt, the faith of the council is that they seal their doom by it."

An elementary school for parents was established, with Brigham Young one of the pupils; primary schools were opened in the second year of most of the settlements, and as early as the winter of 1848-1849 advanced classes were studying Hebrew, Greek, Latin, French, German, and Tahitian. In 1850 the national Congress appropriated five thousand dollars for the foundation of a library in Salt Lake City, and authorized the delegate from Utah to select the books and forward them west. In the same year the church dignitaries made the first appropriation toward a state university. Grandly optimistic as befitted a booming western community, the Council outlined a curriculum to include all living languages spoken by men, and to add Celtic and Teutonic to the instruction in dead languages; to offer all branches of natural science, demonstrating to the confusion of Gentiles the all-pervading presence of the Holy Spirit in scientific phenomena, and rearranging the planetary system in accordance with the Book of Abraham. The *Deseret News* began its honorable existence in June, 1850, as a weekly periodical.

In 1850 there were 11,354 persons in the Territory of Utah, according to the United States census; Salt Lake City embraced somewhat more than half the population. In 1853, by Richard Francis Burton's estimate, twenty-five thousand people lived in the Salt Lake Valley. There was no destitution, and little sickness. The Mormons had made the first conquest of the semiarid frontier; and baffled pioneers in Colorado and in west Texas as late as 1875 were fumbling for their secrets. Captain Howard Stansbury, detailed in 1849 and 1850 to make explorations in the Great Basin and to make the first complete survey of the Great Salt Lake, described the successful technic in broad outline: "Their admirable system of combining labor, while each has his own property, in lands and tenements, and the proceeds of his industry, the skill in dividing off the lands, and conducting the irrigating canals to supply the want of rain, which rarely falls between April and October; the cheerful manner in which every one applies himself industriously, but not laboriously; the complete reign of good neighborhood and quiet houses and fields, form themes of admiration for the stranger coming from the dark and sterile recesses of the mountain gorges into the flourishing valley."

CHAPTER XXIV

LIFE AND LABOR IN THE DIGGINGS

UPPER CALIFORNIA had been simply a buffer province to Spain; spurs of settlement had been thrust out, a parry in tierce, whenever other nations had approached its borders. Fur traders of England and Russia came nearer each year to the California coast, and sometimes trespassed. A mission and a presidio at San Diego in 1769, a settlement at Monterey in 1770, the Bay of San Francisco occupied by soldiery in 1776, and the village of Yerba Buena established by the civilian hangers-on of the presidio at the Bay—the Spanish occupation of Upper California moved that far northward, and no more. It was a tenuous hold; as late as 1846 there were not many more than six thousand Mexicans or Spaniards in the province. When Mexico proclaimed its independence of Spain in February, 1821, and sustained the proclamation in the events of the next few months, Californians, sweetly isolated from it all, were acquiescent.

When the Republic of Mexico had achieved some stability, upon the Constitution of 1824, California was made a territory. Thereafter the pueblos succeeded the missions as the dominating factor in California, and provincial politics became somewhat turbulent. Commerce, for many years a negligible factor, blossomed in the form of smuggling; and the natives made casual contacts with Americans and others who came by sea. A few sailors deserted from their ships became tolerated residents of California.

In 1839 one Johann August Sutter landed at Monterey, presented his credentials to the governor, discoursed agreeably, shuffled his citizenship—German-born, he had acquired Swiss citizenship, and gave that up for Mexican naturalization so that he might hold land in California—and Governor Alvarado granted him eleven square leagues of land, a domain bisected by the Sacramento River. The colony he proposed to establish, Sutter assured Alvarado, would be a valuable frontier guard against Indians and other possible enemies; but with his stockade, his farms and herds and his cosmopolitan followers, Sutter became a continuous source of apprehension to the Mexican authorities at Monterey. He had no bias against Americans.

In 1840 Joseph Robidoux, fur trader, was back at his post on the site of St. Joseph, Missouri; he had been a trader in Santa Fe, and had followed the Gila River trail of the Mexicans into California. Thousands of wild horses and cattle there, perennial spring, fertile earth: western Missourians listened to him agape. Was there fever and ague in California, too? Well, yes, one man; the people in Monterey found the spectacle so novel that they went eighteen miles into the country to see him shake. A fur trader with a fur trader's soul, Robidoux had none of the colonizer in him; but he communicated his enthusiasm to pioneers of the clearing-making kind.

The Western Emigration Society was the result, born in Platte County, Missouri, but soon with correspondents throughout Missouri and as far east as Kentucky. Five hundred men pledged themselves to meet on the ninth of May, 1841, armed and equipped to cross the Rocky Mountains to California. "Our ignorance of the route," wrote John Bidwell, "was complete. We knew that California lay west, and that was the extent of our knowledge. Some of the maps consulted . . . showed a lake in the vicinity of where Salt Lake now is; it was represented as a long lake, three or four hundred miles in extent, narrow and with two outlets, both running into the Pacific Ocean, either apparently larger than the Mississippi River. An intelligent man with whom I boarded . . . possessed a map that showed these rivers to be large, and he advised me to take tools along to make canoes, so that if we found the country so rough that we could not get along with our wagons we could descend one of those rivers to the Pacific."

But just then Thomas Farnham was in New York, having made his way from Oregon by boat; on his change of boats at Monterey the Californian officials had imprisoned him without reason, and Farnham was irate. To a New York newspaper he gave an account of the oppression of Americans by native Californians. The merchants of western Missouri had the account reprinted in a local scissor-clip newspaper; and the Western Emigration Company dwindled down to John Bidwell.

But at the rendezvous, in a grove across the Missouri, there were at leaving time sixty-nine people, three families from Arkansas, nearly all the rest Missourians. There was probably not one hundred dollars in cash among the whole party; there was hope and determination, the stuff of frontier-builders. Happily supplemented by a missionary party including Father de Smet and captained by Thomas Fitzpatrick, veteran Rocky Mountain trader, the company set out upon the yet unchristened Oregon Trail. Captain Fitzpatrick and the missionary party usually took the lead; but there was much road-making for all of them to do—

steep banks to be shaved down, bowlders to be tumbled aside, gulches to be filled, to let the wagons through. At Soda Springs the emigrants turned off from the road to Oregon; beyond was *terra incognita,* and Fitzpatrick had only fragmentary suggestions to leave with them.

September came before the party reached the northern tip of Great Salt Lake. Through the scraggy underbrush the wagons pushed into the salt-incrusted plain; the animals were jaded with the labor of pulling wagons through the soft ground, and could not eat the luxuriant grass sparkling with salt crystals. The party floundered somehow to the Humboldt River, and followed the river to the tule marshes of the Humboldt Sink. Nerves were at ragged edge, and the party broke up, groups seeking different passes through the Sierras. The main group had reached the San Joaquin Valley before it knew for certain that it was in California. And Bidwell's party, the first company of American settlers to go overland to California, melted into the scant American population of the province.

Frémont's journal and map of his explorations in Utah and California in 1843-1844 was happily timed in its immediate publication. It was, in its way, an emigrants' guide, the first for the journey southwest of that point, Soda Springs, where the Oregon Trail veered to the northwest. In 1844 and 1845 several hundred emigrants came overland; and in 1846, with no regard for the Mexican War, emigrant companies bound for Oregon shared the trail with companies bound for California. This last was the year of the Donner party, the group of eighty-seven pioneers from the Mississippi, led by George and Jacob Donner, which rejected the common judgment and struck out for California from the southern tip of Great Salt Lake. It was more direct, on the map, than the common trail around the northern end; but winter caught the Donner party in the heavy drifts of the Sierras. Almost half of the company were dead before rescuers came from the western slope. That was an incident in the selective process of the frontier in weeding out the not-shrewd and the not-tough; and the procession of prairie schooners kept on. California was in a fair way of becoming another outpost of the farmers' frontier, like Oregon, when suddenly its destiny was twisted.

Johann August Sutter, overlord of the Sacramento Valley, wanted lumber, great quantities of it, but not at the high cost of sending men with whipsaws into the redwoods on the Pacific coast and bringing the lumber up the Sacramento in his vessel. Forty miles above his New Helvetia, up the south branch of American River, was a valley thick with pine, balsam, and oak; at Sutter's orders thither went James Wilson Marshall and a party of workmen, blazing their way with ax. By New Year's Day, 1848, the framework of a sawmill had been erected, and a fortnight later a brush dam had been thrown across the American River, to deflect the water through a tailrace and past the mill. Early in the afternoon of the twenty-fourth of January Marshall was sauntering along the tailrace. Yellow flecks mingled with the wet earth caught his curiosity. Four days later, with three ounces of the yellow flecks in his pouch, he rode into Sutter's Fort, and abruptly asked for a private interview.

Hubert Howe Bancroft, who had many conferences with Sutter, was able to patch together that interview: "I want two bowls of water," said Marshall, and the bowls were brought him. "Now I want a stick of redwood, and some twine, and some sheet copper." "What do you want of all these things, Marshall?" "To make scales." Sutter answered, "But I have scales enough in the apothecary's shop," and brought a pair. Marshall drew out his pouch, and cupped the yellow flecks in his hand. "I believe this is gold," he said; "but the people at the mill laughed at me and called me crazy." Sutter examined the stuff attentively; then the two men tested it. Nitric acid was applied to a few flecks, which obediently disintegrated. The flecks were balanced against silver dollars on the scales, and that test was successful. The article on gold in the *American Encyclopædia* was carefully studied, and the two men knew what these flecks were.

Sutter himself could not keep the secret from his correspondence; his messenger, sent to Colonel R. B. Mason, ranking representative of the United States government at Monterey, to secure for Sutter title to the land about the sawmill, with mineral privileges, could not keep the secret. Workmen at the sawmill, their eyes opened, fumbled about in the earth, and discovered gold at other places than the tailrace. The area of the gold field was gradually enlarged, and gradually there came into the California valleys the first pioneers of the miners' frontier. Most of them came from San Francisco, the rendezvous for Americans in California, where a population of eight hundred Americans was already trading in beach lots, angling for local office, and disputing the merits of two weekly newspapers.

In May several of these first pioneers returned to San Francisco, noisily drunk with love of the contents of the bottles, tin cans, and buckskin bags that they displayed. There was no more incredulity, no caution, nothing but a dazzling vision. One San Franciscan has detailed that first heart-bound, which had far more than personal application: a returning gold digger opened his well-filled bag before him, and "I looked on for a moment; a frenzy seized my soul; unbidden my legs performed some entirely new movements of polka steps—I took several bracers—houses were too small for me to stay in; I was soon in the street in search of necessary outfits; piles of gold rose up before me at every step; castles of marble, dazzling the eye with their rich appliances; thousands of slaves bowing to my beck and call; myriads of fair virgins contending with each other for my love—were among the fancies of my fevered imagination. The Rothschilds, Girards and Astors appeared to me but poor people; in short, I had a violent attack of the gold fever."

First the few available sloops and lighters were chartered to carry miners up the Sacramento, then every little cockleshell in San Francisco Bay was pressed into the same traffic. On horseback, in Conestoga wagons, afoot, gold seekers pushed overland toward the mines. Between June and August the towns south of Sacramento contributed the most of the influx into the ever expanding mining region. In September came adventurers from the Hawaiian Islands at the news of a more exciting frontier, and a much greater number of Oregonians who suddenly decided that they were done with farming. Especially from Sonora, where there were many experienced miners, came a stream of emigration from Mexico; but Americans dominated the miners' frontier from its beginning. When the Chinese came, they mattered less than the Mexicans.

By the close of 1848 nine thousand people, probably more, had taken up the hunt for gold. Their average of success was far greater than for the miners of any subsequent year, although the only methods they knew were primitive, slow, and wasteful. They "creviced" with a knife, prying out the gold from the cracks in the rocks; they "panned" the gold-laden earth, lowering their stiff tin or sheet-iron pans into the water, shaking the pans with a sidewise oscillation that raised the dissolving clay and the light sand above the pan's surface, leaving the flakes of gold among gravel and stones settled at the bottom. Usually the miners in placer diggings—shallow diggings along the rivers and the tributary ravines—worked with a cradle. This was a wooden trough on rockers, on the upper end a riddle, a boxlike device with a bottom of perforated

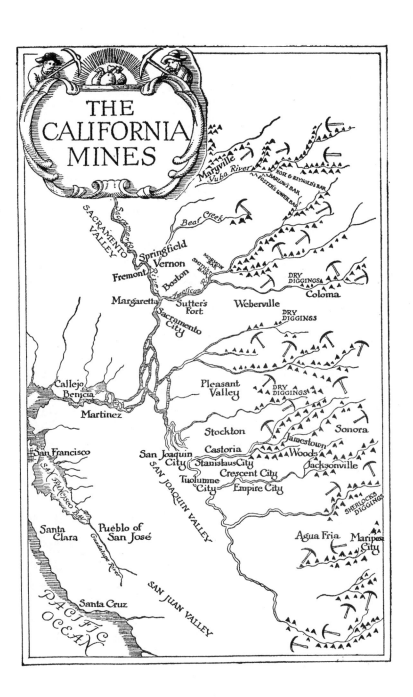

THE CALIFORNIA MINES

sheet iron; strips of wood, "riffle bars;" were nailed across the middle of the trough and at its lower end. The riddle was filled with the "dirt"; then the miner rocked the cradle with one hand, and with the other ladled water into the riddle. Much of the finer gold clung to the canvas-covered "apron" sloping from the riddle to the trough; most of the rest was caught behind the riffle bars, while the water washed out the mud and light gravel.

Hastening from placer to placer, skimming the cream of the virgin diggings, the miners of 1848 gathered ten million dollars' worth of gold. Some miners made a hundred dollars a day for weeks at a stretch, and five hundred or seven hundred dollars for a day's work was not unusual. A correspondent of the San Francisco *Californian* wrote from Dry Diggings, near Placerville, "The earth is taken out of the ravines which make out of the mountain, and is carried in wagons and packed on horses from one to three miles to the water, where it is washed; $400 has been an average for a cart-load. In one instance five loads of earth which have been dug out sold for 47 oz. ($752), and yielded after washing $16,000. Instances have occurred here where men have carried the earth on their backs, and collected from $800 to $1500 in a day." At that time word had just reached the Dry Diggings of newly discovered placers on the Stanislaus River, and two hundred miners were preparing to leave earth worth four hundred dollars a load, in the hope of striking better pay dirt. A miner at the placer diggings on the middle fork of the American River wrote, "I have had in my hands several pieces of gold about 23 carats fine, weighing from one to two pounds, and have it on good authority that pieces have been found weighing 16 pounds." Fevers, dysentery, scurvy, the numbers of luckless, moneyless people in the mining regions, were no check, in the mining regions themselves, in the newspapers, or in the letters to "the States," upon the robust optimism of the scene and the romance of the invitation.

The invitation was widespread by 1849. Mormons carried it over the Sierras to Salt Lake, whence it filtered to the Missouri River towns. Not overland, but by way of Honolulu, it reached the Hudson's Bay people in British Columbia and the American settlers in Oregon. Washington received its official notice in September, 1848. The *Baltimore Sun* on the twentieth of September carried the first sensation-making account of the discoveries. Early in the winter Lieutenant Loeser arrived in Washington from California, with the report of Colonel Mason's own observations in the mining district; and the box of gold-dust he brought was placed on exhibition in the War Department. The *Washington Union* reported: "We are informed that the secretary will send the small chest of gold to the mint, to be melted into coin and bars, and most of it to be subsequently fashioned into medals commemorative of the heroism and valor of our officers. . . . However skeptical any may be, we defy him to doubt that if the quantity of such specimens as these be as great as has been represented, the value of the gold in California must be greater than has been hitherto discovered in the old or new continent; and great as may be the emigration to this new El Dorado, the frugal and industrious will be amply repaid for their enterprise and toil." Everywhere young men believed, and older men who had known failure, or had become embittered at the small results of their constant grubbing, or had the frontier lust in their hearts. Every scrap of information concerning California was in demand, and three guidebooks for emigrants (*California Gold Regions, With a Full Account of its Mineral Resources; How to Get There and What to Take; the Expense, the Time, and the Various Routes, Etc.*, is the title of one, and the subject-matter of them all) appeared before the year of 1848 had ended.

In 1847, in the ordinary routine of business, Congress had authorized the Secretary of the Navy to receive bids for the carrying of the mails to the Pacific Coast—one line of steamships to Chagres, and the other "from Panama to Astoria, or to such other port as the secretary of the navy may select, in the territory of Oregon, once a month each way, so as to connect with the mail from Habana to Chagres across the Isthmus." The promised subsidies were luscious sums; a speculator obtained the contract for carrying the mail on the Pacific, and passed it on to William H. Aspinwall and his just-organized Pacific Mail Steamship Company. On the sixth of October, 1848, the first Pacific Mail ship set out for New York, in ballast. The Straits of Magellan were safely threaded in December, and the ship pointed up the western shore of the continent. In the days of its lonely voyaging in South American waters "California fever" had become epidemic in the eastern states; and ships from New York to Chagres were bringing hundreds of gold seekers to the Isthmus of Panama. When the pioneer ship of the Pacific Mail came into the Bay of Panama on the thirtieth of January, fifteen hundred Americans had crossed the Isthmus, all of them clamorous for passage on the *California*. More than four hundred frantic people somehow clambered aboard—a thousand dollars for a steerage ticket, anything to get to California!

On the last day of February, 1849, the guns of the Pacific squadron boomed salute, the bluejackets manning the yards cheered welcome: the *California* steamed into San Francisco Bay. A second Pacific Mail steamer bringing Argonauts of '49 from Panama arrived on the first of April, a third in May; and thereafter these steamers, supplemented by others, regularly traveled between Panama and San Francisco. But entrance to California by sea re-

quired money, and the typical American pioneer has never
had a dependable surplus of money. The route by way
of Panama was the privilege of professional men, merchants, politicians, gamblers; most of the gold seekers followed the Overland Trail or another of the wagon routes
across the West.

The emigrants who followed the Overland Trail began
the journey either at the old starting points at the northward bend of the Missouri, Independence and St. Joseph,
or, coming from the Middle West across Iowa, they made
final preparations in the Mormon settlement, Kanesville,
at the Council Bluffs, crossed the river and headed immediately for the North Platte. Leaving the Oregon Trail
at Soda Springs or at Fort Hall, the trail to California
led along the Snake River Valley, and up Goose Creek to
the headwaters of the Humboldt. This ill-favored river
was followed to the Sink wherein it disappears. Franklin
Langworthy in 1850 made note of this portion of the route:
"Numerous graves of emigrants are here scattered along
by the wayside, and the effluvia of dead animals fills the surrounding atmosphere." The Humboldt brought emigrants
into the most difficult stretch of the Overland Trail to
California, the crossing of the Sierra Nevada.

Early in 1849 emigrants from at least twenty states
began to assemble in Texas towns; before January was done
the wagon trains were under way. Companies struck out
across Mexico to the port of Mazatlan just below the Gulf
of California, whence they took ship for San Francisco.
Some leaving Texas took the trail through the brush country to Guadalupe Pass (at the southeastern corner of Arizona) and followed the wagon road made by the Mormon
Battalion in the Mexican War from the Rio Grande to
San Diego. Other emigrants from the Southwest crossed
northern Mexico, and from the Pima Indian villages in
Arizona followed the Gila Trail to San Diego. From San

Diego to the mining district—in 1849 the valleys of the Sacramento and its tributaries, the American and the Joaquin—for poor emigrants, the journey followed an overland trail, for moneyed ones the journey was by boat to San Francisco. From Fort Smith and Dallas trails led to El Paso, where emigrants paused for a comfortable few days, and set out with delusive optimism for the Gila River. Whatever route across the southwest territory an emigrant company chose, intense heat, dust-choked trails, a scarcity of water, a paucity of game, were certainties.

Other emigrants left Independence by the caravan trail to Santa Fe, thence to turn off at various points. None of the routes to California were hard and fast. The only way to make a pioneer travel in a set line has been to put him in a railway car.

The number of forty-niners was not much less than a hundred thousand; three-fifths of the number came overland.

Geologists be damned! Californians never trusted them. Some old fellow of imagination greased a shallow iron pot with bacon rind, mixed his bread, clamped the close-fitting iron cover over it, and heaped on coals; with bread enough for several days, and salt, and whisky, he picked up the rest of his grubstake—cup and pan, pick and shovel, and blanket—and set out alone. Perhaps he had a pack pony with him; perhaps he carried all his effects on his back. Across ridges and ravines, through gorges and along mountain-water courses, he followed premonitions that suddenly and unreasonably became convictions.

Likely as not, the prospector struck pay dirt; rumors caught up his exultation, magnified and multiplied the yellow flecks in the earth, and swept over mining camps a hundred miles away. Suddenly lines of brush huts and canvas tents bordered the newly discovered diggings; mule trains came with foodstuffs, whisky, miners' implements, and

[436]

bundles of sawn boards to be ready-fitted into saloons, stores, and hostelries. The history of a new mining town was begun.

The typical mining town of the golden years was reckless, bustling, crude, vigorous. Sunday was its lusty day, the busy period of the stores, the harvest time of the gamblers and tapsters. The few ministers that came to this booming California were more apt to become gold diggers themselves than to cling to their profession. John Steele, himself a renegade from the cloth, remembered the coming of an itinerant preacher to the diggings at Downie's Ravine. Some willing men took sluice lumber, as yet unused, and made seats in the shade of a great live oak. Several old hymns were sung, several earnest prayers offered, and then the minister preached a tear-drawing sermon to his masculine audience. At its close he announced that if the audience would wait till he had dinner he should return in ninety minutes to deliver a second sermon. And the miners of Downie's Ravine willingly enough waited. When the minister returned, he found the benches were being used for tables: the congregation was divided into groups, keeping the playing cards warm.

Professional leeches, Pike County (Missouri) backwoodsmen, arrogant swashbucklers from the southern states, Yankees, Iowans, Irishmen, sailors and soldiers who had deserted ships and forts, Dutchmen, hardened pioneers from the Oregon country, dandies, Indians, and Mexicans, mixed in a jostling money-loose mob. It made a peppery gallimaufry: "Take a sprinkling of sober-eyed, earnest, shrewd, energetic New-England business-men: mingle with them a number of rollicking sailors, a dark band of Australian convicts and cut-throats, a dash of Mexican and frontier desperadoes, a group of hardy backwoodsmen, some professional gamblers, whiskey-dealers; general swindlers, or 'rural agriculturists' . . . and having thrown in a promiscuous crowd of broken-down merchants, disappointed lovers, black sheep, unfledged dry-goods clerks, professional miners from all parts of the world, and Adullamites generally, stir up the mixture, season strongly with gold-fever, bad liquors, faro, monte, rouge-et-noir, quarrels, oaths, pistols, knives, dancing and digging, and you have something approximating to California society in early days."

In the mélange was one conspicuous gap. There were in the mining towns appallingly few women of the home-making, respectable sort, and not many women at all. The census of 1850 placed the female population of California at less than 8 per cent of the total inhabitants of the country, and most of those ladies were recent and dubious accessions of San Francisco. In the mining counties women were less than 2 per cent of the population. A seventeen-year-old youth once rode thirty-five miles from his father's cabin to see a miner's wife—"because I wanted to see a home-like lady; and, father, do you know, she sewed a button on for me, and told me not to gamble and not to drink. It sounded just like mother."

Week days were pretty dull in the town, except when miners who "boarded" left their claims at meal time. When miners neglected their claims during the day, it was only because cabins had to be built against the coming winter, or because dysentery or scurvy had seized them. Cholera raged only once, through the fall of 1850; but then it carried off perhaps 15 per cent of the population of Sacramento, and half that proportion westward.

Practically the only vegetable besides dried beans which miners could buy was potatoes, and that at staggering prices. There were no green stuffs to be had. But the cuisine of the mining towns can be no better understood, in its deficiencies and its charms, than by lingering upon the bill of fare on the tables of the El Dorado Eating Resort at Placerville, in January, 1850:

SOUP

Bean $1 00
Ox tail (short)........................ 1 50

ROAST

Beef, Mexican (prime cut) 1 50
Beef, up along......................... 1 00
Beef, plain............................ 1 00
Beef, with one potato (fair size) 1 25
Beef, tame, from the States............... 1 50

VEGETABLES

Baked beans, plain...................... 75
Baked beans, greased................... 1 00
Two potatoes (medium size) 50
Two potatoes (peeled).................. 75

ENTREES

Sauerkraut 1 00
Bacon, fried........................... 1 00
Bacon, stuffed......................... 1 50
Hash, low grade........................ 75
Hash, 18 karat......................... 1 00

GAME

Codfish balls, per pair.................... 75
Grizzly, roast.......................... 1 00
Grizzly, fried.......................... 75
Jackass rabbit (whole).................. 1 00

PASTRY

Rice pudding, plain..................... 75
Rice pudding, with molasses.............. 1 00
Rice pudding, with brandy peaches.......... 2 00
Square meal, with dessert................ 3 00
Payable in advance
N. B.—Gold scales at the end of the bar.

Each mining town was an out-and-out democracy, and remarkably successful in running its own affairs. Brigadier General Bennett Riley, sent out by the Secretary of War—anomalously—to take over the administration of civil affairs in California, in 1849, saw the mining country for himself, and wrote to Washingtonians that the local *alcaldes* and constables, elected and sustained by the miners, were preserving order and regularity almost everywhere, and that while there had been exercise of judicial powers which no law conferred upon these mining-camp executives, the general results had been to bolster society. "When a new placer was discovered," as Bayard Taylor observed, "the first thing done was to elect officers."

Gold Hill Camp was one of the mushroom upgrowths of the spring of 1850. A band of prospectors stopped in a gulch in the western part of Nevada County, panned in the creek and creviced in the hillside for a few hours, and pitched their tents to stay. Within a week fifteen or twenty men were at work in the gravelly creek bed. Each miner had chosen his own spot. As their widening circles of upturned dirt approached the other, the necessity of some sort of organization became closer. Two circles overlapped, and two miners disputed. The friends of the less belligerent one passed an informal request throughout the camp, which had grown to include fifty miners or more, for a miners' meeting in the evening.

One leading spirit installed himself as temporary chairman, and conducted the election of a permanent chairman. The elected officer put the case: there had been a little trouble about claims, there might easily be more; the time had come for the camp to be put into shape. The bounds of Gold Hill were then decided upon; some regulations were made about the size of claims; a few citizens had some words to say about roughs and thieves; and the meeting adjourned.

Whenever there was occasion, the chairman reassembled the citizenry of Gold Hill. Some further difficulties about claims were decided by vote, and several thieves were convicted and punished as the open ballot decided. Gold Hill never had a recorder or a jury; the regulations were not too complex to be remembered, and the whole meeting constituted a jury. Meetings carried out their own sentences, promptly; and then the miners went back to their diggings. In due time—by coincidence, at the fag end of Gold Hill's prosperity—the civil and criminal law of the state of California stepped in, and easily and without friction took over the powers of the extralegal democracy.

With such general meetings as Gold Hill's, or with a select council, or with the individual rule of an *alcalde* or miners' justice of the peace, the mining camps handsomely demonstrated the talent of Americans—in small settlements —for self-government. The general meeting was the heart of the scheme; councilmen and *alcaldes* well understood the right of the community as a body to interfere if they became arrant or arbitrary. At the same time the lush riotousness of San Francisco, the mounting venality of the municipal officers, was demonstrating just as handsomely how little talent Americans had for government in cities.

Criminal trials at miners' meetings were usually serious affairs, conscientiously handled; lynch-law excitement seldom showed its ugly head, and was so disliked that the excesses of one whisky-glutted community fixed upon that settlement the unshakable name of Hangtown. Whatever legal talent a mining camp possessed was brought into service in a criminal trial; and by 1850 hardly a camp on the Sierra slope did not contain miners who had graduated from law school or were lawyers of experience. The defendant—murderer, horse thief, sluice robber, highwayman—was closely guarded, or tied to a tree; and a cry passed from claim to claim, "They've caught the so-and-so that robbed Barrett's cabin," or whatever the news might be. Within half an hour the miners were assembled; they listened to testimony and speeches, to the chairman's admonition "to do the fair thing accordin' to commonsense," and brought in a verdict. If the mining camp had a population in the hundreds, the case was submitted not directly to the meeting, but to a miners' jury.

In a country without jails, hanging a persistent offender was the only convenient means of disposing of him. Murder and horse stealing were pretty surely capital offenses; and sometimes, as the safety of the community or the freedom of the highway seemed to demand it, miners' courts assessed death sentences for other crimes. Banishment from the camp was a frequent penalty for small thefts and like offenses. Naturally enough in rough times, they fell back upon the characteristic punishment of frontier communities of an earlier day, stripes. There is the story of a fatherly, unctuous-voiced *alcalde* of a mining camp in the northern Sierras, who listened to the open-and-shut evidence against a young man who had stolen a purse of gold-dust: "Would you like to have a jury-trial, my son?" "No, judge; it isn't worth while to do that." "All right, my son. Now you must return the dust you stole." "Certainly judge." "And the court regrets the necessity, but really, my son, you ought to pay costs,—two ounces." "Oh, I can stand that; here it is, and thank ye, judge." "Now the court is fully satisfied, with the exception of one trifling formality. Boys, take him out, and give him thirty-nine lashes well laid on." Barely a handful of miners' verdicts have a recognizable taint of sadism; close to the fountainhead of law as they were, these self-constituted courts aimed to keep their verdict respectable. Another factor added to the conscientiousness of these courts: the serious matter of land laws was also in their hands. Without protection of land titles there would have been anarchy.

Civil law in the mining camps grew out of necessity and experience. The land was free; discovery and appropriation gave the title. The claims in each district were numbered and recorded; local regulations determined their size. "No one was allowed to forestall or to lock up natural resources," as Henry George commented. "Labor was acknowledged as the creator of wealth, was given a free hand, and secured in its reward. The device would not have assured complete equality of rights under the conditions that in most countries prevail; but under the conditions that there and then existed—a sparse population, an unexplored country, and an occupation in its nature a lottery—it secured substantial justice." For all that every educated man in the mining region had been indoctrinated with the idea of individual ownership of land, on the frontier men instinctively adopted the radically different theory that squatters in the Pennsylvania backwoods had worked out for themselves—use of the land, actual occupation, conferred the actual title. And the mining-camp courts stressed that point. Jackass Gulch, belying its guffawing name in the almost unmatched richness of its pay dirt, governed itself by these regulations, a typical statement of the claim laws each mining-camp court adopted:

"*First,* That each person can hold one claim by virtue of occupation, but it must not exceed one hundred feet square.

"*Second,* That a claim or claims, if held by purchase, must be under a bill of sale, and certified to by two disinterested persons as to the genuineness of signature and of the consideration given.

"*Third,* That a jury of five persons shall decide any question arising under the previous article.

"*Fourth,* That notices of claims must be renewed every ten days until water to work the said claims is to be had.

"*Fifth,* That as soon as there is sufficiency of water for working a claim, five days' absence from said claim, except

[443]

in case of sickness, accident, or reasonable excuse, shall forfeit the property.

"*Sixth,* That these rules shall extend over Jackass and Soldier Gulch, and their tributaries."

The land laws varied in details in different localities, of course, as the miners' democracies voted; and they varied as conditions changed. In the lush times in Jackass Gulch, the maximum size of a claim was a space ten feet square; but as the placer miners made off with the surface gold, the legal size of a claim was increased to one hundred feet square. In Jamestown District a claim was required to have, three days after "location," a ditch cut about it and stakes driven at the corners; failure to work the claim within six days after the mining season began caused its forfeiture. In Sawmill Flat, "whenever any dispute shall arise respecting claims or water privileges, each party shall choose two disinterested persons; the four thus selected shall choose a fifth; and the five thus selected shall hear evidence according to the laws of this precinct." Columbia District displayed an early flourish of the chauvinism that was to become California's favorite brand: "Any person who shall sell a claim to an Asiatic or South-Sea Islander shall not be allowed to hold another claim in this district for the space of six months." So run the local variations upon the central theme. When quartz mining began, in the winter of 1850-1851, a claim-governing code similar to the code for placer mining was worked out, and was adopted generally by the miners of the various districts of Nevada County assembled in convention at Nevada City, December 20, 1852; and the laws of that convention were still in force thirty years later.

In the winter of 1850-1851 Congress turned its languid attention to John C. Frémont's senate bill to establish police regulations throughout the mining region, and to levy a tax upon the miners. That measure would have choked off the native initiative of frontiersmen, then building their own institutions to meet their own needs. But Thomas H. Benton and William H. Seward, with keener minds and with a better appreciation of the meaning of the West than Frémont (who may gently be called an egomaniac), insisted upon delay in legislation. A year later the local regulations of the mining camps had so well justified themselves that Congress hesitated to set them aside. The legislature of California in 1851 provided that in all actions respecting miners' claims the courts should take full regard of the proceedings of the miners' meetings, "so far as they are not inconsistent with the laws and constitution of the State," and provided that in all cases of mining claims, whatever their value, the mining-town justices of the peace should have jurisdiction. On July 26, 1866, Congress passed an act recognizing the force of local mining customs; and in subsequent acts, defining the entire subject of mining law, sections referring to locators and their exclusive right of possession and enjoyment of their mining claims, to tunnel rights, to miners' regulations and improvements, to vested rights in the use of water and to rights of way for canals, the cumulative experience of the first mining camps, as expressed in the local laws of their own making, has been written into the national statutes. And the beginning was a signboard on a California gravel bar: "CLAIME NOTISE.—Jim Brown of Missoury takes this ground; jumpers will be shot."

PART VI

FROM ISAAC STEVENS TO GRENVILLE DODGE

There is a power in this nation greater than either the North or the South—a growing, increasing, swelling power, that will be able to speak the law to this nation, and to execute the law as spoken. That power is the country known as the Great West—the valley of the Mississippi, one and indivisible from the Gulf to the Great Lakes. . . . There, Sir, is the hope of this nation—the resting place of the power that is not only to control, but to save the nation.

—STEPHEN A. DOUGLAS

CHAPTER XXV

EXPLORATION ON A GRAND SCALE

IN 1846 citizens of St. Louis projected the building of a railroad to Fayette. Fayette was westward only a hundred miles; but the *American Railroad Journal* announced, "It is thus that our Western brethren are supplying the link of that great chain of railroad communication, which before the end of this century, will probably be unbroken between the Atlantic seaboard and the farthest limits of habitations in the West." For by 1846, in Congress and out, the idea of a railroad traversing the western territories, terminating at no point short of the Pacific Ocean, had become part of the common stock of American optimism. Since 1834 prosperity-conscious editors had been detecting harbingers of the Pacific railroad, and energetic promoters had been attempting to decoy the first robin.

In 1834 Samuel Bancroft Harlow in Massachusetts made use of the press to pump up sentiment for a trans-western railroad to be built by the government; in 1836 John Plumbe, in Dubuque, Iowa, preached a similar gospel in a pamphlet, and two years later organized his townsfolk in a demand for a Michigan-to-Oregon railway. In 1845 Asa

Whitney presented to Congress the first of his indefatigable series of memorials for the building of a railroad, by himself, aided by grants of public land, from the Great Lakes or the upper Mississippi to the Pacific Coast. Hartwell Carver had formulated a definite scheme for a Pacific railway by 1837, and in 1849 and 1850 memorialized Congress for a charter to build a railway from Lake Michigan to the Pacific. Four similar petitions by other promoters had reached Congress by 1850.

And there was much to be said for a steam-and-iron revision of the Overland Trail. A demand for expeditious mail service to the far-western settlements, for military efficiency over a vast region inhabited by roving Indians only sporadically docile, appealed strongly to the national administration and satisfied its occasional qualms that government aid to a Pacific railroad would not be constitutional. Asa Whitney's railway, said the promoter, "would give us the entire control of the commerce of Europe with all Asia, and increase our own far beyond the power of the imagination to estimate." The adjustment of the Oregon question, the taking over of all the Mexican provinces north of Mexico itself, the dauntless surge of emigrants into California and the Pacific Northwest, lent cumulative importance to the idea of a Pacific railway. To encourage the settlement of the subarid Great Plains, to exploit the resources of the mountainous regions of the West, to dilute the local flavor of the frontier sectors with the less specific tinge of the nation as a whole: these things were effects of the Pacific railroad, but were no part of the feeling that demanded the railroad and that built it.

The year of Harrison's election to the presidency began a twenty-year period of zealous railroad-building, and much more zealous railroad-planning, throughout the South and Middle West. The same emotionalism, the same concentrated enthusiasm, that in 1840 had elected a chromo of a log cabin and a cider barrel to the presidency, was put to work in behalf of railroads. After 1845 local conventions to generate enthusiasm for projected local railroads were an unfailing routine of civic spirit. But the prospect of future profits was not a sufficient beginning for railroad-building. There were specific problems to be attacked: how to raise the capital, how to fund the debt, how to control the expenditures, how the railroad should be related to politics and to the state. Practically everything from bond-marketing to roadbed-grading was experimental. Until railroad-building in the Middle West lost its dangerous aspects of instability, such a gigantic plan as the building of a railroad to the Pacific Ocean had to wait.

In 1850 Congress did a great deal to bring about stability: urged on by Senator Douglas, it made grants of public land in Illinois, six sections, alternately placed, for every mile of track, for the benefit of the Illinois Central. Thereafter requests were continually before Congress for additional gifts of public lands to projected railroads; and in nearly every session the requests were granted. In 1852, further, Congress enacted a general statute: any railroad chartered within the next ten years was granted in advance a right of way of one hundred feet through the public domain, with the privilege of taking extra space as needed for its stations, and of cutting timber from the public domain for use in construction.

But for all that Senator Benton, the traditional barrister for frontier demands, could do, for all the distinguished aid that various projects for a Pacific railroad received, the logrolling of sectional interests blocked the authorization of the railroad. The senators elected by southern legislatures were in a compact group, ambitious for itself and playing a dog-in-the-manger policy when projects not southern were presented. When Senator Gwin presented an elaborate bill designed to appease all sectional interests, providing for a main line from San Francisco to Fulton, Arkansas, and branches to Dubuque, St. Louis, Memphis, New Orleans, and Matagorda on the Texas coast, Senator Mason of Virginia denounced the whole thing as a "rape upon the Constitution"; Senator Bell of Tennessee attempted to amend the act by making it exclusively a southern route; and so went the logrolling on every Pacific railway bill.

But the common-sense, conservative impression that the immediately needful thing was to make adequate preliminary surveys of the possible routes across the West was gaining ground in Congress. One other preliminary work, the discarding of the old idea of a domain permanently exclusive to the Indians and the making of new treaties that would move the tribes into smaller reservations in more distant areas, was begun in 1853. In that same year Congress added to the Army-appropriations bill an amendment appropriating $150,000 for explorations and surveys to determine the most practicable and economical route between the Mississippi and the Pacific Coast. Promptly, under the direction of the Secretary of War, Jefferson Davis, qualified civil engineers began the extensive task of surveying and mapping the ways across the West.

Isaac I. Stevens, zealous, thorough, just appointed first governor of Washington Territory, was ordered to conduct the northernmost survey, between the forty-seventh and forty-ninth parallels. Stevens personally was to lead a party from the upper Mississippi to the great bend of the Missouri, and still westward across the Montana table-land to some pass in the Rockies. A far-western expedition under Captain George B. McClellan was to proceed by boat to Puget Sound, and march from the coast across the Cascades Mountains to join Stevens. The instructions were extensive enough: "to collect every species of information bearing upon the question of railroad practicability"—the "lie of the land," astronomical and magnetic observations, the rains and snows of the route, the navigability of the western rivers, whatever else might help. It would be necessary, moreover, to give great attention to the Indian tribes, whose friendship or hostility affected both the building of a railroad and the safety of the explorers.

Stevens made his rendezvous at Lake Amelia, a few miles west of St. Paul. Here his party was assembled, with its multifarious equipment: barometers, odometers, mules, carts, oxen, rations, rubber boots, compasses. On the twelfth of June, "Assembling both officers and men today, I caused to be read the camp regulations which I had prepared for the government of the party, and made a short address in which I informed them that every man would be expected to look to the safety of his comrades; that all alike, whether soldier or civilian, would be expected to stand guard, and in case of difficulties to meet them promptly . . . that in ten days we would reach the Indian country, where heavy guard duty would have to be performed to preserve property and protect lives; that still farther on we would probably be compelled to force our way through the country of the Blackfoot Indians, a tribe proverbially treacherous and warlike; that then the snows of the mountains would have to be overcome, and that every man would be expected to follow where he might be led; and that no one would be sacrificed, nor would any one be subject to any risk, which I would not freely incur; and that whoever was not willing to co-operate with us had better at once retire." He organized his camp into detached parties, each with its lieutenant and its "non-com," so that when he shuffled these groups about on minor scouts and reconnaissances, each man should know his relative position, and know from whom to accept orders. He set a zipping routine: "Cook fires to be made at two o'clock A.M.; the cooks and teamsters called at three; and the animals to be put in good grass; reveille to be sounded at four, and all the

[453]

officers to be called by name; the whole camp to breakfast about four, and the teamsters immediately to start harnessing up; tents struck at half-past four, and camp in motion by five." And he fairly infused his own zealousness into the entire party. The officer of the guard, parading his men about and showing them their positions for the first time, put his orders in the commander's best manner: " 'Your chief duty will be to watch the animals within camp' (here came a pause, he dreading to mention Indians,) 'and *without.*' "

Marching to the Red River, Stevens passed over a gravel prairie, gentle undulations breaking into heavy swells as the party moved westward; the sources of the two great rivers, one flowing into Hudson's Bay, the other into the Gulf of Mexico, he found separated only by a slightly rising prairie that offered excellent facilities for railway construction. The party now followed the Red River Trail, the path of Canadian hunters to the buffalo haunts. On the tenth of July, not quite a month since Stevens had organized his party, "About five miles from camp we ascended to the top of a high hill, and for a great distance ahead every square mile seemed to have a herd of buffalo upon it. Their number was variously estimated by the members of the party —some as high as half a million. I do not think it any exaggeration to set it down at 200,000."

A group on reconnaissance scurried back with word that the country was alive with Indians; but the distant train turned out to be the hunters of the Red River Settlement, an isolated little community of Canadian colonists, on a summer invasion of the plains about the Pembina River— thirteen hundred people, men, women, and children, with eight hundred carts to carry back tons of buffalo meat.

The party moved on through a region of little salt lakes, and salty marshes, then into a series of severe coulees about Mouse River. On the twenty-seventh of July numbers of

Indians rode up; "the first one came toward us with the back of his uplifted hand toward us, as a signal of friendship." An Assiniboine village was near; Stevens gave the order to make camp, and that evening he and several colleagues visited the council lodge.

The pipe was passed, bowls of water and of turnip soup were handed about; and, these ceremonies over, an old chief "with considerable fluency, and, at times, with many gestures," addressed Stevens: "My father, we hear that a great road is to be made through our country. We do not know what this is for; we do not understand it; but I think it will drive away the buffalo. We like to see our white brothers; we like to give them the hand of friendship; but we know that as they come out game goes back. What are we to do?" Stevens explained that the passing of the buffalo herds would be no hardship: that the President would provide the Indians with implements of agriculture, aid them to obtain food with less labor than ever, and would send presents in proof of his kind consideration. The Assiniboines were not satisfied; they did not see how all this jibed with a treaty made at Fort Laramie not long ago, fixing the hunting grounds of the tribe for all time. But the council closed amicably: "My father, our hearts are good; we are poor and have not much, but as a token of our kind feelings, accept those skins and robes on which you are seated." And the next morning was occupied with an exchange of presents.

Onward the expedition pressed, and on the first of August arrived at Fort Union. "We pitched camp," writes Stevens, "and soon after there was an assembling of the whole party at my tent. I congratulated them on the zealous performance of their duty, gave them a cordial invitation to go on, and whatever their determination, should they leave us here, promised them an honorable discharge. All seemed desirous of going on, and not one availed himself of the opportunity to leave the expedition." Lieutenant Donelson, Stevens' aide, was already here with new supplies and equipment brought up the Missouri.

New oxcarts were made, and added teams were brought from the fur company; the women of the post made moccasins, gloves, and other weather guards for the party; dispatches had to be written and sent to Washington. Meanwhile the artist of the expedition was taking daguerreotypes of the Indians, to their high pleasure; and the scientists were no less diligent. Making Donelson the active commandant of the main train, Stevens on the ninth despatched two advance parties to Fort Benton. He himself delayed a day to talk with the Blackfeet and arrange for a general council in the next year to make peace between the Blackfeet and the hunting tribes west of the mountains, and to preserve friendship between Indians and whites. Among the Gros Ventres, he pleaded for peace with the Blackfeet, and distributed presents of blankets, calico and tobacco. "The Indians were invited to come over to my camp and witness the firing of the howitzer, which seemed to give them much pleasure."

The expedition followed the level river bottoms of the Missouri and the Milk Rivers, the route marked out by the American Fur Company's wagons. "There is a singular fact connected with the streams of this country, which become dried up in the summer and fall," Stevens noted. "The fact is, the streams do not dry up; only in the summer and early fall their course is in the sands, and by sinking wells the purest and clearest water would be found at a depth of from two to three feet; and I have no doubt, from my own personal observation, that ample supplies of water would, in the driest season, be afforded by Milk River for the largest emigration, or for the largest business of a double track railroad."

On the first of September Stevens reached Fort Benton,

and detached reconnaissances arrived with their reports in the next few days. Meanwhile Stevens tirelessly questioned the voyageurs and Indians at the post about the country beyond; for a detailed examination of the mountain passes was the real problem of his survey. His aide, Saxton, soon reported his preliminary march from the Pacific Coast to the Rocky Mountains; this report, bolstered by the evidence of his seasoned scout Lieutenant Grover, convinced Stevens that the expedition must move with pack animals, not with wagons, if the Columbia were to be reached before the winter snows had covered up the grass. "Several men whom I was afraid had not strength to make the trip, and whom I had first ordered to accompany Lieutenant Saxton down the Missouri, were so anxious to go on that they brought me a certificate from the surgeon, Dr. Suckley, stating that, in his opinion, they were strong enough for the journey, and accordingly I allowed them to go on."

Stevens' objective, on leaving Fort Benton, was the mountain pass between two famous, towering landmarks, the Crown Butte and the Rattlers. On the twenty-fourth of September the main train crossed the dividing ridge. The Rockies had been surmounted with anticlimactic ease; Oregon waited at the end of the Bitter Root Valley.

Stevens held conferences with the Piegans, Bloods, and Blackfeet, to the east of the divide, and with the Flatheads and Nez Perces of Oregon. "I told them that their rights were the use of their own lands, and that the Great Father desired them to be at peace with the whites, and remain so forever." He directed reconnaissances to the north and south of the Columbia; he sent a reconnoitering party into the Cascade Range, another to the Yakima River, and for the next two years despatched or led scouting parties to explore the mountains and to verify his observations.

"The line of the forty-seventh parallel is central to a vast region of the temperate zone, extending from the water line of the great lakes to the shores of the western ocean," was his final summation. "North of this route there is a vast area, which is habitable, productive, and, at this very moment, increasing in population." His explorations had shown that there was a favorable route from Minnesota to the Rocky Mountains either by way of the Missouri or the Yellowstone; that there was more than one easily graded mountain pass; that there were several practicable passes through the Cascades. His experiences had bred enthusiasm: "The western terminus of this route, central to such a vast geographical area in the temperate zone, and central to the great water lines, canals, railroads, and seats of commerce of the eastern slope, is the most splendid roadstead, admitted in the opinion of all military and naval officers, and all commercial men, on the shores of all the oceans." The pathway of the Northern Pacific had been blazed.

Familiar with barometer and theodolite, with a capital record of frontier service, Lieutenant A. W. Whipple of the topographical engineers was chosen to outline a route along the thirty-fifth parallel. "Repair to the field with the utmost dispatch, and proceed with the survey and reconnaissance," ordered the Secretary of War in May, 1854. But Commodore Perry had just left for the harbor of Tokio; a party was just about to leave for Arctic wastes, in search of Sir John Franklin; Isaac Stevens had already done his shopping. This inquisitive age had outdistanced its instrument-makers, and Whipple had to wait for his barometers to be made.

Meanwhile Lieutenant Ives, his ranking assistant, was despatched to Albuquerque, there to collect information about the country beyond and to complete preparations for the far-westward march of the main party.

Railroads had been chartered which, united, would link Memphis and Fort Smith. This town on the Arkansas

River, at the edge of the Choctaw domain in Indian Territory, seemed the logical starting point. And nearby, at an
outlying barracks, on the fourteenth of July, chain, compass,
and level were unpacked, and the survey of the thirty-fifth
parallel commenced.

Within a fortnight the quartermaster, with long-delayed
stores, and the military escort had caught up with the surveyors. But the added stock of provisions outbulked the
wagons; and Whipple's chainmen were amateurs at packing.
"While employed upon this work, there drove up, in a
wagon drawn by two horses, an odd-looking individual, who
claimed protection. He said that he had traveled across
the country from St. Louis, intending to proceed to Texas,
where his son was residing. In his wagon were dry goods,
and he had in his pocket several hundred dollars. . . . As
our wagons were packed to the bows, and many indispensable articles still lying on the ground, we offered to purchase his wagon and horses, and employ him as driver to
California. He gladly accepted the proposition. His goods
were deposited in a shop for safe-keeping, the wagon was
loaded, and the driver, who had been, in his day, Methodist
preacher, merchant, and pedler, entered upon his new career
with great zeal."

The party traced its course through the Choctaw country
a few miles south of the Canadian, while a reconnoitering
group followed the river itself. Travel was tedious through
the chaparral and over sandstone ledges. Whipple found
Indian guides willing to direct the expedition for a few
days' march, but could find none who would continue to the
headwaters of the Canadian. The season had been unusually dry, and many streams and springs were now waterless.
Jesse Chisholm, the redoubtable Cherokee merchant, slave
owner, and interpreter, was too much the merchant prince
to be interested in the salary the army paid its scouts; and
John Bushman, the Delaware guide, Whipple's last resort,

could not be persuaded: "Maybe you find no water; maybe you all die."

The party had traversed the domain of the semicivilized Choctaws; as they entered the great western prairie they faced the lively prospect of encountering hostile Comanches, and carried the parting advice of Indians who knew the country to New Mexico that the chances of finding enough water were pretty doubtful.

There was an auspicious beginning. Fifty mules strayed away, and reclaiming them from the woods and prairie was a full day's work; on the next day the beef cattle broke loose; on the next morning Whipple was threatened by some very drunken Indians; two Indians were discovered setting fire to the prairie, and the party had to burn a wide space about the camp for protection. Again their progress was arrested by Indians, and again by a burning prairie. This second fire was a lordly menace: "The grass was tall, thick, and dry. The wind had driven the widespread flames over the crest of a hill, directly toward us; and they now came leaping into the air, roaring in the distance, and crackling fearfully as they approached. There seemed to be no safety except in flight. The train, therefore, countermarched in double-quick time, and took refuge behind a watery ravine, where the grass was too green to burn freely. Taking advantage of a comparatively bare spot, the flames were fought, and a temporary opening made, through which we traversed in safety. Mile after mile we trod nothing but cinders." Hard upon the ordeal of fire came a "norther," with rain, wind and sleet. There was no escape from freezing but exercise; so the expedition faced the wind and kept on its march.

The Llano Estacado was in view on the sixteenth of September. The road cut across a jutting tongue of the treeless plateau, then skirted the bluff at its northern limit. Parties of Mexicans and Indians were encountered soon after, as the party turned up the Tucumcari Valley. The valley became a ravine, hemmed by parti-colored bluffs; scrub cedars succeeded scrub cottonwoods. The ravine opened into the long, low range of hills separating the Canadian Valley from the Pecos. Beyond, a few days' march, was the Rio Grande and Albuquerque.

Albuquerque, more central than Santa Fe, had been made the headquarters of the military department of the Southwest. All was excitement here: Indian depredations and anticipated trouble on the Mexican frontier had called out scouting parties, and the troops at headquarters were preparing for active duty. Whipple had to wait until General Garland, the commanding officer of the department, returned from a reconnaissance, as the commissary at the post was unwilling to take upon himself the responsibility of diminishing his stores by furnishing provisions to the expedition. Lieutenant Ives had been here a month, for want of an escort to El Paso across the Comanche-infested plains.

The expedition left Albuquerque on the eighth of November; on the eleventh it left the valley of the Rio Grande and crossed the ridge which led gently into the valley of the Puerco. Across other ridges, across other valleys, always with detached reconnaissances surveying trails on either side of the road of the main train, the expedition proceeded almost due westward. On the twentieth the main train reached the *rancheros* fringing the pueblo city of Zuni. The governor paid Whipple a ceremonial visit, and escorted the surveyors about the town, where the Indians were loathsome with smallpox.

On the twenty-fourth a party under Campbell, the chief surveyor, returned from an advance reconnaissance of the northern passes through the Sierra Madre mountains; directed toward that pass which Campbell had found most favorable, the main train resumed its march. But after a few hours a Zuni war chief overtook them to announce that the governor and councilors had approved of the objects of the expedition, and were sending three guides to lead the party by an easier route to the Colorado Chiquito.

"This morning, Captain Ker, the sutler at Fort Defiance, who had accompanied our party thus far, took leave of us," Whipple wrote in his daybook on the twenty-ninth of November. "We have now broken away from all communication with the civilized world; and, for the first time on the trip, have entered a region over which no white man is supposed to have passed." It was not a formidable country, Whipple found; carpeted with grama grass even in December, it seemed well adapted for grazing cattle and sheep. And where were these waterless deserts the expedition had been expected to encounter? Past a forest of petrified trees, "beautiful specimens of variegated jasper," and nearing the valley of the Colorado Chiquito, even the scrub cedars disappeared, and the evening's camp fire was a puny thing of dry brush; but the grama grass did not fail. With two hundred mules, besides beef cattle and sheep, Whipple's party was able to camp where it pleased without fear of want of grass. The wool of a million sheep, Whipple calculated, would be worth $800,000, and would pay every year a handsome freight to a railroad. "An improved breed of sheep would produce wool of more value, and there scarcely need be a limit to the number that may graze upon this region." And the lieutenant had the courage to predict an abundant agricultural yield for upper Arizona by artesian irrigation. The Navajo Indians were a negligible factor; smallpox was annihilating them by the hundreds.

On the seventeenth of December the party crossed the dividing ridge separating the waters of Colorado Chiquito and the Gila. "We continued our march in the midst of a snow-storm. It was a day of toil for the wagon mules, as snow gathered in balls upon their feet, causing them to slip

[462]

and stumble badly." At a sheltered spot on the side of a forest the party rested for a few days until the mules recuperated. At this camp Christmas Eve was celebrated with éclat. "The fireworks were decidedly magnificent. Tall, isolated pines surrounding camp were set on fire. The flames leaped to the tree tops, and then, dying away, sent up innumerable brilliant sparks. An Indian dance, by some *ci-devant* Navajo prisoners, was succeeded by songs from the teamsters, and a pastoral enacted by the Mexicans."

The march was resumed over crusted snow, so fatiguing to the mules that one wagon was abandoned. Westward the mountain altitudes seemed forbidding; and the expedition swerved to the southwest, curving its way around the high sandstone mesas and the Aztec mountains. Preliminary reconnaissances always revealed a pass. Following the narrow canyon of the little stream called Bill Williams' Fork, on the twentieth of February the expedition reached its confluence. "The Colorado came from the northwest, meandering a magnificent valley, and having received the waters of Bill Williams' fork, entered a chasm among a pile of black mountains below. Upon both sides of it were chains of mountains." An Indian trail followed the valley, but the party could not follow it far; a spur from the mountains, "with a serrated profile like a saw," crossed the valley to the very bank of the river. There was nothing to do but to abandon the wagons, and to load the instruments, with the scientific specimens that seemed most worth saving, upon the mules. The party ascended the spur, threaded the ravine, and kept on, through Piute country, into Mojave domain, across to the west bank of the Colorado. For a blue blanket, a Mexican serape, a shirt, a dragoon's overcoat, and some white beads, a Mojave chief consented to guide the expedition across the gravel plains and the granite ridges to the Mormon Road.

Thence along the fresh wagon tracks of the road between

Salt Lake and the Pacific, the expedition made its final observations. Already independent surveys commanded by Lieutenant R. S. Williamson had described the mountain passes of the Sierra; and without reconnaissances Whipple hurried into Los Angeles and disbanded his party. He had explored virgin territory, given names to rivers, mountains, and passes, had systematized all preëxisting data upon the region of his march; and he had chalked out the course of the Santa Fe railroad.

An expedition under Captain Gunnison set out from Fort Leavenworth in June, 1853, following the emigrants' road along the Kansas River, thence along the Arkansas to Bent's Fort; leaving the Santa Fe Trail as it turned south to find Taos, Gunnison kept on to the west. Across the difficult Rockies the party made its way, and reported vengefully on the region from the Rockies to Green River: "utterly valueless for occupation and settlement by civilized man." The party was now upon an old Spanish trail, kept in constant use by the Utah Indians. The survey followed the eastern base of the Wasatch mountains, and reached the great Sevier Valley. Gunnison was exultant: "On reaching this plain a stage is attained, which I have so long desired to accomplish: the great mountains have been passed and a new wagon road opened across the continent —a work which was almost unanimously pronounced impossible, by the men who know the mountains and the route over them." The Denver and Rio Grande was to be indebted to Captain Gunnison.

His surveyors followed the emigrants' road to California, the trail leading south from Great Salt Lake; but Gunnison did not continue with them far. On October 26, 1853, the commanding engineer and a small escort were ambushed by Indians; the rescue party found Gunnison's body pierced with fifteen arrows, and seven of his men lying dead about him.

William H. Emory, on a military reconnaissance from Fort Leavenworth to San Diego in 1846-1847, had described the western half of the thirty-second parallel route so well that there was no need of another exploratory survey. Secretary Davis directed Lieutenant Parke, who had been the assistant of Lieutenant Williamson in exploring the passes of the Sierra Nevadas, to complete the survey of the southernmost of the proposed routes, beginning from the Rio Santa Cruz, a tributary of the Gila, and working toward the Rio Grande. Eastward, a strange direction for a western exploration!

In January, 1854, Parke set out from San Diego with twenty-eight workmen, whom he had salvaged, with their equipment, from Whipple's and Williamson's expeditions. The party included a military escort, another twenty-eight men. They followed the well-worn road to Fort Yuma, at the strategic point where the Gila joins the Colorado, and kept on eastward, hurriedly, along the line which Emory had described. At the first of the adobe villages on the Santa Cruz the surveyors' actual labor began. The search for a feasible roadbed in this country of scattered little mountain ranges was complicated by another quest, the search for water. Across this Apache country Parke kept on until, at the Pyramid Range, his line of survey struck a tangent to Cooke's Road, the emigrants' wagon trail from Texas to California. He followed Cooke's Road to the Rio Grande.

Captain John Pope carried on the locating work from the Rio Grande to the Red River; from the river to Fort Smith or Memphis, or from whatever point this hypothetical railway should start westward, the country was of course well known in its general features. The combined reports of these thirty-second parallel surveys presented a picture well calculated to confirm a southern gentleman in his amiable opinions: the mountain passes were of low elevation; the table-lands were favorable for railroad construction, as was the surface generally; the temperate climate promised that winter snows would not choke traffic. Not guessing how conditions should change before a Southern Pacific railroad found these reports valuable, Jefferson Davis commended the route along the thirty-second parallel to the attention of Congress.

His recommendation did not affect the deadlock of sectional interests. Although new forces were encouraging Congress—President Buchanan's message in 1853, arguing that government aid would be constitutional and asking the early attention of Congress to the subject, and the propitious state of the national finances—a railway bill providing for three Pacific railroads which squeezed through the Senate in 1855 died in the House. As the Whigs, the old internal improvement party, declined in power, and as the portentous consequences of the Kansas-Nebraska bill threw its shadow over Congress, the movement to authorize and aid a Pacific railroad passed into decline. But meanwhile the Baltimore & Ohio, reaching the Ohio River in 1852, and the Pennsylvania Railroad, running between Philadelphia and Pittsburgh in that same year, ended the honorable service of the Cumberland Road as a trans-Appalachian thoroughfare. Within another year Chicago had rail connection with St. Louis. In 1857 the Ohio and Mississippi was completed from Cincinnati to St. Louis. In the Middle West and in the East was a maze of railroads. By way of a last irony the Democratic party in the campaign of 1856 wrote into its platform "the great importance, in a political and commercial point of view, of a safe and speedy communication through our own territory between the Atlantic and Pacific coasts."

CHAPTER XXVI

SECTIONAL CONFLICT AND THE WEST

IN 1849 advertisements of sales of public lands, paid for by the Department of the Interior, were appearing in the newspapers of New York City, Buffalo, Chillicothe, and St. Paul. The extensiveness of this advertising policy is indicated by the appearance in the Middlebury, Vermont, *Register* of a proclamation announcing land sales in Minnesota. Meanwhile, farmers had entered the region north of St. Paul, making settlements along the banks of the Mississippi and its tributaries. The St. Croix River district, first to develop in Minnesota, was thriving. In the northwest corner of Minnesota Territory Scotch colonists were raising wheat. But the fertile lands along the Minnesota River, "the prettiest country lying wild that the world can boast of," were most favored by pioneer farmers of the fifties.

When Minnesota was organized as a territory in 1849, its population was estimated at a bit over four thousand. In 1854 an estimate of one hundred forty thousand was not far wrong. St. Paul in that year, reported Lawrence Oliphant, contained "four or five hotels, and at least half-a-dozen handsome churches, with tall spires pointing heavenward, and sundry meeting-houses, and a population of seven or eight thousand to go to them, and good streets with side-walks, and lofty brick warehouses, and stores, and shops, as well supplied as any in the Union; and 'an academy of the highest grade for young ladies'; and wharves at which upwards of three hundred steamers arrive annually, bringing new settlers to this favored land, and carrying away its produce to the south and east." In 1857 Minnesota, coupled with Oregon, entered into full statehood.

Access into the rich lands of Iowa had been made easy by the railroads, land companies were making alluring inducements, emigrant guides were being published by the score. The summer of 1854 brought severe drouth to the Ohio Valley and the states eastward, and another epidemic of cholera. And farmers harkened to the literature about healthful, fertile Iowa, sold their old holdings, packed their goods. "The immigration into Iowa the present season is astonishing and unprecedented," reported an Eastern journal in June, 1854; "For miles and miles, day after day, the prairies of Illinois are lined with cattle and wagons, pushing on toward this prosperous state." The ferries at the principal points of the Iowa-Illinois border did business limited only by their maximum capacity; emigrants and their wagonloads of household stuffs and their droves of live stock sometimes waited two or three days for their turn at the ferry. At Burlington "20,000 emigrants have passed through the city within the last thirty days, and they are still crossing at the rate of 600 and 700 a day"; Dubuque, MacGregor, and Keokuk as points of entry recited similar accounts. Over the Chicago & Galena Railroad, it was estimated, more than three thousand emigrants came into Iowa each month. Throughout 1855 and 1856 the invasion continued; in these three years the density of population in Iowa increased from about six to over nine persons per square mile.

Chicago, a city of thirty thousand people in 1850, contained eighty thousand five years later, and one hundred ten thousand at the close of the decade. It had become a cosmopolitan metropolis, the commercial clearing house of the upper Mississippi Valley. In 1854 seventy-four trains a day tapped the Northwest. Its grain trade handled twenty million bushels that year; Chicago had already become the greatest primary wheat depot in the world. But even in Chicago, while the pioneers themselves had passed, frontier conditions had not.

The drains in the streets, the alleys, the casual heaps of refuse in the vacant lots, reeked to high heaven. A "Gehenna of abominations," newspapers christened the Lake shore. Cows settled themselves for a night's rest on the sidewalks of the city. Surrounding massive public edifices and hotels, handsome churches and imposing business-houses, were wooden shanties and sawn-wood cabins. A London newspaperman in Chicago in 1860, when many of the frontier remnants had been removed, described the city as an "extraordinary mélange of the Broadway of New York and little shanties of Parisian buildings mixed up in some way with backwoods life." He could describe it no more definitely; nor could any one else. The frontier was departing; the new industrialism was coming in.

In the lesser towns of Illinois, in the river towns of Iowa and the Mississippi towns farther up the river, that same dubious, erratic transition was a characteristic. Public buildings, waterworks, drainage, refuse-dumping restrictions and "departments of public works," decent hotels, decent roads, better habitations—urban paraphernalia, civic institutions, had to replace the negligent survivals of the vanishing frontier. Nothing in pioneer institutions had tended to cultivate, hardly even to tolerate, a sense of culture and refinement, a flair for the "right thing"—nothing except the downright simplicity and honesty of the West. When a town felt the growing pains of modern urbanity, when an individual realized that he had become

[469]

a Westerner only in a geographical sense and should clothe his new stability in some outward signs, town and individual naturally turned to the East for their models. Both town and individual, unconsciously admitting their inferiority to eastern towns and eastern people in these matters of public buildings and private houses, decorations and color, and the like, promptly discarded that standard of downright simplicity and honesty—a standard they never needed so badly as in those days when they went shopping for modernization. The result was that they chose the most common and most obtrusive devices of eastern cities and the city dwellers—probably the most efficient devices, and probably the ugliest. Parvenu millionaires have generally done just that. The tragedy of the towns in the Ohio Valley and the Mississippi Valley is that they were not parvenu: they were ready and willing to adopt the best techniques in architecture and in civic dressing-up. But the East had such miserable standards to offer them; and they simply didn't know.

Illinois received tremendous accessions of emigrants during the transitional decade. In 1850, a population of 851,840; in 1860, no less than 1,711,951 inhabitants. And simultaneously the state contributed largely to the development of regions farther westward—California, Kansas, Nebraska, and Colorado.

Minnesota's population of 172,023 in 1860 represented an increase of 2730 per cent within the decade; Iowa's accession of almost half a million settlers was an increase of 251 per cent. The eight states of the Old Northwest and the Mississippi showed a gain of three and a half million people in the census of 1860. Impelled not so much by the hectic politics of the time as by its own momentum, the frontier was pushing toward the Missouri, claiming the lands of western Iowa, Kansas, and Nebraska.

When the enactment of Clay's compromise measures had

divided the spoils of the Mexican war into one state, California, and two huge territories, Utah and New Mexico, the only part of the United States without an organized government was the Indian country, extending from Texas to Canada and from the Missouri border to the Rocky Mountain Divide. The Indian Intercourse Act of 1834 was the gilt-edged deed whereby this expanse was delivered to the American Indians in perpetuity, and white persons without license from the Indian Commissioner were forbidden to set foot in the Indian country. Emigration into the far West had begun while the myopic statesmen who had erected the "barrier" were still congratulating themselves.

To pioneering Americans the legal entity of the Indian country was a transparent myth. The western attitude toward statutory and constitutional hindrances was effectively stated by an unknown philosopher who wrote to the *Sacramento Union* in 1859, when the constitutionality of a Pacific Railroad was then being quibbled over: "I respect the Constitution as an old friend. It is good in its way. They [the Fathers] were good and wise men in their generation (although they would be accounted rather slow in these times), but they really were not half so well acquainted with us as we are with them; and whatever they might have been once, they are not so good as we are, for a live dog is better than a dead lion. . . . I have a great respect for our ancestors; but I go for non-intervention even from them in our domestic concerns."

It was inevitable that the national government, exercising its sovereign prerogative, should repudiate its guarantee to the Indian tribes. In 1844 William Wilkins, Secretary of War, proposed territorial organization as a preliminary to the extension of military posts for the protection of the overland emigration, and Stephen A. Douglas, then in the House, had made some attempt to have the suggestions carried out. As the demand for a Pacific railroad gathered momentum in the next decade, the cognate demand for the organization of the Indian country—so that constitutional barriers to the routing of the Pacific railroad through the Platte Valley should be removed—dangled in the political air, waiting for a champion.

Surveying expeditions were in the West, assembling bulky data "to determine the most practicable route" for a Pacific railway; General James Gadsden was minister to Mexico, with instructions to secure from Mexico enough territory south of the Gila for the building of a railroad by a far-southern route; Jefferson Davis, Pierce's Secretary of War, was making a speech in Philadelphia advocating the construction of the railway by the southern route. Senator Douglas seized the moment. From January, 1854, until the end of May, Congress was in a furious moil; on May 30, 1854, the territories of Kansas and Nebraska were created, together embracing the whole Indian country except that part which is now Oklahoma.

Two territories, rather than simply one Territory of Nebraska, were provided for in Douglas' revised draft of his bill, not to create a balance between slavery and liberty, but to give an equal chance to both the northern and central routes to the Pacific. "Upon consulting with the delegates from Iowa," Douglas explained when introducing his revision, "I find that they think that their local interests, as well as the interests of the Territory require that the Territory of Nebraska be divided into two Territories. . . . So far as I have been able to consult the Missouri delegation, they are of the same opinion." The slavery issue was forced upon him: the mere mention of territorial organization raised the specter. "The repeal of the Missouri Compromise" and "Popular Sovereignty" were two wicked cups of babies' blood wherewith Douglas hoped to allay the ghost.

Senator Douglas could not openly avow that the building of the Pacific railroad was his dominant motive: if it had become known that the act generally accepted as a concession to the South, in its allowing slavery to come north of the deadline of 36° 30′, was in reality intended to sacrifice southern railway interests to northern railway interests, Douglas would have caused the same furor in Congress, and his constituents in southern Illinois would have knifed his political career at the first opportunity. But his intimate friend, James W. Sheahan, editor of the *Chicago Times,* revealed the Senator's purpose in a memorial address at the old University of Chicago, which Douglas had founded: "Kansas was closed by law to emigration and travel. Like a huge block, it barred the natural pathway to the Pacific. The South was pressing a railroad from Memphis, and southwesterly across the continent. Mr. Douglas wanted a fair chance to have that railroad lead from the north, where it could find communication through Chicago to the Atlantic. Our railroads had already reached the Mississippi, and others were projected, extending to the Missouri. He wanted Nebraska and Kansas opened, and the country made free to the enterprise of the north."

The passions of the five-months' debate over the extension of slave territory did not allow the settlement of Kansas to develop with the normal drift of the frontier. The "Appeal of the Independent Democrats," published on January 19, 1854, spread wide the message that Douglas' bill was "part and parcel of an atrocious plot to exclude from a vast unoccupied region immigrants from the Old World, and free laborers from our own States and convert it into a dreary region of despotism inhabited by masters and slaves." As soon as the slavery advocates discovered that the geographical position of Kansas was no guarantee of Southern dominance, that settlers from New England were fast coming into the territory, they too became excited. Senator Atchison of Missouri yowled to his constituents: "Will you sit here at home, and permit the nigger thieves, the cattle, the vermin of the North to come into Kansas . . . run off your negroes and depreciate the value of your slaves here?" They would not. They would go into Kansas, vote for the "peculiar institution," and come home again.

To Missourians the emigrants who swarmed into the Territory across the Missouri were an army of dangerous abolitionists, smuggling guns into Kansas, intent on driving out every squatter who dared bring in a slave. The "border ruffians" laid a strict embargo on the Missouri River, boarding and searching steamboats, breaking into baggage, insulting and maltreating passengers; but the emigration simply changed its course a bit, coming into Kansas by way of Iowa and Nebraska.

Southerners were hoodwinking themselves again. The New England Emigrant Aid Company had strenuously advertised Kansas as a part of its campaign to save the Territory for the common man. In the good name of antislavery, Kansas acquired beauty, resources, and opportunities that should have brought a blush of envy to every other district in the Union. Throughout the Ohio and the upper Mississippi valleys were thousands of families who needed very little urging to set them out toward the frontier, where conditions might be better. These people were the colonizers of Kansas.

The census of 1860 sums up the migration into Kansas: only 4,208 persons born in New England were in the Territory; 12,794 had come from New York and Pennsylvania. Iowa, alone, had contributed about as many settlers as had the New England states. Eleven thousand settlers had been Missourians. Ohio, Indiana, and Illinois together despatched a handsome emigration of 30,929 people. These were the emigrants who stuck it out.

"Let him expect when he reaches Kansas," a correspondent of the *Chicago Tribune* obliquely addressed the emigrant, "to find a full-sized sandbar in his stomach and general indications of snags. This will not hurt him. The water of the Missouri resembles a tincture of brick-yard, but in the experience of the writer it is entirely beautiful and damages no one who keeps it unmixed with the lava of western bar-rooms. Let our new pioneers come fully prepared to sleep occasionally under the protecting shelter of the stars. A tent or covered wagon one hundred miles west of the Missouri River are luxuries which any person will appreciate. A genuine Kansas man has many a time made up his bed on prairie grass, tied his horse to his boot, slept comfortably and awakened gracefully. While he cheerfully resigns his own mattress and buffalo robe to the comfort of every stranger, he smiles at the regrets which arise from the memory of the maternal warming pan. In brief if you come to Kansas to *make a home* you must go to work and make it." Settlers from the western states, who came with wagon and team, seeds and implements, were better qualified than those emigrants whom the New England Aid Company transported from 'way down east— fare twenty-five dollars, including all expenses of transportation and board. They tackled the capricious natural environment, won a living, and in the passion-torn years defended their tenets superbly against a battering crew of proslavery forces that included the executive power of the United States. In the closing days of President Buchanan's administration Kansas was made a state. Nebraska, still a territory, was given its present limits in that same session.

As the word went out in 1854 that Nebraska would soon be organized as a territorial government and its lands thrown open to settlement, speculators and restive Westerners gathered in Council Bluffs and the other Iowa towns on the Missouri. In March, 1854, Indian commissioners persuaded the Omahas and Otoes to withdraw from the greater part of their hunting grounds; and squatters ventured across the river to blaze the boundaries of some choice field. On the twenty-fourth of June President Franklin Pierce formally let down the barriers, and the land-hungry mob rushed into the Territory. The western bank of the Missouri was their first choice. The land was not yet officially opened for preëmption; committees protected first comers' rights.

Until land offices were opened, the proof of ownership of a claim was a cabin and a shotgun. Boundaries were blazed through the timber and marked by stakes across the prairie. At the corner stakes a scrawled sign gave strangers the data. The first recordings of these claims were quite simple:

George W. Hollister Claim.   *March 5, 1855.*
Bounded on the north by George A. Izard's claim, on east by Missouri river and lands unknown, on south by Flavius Izard's claim, and on west by lands unknown, containing 320 acres.

J. K. Skirvin Claim.   *March 5, 1855.*
Commencing at a tree on the River Platte, running north one mile and from thence half a mile east to a stake marked and from thence one mile south to a tree marked on the bank of the River Platte. It is bounded on the west by G. G. Turner, on north by M. W. Izard, on the east by Francis M. Privit, and on the south by the River Platte. Containing 320 acres.

The territorial legislature was created in haste and aplomb. Nearly all the members of Nebraska's first territorial assembly, apparently, came over from Iowa for the express purpose of being elected. The appointed governor had marked out certain preliminary counties, neatly and arbitrarily; if Burt County, for instance, entitled to two representatives and a councilman, did not contain a single inhabitant, it was simply an act of neighborly kindliness

[476]

that two wagonloads of citizenry from Council Bluffs should make an excursion into Burt County, hold a picnic, and set up the ballot boxes. "Jones County" was one of these preliminary units, its boundaries extending from "a point sixty miles west of the Missouri river, at the northwest corner of Richardson County," thence west along the Platte to the Rocky Mountains, and south to the Kansas line. An agent was sent to determine the number of inhabitants in that vast district, and to arrange for the election of a corresponding number of assemblymen. His report was rather pathetic: "Said county contains no inhabitants at all, save a few in one corner that properly belong in Richardson, and ought to vote there." That description was not quite accurate; but certainly the dwellers in the scattered "ranches" along the Overland Trail, and the few hunters in the more remote west, did not give a whoop for the privilege of voting in Nebraska territorial elections.

The value of Nebraska farm lands was not yet proven; the selling of corner lots, the booming of speculative enterprises, characterized the first few years of the Territory. By 1860 the area of regularly cultivated land did not exceed a half-million acres, although the census of that year revealed a population of 28,841 in Nebraska. The work of the earliest legislatures reflected the speculative zeal: any number of special acts of incorporation were passed, for insurance companies, universities, railroad companies, "cities" where no inhabitants resided, and banks. No less than three universities were incorporated in 1855, and others were chartered soon after.

This multiplicity of colleges, characteristic of western states, was no doubt intended to hasten the day when the West should contain population and wealth, "with their natural accompaniments of literature and science," superior to any society past or present; it was also an inducement for respectable emigrants, and a site marked "university"

[477]

in the town plat was worth four or five churches to a municipal-bond agent. Charles Lindsey, a shrewd fellow who toured the West in 1859, discovered another aspect of the western idea in higher education: "It appears that in all these Western States there are numbers of petty denominational colleges, with university powers. . . . A diploma conferring the degree of D.D. was forwarded to a preacher, accompanied with the hope that he would appreciate the honor, and hinting that in such cases, the recipient generally enclosed a $10 bill. . . . Each institution considers it its chief mission to send forth as many graduates as possible. . . . One does it—lets the students through easily—and another has to do the same, or its chances of competition would be lost."

But territorial legislatures were always prompt to establish a common school system; and frontier communities often anticipated this official beginning, hiring a teacher whose small salary was met by a general collection.

Each western state, apparently, had to take a financial spree; the experiences of other states in their frontier years left no moral for later frontier legislatures. The first charter of incorporation enacted by Nebraska created the "Western Fire and Marine Insurance and Exchange Company," with powers to deal in all sorts of exchange; and thereby a wild-cat bank almost immediately came into existence. On one day (January 18, 1856), no less than five banks were chartered. The stock of each company was fifty or a hundred thousand dollars, to be increased at will to a half million; when twenty-five thousand dollars of the stock had been subscribed—it was not even required that the subscriptions be paid in—the bank could organize and operate! None of the banking bills demanded the maintenance of a fixed specie reserve, nor erected any other guard against incompetence or rascality. Each Nebraska bank was to make an annual report under oath to the territorial auditor, to be published in three newspapers in the territory; but no such reports ever were made.

In September, 1857, a large banking and insurance company in Cincinnati failed, a famous broker in New York collapsed. These storm signals presaged nothing to western optimists. The *Chicago Times* applied the West's conviction of its superiority over the East to the financial situation: "Even should there be a much greater tumbling among these institutions than we now have any reason to expect, our western banks will' scarcely feel the shock. Wall Street may be the money center, the great stock and currency regulator, but the money strength of the country is in the West."

Alexander Hallam, cashier of the Nemaha Valley Bank at Brownsville, Nebraska, walked into the office of a friend; he was morose and preoccupied. "What's the matter, Hallam, bank closed?" "Well, not closed exactly. No use of closing, nothing to close up on." That simple state of affairs was far from unique. The only record of the assets of the Bank of Nebraska, for instance, is in the return of a writ of execution by the sheriff of the county, reporting his having levied upon and sold the following items: "Thirteen sacks of flour, one large iron safe, one counter, one desk, one stove drum and pipe, three arm chairs, and one map of Douglas County." The notes of only one Nebraska bank of issue were redeemed at par, in the headache-months after September. In the Mississippi Valley states the story was almost as tragic.

Late in the winter of 1857-1858 business in the manufacturing districts of the United States began a cautious revival, as capital became available at low rates but at short terms. Recovery was rapid in the South, thanks to the abundant cotton crop of 1857. In the West, where state control of banks had been most careless, and the mediocre crops of 1857 and 1858 were of little aid in lifting mortgages, recovery was slower. But three years had not passed since the crisis year when the pursuit of wealth was as eager and confident as ever; and the United States, east and west, was well advanced in the inevitable cycle, "Quiescence,—next, improvement,—growing confidence,—prosperity,—excitement,—overtrading,—convulsion,—pressure,—stagnation,—distress,—ending again in quiescence."

During President Buchanan's administration railroads received no grants of public land; and attempts to take the revenue idea out of the national land policy were frustrated by sectional opposition. A free-homestead law was urged by the Free Soil Party, and was therefore tainted; it would sacrifice American lands to a rush of European immigrants; it would draw especially the white laborers from the Old South to the free territories; it was unfair to the railroads which had received land grants; it would make people thriftless: *ad infinitum.* To one cavil, that such a policy was contrary to the military bounty system, whereby gifts of lands were reward for service, Galusha A. Grow, addressing the House on February 21, 1862, made reply in the finest traditions of the forum: "But there are soldiers of peace—that grand army of the sons of toil, whose lives, from the cradle to the grave, are a constant warfare with the elements, with the unrelenting obstacles of nature and the merciless barbarities of savage life. Their battle-fields are on the prairies and the wilderness of your frontiers; their achievements, felling the forests, leveling the mountains, filling the valleys, and smoothing the pathway of science and civilization in their march over the continent. While we provide with open hand for the soldier on the tented field, let us not heap unnecessary burdens upon these heroes of the garret, the workshop, and the wilderness home. They have borne your eagles in triumph from ocean to ocean, and spanned the continent with great empires of free states, built on the ruins of savage life. Such are the men whom the homestead policy would save from the grasp of speculation."

Since 1846 the subject of free-homestead legislation had been before Congress, a period strewn with rejected bills. By 1860 the pressure upon western congressmen was unrelenting; and they in turn, with the support of practically every Republican in either House, were determined to end the long battle with an immediate victory. On March 6, 1860, the House Committee on Public Lands reported a homestead law drafted by Mr. Grow; after six days' sparring the measure passed by a comfortable majority. The Senate gave the bill precedence over one of its own that Andrew Johnson, a veteran worker for a more generous land policy, had introduced. Protracted, vituperative debate, rehashing the ever present background of the slavery controversy, ran its course for several weeks; the outcome was a compromise measure on which both Houses agreed, providing that homesteads should be sold only to heads of families, at the rate of twenty-five cents an acre.

Rumor spread that President Buchanan would be required by his political friends to veto the bill; and veto the bill he did. The gist of his explanation was that the measure put the ax to the root of the existing admirable land system, and would most likely introduce dangerous doctrines of agrarianism and pernicious social theories. The unscarred insurgent who was editor of the New York *Tribune* made a wry face—"Mr. Buchanan must be a near relative of him whom the Yankee characterized as having 'remarkably winning ways to make people hate him' "; and Greeley, with other Republican leaders, set about making the public land policy a party issue in the presidential campaign of 1860.

With the Republican Party in power, the homestead measure was in the hands of its friends. But western congressmen had to meet protests that a revision of the public

[481]

land policy, however desirable, was unwise at that precarious time. The Senate on May 6, 1862, approved a homestead bill by a vote of thirty-three to seven. These seven votes, with the exception of one from Oregon, were cast by senators from slavery states—the last protest of the prewar South against the plan of turning over the public domain to the common man. On the twentieth of May, President Lincoln signed the act donating a quarter section of the public lands to the settler who entrenched his right by five years' residence upon his homestead.

Thirty-one thousand miles of railway had been built in the United States by 1861—built by private initiative, directed by commercial opportunity. All but nine thousand miles lay above the Maryland boundary and the Ohio River; and only one railroad—the Louisville & Nashville—linked the northern system with the southern. The twenty-two thousand miles of railway in the north constituted one vast interweaving of eastern interests with western interests. In 1850 one railroad connected the Ohio River with the Great Lakes; a decade later there were ten. Eight railways linked the Mississippi with Lake Michigan or Lake Erie in 1860; ten years before not even a local railroad touched the Mississippi above Memphis. Four trunk lines crossed the Appalachians; on them depended the greater part of the commercial exchange between East and West, and with that commercial exchange the intangible, sentimental alliances that are rooted partly in commerce. They were adequate.

The optimism of the early fifties had overbuilt the northern railway system; future settlement and future traffic were capitalized, financing construction that maintained its growth and enthusiasm to the moment of deflation—the panic of 1857. The four years after the panic were years of reorganization, consolidation, and improvement. When the Civil War began, the railroads for the first time were asked to carry increased responsibilities, to carry increased business. Carl Russell Fish expressed the gain to the nation: "The railroads were ready, were panting, for an increase of business. The war saved them. In return they saved the country. At least, civil war in 1850 would have meant that the valleys of the Mississippi and Ohio would have been bottled up; the railroads could not have carried their products to the East or to the Lakes, nor could the canals. The harvests which in 1861 saved our foreign credit could not have been sold. . . . It is not so important that there were thirty thousand miles of railroad in the United States in 1861, as that twenty thousand of them had been built in the last ten years. In those ten years greater progress had been made in transportation than in any other twenty of our existence to the present time."

The development of the Ohio Valley and the Mississippi Valley had by 1860 increased the American production of wheat 73 per cent in ten years—from 100,000,000 bushels in 1849 to 173,000,000 bushels a decade later. The southern states annually purchased some ten million bushels from the North, the excess of their needs over local production. The Civil War cut off the southern market, leaving the North with a rapidly increasing surplus, available for shipment to England. The effective blockade of the southern ports by the Union navy stopped the spindles of the British mills, after their large surplus of Southern cotton was exhausted; but at the time when the cotton famine in England was at its height, a more elementary and more pressing famine stared at the British people—a shortage of wheat. In 1860 crops in Great Britain were much below normal. In 1861 the wheat harvest revealed one of the worst crop failures in the history of the country, and the harvest of 1862 was little better.

While in the industrial distress a formidable party de-

[483]

manded recognition of the seceded American states and the use of the British navy to end the blockade of the ports wherein southern cotton had accumulated, wiser men were nodding amen to John Bright's "I maintain, that with a supply of cotton derived mainly from the Southern States, and mainly raised by slave labor, two things are indisputable: First, the supply must always be insufficient; and Second, that it must always be insecure." And British merchants were buying Northern wheat.

In the western states, accordingly, agriculture expanded and prospered. The loyal states and territories increased the total production of wheat from 142,000,000 bushels in 1859 to 191,000,000 bushels in 1863. In 1859 the United States furnished only 11.2 per cent of Great Britain's wheat imports; in the three years of 1861-1863 the North supplied nearly 41 per cent of the imports of wheat and flour into the island kingdom. The produce of the West was the winning counter in the international game.

CHAPTER XXVII

CONCORD COACHES ON WESTERN TRAILS

SAN FRANCISCO in the summer of 1849 was a city
of tents and wooden shanties, with a straggling medley of adobe houses, dingy relics of colonial California. Within the next six months, at least a thousand
frame houses and sheds were built. Any one who could
handle a hammer and saw could get twelve dollars a day for
his labor. The drift sand was leveled, hills tumbled into
the bay; as the slopes of the city were tamed into home
sites, the rapidly advancing piling in Yerba Buena Cove
was filled in, and hundreds of ships sailed from San Francisco Bay laden with California dirt—for ballast on the
return voyage.

The next six years of San Francisco's history are a
unique record of achievement and failure, amazing ambitions realized in defiance of time, and an amazing record of
lawlessness everywhere and peculation in high places: a
history melodramatized by a series of devastating fires, by
duels and murders involving its prominent citizens, by an
organization of thugs and an organization of embattled
citizens. The San Francisco that emerged in 1857 was
vaster and more substantial. Hills were robbed of their
heights, or were half cut away; grades varied from reason-

able inclines to playful imitations of the perpendicular. Brick and granite had become the most-used building materials; in the business center of the town had developed a fortresslike architecture of thick walls, recessed windows, and iron shutters to defy the flames. The business district had followed close upon the piling, advancing six city blocks into the bay within six years. Blotches of ugly hill-cuts and bleak vacant slopes were characteristic of the struggling residence district; rough cabins and boxlike lodging houses were varied with comfortable villas on the preferred slopes, and imposing oddities clapped upon the hilltops. Brick, within the latter half of the decade, went quite out of fashion; a few earthquakes encouraged the residents to take their chances with the increased fire hazard of frame dwellings. Colonies of foreign races, and the slum district with its too-large Australian contingent, were nearer the bay; when the breeze was westerly they could best testify that the city's system of drainage and garbage disposal was very faulty.

Under the increasing gold yield and general development of California, the metropolitan city reached a high mark of prosperity in 1853. By the close of the year its population was about fifty thousand—fully a seventh of the total in the state. But suddenly commerce fell away as home production supplanted the need for importation of foodstuffs; and the golden days of placer mining in the Sierras came suddenly to an end, to be succeeded by the quartz mining era. The crisis passed, business assumed a surer course, regaining strength by the development of manufactures in the Bay area. Within San Francisco's transitional era, the state itself had developed apace.

As the excitement of the gold rush subsided, many Italians and several New Englanders abandoned the pick and pan for the hoe. Salt pork and dried beans, as a steady diet, satisfied neither taste nor health; and the patches of green vegetables that sprang up on the outskirts of the mining towns were amazingly lucrative. A tomato crop raised on an acre and a half near Sacramento in 1850 was valued at eighteen thousand dollars. As if to be worthy of the prices, vegetables grew to enormous size: accounts of potatoes weighing from three to seven pounds, three-pound onions, fifty-pound cabbages, and three-hundred-pound squashes abound in the newspapers of the period, to the despair of the sober historian. Certainly crops were lush, and prices were high—so high that vegetables were imported into the Sierra towns from Oregon to meet the local competition.

The beginnings of American agriculture in California compose one of the rosiest episodes of the farmers' frontier. The importation of grain fell from 740,000 bags in 1853 to nothing in 1855. In 1856 about seventy thousand sacks and barrels of flour were shipped from California to Peru. Almost every crop—vegetable, cereal, tobacco, sugar and tea—was attempted, the zeal of farmers in many cases sustained by prizes offered by the state. Even sericulture had its fling, beginning with successful experiments with mulberry tree and silkworm at San Jose in 1853, and culminating in 1866, when the state offered heavy premiums for California-produced silk. A host of speculators entered the field, hectic and ignorant in their methods; immature trees and diseased cocoons multiplied into the millions, with a prospect that bounties upon miserable silk would swamp the state treasury. The alarmed legislature hastened to revise its bounty offer, and California silk production ended for the time in fiasco.

Stock raising, the chief occupation of colonial Californians, was revived. The cattlemen's frontier of the Far West enjoyed its boom period in the fifties. The demands of the mining towns encouraged special importations, and the deteriorated Spanish breed was built up into a fatter, sturdier animal. In 1850 there were somewhat more than a quarter of a million cattle in California; in 1860 the number had passed the two-million mark. Then, in 1862-1864, came years of disastrous drouth; hundreds of thousands of the cattle were destroyed by starvation or by forced slaughter, and the open range of California never recovered. Thereafter sheep herding was of greater prominence.

As California and San Francisco acquired stability, the history of the state in its placer boom days was being repeated in two districts of the Rocky Mountain country. The beginnings of Colorado and Nevada were enacted with that rapidity characteristic of the miners' frontier—so rapid that before the Civil War began both districts were in the territorial stage.

In the summer of 1858 two or three hundred prospectors were searching with pick and pan in the Colorado Rockies. Some of them were old-timers, men who had caught the fever in California, inveterate rovers who, if they found gold in the mountains, kept mum. Others were companies from the States, whose purses had been flattened by the "hard times." One group was from Lawrence, Kansas Territory. A company of Georgians found gold in paying quantities in the headwaters of the South Platte. Rumors of the find brought the prospectors from Lawrence to the new diggings: "There we found five or six men engaged in mining, and although they had very inferior tools, they were making respectable wages. We immediacely went to work, and found that although things had been considerably exaggerated, we could do well, and had a good prospect for the future."

By July gold had been found in the streams near the present site of Denver. As new rumors and reports sifted across the Missouri, when John Cantrell made a dramatic reappearance in Lawrence with three ounces of gold "dug with a hatchet in Cherry Creek and washed with a frying pan," hundreds of westerners took up the call. Before winter set in, Denver City was in existence. The newspapers were printing itineraries of the course to Denver, and volunteer correspondents in the mines were sending the home papers good copy. Merchants in the border towns bought heavy stocks in anticipation, wheelwrights built prairie schooners; in the gold region speculators laid out strategic townsites, and hundreds of log cabins were built, ready to be rented or sold when the spring rush of emigrants should arrive. And the rush came—an overwhelming horde, disorganized and hectic, in light wagons and heavy prairie schooners, on horseback leading pack mules; men afoot and unencumbered, pulling handcarts and pushing wheelbarrows. "Those who observed the character of the emigration this spring," wrote an onlooker, "must have noticed the vast number who were totally unprepared for an expedition of this kind. A black carpetbag, an extra pair of boots, and a substantial suit of clothes, with, in every case almost, a rifle and gun, and perhaps six-shooter, generally constituted their outfit for a trip of one thousand miles. Of mining implements, or anything to aid in separating the particles of gold from the earth, the exhibition was a scanty one." The answer: discouraged men from the older frontiers, who could farm forty acres but hadn't the adaptability to make a successful invasion of the mines.

The gold in the new diggings was placer gold, scaly and tiny. To these men working independently, most of them without equipment for any mining work but panning, it didn't pay. Libeus Barney, with the saving gift of a sense of the absurd, chronicled the results of his first three days' work: "The first didn't reach the auriferous color, though I washed out about a thousand panfuls. The second day about the same number with a shade of yellow dirt, which inspired courage. Third day, near as I can judge, having no means of measuring or weighing, I secured about the sixteenth part of a new cent's worth of the genuine article."

By May the tattered invasion—William Tecumseh Sherman, at Fort Leavenworth in April, estimated that twenty-five thousand people had gone to the Colorado diggings—was in stampeded retreat into the Missouri Valley.

And then pay dirt was discovered in Colorado. "Immense gold discoveries! Pike's Peak a Glorious Reality!" was the streamer line on the *Leavenworth Times* extra edition, June 10, 1859. Two prospectors, separately working into the mountains away from the foothills, discovered lodes of disintegrated quartz, rich with gold. Below the loose ore was the hard rock, refractory, not to be mined or smelted without great outlay of labor and capital. But until the loose quartz was exhausted, the mountain region was fair ground for any miner who knew how to run a sluice and use quicksilver. In July some twelve or fifteen thousand gold seekers had come into the mountains. Tents gave way to cabins; in favored spots the pine trees were leveled, streets were opened, substantial little towns were built. Optimists without assets of talent or tools drifted into the mining region, worked hard for little gold, half starved, and drifted out again; but the foundations of Colorado had been established.

Ten inches of snow fell on October 31, 1858; and the miners, in enforced idleness, gravitated to talk of politics. A week later a convention determined to demand a government for the Pike's Peak country. "Just to think that within two weeks of the arrival of a few dozen Americans in the wilderness," wrote one of these pioneers, "they set to work to elect a Delegate to the United States Congress, and ask to be set apart as a new Territory! But we are of a fast race and of a fast age and must prod along." They prodded along; and when on March 28, 1859, Denver camp elected its local officers, eight hundred men voted.

And in April the deliberations of delegates from six mining towns brought forth a call for a constitutional convention, to erect a legal framework for a new state—Jefferson. "Shall it be the government of the knife and the revolver," the delegates inquired of the goddess Echo, "or shall we unite in forming here in our golden country, among the ravines and gulches of the Rocky Mountains, and the fertile valleys of the Arkansas and the Platte, a new and independent State?"

By August Colorado had survived the optimistic flow and the discouraged ebb of novice prospectors, and there was no longer doubt of the permanence of settlement in the region. The constitutional convention split sharply into irreconcilable divisions: should the demand for immediate statehood be carried forward, or should the settlers unite instead on a petition to Congress for territorial organization? Two documents were drafted, a state constitution and a memorial to Congress; on September 5, 1859, the sovereign will made its choice. The prospect of the heavy taxation incident to the establishing of a state government was unlikable; on the other hand, pioneers preferred to have their democracy in full measure. Pocketbook prudence won out in the balloting, and in October Beverly D. Williams, local agent of a stage company, was despatched to Washington as territorial delegate—to represent the people of the future state of Jefferson, and to keep an eye on government mail contracts in the interest of the Leavenworth and Pike's Peak Express Company.

On November 7, 1859, the territory of Jefferson, "a provisional government of Rocky Mountain growth and manufacture," came into existence. It was a government similar to the highest type of official territorial structure, with a full-blown constitution drawn up by the people's delegates and ratified by the people themselves, with an elected legislature and executive staff. Of all governments created by pioneers on their own authority and initiative, none had been organized with more deliberateness and care than Jefferson. After having taken a leading part in the building of that government, William N. Byers, editor of the *Rocky Mountain News,* formulated the frontier's theory of first action in politics: "We claim that any body, or community of American citizens, which from any cause or under any circumstance, is cut off from, or from isolation is so situated, as not to be under any active and protecting branch of the central government, have a right, if on American soil, to frame a government, and enact such laws and regulations as may be necessary for their own safety, protection, and happiness, always with the condition precedent, that they shall, at the earliest moment when the central government shall extend an *effective* organization, and laws over them, give it their unqualified support and obedience."

The sectional warfare in Congress blocked all measures to erect a territorial government in the Rocky Mountain region. Meanwhile, in 1859-1860, the legislature of Jefferson passed comprehensive laws for the regulating of land titles, water rights, and mining rights, and promulgated civil and criminal codes of law. But the government was moneyless, without ability to collect taxes; and outside Denver, as the mining camps attended to their own affairs in their own way, loyalty to the government of Jefferson was on the wane. On December 7, 1860, the legislature adjourned, not to meet again. Within the next two months the southern members of the national Congress had struck their last hand-on-desk, chin-tilted-upward attitudes, removed their togas and shaken off the dust of Washington. Immediately, on January 30, 1861, the Senate began consideration of a territorial government for the Pike's Peak country. Neither the name of Jefferson nor the very generous boundaries which the unauthorized government had described were recognized. There was no serious debate; and on the twenty-eighth of February, when President Buchanan signed the measure, the Territory of Colorado became a legal fact.

The Territory of Utah, as organized by Congress on September 9, 1850, extended from the Rockies to the California line. In that summer two members of a Mormon emigrant train passing through the western part of the territory discovered gold in a canyon of the Carson Valley. Placer miners drifted into western Utah, acknowledging no Mormon officers and organizing their scattered camps in the independent custom of the Sierras. From 1850 to 1857 the number of miners in Gold Cañon, the most prosperous of the camps, varied from twenty to two hundred; the yield of the drift rock washed through their rockers and long toms diminished to about two dollars a day. The pioneers were losing hope; Nevada seemed to be a "played-out country." Two brothers in this district, the Lake Washoe diggings, had found evidence to the contrary; but they kept their own counsel. Writing to their father from California in 1856, the Grosh brothers give the first hint of Nevada silver: "Ever since our return from Utah we have been trying to get a couple of hundred dollars together for the purpose of making a careful examination of a silver lead in Gold Cañon. . . . Native silver is found in Gold Cañon; it resembles thin sheet-lead broken very fine, and lead the miners suppose it to be." They had struck the great lode, or properly series of lodes, that came to be known as the Comstock.

One of the brothers, his resistance sapped by poor food and overwork, contracted a mortal blood poisoning from the crushing fall of a heavy pick upon his foot; the surviving one died in that same year, 1857, from exposure to a blizzard in the Sierras. Other miners worked the lode, taking out the placer gold in incredible quantities,

[493]

throwing out the chloride ore that contained the silver. Settlers along the eastern slope of the mountains poured into the new gold region. On the street of the most important camp in the Mount Davidson district, a bibulous, hilarious old ex-teamster, whose name, James Fennimore, had been discarded for the tag of "Old Virginia," fell down, broke his bottle, and rose waving the bottle neck: "I baptize this ground Virginia Town." And Virginia City became the metropolis of the Nevada mining country.

Late in the season of 1859 a lump of the discarded "blue stuff" was submitted to expert assay: a ton of it, was the verdict, would yield $1,595 in gold and $4,791 in silver. Long before the Sierra snows were melted in the spring the rush to Washoe was under way, the miners from Placerville in the lead, through snow and slush, across deep drifts alternating with stretches of wind-swept rock, prospectors and speculators venturing the ascent in saddle caravans before stages could pull through. At Placerville hundreds of tons of Washoe freight were stacked on the hillside, waiting until the blockade of snow should relent. Within a few months twenty thousand people came into Washoe, and half that number stayed. Other thousands scattered into new districts. The "wondrous city of Virginia" in the spring of 1860 was a hectic mess, described by one of the mob: "Frame shanties pitched together as if by accident; tents of canvas, of blankets, of brush, of potato sacks, and old shirts, with empty whisky barrels for chimneys; smoking hovels of mud and stone; coyote holes in the hillsides forcibly seized by men; pits and shanties with smoke issuing from every crevice; piles of goods and rubbish on craggy points, in the hollows, on the rocks, in the mud, on the snow—everywhere—scattered broadcast in pell-mell confusion."

Speculation was universal; while unworked claims were still snowbound, owners issued prospectuses, quoting the handsome results of mythical assays, unloaded the stocks, and printed another batch. In 1859-1860 thirty-seven companies were incorporated with a capital stock totaling $30,040,000; in 1861 forty-nine additional Washoe companies were incorporated. The recorder of claims elected by the miners was an illiterate blacksmith; the official records were kept behind the bar of a saloon adjacent to the smithy; leaves were torn out, dates altered, and claim boundaries revised.

As the year of the Civil War began, the huts and makeshift shanties of Virginia City were nearly all replaced by board cabins; over a hundred buildings were being constructed, besides an uncounted number of lesser shanties. Thirty-eight stores, twenty-five saloons, ten livery stables, two quartz mills, and five lumber yards, gave bustle, smoke, and aroma to the city. There were six fair-sized towns in western Utah, three in Washoe and three in the Carson Valley; small camps were scattered through the Washoe Valley and the Truckee Basin.

Beginning in 1859 new trails were being hewn through the Sierras, and the old ones broadened to admit the Washoe wagons—sturdy, effective, with brake blocks a yard long in the arc, products of the utmost skill of the California workers in wood and iron. Mules were the draught animals, bred in Oregon and California stock farms; they pulled in teams of four or multiples of four. Roads were rapidly built into the mining districts, toll roads built by private enterprise and as profitable as a good mining claim. Four hundred mule teams were pulling Washoe wagons across the Sierras in 1860, and six hundred in 1861. As the Comstock Lode demonstrated its amazing richness and the boom frontier maintained the promise of its beginning, the increase of freight offers an index: in 1862 there were nine hundred fifty teams in the business; in 1863 the *Sacramento Union* reported 2,772 teams, consisting of 14,652 animals, crossing into Nevada with nearly twenty million pounds of freight in eight weeks, a third of the season's work.

Nevada Territory was lopped from Utah on March 2, 1861, on the same day in which the Territory of Dakota was created to give reasonable limits to Nebraska. In politics, as in business, Californians were dominant. In the constitutional convention of 1863 all but four of the forty-three delegates had come to Nevada from California. Purposely overlooking the scanty population in its need for votes in the critical election of 1864, the national administration hastened to make Nevada a state; a convention retouched the constitution of 1863, and by executive proclamation Nevada was ushered into the Union on the thirty-first of October, narrowly in time to elect congressmen and presidential electors. Of course the successful candidates were loyal.

For ten years beginning in 1849, the boats of the Pacific Mail Steamship Company carried the United States mails between the Pacific West and the Atlantic seaboard; the ocean way was the standard route of communication. Every fifteen days, by the schedule, a mail steamship came into San Francisco Bay. A flag hoisted on Telegraph Hill, a large black ball of good tidings, announced the vessel's approach. Reporters hurried to the wharf, and hurried back with their budgets of news to start "extras" rolling from the presses; and citizens formed long lines, like World Series bleacherites, before the delivery windows of the post office. When the steamship left, home-going miners leaned against the rail, watching California, the great lottery, recede. In the ship's hold were the mails for the East.

This fortnightly, circuitous channel of communication was too infrequent and laggardly to satisfy Californians, or Missourians, who were almost equally interested in overland communication. Following the lead of the *Sacramento*

Union, the press of California and the governor and legislature pushed the demand. The Post Appropriation Act of 1857 carried authorization for an overland mail to California. Already stagecoach lines were carrying United States mails between Independence and Salt Lake City, Sacramento or San Diego and Salt Lake, from Independence to Santa Fe, and from Santa Fe to San Antonio. An exchange of mails at Salt Lake City might have established a through overland mail between California and Missouri, but that was not the government's policy; and the mail coaches from Salt Lake to Independence, handicapped by an inadequate appropriation, offered poor and unreliable service at all times and practically none in winter. When Hiram Kimball won the mail contract between Salt Lake and Missouri in 1856, the enterprise brightened, Mormons planned to make settlements at intervals along the route— hostility between government officials and Mormon leaders flared into war, an army was sent into Utah, and the mail contract was summarily canceled. In 1857 and 1858 mail stages were running semimonthly from San Antonio to San Diego.

In July, 1857, bids were opened "for the conveyance of the entire letter mail" to California. The postmaster-general was a Southerner; but abetting any local prejudices that may have influenced him was the record of slow, undependable communication over the central route to California. John Butterfield and his associates were awarded the contract to provide semiweekly communication for six years, on the route Butterfield proffered: "From St. Louis, Mo., and from Memphis, Tenn., converging at Little Rock, Ark.; thence *via* Preston, Tex., or as nearly as may be found advisable, to the best point of crossing the Rio Grande above El Paso, and not far from Fort Fillmore; thence, along the new road being opened and constructed under the direction of the Secretary of the Interior, to Fort

[497]

Yuma, Cal.; thence, through the best passes and along the best valleys for staging, to San Francisco."

On September 15, 1858, exactly a year after the contract was signed, one of Butterfield's coaches left St. Louis as another started from San Francisco. These stages were made by the Abbot-Downing Company of Concord, New Hampshire, as were all of the overland mail coaches that followed them. Postage on a letter, ten cents for each half ounce; fare for a passenger, one hundred dollars in gold; distance of the journey, above twenty-eight hundred miles; schedule time, twenty-five days. Both coaches anticipated the scheduled arrival by a day. As news of the arrival at St. Louis was telegraphed east, President Buchanan responded: "It is a glorious triumph for civilization and the Union. Settlements will soon follow the course of the road, and the East and West will be bound together by a chain of living Americans which can never be broken." San Franciscans burned gunpowder, decked the city with bunting, whooped with their brass bands, and inevitably held a public meeting and passed resolutions. Until the outbreak of the Civil War, Butterfield's mail coaches provided dependable service over the swooping curve of the southern route to California.

The first of the Concord stages were capable of carrying four passengers and their baggage, besides five or six hundred pounds of mail; later coaches held six to nine passengers, and could take on a few more if they did not object to seats on the roof. Passengers who traveled in parties, and carried as part of their baggage several cases of better whisky than could be obtained along the route (frontier whisky was maliciously reputed to freeze overnight in winter), survived the monotonous, jolting trip with more success than lone travelers. Passengers alone with their own thoughts were wont to observe the rugged mountain road, the thundering pace of the coach, and to remain for days in anguish punctuated only by the stops at the way stations. Travelers were usually provided with rubber pillows that, inflated, absorbed enough jostles to permit a tired passenger a little sleep.

Frank Root, an express messenger on the stage line from the Missouri border to Denver, has described the cuisine on that line: "There were about twenty-five regular eating stations on the line between Atchison and Denver. The station keepers went more on furnishing passengers the substantials than they did the light, dainty delicacies. . . . Fried bacon and ham were a regular standby at most of the stations on the upper Little Blue and Platte; still there were furnished an ample supply of buffalo, elk, and antelope steaks in their season, for a distance of at least three hundred miles. Along the lower Little Blue, down through southern Nebraska and northern Kansas—the finest agricultural section on the entire line—eggs and chickens, nice cream for the coffee, with fresh butter and plenty of vegetables, were a prominent feature of the every-day diet. . . . Occasionally there would be a passenger who, before starting out from Atchison west, would fill his pockets and grip with crackers and cheese, dried beef, herring, or 'Bologna,' and make the long trip of six days and nights to Denver without eating a meal at a station." Similar stations along the stage lines between Missouri and California differed only in that, as the road led westward, the food was less inviting and the cooks less skilled.

In 1858 mail stages were running again between Salt Lake and Independence; and the postmaster-general agreed to the establishing of through communication to California, with a transfer of the mail bags at Salt Lake City. By July a semimonthly overland mail was in operation between Independence and Placerville, on a thirty-eight day schedule. "Snow-shoe" Thompson's road between Placerville and Carson City was open most of that winter; severe storms in the Sierra Nevada delayed the coaches in only two or three instances, and then, on pack ponies or carried by men wearing snowshoes, the mails came through.

Carrying little mail, and apparently established as a harbinger of progress, a mail route from Kansas City by way of Santa Fe to Stockton, California, was begun in 1858. Six-mule wagons made the trip in a scheduled time of sixty days. In that same year the far-seeing imperialist in the postmaster-general's office established a mail route across the isthmus of Tehuantepec. But Californians were most interested in the central route, handicapped by a thirty-eight day schedule as against Butterfield's twenty-five, with the contractors given so little compensation that they could not afford to compete in time with the southern route. A joint resolution passed Congress to provide additional compensation to the contractors of the central route, but President Buchanan vetoed it. The *San Francisco Bulletin* called the turn: "It is said that the President refused to sign the bill because the projected route was likely to demonstrate the feasibility of a Central Railroad to the Pacific."

In 1860 and 1861 occurred the romantic interlude of the Pony Express. William H. Russell, of the great overland freighting firm of Russell, Majors, and Waddell, was persuaded by Senator Gwin of California that it was necessary to demonstrate the practicability of the central route for year-round travel before the Administration would forego its preference for the southern route. Russell, Majors and Waddell were then operating the semimonthly line from the Missouri River by way of Salt Lake to Placerville. Russell pledged his firm to the establishing of a Pony Express, and drew his partners into that ruinous gesture.

On February 29, 1860, San Franciscans learned from the *Bulletin* that "horses and riders are now being placed on the line for this new enterprise in this fast age." On the third of April a Pony Express messenger left San Francisco, and another galloped away from St. Joseph. California and the Missouri border were alike elated. The *Bulletin* of the sixteenth of April saluted the last pony of the relay from the East: "It took seventy-five ponies to make the trip from Missouri to California in 10½ days, but the last one—the little fellow who came down in the Sacramento boat this morning had the vicarious glory of them all. Upon him an enthusiastic crowd were disposed to shower all their compliments. He was the veritable Hippogriff who shoved a continent behind his hoofs so easily; who snuffed up sandy plains, sent lakes and mountains, prairies and forests, whizzing behind him, like one great river rushing eastward."

Letters between San Francisco and Salt Lake sent by Pony Express cost three dollars a half ounce, and five dollars from San Francisco to points beyond the Mormon capital. This rate limited the mail pouches to letters requiring the utmost urgency; but no rate, that charged nor any other, could have sustained the Pony Express. Station-houses—some of them, in regions where Indians were hostile, practically fortresses—had been built at an average of fifteen miles apart along the trail. Two men were maintained at each station to care for the stock—horses selected for their splendid mettle, California mustangs preferred. The riders were the pick of the frontier. They were all young men, selected for nerve, jockey-weight, and general aptitude for their dangerous business. Emigrants found safety in numbers; the Pony Express rider rode alone.

That very busy Congress of 1860-1861 authorized, on March 2, 1861, the long-demanded daily mail to California over the central route. Already reports had come to Congress of Confederate depredations upon the Butterfield stage route through Texas; and it was enacted that "the contractors on said route shall be required to transport the entire letter mail six times a week on the Central route, said letter mail to be carried through in twenty days time, eight months in the year, and in twenty-three days the remaining four months of the year." For this service, and for the maintenance of a semiweekly pony express, at a scheduled time of twelve days in winter and ten during the rest of the year, John Butterfield and his associates were granted an annual fee of one million dollars.

About three months were needed for moving the stock and equipment, to build new way stations, and get everything in readiness for the opening of the "Central Overland California Route" along the well-worn trail up the Platte Valley and through the South Pass. On the first of July the first through stages left St. Joseph and Placerville. In the same summer the establishing of a daily mail-coach schedule to Central City, Colorado, did similar work in tightening the bonds between the national government and the far frontier.

CHAPTER XXVIII

THE MINERS' FRONTIER OF THE NORTHWEST

CALIFORNIA was the breeding ground of prospectors, wandering with their blankets and burros, their grubstakes and assaying stuffs, over the trailless West; their seasoned eyes examined every odd bowlder, and tried to trace every fragment of "float rock" back to the mother ledge. Across the Sierras into western Utah, across the Cascades into the inland country of the Far Northwest, north into British Columbia, they were the vanguard of an eastward-moving frontier. H. N. Maguire, courageous enough to write poetry in Montana in 1866, signalized the recoil of the new frontier upon the older frontier advancing from the Missouri:

> From Eastern hives is filled Pacific's shore—
> No more inviting sun-set lands are near;
> The restless throng now backward pour—
> From East to West they meet, and stop right here.

Above the great bend of the Columbia, not far below the international boundary, was Fort Colville, for thirty years the chief inland post of the Hudson's Bay Company. Roamers through the wilderness about the post happened on gold in several localities; and in the late summer and fall of 1855, with business stagnant in the Willamette Valley and about Puget Sound, many settlers of Oregon and Washington explored the region, and made encouraging finds. Gold in small superficial deposits, it seemed, could be found almost anywhere in the Colville region—east of the Columbia, between the Spokane and the Pend d'Oreille rivers. Miners with pan and rockers were making three to six dollars a day, and the luckiest were taking out twelve dollars' worth. But there were no suitable roads from Puget Sound to bring supplies to the distant Colville Valley, and the Oregon Steam Navigation Company, with its steamships on the Columbia, was not organized until the sixties. Wheat could be bought from the French settlers in the Colville Valley, and the miners subsisted on flour and coffee.

More baffling an obstacle than the absence of a supply base was the Indian danger. Both frontiers, it was evident, were closing in upon the Indians; Kamiakin, head chief of the Yakimas, was trying as best he could to unite the unorganized tribes against the white advance; and all the tribes of the far Northwest except the Nez Perces were brooding the prospects of an uprising. As the chieftains explained at a council in 1853: "They always liked to have gentlemen, Hudson Bay Company men or officers of the army of engineers pass through their country, to whom they would extend every token of hospitality. They did not object to persons merely hunting, or those wearing swords, but they dreaded the approach of the whites with ploughs, axes, and shovels in their hands." The invasion of the Colville region by miners followed sharply upon a council held by Governor Isaac Stevens at Walla Walla, at which treaties had been engineered placing the tribes upon reservations—treaties that outraged and embittered all Indians except the chiefs that had received presents.

Incessantly during September small bands of Indians attacked lone miners, and hovered about the lines of travel. When an Indian Agent was killed by a Yakima brave, a company of the regular army marched into the Yakima country, and was thoroughly drubbed. Other tribes took the warpath, and the uprising became general. Volunteers in large numbers were raised in Oregon and Washington; until the autumn of 1856 war flared in murderous spurts. General Wool, commander of the Department of the Pacific, had little taste for the war, blaming it upon Stevens' ill-timed treaties, and claiming—with fair truth—that citizen volunteers were eager participants for the pleasure of murdering and plundering the Indians. He issued a military order, significant in its curious exception: "No emigrants or other whites, except the Hudson Bay Company, or persons having ceded rights from the Indians, will be permitted to settle or remain in the Indian country, or on land not ceded by treaty, confirmed by the Senate and approved by the President of the United States. These orders are not, however, to apply to the miners engaged in collecting gold at the Colville mines. The miners will, however, be notified that should they interfere with the Indians, or their squaws, they will be punished or sent out of the country." Custom, apparently, had justified miners' casual trespassing even to a conscientious officer of the army.

Angus MacDonald, the brainy Scotchman who was chief clerk of the Hudson's Bay post at Fort Colville, had advised the miners disappointed with the light "float" gold in that region to prospect further into the north; and after the Indian uprising of 1855-1856 adventurers from Washington and Oregon ranged into the remote, unknown region of the upper Fraser. They found several rich bars; and when the coming of winter forced a retreat to Victoria, the stories of their good luck became the foundations of a gold rush in the following spring. By the end of March mills on the Puget Sound were closed for lack of laborers, vessels were deserted, the floating population of Victoria followed the Hudson's Bay Trail up the Fraser, and ships from California were bringing gold seekers to the northern shore. Some twenty-three thousand California miners came northward by ship in the spring and early summer of 1858; and eight thousand more made the entire journey to the Fraser region overland. Victoria came into flush times; and James Douglas, governor of Vancouver Island, turned resolutely to the difficult task of extending civil and criminal government into the upper country.

In the California mines the condition of the diggings was rapidly changing, and new methods of production were attempting to keep pace. The exportation of gold, which had mounted to fifty-seven million dollars in 1853, had fallen to forty-eight million four years later. Organized capital and corporate methods of production were needed for the sustained prosperity of the Sierra mining region. Since 1850 the "long tom" had come into use in placer mining, a long trough with a capacity fivefold greater than the cradle. Quicksilver machines were adopted for saving the fine flakes that slipped through ordinary rockers. Sluices, some of them several hundred feet long and all of them requiring coöperative enterprise, had gradually been adopted when the placer deposits were being thinned out and miners realized what short tailraces, carelessly watered, had cost them. Quartz lodes were first worked with an "arrastra," a Mexican invention: a circle paved with stones over which a horse dragged a block of granite attached to a sweep. The granite crushed the quartz lumps scattered over the circle into bits fine enough to be panned. This machinery was too primitive for Americans, who attempted, despite enormous obstacles, to construct mills. Within the decade of the sixties quartz mining took rank over the working of placer diggings. From San Francisco and from St. Louis mining machinery was transported to the far frontiers, miners began to work in combination, and the lone prospector took the added burden of enlisting some corporate capital before he could convert his claim into riches.

On November 23, 1857, the miners of the Colville district met in convention, devised a provisional government for themselves, and petitioned that the Department of the Pacific assign a company of soldiers to the Colville Valley. Colonel Steptoe, in command of Fort Walla Walla, influenced by this request and by later news that two miners had been killed by Indians, determined on a reconnaissance; and on May 5, 1858, his expedition, one hundred and seventy-five men, mostly dragoons and mounted artillerymen, set out for Colville. He followed an old Nez Perce trail, to the Snake River crossing just below the site of Lewiston, and turned northward toward the Spokane River—northward into the domain of Indians bitterly hostile because of the miners' invasion and because of rumors that a military road was soon to be constructed through their country. About twenty miles below the present city of Spokane the braves of the Cœur d' Alene tribe blocked his way. The expedition halted and encamped; Colonel Steptoe knew that his troopers were equipped poorly, with old Jaeger rifles or with musketoons, and he now realized that the stock of ammunition was insufficient. In the morning the retreat began; the exultant braves followed to stage a running fight for several miles before the expedition could be rallied to make a stand. By nightfall only two rounds of ammunition were left to each man; the dead were buried, the two howitzers were dismantled, and the expedition rode off under cover of night, reaching Snake River and the friendly Nez Perce Indians the next day.

General Clarke, newly in command of the Department of the Pacific, took up the challenge in earnest. Troops were concentrated from all parts of the Pacific Coast;

Colonel George Wright was put in command. While several companies of Californians bound for the Fraser River country ventured into the hostile territory, and pushed through successfully, Wright was collecting and drilling his forces at Walla Walla. Late in August his company of six hundred, armed with new rifles which had a greater range than the Hudson's Bay carbines of the Indians, took to the field. At Four Lakes, a few miles southwest of the Spokane, braves from many Indian tribes were concentrated for battle: they got it. The long-range fire of the infantrymen held them off; then the dragoons who had been defeated in May dashed out, and the Indians were dispersed pell-mell.

Wright marched on to the Spokane, meeting a skirmishing fight all the way. He captured eight hundred of the enemy's horses, and killed the whole band. By the time the expedition had reached the Cœur d'Alene mission on the Spokane, the Indians were cowed, and came into council. They agreed not to molest the whites, and to give hostages. The vindictive martinet hanged sixteen Indians. His work, with the successful coöperation of an expedition into the Yakima domain, brought peace that was never seriously broken. The way for the frontier advance into the upper interior country had been cleared; Stevens' treaties pushing the tribes into reservations was carried out, and the Walla Walla Valley was officially opened for settlement.

The establishment of new army posts, the necessities of the new reservations, and especially the incoming of miners and the approach of the farmers' frontier, emphasized the problem of transportation and communication in eastern Washington and Idaho. Governor Stevens secured an appropriation from Congress; and Lieutenant John Mullen, who had been with Stevens' railway-surveying expedition and had done more than any other man to explore thoroughly the tangled country between the Missouri River and the Spokane, was put in charge of construction. Work began in 1859; after three years of substantial work, the leveling of forest, the blasting out of rocky stretches, the building of sturdy log bridges, the road was completed, over six hundred miles, from Walla Walla on the Columbia to Fort Benton on the Missouri. The possibilities of navigation on either river, to complete the new transcontinental highway, were being tested. In 1859 Pierre Chouteau, Jr., of St. Louis, sent the first steamboat to Fort Benton, and thereafter steamboats came yearly from the western capital—two to eight a year until 1865, when the Sioux War along the overland trail into Montana gave the Missouri channel new importance. In the four years from 1866 through 1869 one hundred twenty-nine steamboats ascended the Missouri; then the Union Pacific was within competing distance, and the great days of the upper Missouri were over.

As early as 1850 a steamboat was in service on the Columbia, plying between Astoria and Portland. In 1859 the little *Belle* was making regular trips between Portland and the Cascades, and other steamboats were occasionally making the same course. The obstruction of the Cascades surmounted by a portage, goods and passengers could take steamboats from the Cascades to the Dalles rapids. On the upper Columbia—beyond the Dalles—were several sailboats at the turn of the decade. The Oregon Steam Navigation Company, organized in 1860, built up a virtual monopoly of transportation on all three navigable divisions of the Columbia. Ships and portages were put in first-rate shape, profits were enormous, and the prosperity of the company never flagged. It was a genial monopoly, charging all that the traffic would bear and at the same time giving many a poor traveler free passage and meals. In 1871 the Northern Pacific Railroad bought control of the Navigation Company.

Sixty men, veterans at prospecting, spent the winter of

1860-1861 in Canal Gulch, on Oro Fino Creek in upper Idaho. The riffles of their sluice boxes caught a dollar's worth of gold to four pans, not much, but enough to keep the men working. In March one of the miners made his way to Walla Walla on snowshoes, with the eight hundred dollars that was his share. He reported excellent prospects; and this newest excitement found hundreds of followers. Four or five hundred men started from Walla Walla in that same month; by June the Portland newspapers were lamenting the desertion of homesteads in the Willamette Valley. By September the exodus of Idaho-bound miners had appreciably raised the price of labor in the California mines. Pierce City and Oro Fino, in the center of the new boom district, became busy mining towns as the Clearwater River country revealed its mineral riches; the discovery of promising diggings on the south fork of the Clearwater brought Elk City and Lewiston into existence. In the autumn of 1861 excitement was intensified at news of extraordinary prospects on Salmon River. With the miners' accustomed readiness to abandon old diggings for new, the news of the Salmon River discoveries drew hundreds from Oro Fino and Pierce City, in a stampede southward.

A correspondent of the *Portland Advertiser* in Oro Fino vividly captured the moment: "On Friday morning last, when the news of the new diggings had been promulgated, the store of Miner and Arnold was literally besieged. As the news radiated—and it was not long in spreading—picks and shovels were thrown down, claims deserted and turn your eye where you would, you would see droves of people coming in 'hot haste' to town, some packing one thing on their backs and some another, all intent on scaling the mountains through frost and snow, and taking up a claim in the new El Dorado. In the town there was a perfect jam—a mass of human infatuation, jostling, shoving

[510]

and elbowing each other, whilst the questions, 'Did you hear the news about Salmon River?', 'Are you going to Salmon River?', 'Have you got a Cayuse?', 'How much grub are you going to take?', etc., were put to one another, whilst the most exaggerated statements were made relative to the claims already taken up. . . . Cayuse horses that the day before would have sold for about $25 sold readily now for $50 to $75, and some went as high as $100. Flour, bacon, beans, tea, coffee, sugar, frying pans, coffee pots and mining utensils, etc., were instantly in demand. The stores were thronged." Pay dirt was running as high as forty dollars to the pan; men were making, on an average, a hundred dollars a day, and were writing their friends to hasten to the bonanza. Miners left the Colorado diggings for Idaho. By November perhaps two thousand men were working placers in the Salmon River district.

The wide extent of the gold regions of the West had been amply proven; prospectors went farther afield, leaving Florence with its thousand campfires among the "rises" of the Salmon River basin, and the rich placers of Warren's Diggings, twenty-seven miles to the southeast across Salmon River. They explored the gulches of eastern Oregon; and early in the sixties Canyon City, on a creek of the John Day River, and Auburn, on Powder River, were centers of busy miners exploiting rich diggings. From Auburn prospecting parties explored in all directions; their richest find was in the Boisé River basin, where the mines yielded seventeen million dollars in the first four years. In the Basin in 1864 there were some sixteen thousand people, half of them engaged in mining, the other half "merchants, lumbermen, hotel and restaurant keepers, butchers, blacksmiths, saloonkeepers, gamblers, theatrical people, lawyers, ministers, ranchers, stockmen, and transportation companies." That proportion of miners and non-miners was fairly true of any flourishing mining district.

[511]

In the prosperity of the mining advance Portland developed into a commercial city of six thousand people by 1866—a place of busy wharves, steamboats puffing on the Willamette, long lines of drays rumbling between the river front and the warehouses. But San Francisco never lost its advantage; the mining frontier extended into the eastern slope of the Continental Divide, but San Francisco was still its metropolis. Its woolen stuffs were thick, of fine quality, best adapted to miners' wants. It was the natural distributing point for mining machinery; its machinists were personally familiar with mines, and improvements which were demonstrated successes could be adopted more quickly in San Francisco than in the East. Everywhere on the northwestern frontier the miners from the Sierra districts were the veterans to whom tenderfeet looked for advice. "Idaho is but the colony of California," wrote an Idaho City editor in the summer of 1865. "What England is to the world, what New England states have been to the West, California has been and still is to the country west of the Great Plains. Her people have swept in successive waves over every adjacent district from Durango to the Yellowstone."

In the spring of 1861 James and Granville Stuart found fair prospects in the Deer Lodge Valley, on the upper waters of Clarke's Fork of the Columbia. They expected to buy mining supplies from a steamboat coming to Fort Benton; but on the way the boat was burned up. The brothers hired two men to whipsaw sluice lumber, and sent an order, by a merchant's pack train, to Walla Walla for picks and shovels. The pack train did not return until the season was too far advanced for mining operations; and the Stuarts waited out the winter. The Deer Lodge Valley had long been frequented by mountaineers and trappers; but in the floating population that clustered there in the winter of 1861-1862 were several prospectors.

In May they could commence work; but the old method of pick and shovel yielded the prospectors but one to three dollars for a day's labor. While the Stuarts worked their claim, taking out about two dollars a day, they kept their horses picketed on a grassy slope. That hillside, which was known as Bratton's Bar after 1866, was enormously rich in gold; but in 1862 the prospectors never suspected that there was precious metal under a grassy turf. Emigrants from the Missouri border and from Pike's Peak on their way to the Salmon River district found it necessary to enter Deer Lodge Valley to reach the Mullen Road; but after John White's discovery, in August, of a rich bar on Grasshopper Creek, they remained to build a new frontier in the southwestern corner of Montana.

Around White's discovery the first important mining camp in Montana took shape, Bannack City. Far to the north the discovery of rich deposits on Prickly Pear Creek made apparent that the whole region of the headwaters of the Missouri abounded in mineral wealth.

From Bannack, a town of five hundred people by the spring of 1863, Henry Edgar's prospecting party left on an expedition to the Yellowstone. Their intention was to join the Stuart party in its pioneer exploration of that wonder region, but they were delayed, and the Stuarts did not wait at the appointed rendezvous. Edgar's company, attempting to pick up the Stuarts' trail, fell afoul of Indians, who corraled their possessions and presented an ultimatum: "If we go down the river they will kill us; if we go back they will give us horses to go with. . . . A bunch of horses were driven up and given to us. I got a blind eyed black and another plug for my three; the rest of the boys in the same fix, except Bill, he got his three back. We got our saddles, a hundred pounds of flour, some coffee, sugar, one plug of tobacco and two robes each for our clothes and blankets; glad to get so much. It did not take us long to saddle up."

[513]

On the retreat the party crossed the Yellowstone divide into the rugged valley of the East Gallatin. They were in good spirits again, and unhurried. On the twenty-ninth of May they stopped at a little creek; Bill Fairweather's saddle horse was very lame, and needed rest. Bill strolled aimlessly, and came back to camp: "There is a piece of rimrock sticking out of the bar over there. Get the tools and we will go and prospect it."

Henry Edgar took the pan; Bill chipped into the shelf with his pick, getting a handful of rock fragments. " 'Now go,' he says," runs Edgar's narrative, " 'and wash that pan and see if you can get enough to buy some tobacco when we get to town.' " Edgar panned out quite enough—two dollars and forty cents' worth of gold in that one bowl. That evening, as the other men of the company drifted into camp, "they began to growl about the horses not being taken care of and to give Bill and me fits. When I pulled the pan around Sweeney got hold of it and the next minute sang out 'Salted!' I told Sweeney that if he 'would pipe Bill and me down and run us through a sluice box he wouldn't get a color,' and 'the horses could go to the devil or the Indians.' Well, we talked over the find and roasted venison till late; and sought the brush, and spread our robes; and a more joyous lot of men never went to bed more contentedly than we."

Their next concern was to pan out enough gold to outfit them for a return to the gulch and a thorough prospecting. One day's work gave them the needed hundred and fifty dollars; and on the twenty-eighth they staked out the ground. With the natural generosity of these old Westerners, they also staked out several claims for their friends. "Sweeney wanted a water—a notice written for a water right—and asked me to write it for him. I wrote it for him; then 'What name shall we give the creek?' The boys said, 'You name it.' So I wrote 'Alder.' There was a large fringe of Alder growing along the creek, looking nice and green."

In three years Alder Gulch produced thirty million dollars. The gulch was mined from summit to foot; miners' cabins, villages and towns lined its banks. Virginia City was its largest municipality, with a resident population of thirty-five hundred by the summer of 1864, and a floating population quite as large. An Iowan who came into the town in 1864 wrote back to the *Council Bluffs Bugle*, "We happened to arrive on Sunday, the busiest day in the week. The city was densely crowded with people, 'pilgrims' and miners; auctioneers were bellowing at every corner, or galloping madly up and down the main street; heavily loaded teams and fragmentary trains were wending their way through the crowded streets; pack trains were loading for mining districts further up in the mountains." Main Street of Virginia City was a compact double row of buildings extending the better part of a mile: eight hotels, an unnumbered complement of boarding houses and quick-lunch places, "a number of fine stone business houses," two churches (one Methodist, the other open for all comers), a printing office wherein the *Montana Post* was published, a theater, six billiard saloons, one bowling alley, four or five elegant gambling houses, three dance halls, two fire-company stations, swarms of whisky shops. A mile below the metropolis was the town of Central City; a mile further down the valley was Nevada, with a "Main Street" over a half mile long; a mile and a half below Nevada was Junction City. The road connecting these busy ganglia of miners and merchants was bordered with cabins throughout its length.

John Cowan and his party, all Georgians, discovered gold in a certain gulch on the road from Alder Gulch to Fort Benton. The prospects were not satisfying, and they left to putter in localities to the north; they found nothing better, and late in the season returned to begin regular operations in that gulch, which they christened "Last Chance." In October, 1864, the Georgians were taking out rich yields, and the fame of the new diggings was drawing miners from the other camps. The winter of 1864-1865 was very mild, and the mining boom in Last Chance Gulch was uninterrupted. The miners in convention on October the thirtieth settled upon the name of Helena for their rising city, elected commissioners to lay out streets and establish all the necessary regulations, and chose a recorder. There was no "legal" civil law in Helena for eight months after its founding.

The inrush of miners into Montana that winter hastened a flour shortage in the mining camps. A train of freighters bringing in flour was caught in a mountain snowstorm, the teams were lost, and the wagons left stranded until spring. In Virginia City a French Canadian storekeeper, one Beauvais, had cached a supply of flour, while the price rose to one hundred and forty dollars a sack. A committee appointed by a miners' meeting searched the town for secreted supplies of flour, found Beauvais' cache under a haystack, and distributed the flour among the women and children. The miners reached into their own pockets to pay for most of the distributed flour—not at Beauvais' price, but still at the handsome amount of eighty dollars for a hundred-pound sack. From Helena John Grant, one of the pioneer ranchmen who supplied beef to the mining camps, went to Fort Benton with a string of pack horses and brought back ten sacks of flour; he sold out at once for a dollar and ten cents a pound. Meat, supplied by hunters and cattlemen, was the only food that the mining districts had in assured quantity. Flour, beans, rice, and dried apples were the other standard articles of diet—all high in price and uncertain in quantity.

In the late fall of 1865 T. J. Favorite, editor of the *Radiator* of Lewiston, Idaho, dismantled his press, loaded the pieces on pack ponies, and came over the mountains to Helena. Journalism had ample subject matter in Last Chance Gulch: the vigilance committee of Helena had been organized in the summer of 1865, and the lone pine tree in Dry Gulch nearby had already become famous for its grim usefulness.

Leaving the Overland Trail at Fort Hall or at Soda Springs, emigrants from "the States" followed a trail running north, making a clumsy bracket eastward into the mining district of Montana. Travelers were forced to cross the Continental Divide twice, and to prolong the journey by several hundred miles that a cut-off from the Platte Valley directly through northeastern Wyoming would have obviated. Sidney Edgerton, first governor of Montana, and the territorial legislature united in an appeal to Congress for the opening of a direct road into the Northwest. In 1864 Jim Bridger and John Bozeman, anticipating the government engineers, had struck north from Fort Laramie to find a practicable route into Montana. Bozeman's path lay east of the Big Horn Mountains and west of the Black Hills, up the Powder River and the Yellowstone, into the Gallatin Valley; Bridger pushed farther to the west, leaving the Big Horn on his right, entering Montana from the south. The government, acting promptly upon the legislature's memorial, chose Bozeman's trail as the most feasible, and in 1866 federal troops were despatched to make the road safe for emigrants and freighters.

Territorial government was fairly prompt in following the eastward advance of the mining frontier. The rush to the Nez Perce mines in 1861 and the Salmon River diggings in 1862 resulted in the formation of the Territory of Idaho in March, 1863; and after the rush into Alder Gulch the Territory of Montana was established, in May, 1864. During the course of the Civil War these Westerners of the mining country attended to their own business, with their most active political concern the election of the territorial delegate to Congress. "I heard but little of Union or Disunion," wrote a newspaper correspondent in Montana in 1861. "Those from the Seceding States had not much to say beyond sad regrets that the country should deliberately go to war with itself." Of course there were brawls in the barrooms, and several duels with fists or pistols. To shout openly for Jeff Davis or Abe Lincoln was simply to invite hostilities; and there was usually some one among the listeners ready to take up the invitation. Volunteers were raised in each territory, chiefly for defense of their own frontiers against the Indians.

The pace of migration into the far West was not slackened a whit by the Civil War. The far frontier was a place for refuge for many a draft-evader; families from the border states escaping from the oppressive atmosphere of war time, and from the South, sickened by the ravages of their districts, lent a harassed respectability to the emigration. The rush to the far West became alarming to patriots. In February, 1864, the governor of Iowa attempted to stop up the sieve of the Western boundary: "Large numbers of men qualified for military duty, are preparing to depart at an early day, beyond the Missouri. It is useless to disguise the plain object of their sudden hegira westward, in the midst of winter, and months before the season at which vegetation appears on the plains. . . . Men who are capable of an undertaking so arduous, and able to delve in the golden mines of Colorado, Nevada, and Idaho would make excellent material for filling up the wasted ranks of the Union Army." The draft went into effect on May 10, 1864; but the few troops along the Missouri were inadequate to sift draft-evaders and deserters from among the migrants.

During the winter of 1865-1866 the commandants of frontier posts reported that their hospitals were filled with frost-bitten teamsters and emigrants—the late starters in a season of memorable emigration, whose mules and oxen had frozen to death, and whose stalled wagons were buried under the snow. Demas Barnes, describing a transcontinental trip in 1866, exclaimed: "It is wonderful to see the numbers of farmers with their families and household goods thus migrating to further western homes. Those we saw were principally from the states of Illinois, Indiana, and Missouri, and were either bound for Utah, Oregon, or Washington Territory. We estimated from four to five hundred wagons passed each day—one day at least a thousand. This is only *one* route."

Emigrants' wagons shared the western trails with the caravans of the freighters, and with the stagecoaches. Freighting supplies by ox team from Missouri towns to frontier posts had become an extensive business in the fifties; the brisk times of the bullwhackers began with the springing-up of mining towns in Colorado, and through the years of the Civil War hundreds of trains of ox-drawn wagons brought supplies to the soldiers, mountaineers, and miners of the far frontier. From Atchison, St. Joseph, Leavenworth, Omaha, and Nebraska City trains were constantly outfitting and departing. It was slow business: from Atchison to Denver the ox trains took five weeks; a span of horses or mules could be driven that distance in twenty-one days without putting the stock in poor condition. Freighters were seventy to seventy-five days on the road from the Missouri border to Salt Lake City. Bullwhackers, the teamsters of these ox trains, ranked low in the grades of frontier aristocracy, but they had their pride of profession, symbolized in their fierce attachment for their whips, "three feet stock and twelve feet lash, with buckskin poppers at the tip."

In 1862 Ben Holladay, supply contractor in the Mexican War, freighter, and promoter in general, had come into control of the Central Overland California and Pike's Peak Express Company, operating the daily overland mail from its eastern terminus to Salt Lake under a sublease from the Butterfield company. "Tall and thin, of large grasp and quick perceptions, of indifferent health but indomitable will, fiery and irascible when crossed and a Westerner all through"—so Holladay impressed a passenger in one of his stagecoaches in 1866. Under Holladay's supervision the overland mail took on organization and efficiency. Yet deep snows and mountain blizzards annually triumphed over stage drivers' schedules. The *San Francisco Bulletin* was a useful apologist: "An overland daily mail has always been a favorite of the California public. That when it fails during a month or two in the winter to serve us as handsomely as it always does in summer, it does so from no fault of those who undertake to maintain it, is a gratifying conclusion. . . . It would be a misfortune indeed if, for any cause save and except the completion of long sections of railway between the Missouri and the Pacific we should be deprived of this method of getting to and from the Atlantic States in person or by correspondence."

In 1866 Wells, Fargo and Company absorbed Holladay's lines and other western stage companies in a giant consolidation that gave Wells, Fargo practically exclusive control of the express and stage routes of the West, including the many branch lines that had been built into the most populous districts of the mining frontier. Within the next decade the stagecoaches played a smaller part in the drama of western transportation. They bridged the diminishing gap between busy mining towns and the end o' track of railroads building westward; when the gap was closed the stagecoaches vanished, and before American museums awoke to the significance of their disappearance Concord coaches were dust and rusted iron in village junk heaps.

PART VII
RAILWAYS, CATTLE TRAILS, AND PLOW FURROWS

. . . When
Adown the shining iron track
We sweep, and fields of corn flash back,
And herds of lowing steers move by,
I turn to other days, to men
Who made a pathway with their dust.
—Joaquin Miller

CHAPTER XXIX

GANGS OF PADDIES AND CHINKS

WHEN the handsome new side-wheeler, the *Emilie*, Joseph La Barge, captain, churned its way to dock at Council Bluffs, in August, 1859, Abraham Lincoln picked up his carpetbag and stepped ashore. He was there to see about a little investment in real estate; but he amiably consented to apply the political scalpel to the Democratic carcass, before a full house at the Concert Hall that evening; and he found time for a long conversation with Grenville Dodge, who was taking his ease on the stoop of the grandiose hostelry, the Pacific House, when Abraham Lincoln sat down beside him. The distinguished engineer had in 1853 examined the country to the west; the Mississippi & Missouri Railroad had staked its location of its western terminus on Dodge's shrewd guess that the Pacific railroad would be built along the line of the Platte Valley, beginning somewhere very near Council Bluffs. Lincoln "drew from me all I knew of the country west, and the results of my reconnaissances," Dodge related. "As the saying is, he completely 'shelled my woods.'"

And on July 1, 1862, this President, who fully realized the importance to his Union of a railroad spanning the West, affixed his signature to the Pacific Railroad Act. "A.

Lincoln" is his signature upon almost all official documents; on this enactment, and upon all Union Pacific documents which he signed, there is inked: "Abraham Lincoln."

The Union Pacific Railroad & Telegraph Company was to be a semiprivate corporation, authorized "to lay out, locate, construct, furnish, maintain and enjoy a continuous railroad and telegraph, with the appurtenances," westward from a point on the hundredth meridian, about sixty miles west of Kearney, Nebraska. This nominal beginning of the Pacific railroad was placed in the Territory of Nebraska, to avoid any conflict with States' rights. At this point several railroads from the borders of Iowa and Missouri were to meet. One of these roads was to be built by the Union Pacific itself, to begin from the western boundary of Iowa, the exact location to be fixed by the President. Lincoln called Grenville Dodge, now Brigadier General, from the battlefield; that conversation on the stoop of the Pacific House was recounted, and on November 17, 1863, an executive proclamation fixed the eastern terminus of the Union Pacific at Council Bluffs. The Union Pacific was to build westward to the boundary of California; if the Central Pacific Railroad Company of California, organized by private initiative in 1861, had not reached the boundary, the Union Pacific was to continue its westward course until the lines were joined.

The railroad was to be built with money raised from three sources: a government subsidy, first mortgage bonds, and popular subscriptions to the capital stock. The United States granted a right of way through the public lands, and five full sections on each side of the track for every mile of railroad that was built; the government was to clear away Indian titles wherever they conflicted with the interests of the railroad. As each consecutive forty miles of track were completed, and the construction approved by the government's commissioners, the United States bonds were to be issued to the railroad, to finance further progress. After the railroad was completed, 5 per cent of the net earnings were to be applied annually toward extinguishing its debt to the government.

This was handsome largess; it seemed that in its war-stirred enthusiasm for Union, the East had caught the optimistic generosity of the frontier. "I give no grudging vote in giving away either money or land," declared Henry Wilson, Senator from the old Federalist state of Massachusetts. "What are $75,000,000 or $100,000,000 in opening a railroad across the central region of this continent, that shall connect the people of the Atlantic and Pacific, and bind us together? Nothing. As to the lands, I don't begrudge them."

In December, 1863, ground was broken at Omaha, in ceremonial pomp; but the Union Pacific could make little progress beyond this display, because subscription to the capital stock was lagging woefully, and the great business of the Civil War was making its drastic demands upon money, men, and energy. In the spring of 1864 Thomas C. Durant, vice president of the Union Pacific, its most active executive, and some of his associates were in Washington to appeal for further aid. Almost half a million dollars was spent for dark and devious purposes, and the promoters were successful: the land grant was doubled; the government changed the lien securing its loans to the railroad from a first mortgage to a second mortgage; and, among other concessions, the company was entitled to receive its subsidies of land and money at the completion of each twenty miles of railroad. The benefit of these revisions was extended also to the directors of the Central Pacific.

The financial problems of the Union Pacific were solved by a clever stroke: Durant purchased the charter of the Pennsylvania Fiscal Agency, which had been incorporated

under the lenient laws of Pennsylvania to engage in practically any kind of business. He changed the name of the
corporation to the Credit Mobilier of America, and with
several other financiers formed a small inside ring who
acquired, directly or indirectly, the construction contracts
of the Union Pacific. Stockholders of the Union Pacific
who were also members of the Credit Mobilier were thereby
assured of an excellent profit. The only parties who could
complain were the small stockholders of the Union Pacific,
the "lambs," whose bleatings were unheeded, and the government, which deferred its criticisms until the road was
completed. Peter A. Dey, chief engineer of the Union
Pacific in 1864, found the juggling of specifications and
prices in the first important construction contract too un-
savory for his conscience and resigned. In 1865 Oakes and
Oliver Ames, successful Massachusetts manufacturers, offered their public influence and private fortunes to the welfare of the Union Pacific. Their help was badly needed;
but until the furious factional disputes between the Ames
brothers and Durant were amicably settled, in 1867,
whole-hearted construction of the Union Pacific could not
begin.

The Central Pacific Railroad Company of California
was born in the back room of a hardware and miners'
supply store in Sacramento. The storekeepers were Collis
P. Huntington and Mark Hopkins. Huntington became the
vice president of the road, his partner, treasurer. Leland
Stanford, just nominated on the Republican ticket for governor of the state, was chosen president. Theodore Judah
was the enthusiast whose ability these men hoped to capitalize; a capable engineer, he had explored the Sierra Nevadas
for a railroad route across California. The prize these
capitalists sought in 1861 was the carrying trade of the
Nevada mining regions; but the activity in legislation hall
and lobby that prefaced the passing of the Pacific Railroad

Act found Central Pacific interests well cared for. The House bill which was the foundation of the Pacific Railroad Act, was largely the handiwork of Theodore Judah himself, and was presented by a California senator.

With little preliminary organization to arrange, the Central was first in the field. Taking Charles Crocker, driving executive and construction boss, into its inner circle, the Central Pacific formed two construction firms within its membership; and the directors were thereby assured of immediate profit, as in the case of the Credit Mobilier arrangement. In July, 1863, Judah was pleased to report that six thousand tons of rails, sufficient for sixty miles, had been purchased; and locomotives, passenger cars, flat cars, were also being shipped around the Horn. But before the railroad had done more than begin the first eighteen miles, along the unruly American River, Judah had died, and his assistant, Samuel Montague, became chief engineer. With the beginning of July, 1864, the Central Pacific had opened thirty-one miles of track.

Railroads were building across Iowa in 1865, but Council Bluffs was still far away; of necessity the Union Pacific had to begin across the Missouri, at Omaha. The first spike was driven on July 10, 1865. Materials, machinery and men were brought up the Missouri in steamboats to Council Bluffs; and by the opening day of the new year, forty miles of track had been laid.

With the satisfactory ending of the Civil War, money flowed more readily into such long-pull investments as the Pacific railroads. Amiable amendments of the original Pacific Railroad Act extended the borrowing power of the railway companies. Invigorated after a despondent year, the Central Pacific built a few miles further up the difficult Sierras; end o' track rested in September, 1865, at Illinois Town, fifty-four miles from San Francisco. On its short line the railroad reported earnings of $1080 in gold, a day, for June, 1865. Passenger rates were ten cents a mile, freight rates fifteen cents a ton per mile—no paper currency accepted!

In April, 1866, Durant held a conversation with Grenville Dodge. A successor to Peter A. Dey, some one as well equipped in experience and information, a genius at construction and at managing men, had to be found. Dodge knew his worth; and he made a slow, deliberate speech. "I will become chief engineer only on condition that I be given absolute control in the field. I've been in the army long enough to know the disastrous effect of divided commands. You are about to build a railroad through a country that has neither law nor order, and whoever heads the work as chief engineer must be backed up. There must be no divided interests; no independent heads out West, and no railroad masters in New York."

When General Dodge became chief engineer no one knew whether the Union Pacific would be built out the North Fork of the Platte toward Fort Laramie, or out the South Fork to Denver; no one knew where the road should cross the Rockies; everywhere disorganization was apparent. By the first week of June the Union Pacific was a coördinated, driving force; engineering parties were in action, protected by heavily armed escorts; long-idle construction parties were moving toward end o' track.

Each surveying party included an experienced engineer as chief, two assistants, and rodmen, flagmen, and chairmen, with axmen, teamsters, and herders. As the railroad reached the buffalo range, a hunter was added to the party. Most of the men had been in the Civil War, and knew something about fighting; but in addition each party in a region of hostile Indians was accompanied by a military escort of from ten men to a full company. The party making the final location of the line had the maps and profiles made by the preliminary surveys, and concentrated

upon obtaining a line of the lowest grade and least possible curvature.

Hard upon the locating party came the construction
corps. Each day the grading crew made three or four
miles of roadbed ready for the tracklayers. The bridge
gangs worked five to twenty miles ahead of the track; but
it was seldom that the track waited for a bridge. General
Jack Casement was given the contract for laying the track;
he brought a fine maul-swinging gusto to the task, and could
drive his two-fifty-a-day Irishmen into the same hearty tire-
lessness. Behind the construction corps, on the completed
track, hundreds of freight cars were being hurried to and
from the Missouri. To supply one mile of track with material and supplies required about forty freight cars; for
everything—rails, ties, bridging, all railway supplies, fuel,
food—had to be brought from the increasingly distant town
on the west bank of the Missouri.

The location of the crossing of the mountains had to be
solved at once. Dodge examined personally all the mountain passes and approaches from the Laramie Canyon on
the north to the Arkansas on the south. "The general
examination of the plains along the east foot of the mountains," Dodge reported, "showed that the plains rose from
the Arkansas north until they reached their apex at the
valley of Crow Creek, near where Cheyenne now stands.
Then they fell to the north towards the Laramie, and when
we came to examine the summits of these mountains we
found their lowest altitude was in the vicinity of the
Cheyenne Pass, so that there was no question as to where
our line should run. The line up the Platte and up the
Lone Tree Pass, which I had discovered, was far superior
to any other line, and it forced us to abandon the line in
the direction of Denver."

Ninety miles out of Omaha the track spanned the Loup
River with a long iron bridge, and followed the grading

forces with their "patent excavators" across the grama-grass plains toward the Black Hills. When the road had reached Plum Creek, two hundred miles west of Omaha, the Indians first challenged the advancing rails. Dodge was ten miles farther west, at end o' track, when the hurried word came that a band of Indians had swept down upon a line of freight cars, captured the crew and held the train. Dodge ordered his private car, more an arsenal than a home, hooked to the nearest engine; and with twenty men he raced back. Halting his train, he deployed his men on either side of the track, and in unison they began shooting. The Indians had set fire to the freight cars. At the first volley they mounted their ponies and rode away without show of resistance; but this was the beginning of twenty months' bitter warfare that seriously threatened the existence of the Union Pacific.

At the end of the year 260 miles of track had been laid; and the Union Pacific rested at North Platte, its third division point. This was a town built of tents and un-painted boards, and bathed in whisky, that sprang up with mushroom suddenness; it was, for its brief day, the "Hell on Wheels," as Samuel Bowles christened the shifting town which appeared at each new division point the Union Pacific attained in its western course.

Charles Crocker, superintendent of construction for the Central Pacific, found white labor too independent and too expensive; brought into the Sierras by the railroad company, Irishmen deserted to try their luck at the mines. Crocker answered the problem by hiring Chinamen; at first for twenty-six dollars a month, and later for a top wage of thirty-five, coolies came from Sacramento and San Francisco to work on the railroad. "Efficient as white laborers," Leland Stanford reported of them. "Without them it would be impossible to complete the western portion of this great national highway within the time required by the acts of Congress." The year 1866 was the first in which these Chinese laborers were used; they built twenty-eight miles, up a grade averaging ninety-one feet to the mile, before winter stopped construction.

The spring of 1867 began ominously. The surveying parties, who had wintered in Omaha while they revised their notes, were snowbound for six weeks when they set out to carry on their field work. Durant was acrimonious, and Dodge felt his position insecure; the directors of the road quarreled bitterly. The snow melted into gushing freshets; the Missouri and the Platte were flooded. And from the deep ravines of the Black Hills the Indians swept down Lodge Pole Creek, pulled up the stakes that marked the line of the road, stole the horses, and drove the workmen back. They struck a surveying party on the Laramie Plains, drove away the men and burned their implements and provisions. They braved the military protection of an engineering party, and killed a soldier and a tie-hauler. Dodge tried to keep the facts from the press: it was becoming increasingly difficult to get workmen as disgruntled individuals returned to Omaha or Chicago with tales of the dangers of the railway-builders' frontier. It was safer to work for the Iowa railroads.

Three government commissioners were at end o' track in the last week of May. They had just completed their task of inspecting the finished work, and were in conversation with Grenville Dodge, when more than a hundred Indians suddenly emerged from a ravine, and made a fierce assault upon the workmen; they sent a sudden volley or two of whining bullets, then galloped away. Dodge had jerked out his revolver and run down to the tracks, shouting at the chief graders to get their guns and go after the Indians; but the demoralized workmen had run to the shelter of the freight cars. Dodge stormed about, and returned to the commissioners in an uncooled temper: "We've got to clean

[531]

the damn Indians out or give up building the Union Pacific Railroad. The government may take its choice." Commissioner Frank P. Blair replied that he had seen enough to convince him of the desperateness of the Indians; and shortly afterwards three additional companies of cavalry were stationed along the line for scouting purposes and to keep the Sioux and Cheyenne within the borders of their own ranges.

Seventy miles of track had been laid in the first two working months of 1867. The new terminus was at Julesburg, 377 miles from Omaha. Its nucleus was the old stage-line town of Julesburg, moved across the Platte to the north bank; but Ben Holladay would never have recognized it. In May there were at North Platte fifteen thousand tons of government freight, awaiting transportation; twelve hundred wagons were encamped about the town; cappers, barkers, shills, faro men and blackjack dealers, Jewish clothing merchants, bullwhackers, buffalo hunters, soldiers, odds and ends of humanity, men who lived by brawn, men who lived by wits, and ladies who lived by neither, were in its population of five thousand. In mid-June North Platte contained less than five hundred people, and settled down to begin its undistinguished life as an agricultural community. "Hell on Wheels" had moved to Julesburg.

The Union Pacific had mapped out the town, and laid aside land for its shops. The population that swarmed upon Julesburg believed that the new division point was far enough west to be beyond the pale of law and order; the Union Pacific lots were incidentally preëmpted, as streets were lined with saloons, game rooms, stores and warehouses. Redolent of whisky and gun smoke, Julesburg was a noisy invitation to the construction crews, and a menace to the rapid march of construction. Dodge sent word to Jack Casement to return to Julesburg and restore order. Three weeks later Dodge and Casement were in conversation. "Are the gamblers quiet and behaving?" "You bet they are, General. They're out there in the grave-yard." But, as a matter of fact, most of them had pushed on to the next division point, Cheyenne.

In the late spring Dodge had completed the final loca-tion of the line to Crow Creek, at the foot of the moun-tains, and had named the spot Cheyenne. But the Cheyenne Indians, ignoring the compliment of the christening, hovered on the outskirts. "So they watched Cheyenne's first Fourth of July celebration from afar," writes Dodge's latest biographer, "heard the reverberation of 'anvil-shooting,' heard, though faintly, the playing of the band, saw the shooting of rockets when night came, and if they had been close enough they would have heard General Rawlins deliver the first oration ever given in Cheyenne. On the morning of July fifth, when not a few of the cele-brants were sleeping off the effects of whisky, the Indians slipped down the hills, rushed a party of graders, killed a few, stole the horses, circled the town, and, yelling like mad, vanished up Cheyenne Pass."

In the autumn the construction gangs reached Cheyenne. This was the winter headquarters. Before spring the young town had a population of ten thousand, two two-story hotels, the Headquarters Saloon and ninety-nine others, the Great Western mammoth corral, many another building, hundreds of shanties and tents, and an elaborate history.

In 1866 Congress had given the Central Pacific per-mission to build east as far as it could, till the two roads met. The prize of government subsidies in land and money imbued the officers of each road with a passion for haste; and the directors of the Union Pacific urged Dodge to make final locations as far as possible in 1867, to clear the way for the construction drive of 1868. Dodge plotted his line over the Continental Divide, and on over the Wasatch

[533]

Range toward Salt Lake, and had maps of comforting exactitude to present to the directors in the early winter of 1867, showing that the government subsidies would furnish a handsome excess over the cost of construction. The work of 1867 ended with the track at the crest of the Black Hills, near good timber for ties and bridges; the Chicago & North Western railway reached Council Bluffs in December, giving the Union Pacific a complete rail connection with the East, except for the ferriage across the Missouri. Only two hundred forty miles of track had been built in 1867, but those included all but ten miles of the tremendously difficult ascent to Sherman Pass, the highest altitude in the whole roadway of the Union Pacific. And the elated directors made plans with Dodge to build four hundred eighty miles in 1868.

The decision to leave Denver off the route of the Union Pacific had surprised the people to whom topographical maps meant nothing, and only knew that one of the two cities in the Great West was left, so to speak, on a sidetrack; even more surprising was the decision of the Union Pacific to have the rails touch the northern end of Salt Lake, leaving the Mormon metropolis to the south. Brigham Young fumed, all the more furiously because in the Tabernacle he had told of a divine revelation that the Mormons should assist the Union Pacific. But when the Central Pacific too stood by the recommendation of its engineers that the route north of the Lake was the practicable one, he swallowed his disappointment, and set about making what profits he could out of labor contracts and supply contracts.

During the winter immense quantities of equipment were gathered at Cheyenne. In the Black Hills a thousand lumberjacks were cutting timber to be floated downstream to the railroad line with the spring freshets. Early in the spring gangs of just-recruited laborers tumbled out of every incoming train. On the stretch of track from Omaha to Cheyenne trains were profitably busy; the Union Pacific had in operation fifty-three locomotives, thirteen passenger cars, eight hundred and more freight cars.

The engineering parties set out early, the groups going to Salt Lake crossing the Wasatch mountains on sledges. By the first of April Dodge had returned to end o' track, thundering the constructive gangs into activity. Then the excited financiers in the East, amazingly, hurried up Dodge, told him to get more men, compress his time estimates, disregard expense. The Casement brothers' track-laying contract was changed to read eight hundred dollars a mile for anything less than two miles a day; for building more than that in a day, twelve hundred dollars a mile. The Irish laborers were bucked up by a raise to three dollars a day. The swinging hammers of the Central Pacific crew were ringing too loudly in New York.

When in April the land agent of the Union Pacific arrived at Laramie, the spot selected for the next division point beyond Cheyenne, two hundred people, in wagons, tents, dugouts, cabins made of railroad ties, were camped there waiting for him. Four hundred town lots were sold in the first week; the noisy city that followed the construction camps was ready for another move, and Cheyenne salvaged only fifteen hundred of its ten thousand citizens. On the ninth of May end o' track was at Laramie; on the tenth came the flatcars with those eighty-five hundred people Cheyenne had lost, with their store fronts, bars and tables, wheels and game boards.

In May the Central Pacific tracks entered Reno. A gap in the rails remained at Truckee; on the fifteenth of June that mountain gap had been bridged. Backed by ample capital, propelled by tireless, ambitious directors, the Central Pacific kept an abundance of iron and Chinamen hurrying to end o' track, and the crews moved on into Humboldt

[535]

Valley, aiming directly at the Union Pacific goal of Humboldt Wells, and making no promise to stop there.

Union Pacific gangs sweated and swore; end o' track strode away, a hundred and twenty miles into the Laramie Plains, and the town of Benton, last wild terminus of the road, was born; the feeblest of these terminal towns, it vanished before the first snowfall. What chance to compete with Julesburg and Cheyenne?

The graders were scattered along the more difficult stretches from the Laramie Plains into the Rockies, far ahead of the tie-laying crews who sometimes had to wait for materials. Dodge remained that whole summer between Laramie and the Humboldt mountains, racing between graders and supply trains, driving the work unceasingly. Grasshoppers that year ruined crops, flour had to be sought for, and eight dollars a hundred pounds had to be paid. The Cheyennes struck savagely at a dozen points along the road, killing and scalping. The single track from Omaha was overburdened: forty carloads of material were needed for every mile of railroad-building. But in August the rails were across the Red Desert, where, in the previous summer, a party of fourteen Union Pacific engineers had staved off three hundred Sioux Indians, fighting from morning until night. The rails climbed the Continental Divide, and raced on into Bitter Creek basin. Winter came upon the workmen in the Wasatch mountains; but grading and track-laying went ahead.

The Mormons caught up the work; Brigham Young himself had taken the major contract to grade the last hundred and twenty miles to Promontory Summit; and Mormons, with ten dollars a day and keep for a man with his ox team, and a voracious market for hay at a hundred dollars a ton and potatoes at seven dollars a bushel, reaped profits as the road advanced.

Hard beset by the piling-up snows, the railroad came

to an unwilling halt for the winter at Wasatch, nine hundred sixty-six miles from Omaha. Four hundred twenty-five miles of track had been built since the first of April, and an extra hundred miles of badly needed sidings put in.

But because the Central Pacific was building rapidly across the lowlands, the Union Pacific crews were ordered to battle the snowbound heights, and keep ahead with the track-laying. Huntington of the Central Pacific traveled through the Union Pacific country; and added a postscript to the story of the struggle with nature: "I met some teams with ties in the Wasatch mountains, and I asked what the price was. They said $1.75 each. They had seven ties on the wagon. I asked where they were hauled from, and they said from a certain canyon. They said it took three days to get a load up to the top of the Wasatch mountains and get back to their work. I asked them what they had a day for their teams, and they said $10. This would make the cost of each tie more than $6. I passed back that way in the night in January, and I saw a large fire burning near the Wasatch summit, and I stopped to look at it. They had, I think, from twenty to twenty-five ties burning. They said it was so fearfully cold they could not stand it without having a fire to warm themselves."

Echo Canyon was left behind, the construction gangs moved on into Weber Canyon, and before January was done some one nailed a sign on a lone pine tree beside the track, "1000 Miles"—from Omaha. On the third of March, 1869, the Union Pacific tracks had reached Ogden. The Central Pacific was more than a hundred miles away, and shortening that distance daily.

But the other half of the game was being played in New York and Washington. On the second of March the Secretary of the Interior, a partisan of Huntington's, directed that $1,400,000 worth of United States bonds be issued to the Central Pacific in advance, for the construction of the railway between Echo Canyon and Promontory Point— a line that the Union Pacific had already graded, and on which its track-laying crews were working. This order was the last official act of President Johnson's cabinet. It was a bold coup, but Dodge kept his construction crews at work, and turned to the new president of the United States, General Grant. And the first official act of President Grant was to annul the order, and to prohibit the issuing of bonds to either company until a complete investigation should be made.

While between Ogden and Promontory Point each company was grading a line, side by side, Dodge went directly to Huntington, and bearded the lion. If the two companies did not agree upon a meeting place, he made it plain, the government would interfere to the companies' mutual disadvantage. And shortly officers of the two companies went before Congress, stating their agreement to meet at Promontory Point. Congress, relieved to escape the responsibility of an investigation, solemnly enacted a statute requiring the roads to join at that place: "That the common terminus of the Union Pacific and the Central Pacific Railroads shall be at or near Ogden; and the Union Pacific Railroad Company shall build, and the Central Pacific Railroad Company shall pay for and own, the railroad from the terminus aforesaid to Promontory Point, at which point the rails shall meet and connect and form one continuous line."

The month of April witnessed the fastest track-laying in the history of railroading: daily the distance between the end o' tracks was clipped five miles at either end. Twenty-five hundred men were working for each company, "graders, tie 'shovers,' haulers, bridge builders, track layers, bolters, spikers, train crews and 'cooks and bottle washers.' " Dodge scratched a note to his wife: "I never saw so much needless waste in building railroads. Our own construction department has been inefficient. There is no excuse for not being fifty miles west of Promontory Summit. Everything connected with the construction department is being closed up and closing the accounts is like the close of the rebellion."

On the morning of May 10, 1869, two special trains met at Promontory Point. The special from San Francisco, which had waited three days at Promontory while washouts were being repaired on the Union Pacific, bore the private car of Leland Stanford, president of the Central Pacific, and his nine eminent guests. In their car was the ceremonial "Last Tie," of highly polished hardwood, bound with silver and duly placarded with a silver plate; and the "Last Spike," cast from twenty-dollar gold pieces and capped with a gold nugget. A silver-headed mallet was to be the ceremonial hammer. The meeting of the tracks was not unworthy of the gilt and pomp; the dignity of it was graved upon one side of the Last Spike, "May God continue the unity of our country as this railroad unites the two great oceans of the world."

The Union Pacific special brought Thomas C. Durant, Grenville Dodge, directors and commissions, and a clergyman from Massachusetts to be chaplain to the ceremony. Other passenger trains arrived during the morning. A gap of one hundred feet yet separated the engines of the two specials, to be closed as part of the ritual; and here gathered a cosmopolitan crowd of soldiers, Mormons, Chinese, Mexicans, Indians, Irish workmen, and a few excursionists and journalists from East and West.

The telegrapher at Promontory tapped a readying message to Omaha: "To everybody. Keep quiet. When the last spike is driven at Promontory Point we will say 'Done.' Don't break the circuit, but watch for the signals of the blows of the hammer. The spike will soon be driven. The

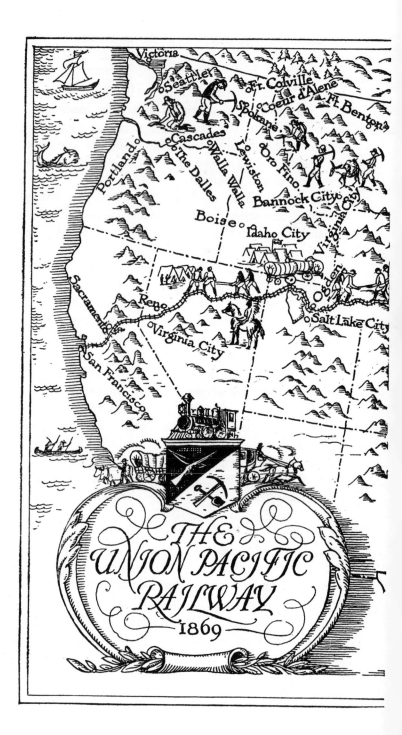

THE
UNION PACIFIC
RAILWAY
— 1869 —

Deadwood

Ft. Pierre

Laramie
Cheyenne
Denver
Julesburg
Omaha
Leadville

Pike's Peak

Santa Fe

signal will be three dots for the commencement of the blows."

A clean-frocked squad of Chinamen carried the Central Pacific rail into place; a gang of scrubbed and shaved Irishmen brought forward the Union Pacific rail—and the gap was closed. The chaplain did his part; then Leland Stanford enounced a vision of three transcontinental tracks, one for passenger trains, one for eastbound freight and one for westbound. Grenville Dodge was reminded of Senator Benton's "There is the East!" speech, and paraphrased a part of it, with acknowledgment.

Ceremonial spikes, offerings of Western states, were presented, and driven into the spike-holes abashedly by the donors as an anticlimax to their presentation speeches. The Last Spike remained untouched. Stanford was nervous. He brought down the silver maul, side-swiped his stroke, and hit the rail a clanging blow. The debonair vice president of the Union Pacific, returning the compliment, purposely missed. The chief engineers, Montague and Dodge, drove the Last Spike into the tie. Then the engines chugged up until their guards touched; each engineer climbed from his cab and broke a bottle of champagne upon the opposite engine. There were a few more speeches; then directors and commissioners assembled in Stanford's car, and the president of the Central Pacific was host to thirsty guests.

To some of these men the Pacific Railroad meant profit; to others, Oriental trade; to some, work done; to some, a bridge between California and the East. But Grenville Dodge foresaw the changing West. In the House of Representatives in 1868 he had outlined the exploitation that the Pacific Railroad made possible: "These mountains are underlaid with gold, silver, iron, copper and coal. The timber ranges that those roads pass will develop an immense lumber trade, and the millions upon millions of Government land that they will bring into the market and render feasible for settlement will bring to the Government more money than all the bonds amount to; and this land and these minerals would not have brought the Government one cent of it were it not for the building of these roads."

CHAPTER XXX

INVITATIONS AND ACCEPTANCES

IN the greater hotels of New York and in many of the city's shops travelers could buy their tickets to the Pacific Coast. There was a diversity of ways to Chicago: the "Allentown" line; the "Great Central Route"; the Erie, and more roundabout connections. The "Great Central Route" was the most attractive in 1869; for its way led by Niagara Falls, the tourists' haven, and it had just added some of Mr. Pullman's palace cars to its rolling stock.

The traveler who chose this forerunner of the present New York Central system left New York in the evening. On the following morning his train arrived at Rochester, where the Pullman cars were attached. One of the three Pullman cars in each train was a "Hotel Car," divided into staterooms and a kitchen. Here was the only water supply for washing and drinking on the train, and an iced wine house. At meal time the conductor walked through the two sleeping cars, taking the passengers' orders; porters set up temporary tables between seats, and brought the food from the kitchen. Travelers were delighted with the novelty of dining in such style while the train was speeding along at thirty miles an hour: "an additional zest is given to the good things by the thought that the passengers in the other cars must rush out when the refreshment station is reached, and hastily swallow an ill-cooked meal. It is proposed to construct dining-cars which will be at the service of all who travel by the train, and when this is done, the limit of improvement will have been reached."

On the tracks of the Great Western of Canada the train slowly crossed the majestic turbulence of Niagara, and sped across lower Canada, arriving in Chicago over the Michigan Central tracks in the next forenoon.

If the Michigan Central express arrived punctually at Chicago, the traveler had seventy-five minutes in which to change stations. Frequently it did not, and philosophical travelers had twenty-four hours wherein to discover the city-soul of Chicago, for there was but one through train a day over the Union Pacific. From Chicago the traveler went to Omaha on the Northwestern or the Rock Island, unless a ticket agent, abusing his innocence, sold him a ticket *via* the Burlington.

After the bustle of getting away ("On such an occasion as this," wrote a harassed English traveler, "the solitary and compassionate man has good reason to rejoice in his loneliness, and to pity those who are accompanied by ladies"), the passenger was embarked upon a twenty-four-hour journey across Illinois and Iowa, through fields of long, rank grass, rolling prairies sparsely dotted with farm-houses.

At Council Bluffs travelers were hustled into omnibuses which filled too soon, and thrust part of their human freight atop with the luggage. Through deep ruts in a foul road the omnibus careened to the river's bank, and was driven onto the deck of a flat-bottomed steamer. So the Missouri was crossed; and the traveler was at the eastern terminus of the Union Pacific.

Omaha was flourishing in 1869. Its population of two

thousand in 1860 had increased tenfold. Within the city were many manufactories, one distillery, several breweries, two daily newspapers, fifteen churches, eleven hotels. Certainly, the West was coming along with a boom! But travelers had to cut their inspection short, and hasten to the Union Pacific depot.

A traveler in this year of 1869, having reserved his Pullman seat by telegraph and consequently amiable when he found other passengers being turned away with the prospect of spending several nights in an ordinary coach, surveyed his fellow-passengers, and wrote: "Some were old Californians returning home after a visit to their birthplaces in the Eastern States. Others were taking the overland route to San Francisco, in order to compare its comforts with those of the route across the Isthmus of Panama. A considerable proportion consisted of adventurers bound for California to seek their fortunes, and a very few were traveling for their pleasure. To nearly every one the journey is a new one, partaking of the character of a daring enterprise. Some who profess to be well-informed misspend their time in endeavors to excite the fears of the timid and the apprehensions of the excitable. They enlarge on the dangers of a line constructed too hurriedly. They draw ghastly pictures of perils to be faced in the event of the wild Indians putting obstructions in the way of the train, and attacking the passengers. It is possible that these tales promoted the sale of insurance tickets."

The journey was soon fairly begun; but passengers who expected to find a desolate West just beyond Omaha were surprised to find farmhouses and tilled fields on either side of the line through most of Nebraska.

A hundred miles from Omaha, at Jackson, travelers saw their first Plains Indians—Pawnees, still living in tepees and hunting buffalo. On to Grand Island, where the train stopped for the supper half-hour; on into the Great Plains, where buffalo were still to be counted in millions; on to Cheyenne, and a halt for breakfast.

"The scenery from this point on," wrote passenger W. F. Rae, who congenitally disliked altitudes, "is tame and uninteresting. In every direction the limitless plains extend to the horizon. Here and there a tuft of wild flowers relieves the monotony of the grass flats. A herd of antelopes bounding along is a sight most welcome to the fatigued eye, while the rare spectacle of two Rocky Mountain sheep, with wild aspect and twisted horns, excites speculation as to how they had wandered so far from their native haunts. Dead oxen by the wayside bear witness to the passage of an emigrant train. . . . A few miles farther on, small patches of white in the crevices of the rocks cause the statement to be made that the country of alkali dust has been reached at last. This, however, is contradicted. The patches in question prove to be traces of snow."

It was a difficult pull, but with slow speed and full power the train pulled up to Sherman, 8,235 feet above sea level. Descending the incline leading into the Laramie Plains by its own weight, a thousand feet of altitude lost in a twenty-mile slide, the train crossed the dizzy wooden scaffolding of Dale Creek bridge, and was soon at Laramie City—"thirty minutes for dinner!"

The Wasatch ranges on the left, the Black Hills on the right, receded, and the line of rail cut through millions of acres of sagebrush. At Carbon station, not far to the west, the construction gangs had cut through a seam of coal; a boon to the Union Pacific, the coal was being mined in quantities of two hundred tons a day for the railroad, and elsewhere in Wyoming Territory engineers had found coal and iron.

Past Fort Steele, an army post chalked with alkali and set in the midst of sagebrush, the train drew up at Rawlins Springs for the supper stop. The Continental Divide was crossed during the night; and at Wasatch the passengers were roused for breakfast. The train was now in Utah Territory; and, for all the "Do not stand on the platform" signs, the passengers clustered to take deep breaths of Echo Canyon and Weber Canyon. Through the sundered rocks of the Devil's Gate, the train raced on—in the distance was the Great Salt Lake—into Uintah, where Mormon lads sold peaches and Mormon ladies tempted passengers to buy embroidered gloves.

At Ogden the passenger for Salt Lake City took a place in Wells, Fargo and Company's Concord coach, and rode for five hours over ruts and stones; but the branch railroad to the Mormon capital had already been begun.

Past Ogden was Corinne, where passengers for Montana Territory took the stagecoach. Beyond, skirting the northern shore of the Lake, the train ascended the steep grade to Promontory Station. Here passengers had to change to the Central Pacific train; the arrangement that made Ogden the junction point was not yet completed. Two hours were allowed for the luggage-hustling and for dinner. In this generous time passengers could stroll down the one street of Promontory, and turn into one of the board or canvas establishments for whisky or three-card monte.

In lieu of Mr. Pullman's excellent cars, the Central Pacific had its own "Silver Palace Cars," of which one traveler wrote, "the name is the best part." Several miles west of Promontory the train began the traversing of the barren Great Basin, then known, so had the phrase shrunk, as the Great American Desert. The line emerged into the Humboldt Valley, and two hundred miles from Promontory stopped at the boom town of Elko, where there were already three thousand people, and a newspaper appeared twice weekly with editorials howling against the Chinese menace. Here there branched off a busy wagon trail to the White

Pine district, where handsome discoveries of silver had just been made.

Along the shrub-fringed Humboldt the Central Pacific approached the base of the Sierras. Reno was the last pause of importance in Nevada; here travelers left to go by stage to Virginia City, the center of the Nevada mining boom. Soon the train crossed the state boundary; and Californians rejoiced, having a great deal to say to other passengers about the sunshine of the Pacific slope. Two engines now puffed together to draw the train up the grade; and at intervals long snowsheds darkened the cars. At Summit Station the crest was passed. Sacramento was a hundred miles away; another hundred miles and a little more of train travel, a short journey in a ferryboat, and the traveler was gaping at the illimitable blue of the Pacific.

Capitalists and congressmen alike were spurred by the building of the Union Pacific to promote other railroad invasions of the West. In 1864 the Northern Pacific Railroad Company was chartered to construct a line from Lake Superior to Puget Sound, and was donated the alternate sections of the public domain in a strip sixty miles wide in the states and one hundred miles wide in the territories. Two years later the Atlantic & Pacific Railroad was chartered, to build along the line of the thirty-fifth parallel survey to California, with a donation of public lands like that of the Northern Pacific. In March, 1871, the Texas Pacific Railroad was chartered, to begin at Marshall, Texas, the head of navigation on the Red River, and extend past Fort Worth and El Paso, thence along the line of the thirty-second parallel survey; it received the same generous grant of territorial lands. The Texas Pacific was the fourth and last of the land-grant transcontinental railways. During the sixties two regional lines, the Denver and Rio Grande and the Kansas Pacific, laid tracks far into the West.

[549]

In 1869 Jay Cooke, invaluable financier of the Civil War, became convinced that Isaac Stevens was right: that the northern strip of territory across the United States needed only a railroad to enable it to become a prosperous agricultural country. Accordingly he became the financial underwriter of the Northern Pacific, and galvanized the lagging enterprise with his own impatience. He gained control of the Lake Superior & Missouri River Railroad, then constructing its line between St. Paul and Duluth, and bought heavily in lands about Duluth as a private investment; near that city, early in 1870, the Northern Pacific began construction.

As a part of this energetic beginning the Land Department of the Northern Pacific was organized, to promote the sale and settlement of the lands of the Company. The land-grant railroads had a double incentive to the work of colonization: the sale of their own lands and, the larger interest, the development of profitable traffic after the peopling of the adjacent lands, government-owned or railroad-owned.

Advertising as a factor in the settlement of the West far outdates the strenuous publicity work of the railroads. The beginning, perhaps, goes back to the old Quaker frontier: pamphlets written by William Penn had sung the advantages of Pennsylvania to a European audience.

After 1850, with the acceleration of American life everywhere as industrial tendencies became more manifest, in the northwestern states the state governments themselves became bureaus of propaganda. "Men who first break up the prairie sod, clear the brush off the slopes, drain the marshes, build the railroads, and do the thousand and one hard jobs incident to pioneer life, and then turn to the building of factories and towns and cities"—the states wanted such settlers, thousands of them, to lop off the frontier years of a state's history and hasten the day when the older commonwealths should yield in prosperity and population to the strident West. In 1852 Wisconsin began the era of organized advertising for immigrants, with the appointment of a commissioner of immigration, who was to reside in New York, maintain profitable contact with the various immigrant protective agencies, consuls, and steamship companies, and to circulate pamphlets in Europe and in New York that provocatively described the resources and opportunities offered by Wisconsin.

In 1853 an additional publicity agent was appointed, to "see that correct representations be made in eastern papers of our great natural resources, advantages, and privileges, and brilliant prospects for the future; and to use every honorable means in his power to induce emigrants to come to this state." And this accomplished press agent visited every important city in the northern states and Canada, and nearly every village in New York and New England; in that year he inserted Wisconsin press matter in more than nine hundred newspapers. The effectiveness of advertising was demonstrated in the report of Wisconsin's commissioner of immigration for 1853: while the entire immigration into the United States was in fact less than the immigration of 1852, immigration for Wisconsin increased 15 per cent in the year. In the commissioner's minimum estimate, sixteen thousand settlers had come into Wisconsin from Germany, four thousand from Ireland, and three thousand from Norway. These were the countries upon which pamphleteering had been concentrated.

The Land Committee of the Northern Pacific had Frederick Billings as chairman, and, to take the immediate task of administering the land grant, John S. Loomis as commissioner. Loomis was also president of the National Land Company, the colonizing agent for the Kansas Pacific in western Kansas and Colorado. Offices were opened in New York and in St. Paul. Loomis drew up a plan of action:

to publish maps and documents describing the railroads and the lands it traversed, to be published in several languages and be distributed by the company's agents throughout Europe and the United States; to cultivate friendly business relations with steamship and rail companies, and to maintain genial relations with the press of Europe and America.

A Bureau of Immigration was organized, its central office in London and branch offices in Germany, Holland and the Scandinavian countries. Through these agencies, and with consular assistance, persuasive literature was scattered broadcast. If in the pamphlet, *Facts about Montana Territory and the Way to Get There,* published by the Northern Pacific in 1872, the writer stated that the only illness which touched the residents of Montana was the distress of over-eating, resulting from excessive indulgence of appetites heartened by the invigorating atmosphere, most other pamphlets wandered little from facts and figures. Circulars and placards had their part in the campaign of persuasion, and special representatives, clergymen favored, were sent into the old countries. In 1872 railroad agents were active in the agricultural counties of England. In 1873 Colonel Hans Mattson, an old hand at such work, was representing the Northern Pacific in Norway and Sweden, organizing colonies to emigrate to Minnesota.

Once groups of colonists were organized for emigrating, precautions were necessary to prevent immigrants bound for the Northern Pacific lands from being shunted off to some other part of the country. The immigrant in New York ran a gamut of high-pressure agents and plunderers; since he knew no English, he was lucky to come through unscathed and headed in his intended direction. The Northern Pacific officials made arrangements with four of the principal steamship lines whereby local agents of the railroad in Europe were furnished tickets for the booking of colonists with through transportation to Duluth or St. Paul.

In the United States Major George B. Hibbard worked among the Grand Army veterans in western New York and the New England states, interesting the officers of the posts in the colonizing work, and distributing Northern Pacific literature. One fruit of this work was the congressional action of 1872 allowing the period of service in the national army or navy to be deducted from the five years' residence required for perfecting title to a homestead.

Expeditions for prospective buyers were organized. Tickets were sold at full fare; but persons who took these excursions were credited with the fare on the purchase price of land bought from the Northern Pacific within two months after the excursion; and they were also entitled to free transportation over the Northern Pacific for themselves and families when they moved to the new home. Reception houses were built at Duluth, Brainerd, and Glyndon, Minnesota, to be used as temporary homes by the immigrants looking about for land. The terms of purchase were made sufficiently flexible to attract moneyless settlers as well as cash buyers. Farm lands could be bought on seven-year payments, with 7 per cent interest. Persons could settle upon and improve the company's lands before they were brought into the market; and when such lands were appraised and ready for sale, the squatters had the first opportunity of purchasing their lands at the regular prices—in 1872, eight dollars to two-fifty per acre graded according to proximity to the railroad.

Reports of the Northern Pacific agents in Europe, in 1873, suggest the part of the railroads in immigration. In the spring a party of sixty-four German emigrants left Bremen for Baltimore, where they were to be met by Northern Pacific agents and escorted to St. Paul. At the same time a company of sixty from Holland had embarked for Minnesota. Another sixty Germans left for St. Paul in mid-April. In May the agent at Liverpool reported the departure of two colonies for St. Paul—one Norwegian, one German. The Swedish agent of the company wrote in late April that he had just despatched fifty emigrants to Minnesota, and that he was giving a first-class ticket to Duluth to a Swedish clergyman who intended to select a location for his prospective colony. In June seventy Swedish families, the Liverpool agent wrote, were setting out for the Northwest. In August a report from Germany announced that eighty-three colonists were ready to embark, and the Swedish agent reported the setting-out of two hundred thirty Finns to the Northern Pacific territory. That summer the vanguard of the Mennonite migration was traveling toward St. Paul, intending to select lands within the Northern Pacific territory.

At the same time the railroad's enterprise in publicity was bringing its reward from New England. The Soldiers' Homestead Colony, organized in Boston by Major Hibbard, founded the settlement of Detroit Lake, Minnesota, in 1871; a year later one hundred houses had been built and occupied at Detroit Lake, and five church societies had been organized. The St. Lawrence Free Homestead Colony of Ogdensburgh, New York, in 1871 took all the railroad and government lands in three townships of Becker County, Minnesota. Four hundred German families came from Michigan. Several other American colonies came into Northern Pacific territory, sharing the tide with European immigration; and the railroad itself had reached Bismarck. Then the years of inflated credits, the years when the European market readily absorbed American securities, came inevitably but unforeseen to an end; and on September 18, 1873, its capital invested to the hilt in Northern Pacific, Jay Cooke's brokerage company closed its doors. Other colonizing enterprises, other western railroads, were halted by the panic; and "prosperity" among the frontier population was a fighting word for the next two years. By

1880 the Land and Immigration departments of the Northern Pacific again were active. Once "official" advertising had been begun, the northwestern states found the results worth a continuance of the state boards of immigration. The board established by Wisconsin in 1867 included the governor, secretary of state, and six others. Committees in each county assisted, securing lists of friends and relatives of the county residents; with the mailing list as a guide, pamphlets were sent into the eastern states and European countries. These pamphlets about Wisconsin were of a high order for this branch of literature; Dr. Increase Allen Lapham, "first scholar of Wisconsin," was engaged to write the official booklet, entitled *Statistics, Exhibiting the History, Climate, and Productions of the State of Wisconsin*. *Statistics* was thirty-two pages of compressed information, in the facts-speak-for-themselves style: topographical features, water power, health, metals, forests, agriculture, live stock, wages, manufactures, railroads, markets, population, cities and towns, newspapers and churches, land tenure and the Homestead Law, schools and libraries, post offices and state institutions, rights of married women.

Minnesota established a Board of Immigration in 1867, with an appropriation of ten thousand dollars a year. It, too, was active in distributing auroral pamphlets and other printed publicity; it sent Swedish, Norwegian, and German agents to meet immigrants in New York and the Canadian ports, to accompany them into Minnesota as guides and interpreters. Colonel Hans Mattson, Swedish-American who had made a reputation for himself in the Civil War, was secretary of the Minnesota board; he was of great influence in bringing Swedes into the state. On one of his trips to the old country he organized a party of eight hundred emigrants. E. Page Davis, agent of the Minnesota board in New York, kept a Broadway office as a bureau of general information; he made an arrangement with the Erie Railway whereby emigrants to Minnesota received a one-third reduction in fare and were permitted an extra fifty pounds of free baggage; and during his tenure a collection of Minnesota products was exhibited at each annual fair of the American Institute at New York.

Iowa's Board of Immigration began its extensive publicity work in 1870, capping the other northwestern states by sending Iowa agents to Europe. In 1871 the post of Commissioner of Immigration became elective in Wisconsin, and suffered the ups-and-downs in the train of that status; for the most part the work of pamphleteering and map-distributing, and more direct persuasion in Europe, was carried on in step with the other northwestern states. The activities of the colonizing boards, maintaining a robust competition for immigrant settlement, accelerated the pace of northwestern development, and to some extent set the tone of that development, in greatly increasing the tendency of Germans, Norwegians, and Swedes to settle in those states.

The loose-dirt days in the Colorado mining regions were quickly passed; and until corporate enterprises with ample capital, organized not for speculation but for actual production, came into the mountain regions, and until improved metallurgical processes came into use, Colorado was a desolate frontier. "Over the hills as far as eye can reach, and up and down the valleys," wrote a traveler in Colorado in 1866, "stand the lonely stamp mills, with their iron chimneys. . . . Now and then from one here and another there came a dull heavy sound, like the falling of a huge weight on some heavy body, showing that some of the stamps were in motion, though most of them were silent as the tomb; no smoke, no sound, and no living thing seen about the innumerable tenements." In 1868, when the Boston and Colorado Company opened its smelter at Black Hawk, the new order in mining was established in Colorado.

Albert Richardson returned to Denver in the late autumn of 1869: "Denver had improved wonderfully during the four months of my absence. Frame and brick edifices were displacing mud-roofed log cabins. Two theaters were in full blast; and at first glance I could recognize only two buildings. When I left there was no uncoined gold in circulation; now it was the only currency. . . . The population was improving, for more families had settled here, but gambling and dissipation were still universal. Nearly all liquors were 'doctored'. . . . The waggish superintendent of the overland mail caught an intoxicated emigrant riding away one of his mules; but instead of having him lynched, boarded the offender gratuitously for a day or two and turned him scot free, on the ground that the whisky sold in Denver would make any man steal."

In June, 1870, the Denver Pacific Railroad linked Denver with Cheyenne and the main line of the Union Pacific; in August the completion of the Kansas Pacific opened rail communication with St. Louis. Both were land-grant railroads; but the old tradition of a "Great American Desert" hit them squarely, and to direct the land seekers into Colorado required organized persuasion.

The National Land Company was the largest of the publicizing and colonizing companies which coöperated with the railroads. These companies, perhaps because the necessity of coöperative irrigation suggested it, concentrated on the founding of agricultural colonies. The first was the German Colonization Company, promoted in Chicago in 1869 by a philanthropic German whose intent was to enable poor German workingmen of the city to take advantage of the Homestead Law. Too much communism, not enough agriculture: in the late summer of 1870 the colony began to disintegrate. In the spring of that year the town of Greeley had been founded, by the most famous of the Colorado colonies. This enterprise, the Union Colony, was the brain

child of the agricultural editor of the *New York Tribune;*
its eight hundred people were hard-working, capable farmers
from the older states.

"In the last year," summed up the *Rocky Mountain News*
in February, 1871, "the National Land Company has transported and located in Colorado and Kansas sixteen colonies;
about half of them from European countries, and the others
from various points in the United States. All have proved
successful and are doing well." And another Colorado
newspaper elaborated, "Colonizing has many advantages.
It secures at the start a community, society, laws, schools,
churches. It enables emigrants to know beforehand the
best places for settlement, by sending out agents to look the
country over. Freights and passage are lower to colonies
than to settlers who come singly. Lands are bought at better advantage."

Within a year after the close of the Civil War, Colorado
had outgrown its dependence on the Missouri Valley for
flour, potatoes, and corn; the territory was agriculturally
self-supporting. In 1867 Colorado farmers sent food to
Montana mining camps, and were bidding to supply the
frontier army posts. In 1870 the production of gold and
silver was estimated at four million dollars; the value of
Colorado's agricultural products that year was only a half
million less. Three years later the zeal of pioneering
farmers in the Great Plains prompted a "Convention of
Trans-Missouri States" at Denver, to demand the interest
of the national government in a grand plan of interstate
irrigation systems.

In 1865 Colorado almost became a state: a popular convention drafted a constitution which the voters approved, a
governor and legislature were elected, and the legislature
made choice of two senators who proceeded to Washington
to urge the admission of Colorado. Congress was willing;
but there was in the constitution of the would-be state a

provision excluding "a negro or mulatto" from the franchise, and President Johnson vetoed the act that would have granted statehood. Perhaps the circumstance that the two senators presented by Colorado would not pledge themselves to vote against Johnson's impeachment accounted for the alacrity of the veto. Colorado's demand for admission was revived periodically for a decade; at last, in 1875, Congress and Grant agreed upon an enabling act for Colorado. In the next year Colorado came into the Union, just in time to express its appreciation to the Republican administration by casting its three votes in the electoral college for Rutherford B. Hayes.

Until the Union Pacific invaded the region, Wyoming to emigrants was simply a dangerous thoroughfare, a road through the ranging ground of implacable Indians. Cheyenne, at the base of the Laramie Range, near several military posts and nearest point on the Union Pacific within striking reach of Denver, was the most important of towns begun by the railroad. In July, 1867, the land agent of the Union Pacific hammered some boards together, called his structure a land office, and exhibited a plat of the future city. Purchasers stormed his shack, paid two or three hundred dollars for a town lot, and the wild town of Cheyenne was born forthwith, lusty and yowling from the moment of its birth.

Morton Post's transaction in real estate is indicative of its progress: in July he bought two lots from the railroad land agent for three hundred dollars; in August he built a store at the intersection of his lots, and sold the fractional remainder of his real estate for five thousand, six hundred dollars. A city government was established in autumn, with a police system that was valiantly busy in ignoring the prevalent rowdiness. On the twenty-seventh of September the citizens assembled for the purpose of organizing a county. Laramie County was given its bounds at that time.

Twelve days later county officers and a delegate to Congress were elected; ten days' residence made a citizen an eligible voter. On the nineteenth of September the first issue of the *Cheyenne Evening Leader* was published; five weeks later another daily newspaper put in an appearance. Telegraphic communication with Council Bluffs and with Denver was completed before the end of October. And the railroad did not reach Cheyenne until the thirteenth of November! In the summer of 1867 prospectors about the sources of the Sweetwater found gold in paying quantities. A company from Salt Lake City followed the good news to the region of the South Pass. Before winter set in miners whose only device for breaking the quartz was a hand mortar had taken fifteen thousand dollars from the first discovered lode. Placer mines were discovered in the gulches nearby. South Pass City was the metropolis of the Sweetwater mining district, a region infested by Indians, and none too certain in the value of its ores. Indians continued to infest the Wyoming trails; troops in garrisons and on patrol duty were too few to prevent a number of Indian depredations and killings. But still prospectors made excursions, and a few new mining camps extended the circle of settlement.

The Dakota legislature organized four counties in the Wyoming country. But this distant region was obviously destined for separation from Dakota; and on July 25, 1868, the Territory of Wyoming was created. The official seal of the territory had on its face a Norman shield; the upper half was emblazoned with mountains, a railroad train on the horizon. On the first quarter below, against a white gound, were a plow, pick and shovel, and a shepherd's crook.

Since 1864 Montana prospectors were tapping surface veins of gold and silver around Butte; and in 1872 William A. Clark came to the Butte pits. Gold miners were amused as wagons loaded with "Clark's rocks" started on the four-hundred-mile drive to Corinne, the nearest point on the Union Pacific; but these gray ores contained profitable amounts of copper. Deep pits and steaming reduction plants, and mountains of refuse and slag, came to characterize the Butte district as the copper deposits were exploited on the grand scale set by Marcus Daly in 1879. In the middle seventies the miners' frontier had extended into the Black Hills; Deadwood in Dakota Territory and Leadville in Colorado boomed into notoriety almost simultaneously, two mining towns that became choice examples of the wilderness in the wild, wild West.

In northern Dakota the wheat-growing frontier was each year extending to the westward; and two great frontiers, traveling in opposite directions, met and overlapped in Montana. From Texas a third frontier advanced over the Great Plains and into Montana, the cattlemen's invasion of the open range.

CHAPTER XXXI

THE OPEN RANGE

BETWEEN 1816 and 1819 the War Department linked the northern frontiers with a chain of five forts from Fort Smith, on the Arkansas River, to Fort Snelling at St. Anthony's Falls, the head of navigation on the Mississippi. A military expedition of 1819 resulted in the establishing of a frontier post near the present site of Omaha. In 1827 that post was abandoned and another took its place, Fort Leavenworth, within a few miles of the site of Kansas City. As the rush of the westward movement ignored the factious barrier of the Indian Territory, other garrisons were established to keep belated pace with the movement of emigrants across the far frontier. Interrupted by Indian uprisings here and there, and by occasional reconnaissances into the wilderness, the little armies in the frontier posts went on with their discipline and training, day by day.

The regular soldiers were an alien element to the other Westerners. William Chandless, a traveler in the West, was simply recording the common comment of the natives when he wrote, "As a rule the army is recruited from the riff-raff of foreigners, too stupid or too indolent to get on in industry . . . great contempt is felt for soldiers in the States; if one appears in a town he is watched like a dog given to stealing. . . . West-Point officers, having passed through a very severe ordeal themselves, are not apt to make allowance for human weakness. But the methods of punishment are to my mind far more odious and degrading than the lash; tying a man to a waggon by his thumbs, loading him with a heavy wooden or iron collar (and even in a town like Leavenworth, Kansas Territory, making him stand guard in public with it on)."

The Civil War marked a period of Indian outbreaks throughout the West; and the frontier formulated a specific grievance against the army. The Indians weren't being killed off. If the national administration's attitude toward the Indians was frequently corrupt and unnecessarily heartless, it was far too tepid to satisfy the frontier. Each amicable treaty with a once hostile tribe of Plains Indians disgruntled the border folk. The editor of the *Council Bluffs Bugle* burst out, in his issue of September 3, 1868: "The whole history of the settlement of this country proves, that after a tribe commenced fighting the whites, they could never be treated with so as to make a permanent peace until after they had been thoroughly whipped and about one-half the number exterminated. This being proved to be the only way a peace on a permanent basis can be obtained, the sooner the plan is adopted and carried into execution, the better for the white people, the better for the Indians and the better for the purse of the nation. Offer a reward of $500 for each Indian's scalp brought in, and in less than six months we will have an end of the Indian war, and will have peace with the red devils on a permanent basis."

The frontier had to have its way; and the best that the

government could do was to attempt to remove the Indians from the path of the westward movement by peaceful means. Congress created a peace commission in the summer of 1867, with instructions to quiet the hostile tribes on the plains, and to secure an unimpeded right of way for the Union Pacific. Two years later a volunteer, non-political Board of Indian Commissioners was organized as a permanent adjunct of the Indian Bureau. In 1871 Congress abolished the system of making treaties; the tribes were no longer recognized as semisovereign nations, and negotiations for their removal were simpler and more effective. The tribes were concentrated upon reserves, and the Indian problem after the middle of the seventies had lost its larger meanings.

Coincidentally with the removal of the tribes from the Great Plains, the herds of great game animals, the buffaloes, were eradicated. As long as these huge, gregarious beasts roamed the prairies, Indians had other subsistence than their own crops and the doles from the government's agencies; they could maintain their independence against any coercion but warfare. When professional hunters invaded the ranges, ruthlessly destroying entire herds, they were in many instances trespassing upon Indian domain. If the army did not eject the trespassers but many times aided them, if the Indian agents and the Secretary of the Interior made no attempt to arrest the devastation, if the half-dozen bills introduced into Congress for the preservation of the buffaloes were sidetracked in committee or otherwise disposed of—if, when in 1874 Congress enacted a bill making unlawful the killing of buffaloes for commercial purposes, President Grant chose not to sign the measure, the explanation of these laxities is no puzzle. Columbus Delano, Secretary of the Interior, put his attitude quite simply in 1873: "I would not seriously regret the total disappearance of the buffalo from our western prairies, in its effect upon the Indians, regarding it rather as a means of hastening their sense of dependence upon the products of the soil and their own labors."

Almost seven million buffaloes ranged the Great Plains in 1870, touching the Canadian plains and southwest Texas at the extremes of their migratory waves. The roadway of the Union Pacific gave limits to a northern herd of almost two million buffaloes and a southern herd of about five million. The precursors of these harassed beasts had ranged as far eastward as the coastal plains; from the beginnings of colonial settlement hunters had taken toll, clearing the Appalachians, the Ohio Valley, the Mississippi Valley, of the game animals. In the mid-thirties the winter pelage of the buffalo had become one of the two most valuable items of the fur trade, and the rate of destruction had been accelerated. Yet, in 1870, there were seven million left.

At Fort Hays, Kansas, in 1870, John Wright Mooar, a young adventurer fresh from New York City, was making his living supplying the army post with wood; James White sold buffalo meat to the post commissary. The hides of the buffaloes White killed he threw away. Mooar suggested that they attempt to find a market for the hides, and a pack was sent east, ultimately to fall into the possession of a Pennsylvania tannery. The tanners experimented, were satisfied, and made an initial contract for two thousand hides at three dollars and fifty cents each. Other tanners, English and American, soon entered the field, sending agents to Hays City and to other points on the fringe of the frontier. This dual demand for buffalo skins—skins taken in winter wanted by the furriers for coats and carriage rugs, skins taken in summer wanted by leather-product companies—meant that buffalo hunting would be carried on incessantly, that there would be no respite in the breeding season or at any other time. Winter robes, at

New York prices in 1870, were bought at about sixteen dollars and a half for a "Grade A" skin, and thirteen and eight dollars for second-grade and third-grade skins. Hides, taken in the seasons when the fur was worthless, brought about two dollars each. There was a restricted but profitable market for buffalo tongues, salted and packed in barrels, and for the "mop," the bunch of long hair that drooped over the buffalo's horns and eye. Buffalo hunting was no longer a local avocation for frontiersmen; it was a professional occupation.

Western Kansas was the first frontier of the devastation: Wright, Beverly and Company of Dodge City, Kansas, Bates of St. Louis and Durfee of Leavenworth, the largest commission companies to seize upon the business, shipped hundreds of thousands of buffalo hides in 1871 and 1872. William Blackmore, English sportsman, reviewing these years, wrote: "When in the West in 1872, I satisfied myself by personal inquiries that the number of buffalo being then annually slaughtered for their hides was at least one million per annum. In the autumn of 1868, whilst crossing the plains on the Kansas Pacific Railroad—for a distance of upwards of 120 miles, between Ellsworth and Sheridan, we passed through an almost unbroken herd of buffalo. The Plains were blackened with them, and more than once the train had to stop to allow unusually large herds to pass. A few years afterwards, when traveling over the same line of railroad, it was a rare sight to see a few herds of from ten to twenty buffalo." In 1873, when the settlers in eastern Kansas were suffering from the destruction of their crops by the ravages of the grasshoppers, orders from Washington despatched several companies of soldiers to the Republican River Valley to kill buffalo for the starving families; the troops found very little meat for them to kill, for the hunters had slaughtered nearly every buffalo in the region.

When construction work on the Santa Fe was stopped in the fall in 1872, hundreds of men were stranded in the Plains without work. All who could rustle a team and horses on their own account, or who could get a merchant to stake them to an outfit, became buffalo hunters. During the winter of 1872-1873 there were more buffalo hunters on the range than ever before or afterwards. The result was a glutting of the market, the small returns frightening many of the newcomers from the field. Prices quickly bounded upwards again; and the fall of 1873 saw an accession of many "hard cases" from the East, who wanted the excitement and the profits of buffalo hunting. By that time the western merchants, thanks to their credit system, had the business pretty well in hand. They sent large, well-organized parties into the range, established central stations near the hunting grounds, and built smoke houses to preserve the meat while it was still fresh from the slaughter.

The most approved party consisted of four men—one shooter, two skinners, and one man to cook, stretch hides, and take care of camp. A light wagon, drawn by two horses or mules, took the outfit into the wilderness, and was sent out each day from camp to bring in the skins upon the field. The supplies were small; the meat of the buffalo was to be the hunters' mainstay. A sack of flour, five pounds of coffee, ten pounds of sugar, a little salt, a side of bacon, and a few pounds of beans, was a month's supply. The wagon carried a "Dutch oven," a frying pan, a coffeepot, four tin plates, and four tin cups. The fastidious could impale their food on their skinning knives; the democrats used their fingers. There was also in the wagon a ten-gallon keg of water. Lead, powder, shells, paper caps, and other accessories for ammunition-making were carried in the wagon: good hunters did not buy many shells, but refilled the cartridges themselves. Knowing hunters chose the Sharp's rifle, guns of .50 or .55 caliber that would kill a buffalo at fifteen hundred yards.

As long as the hunter kept alee of the buffalo—these animals were of short sight but keen scent—he might shoot down a score or more before the stupid, easily bewildered beasts had outdistanced him. The amazing extent of the slaughter is told in the reports of the Western railroads: the Atchison, Topeka & Santa Fe in 1872 and 1873 carried east about 424,000 buffalo robes and hides, and the Kansas Pacific and Union Pacific each carried as many—in all, about 1,250,000 buffalo skins transported by three railroads within two years. In 1874, of necessity, the hunters went southward, past the Cimarron and into the Canadian Valley; western Oklahoma and northwest Texas became the depots of the business. By the close of 1875 the great southern herd had ceased to exist. A remnant of fifteen or twenty thousand roamed in frightened bands across the desolate country from southern Colorado to the Pecos River in west Texas; this remnant was hunted down and exterminated within the next few years.

Between 1879 and 1883 the hundreds of thousands of buffaloes ranging through Dakota and Montana, that had escaped the first fury of the business, were systematically hunted down. Hunters' camps lined the Missouri, the Yellowstone, and their tributaries, cutting off the buffaloes from water; and a cordon of camps along the international border prevented the herds from escaping into Canada. The Northern Pacific was the great carrier of the hide trade; one scant carload transported east in the spring of 1884 signalized the almost complete extermination of the northern herd.

The white, bare skeletons of the slain buffaloes were strewn over the Great Plains. Homesteaders got a start in their new existence by collecting the bones, used by fertilizing plants in the manufacture of phosphates, and by sugar refineries to make carbon. Stacks of buffalo bones towered above the railway freight cars; the resources of the railways were strained to move this tremendous tonnage. There is record of "a rick of buffalo bones, on the Santa Fe right of way, and twenty miles ahead of the track from Granada, Colorado, packed twelve feet high, nearly that wide at the base, and one-half mile long."

The breaking up of the large tribal reservations, the disappearance of the big game herds, and the building of railroads into the West faster than the farmers' frontier was keeping pace, allowed the cattlemen's frontier to extend over the Great Plains and into the rugged wastes of the northern territories.

In Texas, millions of cattle—Longhorns, half-wild beasts of lean flanks and fiery temper; millions of cattle, and a pitifully inadequate local market. In Chicago, the Union Stock Yards, a fenced-in half-section of prairie lands on Halsted Street; and in St. Louis and Kansas City, more modest beginnings of the packing industry. In the Great Plains, the open range, unoccupied and unfenced. These were the elements of the cattlemen's frontier, elements that the building of the Union Pacific, the Kansas Pacific and the Santa Fe linked into coherence.

Drives of cattle northward from Texas became an established institution in 1867, when the Kansas Pacific had been constructed two hundred miles to the west of Kansas City. Abilene, on this newly built stretch of rail, had a vigorous mayor, Jim McCoy; with his exhortations Abilene attained a "cow-town consciousness," and despatched press agents southward to urge the advantages of bringing herds of Texas cattle to Abilene. This year marked the beginning of organized and extensive trail-driving, an institution that throve during the seventies, and lingered in diminishing importance until the nineties. In 1880 the Chisholm Trail, the customary route of the cattle drovers from the Texas-

Oklahoma border into Kansas, was closed by the invasion of homesteaders, whose claims blocked the trail at the Kansas border. In 1884 railways had been built into the Southwest, and were transporting Texas cattle to the northern packing houses.

In that same year a foreman of the trail-drive complained, "Now there is so much land taken up and fenced in that the trail for most of the way is little better than a crooked lane, and we have hard lines trying to find enough range to feed on. These fellows from Ohio, Indiana, and other northern and western states—'the bone and sinew,' as politicians call them, have made farms, enclosed pastures, and fenced in water-holes till you can't rest; and I say, damn such bone and sinew!" By 1885 Nebraska, Kansas and Colorado had enacted laws prohibiting the transportation of Southern cattle across the state borders, and there came an end of the great drives. Ten million cattle and one million horses had been driven from Texas to the cow towns along the railroads. The end of the open range was the end of the Texas trail; and the gradual change from the open range to an era of surveys, homestead claims, and fences, brought the end of the great days of the ranching industry in the Great Plains. There has not been a more colorful frontier than the Wild West of the cattle country; and the frontier never produced a more distinctive craftsman than the cowboy. It is no wonder that romancers have magnified him into a legend.

He was, in his avatar, a Texan. He wore a Stetson, with a huge crown and a wide brim; a flannel shirt, with a bandanna handkerchief loosely encircling his neck; his pants were butternut color, store-bought; his boots high-heeled, small-footed, expensive. He wore a vest, largely because of the storage room of its pockets; he had an extra vest, a sartorial masterpiece of color, worn for the eyes of his lady-love and to dances and celebrations. He wore gloves all year, in summer to protect his hands against the sting of the lariat; leather or goatskin chaps were put over his trousers when there was riding to be done, and for ceremonial occasions. Here and there were decorative gewgaws. He carried a Colt revolver.

He was an untiring worker, skilled in horsemanship, and acquainted with the ways of cattle, as a Mississippi pilot intuitively knew the vagaries of the river. He was loyal when his boss was a product of the West, indifferent and swaggeringly superior before "outsiders"; he was senti-mental, taciturn, terse in thought and expression. He was the possessor of a code, a tradition, and a rich lore of yarns and ballads. He was a hard drinker when he had the chance. And he was damned fond of his horses.

Recruiting their herds from discouraged emigrants, buy-ing footsore cattle along the Overland Trail, pioneers in Montana and Colorado had by the close of the Civil War built up little cattle businesses about the mining camps. In the little towns that sprouted along the roadway of the Union Pacific settlers established small ranches, supplying the army posts on the frontier and occasionally sending a cattle car east. The timely invention of the ice machine, the refrigerator car, and food-canning processes coincided with the beginnings of cattle drives from Texas breeding grounds to northern railway stations. To the pioneer stock-men in the western territories, this combination of circum-stances in a quickening world meant a golden opportunity: to make a ranchmen's domain of the Great West between the farmers' frontier and the Rockies.

"The feeding ground for mighty flocks, the cattle pasture of the world": that was the Westerner's faith in his coun-try, and he bought the lean Texas cattle for fattening and sale, and for breeding. The prolific and resourceful female Longhorn stock was preserved; imported bulls, Hereford, Polled Angus, Short Horn, and Galloway, were bought for

[571]

sires. The growing live stock market of Denver was the first point of contact between the Texas cattlemen and the Westerner. By 1869 a million cattle were grazing within the borders of Colorado Territory, more than half of them in the northern region from Denver to the Wyoming boundary. Longhorns had come into the Wyoming ranges; and the Union Pacific was distributing brochures enthusiastic over the stock-fattening qualities of the "succulent grasses" of the Great West. Early in the seventies Cheyenne, Omaha, and Kansas City, enlivened with the energy born of competition, were bidding for the shipping trade of the western ranches.

Congress did not adapt its land laws to aid the cattlemen. A ranchman could secure no more land than a farmer, and then only by representing himself as an actual settler. The most land that could be claimed from the public domain by any one settler was four hundred eighty acres: one quarter section under the Homestead Act; another hundred and sixty acres at $1.25 an acre under the Preëmption Law, which was not repealed until 1891; and a third quarter section of land under the Timber Culture Act of 1878, which enabled settlers to obtain additional land by planting a certain number of trees on the public domain. Grazing a herd of profitable size required thousands of acres; because he could not get his acreage legally, the cattleman was forced to become a trespasser, and as his ranch was menaced by the encroaching frontier of the dry-farmers, was practically forced to make illegal entries upon the tracts wherein his herds were grazing—that, or to fence off lands of the public domain.

Water rights controlled the range. As a Colorado stockman testified, "Wherever there is any water there is a ranch. On my own ranch I have two miles of running water; that accounts for my ranch being where it is. The next water from me in one direction is twenty-three miles;

now no man can have a ranch between these two places. I have control of the grass, the same as though I owned it." For the carrying out of this code, and because of the necessity for coöperation among stockmen in a vast region in which there were no fences, and over which cattle drifted far from the home ranch, and in protection against thieves —Indian and white—western cattlemen naturally banded themselves into associations. On November 14, 1871, the Wyoming Stock Grazers' Association held its first—and probably its only—annual meeting, at Cheyenne. Two stock growers' associations were in existence in Colorado by 1872. The Laramie County Stock Growers' Association was organized in 1873. Of the several such associations that were organized throughout the cattle country within the next few years, one emerged the most prominent— powerful, far-reaching, and, on occasion, unscrupulous: the Wyoming Stock Growers' Association. In 1884 the legislature of Wyoming Territory made the Association a quasi-public institution, with full control over the cattle industry of Wyoming and with legal means of enforcing its regulations.

In the first years of the open range cattle were dealt in by thousands, on contracts which were simply verbal agreements; or if the formalities of business were to be observed, a few figures might be penciled on the back of a tomato-can label. Buying by "book count" was the common method. Gathering and rebranding to determine the exact number of cattle in a herd was a time-wasting, costly process. "It is safe to say that in many cases not half of the cattle represented on the books were in actual existence," writes an old cattleman. "The owners were honest but the wastage was far greater than any of us expected." But in the fervor of speculation, book counts were the basis of transactions, and were accepted as security by the banks. It was an era of optimism and honesty; in the words of a

[573]

loan agent, "It is fair to say that in those early years we never had a wilful misrepresentation, a single dirty act such as a mean debtor can play up against you."

In the fall of 1871 the plains of western Kansas were stocked with cattle by newcomers who had read that a start with five or eight hundred cattle in this western country, where grass and water were as free as the air, would bring tremendous wealth in four or five years. There was not one of these men who rode the Kansas plains that autumn who did not believe that his fortune was made; the height the prairie grass would surely be by the first of March was measured on table legs as men met to exchange gossip on prices and markets. The Kansas winters were so mild, it was said, that there was hardly any need for coats; and some enthusiasts cited statistics to show that an increase of population in a region brought about an increase in the rainfall. And when the terrible winter was over, the owners rode out from their snowbound ranch houses, and found a half, perhaps a fourth, of their cattle still alive.

The story of the cattle country for the next few years is largely a repetition of the story of these two, with boom times bringing overspeculation and overstocking, to be followed by a devastating winter or a crash in the market. But the influx of cattlemen and cattle continued. Montana and Arizona alike were occupied. Englishmen sought out the plateaus of Colorado, and Americans learned of a new cattle-raising country through English newspapers and magazines. Then from the overcrowded East began an exodus of would-be cattle barons. The excitement of the discovery of precious metals in Dakota Territory and the Indian hostilities in that region in the mid-seventies brought the northern frontier to the attention of the country. Many a gold seeker remained to become a ranchman. The Northern Pacific thrust its way through this northern domain; and its prospectuses described glamorous prospects for live stock ranching along its route. In 1881 General James S. Brisbin, a wizard at multiplying figures, published his *The Beef Bonanza; or, How to Get Rich on the Plains,* a pillar of fire leading optimists into the West.

In the early eighties the demand for stock cattle on the northern ranges transcended the supply. "Every day brings news to the effect that the bulk of the cattle on the northern trail are under contract before leaving Texas," reported the *Breeder's Gazette* in May, 1884. Eastern capital rushed into ranching enterprises; cattle companies multiplied. By 1885 two tendencies were evident: the business was taking on organization from distant headquarters, ceasing to be a frontier enterprise; it was falling a victim to overexpansion.

The rustler, cattle thief and horse thief, was in the new cattle country from its beginning. The simple process of roping and branding an unmarked cow, a "maverick," was soon supplemented by a complex technique of brand-blotting and rebranding, and thievery on an audacious organized basis. Some of the big corporations, in attempting to swell their herds at the expense of the small cattlemen, offered a bounty on each maverick branded for the home ranch; this brought cowboys within one step of actual rustling, and many of them crossed the pale. The next "business step" of the big companies was to permit no cowboy to own a brand of his own, and to pay no more commissions on mavericks. For many high-tempered cowboys this was the final insult. Most rustlers were renegade cowboys.

In the upper Rio Grande country, just west of the Staked Plains, the scum of the frontier—rustlers, outlaws, and refugees from justice—had congregated by 1876. The outcome of the meeting of this backwash of the border country with the cattlemen just then occupying the range was the vicious "Lincoln County War," a series of indiscriminate killings that had the incidental effect of launching Billy the Kid on his bloody notoriety.

After the middle seventies rustlers infested the ranges of Montana and Wyoming; organized in a loose recognition of kinship, they stole horses and ran off cattle almost as they pleased. These gangs were met by Vigilance Committees and by the stockgrowers' associations. Designed first to protect their members at the central markets and to arrange for systematic round-ups, these associations turned naturally to problems of range protection. In 1891 the Wyoming Stock Growers' Association announced, "There has been made public, although it was known to many intimately connected with the range, a system of stealing which in its effects has been not only disastrous to those engaged in the business of cattle raising, but has had a disheartening effect on investors. . . . It is a matter of life or death." Behind the screen of a number of small ranchmen whose herds mingled on the open range with those of the larger companies, homesteaders were filtering into the range. Juries composed of small ranchers and grangers would not convict a rustler accused of stealing stock from the great corporations. In four years cattlemen brought one hundred and eighty suits against rustlers in Johnson County, securing one conviction—that of a rustler who had killed a cow and taken home a quarter of beef, for which offense he was pronounced guilty of petty larceny and assessed the value of the beef. "Cattle baron" was the most odious title in the galaxy of plutocracy.

In the fall of 1891 the Wyoming Stock Growers' Association rallied its strength for one last effort to save the range industry. The state live stock commission, which they dominated, made inspection so stringent that public sentiment was inflamed. In November news came from Johnson County, in northern Wyoming, that two men suspected of rustling had been murdered from ambush; an ex-inspector of the Association was suspected. Matters had taken a more serious turn; and by the spring of 1892

Johnson County was in open revolt against the large ranch-men.

On April 4, 1892, the Association held its regular annual meeting in Cheyenne. On the following afternoon a special train was parked in the Cheyenne yards, composed of a chair car with curtains tightly drawn, three stock cars loaded with saddle horses, and a flat car bearing wagons and camping stuffs. Early the next morning it arrived in Casper, the railway point nearest Johnson County. That day the telegraph wires about Casper were cut.

Twenty-five frontier roustabouts, recruited in Denver, had been imported into Johnson County; with them from Cheyenne had come several leading members of the Wyoming Stock Growers' Association. On the ninth of April the invaders surrounded two suspected rustlers in an isolated ranch house; both were killed. The band started on the next morning for the town of Buffalo, the hotbed of opposition. But the population of the little town met them on the way—a formidable crowd of about two hundred men ready to fight. The cattlemen and their thugs retreated, and were besieged in a ranch house. Word of the plight of some of Wyoming's leading citizens sped to the governor, who wired frantically to President Harrison to order out the federal troops at Fort McKinney, twenty-five miles from Buffalo. On April the thirteenth, just as the embattled citizenry was about to push a buckboard loaded with dynamite against the ranch house, three companies of cavalry rode into the scene; and the Johnson County War was over. The decline of the range cattle industry in Wyoming could not be arrested; and in Montana, where the decline was attended by no such pyrotechnics as in Wyoming, the center of the cattle industry shifted from the eastern ranges back into the central part of the state. Privately owned hay lands and pastures, settlers' dogs and ubiquitous sheep harassed and reduced the

[577]

range industry. John Clay told an editor of the *Montana Stockman and Farmer,* in the late fall of 1897: "The granger and the sheepmen are gradually, but no less surely surrounding the open country. As the red man disappeared, as the buffalo disappeared, so the days of open ranging—that life of rollicking work in summer and loafing in winter —is fast approaching dissolution. The southern part of the state, outside of Custer County, has no large herds left. The farmer has taken up so much of the best valley lands, and is prospering. The large and small cattlemen are getting together, so that it is now a pasture and hay proposition in winter, while there is yet a good deal of summer grazing in the open."

Sheep-ranching after 1870 shifted to the open range, as rising land values and competition with other farm enterprises thinned out the sheep from the East and from most of the Mississippi Valley, sending them into the frontier. Sheep from Utah, California and Oregon were driven to the northern ranges. Mexican breeds were the foundation stock on the open range; Mexicans, for the most part, were the first herders.

In 1880 two-fifths of the country's sheep, and in 1890 nearly one half, were in the West. Within the last decade of the century the sheep industry was concentrated in the Rocky Mountain region. The census of 1900 reported a total of almost forty million sheep in the United States; over twenty-three million were in the Rocky Mountain states, from Montana to New Mexico.

The cowboy despised the sheep herder, and the sheep that in their wanderings nibbled the grass close to the earth and trampled the roots with their sharp hooves, and left about watering places an odor that cattle seemed to like as little as did cowboys. With the beginning of this century came the crisis in the struggle for free range between sheepmen and cattlemen. In the nineties the unwritten law of priority had been invoked in drawing a dead line between sheep range and cattle range. There might have been no more open conflict than the unspoken hostilities which had always existed, if "nesters," irrigationists and dry-farmers, had not preëmpted lands that had seemed destined for grazing or for nothing. Sheepmen and cattlemen were forced close together on a smaller range; and sporadic warfare was the result.

In western Wyoming the sheepmen decided to ignore the dead line set by the cattlemen. An army of cowboys rode in upon the trespassing sheepmen and ousted one hundred thousand sheep from the cattle land; the sheepmen's wagons were burned and the herders given warning never to return. When the sheep were again driven into the Green River country the cowboys met them again, clubbed four thousand to death, and drove the rest across the dead line. Later, at Big Piney, after another invasion of the cattle country, the sheep herders were tied to trees and forced to watch the clubbing of their flocks and the burning of their wagons. In 1907 and again in 1908 sheepmen attempted successfully a mass invasion of the cattle country, on the drive to winter ranges. The cattlemen attempted a few legal prosecutions; and when in January, 1909, these cases were thrown out of court, the cattleman-sheepman conflict came to a long overdue close. The sheepmen had won. On the semiarid ranges, including Federal preserves, sheep are now predominant.

Jonathan Doak, Texan ranchman, brought a rambling interview to a close: "All old-time cattlemen will know why, after running cattle for years, I changed to, or mixed them with, the sheep business. With wool going up and beef going down, with voting a Democratic ticket and electing a Republican President, what could a fellow do but line up for protection? But while I must admit that sheep bring in the 'iron men' I'll always be, at heart, a cattleman.

WESTWARD

A man can never trail a herd across the broad reaches of the great outdoors, lie on his blanket and watch the stars, as the night wind brings the songs of the night guard; hear the welcome, 'Come and get it,' when he feels like a drouth cow looks, nor listen to the honest 'sure will miss you,' of an old-time cowpuncher and ever be anything else at heart but a cowboy and glad of it."

CHAPTER XXXII

LAST SKIRMISHES OF THE CONQUEST

H ALL County, Nebraska, is on the Platte River, where on the north bank the rich bottom lands stretch inland from five to twenty miles. After the Nebraska lands nearest to Iowa markets had been taken up, settlers and speculators turned to the valley of the Platte. Hall County itself, it seemed to a banking house of Washington, D. C., after its executives had done some fevered calculations with a map and a pair of calipers, was the logical location of the permanent capital of the United States; and in July, 1857, the first settlers, a party of thirty-seven sent under the bankers' auspices, came into the region. Immediately they were at work, staking out claims, building cabins, breaking sod. Winter caught them far distant from supplies, with the roads impassable; but there was game in the wilderness, and the emigrants pulled through. The ambitious firm of Chubbs Brothers and Barrows, bankers of Washington, D. C., did not: when hopes were highest, the panic of 1857 suddenly jounced the optimists into bankruptcy.

In July, 1858, twenty emigrants came into the township. Crops had already been planted by the first comers, and the yield was encouraging. In the fall of 1859 the problem of a market was happily solved when the colonists obtained a contract to supply Fort Kearney, forty miles distant, with two thousand bushels of corn. And after the discovery of gold in Colorado, emigrants from Iowa were following the Platte through Hall County; the colonists along the trail quickly learned to sell cabbages at fifty cents each, watermelons for a dollar, and to buy the lame cattle and young calves that encumbered the emigrant trains.

By 1860 there were a hundred and sixteen residents in the county. The Indian wars that seared the West during the years of the Civil War drove almost all the settlers in the Platte Valley back, for a time, beyond the Missouri; but the pioneers in Hall County had built themselves a stockade, and withstood the savage fury. With the end of the Civil War, settlement regathered momentum. In 1866 the Union Pacific invaded the Platte Valley, ruthlessly destroying the timber along the stream, but bringing in its wake confidence and the promise of a market, that populated the lands several townships back from the river. By 1870 over a thousand settlers were in Hall County—two-thirds of them men—and almost six thousand acres were under cultivation. During 1872 practically all the "government land" in Hall County was entered, by homestead or preëmption, and newcomers had either to buy from an old settler or purchase railroad land. Cattlemen preempted two quarter sections in the northern part of Hall County, hoping to use the thousands of acres of unclaimed land about their sections for grazing their herds; but the rapidity of settlement so disgusted them that they gave up their claims and moved westward.

A home seeker's expenses began with his migration into the frontier. To follow the magnet of cheap land required money—a wagon and team, provisions, sundry things. Many an emigrant borrowed from a relative or a friend the money that enabled him to make the journey into the

West and to care for the purchase or registration of his lands. It was thereafter, to an extent that pioneers never previsioned, that money was needed—money to convert the rough prairie into a home and an income-producing farm. Horses and implements, the building of a house (even a sod house) and stables, buying seed and some live stock, breaking the sod, sustenance for the emigrant and his family for the year or so before regular crops could be raised. . . . There were additional financial hardships that first settlers on the prairie had to face: the danger of prairie fires in late July and August; the cost, and uncertainty of getting a physician when one was needed; and, in the Great Plains, the grasshoppers.

But the standard of living was practically the same with all settlers; there was no expensive social competition. And the settlers had the inestimable bond of having the same things to complain of.

In 1869 the grasshoppers brought heart-breaking destruction. After the panic of 1873 banks were in straitened circumstances and chary with their loans. Late in July, 1874, grasshoppers swarmed again over the Great Plains, and devoured almost all the growing corn. And the pioneers' technique had not yet mastered the Great Plains; that mastery has never been complete, and has been attained in its present degree after infinite disappointment and endless struggle. The gasoline engine, barbed wire, water conservation, many another device and adaptation, have marked advances in the conquest of the most stubborn of frontiers, the subhumid regions of the Great Plains.

Generally unfavorable conditions—destructive pests, drouth, financial depression—have at times almost completely stopped the westward movement of pioneers. But unfavorable local conditions—the hail storms in Hall County in 1878, for instance—were discounted by pioneers' optimism. In 1879 the number of newcomers into Hall County was greater than in any year since 1872; but the number of residents who removed from the county was much greater than the average, and the majority of settlers had slipped far back in their struggle for prosperity.

In 1892 a student at Johns Hopkins University carefully assembled data upon the settlement of Hall County, and particularly of Harrison Township within the county, a typical district of the farmers' frontier. North several miles from the Platte, in the "second bottom" lands, the first settlers came into the township in 1872; by the end of that year, entries of some kind had been made on all the government lands. In all, with the abandoning, the forfeiture, and the transfer of interests, one hundred fifty-nine entries were made on those government lands, the last entry being made in February, 1884. Ninety-seven of these claims had been homesteaders'; fourteen others were homestead claims made by soldiers, whose time of service in the army was deducted from the regular requirement of five years' residence; twenty-five claims were preëmptions, twenty-three were timber claims. Of the one hundred ninety settlers who purchased land in the township between 1872 and 1892, one hundred six sold their farms; of the eighty-four who stayed, by 1892 ten had entered the landlord class and were living outside the township.

When Harrison Township was first settled, the Union Pacific was asking four dollars an acre for its railroad lands. In 1878 and 1879, five or six dollars an acre was the current price; within the next five years, land of average quality brought from six to eight dollars an acre. These, of course, were prices for unimproved land sold on long-time installment payments. In 1892 land with good average improvements sold at twenty-five dollars an acre. But at that time 67 per cent of the farms in Harrison Township were mortgaged, 15,720 acres in all, with an average debt against each acre of $8.78, an average debt against each mortgagor of $1,517.32.

Harrison Township was the microcosm: the agricultural West was the greater world mirrored in the little. In these days when the frontier was disappearing, and with it something of the old opportunity and the old liberty to "pack up an' git," discontent was deepened by the discovery that the railroads were a Janus to the West, and that the other face was quite ugly. Townships and farmers along the rights of way had, to encourage railroad-building, subscribed heavily to the stock; when these railroads entered receivership or a reorganization or a merger —and hardly one of them had a level financial history—the original stockholders usually were the sufferers. Where competition was slack, freight rates were pushed upward as high as the traffic would bear. Land withdrawn from the public domain and presented to the railroads was being held for speculative purposes, or was being offered at prices much higher than the government had asked for adjacent lands.

In the first phase of the crusade against the economic ills besetting the agrarian districts of the Mississippi Valley and the Great Plains, the farmer was a member of the National Grange of the Patrons of Husbandry. When in 1872 the real spread of this agrarian society began, the state Granges invaded politics, to win statutory limitations of railroad rates. These enactments were of very diverse efficiency and practicability, but generally were successful in passing the scrutiny of the supreme courts and in establishing the principle that "when private property is devoted to a public use, it is subject to public regulation," in the basic decision of Chief Justice Waite of the United States Supreme Court in 1877. When, encouraged by these victories, the Granges sought further revisions of the economic order, attempting coöperative buying and selling, and even

[585]

the coöperative manufacture of farm machinery, the National Grange walked into the valley of shadows.

Beginning in 1876 and in every national election thereafter (except the election of 1888), through the debacle of Bryan's candidacy in 1896, embattled farmers drove against the top of the national structure. "A new political organization of the people, by the people, and for the people, to restrain the aggressions of combined capital upon the rights and interests of the masses, to reduce taxation, correct abuses, and to purify all departments of the Government," as the National Greenback party announced itself, made a half-hearted rush at the heights in 1876. In 1880 General James B. Weaver of Iowa, one of several Greenbackers elected to Congress in 1878, took up the presidential standard and made an honorable attempt "to visit the various sections of the Union and talk to the people": large crops and good prices lulled western farmers into content, and Weaver received far fewer votes than he deserved. The nomination of General Benjamin F. Butler by Anti-Monopolists and Greenbackers in 1884 was everybody's mistake.

"The limiting of the legal-tender quality of greenbacks, the changing of currency-bonds into coin-bonds, the demonetization of the silver dollar, the excepting of bonds from taxation, the contraction of the circulating medium, the proposed forced resumption of specie payments, and the prodigal waste of the public lands" was the list, drawn up by an insurgent convention of 1878, of economic tendencies that every good farmer should denounce. In the "heart-breaking nineties" this *strafe* list, little modified, had reënforced significance; for the prices of grains were at low levels, and the cost of transportation and the interest on mortgages maintained their old adamant uniformity. The People's Party, committed to paper-money panaceas and, perhaps, to Mary Elizabeth Lease's advice to Kansas farmers, "raise less corn and more HELL," elected two United States senators—from South Dakota and Kansas—in 1890; and in 1892 its candidate, General Weaver, polled more than a million votes. Fusion in state elections with the under-dog Democrats allowed Populists to sweep the field in Colorado, Idaho, Kansas, Nevada, and North Dakota. In 1896 the strength of the malcontents was augmented by the political influence of silver-mining interests. Unrestricted coinage of silver was another way to obtain "cheap money"; and the agrarian crusaders readily followed the free-silver interests when those interests captured the Democratic party. But not the agrarian crusaders of the Northwest, Iowa, Minnesota, and North Dakota: dusting themselves free of Bryan's alliance of the Old South with the agrarian and mining frontiers of the West, they joined with the Old Northwest and the conservative East to settle the election of 1896.

After the admission of Colorado in 1876, no stars were added to the national flag for thirteen years. Western territories ripened; but they remained territories. They were restive under the restraints of their inferior status. Congress could interfere in local affairs even to the extent of vetoing a legislative enactment. All the important executive and judicial officers of a territory were appointed by Congress; and, owing nothing to the people whom they governed, they reflected that detachment in their official acts. And all the political carpetbaggers were not in the South.

Democrats in Congress were resolved not to increase the strength of their political opponents by creating new states. The West was the stronghold of nationalism; and, for all the peccancies of Grant's administration, the Republican party was popularly identified as the protector of the nation. Remembering those three votes of Colorado's electors for Hayes, a partisan block barred the way of Western territories. The Democratic majority in the House of Representatives was overthrown in the elections of 1888; and the blockade was lifted. Dakota, by human and physical geography evidently designed to become two states; Washington, thriving with the exploitation of its natural resources, the mines, the salmon, the timber, and the development of wheat growing and sheep herding; Idaho, Montana, and Wyoming, territories created by the eastward push of the miners' frontier and developed by the live stock industries, were awaiting full statehood. So was Utah, aspirant for statehood for forty years, but barred out by social prejudice against the Mormon doctrine of plural marriage. So was New Mexico, organized as a territory in 1850 and given its present limits by the creation of Arizona Territory in 1863.

The "Omnibus Bill," enacted on February 22, 1889, was an enabling act for four prospective states—North and South Dakota, Washington, and Montana. In Wyoming and Idaho constitutional conventions were blithely assembled, just as if Congress had authorized them; so that in the summer of 1889 constitutional conventions were in session in six western towns. One of these, the convention in South Dakota, ratified a constitution devised and adopted in 1885; the others framed new documents.

Each state was required to embody in its constitution "irrevocable pledges": that claims to public lands and tribal lands should expressly be renounced; that there should be perfect toleration of religious sentiment; that systems of public schools "free from sectarian control" should be established. These and other guarantees required by Congress were complaisantly written into the six constitutions. These constitutions had much else in common. Most of the state boundaries were highly artificial; most of the citizens had been born in other states. Gwin Hicks of Washington was the only delegate at any of these conventions born within

[588]

the territory whose future constitution he was helping to frame. The constitutions drafted in 1889 were only incidentally concerned with purely local matters. They attacked the broader problems of state government; together these constitutions offer a résumé of western ideas at that moment when the frontier line disappeared from government maps.

Territorial legislatures had been unnecessarily lavish in their expenditures; unchecked by constitutional restraints, they had become brazen in their peccadilloes. They had failed to represent even the average sentiment of their constituents. Delegates in 1889 were eager to reduce legislators' perquisites, and to engird the legislative power with prohibitions. Declared a member of the South Dakota convention, "The object of constitutions is to limit the legislature." The constitutions, therefore, were bulky documents, crammed with legislation that ordinarily would have been in the statute books rather than in the fundamental law. There were to be commissions and bureaus in abundance— of public lands, of public instruction, of agriculture and labor, of railway relations, boards of water control, of arbitration, of pardons, of charities, bureaus of statistics, of immigration, of public health. To the officers of these bureaus the people of the western states entrusted a great part of the affairs of government—to set these highly important affairs out of the reach of the legislatures. Legislators were barred from any personal interest in contracts for supplies for the state departments; and members personally interested in the outcome of any bill were generally required to announce the fact and to refrain from voting. Elaborate clauses were framed to prevent the trading of votes, logrolling by legislators, and "corrupt solicitation" by outsiders. Three constitutions struck at legislators who accepted passes from the railroads.

The power of the executive was invaded: he was entrusted

with almost no privileges of appointment. The judiciary, the ordinary administrative offices, most of the commission chairmanships were elective posts. Each of the constitutions modified in some way the traditional method of trial by jury. In South Dakota, Idaho, and Washington, a three-fourths majority was made sufficient for a verdict in all civil cases; in Montana, a two-thirds majority in civil cases and in criminal misdemeanors. Governors and judges were hedged about to keep them out of politics. It was an "epoch of reforming human nature by constitutional limitation."

Each state made generous provision for a university as the apex of its educational system. "Practical" colleges in agriculture, forestry and metallurgy were especially favored. Wyoming and Idaho sponsored a novelty: the legislature was authorized to require at least three years' public school attendance of every child not educated by other means.

The rapid unification of the country through railway development had created many a monopoly; and banks and common carriers were destined for particularly rigorous treatment at the hands of these delegates of 1889. No corporation was permitted to issue stocks or bonds "except for labor done, services performed, or money or property actually received." As natural corollaries to anticorporation legislation were a number of measures designed to protect the laborer. Legislatures attempted to protect the miner from unsafe working conditions, and were especially solicitous for laboring women and children. Idaho and Wyoming made eight hours a lawful day's work on all state and municipal enterprises. The Wyoming constitution hinted at a minimum wage in its declaration that the rights of labor should have "just protection through laws calculated to secure to the laborer proper rewards for his service." The importation of Pinkerton "detectives" by capitalists to overawe strikers invoked in five of the six states measures to prevent such outrages.

Prohibition and female suffrage were ardently discussed in the constitutional conventions. In Wyoming female suffrage was given its first constitutional recognition. Every safeguard that could be devised was called into use in an attempt to insure the people against excessive public indebtedness, excessive taxation, and wastage of public revenue.

Early in November, 1889, the four states of the Omnibus Bill were by presidential proclamation introduced into the Union. Wyoming and Idaho were admitted in the next July.

The work begun by the Land Act of 1785 and the Ordinance of 1787 was substantially completed. Since the state of Kentucky had been created out of the back country of Virginia, twenty-nine states had been admitted into the Union. Only four additional states were to be anticipated; and one of these, Utah, was well past its frontier years.

Oklahoma comprised the southern tip of that vast tract which had once been set aside as the permanent home of the Indians. With the passing of the buffalo, the seventeen thousand Indians who occupied this area of twenty-five million acres had no use for the greater part of the lands; and cattlemen invaded the Territory, leasing grazing room for their herds. Railways entering Texas from the north had to cross the Indian Territory, profitless trackage until the country should be developed by white settlement. Two lobbyists in Washington began a campaign of advertising, agitation, and chicanery to open the Territory, in 1879; and a third, David L. Payne, developed his own fortune by promoting a sievelike "association" of prospective land buyers. Several times Payne and a group of followers attempted to crash the military barrier, but each time the soldiers found them and ejected them.

In 1885 the Oklahoma "boomers" succeeded in a bit of spite work, the eviction of the cattlemen from their leased lands by presidential proclamation; and in the same year Congress passed a resolution authorizing the President "to open negotiations with the Creeks, Seminoles and Cherokees for the purpose of opening to settlement under the homestead laws, the unassigned land in the Indian Territory." Thereby Congress gave the first definite encouragement to the demand for the opening of Oklahoma. The agitation gained momentum in the western states; legislatures passed resolutions in favor; but two attempts to gain action from Congress failed, as the opposition maintained that to organize Oklahoma into a territory before a clear title had been procured from the Indians was equivalent to coercion. In 1889 treaties with the Creeks and the Seminoles ceded a large section of the Indian Territory to the United States; and President Harrison proclaimed the country open to homestead entry at noon, April 22, 1889. At that hour the cordon of soldiers along the boundary gave way to the rush of home seekers. A year later Congress established the Territory of Oklahoma, whose limits were extended from time to time as additional Indian lands were made available.

At the Latter-day Saints' convocation of 1890 polygamy was formally renounced. That unique barrier disposed of, Utah was admitted as a state in 1894. Oklahoma, having aggrandized the whole of the Indian Territory by a complex arrangement with the tribes, was admitted to full statehood in 1907. There remained New Mexico and Arizona; these were belatedly admitted in 1912, Arizona trailing last because President Taft demanded that the provision of its constitution authorizing the recall of judges be stricken out.

That year, 1912, marked the end of the frontier in another sense; then, embodied in the Progressive Party, the political ideas of the pioneers reached the climax of their

rise and the beginning of their fall. Geographical section-
alism as a political force entered its present decline, and
slowly, at first covertly, then openly, another line of political cleavage assumed primary importance: rural interests
against urban interests. If the West—the states that are
closest to their frontier days—seems to persist as a frontier
entity, that mirage exists because most of these states are
predominantly agricultural. The frontier is transitional:
hunter, fur trader, Indian fighter, freighter, prospector,
scout, river pilot, lumberjack, stagecoach driver, cowboy,
have their day; and the farmer survives. The last of the
pioneers, the farmer holds fast to the earth; the vanguard
of the conquest is gone, and the army of occupation is
entrenched.

The national land policy gave the farmer an incalculable
advantage. The public domain was tendered, in fee simple,
to the homesteader; and he grabbed it, with small thanks.
As, after 1889, the long-generous vessel of national wealth,
the public domain, approached low depth, land lust did not
diminish. The opening of an Indian reservation to settlement, the completion of an irrigation enterprise, brought
crowds of home seekers ready to claim their quarter sections
of government land. Politicians in the western states found
the surest way to the hearts of constituents to be the bring-
ing-in of federal capital to make subarid districts of the
national domain into arable lands.

The first attempt of the national government to open its
arid regions to settlement produced the Desert Land Act
of 1877, whereby tracts of six hundred forty acres were
offered at $1.25 an acre on condition that irrigation be
introduced—an act that gave ranchmen, little interested in
irrigation, opportunity to get title to the nucleus of a ranch,
and gave shady individuals a chance to organize irrigation
companies for speculative purposes only. An act of 1894
made water rights inseparable from landrights, and pro-

vided for the organization of extensive irrigation enterprises, the private company ultimately to surrender ownership to the water users' associations, under the supervision of state land commissions. By the Reclamation Act of 1902 the revenue from sales of public land was set aside for use in irrigation projects conducted by the government itself. The provisions of the Homestead Act were made to apply to the settlement of lands made arable by federal enterprise.

The revival of western railway construction after the Panic of 1873 hastened the disappearance of the frontier. The "Golden Spike Special" of the Northern Pacific sped across the continent in 1883. The Canadian Pacific was finished in 1885, and the Great Northern in 1893. To the south the Southern Pacific spanned the West in a great network. Every fair-sized section of the West was brought within reach; and with greater access the railroads brought wider publicity. Behind the advance line of pioneer farmers, other settlers were coming into uncrowded regions.

Even the XIT ranch of the Texas panhandle, three million acres in expanse, surrendered to the grangers. Tascosa, on the rim of the XIT ("ten counties in Texas") domain, was reached by the Fort Worth & Denver Railroad in November, 1887; and the Santa Fe ran its first scheduled train into the panhandle on January 1, 1888. An extension of the Rock Island was expected; and the *Tascosa Pioneer* crowed, "When the Rock Island hits the Panhandle, when Greek meets Greek, then look out all about you. . . . Tascosa will sell more whiskey than for any previous two years in her history—when the Rock Island comes." The cattlemen of the panhandle recognized the signs of the times, and did not attempt to stay the transition.

"Wagons and wagons with white tops, rope-bottomed chairs, tow-heads, brindle cows, yellow dogs and a pervading air of restlessness have poured through this week in the direction suggested by Horace Greeley," reported the *Pioneer* on June 9, 1888; and the two railroads, with active colonization bureaus, were bringing in other imigrants. And the *Pioneer*, bravely clinging to its western flavor in the face of the immigration that was to demand dullness in its newspapers, announced:

IT IS COMMON TALK
That the laying in of a line of baby carriages by our merchants is a pointer as to the gradually changing order of our population and indicates that it is generally understood whither we are drifting.

The XIT Company began in 1901 to sell tracts to cattlemen, making commensurate reductions in its herds. In 1905, when newspapers over the country were reciting the beauties and opportunities of Texas in an endeavor to check the immigration of American farmers into Canada, the company began the sale of small tracts to farmers; eight hundred thousand acres were disposed of in plots averaging about two hundred acres. One high-pressure worker for the XIT Company, George C. Wright, was caught in action by one who wrote, "I never saw anything to equal Wright's organization. He shipped down a lot of automobiles for use in showing his prospectors [*sic*] around. He would unload five and six hundred prospectors at a time, most of whom were from Illinois, Iowa, Indiana, Oklahoma and Missouri. I don't think he sold any land to men who did not see it, but I don't believe he ever tried to sell to one who did not buy. Wright paid five dollars an acre for this first land and paid his agents five and six dollars for selling it. It was sold at twenty-five dollars an acre. Besides additional options from the Syndicate [who owned the XIT ranch], Wright bought 100,000 acres from Bill Halsell at Spring Lake, four leagues from C. F. Harding, and 80,000 acres from Tom Kelly. He sold

[595]

every acre of this in a little over two years and must have cleaned a million dollars on it."

But since too much of their lands entrusted on option to development companies was bought by bankers and capitalists, and the Company wished to do its own speculating, the office of Land Commissioner for the XIT was created. Hotels were built for the convenience of home seekers, and sustained colonization work was carried on. In 1912 the last remnant of the XIT herds was sold.

The displaced frontier has this revenge upon the survivor, the farmer: the symbol of the West, the romantic image that instantly the mind's eye sees when the West is mentioned, is the cowboy.

The final skirmish in the conquest of the frontier will be a cultural one. But the present skirmish in the mountain ranges of the Northwest is not that: it is physical war, a war of extermination against the wild horses, and the tale of it is dust in a gentleman's throat. There are now five slaughterhouses licensed especially for this business. The work began in 1920. As a person in Montana, one E. W. Wayman, has just announced, "Range horses do not contribute their just share of maintenance for county and state government through taxation as compared with other live stock interests, but consume a large portion of the grasses which are needed by the livestock interests which pay the greater proportion of livestock taxation."

The proprietors of these slaughterhouses don't like to admit visitors. They seem uncomfortable. Cranks write them letters, they say; sentimental old women come sniffing around, and reporters distort what they're told. It's a business—that's all, just a business. Horses were captured on the range, and brought by rail to the canning house. Five dollars for the general run above yearlings, two dollars and a half for yearlings. They were shot—behind the ear—quartered, slashed, and cured, pickled, or frozen, and packed in tin cans. There is a dependable market for them in Europe.

Russell Lord was talking to a railroad man in the freight yard of one of these canneries. "A band of some sixty horses was being driven up the road. They were not of the bunch that had come off the box cars but horses rounded up within a hundred-mile radius by these riders, the railroad man said, and marched in slowly afoot. 'Three hundred dollars will keep those five birds in liquor a week or so,' he estimated. 'Then they'll ride out again.' One man rode ahead of the herd, four in the rear. It was a sorry group of horsemen. They rode heads down. The demeanor of the driven horses was in kind—shambling, beaten."

This is a casual episode at the fag end of the war against the wilderness—an episode that happens to emphasize the casual cruelty which is a vagrant by-current of the westward movement. But the pioneer's conquest was no more cruel than the Nature it vanquished, and not remotely as harsh as the industrial conquest of men. The frontier had, all its own, a glamor and a dignity; and it nurtured in the men who loved it two splendid things—honesty and personal liberty.

NOTES ON MATERIALS

These jottings make no pretense to completeness in any sense. The handbook which F. J. Turner and Frederic Merk devised for the use of their Harvard students, *List of References on the History of the West* (Cambridge, 1922, rev. ed.), is at present the closest approach to a bibliography of the westward movement; and the following paragraphs may play a double part: casual footnotes to my narrative, and marginalia to the Turner-Merk handbook.

A few books may be called generally useful: F. L. Paxson, *History of the American Frontier, 1763-1893* (Boston and New York, 1924); Seymour Dunbar, *A History of Travels in America* (Indianapolis, 1915); P. W. Bidwell and J. J. Falconer, *History of Agriculture in the Northern United States, 1620-1860* (Washington, 1925); B. H. Hibbard, *A History of the Public Land Policies* (New York, 1924); Cardinal Goodwin, *The Trans-Mississippi West, 1803-1853* (New York, 1922). These last two titles express personal choices in somewhat crowded fields.

PART I

A. H. Buffinton, "The Policy of Albany and English Westward Expansion," *Mississippi Valley Historical Review,* VIII (March, 1922), 327-366, and "New England and the Western Fur Trade, 1629-1675," *Publications of the Colonial Society of Massachusetts,* XVIII (January, 1916), 160-192, are excellent studies. Supplementing the former monograph are Peter Wraxhall's *An Abridgement of the Indian Affairs* . . . , edited with a valuable introduction by C. H. McIlwain (Cambridge, 1915), and Helen Broshar's paper, "The First Push Westward of the Albany Traders," *Mississippi Valley Historical Review,* VII (December, 1920), 228-241. W. B. Weeden, *Economic and Social History of New England, 1620-1789*

(Boston, 1891), includes scattered paragraphs on the fur trade. Thomas Morton's *The New England Canaan,* edited by C. F. Adams, Jr. (Boston, 1883) is worth any one's time.

A. J. Morrison, "The Virginia Indian Trade to 1673," *William and Mary Quarterly Historical Magazine,* I (2nd ser., October, 1921), 217-236, loosely strings together an assortment of quotations; and C. A. Hanna, *The Wilderness Trail* (New York, 1911), offers the fullest account of the earliest Pennsylvania traders.

F. J. Turner, "The First Official Frontier of the Massachusetts Bay," *Publications of the Colonial Society* of Massachusetts, XVII (April, 1914), 250-271, and "The Old West," *Proceedings of the State Historical Society of Wisconsin* (1908), 184-233, are invaluable. It should hardly be necessary at this date to refer to Mr. Turner's essay upon "The Significance of the Frontier"; its influence is unescapable.

P. A. Bruce, *Institutional History of Virginia in the Seventeenth Century* (New York, 1910) devotes a chapter to the military frontier. An anonymous description of "The Present State and Government of Virginia," *Collections of the Massachusetts Historical Society* V (1st ser., reprint, 1835), 124-166, was written between 1696 and 1698. The extension of the Virginia frontier in the eighteenth century is the subject matter of Fairfax Harrison, "Western Explorations between Lederer and Spotswood," *Virginia Magazine of History and Biography,* XXX (October, 1922), 323-340; C. E. Kemper, "The Settlement of the Valley," *ibid.,* XXX (April, 1922), 169-182; L. K. Koontz, *The Virginia Frontier, 1754-1763* (Baltimore, 1925). The two most valuable studies of the southern frontier are C. W. Alvord and Lee Bidgood, *The First Explorations of the Trans-Allegheny Region by the Virginians, 1650-1674* (Cleveland, 1912), and V. W. Crane, *The Southern Frontier, 1670-1732* (Durham, 1929).

Ann Maury, *Memoirs of a Huguenot Family* (New York, 1853), contains, in the diary of John Fontaine, the only account of Spotswood's expedition of 1716. Spotswood's own letters comprise the first two volumes of the *Collections of the Virginia Historical Society.*

PART II

Joseph Doddridge, *Notes on the Settlement and Indian Wars, of the Western Parts of Virginia and Pennsylvania for the Years 1763 until 1783* (Wellsburg, 1824) and Philip Tome, *Pioneer Life;*

or *Thirty Years a Hunter* (Buffalo, 1854) have such merit as pictures of backwoods life that local historians have indolently quoted entire chapters from one or the other—sometimes without the bother of quotation marks. These volumes are useful corollaries: U. J. Jones, *History of the Early Settlement of the Juniata Valley* (Philadelphia, 1856); I. D. Rupp, *The History and Topography of Dauphin . . . and Cumberland Counties* (Lancaster, Pa., 1846); A. W. Patterson, *History of the Backwoods, or the Region of the Ohio* (Pittsburgh, 1843); J. B. Walker, *Experiences of Pioneer Life* (Chicago, 1881); W. J. McKnight, *Pioneer History of Northwestern Pennsylvania* (Philadelphia, 1905); James Veech, *The Monongahela of Old* (Pittsburgh, 1858).

Old misconceptions about John Peter Salley are dispelled by Fairfax Harrison, "The Virginians on the Ohio and Mississippi in 1742," *Virginia Magazine of History and Biography,* XXX (April, 1922), 203-222. A. J. Withers, *Chronicles of Border Warfare* (Clarksburg, W. Va., 1831), details one of these folk-recollections of Salley's journey, and R. G. Thwaites, in his edition of the *Chronicles* (Cincinnati, 1895), adds variants told to Lyman Draper.

A list of the western land grants of the governor and council of Virginia, 1745-1754, evidently written by the clerk of the council, is in the Manuscript Division of the Library of Congress.

The original journals of Christopher Gist and Dr. Thomas Walker make up the thirteenth volume of the Filson Club series: *First Explorations of Kentucky* (Louisville, 1898). The Loyal Land Company settlements have been described by Lyman Chalkey, "Before the Gates of the Wilderness Road," *Virginia Magazine of History and Biography,* XXX (April, 1922), 183-202.

J. S. Bassett, "The Regulators of North Carolina (1765-1771)," American Historical Association *Report* for 1894, 141-212, is a classic of careful research. The weird and wonderful sketch of the Regulation in Miss C. S. Skinner's *Pioneers of the Old Southwest* (New Haven, 1919), is not. Archibald Henderson, *The Star of Empire* (Durham, 1919), is useful.

These excellent publications of the Filson Club have contributed largely to my sketch of the beginnings of settlement in Kentucky: G. W. Ranck, *Boonesborough* (Louisville, 1901); Thomas Speed, *The Wilderness Road* (Louisville, 1886); and the memorial volume, *The Century of Kentucky, Wednesday, June 1, 1892* (Louisville, 1892). Later in this section I have made use of Thomas Speed, *The Political Club [of] Danville, Kentucky* (Louisville, 1894).

Of the several semipopular accounts of Boone and his fellows, H. A. Bruce, *Daniel Boone and the Wilderness Road* (New York, 1910) is the best. Temple Bodley's *George Rogers Clark, His Life and Public Services* (Boston and New York, 1926), is practically a compilation from Clark's own writings, punctuated by keen analyses. Of the several biographies of Clark published within the last few years, J. A. James, *The Life of George Rogers Clark* (Chicago, 1928), shows the most extensive research.

PART III

B. A. Hinsdale, *The Old Northwest* (New York, 1888), Jacob Burnet, *Notes on the Early Settlement of the Northwestern Territory* (New York and Cincinnati, 1847), and J. A. Barrett, *Evolution of the Ordinance of 1787* (New York, 1891), are supplemented by the published letters of Manasseh Cutler, Rufus Putnam, and John Cleves Symmes. Of the several monographs dealing with the importance of the West in this transitional era, an outstanding one is A. C. McLaughlin, "The Western Posts and the British Debts," *Yale Review,* III (February, 1895), 408-424, and IV (May, 1895), 58-79.

S. C. Williams, *History of the Lost State of Franklin* (Johnson City, Tenn., 1924), replaces G. H. Alden, "The State of Franklin," *American Historical Review,* VIII (January, 1903), 271-289, and every other account. Archibald Henderson, *The Conquest of the Old Southwest* (New York, 1920), is the best of several unimpressive semipopular histories of the Old Southwest. Mr. Williams has just published his *Beginnings of West Tennessee* (Johnson City, 1930).

Francis W. Halsey's *The Old New York Frontier* (New York, 1901) is the most useful of his several excellent volumes. The Phelps-Gorham purchase, reviewed by Henry O'Reilly, *Settlement in the West: Sketches of Rochester, with Incidental Notices of Western New York* (Rochester, 1843), is the starting point of Paul D. Evans' intensive study, *The Holland Land Company* (Buffalo, 1924). William Cooper, *A Guide in the Wilderness,* a compilation of letters written by Judge Cooper to an Irish friend, was originally published in Dublin in 1810; a reprint (Rochester, 1897) is not quite so rare. James Fenimore Cooper, "Chronicles of Cooperstown" is available in S. T. Livermore, *A Condensed History of Cooperstown* (Albany, 1862). The political significance of the concentration of western New York lands in the hands of gentlemen

is discussed in D. R. Fox, *The Decline of Aristocracy in the Politics of New York* (New York, 1919).
Of the numerous articles upon frontier influences in American religion, probably that by J. M. Thomas in the New Jersey Historical Society *Proceedings,* XI (January, 1926), 1-18, is the sanest. In describing the Revival of 1800, I have made particular use of Richard M'Nemar, *The Kentucky Revival* (Albany, 1808); C. C. Cleveland, *The Great Revival in the West, 1797-1805* (Chicago, 1916); David Elliott, *The Life of the Reverend Elisha Macurdy* (Allegheny, Pa., 1848); and Z. F. Smith, "The Great Revival of 1800," *Register of the Kentucky Historical Society,* VII (May, 1909), 19-35. Revivals are discussed, very respectfully, in F. G. Beardsley, *History of American Revivals* (New York, 1904), and less respectfully in G. C. Loud, *Evangelized America* (New York, 1928). A careful monograph has just been published: W. M. Gewehr, *The Great Awakening in Virginia, 1740-1790* (Durham, 1930).

In H. M. Brackenridge, *History of the Western Insurrection in Western Pennsylvania* (Pittsburgh, 1859), Judge Brackenridge's own published account, written mainly to defend his own part in the Insurrection, is revised and extended by his son. William Findley's *History of the Insurrection in the Four Western Counties of Pennsylvania* (Philadelphia, 1796), is spirited account by a participant. A third participant, General John Neville, is indirectly represented by a lineal descendant, Neville B. Craig, who devoted much space in his curious periodical, *The Olden Time* (Pittsburgh, 1846-1847) to whitewashing the family tree.

Resolutions and remonstrances of Westerners affected by the Spanish control of New Orleans have been reprinted in the *William and Mary College Quarterly,* II (2nd ser., October, 1922), 239-256; and others, with an introduction by Mr. Bodley, in the thirty-first volume of the Filson Club publications (Louisville, 1926). I. J. Cox and J. C. Parish have been the busiest of several historians who have attempted to ferret out the Spanish intrigues with the American border folk. A. J. Whitaker's study, *The Spanish-American Frontier: 1783-1795* (Boston and New York, 1927), has enough valuable information to excuse its pomposity. F. A. Ogg, *The Opening of the Mississippi* (New York, 1904), obstinately refuses to become antiquated. Louis Pelzer, "Economic Factors in the Acquisition of Louisiana," *Mississippi Valley Historical Association Proceedings,* VI (1912-1913), 109-128, is a thoughtful interpretation.

NOTES ON MATERIALS

A biographical sketch of Arthur St. Clair, by Ellis Beals, is in the *Western Pennsylvania Historical Magazine,* XII (April, 1929), 75-96; in the same issue are several pages of advertisements taken from early Pittsburgh newspapers. S. J. Killikelly, *The History of Pittsburgh* (Pittsburgh, 1906), is one of the best of local histories; but N. B. Craig, *History of Pittsburgh* (Pittsburgh, 1851) still holds interest.

A. B. Hulbert, *Waterways of Western Expansion* (Cleveland, 1903) amiably discusses early navigation upon the Ohio. Zadoc Cramer's occasional *Navigator* (Pittsburgh, v. d.) is invaluable. O. A. Rothert, *The Outlaws of Cave-In-Rock* (Cleveland, 1924), develops a restricted topic exhaustively.'

PART IV

F. G. Teggart, "Notes Supplementary to Any Edition of Lewis and Clark," American Historical Association *Report* for 1908, I, 185-195, and A. P. Nasatir, "Anglo-Spanish Rivalry on the Upper Missouri," *Mississippi Valley Historical Review,* XVI (December, 1929-March, 1930), 359-382 and 507-528, present the Spanish precedents for the expedition of Lewis and Clark. That epochal exploration is best followed in the edition of the *Journals* edited by R. G. Thwaites (New York, 1904-1905). Contemporary explorations are described in I. J. Cox, "Exploration of the Louisiana Frontier, 1803-1806," American Historical Association *Report* for 1904, 151-174; and in *Documents Relating to the Purchase and Exploration of Louisiana* (Boston and New York, 1904). H. E. Bolton, "Papers of Z. M. Pike," *American Historical Review,* XIII (July, 1908), 798-827, brought forward new materials but settled no questions.

J. W. Pratt, *Expansionists of 1812* (New York, 1925), with D. R. Anderson, "The Insurgents of 1811," in the American Historical Association *Report* for 1911, I, 167-176, and C. B. Coleman, "The Ohio Valley in the Preliminaries of the War of 1812," in the *Mississippi Valley Historical Review,* VII (June, 1920), 39-50, establish the western influences toward the declaration of war.

The five volumes comprising *The Centennial History of Illinois* (Springfield, 1917-1920) are the most comprehensive and scholarly history of any state. The first two—S. J. Buck, *Illinois in 1818,* and T. C. Pease, *The Frontier State*—admirably describe the frontier era; and the third, A. C. Cole, *The Era of the Civil War,* begins with a chapter upon "The Passing of the Frontier."

The journals of David Thomas, *Travels through the Western Country in the Summer of 1816* (Auburn, N. Y., 1819); Estwick Evans, *A Pedestrious Tour* (Concord, N. H., 1819), and William Faux, *Memorable Days in America* (London, 1823), offer pictures of life and labor in the Old Northwest between 1816 and 1820. I have borrowed Mr. Burke Williams' conversation from John Regan, *The Western Wilds of America* (Edinburgh, 1859).

L. K. Mathews, *The Expansion of New England* (Boston, 1909) and R. I. Purcell, *Connecticut in Transition* (Washington, 1918), are pioneering monographs in a field which scholars are just now invading.

Daniel Boone's western "palatinate" has been described by W. S. Bryan, in the *Missouri Historical Review,* III (1909), 89-98 and 198-205. Of the many other useful articles in that quarterly, two have been of particular value to me: Jonas Viles, "Missouri in 1820," XV (October, 1920), 36-52; and W. B. Stevens, "The Travail of Missouri for Statehood," *ibid.,* 3-35. Mr. Stevens' amazingly malwritten history of his state takes none of the charm from W. F. Switzler, *History of Missouri* (St. Louis, 1881); and J. T. Scharf, *History of St. Louis City and County* (Philadelphia, 1883), is as unique in its own field as the classic work of H. M. Chittenden, *The American Fur Trade of the Far West* (New York, 1902).

T. B. Searight, *The Old Pike* (Uniontown, Pa., 1894), is the bulwark of later studies of the Cumberland Road. A. B. Hulbert, *The Cumberland Road* (Cleveland, 1904), traces construction west of Pennsylvania; and J. S. Young, *A Political and Constitutional Study of the Cumberland Road* (Chicago, 1904), describes its legislative history. F. L. Paxson, "The Gateways of the Old Northwest," *Michigan Pioneer and Historical Collections,* XXXVIII (1912), 139-148, points out the common significance of the Cumberland Road and the Erie Canal.

Journals of travel upon the Santa Fe Trail are reproduced in *The Journal of Jacob Fowler,* edited by Elliott Coues (New York, 1898); "Captain Thomas [!] Becknell, 'Journal from Boone's Lick to Sante Fe,'" *Missouri Historical Review,* IV (January, 1910), 65-81; Major Alphonso Wetmore, "Journal," *ibid.,* VIII (July, 1914), 177-197; M. M. Marmaduke, "Journal," *ibid.,* VI (October, 1911), 1-10. T. J. Farnham describes an expedition in 1839 in his *Travels in the Great Western Prairies* (London, 1843). Most invaluable is Josiah Gregg, *The Commerce of the Prairies* (2nd ed., New York, 1845). J. T. Lee, "The Authorship of Gregg's *Commerce of the Prairies,*" *Mississippi Valley His-*

torical Review, XVI (March, 1930), 451-466, demonstrates that the pioneering merchant did not write his own book, but that "John Bigelow took the 'log of the ship,' or field notes of a busy explorer and created therefrom a readable book." Pedro Vial's journal is translated in Louis Houck, *The Spanish Regime in Mexico* (Chicago, 1909). The military and economic effects of the Santa Fe trade are described in F. F. Stephens, "Missouri and the Santa Fe Trade," *Missouri Historical Review,* X (July, 1916), 234-262, and XI (April, 1917), 289-312. Fred S. Perrine, "Military Escorts on the Santa Fe Trail," *New Mexico Historical Quarterly,* II (April, July, 1927), 175-193 and 269-304, is a convenient summary; original records in this connection are found in P. St. George Cooke, *Scenes and Adventures in the Army* (Philadelphia, 1857), and "Report of committee appointed to prepare a correct map of the old Santa Fe Trail across Kansas," Kansas State Historical Society *Report* (1913), 107-125.

PART V

E. C. Barker has embodied several of his earlier monographs in *The Life of Stephen F. Austin* (Dallas, 1925). M. A. Hatcher, *The Opening of Texas to Foreign Settlement, 1801-1821* (Austin, 1912) has been particularly useful to me. W. C. Binkley, "New Mexico and the Texan Santa Fe Expedition," *Southwestern Historical Quarterly,* XXVII (October, 1923), 85-106, and T. M. Marshall, "Commercial Aspects of the Texas Santa Fe Expedition," *ibid.* (January, 1917), 242-259, are scholarly footnotes to G. W. Kendall, *Narrative of the Texan Santa Fe Expedition* (New York, 1844). The relation of land speculation to the acquisition of Texas is discussed in C. A. and M. R. Beard, *The Rise of American Civilization* (New York, 1927).

The *Quarterly of the Oregon Historical Society* has printed, in addition to several valuable journals and documents, some unusually good studies: F. G. Young, "The Oregon Trail," I (December, 1900), 339-370; H. C. Dale, "The Organization of the Oregon Emigrating Companies," XVI (September, 1915), 205-227; J. R. Robertson, "The Genesis of Political Authority and of a Commonwealth Government in Oregon," I (March, 1900), 3-59; J. R. Wilson, "The Oregon Question," I (June, September, 1900), 111-131 and 215-252.

Cardinal Goodwin has written compact accounts of the trend of

settlement into the Mississippi Valley: "The Movement of American
Settlers into Wisconsin and Minnesota," *Iowa Journal of History
and Politics,* XVII (July, 1919), 406-429; and "The American
Occupation of Iowa," *ibid.,* XVII (January, 1919), 83-102. More
intensive is G. N. Fuller, *Economic and Social Beginnings of
Michigan* (Lansing, 1916). L. P. Kellogg, "The Story of Wisconsin, 1634-1848," *Wisconsin Magazine of History,* III (1919-
1920), in four installments *passim,* is a summary introduction.

The land claim associations are most fully described for Iowa:
B. F. Shambaugh, editor, *Constitution and Records of the Claim
Association of Johnson County, Iowa* (Iowa City, 1894); and
Dr. Shambaugh's monograph, "Frontier Land Clubs, or Claim As-
sociations," American Historical Association *Report, 1900,* I, 67-84.
A similar monograph is C. J. Richey, "Claim Associations and
Pioneer Democracy in Early Minnesota," *Minnesota History,* IX
(June, 1928), 85-95. A valuable picture of the equipment and am-
bitions of the incoming settler is comprised in an editorial article,
"Advice to Emigrants," *The North-Western Review* [Keokuk,
Iowa], I (November, 1857), 1-7.

John Steele, *In Camp and Cabin* (Chicago, 1928); E. G. Buffum,
Six Months in the Gold Mines (Philadelphia, 1850); and C. D.
Ferguson, *Experiences of a 49'er* (Cleveland, 1888), are repre-
sentative of many journals of life in the California mines. H. H.
Bancroft's chapters and C. H. Shinn, *Mining Camps* (New York,
1885), offer the best general résumés. Franklin Langworthy,
Scenery of the Plains, Mountains and Mines (Ogdensburgh, N. Y.,
1855) and L. V. Loomis, *A Journal of the Birmingham Emigrating
Company* (Salt Lake City, 1928) include fairly detailed accounts of
the Overland Trail to California. C. H. Shinn, *The Story of the
Mine* (New York, 1896), is an account of the Comstock Lode in
Nevada.

PART VI

The thirteen volumes of *Reports of explorations and surveys for
a Railroad From the Mississippi River to the Pacific Ocean* (Washington, 1855-1860) are lavish memorials of a bygone era in government printing. These volumes were once digested by G. L.
Albright, *Official Explorations for Pacific Railroads* (Berkeley,
1921) very inadequately and with practically no supplementary research. There are quite a few short monographs on the history of

the Pacific railroad movement in Congress, all harmlessly repeating the others' labors.

F. H. Hodder, "The Railroad Background of the Kansas-Nebraska Act," *Mississippi Valley Historical Review*, XII (June, 1925), 3-22, is a convincing explanation of Senator Douglas' motives. W. O. Lynch, "Popular Sovereignty and the Colonization of Kansas," *Mississippi Valley Historical Association Proceedings*, IX (1917-1918), 380-392; M. J. Klem, "Missouri in the Kansas Struggle," *ibid.*, 393-413; and Roy Gittinger, "The Separation of Kansas and Nebraska from the Indian Territory," *Mississippi Valley Historical Review*, III (March, 1917), 442-461, relate the consequences of the Act in Kansas.

L. B. Schmidt, "Influence of Wheat and Cotton on Anglo-American Relations during the Civil War," *Iowa Journal of History and Politics*, XVI (July, 1918), 400-439, and C. R. Fish, "Northern Railroads, April, 1861," *American Historical Review*, XXII (July, 1917), 778-793, are revealing interpretations of the importance of the West in the Civil War. D. E. Clark, "The Movement to the Far West during the Decade of the Sixties," *Washington Historical Quarterly*, XVII (April, 1926), 105-113, describes the continuation of the westward movement during these years of war.

F. L. Paxson, "The Territory of Colorado," *American Historical Review*, XII (October, 1906), 53-65, and essays by J. F. Willard and C. B. Goodykoontz in *Colorado: Short Studies of its Past and Present* (Boulder, 1927), have been particularly useful.

F. A. Root and W. E. Connelley, *The Overland Stage to California* (Topeka, 1901), is a unique compilation of statistics and gossip; L. R. Hafen, *The Overland Mail* (Cleveland, 1926), has brought order into chaos. William and G. H. Banning, *Six Horses* (New York, 1930), is a lively narrative.

W. J. Trimble, *The Mining Advance into the Inland Empire* (Madison, 1914), follows the eastward recoil of the frontier across the Pacific Northwest. Of the many articles in the *Contributions to the Historical Society of Montana* written by pioneers themselves, Henry Edgar's "Journal," III (1900), 124-142, and the narratives by Peter Koch and by Granville Stuart are noteworthy. H. M. Chittenden, *History of Early Steamboat Navigation on the Missouri River* (New York, 1903), is complemented by I. L. Poppleton, "Oregon's First Monopoly—the Oregon Steamboat Navigation Company," *Oregon Historical Society Quarterly*, IX (September, 1908), 274-304.

The letter written by an Iowan newly arrived in Virginia City,

WESTWARD

from which I quote, appears in the *Council Bluffs Bugle,* April 20, 1865. L. F. Crawford, *Rekindling Camp Fires* (Bismarck, 1926) contains a spirited description of Virginia City in 1864.

PART VII

G. M. Dodge told his own story in *How We Built the Union Pacific Railway;* J. R. Perkins, *Trails, Rails, and War* (Indianapolis, 1929), is an admirable biography. L. H. Haney, *Congressional History of Railways* (Madison, 1908-1910) and R. E. Riegel, *The Story of the Western Railroads* (New York, 1926) are scholarly; E. L. Sabin, *Building the Pacific Railway* (Philadelphia, 1919), is popular but substantial. In the *Union Pacific Magazine* for February, 1922, is an anonymous article, "Abraham Lincoln and the Union Pacific." W. F. Rae, *Westward by Rail* (New York, 1871) is an account of a transcontinental journey in 1869. F. L. Paxson, "The Pacific Railroads and the Disappearance of the Frontier in America," American Historical Association *Report* for 1907, I, 105-122, is an excellent summary.

T. C. Blegen, "The Competition of the Northwestern States for Immigrants," *Wisconsin Magazine of History,* III (September, 1919), 1-29, and J. B. Hedges, "The Colonization Work of the Northern Pacific Railroad," *Mississippi Valley Historical Review,* XIII (December, 1926), 311-342, I have used freely.

My *The Cowboy and his Interpreters* (New York, 1926), and my *The Hunting of the Buffalo* (New York, 1929) are the basis of the present chapter upon "The Open Range." L. G. Connor, "A Brief History of the Sheep Industry in the United States," American Historical Association *Report* (1918), I, 89-197; E. S. Osgood, *The Day of the Cattleman* (Minneapolis, 1929); Louis Pelzer, "A Cattlemen's Commonwealth on the Western Range," *Mississippi Valley Historical Review,* XIII (June, 1926), 30-49; and R. S. Fletcher, "The End of the Open Range in Montana," *Ibid.,* XVI (September, 1929), 188-211, have been useful.

J. E. Haley, *The X I T Ranch of Texas* (Chicago, 1929), is a first-rate narrative, which describes a frontier area in transition.

I have drawn upon A. F. Bentley, "Condition of the Western Farmer . . . ," *Johns Hopkins University Studies in History and Political Science,* XI (1893), for my sketch of a western agrarian community. S. J. Buck's *The Granger Movement* (Cambridge, 1913) and his *The Agrarian Crusade* (New Haven, 1920) are standard in their field. F. E. Haynes, *Third Party Movements*

[608]

Since the Civil War (Iowa City, 1916), is a narrative of the turbulent West in politics. J. D. Hicks has written a flock of monographs upon the Populists. His *The Constitutions of the Northwest States* (Lincoln, Nebr., 1923) is a very convenient summary.

INDEX

[611]

INDEX

INDEX

Campbell, Col. Arthur, Revolution, 136.
Campbell, Col. John, Revolution, 130.
Campbell, Thomas, religious leader, 215.
Canada, frontier attitude toward, 276, 278; War of 1812, 279-81; emigration from U. S., 595.
Canadian Pacific Railroad, 594.
Canals, Ohio Valley, 396. *See* Erie Canal.
Canandaigua, N. Y., land office, 186.
Cantrell, John, miner, 488-9.
Canyon City, Ore., mining, 511.
Cape Ann, settlement, 6.
Carmichael, William, commissioner, 254.
Carolina, charter, 18; settlement, 18; traders, 34-5, 39-40.
Carver, Hartwell, railroad project, 450.
Casa-Calvo, Marquis of, opposes Americans, 267-8.
Casement, Gen. Jack, Union Pacific, 529, 532-3, 535.
Cass, Lewis, 347, 386, 389, 390.
Cattlemen's frontier, 561; colonial, 41; western ranges, 55-7; California, 487-8; trail-driving, 569-70; decline, 570-7; rustling and reprisal, 575-7; and sheep, 577-9. *See* XIT Ranch.
Cayuse War, 383.
Cazenove, Theophile, buys lands, 187.
Cazenovia, N. Y., 188.
Central City, Colo., mining, 502.
Central City, Mont., mining, 515.
Central Pacific Railroad, organized, 526; and Pacific railroad acts, 524-5, 527, 533; construction, 1863-5, 527; Chinese labor, 530; 1866, 531; 1867-8, 535; 1869, 537-9; completion, ceremonies, 539-42; journey upon, 548-9.
Champoeg, Ore., meeting, 380.
Chandless, William, 562-3.
Charleston, center fur trade, 40.
Cherokee Indians, 30-1, 35, 109, 110-1, 139, 362, 460, 592.
Cherry Valley, N. Y., laid waste, 142.
Cheyenne, founded, 559; growth, 560; and Union Pacific, 533, 534, 535, 557; cattle trade, 572, 573.
Cheyenne Evening Leader, 560.
Cheyenne Indians, 532, 536.
Chicago, development, 395, 468-9; railroads, 466, 545.

Chicago & Galena Railroad, 468.
Chicago Times, 479.
Chihuahua, fair at, 330, 332; expedition from, 364.
Chillicothe, founded, 161; capital Northwest Territory, 162.
Chippewa Indians, 67.
Chisholm, Jesse, 459; Chisholm Trail, cattle, 569.
Chittenden, Hiram M., 302.
Choctaw Indians, 56, 459-60.
Chouteau's Island, 339, 345.
Chouteau, Pierre, fur trader, 302.
Christian Church, denomination, 214-5.
Chubbs Brothers & Barrows, 581.
Ciboleros, 332.
Cincinnati, founded, 158; capital Northwest Territory, 162; in 1834, 327.
Circuit riders, 216.
Civil War, importance of West, 482-4; in Northwest, 517-8; Indian troubles during, 509, 563, 582.
Claiborne, W. C. C., 266, 267, 268; as governor, 259-60.
Claim Associations, Iowa, 397-9; Nebraska, 476.
Clark, Daniel, consul, 266.
Clark, George Rogers, to Kentucky, 120; Indian war, 122, 124-5; Old Northwest, 129-134; intrigue rumored, 232-3.
Clark, John, 218-20.
Clark, William, fur trade, 302. *See* Lewis and Clark.
Clarke, General N. S., 507.
Clay, Henry, 317, 386-7; "War-hawk," 275-6, 278; Compromise of 1820, 299-300; of 1850, 470-1.
Clay, John, cattleman, 578.
Clearwater River, mines, 509-10.
Cleaveland, Moses, 161.
Cleveland, founded, 161.
Clinton, De Witt, Erie Canal, 315.
Clinton, George, Gov. N. Y., 141, 185.
Clothing, frontiersmen's, 85.
Coashutta Indians, 269.
Cœur d'Alene Indians, 508.
Colorado, settlement, 488, 551, 556-8; Jefferson Territory, 490-2; Colorado Territory, 492-3; constitution, 558-9; statehood, 559; agriculture, 557-8; ranching, 571, 572. *See* Mining frontier.

INDEX

De Smet, Pierre de, 375, 426.

Detroit, in Revolution, 127, 132, 134, 145; and fur trade, 159; War of 1812, 279-80; in 1818, 389; 1825-31, 390; 1836, 394-5.

Detroit Lake, Minn., 554.

Dewees, W. B., Texas, 361.

Dey, Peter A., Union Pacific, 526.

Dinwiddie, Robert, opposes French, 68-70; bounties, 71.

Discontent, frontier, absentee proprietors, 10; outbreaks of, 105; causes, 106; economic burden, 583-5; "agrarian crusade," 585-7; territorial government, 587, 589. *See* Bacon's Rebellion; Mississippi, free navigation; Whisky Insurrection; *passim.*

Doak, Jonathan, cattleman, 579-80.

Dodge, Grenville, and Lincoln, 523; joins Union Pacific, 528; directs construction, 528-39; at Promontory Point, 539-42; on effects of Pacific railroad, 542-3.

Donelson, Lt. A. J., with Stevens, 456.

Dongan, Gov. Thomas, expansionist, 26-7.

Donner party, to California, 417, 427-8.

Dorchester Company, settlement, 6.

Douglas, Sir James, 506.

Douglas, Stephen A., railroad land grants, 451; Pacific Railroad, 471-2; Kansas-Nebraska Bill, 472-3.

Douglass, Gen. Ephraim, 163.

Downie's Ravine, Calif., mines, 437.

Dry Diggings, Calif., mines, 432.

Dubuque, Iowa, 468.

Duer, John, lands, 187.

Duer, William, lands, 156.

Duluth, railroad, 550.

Dunbar, William, scientist, 266; exploration, 266-7.

Dunmore, Lord, in Revolution, 118, 125.

Duquesne, Marquis de, 68-9.

Durant, T. C., Union Pacific, 525-6, 531, 539, 542.

Dwight, Timothy, 205.

Edgar, Henry, miner, 513-5.

Edgerton, Sidney, Gov. Montana, 517.

Education, and Ordinance of 1787, 155; on frontier, 197, 283, 294-5, 477-8.

El Dorado Eating Resort, menu, 438-9.

Elk City, Idaho, mining, 510.

Ellicott, Joseph, and Holland Company, 190; quoted, 201.

Elm Grove, outfitting point, 377-8.

El Paso, Texas, trail through, 436.

Emilie, steamboat, 523.

Emory, Capt. W. H., reconnaissance, 465.

England, Oregon claim, 372, 385-6, 387-8; and Western wheat, 483-4.

Episcopal Church, in West, 203.

Erie Canal, built, 315-6; stimulates settlement, 316, 390; impetus to canal-building, 396.

Erie Railroad, 404, 544.

"Erocoise," Lake, fur district, 13-4, 15.

Evangelists, methods, 207.

Evans, John, trader, 262.

Fairfax, Lord, landowner, 58, 69.

Fallam, Robert, exploration, 22-3.

Fallen Timbers, Battle of, 160.

Fanning, Edmund, in Regulation, 95, 96-7, 100, 102.

Farmer, John, maps, 390.

Farnham, T. J., to Pacific West, 375-7, 426; on Santa Fé Trail, 336, 338; *Travels,* 377.

Farrar, John, attorney, 118.

Far West, Mo., Mormons, 412-3.

Faux, William, traveler, 284-5.

Fayette, Mo., railroad, 449.

Fayetteville, N. C., mart, 93.

Femme Osage region, settled, 292, 294, 296.

Ferguson, Patrick, in Revolution, 140.

Ficklin, O. B., Representative, 392.

Filson, John, with Symmes, 158.

Findley, William, Whisky Insurrection, 221-2, 229.

Fink, Mike, boatman, 248.

Finley, John, exploration, 111-2.

Fish, Carl Russell, on railroads, 483.

Fitzpatrick, Thomas, 378, 426-7.

Flatboats, Ohio River, 244.

Flathead Indians, 457.

Flint, Timothy, 309.

Florida, boundary fixed, 255; and expansion-fever, 256-7, 276; purchase, 372; lands donated, 400. *See* West Florida.

Floyd, John, frontiersman, 116.

INDEX

Gregg, Josiah, Santa Fé trade, 303, 336, 338-9, 347, 348, 364.

Griffin, E. D., 205.

Griffith, David, bishop, 203.

Grosh brothers, miners, 493.

Grover, Lt. Cuvier, with Stevens, 457.

Grow, G. A., and homestead law, 480-1.

Guadalupe Pass, 435.

Gunnison, J. W., survey, 464.

Gwin, Senator W. M., railroad, 451; overland mail, 500.

Haldimand, Sir Frederick, and British posts, 159.

Hall County, Nebr., agriculture, 581-5.

Hamilton, Alexander, land speculation, 184; sponsors Excise Act, 220; and Insurrection, 229, 230; favors free navigation, 234.

Hancock, Stephen, frontiersman, 135.

Hand, Gen. Edward, Pittsburgh, 127-8.

Hannegan, Edward A., Senator, 386, 387.

Hannan, Adam, lands, 59.

Harlow, S. B., railroad project, 449.

Harr, David, wagoner, 319.

Harris, William, with Lederer, 20.

Harrison, Benjamin, President, 577, 592.

Harrison Township, Nebr. See Hall County.

Harrison, W. H., career, 272-3, 274; Land Act, 273; Tippecanoe, 277-8; War of 1812, 280-1; President, 369, 400.

Harrod, James, in Kentucky, 115-6.

Harrodstown, founded, 115-6; and Indians, 124.

Hastings, Lansford, to Oregon, 378.

Hastings, S. C., Iowa, 398.

Hayes, R. B., President, 559, 587.

Heald, Capt. Nathan, at Fort Dearborn, 279.

Helena, Mont., mines, 516.

Henderson, Richard, character, 110; and Regulation, 102, 110; Transylvania, 110-8; French Lick, 139.

Henry Andrew, trader, 408.

Henry, Patrick, Transylvania, 115; aids Clark, 129.

Hibbard, G. B., railroad lands, 553, 554.

Hicks, Gwin, 588.

Hillsboro, N. C., mob, 102-3.

Hodge, Rev. William, 208.

Hogg, James, Transylvania, 119.

Holladay, Ben, stage lines, 519-20, 532.

Holland Land Company, 187-192.

Holston Valley, settlements, in Revolution, 130, 136.

Homestead Act. See Land Act of 1862.

Hooker, Thomas, Hartford, 9.

Hopkins, Mark, Central Pacific, 526.

House-raising, 84.

Houston, Sam, President of Texas, 363.

Howell, Rednap, in Regulation, 95, 103.

Howard, John, exploration, 52-5.

Hudson's Bay Company, 18, 372, 373, 388, 503.

Hull, Gen. William, War of 1812, 279-80.

Hunt, William Price, to Astoria, 304-6.

Hunter, George, exploration, 266-7.

Hunter, James, at Alamance, 95.

Hunter, Robert, and German immigrants, 47.

Hunters, pioneer, characteristics, 88-91.

Huntington, Collis P., Central Pacific, 526, 537, 538.

Husband, Hermon, in Regulation, 95, 97, 99-100, 103, 104-5.

Hussey, Obed, reaper, 404.

Hutchins, Thomas, surveys, 153.

Idaho, settlement, 509-11; Territory, 517; constitution, 588-91; statehood, 591.

Illinois, settlement, 283-4, 288-9; growth, 316, 470; statehood, 284, 297, 298.

Illinois Central Railroad, land grant, 451.

Immigration, Boards of, railroad, 550, 551-5, 595; state, 550-1, 555-6.

Imperialism, frontier trend, 276, 337, 363, 374, 386-7.

Independence, steamboat, 297.

Independence, Mo., Mormons at, 412; outfitting point, 336, 373, 381, 435, 497-9.

Indiana, settlement, 274, 284, 316; Territory, 162; statehood, 284.

INDEX

Indian Commissioners, Board of, 564.
Indian Intercourse Act (1834), 407, 471; nullified, 471.
Indians, hostilities, 78, 237, 338, 408, 416; Revolution, 122, 124-45 *passim;* Old Northwest, 160-1; Tecumseh, 276-8; Santa Fé Trail, 343-6; Black Hawk War, 391-4; Pacific Northwest, 504-5, 507-8; Civil War, 509, 563, 582.
Indians, land cessions, 7-8, 10, 76, 111, 150, 158-9, 160, 234, 276, 394, 564.
Indians, pioneers' hatred of, 343, 471, 563.
Indians, removal of, to Great Plains, 407, 471; to smaller reservations, 452; and destruction of game, 564.
Indian Territory. *See* Oklahoma.
Innes, Harry, urges separatism, 234.
Iowa, settlement, 396-7, 468; Territory, 397; railroads, 545; Board of Immigration, 556.
Iroquois Indians, 24-5, 70, 111, 185, 189.
Irrigation, Colorado, 558; Utah, 418, 423; land acts, 593-4.
Ives, Lt. J. C., with Whipple, 461.

Jackass Gulch, mining laws of, 443-4.
Jackson, Andrew, President, 274, 278, 317, 345, 346, 369.
Jay, John, to Spain, 147; Treaty of Paris, 147-8; Mississippi closure, 232-3.
Jefferson, Territory of. *See* Colorado.
Jefferson, Thomas, 161, 163, 298; Transylvania, 115; Ordinance of 1784, 152; and religious liberty, 202; favored by West, 234; Louisiana Purchase, 256-8; sponsors explorations, 260-1, 262, 266, 267; and Pike's expedition, 264; National Road, 311, 312-3.
Johnson, Andrew, and homestead law. 401, 481; and admission of Colorado, 559.
"Johnson County War," 576-7.
Johnston, Edward, on pioneers, 7.
Johnston, Sir William, Indian affairs, 67, 237.
Judah, Theodore, Central Pacific, 526-7.
Julesburg, railroad town, 532-3.

Juniata Valley, squatters in, 75-6; mob, 218-9.
Junction City, Mont., mining, 515.

Kamiakin, conspiracy, 504.
Kansas, Territory, 472; settlement, 473-5, 551; statehood, 475.
Kansas City, 569, 572.
Kansas-Nebraska Bill, 466, 472; and Pacific Railroad, 473.
Kansas Pacific Railroad, 549, 551, 557, 566, 568, 569.
Kaskaskia, in Revolution, 128, 130-2.
Keefer, William, wagoner, 319.
Keelboats, on Ohio, 245, 307.
Kelley, Hall J., in Oregon, 374.
Kendall, Amos, 321; on militia, 279.
Kentucky, explored, 61-3, 66, 112, 113; settlement, 113-7, 119-20, 122, 126; in Revolution, 124-5, 126-7, 135-8, 145; separatism, 176-181, 233-5; statehood, 181; religion in, 203-14 *passim.*
Keokuk, Iowa, 468.
Keokuk, Sauk chief, 391.
King's Mountain, Battle, 140.
Kirtland, Ohio, Mormons, 412, 420.
Kittaning Path, war-trail, 79.
Knox, Gen. Henry, lands, 184.

La Concha, Fernando de, 330.
Lake Superior & Missouri Railroad, 550.
La Lande, Baptiste, to Santa Fé, 333.
Lamar, M. B., Texas, 364-5.
Lands, public: *See* Ordinance of 1784, of 1785; act of 1796, 272; of 1800, 273; of 1820, 359; of 1841, 400, 572; bill of 1860, vetoed, 481; act of 1862, 150, 572, 594, agitation for, 401-2, 480, passed, 481-2, soldiers' exemption, 553; act of 1877, 593; of 1878, 572; of 1894, 593-4; of 1902, 594; grants to railroads, 451, 480, 524-5, 549; speculators, methods, 395-6.
Lands, tenure of, colonial, 7-8, 24, 40-2; Holland Company, 191; railroad's terms, 553.
Lands, western, ceded to nation, 146.
Langlade, Charles de, 67.
Langworthy, Franklin, to California, 435.
Lapham, Dr. I. A., as publicist, 67.

[618]

INDEX

INDEX

Natchitoches, La., 267, 268, 354.
Nationalism, frontier trend, 231.
National Land Company, 551, 557.
National Road, "2 per cent fund,"
310-11, 315; and Constitution, 311.
See Cumberland Road.
Nauvoo, Ill., Mormons, 413, 416.
Navigator, river guide, 246; an-
nounces steamboats, 249.
Nebraska, Territory, 472, 475; settle-
ment, 475-6, 477; claim associa-
tions, 476; legislature, 476-7; wild-
cat banks, 478-9; agriculture,
581-5.
Nebraska City, outfitting point, 519.
Needham, James, exploration, 28-31;
killed, 31.
Nemaha Valley Bank, fails, 479.
Nevada, settlement, 493-5; statehood,
495.
Nevada, Mont., mining, 515.
Nevada City, Calif., mining, 444.
Neville, John, at Fort Pitt, 127; and
Whisky Insurrection, 224-5.
New England, colonial, 3-16; emigration from, 161, 183-4, 274, 282-3,
284, 316, 474; railroad land
agents in, 553, 554; settlement in,
1783-1800, 183.
New England Emigrant Aid Company, 474-5.
New France, fur trade, and Iroquois,
24-5, 26, 35, 67; extension of, 25,
35-6; *coureurs du bois* to Carolina,
26; explorations and fur trade,
35; settlement in lower Louisiana,
39. See French and Indian War.
New Jersey, colonial, immigration,
40.
New Madrid, Mo., founded, 354.
New Mexico, Spanish, 329; Territory, 471; ranching, 575, 578; statehood, 592.
New Netherlands, opposes new English expansion, 14-6; taken by
England, 18, 25; Fort Orange, 24.
New Orleans, and Claiborne, 259-60;
individuality, 270.
New Orleans, steamboat, 325.
New Orleans Times, 395.
New York, western lands, arrange-
ment with Massachusetts, 185;
Phelps-Gorham purchase, 185-6;
Morris purchase, 186; Holland
Land Company, 187-192; Pulteney,
192-3; Cooper, 193-9; errors of
proprietors, 199-201; effect on

politics, 200-1; later settlement,
316.
New York Central Railroad, 404,
544-5.
New York Missionary Magazine,
216-7.
Nez Perce Indians, 457, 507.
Nicholson, Gov. Francis, and fur
trade, 36.
Nicolls, Gov. Matthias, and Albany
traders, 25.
North, Lord, and evacuation of
British posts, 159.
North Dakota, constitution, 588-91;
statehood, 591.
Northern Pacific Railroad, 409, 458,
549, 554; Land Department, 550,
551-5; carries buffalo hides, 568;
opens Dakota, 574.
North Platte, Nebr., on Union Pacific,
530, 532.
Norwegians, and railroad publicity,
554.

Occaneechi Indians, 30, 31.
Ogden, on Union Pacific, 537, 538.
Ohio, statehood, 273; constitution,
273-4; settlement, 274, 284, 316.
See Old Northwest.
Ohio Company (1749), 59, 63-4, 66-7,
69.
Ohio Company (1786), organized,
153-4; land purchase, 156; Marietta, 157-8.
Ohio River, navigation of, course described, 241, 326-8; seasonal peaks,
243-4; barges, 244; flatboats, 244;
Zadoc Cramer on, 244; keelboats,
245; packets, 246, 248; emigrants,
246, 249, 325; boatmen, 246-8;
banditry, 248-9; steamboats, 249,
325.
Ohio Valley, explorations. See Viele,
Gist, Walker, Howard; French
claim to, 67. See New France.
Oklahoma, settlement, 591-2; statehood, 592.
Oldham, John, Connecticut, 9.
Old Northwest, Clark in, 130-4, 146;
lands ceded to nation, 146, 148-9;
and Treaty of Paris, 146-8; Indian
title extinguished, 151, 158-60;
evacuation of British posts, 159.
See Ordinance of 1784, of 1785, of
1787.

[621]

INDEX

Oliphant, Lawrence, on St. Paul, 467-8.

Omaha, outfitting point, 519; Union Pacific, 527, 531, 539; in 1869, 545-6; cattle trade, 572.

"Omnibus Bill," 588; states admitted under, 591.

Orange County, N. C., Regulators in, 95-105.

Ordinance of 1784, 151-2.

Ordinance of 1785, 152-3, 154.

Ordinance of 1787, 154-6.

Oregon, admission to Union, 370, 386-7; treaties involving, 371-2, 385-6, 388; settlement, 373-9, 381-5, 388; government, 379-80, 382-3; Territory, 388; statehood, 468.

Oregon Steam Navigation Company, 504, 509.

Oro Fino, Idaho, mining, 510.

Osage Indians, 302, 335.

Otoe Indians, 293.

Otsego County, N. Y., created, 196.

Otsego Herald founded, 198.

Overland Mail, urged, 496-7; stage mails in West, 1856, 497; Butterfield, southern route, 497-8; coaches *via* Salt Lake, 499-500; Pony Express, 500-1; daily schedule coaches, 501-2; Holladay's coaches, 519-20; Wells, Fargo, 520.

Overland Trail, to Oregon, 373, 375, 378-9; Mormons, 417-8; overland routes, southern, 425, 435-6; to California, 426-7, 435; to Northwest mines, 517.

Pacific Mail Steamship Company, 434, 496.

Pacific Railroad, agitation for, 449-52; bills in Congress, 451-2, 466; surveys (1853-5), 452-66; and Kansas-Nebraska Bill, 472-3; effects of, Dodge quoted, 542-3. *See* Central Pacific, Union Pacific.

Packet boats, on Ohio, 246.

Palmer, Joel, on Overland Trail, 388.

Panic of 1819, 359; of 1837, 395-6; of 1857, 479-80; of 1873, 554, 583.

Parke, Lt. John G., 465.

Parsons, Samuel, Ohio Company, 154.

Pastorius, F. D., leads colonists, 46.

Patterson, James, frontiersman, 76-7.

Pattie, James Ohio, to California, 410.

Pattie, Sylvester, 410.

Pawnee Indians, 308.

Payne, David L., "boomer," 591.

Paxson, F. L., 370, 396.

Peck, J. M., on immigration, 297-8.

Penn, William, promotes immigration, 40, 46.

Pennsylvania, colonial, Scotch-Irish and Germans to, 46-49 *passim;* western, settlement, 316. *See* Juniata Valley, Pittsburgh.

Pennsylvania Fiscal Agency, 525.

Pennsylvania Railroad, 466, 544.

People's Party, 586-7.

Peoria, Ill., emigrants from, 375.

Pequot War, 8-9.

Perry, O. H., War of 1812, 281.

Peters, Richard, evicts squatters, 75-6.

Phelps-Gorham Purchase, New York Lands, 185-6.

Phelps, Oliver, 185, 186.

Pickawillany, fur post, 67.

Piegan Indians, 457.

Pierce, Franklin, opens Nebraska, 576.

Pierce [City], Idaho, mining, 510.

Pike, Z. M., Mississippi expedition, 263-4; western expedition, 264-6; intricacy of motives, 264-5; on Purcell, 333.

Pinckney, Thomas, envoy, 254-5.

Pioneers, institutions, progmatic test, 11, 202-3; political demands, 33, 101-2, 106, 231; characteristics, 80, 84-5, 95, 105-6, 287-8, 289-90, 375-6, 597. *See* Discontent, frontier; political thought, 274, 275, 471. *See* Constitutions, Imperialism; social life, 80-7, 121-2, 289-90. *See* Agriculture, Crime and punishment, Religious interest, Women; *passim.*

Pittsburgh, in Revolution, 125, 126; Virginia-Pennsylvania dispute, 125, 237, 238; in Whisky Insurrection, 225-7, 229-30; early years of, 236-43; in 1770, 237; in 1784, 239; in 1792, 240; in 1800, 242; in 1834, 325. *See* Fort Duquesne, Fort Pitt.

Pittsburgh Gazette, 224, 229; founded, 239; advertisements from, 243.

Placerville, Calif., 438, 441, 494, 499, 502.

Plantations, southern, westward pressure, 92, 360.

Plumbe, John, railroad project, 449.

[622]

INDEX

Plymouth Trading Company, 9.
Political thought, frontier. *See under* Pioneers.
Polk, James K., 317, 348, 370, 386, 387.
Ponca Indians, 262.
Pontiac's Conspiracy, 237.
Pony Express, 500-1.
Pope, Captain John, survey, 465.
Portland, Ore., 510, 512.
Portland Advertiser, on rush to mines, 510.
Potawatami Indians, 393, 394.
Potomac Company, canal, 312.
Potomac River, south branch, settlement, 79-80.
Prairie fire, described, 460.
Prairie lands, occupied, 403-4.
Pratt, Orson, Mormon, 417.
Pratt, Parley, Mormon, 418.
Praying societies, 204.
Preëmption, 400, 572. *See* Squatters, Claim associations.
Presbyterians, in Watauga, 109; in 1800, 205; loss of strength, 208-9, 215. *See* Scotch-Irish, Religious interest.
Preston, Texas, stage route, 497.
Pringle, John and Samuel, frontiersmen, 79.
Proclamation of 1763, 78, 119.
Progressive Party, 592-3.
Promontory Point, Pacific railroads meet, 538-542.
Provot, Étienne, 408.
Pullman cars, in 1869, 544-5.
Pulteney, Sir William, lands, 192-3.
Purcell, James, in Santa Fé, 333.
Putnam, Rufus, and Ohio settlement, 153-4, 157.
Pynchon, William, and Springfield, 10.

Quitrents, 149-50; difficulty of collecting, 40-1, 78; demand for remission, 50.

Rae, W. F., railroad journey, 547.
Railroads, across Appalachians, 404-5, 446; 1850-61, 450-1, 469, 482-3; transcontinental, 594; land grants to, 451, 480, 524-5, 549. *See* Pacific railroad, Central Pacific, Union Pacific.
Raisin River Massacre, 281.

Randolph, Edmund, on western discontent, 228.
Randolph, John, 300.
Rangers, Virginia, at Fort Henry, 12; cross Blue Ridge, 43.
Red River (South) explored, 266-9.
Red River Settlement, 454.
Reeside, James, stage line, 321.
Regan, John, traveler, 287.
Regulators, North Carolina, abuses in provincial government, 93-4; other distresses, 94-5; protests, 95-6; Orange County, outbreak in, 95-6, 101-2; riots, 96-7, 102-3; Tryon moves against, 98-100, 103-5; Alamance, 104-5.
Religious interest, of West, 197, 202-17, 342; Missouri, 296; and colonization of Texas, 354, 357, 360; Oregon, missionaries, 373-4; mining camps, 437. Great Revival: portents, 205; McGready, 205-7; philosophy of, 206-7; effects of, 208-9, 213, 215-7; frenzies, 210-12; compared with Great Awakening, 212.
Rensselaer, Stephen van, lands, 184.
Republican Party, and free lands, 481. *See* Free Soil Party.
Restoration, the, effect upon frontier, 18.
Revolution, American, frontier's part in, 118, 124-43, 145; Treaty of Paris, 146-148.
Rhea, John, president West Florida, 270.
Richardson, Albert, on Denver, 557.
Riley, Bennett, escorts traders, 345; in California, 440.
Robertson, James, and Watauga, 107-9; to French Lick, 139; federal appointee, 234.
Robidoux, Joseph, trader, 425.
Rocheblave, Chevalier de, at Kaskaskia, 128-9.
Rocky Mountain Fur Company, 303.
Rocky Mountain News, 558.
Rooseboom, Johannes, to Michilimackinac, 26-7; captured, 27-8.
Roosevelt, Nicholas, steamboat building, 249, 325.
Root, Frank, on food at way-stations, 499.
Rowan County, N. C., Regulators in, 100.
Russell, Majors and Waddell, freighting, 500.

INDEX

Tupper, Benjamin, Ohio Company, 153.

Tuscarora Path, traders' road, 76.

Tyler, John, President, 348, 369.

Underhill, John, Indian war, 9.

Union Colony, Colo., 557-8.

Union Pacific Railroad, carrying trade, 509, 568, 569, 571, 582; authorized, 523-4; amendments to charter, 525, 527; Credit Mobilier, 526; construction in 1865, 527; surveying corps, 528-9; construction corps, 529; in 1866, 530; Indian menace, 530-2; in 1867, 531-4; in 1868, 535-7; in 1869, 537-9; completion, ceremonies, 539-42; effects of, 540, 542-3; journey upon, 545-8.

Union Stock Yards, Chicago, 569.

Utah, see Mormons; Territory, 471, 493; statehood, 592.

Utah Indians, 464.

Venango, fur post, 68.

Vermont, independent state, 184.

Vial, Pedro, exploration, 330-2.

Victoria, B. C., and mining frontier, 505, 506.

Viele, Arnout C., exploration, 28.

Vincennes, in Revolution, 130, 132-4; Harrison at, 277.

Virginia, explorations, 6, 17-24, 28-31, 33; westward recession of frontier, 12, 32; Valley of Virginia, settlement in, 50-1, 52.

Virginia City, Mont., 515, 516.

Virginia City, Nev., 494, 495.

Virginia Military Reserve, in Ohio, 161.

Wagoners, Cumberland Road, 319-20.

Walker, Felix, to Boonesborough, 112, 113.

Walker, Thomas, exploration, 60-3.

Walla Walla, mission, 376, 383.

War of 1812, wanted by West, 275-6, 278-9, and Congress, 278; campaigns, 279-81.

Warren, Capt. William, on Indian ravages, 142.

Warren's Diggings, Idaho, 511.

Washington, Territory, 401; constitution, 588-91; statehood, 591. *See* Oregon; Mining frontier.

Washington, George, opposes French, 68-71; buys western lands, 71; on rage of speculation, 151; appoints Wayne, 160; on free navigation, 253; on Pittsburgh in 1770, 237.

Washington, Lawrence, Ohio Company, 63.

Washington Union, 433.

Washoe, Lake, mining region, 493-6.

Watauga, settlements, 107; Association, Articles, 108; government, 108-9; ended, 110; emigration from, 139.

Watson, Senator James, lands, 184.

Wayne, Gen. Anthony, Indian campaign, 160.

Weaver, James B., candidate, 586, 587.

Webster-Ashburton Treaty, 385-6.

Weiser, Conrad, Pa. agent, 75.

Weiser, J. C., German colonizer, 47.

Western Emigration Society, 425-6.

Western Fire and Marine, wildcat bank, 478.

Western Pilot, river guide, 325-7.

Western Reserve, Conn., in Ohio, 161.

West Florida, becomes American domain, 270; addition to Louisiana, 271.

Westward movement, forces impelling, 4, 9; from Massachusetts coast, 9; succession of frontiers, 16, 593; at close of Revolution, 183; after War of 1812, 281; "Great Migration," 282-4, 286; into Missouri, 297; to Far West, 381; into Mississippi Valley, 385, 394, 470; during Civil War, 518; accelerated by railroads and state publicity, 550-6; *passim.*

Wetmore, Major Alphonso, 337-8.

Wheeling, W. Va., in 1834, 326.

Whipple, Lt. A. W., survey, 458-64.

Whisky, in backwoods economy, 220-1; as social institution, 82, 84, 200, 210.

Whisky Insurrection: excise in colonial Pa., 220; Act of 1791, 220, 222-3; denounced, 220, 223; excise in Penn. (state), 221; outbreaks, 221-2, 223, 224-5; modified, 224; mob spirit, 224; Braddock's Field, 225-7; suppression of, 228-30.

White, Elijah, Oregon, 377-9.

White, James, buffaloes, 565.

INDEX

White, John, Dorchester Company, 6.

White, John, miner, 513.

Whitman, Marcus, missionary, 375, 376, 383.

Whitney, Asa, railroad project, 449-50.

Wight, Lyman, Mormon colony, 413-6.

Wilderness Road, traced, 112-3; importance, 119, 121, 122.

Wild horses, extermination, 596-7.

Wilkins, William, Secretary of War, 471.

Wilkinson, James, intrigue with Spain, 233, 235, 253; promotes separatism, 234; and Pike's expedition, 264-5.

Willamette Falls, Ore., 373, 379.

Willamette Valley, Ore., settled, 504, 510.

Willard, Simon, and founding of Concord, 7-8.

Williams, Burke, backwoodsman, 287-8.

Williams, John, land agent, 120.

Williamson, Charles, land agent, 192-3.

Williamson, Lt. R. S., survey, 464, 465.

Willing, Capt. James, in Revolution, 131.

Wilson, Henry, Senator, 525.

Wilson, James, and Constitution, 311

Winnebago Indians, 392, 393, 394.

Winslow, Edward, in fur trade, 7.

Wisconsin, settlement, 316, 396; immigration boards, 551, 555, 556.

Withers, A. S., on pioneers, 80.

Women, on frontier, and religious interest, 204, 210; rôle of, 381-2.

Wood, Abraham, and Fort Henry, 12-13; sponsors explorations, 17, 21-2, 28; deplores indifference, 31-2.

Wood, Thomas, with Batts, 22.

Woodruff, Wilford, Mormon, 418.

Woodward, Henry, in Carolina frontier, 18-9.

Wool, Gen. J. E., in Northwest, 505.

Wool fulling, primitive, 85.

Wright, Beverly and Co., 566.

Wright, Col. George, Indian war, 508.

Wright, G. C., land agent, 595.

Wyandot Indians, 64, 151.

Wyeth, Nathaniel, trader, 373, 376.

Wyoming, Territory, 560; mining, 559-60; ranching, see Cattlemen's frontier; railroad, see Cheyenne, Laramie; constitution, 588-91; statehood, 591.

Wyoming, Penn., laid waste, 141.

Wyoming Stock Growers' Assn., 573. See Johnson County War.

XIT Ranch, breaking up of, 594-6.

Yakima Indians, 504, 508.

Yellowstone region, Stuart expedition, 513.

Yorktown, surrender at, 145.

Young, Brigham, Mormon leader, 414-22 *passim;* and Union Pacific, 534, 536.

Zuni Indians, 461-2.

(1)

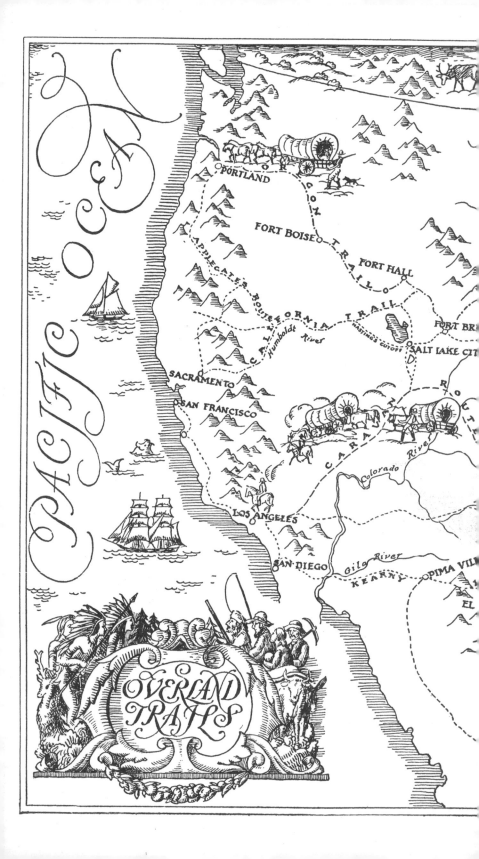

PACIFIC OCEAN

PORTLAND

FORT BOISE

FORT HALL

APPLEGATE ROUTE

CALIFORNIA TRAIL

Humboldt River

HASTINGS CUTOFF

FORT BRI

SALT LAKE CITY

SACRAMENTO

SAN FRANCISCO

ROUTE

CARA

Colorado River

LOS ANGELES

SAN DIEGO

Gila River

KEARNY

PIMA VIL

EL

OVERLAND TRAILS